Michael Curtis

SHOULD ISRAEL EXIST?

A Sovereign Nation

Under Attack by the

International Community

SHOULD ISRAEL EXIST?

A Sovereign Nation Under
Attack by the International
Community

Michael Curtis

First printing: January 2012

Balfour Books
Customer Service: +1 877 887 0222
P.O. Box 2180
Noble, OK 73068
www.balfourstore.com

ISBN: 978-1-933267-30-2

Cover and Interior by Brent Spurlock, Green Forest, AR

Printed in the United States of America

To William J. Flynn

In admiration

Foreword

The title of this book poses two related questions, 1) Does the State of Israel have a valid right to exist as a sovereign state, a member of the family of nations participating as an equal member with other sovereign powers; and 2) Does the international community adequately perceive that Israel plays a vital role for the success and defense of freedom and democracy and western values? Professor Curtis' thoroughly researched effort is a tour de force which refutes the legal, political and historical attacks on Israel's right to exist that have been launched by Israel's enemies and detractors. He also demonstrates that Israel is like an avatar, a defender of freedom and human rights in a world under attack from Islamic terror and extremism. Professor Curtis conceives of Israel as the metaphoric canary in the mineshaft, placed there to warn miners of the presence of odorless deadly fumes; if the canary dies, the miners know that they, too, are in danger of succumbing to the fumes. While the canary lives, they are safe. So, too, as long as Israel remains a sovereign country, the democratic nations are safe.

Professor Curtis' underlying thesis is that Israel's enemies and detractors employ arguments and historical narratives that are lacking in truth and validity in many cases. His careful scholarship and authoritative use of sources provide answers essential to understanding the complexity of Middle East history and politics. This book addresses the need, and provides an added voice to define and defend the struggle the free world faces in the attack on western civilization by Islamic radicalism. It is a worthy effort to combat the fervor and hatred, and indeed, the anti-Semitism which pervades much of the dialogue in the attempt by Israel's enemies to achieve its destruction. Professor Curtis is quite correct in raising international anti-Semitism as an element in the assault on Israel's legitimacy.

The Middle East is presently aflame with protest and violence; rulers and governments have fallen, civil wars threaten and the results are not yet knowable. History is in the making, but historians have no guidebooks ready. Change is certainly to be predicted, but its dimensions are not yet charted. The protestors' complaints and demands are varied and include cries for economic, social and political reform, jobs, education, participatory democracy and economic justice. Religious conflicts and claims pervade the scene, including calls for restoration of a caliphate; violence and cruelty is a common companion.

In all of this tumult, the Arab/Israel/Palestinian conflict remains largely on the sidelines, practically moribund. Demands and counter-demands for negotiations abound, but that conflict seems to be outside the center of the concerns of the active participants in the Arab Revolt. Will that change when the present contestants leave the field of conflict? It is probably too much to hope that the almost uniform rejection by the Arab and Islamic world (save Egypt and Jordan) of Israel's right to exist will for long be neglected as the favorite obsession of Israel's enemies.

There is a simple and plain reason that the present iteration of the Arab/Israel/ Palestinian conflict remains unsolved. It lies in the fact that the Palestinians have refused, or are unable, to accept and recognize Israel's right to exist. And Israel for its part refuses, or is unable, to assume the risks to its existence, safety and security it would face if it yielded to the demands for concessions made by the Palestinians.

Professor Curtis puts the conflict in historical context, not only for the last hundred years, including the Ottoman Empire, but also from the dawn of civilization when Abraham received the Covenant and began the rise of the three Abrahamic religions, Judaism, Christianity and Islam. In the sweep of twenty-six chapters, we see how the conflict evolved through two world wars and into the modern era where it is certainly touched by the resurgence of Islamic radicalism.

This book also weaves the existence of anti-Semitism into the problems faced by Israel in the current assault on its legitimacy. Anti-Semitism has been faced by the Jewish people from the very beginning, back to the earliest times. It continues today, perhaps most virulently in parts of the Arab world, and is fueled by organized incitement by many governments and powerful religious leaders. Considering the treatment of Israel by elements of the international community, by the huge majorities against Israel in the United Nations and agencies and groups related to the U.N., it is hard to escape the question of whether the animus against Israel in those circles may be a reflection of latent or historic anti-Semitism. Professor Curtis includes among his twenty-six chapters the suggestion that no small part of the animus against Israel derives from the persistence of this ancient scourge.

Kenneth Bialkin

Contents

Introduction ,,8

1. The Obsession with Israel ,, 13

2. The International Assault: ,,23

3. Lawfare and Universal Jurisdiction ,,,60

4. The Charge of Racism,, 74

5. The Charge of Apartheid: the Big Lie,,,88

6. The Charge of Colonialism,, 106

7. On the Road to a State ,,116

8. No Compromise,, 129

9. The Mufti of Jerusalem and the Nazis ,, 138

10. The State of Israel Established ,, 161

11. Original Sin,, 170

12. The United Nations Relief and Works Agency,,,,,,,,,,,,,,,,,,,,,,,,,,,,,, 180

13. The Right of Return,,, 188

14. The Captured Territories ,,, 196

15. The Charge of Occupation ,,,204

16. The Issue of Settlements,, 210

17. The Charge of Discrimination ,, 218

18. Palestine and the Mandate ,,,225

19. Land Ownership ,,236

20. Nationality and Citizenship ,,, 240

21. The Importance of Peoplehood,,,247

22. Israel, Jews and the Diaspora,,253

23. The Need for Security and Defense ,,,256

24. A Jewish State,,272

25. A Jewish and Democratic State,,,283

26. Conclusion ,,291

Notes ,,, 326

Index,,341

Introduction

If the trumpet gives an uncertain sound, who shall prepare for the battle? This book is concerned with the battle being fought in the Middle East in which the democratic state of Israel, the David in the encounter, has been deceptively portrayed by numerous hostile forces as the Goliath. Directly or indirectly, the ultimate objective of the hostile attacks is the elimination of the Jewish state of Israel. Furthermore, some of those attacks, from Islamic extremists and from others, emanate from antisemitism, the hatred of Jews. One result of this has been the present difficulty in distinguishing condemnations and criticisms of Israel and expressions of anti-Zionism, from antisemitism, or judeophobia, and words of hatred and contempt directed at Jews.

This book is a response to the relentless onslaught against the state of Israel and the rights of the Jewish people waged, not only by hostile countries as might be expected, but also by international organizations, non-governmental organizations, human rights bodies, members of the media and academics. This tendentious warfare—political, diplomatic, and legal—has little to do with appropriate or warranted criticism of specific actions or decisions of Israel and its citizens, all of which have been subjected to a critical microscope beyond anything experienced by other countries in the world. Rather, this campaign seeks to demonize the country by launching spurious accusations against Israel as a racist, colonialist, discriminatory, apartheid state, and a violator of human rights.

With a decent respect to the opinions of openminded people when presented with the facts, this book offers a corrective to the biased and unfair narrative and to the inaccurate and politically motivated historical picture presented by groups and individuals hostile to Israel, regarding the conflict between Israel, Arab states and Palestinians. It calls upon the reader to exercise fair and independent judgment concerning the very existence of Israel and other issues related to the realities of the Middle East, rather than unreservedly accept the fashionable opinion of the moment or adhere to outmoded and ideological beliefs. This book challenges the negative images, myths, false narratives, misrepresentations, and malicious stereotypes about Israel and Jews. It tries not to accord the status of axioms, to what are little more than opinions.[1]

Although one can agree that the conflict between Israel and its opponents is not a Manichean contest between good and evil, it is also not one of moral equivalence. It is a conflict between a state, about which genuine criticism might and has frequently been made, and the antagonistic entities, those nations, groups, and individuals who are unwilling to accept its existence as a legitimate state in the Middle East or to recognize its sovereignty and territorial integrity. The paradox in this situation is that the condemnations and attacks on Israel, a democratic country, often come from regimes led by autocratic rulers or members of military juntas who themselves lack any real legitimacy, and from groups and individuals, who defend or support corrupt and stagnant political and social systems characterized by dishonest institutional behavior, inequality in laws, and suppression of human rights.

In view of these realities, people who are genuinely interested in promoting humanitarian concerns will be disconcerted to realize that in the battle waged against Israel the language of human rights, a cause in which they are interested, has been misused. The constant repetition of untruths and distortions has perverted international law and the operation and activity of international organizations, above all the United Nations and its various units. How can the reader excuse the misnamed United Nations Human Rights Council for spending its time passing fully half of all its critical resolutions against one state, the state of Israel, while virtually ignoring the violations of human rights committed by other states, including those who are members of the Council? What can explain the decision of UNESCO, the United Nations Educational, Scientific, and Cultural Organization, in October 2010 to declare that Jewish sites, which many regard as holy, the Tomb of the Patriarchs in Hebron, and the Tomb of Rachel near Bethlehem, could not be added to Israel's National Heritage List? Instead, Rachel's Tomb is to be re-labeled as an Islamic mosque. This decision, approved by a vote of 44 to 1 with 12 abstentions, was the result of proposals by five Arab states and the pressures they imposed on others.

No doubt for many oil-importing countries, self-interest in continuing to obtain supply of Middle Eastern oil may well be the motivating factor propelling support for this decision and for other criticisms of Israel, and challenges to its existence. Yet, as open minded people may recognize, those hostile to Israel may be infected by what Emile Zola, in his great article "J'Accuse" of January 13, 1898 castigating those who had falsely accused the Jewish Captain Alfred Dreyfus of espionage, called "the spirits of social evil," or outright antisemitism. Conscious of a necessary distinction to be made between Islam as a religion and Islamism, meaning radical and extremist Islam, a political ideology which is regarded as a distortion of true Islam, this book explores both the impact of that ideology which includes antisemitic rhetoric and the role that German Nazism played in its formation.

For purposes of rational discussion, the following chapters offer a challenging series of propositions. First, the actions and policies of Israel are not the basic root cause of the Israeli-Arab conflict, now the Israeli-Palestinian conflict, nor are they responsible for instability and conflict in the Middle East. That instability and the unwillingness of non-Israelis to solve the conflict, and the use made of the Palestinian issue by Arab states for their own agenda are discussed in a number of chapters. A posture of apologetics by Israel is neither necessary nor helpful for advancing the peace process. Second, Israeli policies are not responsible for the persistence of the Palestinian refugee problem, which is much more the result of the indifference of Arab states and of the operation of the United Nations Relief and Works Agency (UNRWA), essentially running a welfare state for Palestinian camp refugees. Third, the existence and legitimacy of the state of Israel should be universally accepted on the basis of the historic relationship of the Jewish people and the land, whether defined as Palestine, the Holy Land, or *Eretz Israel*. Denial of the Jewish people's right to national self-determination or of the historic connection to Palestine is unacceptable. Israel is not a colonial power, nor did it launch a campaign to propel Palestinian Arabs to move from their homes.

Fourth, the complex issues of nationality, citizenship, and land ownership are examined in the context of that historic relationship and the right of Jewish self-determination. Fifth, in the existing hostile environment, the Israeli need for security and defense is paramount and explains restrictions imposed in some areas of physical space and behavior. Sixth, there is no inevitable incompatibility between a Jewish state and a democratic state. Seventh, as already suggested, international law has been misused and international organizations have been perverted for anti-Israeli partisan purposes, and that has been done in the name of worthy causes such as that of human rights. The language of human rights has been misused to portray Israel as the source of injustice in the world. Eighth, double standards have been adopted in evaluating Israeli behavior, attitudes, and actions, while violations of codes of behavior, social and legal, by other nations have been mostly ignored, and few resolutions have referred to the absence of human rights, women's rights, and freedom of expression in Arab countries. Ninth, Israel has been subjected to unwarranted discriminatory calls for boycott, divestment, and sanctions against it, and above all calls to delegitimize and eliminate the state. Tenth, an ideological campaign stemming partly from a credo of Third Worldism and partly from styles of thought such as postmodernism, cultural relativism, and multiculturalism has sought to undermine the moral fabric of Israel. This is often accompanied by moral indifference or intellectual apathy about the reprehensible activities of non-Western regimes. Indifference, as Elie Wiesel once said, is a strange and unnatural state in which the lines blur between light and darkness, good and evil.[2] Eleventh, many in the media and the academic world have engaged in biased and inaccurate reporting and in what Julien Benda called the "intellectual organization of political hatred."[3] Some of that reporting may be motivated, consciously or not, not only by a hatred of Israel, but also by antisemitism. Those reporters might be reminded that antisemitism was the most important weapon in Hitler's propaganda arsenal, and almost everywhere it was a deadly and efficient one.[4] Hitler also commented that in view of the "primitive simplicity" of the minds of people "they more easily fall a victim to a big lie than to a little one."[5]

Finally, this book rests on the premise that the attacks on Israel and the animosity and hatred towards it are also directed against other democratic countries, particularly the United States, and Western culture in general. The Israeli canary in the political coal mine must continue singing to give voice to Israel's existence and to take pride in its accomplishments. If it dies, it would act as a warning of existing dangers to the democratic countries in the world, countries that also uphold principles of freedom and justice, and welcome diverse faiths and ethnicities. Those countries are now faced by Islamist extremists who seek to overthrow or weaken secular states, and replace them by theocratic regimes. The canary must sing on behalf of freedom, pluralistic democracy, universal human rights, and true principles of international law. Senator John F. Kennedy, as a presidential candidate, recognized this in his speech of August 26, 1960 in New York to the Zionists of America Convention, when he said that Israel "carries the shield of democracy and it honors the sword of freedom." It still remains true, as Reinhold Niebuhr, the Christian theologian, asserted in 1967 that the survival of Israel is "a strategic anchor for a democratic world...and an asset to America's national interests in the Middle East."[6]

Chapter 1

The Obsession with Israel

On May 14, 1948, in Tel Aviv, the State of Israel was established upon the termination of the British Mandate of Palestine entrusted by the League of Nations in 1922. Its Declaration of Independence proclaimed, "We offer peace and amity to all neighboring states and their peoples, and invite them to cooperate with the independent Jewish nation for the common good of all. The State of Israel is ready to contribute its full share to the peaceful progress and reconstitution of the Middle East." It is an enticing notion to envisage the Middle East today if the Arabs and the Palestinians had accepted the presence of Israel on that day and recognized its right to exist. However, by dawn the next day Egyptian planes had bombed the new State and five Arab armies invaded it. Over 60 years later Israel has still not been able to be at peace with its neighbors, except Egypt and Jordan. If its last conventional war with Arab states was fought in 1973, Israel, from the Lebanon war in 1982 to Operation Cast Lead in Gaza in 2008-2009, has been obliged to respond militarily to attacks on its civilian population.

Nor has Israel received a warm welcome over those years by the majority of the international community. On the contrary, unrelenting animus, physical assaults, verbal propaganda, and religious dogma, from many political and geographical directions, have been directed against Israel. Moreover, in recent years the hostility against Israel, regarded by enemies as a bastion of the West, can now be seen as part of the struggle mounted against democratic countries and Western societies in general. That struggle may best be seen as the organization, intellectual and physical, of political hatred. The moment has come to speak truth to those who are misguided, willfully ignorant, or hopelessly prejudiced, and to give, as George Washington wrote in his letter of August 21, 1790, to the Truro Synagogue in Newport, "to bigotry no sanction, to persecution no assistance."

James Madison, in *Federalist Paper 37*, understood the problem. He wrote it was a "misfortune, inseparable from human affairs, that public measures are rarely investigated with the spirit of moderation which is essential to a just estimate of their real tendency to advance or obstruct the public good." What can explain the virulence of the immoderate attacks on Israel and the obvious hatred, with no concern for the public good, underlying them? The threats of the President of Iran and of Islamist movements in Arab countries to eliminate the state of Israel have been pronounced on numerous occasions. What is less acknowledged, even by some well intended persons, is that Israel has a legitimate point of view, and their refusal to take account of this, and simply regard all of Israeli actions as unjustifiable or as crimes against humanity, is tantamount to a call for delegitimization or elimination of the state of Israel. In his last speech on the Middle East to the United Nations Security Council on December 12, 2006, Kofi Annan, the outgoing Secretary-General, said that "Palestinians and their supporters will never be truly effective if they focus solely on Israel's transgressions, without conceding any justice or legitimacy to Israel's own concerns, and without being able to admit that Israel's opponents have themselves committed appalling and inexcusable crimes."

In his remarks in November 2006 at a memorial service for Yitzhak Rabin, the assassinated Israeli Prime Minister, the distinguished Israeli writer, David Grossman, said "The very existence of the State of Israel is a miracle of sorts that happened to us as a nation, a political, national, human miracle." This book contends that the miracle in the desert must survive, and that in the face of incessant international hostility it can clarify the path for other democratic nations faced by similar danger. As with the canary, signs of suffocation or danger to the existence of Israel serve to warn the world of the life-threatening danger to all democratic societies from unwarranted and obsessive condemnation. The animus against Israel must be fully understood in the context of a danger, in both a religious and secular form, to the West, especially to the United States, and an endless challenge to its democratic values.

Israel, the only democracy in the Middle East, whether regarded as a bastion of the West or not, has faced that danger in five wars since 1948, each a threat to its existence, with courage and imagination, and also at crippling costs of defense. In spite of this Israel has not developed a siege mentality. It has tried to act in a self-sufficient and independent manner, and to foster the normalization of the Jewish people as a nation among nations. It does not blame itself because others want to destroy it. Instead, it is a vibrant democracy, including the rule of law, independent court system, a free press and media, political and legal equality, a culture of openness, regular elections, freedom of speech, freedom of religion, a pluralistic society, equal protection guaranteed by law, and legal equality for women in work, education, health, and social welfare, as well as recognition of their significant role in public life, in academia, and in the economy. The nature of the democracy was exhibited in manifest fashion when in January 2011, Moshe Katsav, the former President of Israel, was found guilty of charges of rape and harassment by a three-judge panel composed of two women and a Christian Arab, and sentenced to seven years in prison. The sentence on appeal was upheld on November 10, 2011 by the Israeli Supreme Court, sending a clear message that Israel upheld the principle of equality before the law.

Israeli society has produced considerable achievements in science, literature, art, and culture. It combines a spirited secular life style, symbolized by Tel Aviv, and a more official and religious life as exemplified by Jerusalem. The social and demographic mix of the population, and the nature of the economy has been changing while the country has been absorbing citizens coming from over a hundred Jewish communities, most from backgrounds that lacked democratic traditions. The democratic nature of the system has been enhanced by the significant role of the Supreme Court and its willingness to overrule the government and the Knesset (Israeli Parliament) on issues of public policy when it thinks it necessary to do so.[7]

In his speech at the 1937 Zionist Congress in Zurich, David Ben-Gurion was realistic about a future state. The Zionist vision he said "is rooted in the historical reality of the Jewish nation; but the external forces and circumstances condition the possibilities and methods of its realization."[8] The drama of the history of Israel has borne this out. In spite of the celebrated feats of commercial, scientific, and technological creativity, the nation-building and integration of Jews from so many countries, and the entrepreneurial innovation of the small population of a little over seven million, of whom one million are Arab, Israel has been perplexed by the reality and the intensity of hostility resulting from the Arab-Israeli and the Palestinian-Israeli conflict.[9] A nation that sought peace and friendship with neighbors has now to deal not only with Arab hostility and statements calling for the destruction of Israel, but also with defamation, glib and false rhetoric, by many in the international community.

In one of the cases of Sherlock Holmes, the crucial fact that led to the solution of the problem was that the dog did not bark. The most striking fact about the United Nations and many international organizations is that their barking, and occasional biting, is mainly directed against one member state. The bitter truth is that the State of Israel has been subjected to more constant criticism and condemnation since its establishment than has any other country in the world, not simply for its specific policies, decisions and actions, but also over its legitimacy and very existence. It is the only state that has been the object not only in Arab countries, but also throughout the world of obsessive accusations of gross violations of human rights, of conspiratorial activity for world domination, and blood libels. Many of those countries have registered automatic disapproval of any Israeli actions, even those taken in self-defense. Their attitude is reminiscent of the French witticism: *cet animal est fort méchant; quand on l'attaque il se défend* (this animal is very wicked; when it is attacked it defends itself). Diogenes with his lamp searching for evidence of firm moral principle in some of those countries would come away disappointed.

As an open society Israel has experienced both internal and external criticism: internally because of the considerable number of human rights groups and other organization preoccupied with perceived faults, and externally as a result of Arab and international hostility. This hostility has been exacerbated by the large number of representatives of the foreign media in Israel, about 350 permanent news bureaus; probably a larger number than in any other city except New York and London. The bureaus have given considerable publicity, often negative and prejudiced in character, to the staged events by Palestinians protesting about some activity by Israelis, acting either officially or privately. After a moving visit to Israel the British playwright, David Mamet, not previously sympathetic to Israel's difficulties, commenting on the prevalence of negative reporting, wrote that "Israel was fighting against terror, misthought public opinion, as well as against disgracefully biased and indeed fraudulent reporting... the Western world is (about Israel) deeply confused between the real and the imaginary."[10] That "misthought" opinion and reporting in recent years has focused with intense light on the nature of the state, on the alleged impurities, imperfections, and lack of moral righteousness in the character and behavior in the diverse Israeli society and politics.

Within Israel, strong criticism of this kind is not unfamiliar. One of the prominent Israelis disturbed by the present nature of his country is David Grossman who, despite his positive comment quoted above, said that "The state of Israel has been squandering, not only the lives of its sons, but also its miracle; the miracle has broken down to routine and recklessness, to corruption and cynicism." Outside Israel, and more specifically in recent years, politicians, writers and journalists, the global media, religious leaders, academics and students in and outside of universities, the theatrical and publishing worlds, established churches, members of national and international bodies and non-governmental organizations (NGOs), and human rights organizations, have concentrated on what they conceive as the racism, discrimination, colonialism, improper occupation of territory inherent in an Israel which they designate as an *apartheid* (a Dutch-Afrikaans word for separation) state. The very language used in the persistent characterization of Israel and its actions as "illegal" or "illegitimate" or "disproportionate" or as "ethnic cleansing" or even as "genocide" has influenced international opinion. That language, distorted as it is, has shaped perceptions and factual premises about Israel.[11]

The more extreme of these critics liken Israeli actions to those of Nazi Germany, or compare Islamic terrorism against Israel to European resistance against the Nazis. Israeli operations against terrorists in Gaza have been equated with the destruction of Guernica in the Spanish Civil War. Some individuals in international arenas who accuse Israel of "crimes against humanity" at the same time deny the existence of, or minimize, the scope of the Holocaust. Others deny the historic fact of Jewish ties to Jerusalem or the existence or meaningfulness of the Jewish Holy Places in Palestine, though excavations in the City of David, the six hectare ridge that is regarded as the main location of biblical Jerusalem, in the area of the Western Wall, and in Jewish ritual baths in Jerusalem indicate Jewish habitation there for thousands of years. Recent findings include the Siloam Inscription, an 8th century B.C. Hebrew inscription that commemorates the building of a water tunnel under the ridge, and the Pool of Siloam, which dates from the Roman period, and the street that connected it with the Temple Mount, and a well preserved site from the First Temple period called the Ophel City Walls Site, which includes royal buildings, store rooms, a watchtower, and ritual baths. It is believed to be the Water Gate mentioned in the Bible (Nehemiah 3:26).

This concern about deficiencies, anguish about the defective "soul" of Israel, and disenchantment with the small country about the size of New Jersey, whether sincere or inspired by partisan motives and which often goes far beyond honest, principled criticism, is both surprising and unwarranted. The founders of the State of Israel, and indeed the principles of Zionism, the word coined, probably by Nathan Birnbaum in Vienna in 1890, to designate the Jewish liberation movement, never suggested that the recreation of a Jewish state in its ancient homeland where the kingdom of Judea under David was established circa 1010 B.C., would resemble a city on the hill, a shining beacon devoid of blemishes or of the necessary compromises required for survival. Israel, in theory and in practice, has not, in Alexander Hamilton's words in *The Federalist Papers 85*, engaged in "the chimerical pursuit of a perfect plan." Israel or Zion, the word for the old fortress or hill in Jerusalem, was never intended to embody the moral consciousness of the world, or be a light unto the nations. Nor, again in the words of Hamilton (*Federalist, 6*) did Israel indulge in idle theories promising exemption from "the imperfections, weaknesses, and evils incident to society in every shape."

Nevertheless, both for those with millenarian and even utopian beliefs, and others with less high-minded and more partisan motivation, Israel has been held to an impossibly high standard for over sixty years, a standard or double standard that has ~~been~~ not been applied to any other country. In the case of Israel its alleged deficiencies have been the justification for the prejudice against it and the fervor with which it is denounced, demonized, and ostracized in the international community. Whatever the ostensible reasons for the extravagant animosity against Israel, which in its most explicit form denies Israel's right to exist, it may in reality be based on traditional antisemitism that has existed for centuries, historical jealousies concerning the Jewish people, and falsely grounded apprehensions of Jewish behavior. The contemporary animosity and expressions of what have been the overtones of antisemitism resemble the prejudice of the Pharaoh of Egypt, "behold the people of the children of Israel are more and mightier than we." (Exodus 1:9)

Certainly it remains logically inexplicable that a people that historically has been the victim of prejudice and aggression and worse should be falsely and relentlessly condemned for supposedly victimizing others and for jeopardizing peace. It is equally inexplicable that some historians who in general are reluctant to make categorical judgments have no hesitation in condemning Israel. Even more perplexing is the spectacle of conscientious humanists showing so little concern for human suffering in the world other than on occasions involving Israel and its actions. Part of that spectacle is the facile sentimentalizing by some in the international political left excusing or disregarding the lawless and inhumane brutality in countries about which they know little, simply because those countries were subjected at one point to Western rule.

Another rationale for this behavior is the commitment to political correctness that disregards or ignores political reality. That political correctness whether, genuine or sanctimonious, may adhere to the false dogmas that the main problem in the Middle East is the Israeli-

Palestinian conflict, that the explanation for a lack of solution is Israeli occupation of disputed land, that Israeli settlements are illegal and that they are an obstacle to the achievement of peace. This is to ignore the other conflicts in the area that affect the dynamics of politics; historic animosities, personal rivalries, religious differences, territorial disputes, the Arab poverty and unemployment, the lack of freedom and human rights in Arab systems, all of which have played a role in the pattern of continuing violence in the area. The area is marked by a number of vexing characteristics: wars among ethnicities, wars among sects, dysfunctional sharing of power preventing any possibility of common citizenship, inability to rally around a common purpose, authoritarian governments and praetorian states of various kinds, political uncertainty, frequent resort to violence, unpredictability, and challenges to the legitimacy of state boundaries and the internal stability of various states.[12] To these factors can be added the restless young citizens in Arab countries where about a third of the population is under fifteen, and where the new technology, the Internet, Facebook, Twitter, and You Tube, provides information for social and political networking which can challenge state-run media and propaganda.

The opinion of so many in the international community that Israel is the most troublesome issue in the Middle East was belied by the views of many current Middle Eastern leaders and the actions of many of the population of the Middle Eastern countries in the winter and spring months of 2011. Arab demonstrators were not bemoaning the fate of Palestinians, but were concerned with the deficiencies in their own societies. In her speech to the League of Arab States in Cairo on March 15, 2010, Catherine Ashton, the High Representative for Foreign Affairs and Security in the European Union, and former British Labour Party politician, spoke of the "continued importance that the European Union attaches to the resolution of the Arab-Israeli conflict. This is a vital European interest and is central to the solution of other problems in the region."

These typical remarks were doubly inaccurate. The revolts of Middle East populations in the early months of 2011, when the so-called "Arab street" erupted spontaneously, were focused on poverty, unemployment, rising prices, and poor economic conditions, and on the repression, corruption, the inferior status of women and minorities, in their societies, not on concern for Palestinians, the peace process, or opposition to building some housing in Ramat Shlomo or other Israeli settlements. The masses in Egypt, Libya, Yemen, Tunisia, and Bahrain demonstrating violently in those months against their rulers were more immediately concerned with their own freedom, ability to participate in decision-making, and economic opportunities than with Jewish housing in the West Bank, even if they disapprove of Israeli policy. The leaders themselves have been less focused on Israel than on the danger of Iran's nuclear program, its apocalyptic mullahs, its influence in Lebanon and Syria and probably in Shiite southern Iraq after the American departure, and Iranian support for radical political movements and terrorism in the Middle East and in the Balkans, and on the threat of the Muslim Brotherhood. Iran is feared as an octopus whose tentacles are reaching out to manipulate, foment, and undermine moderates in the Middle East.

Unlike the views of Catherine Ashton, who declared that Israeli settlements are illegal and constitute an obstacle to peace, the Palestinian leadership, as reported in leaks about negotiations with Israel, privately accepted that the majority of Israeli settlements can be considered legitimate and are not a major obstacle. Nor were the demonstrators in the uprisings against their rulers in the Arab countries in the spring of 2011 concerned about "Palestine," as they risked their lives for their own freedom and human rights. One might well conclude that since the Palestinian issue has apparently become less important, if still an emotional issue, for most Arabs it has become more symbolically important for the Western political left which is now is more royalist than the king in its emphasis on Palestinian rights, or more precisely on an anti-Israeli disposition. Moreover, that political attitude, by addressing the Israel-Palestinian conflict as central to Middle East issues and to world peace, is counter-productive because it neglected or minimized criticism of Arab leaders for their violations of human rights and the repression in their countries, thus contributing to the continuation of the authoritarian or dictatorial regimes. The left is less concerned with the slow and inadequate political and economic development, the low economic growth, the poor public services, high unemployment, the corruption of Arab rulers, internal differences within Islam, the elimination of inequities in Arab societies, and the threat of Iran, than with seeing Palestinians as the personification of ultimate victims. In this narrative, all Palestinians, irrespective of facts or behavior, become part of a privileged group with the status of victimhood.[13] This narrative also equates the suffering caused by the Arab military defeat in 1948-49 with the suffering of Jews in the Holocaust.

Chapter 2

The International Assault: Hypocrisy on Display

International politics is not a morality play, nor a branch of theology. The national interest of countries, however defined, inevitably sets limits on "messianic passions."[14] Those idealists who had hoped that the United Nations and auxiliary organizations created after World War II would foster peace and play a prominent role in ending the use of force in international politics must be disappointed that instead the ontological character of these international bodies is more a political battlefield, displaying an insatiable enthusiasm for anti-Israeli resolutions, than a model of objective deliberation aiming at genuine principles of international law. The experience of over sixty years has shown that the United Nations and other international bodies have frequently been used as forums for waging a conflict in public, rather than promoting normative behavior and the solution to problems. What is distinctive about the political war against Israel is that it has been waged in so many forums, international and otherwise, and at every opportunity. The ritualistic resolutions passed by the UN and other international organizations result from political advocacy, deliberate machinations, fear of consequences of doing otherwise, and traditional antisemitism, rather than from a concern to create an improved moral order. In his book, *Defending Identity,*[15] Natan Sharansky wrote of the hypocrisy and double standards of the international human rights organizations, which reflect the disappearance of clear moral criteria that alone can guard human rights. The institutional culture of the UN and related organizations, with their bizarre priorities and misuse of time and resources, views Israel, at a minimum, as a terrible embarrassment and nuisance.[16] That culture and behavior embody what Maimonides regarded as the most derogatory form of utterance, *motzi shem ra*, the spreading of evil falsehoods.

Stereotypical and biased generalizations about Israel are made in those bodies by hostile countries taking a particular partisan view, and emphasizing undesirable traits or characteristics or behavior patterns with unreflecting regularity and without subtle distinction. The kindest thing one can say of these generalizations is that they are functional elements reducing the complexity of international affairs and relationships to a simple level. After all, we all have a limited capacity to absorb and process information about the political and social world.[17] Analysts of international relations studying decision-making sometimes posit the concept of "group think."[18] They suggest that a group of people coming together to discuss a particular problem may develop a consensus and an accepted and uniform way of looking at the problem that they see as justifying their action. However, the generalizations, manufactured for political advantage, are often based on simple archetypical myths portraying Israel as a conspiratorial enemy. Those hostile generalizations for some thirty years have increasingly been focused on four main charges against Israel: it is racist, it is colonialist, it is an oppressive occupier, and it is an apartheid state.

No one will gainsay that honest, principled criticism of Israeli political policy making, and genuine critiques of imperfections and inequalities in the character and behavior of Israel's diverse society are not only perfectly appropriate but also are a crucially desirable feature of dialogue in democratic culture. Commentary of this kind, in the Israeli domestic scene, in international publications, radio, and television, by a multiplicity of political and non-governmental organizations, and in the halls and classrooms of the academy, is not scarce. However, at times the search for misdeeds in Israeli politics and society resembles enthusiastic, if bumbling, inquiry by short-sighted detectives with the result that the line between sincere criticism and prejudice becomes difficult to discern. The moral fervor exhibited by that criticism often discounts judgments about the realistic consequences of the exercise of power, the rules, organization and coercion in a beleaguered country. The Israeli writer, Aharon Megged, speaking of fellow Israeli writers, even commented that since the Six-Day War the country had witnessed "an emotional and moral identification by the majority of Israel's intelligentsia with people openly committed to our annihilation."[19]

It was Ben-Gurion who explained, soon after the establishment of Israel, "we must learn to think like a state," and coined the word *mamlachtiyut*, that expressed the need to act as a responsible sovereign power, politically and militarily. Sadly, there is no manual on how to run a Jewish state. Jews, for several thousand years, lacked the power to act in history.[20] Ben-Gurion's great contribution was to answer effectively the troubling question of whether a people that had been powerless for so long could now wield it and take responsibility for it. Though ultra-Orthodox Jews and many assimilated Western Jews were troubled by his answer, Ben-Gurion led the transformation of a nation into a state.[21] In reply to critics, such as the historian Jacob Talmon, who was concerned about possible trends that could lead to totalitarian democracy, he argued that the use of necessary power and coercion for collective purpose in Israel, and mobilization of resources for Zionist ends would not lead to dictatorship or despotism.[22] Some more recent Israeli writers, such as Adi Ophir, have become concerned, not only about Israel in particular, but also about the modern state as such, which they regard as a "totalizing structure" because of the power it can exercise.[23] Since the establishment of Israel, its people have been divided over the degree to which the power of the state should be employed, especially concerning foreign policy. This problem of the Jewish ambivalence towards the use of power has been relevant to the nature of the Israeli response to the attacks of armies in the past, and more recently against those terrorists who use civilians and densely populated areas for protection.

The radical and negative answer to the view of the state exercising power is familiar from the assertion of Michel Foucault that politics comes from "resistance to 'governmentality'."[24] In practice, this outlook has meant not simply impassioned criticism of Israel and its alleged collective misdeeds and moral crimes by outsiders, but also confrontation by some of its own citizens; detachment, refusal to engage in civic affairs and obligations (such as refusal to perform military service), providing support for the international efforts in various ways to boycott Israel, exhibiting intense solidarity with the Palestinian cause, and expressing detestation of compromise with principles. Again, this attitude is familiar from the writings of another French philosopher, Jean-Paul Sartre, who applauded the Algerian "freedom fighters" for their killing of French settlers.[25] His approval of revolutionary violence, both in terms of its utility and for the self-realization and the emotional life of its perpetrators, was to have an important influence on the psychology of those hostile to Israel. In recent years the international radical left's general approval of "the wretched of the earth" has become affected by interest in and some approval of Islamic fundamentalism, a danger to the West and to Islam itself as well as to Israel. Hamas in Gaza is the local embodiment of that fundamentalism. Its ideology as an Islamist jihad movement has not been altered by its responsibilities as the governing power in Gaza.

Because of the outpouring of censure on every occasion of Israeli action, one might well conclude that some of the more extreme of the individuals who so relentlessly express such prejudice have a deep antipathy not only towards the policies of the State of Israel, but also towards Jews in general. They may or may not regard themselves as antisemitic, or perhaps as accepting the conclusions of the infamous *Protocols of the Elders of Zion*, the forgery fabricated by a Russian journalist associated with agents of the Russian secret police at the end of the nineteenth century, which portrays an imaginary meeting of a few Jewish leaders plotting an international Jewish conspiracy to take over the world.[26] The volume of their rhetoric, however, does suggest that they see, or pretend to see, the actions of Israel as a fulfillment of some Jewish conspiracy to dominate the world. One of the more bizarre consequences was the assertion by an Egyptian cleric in June 2010 that one of the protocols was the Jewish plan to keep non-Jews preoccupied with songs, soccer, and movies.

It has long been apparent to any objective observer that criticism of Israeli behavior has often gone far beyond any reasonable measure, and has taken a direction that is strident, tendentious, disproportionate, and particularistic. That criticism has often been couched in shrill or emotionally polemical terms and has called for ideological demonstrations and boycotts in many areas: economic, medical, sports, architectural, cultural such as film festivals, and academic. In the economic sphere, calls have been made for a consumer boycott of all Israeli goods, bans on importation of Israeli products, divestment from companies investing in Israel and from Israeli companies, and boycotts on tourism to Israel.

Particularly surprising have been the calls by academic bodies, journalists and trade unionists in Britain, France, all three Scandinavian countries, and the United States, purportedly believers in free speech and open exchange of ideas, for some forms of intellectual boycott. These might include refusal to participate in academic and cultural cooperation, collaboration or joint projects with Israeli institutions and academics, promotion of divestment from Israel, ending study abroad programs in Israel, stopping collaborative research, refusing to review work of Israeli scholars, preventing publication of articles by Israeli academics, preventing defenders of Israel from speaking, and protests, such as sit-ins at Western universities.

Particularly surprising is the blanket censorship of, and boycotts against, Israeli academics regardless of their political orientation or connection with governmental or military policies. This must be a unique case in the world; a boycott of universities in the name of academic freedom. This is not only a stance that abuses individuals and institutions indiscriminately, but also one that is the antithesis of the whole academic purpose and is antithetical to the fundamental values of the academy: the fostering of scholarship and intellectual exchange. The censorship has had its farcical moments. Mona Baker, the Egyptian born professor and editor of journals in Britain, dismissed two distinguished individuals from her editorial board for being Israeli citizens; one was Professor Miriam Schlesinger, herself a peace activist and a leading figure in Amnesty International in Israel, often critical of the state. A similar miscalculation was made in March 2011 by the Senate of the University of Johannesburg in South Africa, which decided not to renew a research agreement with Ben-Gurion University, ostensibly for "aiding and abetting the occupation." The Senate had forgotten that the research dealt with water reclamation, a subject that Ben-Gurion University was exploring together with Palestinian and Jordanian researchers.

Equally surprising has been the harsh criticism of Israel, not only by democratic governmental bodies such as most of the European Union in the 1970s and especially since its Venice Declaration of June 1980, but also by non-governmental organizations, by social and religious bodies, and by religious dignitaries. Amnesty International has called for an embargo of arms to Israel; both the War on Want and the Amos Trust have attacked the security fence built by Israel; churches such as the Presbyterian (US), United States Methodist, United States Church of Christ, United States Church of Canada, Church of England Synod, and World Council of Churches in Geneva; Unions such as Unison, the largest public service workers Union in Britain; Unite, the largest overall British trade Union with 2 million members; the British National Union of Journalists, the British National Association of Teachers in Further and Higher Education and the Association of University Teachers, which merged in 2007 to become the University and College Union; the British Trades Union Congress (which in August 1917 had declared its support for a Jewish homeland in Palestine); the Scottish Trade Unions Congress; the National Union of Students, the Canadian Union of Public Employees, the Canadian Union of Postal Workers, the main Norwegian Union, LO; and the Irish Municipal, Public and Civil Trade Union, have all called for some form of pressure on Israel. In October 2010, Archbishop Desmond Tutu of South Africa, repeating his equation of Israel with the former South African system, called on the Cape Town Opera Company not to go to Tel Aviv and perform George Gershwin's *Porgy and Bess* at the opening of the Israeli Opera season the following month. More openminded than the Archbishop, the Company did perform.

Some of the manifestations of the rhetorical and practical discrimination against Israel, which have become increasingly numerous, have been relatively mild, but they nevertheless display acquiescence in the campaign to delegitimize and demonize the state of Israel. A few examples are sufficient to appreciate the international extent of the prejudice. Language has provided a falsification of the real nature of Israel with frequent references to illegal occupation, ethnic cleansing, violation of human rights, Palestinian right of return, settler-colonial, racist power, policy of extermination of a people. The critical rhetoric has led to numerous actions that impose obstacles on Israel. The Norwegian government forbade a German shipbuilder based in Norway from using Norwegian waters to test a submarine being built for the Israeli navy. Some Israeli tennis players were only able to compete behind closed doors in a Swedish stadium. Israeli academics have been not invited or have been prevented from attending university conferences. Israeli films have not been shown at international festivals. The Israel Antiquities Authority was excluded from an international conference held in 2009 in Ramallah, by the World Archeological Congress. Israelis were barred from taking part in the gay pride parade in Madrid in June 2010. Only tortuous logic could identity a chamber music performance by the Jerusalem Quartet in London in 2010 with alleged commission of Israeli war crimes and human rights violations. Yet its performance was disrupted. Similarly, a performance in London in September 2011 by the Israel Philharmonic Orchestra was disrupted by pro-Palestinian protestors to the point that the BBC cut off the live broadcast of the concert. This was the first time since BBC broadcasts began in the 1930s, that one has been disrupted. Such behavior may appropriately be regarded, not simply as a political gesture, but also as antisemitic, because it condemns Israel while it is indifferent to the actions of other countries that have actually committed serious crimes.

It is worth repeating that Israeli behavior has been evaluated by a standard not applied to any other country, and one which no nation, past or present, has ever sustained or been asked to sustain. Positive statements about admirable features of Israel culture and achievements are either non-existent or less prominently mentioned in contemporary discussion; rather, they are almost exclusively confined to critical comments. Even statements expressing understanding or sympathy for Israel's predicament in the Middle East may be qualified by other statements which posit an argument of "moral equivalence," a disease of the sophisticated, between the two sides. Terrorist attacks against Israeli citizens may be viewed as no more iniquitous than Israeli attempts to stop them. In this equation both sides are said to be contributing to the "cycle of violence" in the Middle East, and thus should be condemned.[27]

EYELESS IN GAZA AND ELSEWHERE

By dint of the constant reiteration of a biased narrative of events in the Middle East, particularly of the interactions between Israel and Palestinians, and the deliberate unsympathetic interpretation of Israeli actions, the world is well aware of problems in the West Bank. One may ask if it is similarly aware of much worse problems in East Timor. Advocates of human rights have frequently been culpable of selective morality in their analysis of instances of injustices and flagrant violations of rights. Shylock may not have been completely accurate in his line, "What judgment shall I dread, doing no wrong?" He was more correct in his following lines, "You have among you many a purchased slave, which, like your asses and your dogs and mules you use in abject and in slavish parts."

Consider the outrage expressed by international bodies over actions by Israeli authorities compared with the response, either minimal or nonexistent, to those in an endless list of actions in other countries in recent years: the 20,000 civilians, part of the total of 70,000, killed by Sri Lankan troops fighting against the Tamil Tigers; the estimated 100,000 Uzbeks who in June 2010 fled ethnic violence in Kyrgystan; the invasion of Georgia by Russia in 2008; the "cleansing" of Bahais in Iran; the killing in Syria in March 2010 of Kurds celebrating the festival of Nowruz and the deprivation of the human rights, including travel, property and work, of the Kurds in Syria who constitute ten per cent of the country, but are regarded as foreigners (*ajanib*) and about 300,000 of whom have been stripped of Syrian citizenship; the liquidation of the Assyrian minority in Iraq; the massacre in February 1982 of at least 20,000 by Syrian bombing of its citizens in Hama; the killing of Kurds and machine gunning in July 2008 of prisoners in Saidnaya jail; the murder of over thirty Lebanese leaders and personalities by Syria since the 1980s; the killing by Turks of over 30,000 Kurds in Anatolia and northern Iraq and the refusal by Turkey to recognize the existence of a separate Kurdish identity; the expulsion of Americans in 2010 by Morocco for Christian proselytizing; discrimination against Berbers in North Africa; the slaughter of Christians by Muslims in the Sudan and in Nigeria; the killing of over 2 million in Darfur; the murder of over 700 people by Boko Haram, the Islamist militant group in Nigeria; the murder in 1994 of over 800,000 people, primarily members of the ethnic Tutsi group by Hutus in Rwanda; the turmoil in Zimbabwe; the slavery still existing in parts of Mauritania and the female genital mutilation to which most baby girls there are subjected; the slaughters by the al-Shabab group in Somalia and the Horn of Africa; the brutal killings of civilians and police by the Maoist guerrillas, known as the Naxalites, in the state of Chhattisgarh in India; the lack of freedom in North Korea, the world's remaining totalitarian state where over 150,000 political prisoners are incarcerated in five large camps; violence and gang rapes in the Congo where over four million have been killed or driven from their homes; the more than 150,000 estimated killed in Chechnya; discrimination against Tibetans; the elimination of opponents in China and its violent repression of Uyghurs in Urumqi; massacres in July 1995 of 8,000 Muslims by Bosnian Serbs in the Balkans, especially around Srebrenica in an area supposedly protected by UN peacemakers; the bombing by Jordan in Black September 1970 of Palestinian refugee camps killing thousands of Palestinians; the slaughter in 1971 by Kuwait of Palestinians living there; and the discrimination and oppression within the Arab world, particularly against women and children, and also against Christians in Lebanon and Egypt. Since the end of World War II hundreds of thousands of Muslims have been killed or murdered in the Algerian civil war, the Iran-Iraq war, in Darfur, Somalia, the Philippines, Chechnya, Pakistan, Yemen, and in the Lebanese civil war.

The international community has paid scant attention to the practice in Syria and other Arab countries of the murder by men of their female relatives for besmirching the honor of the family by having sex outside marriage, by having been raped, or by wearing what they deem to be immodest clothes. That community has paid little heed to the fact that males are in every way privileged over females in the Muslim world: men inherit more than women; women are disadvantaged in custody disputes; and women may be unable to exercise free will to initiate arbitration. Nor has attention been drawn to the virtual form of slavery of the million and a half migrant workers, enduring long hours, poor pay, and mistreatment in Saudi Arabia, and to the lack of freedom of travel and choice of residence in that country. Attention has not been given to the similar fate of the 660,000 migrants in Kuwait. Nor has international opinion focused on the fact that Islamic law treats conversion from Islam to Christianity as apostasy, with dire consequences: the penalty for apostasy is death, even if the individual recants.

Surprisingly little attention has been paid by the international bodies interested in violations of human rights and by those ostensibly concerned about the treatment and condition of Arabs in Middle East countries to help remedy the deficiencies pointed out by the Arab intellectuals who wrote the United Nations Arab Human Development Report of 2002, which has largely been ignored. That report concluded that Arab nations suffer not so much from any actions of Israel, as from a deficit of freedom, gender inequality, weak commitment to education, and from denial of human rights in their own countries. Those nations apparently are reluctant to tackle their own domestic economic and political problems. A glaring problem is the inferior role of women in society and in political participation. According to the 2009 UN Development Report, Arab countries are less industrialized today than they were four decades ago, and have made only slight progress in human development over the last decade. Poverty has increased, wealth in those countries is poorly distributed, and unemployment is high. The report also stated that knowledge in the Arab world was hampered not only by the "linguistic isolation" of the Arabic language, but also by religious extremism and intolerance, and by restraints on political, press, and economic freedoms.

The thrust of the 2002 Report is buttressed by objective scholarly analysis, such as that by Timur Kuran.[28] Arab and Muslim propaganda has blamed Israel for all the problems in the Middle East. However, the present state of underdevelopment in the area results from the slow adaptation of key institutions of the modern economy. The failures of the Arab countries include a weak private sector and civil society, uncompetitive industrial products and services, few political checks and balances on non-democratic rulers, lack of mass mobilization of productive resources and savings, few long term individual planning objectives, inadequate exploitation of new technologies, and Islamic law. Outsiders, particularly Israel, are not responsible for the underdevelopment and lack of modernization in the Arab world.

THE USE AND ABUSE OF LAW IN THE INTERNATIONAL COMMUNITY

In an article published in 1990, Adam Roberts warned that the "language of law can become a language of right and wrong, of moralistic reproach."[29] Theoretically, international law has been formulated to prevent hostilities, to regulate armed conflict, and to suggest alternative methods of settling disputes among nations, but in reality it has also been a mechanism to institutionalize partisan political positions. It would be unrealistic to expect otherwise, whether one takes a realistic (Hobbesian) or idealistic (Kantian) view of international relations. What is different in the case of Israel is that the application of such law is infused with an animus that exceeds the usual boundaries of differences of opinion, while paying scant attention to the realities of the conflict between Israel and Arabs. The selective and intemperate language alone, by international bodies as well as others, indicates the animosity towards the state of Israel; phrases such as criminal responsibility, oppressive occupation, crimes against humanity, violation of principles of criminal accountability laid down at the Nuremberg trials, are commonplace in the international discourse.

For any reasonably objective analyst, it is difficult to avoid cynicism about the critical judgments of the policies and actions of Israel made by international bodies, ostensibly created for and purportedly engaged in furthering the existence of peace and justice in the world, but in reality weaving a fabric of baseless allegations. To paraphrase Lord Macaulay, no spectacle is as ridiculous as the international community in its periodical fits of morality. The spectacle of this morality also carries a high price; in fiscal year 2009 support of the UN cost the United States $6.35 billion or twenty-three per cent of the UN's total budget. Witnessing today the masquerade of international bodies, born after the successful struggle against Nazi Germany, in dealing with human rights issues, it is dispiriting to recall the high hopes that have been perverted.

A simple comparison shows the change of opinion and international mood. The Council of Europe, set up in 1949, displayed in its early years photos of David Ben-Gurion, who was lauded and accorded guest status among the European leaders. Twenty-five years later, as a result of the working alliance of the former Soviet bloc, the so called non-aligned nations, and the Arab world, Yasser Arafat, head of the Palestine Liberation Organization (PLO) was received as a head of state and spoke at the United Nations General Assembly (UNGA) on November 13, 1974, delivering his "gun and olive branch" speech with a pistol holster in his clothes. The UNGA had, in October 1974, accepted the PLO as "the sole representative of the Palestinian people," and on November 22, 1974, by Resolution 3236, would recognize the Palestinian people's right to self-determination. By Resolution 3237 (November 22, 1974), it granted "observer status" to the PLO. This was the first time that such status was given to a non-nation. The PLO thus had the image as liberation fighters, not guerrillas.

A year later the PLO was given similar recognition by the UN Food and Agriculture Organization. It was also given observer status in October 1977 at the UN Civil Aviation Organization, even though it had no planes of its own. Even more, the UNGA in 1977 set the day of November 29 as the annual official celebration of "Palestine Day." Two years later, the then UN Secretary-General, Kurt Waldheim, the former Austrian lieutenant who lied about his actions regarding Jews as an officer in the Nazi army stationed in the Balkans, was conspicuously absent from the signing of the Egyptian-Israeli Peace Treaty on March 26, 1979, explaining while in London that the Palestinian issue was "the crux of the problem" and that the Treaty had not dealt with it sufficiently. In December 1980 Waldheim allowed two mayors from the West Bank to stage a hunger strike in the UN building in New York to protest Israeli policies.

High expectations of the role of the UN have been tempered. Its history so far resembles the commentary on the changing French Revolution by Edmund Burke that "very plausible schemes, with very pleasing commencements have often shameful and lamentable conclusions."[30] It has not been able to maintain international peace and security as its founders hoped, nor brought "the end of the system of unilateral action, exclusive alliances, and spheres of influence and balance of power" as President Franklin Roosevelt desired. It is not a nascent world government. Certainly the UN has made important contributions on some issues: the elimination of certain diseases, technical standards for safety, environmental management, economic and technical assistance, relief of famine, and peace-keeping forces, though the last were not successful in Rwanda or in Bosnia. But it has also been the forum where Zionism is described as racism in situations that have no bearing on the issue of peace in the Middle East, or anywhere else, and it has been used as a weapon for political pressure rather than as a vehicle for solution of problems.

The United Nations has greatly changed since its formation by fifty-one nations immediately after the end of World War II. Today, non-Western countries, many who seem to be automatically hostile to Israel, constitute about two-thirds of the total of the 192 members. Changes in the composition of the UN Security Council, which includes non-permanent members from Africa and Asia, have meant more opportunities for voices critical of Israel to be heard. It is conspicuous that the Security Council has never condemned any Arab state for military or terrorist attacks against Israel. With the constant resolutions condemning Israel, it is apparent that the UN is not acting, according to its charter, as "a center for harmonizing the actions of nations."

It is a sad reality that the United Nations and its various agencies have become a battleground for political advantage for the non-Western bloc, rather than the epitome of international peace and justice. All of those bodies have been misused for political purposes extraneous to the professed reason for their existence. The structure of international organizations now rests on frail pillars. The whole foundation is imperiled by the constant and perverted abuse of the organizations, official and unofficial, in the unremitting warfare against Israel.

Almost all the UN organizations have, to varying degrees, been party to this warfare. Only in the UN Security Council has the stream of hostile resolutions against Israel been checked. This has largely resulted from the use by the United States of the veto. Starting with the administration of Richard Nixon in September 1972, when the United States vetoed two resolutions, every US President has followed this tactic; Gerald Ford four, Ronald Reagan eighteen, Jimmy Carter one, George H.W. Bush four, Bill Clinton three, George W. Bush nine. In all, seven presidents of the United States have exercised forty-one vetoes in defense of Israel. Other hostile resolutions have been blocked or never came to the floor.[31]

UNITED NATIONS GENERAL ASSEMBLY (UNGA)

The most flagrant examples of the disproportionate criticism of Israel in the UN bodies come from the United Nations General Assembly (UNGA) and the United Nations Human Rights Council (UNHRC), whose missions are to promote universal respect for the protection of human rights and fundamental freedoms. Some striking comparisons that can be made are that the UNGA has not condemned the Turkish occupation of Northern Cyprus that has existed since 1974; the creation of a separate Turkish-speaking republic there, that no country other than Turkey recognizes; the occupation of Tibet by China; or the occupation of Western Sahara by Morocco.

What is apparent in the UN is the larger role of the UNGA, a body in which the non-Western countries have a considerable majority. Most of the policy resolutions in the area of human rights have come from the UNGA, in which, unlike the Security Council, all nations have a vote. The consequences of the majority role of non-Western countries have been that resolutions supporting Western concerns cannot obtain agreement, that the non-Western states can block actions antithetical to their interests, that Western democracies have usually been in a defensive or reactive position, and that the Soviet Union, and now Russia, have taken advantage of the anti-colonial disposition to form coalitions in their own interest. Constitutional rules do provide that only the Security Council can impose sanctions or other forms of coercion to resolve a dispute, while the UNGA is mandated only to discuss matters and make non-binding recommendations. However, the UNGA has expanded its role and has succeeded in transforming the UN into a global political actor, able to affect the international political environment as well as providing an arena for individual political maneuvering of member states. The UN has therefore become a weapon for the non-

Western bloc in international relations and a venue to which that bloc brings disputes to weaken Western countries.

One must allow that the UN has played or tried to play some role in the search for settlement of the conflict between Israel and Arabs, but that role in practice has been minimal. It set up the Disengagement Observer Force in the Golan Heights; UNIFIL (the Interim Force in southern Lebanon) whose mission according to Security Council Resolution 425 was to "confirm the withdrawal of Israeli forces from southern Lebanon" (the "Interim Force" has been there since 1978); and military observers of its Truce Supervision Organization. Yet the UNGA in November 1979 and December 1980 passed resolutions condemning the Camp David Accords that might otherwise have been an initial step forward in the peace process.

It is startling to recall that Israel has been the subject of more critical resolutions in the UNGA than any other nation. In 2008, Israel was the subject of 120 resolutions, compared with forty-seven on Sudan, the second country on the list, with thirty-seven on the Democratic Republic of the Congo, and with thirty-two in Myanmar. While the UNGA has passed over a hundred resolutions on Palestinian refugees, it has not addressed a single one to Jewish refugees from Arab countries. About 800,000 Jews fled or were driven from Arab countries both before the establishment of the state of Israel, and especially after the state was established, leaving behind valuable assets and property, the exact amount of which has been subject to different calculations.[32] Operation Magic Carpet brought almost all of Yemen's 50,000 Jews to Israel. Specific laws in 1950 and 1951 in Iraq deprived Jews of their nationality and their property.[33] The international community has remained silent about the destruction of Jewish communities in Arab lands and the reasons for the absence of Jews in Cairo, Baghdad, Alexandria, Damascus, and Aleppo, once thriving Jewish communities. Few recall that the Jewish population in Egypt, which in 1922 was 80,000, is now less than 100, or that Maimonides, the twelfth century rabbi and philosopher and the first person to write a systematic code of all Jewish law, was also physician to the ruler of Egypt. In 1956 Egypt expelled about 25,000 Jews and seized their property. The issue of Jewish refugees from Arab countries has been largely ignored by the international community. However, the US House of Representatives did in 2008 touch on it by adopting Resolution 185, which resolved that "for any comprehensive Middle East peace agreement to be credible and enduring it must address all outstanding issues relating to the legitimate rights of all refugees, including Jews, Christians, and other populations, displaced from countries in the Middle East."

In similar fashion to its attitude on refugees, the UNGA has been silent on the issue of terrorism. Not only has it been unable to frame an accepted definition of "terrorism." In spite of the creation of the Counter-Terrorism Committee, set up by a unanimous vote approving the Security Council Resolution 1373 on September 28, 2001 to prevent and combat terrorism after the terrorist attacks two weeks earlier on the United States, the United Nations has also been unable to name a single terrorist, terrorist organization, or state sponsor of terrorism.[34] Noticeably, the same Resolution also called for respect for human rights and the rule of law while countering terrorism.

THE UNITED NATIONS HUMAN RIGHTS COUNCIL

The most consistently hostile body has been the UNHRC that replaced the Commission on Human Rights in March 2006. This original Commission was set up as a result of Article 68 of the UN Charter. In its Preamble, the Charter "reaffirms faith in fundamental human rights, in the dignity and worth of the human person." In Article 1 it called for "promoting and encouraging respect for human rights and for fundamental freedoms for all without distinction to race, sex, language or religion." It therefore was to implement the aspirations of the Charter. The concept of human rights had become important in the post World War II world.

But a considerable gap emerged between concept and realty. The rhetoric of human rights has sometimes become a subterfuge for an anti-Israeli agenda. The bias of this original Commission on Human Rights was evident in its proceedings, which between 1946 and 2006, devoted about fifteen per cent of its time and about one-third of its resolutions devoted to specific countries to condemning Israel. Many of those resolutions condemned Israel for violations of human rights. One state, Sudan, which was not similarly condemned in spite of the slavery and genocide in the country, was elected to the Commission in 2004.

One of the more bizarre incidents at the Commission on February 8, 1991 was the speech by Nabila Chaalam, the Syrian representative, who urged members to read the 1985 Arabic book, *The Matzah of Zion*, written by Mustafa Tlass, the Syrian Minister of Defense, which purports to prove the blood libel that Jews kill non-Jews and take their blood to make matzos for Passover. These fulminations appear more bizarre in the light of objective analyses of Syrian government behavior. The 2009 US State Department report on human rights in Syria observed, among other things, numerous serious human rights abuses, arbitrary or unlawful deprivation of life, enforced "disappearance" of some 17,000 persons, "suspicious" deaths, torture of a repulsive kind and abuse, corruption, and arrests for insulting the president and the judicial system. Almost as equally bizarre as the speech by the Syrian representative was the election, by a vote of 33-3 and 17 abstentions, of Libya in 2003 as chair of the Commission, a position it held until 2006.

The UNHRC with a budget of some $150 million in 2009, has a staff of about 1000 working in fifty countries and a High Commissioner for Human Rights. Since 2008, Navanethem Pillay, a South African woman of Tamil descent who served as a judge, and for four years as president at the International Criminal Tribunal for Rwanda, has occupied the position. Her views are not unknown; on January 9, 2009, she argued that Israel was guilty of "egregious violations of human rights." She then called for "credible, independent, and transparent investigations (of the Gaza fighting)…to identify violations and establish responsibilities." Her comment on the killing of Osama bin Laden by US Navy Seals on May 1, 2011 was that in compliance with international law counter-terrorism activity does not allow committing "extra-judicial killings."

UNHRC also has an Advisory Committee of eighteen persons. Among them are at least three seemingly inappropriate individuals, whose impartiality may be questioned. Halima Warzazi, a former Moroccan diplomat, is chair of the Committee. She was instrumental in preventing the censure in 1988 of Saddam Hussein, who had used gas against thousands of Kurds in Halabja. She is well known for her attacks on the United States. Jean Ziegler, Swiss former professor of sociology and socialist politician, is vice-chair of the Committee. In 1989, a year after the Libyan attack on the Pan Am plane at Lockerbie, he was the co-founder, with a $10 million subsidy from Libya, of the "Muammar Gadhafi International Prize for Human Rights." The Prizes have gone to Fidel Castro, Hugo Chavez, Roger Garaudy, a French Holocaust denier, and Louis Farakhan, head of the Nation of Islam. Ziegler, an admirer of Fidel Castro, Che Guevara and other revolutionary political personalities and groups, has been one of Europe's anti-American and anti-Israeli ideologues.[35] The third individual, Miguel d'Escoto Brockmann, former Nicaraguan foreign minister in the Sandinista regime of Daniel Ortega and a former president of the UNGA, 2008-2009, has termed Castro a "World Hero of Solidarity" and accused Israel of being an apartheid state.

In its first five years the UNHRC condemned Israel in thirty-five resolutions (about two-thirds of the total), while the rest of the world was condemned only twelve times. The Council also has Special Sessions. Of the twelve such Sessions devoted to criticisms of individual countries, six were on Israel and the others on the rest of the world. In somewhat extraordinary behavior the Council, when confronted by a draft resolution in 2009 to discuss the killing of 20,000 civilians in Sri Lanka, concluded by praising the Sri Lankan government for its "promotion and protection of all human rights." The Council also set up five fact-finding missions or inquiries. All of them were directed against Israel.

During the 14th session of the Council, 2009-2010, Israel was condemned more times than the rest of the world combined. In 2010 about eighty per cent of the resolutions (twenty-two in number) were concerned with alleged Israeli violations of human rights; the rest were devoted to six other states. Similarly in 2011, by March of that year there were six resolutions on Israel, one on each of four countries, and none on the other 187 nations. One indication of the blatant partiality of the Council was made plain in 1993, when the UN appointed a Special

Rapporteur "to investigate Israel's violations of the principles and bases of international law, international humanitarian law and the Fourth Geneva Convention (of August 1949) ...in the Palestinian territories occupied since 1967." So far five people have held that position. One of these Special Rapporteurs, John Dugard, stated in 2005 that the mandate to investigate did not extend to violations of human rights committed by the Palestinian Authority.

Not surprisingly, in 2009, Libya, a country characterized by the US State Department as engaged in torture, imprisonment of political opponents, and criminalization of homosexuality, was re-elected by 155 of 192 votes to become a member of the UN Human Rights Council. It accepted the statement by Libya that "The Libyan Arab Jamahiriya (rule by the masses) is fully committed to the promotion and protection of human rights principles...including the right to direct participation in public life...it has paid great attention to human rights over the past 30 years." The Council appeared oblivious of the human abuses perpetrated over a forty year period by Libya, particularly its violence against an estimated 1,200 individuals, mostly opponents of the regime who were arrested and killed in 1996, in Tripoli's Abu Salim prison. It did not inquire into the mysterious disappearance in 1978 of the Iman Musa al-Sadr, leader of Shiites in Lebanon, while on a visit to Libya. Nor was the Council concerned with the reality that Libya had no parliament, no trade unions, no political parties, and no real civil society. Nor was it troubled by Libya's involvement in wars in Liberia, Sierra Leone, and other African countries. The country had been under the tyranny of Moammar Gadhafi since he and fellow officers had ousted Libya's King Idris in a bloodless coup in 1969. Gadhafi, who came from a Bedouin family from the Gadhadfa tribe which has dominated the area around Tripoli, referred to himself in grandiose terms as "Imam of all Muslims," "Dean of Arab Rulers" and "King of Africa's Kings." Less grandiosely, he was behind the killing of a British policewoman in London in April 1984, the killing of several Americans and the wounding of 229 people in Berlin in 1986, and was ultimately responsible for the bomb that bought down Pan Am flight 103 in Lockerbie in 1988, killing 270 people, including 190 Americans. Gadhafi had long discriminated against the Libyan minority Berbers, the non-Arab ethnic group of mostly Ibadi

Musims, who were neglected economically and also forbidden to teach the Berber language in their schools or to celebrate Berber festivals and holidays. Nevertheless, Libya, a country of mostly Sunni Muslims, was in 2009 made chair of the planning and the main committees of Durban II, the so-called world conference on racism. More sordidly, Libya, under Gadhafi, became a multi billion dollar kleptocracy in which his family or allies led a lavish life style and had a direct stake in anything valuable, including portfolios of fashionable properties and luxury mansions in Britain and in Austria, shares in publishing houses, and monetary accounts, over $35 billion in banks around the world that are in the names of members of Libyan tribes loyal to the leader. Gadhafi, who was personally involved in lucrative business deals, was able to conceal his money and investments for a long time.

In an act of righteous indignation on February 25, 2011, the UN General Assembly, based on its authority to suspend rights of membership in the UNHRC if a member had committed gross and systematic violations of human rights, suspended the membership of Libya. Gadhafi had by then deployed troops, tanks, fighter jets and helicopters against his own people and killed hundreds of them. His son Saif, in a television video, had brandished a semi-automatic weapon and declared he would do anything to perpetuate his father's regime. The "indignation" of the international organizations was ironic political theater, since a month earlier in January 2011, the universal periodical report of the Council had noted that many countries, including not only North Korea and other non-democratic countries, but also Australia, Canada, and Poland, while expressing some concerns, had spoken of Libya's commitment to and progress in human rights. Even the United States, though troubled by reports of the torture of prisoners and other human rights violations by Libya, supported Libya's "increased engagement with the international community." This view was shared by Harvard Professor Stephen M. Walt, who earlier had written that Libya had been a valuable ally in the "war on terror," and that the remarkable improvement of US-Libyan relations was "one of the few (only?) success stories in recent US-Middle East diplomacy."[36]

A comparison between the attitude of the UNHRC toward Israel and toward the Congo, the scene of countless horrors where between four and five million have been killed in fighting since 1998, is revealing. Even though the US State Department in 2009 reported that in all areas of the Congo the government's human rights record remained poor, and security forces continued to act with impunity, the UNHRC in June 2009 characteristically decided that it would discontinue consideration of the situation in the Democratic Republic of the Congo. Of the thirty-three charges of violations of human rights issued by the Council between 2006 and 2009, twenty-seven have been against Israel. At its eleventh session in 2009, the Council spent six hours in critical discussion of Israel; it spent one minute on the Congo. In another report, Israel was, next to the Islamic Republic of Iran, declared guilty of the largest number of violations of human rights in the world. In early 2010 the Council condemned Israel in five resolutions, while the entire rest of the rest of the world was mentioned in only four resolutions. None of the world's other 187 states were mentioned.

None of this barely disguised partiality or unsubtle hypocrisy is surprising in view of the membership of the UNHRC, which in 2011 included Libya, Saudi Arabia, Angola, Uganda, Qatar, Cuba, China, Kyrgystan, and Burkina Faso, most of whose female population has undergone female genital mutilation. Members are elected on the basis of the five regional group system of the UN, with each group being allotted a certain number of seats. In the UNHRC, the Africa and Asian regional groups have the majority of the forty-seven seats; the majority of those two groups are in the Organization of the Islamic Conference (OIC), the member states of which thus have about seventy per cent of seats allotted to the two regional groups. The OIC has fifty-seven members, fifty-six states and the "State of Palestine" since 1969. Given the attitude of Islamic states on equality of women, it was a striking instance of duplicitous moral principle or theatrical farce for the UN in 2010 to elect Iran to be a member, which it became in March 2011, of its Commission on the Status of Women, which terms itself the principal global policy making body to promote gender equality and advancement of women worldwide. The electors ignored the fact that in Iran women face corporal punishment for wearing the wrong clothes and, even worse, stoning for adultery, in which the female is always considered the guilty party. Iran has joined the Democratic Republic of

Congo on this Commission. What was important was not the issue of the status of women, but increasing the power of the anti-Israeli bloc.

UNESCO AND OTHERS

The United Nations Educational, Scientific, and Cultural Organization (UNESCO) has also been less than impartial in matters referring to Israel. Founded in November 1945, article 1 of its constitution states that its purpose was "to contribute to peace and security by promoting collaboration among nations...to further universal respect for justice, for the rule of law and for the human rights and fundamental freedoms which are affirmed for the peoples of the world." Over the years UNESCO, echoing those countries in which justice, the rule of law and human rights are conspicuously absent, has condemned Israel for "altering the historical features of Jerusalem by its archaeological excavations...and threatening the historical and cultural sites" of the city, a statement that was made despite the fact that its own experts and commissions of inquiry found that the excavations were technically efficient and not harmful to any sites. It denied Israel membership in its European regional group. Archaeological digs have thus become symbols of political machination. As early as November 1974, UNESCO voted to withhold assistance from Israel in the fields of education, science, and culture, because of "Israel's persistent alteration of the historic features of Jerusalem." In 1989 it claimed that "Israel's occupation of Jerusalem" was destroying the holy city by its actions.

In 2009 UNESCO designated Jerusalem as the "capital of Arab culture." In October 2010, UNESCO passed a number of resolutions. One, in response to proposals by Arab member states, and passed by a vote of 44-1-12, called for Jewish landmarks (Rachel's Tomb, near Bethlehem and the Tomb of the Patriarchs, centered around the Cave of the Machpelah (double cave) in Hebron, the site bought by Abraham about 3,800 years ago as a grave for his wife Sarah, himself and their future generations), not to be added to Israel's National Heritage list. Instead, they were declared to be "integral parts of the occupied Palestinian Territories and any unilateral action by the Israeli authorities is to be considered a violation of international law." These landmark historic sites were thus removed from Israeli sovereignty. The declaration also explicitly challenged the connection of the state of Israel to the land in which it exists. UNESCO had forgotten that Hebron was the birthplace of three Jewish Patriarchs, Abraham, Isaac, and Jacob, and three Jewish Matriarchs, Sarah, Rebecca, and Leah, and that the Tomb of the Patriarchs is the oldest Jewish shrine and is generally regarded as the second holiest site in Judaism. Architecturally, the cave, built by Herod the Great, is the only fully surviving Herodian structure from the 1st century B.C. The UNESCO decision also relabeled the Tomb of Rachel, Judaism's third holiest site, as an Islamic mosque. That decision ignored the fact that Hebron contains, in addition to the cave, the tombs of confidants of Kings Saul and David, and of Ruth and Jesse, David's ancestors.

Four other resolutions passed at the same time in 2010 included a demand for Jordanian and Wafk experts to be given access to Israeli work at the Ascent to the Mughrabi Gate which links the Western Wall plaza and the Temple Mount in the Old City of Jerusalem; the right to protest at Israeli excavations on the Al-Aksa Mosque compound in the Old City; a statement of concern about "the harmful impact of the separation Wall" on cultural and educational institutions in the West Bank; and a statement deploring "the continuous blockade on the Gaza Strip." The US was the only dissenting vote in four of the resolutions. Later, UNESCO adopted a resolution that Israel should cease all archeological works in the Old City of Jerusalem.

The partisan nature of UNESCO functioning was shown in October 1980, when Yasser Arafat, an individual not particularly knowledgeable about education, science or culture, was invited to address its General Assembly, held that year in Belgrade. His speech on these subjects was largely confined to denouncing Zionism. In 1982 the UNESCO Conference on Culture in Mexico City sponsored the writing of a Palestinian history from the time of Jesus, thus eliminating Jews from the historical accounts of the area. Consonant with this anti-Israeli bias, Farouk Hosni, artist and Egyptian Minister of Culture for over twenty years, who threatened to burn Israeli books if he found them in Egyptian libraries, was a candidate, though unsuccessful, in 2007 for the directorship of UNESCO. The successful candidate, and the new Director-General of UNESCO, is Irana Bokova, a left-wing Bulgarian politician, who was mostly educated at the Moscow State Institute of International Relations.

The bias against Israel exists not only within the UN but also in other international agencies, such as the International Telecommunication Union conference and the International Atomic Energy Agency. The Red Cross, though it recognized the Turkish crescent and other emblems, arbitrarily discriminated against Israel by refusing recognition of the Magen David Adom (the Red Shield of David) as an emblem and excluding the MDA Society from full participation in the International Red Cross until June 2006. In 2010, after Israel was admitted to the Organization for Economic Co-operation and Development (OECD), it was made the venue for the annual tourism conference of the organization; Israel had agreed that no part of the conference would be held in east Jerusalem, but nevertheless Spain boycotted the meeting.

The lack of partiality regarding Israel has been institutionalized within the structure of the United Nations itself. In 1968 a new unit was established, a UN Special Committee to investigate Israeli practices affecting the human rights of the Palestinian people and other Arabs. The assumption that those rights were being violated by Israel was assumed and decided before any investigation took place. The Committee soon showed its partisan character by its early reports. It condemned Israel "for pillaging of archaeological and cultural property in the occupied territories," and it decided that Israeli practices constituted "grave violations" of the UN Charter. In addition, the UN also set up a Special Rapporteur to investigate Israeli practices. One of the General Assembly's secretarial units, the Division for Palestinian Rights, serves as staff for the UN Committee on the Exercise of the Inalienable Rights of the Palestinian People (CEIRPP), created in 1975. This Division, together with some other UN offices, disseminates information critical of Israel, and has as its main function advocacy of Palestinian rights and the mobilizing of international support for that policy. The CEIRPP in July 2005 endorsed a declaration for a "global campaign of boycotts, divestment and sanctions" against Israel.

Within the UN at large the bias is reinforced by the exclusion of Israel from full UN participation. A very considerable part of the operations of the UN occur in the context of five regional groups. Every member of the UN is a full member of one of these five groups, except Israel, which had for long been excluded from them. The Muslim countries opposed Israeli membership of the Asian group, though "Palestine" is a member. "Palestine" obtained official observer status in the UN in November 1974, and became a super-observer in 1998, able to take part in debates in the General Assembly and to present points of order. The following year attempts were made to deprive Israel of its status as a member of the UN.

Some change in international approval of Israel and understanding of its difficulties has occurred. In 2000 Israel was permitted to become a temporary member, for limited purposes, of the Western Europe and Others Group (WEOG), and in 2004 was made a permanent member. In 2005 the UNGA approved the establishment of an annual Holocaust Remembrance Day, and in January passed a resolution that Holocaust denial could be seen as approval of genocide. In spite of this, Arab newspapers, journals, and books not only persist in Holocaust denial, some even justify the genocide.[37]

ISRAEL AND GAZA

Two important recent examples of international bias are the attitudes regarding the Israeli response to the Hamas shelling in Gaza in 2008, and its action against the flotilla attempting to break the blockade of Gaza in May 2009. Given the "moral conscience" of the world, the general response to the action of Israel, Operation Cast Lead, in December 2008 in Gaza against the forces of Hamas, which had shot what some calculate as 12,000 rockets against about 800,000 Israeli civilians who were within their range, was entirely predictable. Rather than seeing the Israeli action as a legitimate response to aggression, many commentators saw it as an unprecedented use of force and as collective punishment or, in moderated language, as a "disproportionate" attack. Those commentators have not yet defined what a "proportionate" response might be to unprovoked Arab attacks on innocent civilians. Nor have they often referred to the articles in the Hague Regulations and in Protocol 1 of 1977 additional to the Geneva Convention of 1949 which forbid military assets or personnel being placed in populated areas, as Hamas has done. After the flotilla incident in 2009, a Resolution introduced by Pakistan and Sudan titled "The Grave Attacks by Israeli Forces against the Humanitarian Boat Convoy" was adopted and called for an investigation into the actions of Israel. The familiar attitude of the UNHRC in response to this condemnatory Resolution was to report that Israel had committed an outrageous attack, and had engaged in "violence against civilians as part of a deliberate policy;" it also criticized the Israeli legal system for inaction.

THE GOLDSTONE REPORT

A second indictment of Israel came in September 2009 from the Report of the United Nations Fact Finding Mission on the Gaza Conflict, usually referred to as the Goldstone Report, after the name of the chairman, Justice Richard Goldstone, former member of the South African Supreme Court. This Report was the outcome of Resolution S-9/1 of the UN Human Rights Council (UNHRC), which was adopted by 33-1-13 on January 12, 2009, after being introduced by Cuba, Egypt, and Pakistan. It called for an international "fact-finding mission" to investigate "all violations of international human rights law and international humanitarian law by the occupying Power, Israel against the Palestinian people throughout the Occupied Palestinian Territory, particularly in the occupied Gaza Strip due to the current aggression." It also called on Israel not to obstruct the process of investigation and to cooperate fully with the mission.

About this Resolution two observations are pertinent. One is that it assumes an equivalence, moral or otherwise, between the actions of Israel in its self-defense and those of Hamas in Gaza in its sustained barrage of rocket attacks for eight years on innocent Israeli civilians, and its relentless pursuit of the destruction of Israel. The other is that the UNHRC, as we have seen, is not an impartial body concerned as it should be with protecting global human rights. Rather it, like its predecessor the UN Commission on Human Rights, has been a major weapon in promoting the bias exhibited by international organizations towards Israel. This misuse of human rights as a political tool stems from improper application of law, from the political atmosphere and orthodoxy, from the manipulation of facts as a result of non-objective reports, from political opportunism, and from the adoption of double standards.[38]

The bias and unbalanced nature of the UNHRC Resolution is evident in the language. It was passing judgment before any inquiry was held and mostly focused on criticism of Israeli actions, virtually disregarding that it was responding to provocation. The four members of the fact-finding Mission, which was set up on April 3, 2009, were chosen by the president of the UNHRC. Besides the chair, they were Professor Christine Chinkin of the London School of Economics; Hina Jilani, Pakistani lawyer, one of the founders of the Human Rights Commission of Pakistan, and UN Secretary-General's Special Representative on Human Rights Defenders; and Colonel Desmond Travers of the Irish Defense Forces and former Commandant of its Military College. They were not models of impartiality. Professor Chinkin had co-signed a letter to *The Times* of London dated January 11, 2009, saying that Israel's actions in Gaza amounted to "aggression, not self-defense;" those actions were collective punishment of Gaza's citizens. Those actions were contrary to "international humanitarian and human rights law… and are prima facie war crimes." The letter asserted that the "rocket attacks on Israel by Hamas, deplorable as they are, do not in terms of scale and effect amount to an armed attack entitling Israel to rely on self-defense."

Ms. Jilani and Colonel Travers had signed an open letter of March 16, 2009, to UN Secretary-General Ban Ki-moon stating there was a need for an investigation of violations committed by all parties to the Gaza conflict, that they were shocked by the events in Gaza, and that the truth must be established about crimes perpetrated against civilians on both sides. Ms. Jilani had previously been quoted in *The Jurist* in 2005 that "Israel is depriving Palestinians of their basic human rights using security as an excuse."

The distinguished Judge Goldstone accepted the chair of the Mission. The chair had already been refused by Martti Ahtisaari, former president of Finland, and by Mary Robinson, former UN Commissioner for Human Rights. The latter, no friend of Israel, explained in February 2009 her refusal by saying the Resolution only "looked at what Israel had done, and I don't think that's a human rights approach. We need an inquiry to look at the violations of international humanitarian law by all sides." She "felt strongly that the Council's resolution was one-sided and did not permit a balanced approach to determining the situation on the ground." She criticized the UNHRC for adopting resolutions guided not by human rights, but by politics. This pattern of behavior gave credence to the view "that the UN's highest human rights body is inherently anti-Israel."

Goldstone claimed that the mandate of the Commission was to "investigate all violations of international human rights law and international humanitarian law that might have been committed at any time in the context of the military operations" conducted in Gaza between December 27, 2008, and January 18, 2009. In fact, he had softened the UNHRC Resolution, which had limited the mission to investigations of the actions by "the occupying Power, Israel, against the Palestinian people."

The function of the Mission was to inquire into the conduct of the participants in the conflict (*jus in bello*), not to discuss the right to resort to hostilities (*jus ad bellum*). An immediate problem was whether the Fact-Finding Mission should confine itself to uncovering the relevant facts, since it was not a criminal investigation, or whether it should go further and draw conclusions from them. This issue then became related to the assessment of the facts and violations of law on conduct of hostilities in the context of international humanitarian law, rules which can be subject to different interpretations.[39] The critical differences of opinion about Operation Cast Lead, the Israeli military action that began on December 27, 2008, clearly show the problems of assessing armed conflict in relation to international law, and balancing military necessity and protection of civilians in war.[40]

Irrespective of the contentious details of the actions dealt with in the long Report, and criticism of the improper procedures of the Mission, two assumptions are of particular concern; the inherent concentration on alleged Israeli misconduct and bias against Israel in the conflict; and the mistaken view that Israel had not and would not investigation alleged violation of its armed forces. Though it did make minor critical remarks about Hamas, perhaps an attempt at moral equivalence, the main thrust of the 575 page Report was critical of Israel. The Report acknowledged that there was evidence that "Palestinian armed groups committed war crimes, as well as possibly crimes against humanity." It said that "launching (by Hamas) of attacks from or in the vicinity of civilian buildings… are serious violations of the obligation on the armed groups to take constant care to protect civilians from the inherent dangers created by military operations." (para 495).

However, two remarks are pertinent to this statement. The first is that the Report minimized the use that Hamas made of hospitals, mosques, and houses for military purposes. The other, crucial for this analysis, is that more emphasis was put on Israel's actions; the Report stated that Israel "acted disproportionately in its attacks on Gaza in Operation Cast Lead" and had intentionally and deliberately targeted civilians. The strongest statement (para 1690) was its sweeping conclusion that Israel had launched "a deliberately disproportionate attack designed to punish, humiliate and terrorize a civilian population, radically diminish its local economic capacity both to work and to provide for itself, and to force upon it an ever increasing sense of dependency and vulnerability."

The Report also held there were major flaws in Israel's system of investigations and prosecutions of serious violations of human rights and humanitarian law. This is a startling conclusion, because Israel had indeed been concerned with investigating its military actions. A notable example was the decision of the Israeli Supreme Court, sitting as the High Court in 1996, that approved of the procedures. It held that the normal command investigations of the IDF were the appropriate way to deal with an inquiry into an incident that had occurred during military operations (Moir Haim v. Israel Defense Forces, HCJ 6208/96).

In an extraordinary way the Report went further than the infamous 1975 "Zionism is Racism" Resolution of the UNGA, which was "revoked" by a vote of 111-25-13, in indirect fashion on December 19, 1991. It went beyond its mandated "fact-finding" mission by expressing legal opinions. It called for criminal charges to be brought against Israelis through the use of universal jurisdiction, and also recommended that the UN Security Council refer "the situation in Gaza to the prosecutor of the International Criminal Court," to which Israel does not belong, if Israel did not conduct its own investigation.

The prejudgment evident in the mandate given to the inquiry was echoed in the Goldstone Report, when it declared Israel's "guilt," accusing it of violating international law through the use of "disproportionate force" and deliberate targeting of civilians. The Report virtually disregarded the Hamas provocations; the use that Hamas made of civilians as human shields, its operations from schools, mosques, and hospitals; its use of humanitarian symbols, such as ambulances, for military purposes; the assistance given to Hamas by Syria and Iran; and the considerable efforts of the Israeli military to minimize civilian casualties in Operation Cast Lead. It ignored the reality of the strategy of Hamas. Surprisingly, though there was ample photographic evidence to the contrary, it found no evidence that Palestinian combatants had mingled with the civilian population to shield themselves from attack. It also found no evidence that Palestinian armed groups, which had launched rockets from urban areas, had done so in order to be shielded from Israeli counter-attacks. Even more surprisingly, the Report of the "fact-finding" mission alluded to Israel's political policy. The Operation (para 1674) "fits into a continuum of policies aimed at pursuing Israel's political objectives with regard to Gaza and the Occupied Palestinian Territory as a whole." The Report was critical of Israel's objectives, of its blockade of the Gaza Strip, and of the behavior in the West Bank. Indeed, the very title of the Report presented to the UNHRC on September 15, 2009 is "Human Rights in Palestine and Other Occupied Arab Territories: Report of the United Nations Fact Finding Mission on the Gaza Conflict." It was approved, by a vote of 25-6, by the UNHRC, and forwarded to the UNGA.

Perhaps the kindest remark to make of the Goldstone Report is that it is a parody of the Queen in *Alice in Wonderland,* "Sentence first-verdict afterward." The Goldstone Report was endorsed by the UNGA, by a vote of 114-18-44 on November 5, 2009, and approved by the UNGA, 98-8-33, in a vote conducted on February 26, 2010, during a snowstorm which prevented some delegates from attending. The vote called for states to conduct investigations into violations of international humanitarian and international human rights law. The Report held that major structural flaws existed regarding Israel's system of investigations and prosecutions of serious violations of human rights and humanitarian law. Both the Report and the UNGA refused to acknowledge that Israel had in fact, taken such investigations seriously, in the High Court Moir Haim case in 1996, in the Winograd Commission Report of January 2008, and was to do so in the Turkel Commission Report of January 2011.

The Goldstone farce continued with an astonishing mea culpa by the author of the 575 page Report. Goldstone, in an article in the *Washington Post* on April 1, 2011, confessed "We know a lot more today about what happened in the Gaza War of 2008-09 than we did when I chaired the fact-finding mission...If I had known then what I know now, the Goldstone Report would have been a different document." He disavowed the main point of the Report and now accepted that Israel had not engaged in intentional killing of Palestinian civilians; "civilians were not intentionally targeted as a matter of policy." Goldstone had accepted the unverified Palestinian testimony by Hamas, a group that does not tolerate dissent, and others to his committee as valid evidence. He confessed that the allegations against Israel were based on situations "where our fact-finding mission had no evidence on which to draw any other reasonable conclusion." He had essentially ignored or minimized the nature of Hamas in Gaza, and its ideological call for the elimination of Israel. He had not recognized the deception of Hamas fighters dressed as civilians or their use of civilians for military purposes; this recognition would have made invalid the charge against Israel of attacking civilians. He appeared unaware of the use made by Palestinian fighters of civilians, especially women and children, to accompany them or to act as human shields in order to protect themselves from attack by Israel. His report had failed to make the distinction, crucial in international law and analyzed in a later chapter, between fighters and civilians, and had misapplied the concept of proportionality. The report had also misapplied the concept of "proportionality."

Goldstone had hoped, unrealistically, that Hamas would conduct its own investigations of its actions, and that it would curtail its attacks on Israel; "sadly that has not been the case." What is most surprising in the Mission chaired by an astute jurist was the failure to recognize the political context, the conflict between a democratic state and a terrorist organization. The astute Goldstone, however, did acknowledge in his article of April 1, the character of the UNHRC "whose history of bias against Israel cannot be doubted." He did not comment on the statement by High Commissioner Navi Pillay to the UN Security Council on July 7, 2010, that it supported the recommendations of the Goldstone Report. She was reiterating the call by the UNHRC for the Security Council to consider action on the Report, including "referral of the situation in the Occupied Palestinian Territory to the prosecutor of the International Criminal Court."

After receiving the Report, the UN Human Rights Council voted on November 5, 2009 to endorse it and to send it to the UN General Assembly with the recommendation that the UN Security Council be asked to send it to lawyers at the International Criminal Court for prosecution of Israel for war crimes and crimes against humanity. The UNHRC endorsed it again in February 26, 2010.

Belatedly, Goldstone recognized the essential asymmetrical behavior, both during and after the fighting, of the two sides after the completion of two reports. The first came from the legal corps of the IDF and the Israeli military police which had investigated all allegations of misconduct during the Gaza conflict and reported its findings to the UNHRC. The second was the final report by the UN committee of independent experts, chaired by former New York judge Mary McGowan Davis, that followed up on the recommendations of the

Goldstone Report. That report, issued on January 24, 2011, made clear that Israel had investigated over 400 allegations of operational misconduct in Gaza, while Hamas had not conducted any investigations into the launching of rocket and mortar attacks against Israel. Civilians were not intentionally targeted by Israel as a matter of policy, though some were killed by military mistake. No accountability was obtained from Hamas, which had made no effort to investigate the allegations of its war crimes and possible crimes against humanity.

MAKING WAVES

Following the Goldstone Report, another highly critical statement on Israel was issued by the UN Human Rights Council in 2010, which discussed the incident in May 2009 concerning the flotilla that attempted to break the blockade of Gaza. To prevent this, Israeli forces intercepted the Turkish registered ship *Mavi Marmara* which was carrying some sophisticated arms, as well as steel pipes and slingshots. With these weapons, this ship of "peace" attacked Israeli naval commandos. Nine passengers were killed and several Israeli soldiers were wounded during the fighting. Though the fact finding Report by the Council on the incident did recognize that the primary object of the flotilla was political, not humanitarian, it nevertheless concluded that since the blockade was inflicting "disproportionate damage on the civilian population in the Gaza Strip" the interception of the flotilla by Israel could not be justified and therefore had to be considered illegal. Going far beyond its mandate, the Council Report editorialized about the "regrettable reputation which Israel has for impunity and intransigence in international affairs." More regrettable was the political bias exhibited by the Council. Not coincidentally, the flotilla event was the most covered news story about the Middle East in 2010. Less covered was the declaration by the delegation of people connected with *Mavi Marmara* at their meeting with President Ahmadinejad in Teheran in February 2011, that its purpose was to build a Middle East without Israel and America.

Was the Israeli action in accordance with international law? In June 2010 the Turkel Commission, headed by the former Israeli Supreme Court Justice Jacob Turkel and including three other Israelis and two international observers, one of whom was Lord Trimble who was accorded the 1998 Nobel Peace Prize Award, was set up in response to demands for an international investigation into the Gaza flotilla event. In its report issued in January 2011, the Commission decided that the Israeli naval blockade of the Gaza Strip, in view of the security circumstances and Israel's efforts to comply with its humanitarian obligations, was within the bounds of the rules of international law. The purpose of the blockade was primarily a military-security one, and did not constitute collective punishment of the Gaza population, though "the affected population will generally feel the effects" of pressure. Though the economic life of the civilian population of Gaza might be adversely affected as a result of economic warfare, this did not constitute collective punishment. The Commission also defended the action of the Israeli forces who acted against the extensive and manipulated violence launched by the participants in the flotilla.

Those participants claimed they were trying to bring publicity to the humanitarian situation regarding Palestinians in Gaza. But among them were about forty activists who were armed with a wide array of weapons, including firearms, capable of causing death or serious injury. The Commission also held, what is more important for the thrust of this book, that the Gaza Strip was not occupied territory, that Israel did not maintain total control over land access to Gaza, and that neither control of airspace nor a naval blockade constituted effective control over the territory.

The international community at large, as well as the UN, showed its partisan nature by the immediate condemnation of Israel for its action in boarding the Gaza bound ship. However, this hostility was not shown by a report, the Palmer report named for Geoffrey Palmer, former New Zealand prime minister and chair of the inquiry commissioned by the UN Secretary-General to investigate the flotilla incident, which was issued in September 2011, and was a more balanced statement than the usual UN documents concerning Israel. The report rebutted many of the allegations made about Israeli behavior. Though it held that Israel had used excessive and unreasonable force in the action, it also held that the naval blockade of Gaza was legal and that Israel was entitled to take reasonable steps to prevent the influx of weapons into Gaza. Hamas had been firing projectiles into Israel or permitting others to do so. The report did not accept the view that the flotilla was engaged in a humanitarian mission. Though the report was largely a vindication of Israeli action, the immediate response of the Turkish government was to withdraw its ambassador from Israel and to expel the Israeli ambassador from Turkey.

Even before the Palmer report, it was clear that international critics had ignored two relevant issues. One is the intransigent belligerence of Hamas, which has never been a part of the PLO and does not regard the PLO as "the sole legitimate representative of the Palestinian people," and thus does not accept any agreements made by the PLO with Israel. Hamas was founded in 1987, as an offshoot of the Muslim Brotherhood (Ikhwan) with the aim of "liberating Palestine from Israeli oppression" and establishing an Islamic state from the Mediterranean Sea to the Jordan River. It contains a military wing, the al-Qassam Brigades, which to some extent operates independently from the main organization. Hamas was listed in 1993 as a terrorist group by the United States, and in 2003 by European countries.

Hamas, now in control of Gaza, still refuses to recognize the legitimacy of Israel. Indeed, the Hamas Charter, written in 1988, declares that "the struggle is against the Jews," that the whole of historic Palestine is an Islamic endowment, and that it is a religious duty to liberate it by jihad. Mahmoud al-Zahhar, co-founder and leader of Hamas, in an interview on June 23, 2010, was unequivocal on this point, "Our ultimate plan is to have Palestine in its entirety...We will not recognize the Israeli enemy." The 12,000 rockets and mortar shells that were fired from Gaza at Israeli civilians between 2000 and 2008 were usually launched from within Gaza's densely populated civilian areas, near schools and UN facilities, contrary to international law. Hamas' arsenal of weapons now includes long-range rockets, with greater precision than earlier missiles. They now include the Iranian Fajr-5, with a range of forty-five miles, which is capable of hitting Israel's main cities, surface to air missiles, within ninety seconds of launching. It also includes the Russian AT-5 Kornet anti-tank guided missile, which can penetrate the armor of an Israeli Merkava tank.

In addition to its launching of rockets, Hamas was also responsible for suicide bombings against Israeli civilians on buses, in markets, and other public places. Moreover, in its efforts to be the dominant power among Palestinians, Hamas has attacked fellow Arabs; in May 2007 it initiated a coup against the Fatah executive headquarters in Gaza, killing thousands and executing political opponents.

A second relevant fact, largely ignored by critics of Israel, is that the ship had been sponsored by the Turkish group IHH (Insani Yardim Vakfi), a member of the "Union of the Good," an Islamic umbrella organization based in Saudi Arabia. It was established in 1992, euphemistically termed "Humanitarian Relief Fund" and labeled as a charity, but it is connected with the Muslim Brotherhood, al-Qaeda, and other terrorist organizations, and is opposed to the existence of the state of Israel. It has provided assistance to Islamic militias in Afghanistan, Chechnya, and Bosnia. Like organizations such as Hamas and Hezbollah, the IHH in addition to its militant activities, does provide some effective social and other services for people, in order to develop and sustain their loyalty. In the case of the Gaza flotilla, the IHH participation was a deliberate attempt to provoke Israel, rather than a genuine humanitarian mission. The real purpose of the flotilla was to challenge Israel's policy regarding the Gaza Strip, rather than convey humanitarian aid. This was borne out by the fact that the flotilla did not carry a single crate of humanitarian goods. In what might be regarded as a parody of moral outrage, UN Secretary-General Ban Ki-moon, echoing the words of the police chief in the film Casablanca, said "I am shocked by reports of killing of people in boats carrying supplies to Gaza." He was curiously silent about the copious availability of supplies and the conspicuous consumption displayed in the new large, 9,700 square feet air-conditioned shopping mall in Gaza. Nor was the international media conspicuously vocal about the 800 or more tunnels built into Egypt by Hamas, allowing it to smuggle in food, fuel, cement, and luxury items. No humanitarian emergency was apparent.

Other commentators have been similarly "shocked" by the imposition of an Israeli blockade, the aim of which was not to stop foodstuffs from entering Gaza, but to prevent Hamas from obtaining weapons and ammunition. Yet historical precedents for blockades date back to the fifth century B.C., when Spartan forces surrounded Athens first by land and then, successfully, by sea. Similar actions followed throughout history: Alexander the Great blockaded Tyre in 332 B.C.; the Ottoman Empire blockaded Constantinople; the Dutch Republic blockaded the Scheldt; Britain blockaded France during the war with Napoleon, and the United States in 1812; the Union blockaded the coasts of the Confederacy during the Civil War; the United States blockaded San Juan in 1898 during the Spanish American war; during World War I and II the Allies blockaded Germany and Japan; Egypt blockaded the Straits of Tiran in 1956 and Israel in 1973: the US, under President Kennedy, blockaded Cuba; India began a blockade, when Bangladesh tried to secede from Pakistan; and during the Iran-Iraq war, 1980-1988, there was a blockade of the Shatt el-Arab.

Today, a naval blockade to prevent weapons and materials from reaching a party engaged in armed conflict is acknowledged as appropriate if it is conducted in accordance with the rules of international law and consideration of the humanitarian needs of the population involved.

Chapter 3

Lawfare and Universal Jurisdiction

It is a truism that law and judicial systems have historically been employed to achieve political or military objectives. What is particularly disconcerting in recent years has been the exploitation of law for negative purposes, above all for condemnations of Israel. This can be summarized in two ways: lawfare, the pursuit of strategic aims and political objectives, and the waging of war, by legal methods as a substitute for traditional military means to defeat or weaken the enemy; and universal jurisdiction, the ability of national courts to investigate or hear charges of "war crimes" or crimes against humanity allegedly committed in other countries. Henry Kissinger gave early warning of the problem caused by the increasing trend to use courts to prosecute alleged violations of human rights, and of the submitting of international politics to judicial procedures: the danger was the risk of "substituting the tyranny of judges for that of governments; historically, the dictatorship of the virtuous has often led to inquisitions and even witch-hunts."[41]

Lawfare, a term which apparently was first used in an article written by two Australians in 1975, has been defined, particularly by military lawyers, in various ways.[42] It can indicate the use of law as a weapon of war, as a means of pursuing a strategic objective, the traditional domain of warfare, through legal mechanisms. A useful starting point is to see lawfare as a strategy and tactic of using, and more often misusing, the law as a substitute for traditional military means to achieve an objective.

Often it has become a travesty of due process and of the rule of law. The strategy and tactics are the modern version of the principle of the Prussian military theorist Carl von Clausewitz, the continuation of war by legal means.[43] It was understandable that after the horrors of World War II some regulations would be made, through international law, to constrain military actions by states, to use universal codes of conduct and human rights to put limits of a normative kind on the use of military power, and to add to the laws governing military occupation. It is also apparent that political and military leaders of democratic countries, concerned with the degree of public support for their actions, are aware in the contemporary climate that the support might decline if public opinion believes that war is being conducted in an unfair, inhumane, or iniquitous fashion. Equally apparent is the present reality that lawfare is being used by Arabs and their supporters not only to make Israel's military response to attacks more difficult, but also in increasing mode to weaken international respect for the country. Thus, there are inaccurate reports by international bodies of "massacres" by Israeli forces; allegations of war crimes; campaigns for boycott, divestment, and sanctions; and, in contravention of the Geneva Conventions, use by Palestinians of civilians, some of whom become casualties when Israel responds to terrorist attacks, behavior which leads to criticism of Israel.

However desirable the intent to use international law to obtain general desirable conduct and behavior concerning the use of force or to punish violators of human rights, a number of practical problems have arisen, in addition to a general theoretical issue. This last issue, beyond the scope of this book, is the question whether international law sanctions the right of humanitarian intervention, including the use or threat of force, by a state or group of states to protect basic human rights of persons who are subjects or residents of another state.[44] A liberal view would be that the "legitimization of humanitarian intervention is a natural concomitant of human rights law."[45] This suggests that the international community has an obligation to intervene to stop or to prevent atrocities, as in Rwanda or Bosnia, and in Middle East countries.

Three issues arise. The first is the compatibility of this obligation with Declarations of the UN General Assembly, including Resolution 2131(XX) of December 21, 1965, and A/Res/36/103 of December 9,

1981, that no state or group of states has the right to intervene in any form or for any reason whatsoever in the internal or external affairs of other states. Related to this is a second problem that an ideology of humanitarian intervention may not be consonant with the principle of national self-determination. Intervention, in the context of civil war or internal upheaval, may result in a regime change or introduction of different political or cultural values. The third issue is the question of whether foreign policy of the intervening country should be motivated by moral outrage as well as by strategic national interests. Moral questions are inevitably related to considerations of power politics. The choice has to be made about the desirability of, and the response to, intervention to bring about desirable change in principles and values, especially in Middle Eastern countries where regions have brutalized their own citizens and where cultural and social modernization has been slow to develop, and where religion may have been perverted to some extent to encourage fanaticism.[46] Western countries have to balance an effective and strong policy with the need not to appear arrogant and colonial.

The first practical problem is that the restrictions imposed by international law on military actions have produced problems rather than solutions, as lawfare has affected actions and become a decisive element in 21st century conflicts. Lawfare, in both a strategic and tactical sense, has been used to obtain a victory or to impose constraints on an opponent. Strategically, lawfare has been used to stop the building of the separation fence in the West Bank, to condemn the Israeli blockade of Gaza, and to block the adoption of a general prohibition of terrorism in the UN General Assembly. Tactically, lawfare has been used by Palestinians to justify use of civilians for military purposes, false reports of massacres, and misleading reports of alleged war crimes.[47] In all these ways the traditional rule of law concept has given way to misuse of the law, the abuse of law for the benefit of a particular party to a conflict, thereby discrediting the authority of the international legal system.

In discussing the NATO campaign in the Balkan War in the late 1990s, Richard Betts asserted that NATO's "hyperlegalism" made the conflict "reminiscent of the quaint norms of premodern war." The NATO lawyers put constraints even on the preparations for action. The direct role played by lawyers in managing combat operations in the campaign and trying to avoid allegations of violations of the laws of war, was so considerable that it meant, in effect, that they became tactical commanders.[48] To avoid such allegations, in recent years, Israeli army units have had specially trained teams equipped with video cameras and tape recorders to document ongoing military action. The growing problem was enunciated by the Commission, headed by the retired Judge Eliyahu Winograd, and set up to examine the events before and during the 2006 Israeli War with Lebanon. It reported in April 2007, not only on problems in the Israeli political and military decision making process, but also on the issue of legal advice during military operations. It expressed concern over the increasing reliance on legal advisers, "judicialization," which might shift responsibility from commanding officers to advisers and thus divert the attention of military commanders from operational matters.

The new international law is also being used as a weapon against democratic countries, such as the United States and Israel, through the setting of unrealistic standards, containing unrealistic norms in conflict, especially about collateral damage, which make military actions more difficult.[49] Moreover, the negative aspects of lawfare are manifest not only in the realm of military conduct, but also in restrictions on behavior customary in democratic countries. Laws have been used to silence and punish free speech when it is critical of radical Islam or terrorism. Blasphemy laws have made it a libel offense to criticize Islam or the Prophet Muhammad. Such criticisms are said to be hate speech or defamation of religion, a subject dealt with in a later chapter.

The new international laws have made the countering of terrorist aggression more difficult by using concepts such as disproportionate or inhumane behavior to prevent action. It was noticeable that the Israeli Defense Forces in Operation Cast Lead, in its attempt in 2008 to counter terrorism from Gaza, sought to minimize civilian casualties in a number of ways: by dropping hundreds of thousands of leaflets to warn inhabitants to leave areas it intended to attack; making over a hundred thousand telephone calls; and by radio broadcasts.[50] Israeli observation of the international law restrictions not to attack civilian places meant it was handicapped by the realities that the Gaza-based leadership was secreted in underground housing underneath the largest hospital in Gaza, and by the use by Hamas of mosques as armories, assembly points for fighters and command and control centers.

International and Palestinian groups, and Western non-governmental organizations (NGOs) claiming to promote human rights and humanitarian concerns, such as Oxfam, Christian Aid, and War on Want, have pursued political goals aimed at demonizing and delegitimating the State of Israel by using international law. Other NGOs, consciously or inadvertently, may contribute to that end. One example of this is the Interchurch Organization for Development Cooperation set up in the Netherlands in 1964 to provide assistance in social services and economic development to over fifty countries in the world. It is financed by the Government of the Netherlands and the European Commission of the European Union, and in its turn since 2007 has contributed to the financing of Electronic Intifada which states openly that it publishes information about the Israeli-Palestinian conflict from the Palestinian perspective. In his writings the executive director of this group, Ali Abunimah, equates Israel to Nazi Germany and compares the Israeli press to *Der Stürmer*, the obscene antisemitic weekly tabloid published in Germany by Julius Streicher from 1923-1945, which called for the extermination of Jews.

The Western groups, with their singular compassion for what they perceive as the sufferings of Palestinians, have made Israel a scapegoat, foisting on it the supposed past sins of Western imperialism, fascism, and racism.[51] This attitude may kindly be defined as the politics of pity, or less benignly as masochistic gratification in blaming their own democratic civilization in which Israel is included. These NGOs have in recent years been playing an increasingly important role in influencing international relations, and in taking advantage of the increase in legislation and jurisprudence and in international legal institutions such as the International Criminal Court (ICC).

The ICC was created in 1998 by the Rome Statute which was adopted, 120-7, at a diplomatic conference convened by the United Nations General Assembly, and came into force in July 2002. Its purpose is stated to be to investigate and exercise jurisdiction over core international crimes; genocide, crimes against humanity, and war crimes.[52] Israel did not ratify either the Rome Statute, or the ICC, largely because the Statute included in its definition of war crimes an article referring to the transfer by an occupying power of some of its civilian population into territory it occupies. Israel feared that every action by Israeli personnel regarding occupation could henceforth be investigated to see if it were a war crime or a serious breach of humanitarian law, with charges brought against its officials under the rubric of universal jurisdiction.

UNIVERSAL JURISDICTION

Universal jurisdiction stems from the historic need for countries to be able to deal with pirates, and more recently, perpetrators of crimes against humanity, or violators of human rights. The idea of the United Nations organization really occurred on January 1, 1942, in Washington, when twenty-six Allied countries, led by President Roosevelt and Prime Minister Churchill, issued a declaration to pursue the war against Germany, Italy, and Japan. The preamble of the declaration justified the call for complete victory over the enemies by claiming, among other matters, that it was essential "to preserve human rights and justice in their own lands as well as in other lands." In his State of the Union Address to Congress on January 6, 1941, Roosevelt had ended by saying "Freedom means the supremacy of human rights everywhere." The freedom of which he spoke would be "a definite basis for a kind of world attainable in our time and generation." The assertion of human rights was to become prominent in the agenda of the international community, though also misused in practice.

Speaking about the 1942 declaration Roosevelt uttered the phrase "United Nations" to describe the Allied military coalition. One immediate practical result was to enable the United States to send supplies to Britain and the Soviet Union as part of the Lend-Lease Agreement. Two other results followed. One was a statement accusing Germany of massacring Jews in Poland, perhaps the first acknowledgement of genocide by the Nazis. The other was the first multilateral agreement on a range of international crimes. The Allies agreed on the preservation of human rights and justice in their own countries as well as in other lands. Seventeen countries in October 1943 set up the United Nations War Crimes Commission (UNWCC) to investigate war crimes, including those perpetrated by rulers against their own citizens, and to help prepare indictments. It could not itself prosecute war criminals, but presented lists of those accused to member states; these amounted to eighty lists with over 36,000 suspected individuals. The UNWCC, which lasted until 1948, went beyond the principle of non-interference in the domestic affairs of individual countries by formulating principles relating to the commission of war crimes and the liability of perpetrators.[53] It argued that the category of war crimes should include acts committed by rulers against their own subjects. But as a result of the conflicts and struggles in post-war international politics, no consensus was reached on whether moral aspirations could be regarded as a source of law.[54] Nevertheless, the issue of human rights has been used rhetorically as a measure and standard of international morality, as a universal principle applicable to all peoples and cultures. This remains the case in spite of the gap between these lofty international aspirations and the reality of abuses and brutal practices in individual countries.[55]

An important moment in the implementation of universal jurisdiction were the Nuremberg Tribunals, 1945-46, which, in a form beyond national courts, tried war criminals of the Axis countries, primarily Nazi Germany, for violations of international law and the laws of war. Since then, international legal prescriptions applying directly to individuals as well as to states have been established against violations of human rights. With great, if pious, expectations, compliance with human rights was supposed to become a major normative feature of the conduct of states.

Now in recent years, universal jurisdiction has been regarded as a method ostensibly to be used to promote not only the broadening of human rights, but also international justice in general. Some legal theorists, in the search for a just society, have thus argued for "transitional or transnational justice," allowing judicial decisions to be grounded on treaties, laws, and court decisions of other countries or academic writings.[56] This point of view became better known with the creation of two *ad hoc* tribunals, the International Criminal Tribunal for the former Yugoslavia in 1993, and a similar Tribunal for Rwanda in 1994. These were followed by a Special Court for Sierra Leone in 2002, a Court of Cambodia, and a Special Tribunal for Lebanon in 2007, which has been slow to function. These tribunals are not only slow to act, but are also expensive, largely because they require a considerable number of investigators on the ground. They are likely to be limited in number, partly because a prosecutor can investigate only at the request of the country involved or of the UN Security Council, and partly because of the problem of entering a war zone. What is recently important in international law is the movement from war crimes trials to concentration on serious violations of human rights, on crimes against humanity, and genocide.

The view that abuses of human rights and war crimes should be investigated has become more pronounced. Since the International Criminal Court in The Hague possesses limited jurisdiction, an alternative method is to allow individual states to investigate alleged abuses on the basis of universal jurisdiction. This principle allows a national court in a particular state, rather than an international court, to adjudicate actions and serious crimes committed by foreigners outside the territory of that state regardless of their nationality; it is applicable to actions considered to be of exceptional gravity that affect the fundamental interests of the international community as a whole.[57]

States can start criminal procedures against individuals accused of international crimes, can investigate, and can bring the accused to trial, going beyond the normal practice for states to have jurisdiction only over crimes committed in their own territory. By this method national court cases have been brought against dictators such as Augusto Pinochet of Chile and some of those responsible for the massacres in Rwanda. The case against Hissène Habré, former leader of Chad for eight years during which he is alleged to have been responsible for 40,000 politically motivated murders and 200,000 cases of torture, was considered in Senegal.

The concern with human rights was admirably illustrated with international intervention in rogue states such as Somalia and the former Yugoslavia. However, the essential problem with universal jurisdiction is the fact it is being abused, especially by the cynical manipulation of the concept of the rule of law. The claim to uphold human rights became a rationale for anti-colonialism. British Law Lord Nicolas Browne-Wilkinson was prescient about the concept of universal jurisprudence: he wrote that "If the law were to be so established, states antipathetic to Western powers would be likely to seize both active and retired officials and military personnel of such Western powers and stage a show trial for alleged international crimes."[58]

Lord Browne-Wilkinson was rightly concerned. Investigative procedures are being used for political ends. The principle target of these procedures has been Israel. One example is the suit in Madrid in 2008, filed by a Palestinian non-governmental organization which asked for arrest warrants against Israeli officers alleged to have been involved in the killing of a Hamas leader in Gaza. A number of similar cases have been filed in various European countries, in the United States, and in New Zealand. Instead of using violence and traditional weapons, groups have sought to intimidate and silence opponents and to lessen the ability of democracies to defend their systems against terrorism by using prosecutions, civil and criminal, in the courts as a battlefield.[59] These lawsuits have been used to wage legal battles not only against politicians and officials, groups supportive of Israel, and those acting to counter terrorist activity, but also against those who criticize the activity of terrorists in their violation of human rights, and question the sources of their financing. Manipulating the terminology of human rights, they attempt to prevent or limit free speech or legitimate criticism of religious extremism or Islamic terrorism made in statements and publications by people in democratic systems. The hidden agenda behind the use of lawfare against Israel is to limit the ability of the Israeli defense forces to defend the country against terrorism and respond effectively against attacks on its citizens. More generally, by the constant repetition of falsehoods, it reduces, even eliminates, respect for due process of law.

In a major way, those hostile to Israel have begun exploiting the courts, often in frivolous suits, in European countries and in North

America. They have harassed Israeli civil and military officials, and also companies, groups and individuals friendly to Israel by using civil lawsuits and criminal complaints for alleged violations of international law, behavior as "war criminals" or perpetrators of international crimes against the Palestinian people. They have attempted to have the charity status and tax exemptions of bodies giving financial assistance to Israel removed.

These critics refuse to acknowledge that various codes of international law allow all states to restrict rights for purposes of "control and security," "public order and safety," and "national security, public order, public health or morals or the rights and freedom of others." The codes include the Fourth Geneva Convention, Hague Convention, and the International Covenant on Civil and Political Rights. They argue either that Israel cannot claim the "inherent right of individual or collective self-defense if an armed attack occurs against a Member of the United Nations," which is enshrined in Article 51 of the UN Charter, if it responds to attacks in occupied territory, or that such Israeli actions are violations of international law.

Those actions have sometimes been criticized as violations of Israel's own moral principles about the use of force, and as being outside the rule of law. First, even admitting that the concept of "just war" lacks clear definition regarding the nature of targets chosen and the acceptable and proportionate degree of response to attacks, Israel can fairly claim, as in case of Operation Cast Lead, that its offensive in retaliation against Hamas, when Hamas launched rockets from Gaza against Israeli citizens, was not only justifiable but an example of the international law concept, *jus in bello*. Though some have criticized the behavior of the Israel Defense Forces, and doubtless some aberrant behavior did occur, it is still largely true that the IDF retains and tries to adhere to its code of military conduct, *Tohar HaNeshek* (purity of arms), meaning that Israeli soldiers will not use force against non-combatants and prisoners of war, and will do all they can to avoid causing harm to civilian lives, bodies, dignity, and property. During Operation Cast Lead, the IDF distributed leaflets to civilians in Gaza saying they should leave a potential conflict area. Unlike its adversaries, Israel, in this non-classic war situation, tried to minimize collateral damage. Under the Israeli

Law of Armed Conduct, members of the Judge Advocate General officer corps can investigate and bring criminal charges against fellow soldiers for committing war crimes. Military experts such as Colonel Richard Kemp, a former commander of British troops in Afghanistan, and Anthony Cordesman of the Center for Strategic and International Studies have held that the performance in 2009 of the IDF in Gaza was an illustration of an attempt to avoid civilian casualties. Indeed, Colonel Kemp made a striking statement about the operation of the Israel Defense Forces in Operation Cast Lead in Gaza. In a broadcast on the BBC on January 9, 2009, he said, "I don't think there's ever been a time in the history of warfare when any army has made more efforts to reduce civilian casualties and deaths of innocent people than the IDF is doing today in Gaza." In remarks to the UNHRC on October 16, 2009, Colonel Kemp repeated his point; "The IDF did more to safeguard the rights of civilians in a combat zone than any army in the history of warfare."

Though Israel has been accused of acting in defiance of the rule of law, the behavior of its authorities suggests otherwise. All persons detained as a result of hostilities and warfare have a right of access to counsel and to independent courts. The Israeli judiciary reviews the cases and, where appropriate, orders the release of the detainee. In May 2002, in operations in the West Bank, about 6,500 were detained; 5,000 were released and the others had a speedy trial.

PARTISANSHIP BY LAW

It is now a familiar occurrence for the law of libel to be used, or threatened to be used, to intimidate Israelis and defenders of Israel. Punishment and penalties have been called for in international forums through this misuse of international law, and by the use of universal jurisdiction statutes in courts in over 125 countries including Britain, Canada, Spain, Netherlands, New Zealand, Switzerland, Belgium, and the United States. One lawsuit in Belgium in 2001 related to the events in 1982, when Christian Phalangists, a Maronite group, retaliating for the assassination of their leader Bashir Gemayel two days earlier, killed

800 Palestinians in the Sabra and Shatila camps in Beirut. Ariel Sharon, Israeli Minister of Defense at the time, and who was obliged to resign from the post after criticism by the Israeli Kahan commission of inquiry report of February 1985, and Israeli military leaders were accused in this lawsuit of grave violations of international humanitarian law (the law of armed conflict), genocide, crimes against humanity, and war crimes. The case was ended when, after some legal maneuvering, the law incorporating international crimes into the Belgian Criminal Code was repealed in August 2003.

Court warrants, or applications for them, have been sought in a number of European countries for Israeli public figures, including the Israeli President, Foreign Minister, Defense Minister, Chief of Staff of the IDF, Director of the General Security Service, and military leaders, as well as heads of business corporations. A few examples suffice. Doron Almog, former head of the IDF Southern Command, could not leave his plane in London in September 2005 for fear of being arrested on a warrant for violating the Geneva Convention in connection with the destruction of some buildings in Gaza. Moshe Ya'alon, former IDF Chief of Staff, cancelled a trip to London in 2009 for fear of being charged with war crimes. A Spanish court in 2009 considered, but did not conduct, an official inquiry into charges against seven Israeli officials for their role in the killing of the military leader of the Hamas organization. In July 2009 the National Court of Spain issued arrest warrants against six Israelis, including Binyamin Ben-Eliezer, former Defense Minister, for allegations of war crimes committed in 2002, and after. British magistrates in December 2009 issued a warrant against Tzipi Livni, leader of the Israeli Kadima party, former Foreign Minister and for a short time Prime Minister, for alleged war crimes committed in the military operation in Gaza. The issuance of the warrant, which did not need a prosecuting lawyer, prevented her from entering Britain and accepting an invitation to speak at an event in London. The groups seeking British court authority for the arrest of Israeli leaders based their argument on the principle of "universal jurisdiction." According to the 2001 International Criminal Court Act, an arrest warrant for those politicians or officials can be granted by a British magistrate on *prima facie* grounds alone; in reality the warrants have resulted from a political agenda organized by a group of lawyers established by Hamas after the fighting in Gaza in 2008. A similar attempt to arrest Ehud Barak, then Defense Minister, who was attending a British Labour Party conference in September 2009, failed because he had immunity as a diplomatic representative. Threat of being arrested caused the members of an Israeli military delegation who had been invited by the British Army to cancel their visit. The chief spokesman of the IDF, Avi Benayahu, was obliged to visit London incognito in March 2011, for fear of being targeted for alleged war crimes.

What is conspicuous in these censorious indictments of Israel, made by those supposedly acting on behalf of the principle of human rights, is that they are focused on only one side of the Israeli-Palestinian conflict. They are all partisan, anti-Israeli, and implicitly antisemitic. The result has been that Israeli political and military leaders are reluctant to travel abroad.

Officials of other countries, including President George H.W. Bush for US actions during the first Gulf War, have been threatened by this abuse of law, but Israeli officials have been the largest target. As referred to earlier, the inclusion in the jurisdiction of the ICC of the definition of "crimes against humanity" as "the transfer, directly or indirectly, by the occupying power of parts of its own civilian population into the territory it occupies," is clearly aimed at Israel's settlement policy. By contrast "terrorism" is not mentioned as a crime. To this point no prosecution of Israel in the ICC has occurred, but in 2004 the International Court of Justice in The Hague issued an advisory opinion criticizing Israel for building the fence in the West Bank, intended to prevent terrorists from entering Israel. The Court had acted on a request by the UN General Assembly to advise on "the legal consequences arising from the construction of the wall being built by Israel, the occupying Power, in the Occupied Palestinian Territory, including in and around East Jerusalem." Though the Court's opinion was non-binding, it encouraged groups and organizations hostile to Israel to call for the dismantling of the fence, or, using a more captious vocabulary, the barrier, or wall.

Private interest groups have also sought litigation in national courts against Israeli officials and corporations doing business with the Israeli military, purportedly on behalf of the human rights of Palestinians killed or injured in Israeli military activities in actions against terrorists. They seek judgments to punish those involved in those actions, to have the actions declared illegal, or condemned as "disproportionate use of force," or as "collective punishment," or as unlawful targeting of civilians.

The concept of universal jurisdiction was used in the 2009 Goldstone Report as an avenue for states "to investigate violations of the grave breach provisions of the Fourth Geneva Conventions of 1949, prevent impunity and promote international accountability." This was not the first time that the Fourth Geneva Convention, an agreement that was adopted as a *post facto* condemnation of Nazi Germany, was used to condemn the people that the Nazis had persecuted. The UN Security Council on March 1, 1980, adopted a resolution that Israel had been in "flagrant violation" of the Convention; thus, Israel was the first country to be charged with behaving as the Nazis had done. The condemnation was essentially repeated by the UN Human Rights Commission in 1981 which concluded that "Israel's grave breaches of the Geneva Convention...are war crimes and an affront to humanity."

This misuse of law against Israeli senior officials in countries whose legal system allowed prosecution of foreign citizens for alleged crimes not committed in their territory, was not confined to Britain. Not only was a case brought in Belgium in 2003 against Ariel Sharon, as stated above, but also similar cases have been brought in Spain. The allegations continue in political activity by the curious alliance of Islamic fundamentalists and the European political left. Under the title of the International Campaign against US and Zionist Occupation, the alliance has held a number of conferences protesting against the US role in Iraq and expressing solidarity with the resistance in Palestine against Israel. Even more specifically, a similar alliance of Islamicists, lawyers, academics, and peace activists, in December 2009 in London, organized a meeting on "Universal Jurisdiction against Israeli War Criminals."

The following chapters examine the various charges made against Israel since its establishment.

Chapter 4

The Charge of Racism

Some of the charges made against Israel, and discussed in the international media, range from the ludicrous to the malevolent. Perhaps the most farcical were the allegations since the late 1990s that "Zionist" chewing gum had made Palestinian women sterile, that Jews were stealing internal organs of Palestinians for medical experiments, that the Israeli secret service, the Mossad, was behind attacks by sharks on tourists at Egyptian Red Sea resorts, that a vulture detained in Saudi Arabia was an Israeli spy, that President Mubarak of Egypt was an Israeli agent or spy, that Israeli attack dogs were sent into Jericho, that Israelis sent wild boars into the West Bank to destroy agricultural produce, and that rats were placed in areas of Arab habitation in Jerusalem. No Hollywood movie on the Egyptian past would include a statement similar to that on Egypt-TV on November 18, 2010, that the Roman war against Cleopatra was Jewish in essence because the Jews had financed the Romans. More disturbing were allegations that Israeli forces had massacred "thousands" of Palestinian civilians in the refugee camp in Jenin in April 2002 during Operation Defensive Shield, a response to the terrorism of the second *intifada*. The "massacre" did not occur, since, in fact, the true number of Palestinians killed in the fighting is fifty-seven, most of whom were armed combatants, not civilians; the Israelis lost twenty soldiers. Nor have any "massacres" occurred, or organized destruction of people or property, or systematic use of torture, or "ethnic cleansing." Equally disquieting was the statement that a twelve year old Palestinian boy, Muhammad al-Dura, had been killed on September 30, 2000 by IDF gunfire; he became an icon of Palestinian suffering, but in fact, either he was killed by Palestinian fire or, more likely, the whole incident was staged for political advantage. These can be discounted as trivial if disconcerting, but the charge against Israel of "racism" has to be taken seriously.

In the nineteenth century scholars began to construct theories about race, defined as a group of people distinguished from other people by certain characteristics: skin color, facial features, language, ancestry, or national origin. Using philological, philosophical, and scientific approaches, they tried to provide an account of the evolution of civilizations or to explain the origin of humanity through racial theories.[60] However useful the scholarly attempt at racial classification and at formulating biological concepts may have seemed, it had both terminological flaws and prejudicial political, social, and economic consequences.

The first problem is that the term "race" has always been vague and has been used in imprecise, arbitrary, and variable ways. Races were seen as having characteristics which were specific to each one, innate, and unchangeable, assumptions which have been discredited by contemporary molecular analysis. The French scientist, François Jacob, who won the Nobel Prize for Medicine in 1965, wrote in 1979 that the concept of race "has lost all operative value and can only attest our view of a reality that is in constant motion."[61] Terminology was misused: the philological concepts of differences between Aryan and Semitic language groups were transformed into ideological and political doctrine, of irreconcilable ethnic differences.[62] These theories of race led to practices resulting in forms of political and social discrimination, and the development of negative or hostile attitudes and actions towards others. To characterize discriminatory behavior of this kind, the term "racism" began to be used. The term became familiar in the 1930s because of the way in which Nazi Germany, using biological criteria as an excuse, regarded and persecuted its Jewish population. But biology did not cause or explain the Holocaust. Science did not lead to racism and hatred; hatred used science to justify its racism.[63]

Racism went beyond the familiar attitude of xenophobia, the Greek word to indicate fear, contempt, or hostility to strangers. It was not merely a belief that race is the primary determinant of human traits and capacities, but also an assertion that some racial groups are inherently superior to others and that discrimination against those others was morally and scientifically justifiable. This discrimination could therefore be actually implemented in the institutions and structures, and in political and social behavior in the supposedly superior society.

The use made by Nazi Germany of race, which became racism, and resulted in the Holocaust led in the post-World War II world to reconsideration of "man's myth, the fallacy of race."[64] Social scientists and others suggested that "race" was a social construction rather than a concept based on biological differentiation. The post-war world has therefore witnessed attempts to overcome discrimination against improper social construction of race and racism.

It is ironic that following the rise of antisemitic incidents in the world, the UNGA in 1960 adopted a resolution which did not specifically mention antisemitism or define "race," but which condemned "all manifestations and practices of racial, religious, and national hatred." This was followed by the adoption by UNGA in December 1965 of the International Convention on the Elimination of all Forms of Racial Discrimination. It defined racial discrimination and said that its existence would be judged by its effects; this would depend on whether an action had "an unjustifiable disparate impact upon a group distinguished by race, color, descent, or national or ethnic origin." According to the Committee on the Elimination of Discrimination, which began operating in 1969, racial discrimination would occur where human rights and fundamental freedoms in the political, economic, social, cultural, or any other field of public life was nullified or impaired. However, "religious discrimination" was not included in the general formula because of opposition from Arab countries to Western efforts to define antisemitism and Zionism as racism.[65] Further attempts by the United States in the Commission on Human Rights to condemn antisemitism as racism were blocked, especially by Saudi Arabia, which argued for deleting references to any particular form of racism.

Racism today, like fascism generations ago, has become a word that is loosely used. The term is applied to individuals or groups that supposedly exhibit the most repugnant behavior and absence of moral concern towards other people who are different from themselves. Though the term "racism" has not been precisely defined in international law, being accused of racism constitutes a singular kind of opprobrium, not one of definition. Its very use raises the emotional temperature of any communication. In recent years it has infected the dialogue about Israel and its policies. It polarizes any genuine discussion of relevant issues. It uses the classical rhetorical trope of occultation, to call attention to a phenomenon while refusing to explain it. The indiscriminate, hermetic criticism of Israel, especially since the war of 1967, has gone further. It reached its apogee when people began denouncing Israel not simply as a belligerent occupying power, but as a racist, and even more as an apartheid, state, thus evoking the injustices of the former South African regime. This exaggerated criticism first appeared at the conferences and publications of international organizations, largely as a result of the initiatives of the Soviet Union since 1965 and the Palestine Liberation Organization (PLO). Both tried to associate Zionism with racism.

The Arab argument against Zionism usually claims to rest on political analysis, not on antisemitism. No one reading the National Covenant of the PLO can accept this benign explanation for the intransigent hostility to Israel. More likely, readers will recognize that the Arab hostility rests on a deep, emotional base, if not a genuine fear, of a "Chosen People" who, according to some Arabs, are supposed to be planning to create a future Jewish empire stretching from the Nile to the Euphrates. That National Covenant of the PLO adopted in 1964 and amended in 1968, states in Article 19 (1964) and Article 22 (1968) that Zionism is " racist and fanatic in its nature: aggressive, expansionist and colonialist in its aims: and Fascist and Nazi in its ends and means." The charge by the Arabs against Israel of racism is doubly ironic. It is the Arabs who deny Jews, who have a unique connection with a historic homeland, the right of self-determination, while claiming the same right for themselves or for the Palestinians. Palestinians have attempted to deny the Jewish connection with the Western Wall and the Temple Mount in Jerusalem and other historical sites, and have even vandalized some of them, such as Joshua's tomb in the village of Timnat Heres, by covering it with graffiti in Arabic. Moreover, this denial of Jewish self-determination has been made by people in countries and territories which have exhibited the most egregious forms of discrimination and persecution. Even more, Arab media and Islamic political rhetoric has resonated with the routine use of blood libel images, of Jews as vampires, with a deluge of hatred against "Zionists."[66]

THE SOVIET ROLE

For its own political reasons, largely intended at first to diminish British influence and increase its own in the eastern Mediterranean, the Soviet Union after World War II declared its support for partition of Palestine and the establishment of a Jewish state. The Soviets viewed the Zionists as fighting against British imperialism and against the Arab protégés of Britain.[67] At crucial moments, Andrei Gromyko, the Soviet delegate to the UN, in statements issued from the UN in May 1947 and on November 26, 1947, mentioned a possible solution: the division of Palestine into two separate autonomous states, one Jewish and one Arab, if the two sides could not agree on any other solution. He declared that the Jewish people had been closely linked to Palestine for a considerable period in history, and that partition was in keeping with the principle of the national self-determination of peoples. The Arabs, he said, aimed at the suppression of a national liberation movement. The Soviet Union voted in favor of the 1947 UNGA Resolution for partition. In contrast, the Arab Higher Committee argued that this Soviet position, which was also held by the Americans, was "a monstrous distortion of the principle of self-determination in Palestine" since the population of Palestine was largely Arab and therefore on the basis of self-determination, Palestine should become an independent, unitary Arab State.

The Soviet Union was the first country to recognize the new state of Israel, *de jure*, and would, via Czechoslovakia, send arms to Israel when the state was immediately invaded. It hoped, in vain, that Israel would become a pro-Soviet country in the Cold War between the Soviet Union and the West. Since this did not happen the policy of the Soviet Union soon changed. The Soviet Union came to believe that the

Arab states could be an important and more useful player for it in its anti-Western campaign. From the time of Lenin, the Soviet Union had been ideologically opposed to the concept of Zionism. The opposition became more embedded in Soviet ideology as Stalin became negatively fixated on Jews. Perhaps his daughter's marriage to a Jew deepened his prejudice. Stalin's persecution of Jews became more pronounced after World War II. In 1948 the Soviet Jewish Anti-Fascist Committee, which had been the tool he set up during World War II to gain international Jewish support for the Soviet Union, was abolished. Its members, including important Yiddish writers and poets such as Peretz Markish and David Bergelson, were arrested and executed after a secret trial in 1952. Consequent political trials of leading Jewish figures were held in which the accused were termed, *inter alia*, "cosmopolitans without country." Stalin extended the persecution to satellite Soviet countries. At the trials in Prague in November 1952 of fourteen Czech Communist leaders, eleven of whom were Jewish, Israel was accused of being at the service of imperialism. In his last fantasy before his death in 1953 Stalin invented a "Doctors' Plot" in which Jewish doctors were planning "Zionist crimes" and were spies linked to the American Joint Distribution Committee. By portraying Zionists as agents of imperialism, and depicting the Arab war against Israel as part of the world wide struggle against imperialism, the Soviet Union criticized Israel directly and the democratic West, especially the US, indirectly.

The Soviet Union continued to mix political motivations with open antisemitism; Stalin declared in 1953 that "every Jew is a nationalist and an agent of American intelligence."[68] Antisemitism, in literature and political policies, was a traditional phenomenon in the Soviet Union. Writers like Vladimir Begun gave new vigor to it and linked it to anti-Zionism. Begun's 1974 book *The Creeping Counterrevolution* reasserted the themes of the *Protocols of the Elders of Zion*. His next book, *Invasion without Arms*, published two years after the 1975 United Nations General Assembly Resolution 3379, the Zionism as Racism Resolution, stated that there was a unity of the Judaic and Zionist Weltanschaung and that "Zionist gangsterism...has its ideological roots in the scrolls of the 'holy' Torah and the precepts of the Talmud." By 1976 Zionism as racism was present in Soviet textbooks.

The Soviet political polemic against Israel degenerated to a point where anti-Zionism and antisemitism became so intertwined as to be inseparable. Indeed the intensity of Soviet anti-Zionist polemics suggests elemental emotions, especially as the Soviet statements equating Zionism and Nazism became more pronounced. In Soviet propaganda the two were held to share a common opposition to communism; both elevated race and nation into absolutes; both insisted on racial purity and viewed the world as composed of a hierarchy of peoples in which each was the dominant factor and the chosen people. The antisemitic allegations of an international Jewish plot, depicted in *The Protocols of the Elders of Zion*, became transmuted into a Zionist conspiracy to control the world. Influential books by Trofim Kichko and other writers were diatribes against Jews and Zionists, on the basis that both supported the concept that Jews were a chosen people, a superior race destined to rule others. Some of the books were bizarre; according to one, the manuscript of the theory of relativity was stolen by the Jewish Albert Einstein from a non-Jewish Russian. The anti-Israeli activity took an increasing official character. Yuri Andropov, then head of the KGB, set up in 1971 a special minorities section with a Jewish department in it. A committee of the Soviet Academy of Science was established in 1972 to expose and criticize Zionism. In 1974 a directive of the Central Committee of the Communist Party called for "the intensification of the struggle against the anti-Soviet activity of Zionism."

The third edition of the *Great Soviet Encyclopedia* (1969-1978) declared that the "main posits of modern Zionism are militant chauvinism, racism, anti-Communism, and anti-Sovietism." Zionism was addressed as anti-human and reactionary; its adherents were fighting against freedom movements. The Soviet Union publicly positioned itself as the leader of the anti-imperialist camp, while internally it acted aggressively, and imperialistically itself, against ethnic and national groups within its sphere of control. It was to continue this hostility to Israel as it sought to develop close and extensive relations with the Arab world and the Third World.[69] As part of the attempt to prevent Jews in the Soviet

Union from emigrating to Israel, the Anti-Zionist Committee of Soviet Public Opinion was created in 1983 and lasted until 1994; it was headed by Colonel-General David Dragunsky, Hero of the Soviet Union, and, for a time, included the Chief Rabbi of Moscow. Among its polemical pronouncements, the Committee asserted both that Israel was the instrument of American imperialism in the Middle East and was using Nazi methods to achieve its objectives, and that Jews did not want to leave the Soviet Union because they were aware of the evil nature of Zionism.

In addition to its rhetoric, the Soviet Union was actively helping the Arab states militarily during "the war of attrition" in the early 1970s, by positioning surface-to-air batteries in Egypt against Israeli planes along the Suez Canal, by firing Scud surface-to-surface missiles against Israeli troops in Sinai in 1973, and by its threats on two occasions. On the first in 1956, Prime Minister Nikolai Bulganin and Nikita Krushchev, Communist Party general secretary, threatened to send "volunteers" to the Middle East if Israel persisted in its "armed aggression" against Egypt. It may have been an idle threat, but it became ominous since "Russian volunteers" had just cruelly crushed the Hungarian uprising in Budapest. On the second occasion in 1973, the USSR threatened to intervene directly against Israel.[70] In the negotiations in 1964 and 1965 of the International Convention on the Elimination of all Forms of Racial Discrimination, the Soviet Union prevented the UN from condemning antisemitism. Instead, the Soviet Union, which had continually supported the Arab states and the Palestinians in international forums, planned, in collaboration with the Palestine Liberation Organization, to condemn Zionism, to proclaim that Zionism was equated with racism and with the accompanying evils of imperialism and colonialism. For the Soviet Union this attack on "Zionism," that is Israel, was a useful device to deflect agitation for political and human rights by ethnic groups in its own territories, as well as an easy way to gain support from Arab countries in the Cold War period.

The continuous Soviet anti-Zionist campaign, during and after Stalin's rule, was shaped by both internal and external factors. Internally, it was a warning to Soviet Jews who had shown exuberance at the arrival of Golda Meir as Israel's ambassador to Moscow in 1948, and again in 1967 in celebrating Israel's victory in the Six-Day War, not to associate themselves with Israel or to support it. Allowing Jews to behave in this way might serve as a dangerous example for subject peoples in the Soviet Empire and become a threat to Soviet national security. Also, Russian Jewish emigration to Israel would be both a loss of professionally trained men and women, and an incitement to other groups to leave. The Russians also hoped to limit internal difficulties by alleging that almost all the known dissenters were Jews. For many, anti-Zionism was a convenient device to camouflage traditional antisemitism and to appeal to Russian national-chauvinistic sentiments. Jews, as so often in history, were used as scapegoats to divert attention from or to be held responsible for Russian economic and political failures.

Externally, anti-Zionism benefited the Soviet Union in a number of ways. Hostility of this kind gained favor from Muslims in the world, as well as more specifically from its own Muslims who accounted for about fifty million, a fifth of the then Soviet population, and also from Arab nationalists. By portraying Zionism as an agency of imperialism, and by declaring that the Arab war against Israel was part of the world wide struggle against imperialism, the Soviet Union could criticize Israel directly and the democratic West and Western values indirectly. It was thus able to influence the Third World countries and the Non-Aligned Movement, and at the same time divert attention from its own foreign adventures. That Movement, founded in 1961 in Belgrade to group those countries not formally aligned with or against a major power or bloc, has in 2011 a membership of 118 countries and 20 observer countries.

In the continuing Soviet international policy there was an increasing tendency to equate Zionism and Israel with discrimination, racism, and fascism, and to use the parallel with Nazism more openly. At the United Nations on June 9, 1967, the Soviet representative, Nikolai Federenko, accused Israel of behaving like the Nazis and attacked the Israeli leaders as war criminals. Moshe Dayan was presented as a pupil of Hitler, and the Six-Day War as equivalent to the Nazi aggression against Poland in September 1939. Themes appeared accusing Israel of genocide against the Arabs in occupied territories, and of a Jewish *Herrenvolk* establishing concentration camps and behaving like the Gestapo.

Later, the Anti-Zionist Committee of the Soviet Public, set up in June 1983 to fight "against chauvinism or nationalism" and composed of Jews who were part of the Soviet establishment, falsely stated that Jews had collaborated with the Nazis, that the leaders of international Zionism had betrayed Jews to the Gestapo during World War II, and that a Palestinian Jewish office headed by Levi Eshkol, the Israeli prime minister, operated in Berlin during the war.

ZIONISM AS RACISM: RESOLUTION 3379, NOVEMBER 10, 1975

These Soviet polemical assaults and political machinations affected the international climate of discussion about Israel. The UN General Assembly on December 14, 1973, passed Resolution 3151 (72-36-32), the first UN Resolution to associate Zionism with a racist regime. The Resolution stated there was an "unholy alliance among Portuguese colonialism, South African racism, Zionism and Israeli imperialism." In a contrary fashion, another UNGA Resolution in 1974, passed to justify Palestinian actions against Israel, held that nothing in its definition of "aggression" could in any way prejudice "the right of peoples under colonial and racist regimes or other forms of alien domination" to struggle for self-determination, freedom and independence. The next year, in June-July 1975, the delegates to the UN International Women's Year Conference in Mexico City condemned Zionism along with colonialism, neocolonialism, apartheid, foreign occupation, and racial discrimination in all its forms. The next month the Assembly of Heads of State and Government of the Organization of African Unity, meeting in Kampala, July 28-August 1, 1975, compared "the racist regime in occupied Palestine" with the "racist" regimes in Zimbabwe and South Africa. All were said to have a common imperialist origin. Again, the Foreign Ministers of the Non-Aligned Countries meeting in August 1975 in Lima, severely condemned Zionism as a "threat to world peace and security."

In what may well be considered its lowest point, the United Nations in its General Assembly Resolution 3379 (XXX) on November 10, 1975, declared that "Zionism is a form of racism and racial discrimination."

It was carried by a large majority, 72 to 35, with 32 abstentions. It was clearly inspired by the propaganda of the Soviet Union. The adoption of the Resolution reduced the UNGA to a level of cynical opportunism. It lent respectability to the misuse of international forums for the purpose of maligning Zionism, impugned the legitimacy of the state of Israel, and, both directly and indirectly, led to the increase in and legitimization of antisemitism. A terrible lie had been promulgated by states, many of which engaged in racist oppression. The British literary critic, Goronwy Rees, commented on the specters haunting the debate on the resolution: "the ghosts of Hitler and Goebbels and Julius Streicher, grinning with delight, to hear not only Israel, but Jews as such denounced in language which would have provoked hysterical applause at any Nuremberg rally."[71] The Israeli Prime Minister, Yitzhak Rabin, was equally clear in his speech to the Knesset on November 11, 1975: "By denouncing Zionism as a so called 'racist' doctrine, the initiators of the Resolution aim at denying the existence of Israel, which is the product of the creative activities of the Jewish people's self-liberation movement-Zionism."

For many years the Soviet-Arab coalition had attempted to have Israel expelled from international forums. Finding this was not possible, due largely to the opposition of the United States, the coalition attempted to have Israel treated as an international pariah through this Resolution. The coalition was able to persuade a sufficient number of nations to support the Resolution by appeals to ideological convictions, religious identification, Third World solidarity or simply self-interest. Among the supporters of the Resolution were thirty-six states with Muslim majority population, the Soviet bloc of fifteen except Romania, twenty-three African (some of them Muslim), seven Asian, and two Latin American countries, Brazil and Mexico. The majority included the dictatorial and authoritarian countries of the world, while almost all the existing liberal democracies were in the opposition. The non-democratic countries had exhibited their monolithic antisemitism masquerading as moral righteousness.

The aim of Resolution 3379 was to portray Zionism as an evil ideology. That ideology was seen as embodying racist exclusiveness, having colonial intentions, and seeking to occupy the land of Palestine by military means and to dominate the Arabs living there. This extraordinary Resolution ignored or misunderstood the diversity of the Zionist movement, which was never unified, but embraced a number of different streams, political, religious, practical, and cultural. It also disregarded the aspirations for a Jewish independent state in the ancient homeland of the Jewish people which, among other things, would be both national renewal and a safe haven for Jews.

Zionism was only the most recent of the struggles of the Jewish people for self-determination, struggles that had been manifested in the Maccabean Revolt, 167 B.C.-160 B.C., in the war against the Romans, 66-73 A.D., and in the Bar Kokhba Revolt, 132-135 A.D., also against the Romans. Resolution 3379 gave greater political and intellectual credibility to the attack on Zionism, and even endowed that attack with the ostensible moral value and the legitimating function accorded UN resolutions. The concept of Zionism as racism gained sufficient respectability to be mentioned in works on international law. Paul Johnson commented that the real danger about this UN activity was that "paper majorities tended to grow into real policies: the corrupt arithmetic of the assembly...tended to become imperceptibly the conventional wisdom of international society."[72] Following 3379, the pace and extent of UN excoriation of Israel and of Zionism increased. In addition to the hundreds of critical resolutions and proposed actions in the different UN agencies discussed earlier, the majority of votes against Israel increased. Attempts were made to suspend Israel from participating in the various agencies; sanctions against Israel or calls for an end to military, economic and political aid were threatened. Though no UN resolution was ever passed to expel Israel from the organization, the country was nevertheless denied participation in most of UN activity, including the right to speak or debate in certain forums.

Yet, attempts to reject Israel's credentials in the international bodies failed. The Islamic Conference of forty-two members at the time, pressed in 1980 for the expulsion of Israel from the UN. The Non-Aligned Movement meeting in New Delhi in February 1981, urged the credentials of Israel at the UN not be accepted; the Israeli delegation to the international energy conference in New Delhi in September 1983 was banned; and the expulsion of Israel from the World Postal

Union was discussed in June 1984. Though most of these attempts failed, a new code of conduct became implicitly accepted in the efforts of international bodies to isolate Israel politically and diplomatically. All actions or failures to act by Israel were likely to be condemned, and its very legitimacy continued to be challenged. Moreover, Resolution 3379 injected a resurgence of the virus of antisemitism into the international political body, thanks to the Soviet Union.

Resolution 3379 had other consequences. The first was that the UN itself was discredited by this clear example of partiality, the strident language, exaggerated demands, and torrent of unproductive words and resolutions. It meant that the UN deterred, rather than fostered, peaceful negotiation. A second was that Resolution 3379 deepened the antagonism and hostility of many of the Arab parties to Israel. Even King Hussein of Jordan, who had been educated at Harrow and Sandhurst in Britain and was generally regarded as a moderate, felt obliged at the UNGA on September 25, 1979, to speak of "Israel's racist Zionism." The less moderate President Hafez al-Assad of Syria, felt in September 1980 that the proper commentary on President Sadat who had made peace with Israel was that "he had turned into a Zionist." Syria broke all diplomatic relations with Egypt, which was also expelled from membership of the Arab League.

A third consequence was that the Resolution adversely affected the intellectual climate, especially on university campuses and in the media, on the question of Zionism and the actions and policies of Israel. Critics of Israel in seminars, conferences, and in the works of the "new historians," adopting a posture of sophisticated scholarly apparatus and rational, if impassioned, analysis, ransacked Zionist literature for allusions to race. They searched for passages in that literature which exalted Jewry or were derogatory of Arabs, or for those statements that contained Jewish self-criticism or made negative commentaries on life in the Diaspora. In this state of intellectual and political, and sometimes physical, siege the task of examining the complex phenomenon of Zionism and the Jewish movement for self-determination and national liberation in an objective fashion has been more difficult. It is made even more difficult by the double standard applied to this issue. In the post World War II era when the concept of self-determination has been accorded high priority in many instances, the Jewish liberation movement is the only one that has been denounced.

The 1975 UNGA Resolution was followed by numerous other resolutions of similar character in a variety of organizations, including many others in the UNGA itself; the 1980 UN World Conference on Women in Copenhagen, African and Non-aligned bodies, UNESCO, and student groups. At the second UN World Conference on Women in Copenhagen in 1980 the idea of eliminating "Zionism," (the state of Israel) was introduced.

The lead to revoke the 1975 UNGA Resolution was taken by the United States, particularly through the efforts of Ambassador and later Senator Daniel Patrick Moynihan, in 1990. President George H.W. Bush declared at the UNGA in September 1991 that "to equate Zionism with the intolerable sin of racism is to twist history…to equate Zionism with racism is to reject Israel itself." On December 16, 1991, the UNGA in Resolution 46/86, by a vote of 111 to 25, with 13 abstentions and 17 absent, "decided to revoke the determination contained in resolution 3379." Thirteen Arab countries voted negatively, and another six were absent. As a result of strong pressure by the United States the UN had, at least for a moment, cleansed itself of a dishonorable act. Yet the repeal is more explicable in terms of important changes in world politics than in terms of a sudden UN conversion to a politics of probity. Three factors in particular were important at the time: the dissolution of the Soviet Union, the heightened presence of the US in the Middle East after the successful first Gulf War, and the political impotence of the non-aligned countries in world affairs.

Since then, the charge of racism, implicitly antisemitism, has been made in the international community. It was expressed vigorously on the public stage by President Mahmoud Ahmadinejad of Iran on April 20, 2009, with his declaration of "Jews, a small minority who dominate the politics, economy, and culture of major parts of the world by its complicated networks, and establish a new form of slavery to attain its racist ambitions."

Chapter 5

The Charge of Apartheid: the Big Lie

In March 2011, the postal services of Liberia, Gambia, and Sierra Leone simultaneously issued a set of three commemorative postal sheets in memory of Jews who had fought apartheid and racism in Africa. It was disconcerting that a celebrated individual such as Archbishop Desmond Tutu, Nobel Prize winner, while stating that "In our struggle against apartheid the great supporters were Jewish people," should in 2002 have compared the treatment of Palestinians by Israel with the treatment of native Africans by the former South African regime, particularly when he appears to have remained silent about the persecution of, or discrimination against, fellow Christians by Muslims. Others went further than Tutu in criticism. Israel was said to be the embodiment of triple evils: apartheid, occupation, and colonialism. Thus, it could be the object of a boycott, divestment, and sanctions against it. The charge of apartheid erupted in earnest at the NGO meeting associated with the Durban "anti-racism" conference. Its initial impetus was on American and European college campuses. In Britain, the initial call in April 2002 was for a moratorium on European research and academic collaboration with Israeli institutions. Two years later, the Presbyterian Church in the US called for divestment from Israel. In July 2005, at a meeting of Palestinians and others, the boycott, divestment, and sanctions (BDS) movement was launched. The date was symbolically chosen; it was exactly one year after the ruling of the International Court at The Hague in July 2004, that the Israel security fence was illegal according to international law.[73] A wide diversity of groups—academic, church (especially the Presbyterian and British Methodist churches), labor unions, international organizations, courts, commercial groups, and some pop stars—have joined in the movement or promoted the charge against Israel, of being an apartheid state. The Global BDS movement, in which the Israeli Arab philosopher Omar Barghouti is a leading figure, is committed to "strengthening the boycott as a central form of resistance to Israeli occupation and apartheid." In reality it is an attempt to isolate Israel and to alter international public opinion against it. The machination behind this is the argument that the BDS movement is based on the principle of the universal rights of man.

All this prejudice was paradoxically the perversion of reality. Any reasonable observer could appreciate the falsity and absurdity of equating contemporary Israel, faults and all, with the specific and empirical behavior of the former South African regime. Controversial Israeli actions in the West Bank, such as house demolition and some expulsion of people, regrettable though they are, do not constitute a behavior pattern comparable to that in South Africa, where apartheid policy was systematically grounded on legal racism and segregation of people of different races. South Africans were officially recorded on the basis of race ranging from white to seven other population groups. Laws created and maintained a society of legal, economic, and residential discrimination. It was also a system where a minority dominated the majority. Contrary to the situation in South Africa, Israel has never banned mixed marriages or subjected Arabs to forms of servitude or to a lesser form of citizenship.

The very word "apartheid" derives from an Afrikaner term meaning separateness or apartness, but in recent years its definition has been deliberately changed by international bodies to fit the case of relations between Israel and Palestinians. The UNGA on November 30, 1973, defined the crime of apartheid as "inhumane acts committed for the purpose of establishing and maintaining domination by one racial group of persons over any other racial group of persons and systematically oppressing them." This crime, part of "crimes against humanity," was further defined by the 2002 Rome Statute of the International Criminal Court as inhumane acts "committed in the context of an institutionalized regime of systematic oppression and domination by one racial group over any other racial group or groups and committed with the intention of maintaining that regime." In a strong report in February 2007, John Dugard, the United Nations Special Rapporteur on the situation of human rights in the Palestinian territories occupied since 1967, wrote that "Israel is clearly in military occupation of the Occupied Palestinian Territories. At the same time elements of the occupation constitute forms of colonialism and of apartheid, which are contrary to international law." He posed the question, one that he had already answered, "Can it be seriously denied that the purpose of Israeli actions was to establish and maintain domination by one racial group (Jews) over another racial group (Palestinians)" and was systematically oppressing them? The answer was given by Richard Goldstone in the New York Times on November 1, 2011 where he wrote that the charge that Israel was guilty of the crime of apartheid was "an unfair and inaccurate slander against Israel calculated to retard rather than advance peace negotiations."

To illustrate how the accusation of apartheid does not apply to Israel, and to demonstrate the invalidity of Dugard's conclusion, it is helpful to examine the exact nature of apartheid as it existed in South Africa. It was a political and social system introduced in 1948 by the ruling National Party under its leader D. F. Malan and lasted until 1994, when Nelson Mandela, leader of the African National Congress who had spent twenty-seven years in prison, became president of the country.

The first major edict of discrimination was the prohibition in 1949 of mixed marriages between white people and people of other races. A year later, adultery or immoral acts between white and black people were forbidden. In 1950, a national register was created in which each person's race was recorded, and tests were made of physical and linguistic factors to define race. In the same year different residential areas were established for different races. Over three million people were relocated by forced removal. According to other statutes, blacks could not perform any skilled labor in urban areas except in those areas designated for black occupation, and they could be removed from public or privately owned land and resettled in special camps. Starting in the 1950s, statutes created a system of territorial segregation. In 1951 black homelands, or Bantustans, with some measure of self-government and regional authority, were set up in South Africa and in Southwest Africa (now Namibia). In time, the area of the Bantustans constituted about thirteen per cent of the country. As a corollary, the possibility of blacks having the right of permanent residence in towns was narrowed to those who had lived or worked there for not less than fifteen years.

By the Pass Laws of 1952, black people over sixteen were obliged to carry identification at all times. Anyone unable to produce a pass could be arrested. No black could leave a rural area for an urban one without official permission; in urban areas a black had to obtain a work permit within seventy-two hours of arrival. By the Bantu Education Act of 1953, a curriculum was to be compiled to suit "the nature and requirements of the black people." The aim of this was to limit educational opportunities for blacks through schooling, that would provide them only with skills to serve their fellow blacks in the homelands or to work in jobs under whites. Probably the most egregious of the statutes was the 1953 Reservation of Separate Amenities Act, which imposed forced segregation in all public amenities, public buildings and transport, in order to prevent contact between white and other races. Facilities provided for the different races did not have to be of equal quality. By an act of 1959, black students could no longer attend white universities.

The Promotion of Bantu Self-Government Act of 1959 codified even further the establishment of Bantustan. This Act classified black people into eight ethnic groups. Each was to live in a homeland developed for it and could govern itself without white intervention. The overall objective was to segregate the black homelands by making them self-governing political units. People became citizens of their homelands and thus were deprived of South African citizenship. The 1970 Bantu Homelands Citizens Act went even further. All black people were compelled to become citizens of the homelands relevant to their ethnic group, irrespective of whether or not they lived there. They would now officially be considered aliens, without South African nationality or the right to live or work in South Africa. Between 1976 and 1981, four of the ten Bantustans set up were granted independence, with a government and a flag of their own. But they were not recognized internationally. The apartheid legislation affected all aspects of life and institutional behavior. It also led to severe restrictions of freedom of speech and press.

For forty years no genuine negotiations were undertaken to change or modify the oppressive laws. Beginning in the mid 1980s some of the restrictions began to be removed and the dismantling of the apartheid system began. After the release of Nelson Mandela in 1990, and the first democratic election in 1994 with all people able to vote which led to the establishment of the National Unity government apartheid was officially ended.

Can the reality of relations between Israel and Palestinians be justly or even remotely compared with this picture of the nature of an apartheid regime? Israel has been criticized for the unequal treatment of Israeli Arabs within its territory, for the existence of separate roads, checkpoints, roadblocks, permits, temporary residence cards, curfews, clearing of olive groves used for ambushes, and border defenses outside the Green Line (the cease-fire line between Israel and Jordan in 1949), for limited access by Palestinians to land and resources, and for Israeli settlements in the disputed areas of the West Bank and Golan Heights. What is generally ignored in the criticism of these restrictions is that they were all imposed for security reasons, not for purposes of discrimination.

It is true that the *Teudat Zehut* (compulsory national identification card) contains the Hebrew calendar date of birth of all legal residents of Israel, including Arabs, over sixteen. But to term this "apartheid" or "foreign occupation" or discrimination against Arabs may be deemed rhetorical excess or linguistic partisanship. Whatever the validity of some or all of the criticisms, Israeli policies are not based on racial criteria, nor animated by racist ideology, nor do they seek to create Bantustans. Israeli Arabs have not been deported to the West Bank or Gaza or elsewhere. They have not been denied access to universities, hospitals, restaurants, transport, shopping malls, cinemas, or political organizations, or to international bodies, or movement to and from the outside world without cause.

The Israeli system embodies the definition of citizen by Aristotle, "a man (person) who shares in the administration of justice and in the holding of office." (Aristotle, *The Politics*, 1274a). Israeli Arabs are entitled to citizenship and have all the rights of citizenship, including voting. All public facilities are open and available to them. Some policies of affirmative action for housing Israeli Arabs have been considered, and free professional advice has been given to help with housing permits. The Palestinians in East Jerusalem are regarded as permanent residents, most of whom are not citizens of Israel; they have the right to vote in municipal elections. As holders of "blue cards" they have access to schools, jobs, medical care and welfare benefits.

The struggle of local Africans against the oppressive Afrikaner colonial system cannot be considered comparable to the friction between Palestinians and Jews who have returned to their ancient homeland. A deliberate legal policy of segregation and discrimination in South Africa is not equivalent to a tragic clash of two national movements competing for self-determination of peoples in the same area. In contrast to the South African case, negotiations have been sought by Israel since 1949 to reach a just and lasting peace between the two sides. Israel is not an outpost of European imperialism, nor do the Palestinians personify an anti-colonial ideology. The Zionist movement was not a colonial project seeking to dispossess local indigenous Arabs from their land.

Indeed, mainstream Zionist assertions have always called for full rights to be given to non-Jews in any Jewish state. Theodor Herzl expressed this in his fanciful utopian novel, *Altneuland*; membership in the new society he envisaged was open to people no matter "what race or creed...you must hold fast to the things that have made us great: to liberalism, tolerance, love of mankind." One character in Herzl's novel says that the new society must also include "freedom of thought and expression, generosity of spirit and love of humanity." Similar views were expressed by Zionist leaders such as David Ben-Gurion and Vladimir (Zeev) Jabotinsky, even though the two individuals disagreed on other issues. For Ben-Gurion, the social democrat, in

Our Neighbours and Us, the "vision of social justice and equality (of the Jewish people) absolutely and unconditionally require the rights and interests of the country's non-Jewish residents to be scrupulously preserved and respected."[74] For Jabotinsky, the leader of the Revisionist Zionists, "the law of the Land of Israel must guarantee the equality of citizens, languages, religions, and a very large degree of 'personal autonomy' for every group of citizens who wish for it." In an article of November 4, 1923, originally published in Russian, he wrote, "we shall never do anything contrary to the principle of equal rights, and (that) we shall never try to eject anyone." He proposed equal rights for all citizens, irrespective of race, religion, language or class, without any restriction, in all walks of the country's public life. The Israeli Declaration of Independence, fulfilling this aspiration, states that Israel "will ensure complete equality of social and political rights to all its inhabitants irrespective of religion, race, or sex."

THE POLITICAL USE OF "APARTHEID"

Lewis Carroll, in *Alice in Wonderland,* immortalized the adage that words mean what you want them to mean. The adage has been fulsomely demonstrated in contemporary times by the misuse of the word "apartheid" as an ideological slogan, employed in rhetorical fashion to accuse opponents of racial or ethnic discrimination. Distinctions between people, inevitable in political and social life, have in this way been categorized as improper or immoral or illegal forms of discrimination. In November 1973 the UN General Assembly (Resolution 3068) adopted the International Convention on the Suppression and Punishment of the Crime of Apartheid, which became enforced in July 1976. Implicit in it was that a condition of apartheid was not limited to the South African regime, but was to be considered a crime against humanity. As described earlier, it was now defined as policies and practices of racial segregation and discrimination that have the purpose of establishing and maintaining domination by one racial group of persons over another group of persons and systematically oppressing them, in particular by means such as segregation, expropriation of land, denial of the right to leave and return to one's country, the right to a nationality, and the right to freedom of movement and residence.

Drafted by the Soviet Union, with the support of the Islamic and "non-aligned countries" in the Cold War period, the Resolution 3068 is implicitly directed against the Western alliance of democratic societies with Israel, as was made clear by those who voted for it. It became a statement by which the non-West could attack Israel and Israel's allies or friends, the western democracies. Most of the "non-aligned" Arab and Islamic countries remain aligned against Israel and they garner support from those individuals who agree with the stance of anti-colonialism of the international political left, for whom Israel has become the pariah nation.

A familiar feature of international politics is that countries, like individuals, frequently respond as powerfully to fictions as they do to realities.[75] This was clearly demonstrable in the changing public perception of Israel by black African countries. The charge of apartheid against Israel introduced by the Soviet Union and the Palestinians was an important, if not the only, reason for the change in attitude of African countries, a number of which broke official diplomatic relations with Israel. Early in its history, the state of Israel was committed to humanitarian action in Third World countries, especially in Africa.[76] This was partly the outcome of enlightened self-interest and hopes that newly independent African states would become friendly to Israel, but even more an illustration of a concern for social justice and a demonstration of genuine sympathy for other new developing nations engaged in nation-building. These countries benefited from 5,000 Israeli agricultural and other experts, and from Israel's experience in various areas: agriculture, regional planning, zone development, water management, community development, education, youth, and health programs. Israel provided African countries with expert help, trainee programs, and military training.

Starting in 1957, when it established diplomatic relations with newly independent Ghana, Israel set up thirty-two diplomatic missions in Africa. The cordiality was beneficial to both sides, politically and economically, with Israel purchasing raw materials from the African countries and setting up construction projects in a number of them. By a set of cooperation agreements signed with twenty-one African states, over 9,000 African students attended Israeli academic and training institutions; many were given scholarships at those institutions. A variety of projects primarily concerned with community development and agricultural assistance were set up by over 2,000 Israelis. The earliest significant one was the Black Star Shipping Line, established in 1957 by Zim Lines in Ghana. Other projects included low cost housing in the Ivory Coast, roads in Nigeria, cotton plants in Swaziland, and pharmaceutical works in Ethiopia. Israel trained African pilots, military and police officers, and helped establish a military academy in Sierra Leone. Golda Meir saw Israel's African policy as "a continuation of our own most valued traditions and as an expression of our deepest historic instincts."[77] For their part, African countries saw Israel as an example of a newly independent nation pointing a way to economic modernization and political development. They recognized common features: a history of past persecution, a country with a mixed economy, and a state facing danger of aggression by external forces.

The harmonious relationship began to change after 1967 for a variety of reasons: the changed image of Israel as a result of the Six-Day victory, the direct pressure of Arab states, Arab threats to African regimes or to the lives of individual leaders, appeals for Islamic unity to those countries that were predominantly Muslim, common opposition of Arabs and Africans to colonialism, promises of oil supplies at reduced prices, and the supposed close connection of Israel with South Africa. Resolutions calling for Israeli withdrawal from Egyptian territory were introduced at meetings of the Organization of African Unity (OAU), and the occupation of Sinai was held to be "a serious threat to the regional peace of Africa." Twenty-nine African countries broke off diplomatic relations with Israel. Many of them lent support to criticism of Israel in its conflict with the Arabs. Their change of heart showed in the 1975 UNGA Resolution, Zionism as racism, when twenty-three African countries voted in favor, five voted against, and twelve abstained.

Besides the effect of Arab pressure, the main reason given for the break in African-Israeli relations was the alleged close tie and affinity between Israel and South Africa. A particularly flagrant and sustained attack on Israel came from the Special Committee on the Policies of Apartheid of South Africa, generally known as the Special Committee against Apartheid, set up by the UN in 1962. This Committee made repeated references to "systematic collaboration between South Africa and Israel," a number of special reports on the relationship between the two countries. The Committee collaborated with a number of groups— the Afro-Asian People's Solidarity Organization, the Organization of African Trade Union unity, and the World Peace Council (a Soviet front group)—in organizing a conference on the alliance of Israel and South Africa, which was held in Vienna in July 1983. The conference condemned Israel for its "collaboration with the racist regime of South Africa." It concluded that the "alliance" was serious and was a menace to the people of southern Africa (UN Document A/38/311, July 25, 1983).

As a result of Arab insistence and obviously aimed at Israeli settlements, the International Criminal Court (ICC) included in its definition of crimes against humanity the words, "the transfer, directly or indirectly, by the occupying power of parts of its own civilian population into the territory it occupies." The Rome Statute of the ICC listed in its Article 7 states that apartheid was one of the crimes against humanity and defined it as inhumane acts "committed in the context of an institutionalized regime of systematic oppression and domination by one racial group over any other racial group or groups, and committed with the intention of maintaining that regime." Accordingly, members of organizations and agents of an apartheid state are subject to criminal prosecution, irrespective of motives involved.

The crucial change in definition of apartheid from the 1973 formula was that persecution was now said to be on political, national, ethnic, cultural and religious grounds, not merely racial ones. This definition could thus be seen as applicable to Israeli actions in the territories. One perhaps unintended consequence was that Jimmy Carter entitled his 2006 book, *Palestine: Peace not Apartheid*. Though Carter admits that Israel does not practice apartheid policies, the loose use of the word in his title allows the analogy of Israel and the former South Africa to be insinuated. He and others do not sufficiently appreciate that the essence of the Israeli-Palestinian problem is not one of domination of one group over another, or enforced inequalities, or refusal of the regime to engage in compromises as in South Africa, but rather two nationalist movements wanting to establish states on the same land.

What is ironic in the stage managed posturing of righteous moral indignation and censorious edicts about the actions or non-actions of Israel, is that it stems from countries like Saudi Arabia, where the charge of apartheid might more properly be applied. Christians who live in Saudi Arabia are not allowed to practice their faith. Display of items and articles belonging to non-Muslim religions are prohibited. Non-Muslim clergy are not allowed to enter the country for the purpose of conducting religious services, and non-Muslims are forbidden to enter the cities of Mecca and Medina. In view of this intolerant behavior, once again a fair commentary would be that international law has been used, or misused, for partisan purposes to attack only Israel.

To emphasize this partisanship even more, it is worth pointing out in this connection that since 1999 the UN, at the urging of the Organization of the Islamic Conference of 57 (56 states and the Palestinian Authority) has every year passed a resolution on Combating Defamation of Religions which in effect attempts to prevent criticism not of all religions, but only of the "defaming" of Islam."[78] For political reasons, the original framing of the resolution, "defamation of Islam" was changed to "defamation of religions" or "vilification of religions" and the resolutions condemn anyone "perpetuating stereotypes about certain religions," but the intent to prevent criticism of Islam is evident. The resolution proposed in 2009 stated that Islam was frequently and wrongly associated with terrorism, and that it was the "obligation of all states to enact the necessary legislation to prohibit the advocacy of incitement to discrimination." The resolution passed on March 25, 2010, by the UN Human Rights Council called for restrictions on speech regarding Islam in order to fight intolerance and promote "human dignity." Pakistan, which introduced the resolution, accused Western countries of targeting Muslims, using pressure to do so.

It is somewhat encouraging to record that unlike previous resolutions in the UNHRC, it was passed by a narrow majority, 20 to 17, with 8 abstentions, and that in the UNGA in 2010 a similar resolution was passed by only 79-67-40. The continuing resolutions, supposedly addressing human rights violations, in reality justify censorship, because in effect they restrict free speech and the rights of individuals to express their ideas and beliefs, concepts which are proclaimed in the non-binding resolution, the Universal Declaration of Human Rights of December 10, 1948, and in two international human rights covenants of 1966, which are regarded as binding in international law. Violations of human rights were declared by the UN Security Council (Resolutions 794, 940, 1199) to be a threat to peace.[79] One notorious consequence of these restrictions on free speech was the decision in November 2010 of V.S. Naipaul, who won the Nobel Prize for Literature in 2001, to withdraw from an international writers conference to be held in Istanbul, because of objections to his criticism of "the calamitous effect" of Islam. He had remarked that Islam had both enslaved and attempted to wipe out other cultures. Turkish participants threatened to boycott the event, saying that Naipaul had insulted Muslims. By contrast, criticism of Islam is, at best, unwelcome in Arab, and now in some Western European countries, and at worst deadly. The worst is the rule in Saudi Arabia, where persons who insult Islam may be beheaded. Death threats, as well as lawsuits against critics of Islam, such as Salmon Rushdie a generation ago and Susanne Winter, member of the Austrian parliament who was sentenced to three months in prison, are not uncommon. In a notorious and absurd episode in Sudan, a British teacher who gave the name Muhammad to her teddy bear was threatened with imprisonment and death.

In Europe, a serious problem has arisen with the passage of laws and European agreements that have had the effect of limiting free expression and punishing criticism of Islam. Much of this is based on well-meaning documents of international law concerned with tolerance. However, a brief look suggests that the intention has led to restrictions on free speech about Islam. The 1950 Convention for the Protection of Human Rights and Fundamental Freedoms, issued by the Council of Europe, includes Article 10 which grants freedom of expression, but, among things, conditions that particular freedom on "the protection of the reputation and rights of others." The UNGA Resolution 2106 (XX) of December 21, 1965, which entered into force on January 4,

1969, in its International Convention on the Elimination of all Forms of Religious Discrimination, states in Article 4(A) that "all dissemination of ideas based on racial superiority or hatred" is punishable by law. The UNGA Resolution 2200A (XXI) of December 16, 1966, which issued the International Covenant on Civil and Political Rights, and entered into force on March 23, 1976, proposes a prohibition. Its Article 20 says that "Any advocacy of national, racial, or religious hatred that constitutes incitement to discrimination, hostility, or violence shall be punishable by law."

Prosecution of those who have made critical remarks about Islam has taken place in a number of European countries. The most well known is the case of Geert Wilders, a member of the Dutch Parliament, founder and leader of the Dutch Freedom Party (PVV), who has had to face legal charges of hate speech and "incitement to hatred," and threats against his life which have forced him to travel with bodyguards and live in safe houses. It is true that Mr. Wilders, an outspoken man, directed a film that criticized the Koran as an incitement to violence, compared the Koran to Hitler's *Mein Kampf*, and referred to Muhammad as "the devil." Yet more telling is the fact that a Western parliamentarian is prosecuted for political opinions in a country in which Muslims are prominent in the country's four major cities and now constitute a powerful political force. Accusation of blasphemy about Islam was given higher priority than sustaining free speech. In addition, Wilders was denied entry into Britain as a result of his opinions. Wilders was acquitted in June 2011 by an Amsterdam court, of all charges of hate speech, after a legal ordeal that lasted almost two years and during which leftist and Islamic organizations had tried to silence him.

The Dutch filmmaker, Theo Van Gogh, was murdered in November 2004 by a Dutch-Moroccan Muslim for his criticism of the treatment of women in Islamic countries. The former sex-kitten Brigitte Bardot was tried and fined for "insulting racial hatred" for her critical remarks about Muslims in France. The American writer Rachel Ehrenfeld was forced to pay for expensive lawsuits in a case in London, brought by a Saudi businessman who successfully sued her for alleged libel in a book that had been published in the United States and which had sold only a few copies in Britain. Flemming Rose, the Danish journalist and editor, has encountered harsh criticism for publishing twelve cartoons of Muhammad in his newspaper, *Jyllands-Posten*, in September 2005; while the cartoonist himself, Kurt Westergaard needed police protection. A number of Danish embassies were attacked. One of the cartoons portrayed Muhammad wearing a turban shaped like a bomb with a lit fuse. The OIC demanded that the United Nations impose sanctions on Denmark because of the cartoons.

Freedom of speech is limited by these threats and by the strict blasphemy laws in a number of Muslim countries. Jesper Langballe, a Danish Member of Parliament, was convicted of hate speech and racial discrimination for discussing honor killings in Muslim families. Lars Hedegaard, the President of the International Free Press Society, was indicted for discussing the persecution of Muslim women and rapes within Muslim families. Both of these gentlemen were charged under a Danish law which punishes pronouncements "by which a group of persons are threatened, insulted or denigrated due to their race, skin color, national or ethnic origin, religion or sexual orientation." Truth of the pronouncements is not mentioned. Pascal Bruckner cogently argued regarding these efforts to make criticism of Islam a punishable offense, that "we are abetting the construction of a new thought crime, one which is strongly reminiscent of the way the Soviet Union dealt with the 'enemies of the people.'" Even the Pope, Benedict XVI, was reprimanded for remarks he made at a speech at Regensburg in September 2006, when he quoted the late 14th century Byzantine emperor Manuel II Paleologus as saying, "Show me just what Muhammad brought that was new, and there you will find things evil and inhuman, such as his command to spread by the sword the faith he preached."

Almost certainly the threat of lawsuits brought by Islamic groups has led to self-censorship by Western writers. It did not encourage free speech or a free press that the OIC, in its 1990 Declaration of Human Rights in Islam, stated that expression of opinion should be "in such manner as would not be contrary to the principles of the sharia." By its Charter of 2008, the OIC claims to be the protector of Muslim immigrants living in non-Muslim countries. It appears less concerned with the Islamic practice of legal beating of Muslim women, or honor killings in the Arab countries by blood relatives of females who are said to have besmirched the good name of the family or acted "dishonorably." For the women murdered because of "family honor," there is no funeral or gravestone. In Syria the penal code enshrines the inequality of women in marriage and inheritance rights and allows lower penalties for murder and other violent crimes against women in defense of family "honor."

Western publishers have in recent years been careful in their publication of books on Islam, its history or culture. Both scholarly and popular discussion of the subject has become a somewhat perilous enterprise. The celebrated publishers Random House, in 2006 withdrew the book *The Jewel of Medina*, which discussed Muhammad's child bride, for fear of offending Muslims. The Yale University Press in 2009 refused to publish the twelve Danish cartoons of Muhammad in a book on the subject, *The Cartoons that Shook the World*, by Jytte Klausen, as well as any images of Muhammad, including those by Gustave Doré and Salvador Dali. In the same year the German publisher Droste withdrew a novel, *To Whom Honor is Due*, by Gabriele Brinkmann, because of passages deemed controversial.

Moreover, religious freedom is limited in a number of Arab countries; Saudi Arabia bans non-Muslims both from having their own house of worship in the country and also from practicing their religion. Jordan does not allow Israelis entering the country to carry or wear Jewish religious artifacts. There are mosques in Rome, but there is no expectation of reciprocity: no churches, let alone synagogues, exist in Mecca, Jeddah, or Riyadh. Nor is it easy to build churches in Egypt, which sets a number of conditions before construction can begin. Certainly, some violations of religious freedom exist in the Christian world, but it is equally certain that Muslim states are responsible for far more pervasive and severe violations of religious rights of Christians and Jews. In many of those states, Christians are not allowed to proselytize and Muslims are forbidden to convert to Christianity.[80]

Can the behavior of countries, such as Saudi Arabia, Pakistan, Egypt, and Iran, be equated with racism or acting as apartheid states? Many of them calling for limits on "defamation of religion," have high levels of restriction on freedom of religion, and threaten or punish the freedom of speech of human rights activists and religious minorities. In the 1970s, to prevent criticism of the political ideology of Islamism, Iranian fundamentalists, imitating Leon Pinsker's use of "Judeophobia," coined the word "Islamophobia," essentially implying an outlook or world view involving an unfounded dread and dislike of Muslims, which results in practices of exclusion and discrimination. No doubt some prejudice against Muslims does exist, but the Iranian use of the word as a derogatory term is in essence an attempt to silence those who criticize Islamism, or radical Islam; both those Muslims those who question the rigidity of the interpretation of the Koran and the restrictions on dress and behavior, and those non-Muslim Westerners who are concerned with the activities of radical Islamists in their countries and who are therefore called racists. The Cairo Declaration on Human Rights, enacted by the OIC in August 1990, is unequivocal on the issue of rights and free speech. Article 24 states that all the rights and freedoms in the Declaration "are subject to the Islamic Sharia" and Article 25 states that the Islamic Sharia is "the only source of reference for the explanation or clarification of any of the articles of this Declaration." Its edicts are therefore, superior to the universal Declaration of Human Rights. In addition, it declares (Article 22) that information "may not be exploited or misused in such a way as may violate sanctities and the dignity of Prophets." These actions restrain or prevent individual judgment of the nature of Islam and its adherents. John Stuart Mill, in his advocacy of free speech, thought it was preferable for people to seek the truth for themselves rather than have it imposed on them. Islamic fundamentalists view elections not to promote democracy or individual freedom, but as a way to promote Islam.[81]

THE DURBAN FOLLIES

Inherent bias by the non-Western international community was again illustrated in the campaign of political warfare conducted in the two World Conferences against Racism, Racial Discrimination, Xenophobia, and Related Intolerance. The first was held in Durban in September 2001. The second, Durban Review Conference (Durban II), was held in Geneva in April 2009. The objective of this second Conference was to examine the effective and comprehensive implementation of the conclusions and recommendations of the UN Durban 1.

Durban I was hosted by the UNHRC. Among the participants in 2001 were representatives of states, Palestinians and groups sympathetic to their interests, and about 1,500 non-governmental organizations (NGOs), some of which helped to shape the critical language about Israel later used at the Conference. As in UNGA Resolution 3379 of 1975 (the Zionism as Racism Resolution), the main thrust of the Durban Conferences were the charges against Israel of racism, apartheid, and domination of occupied territory. The Durban process was concerned with "the plight of the Palestinian people under foreign occupation." One of its consequences was the impetus given to the campaign for boycott, divestment, and sanctions against Israel. Not only were there to be fewer specific contacts with Israel, but in a more general sense Israel was to be isolated from the world community.

The first Durban Conference was accorded legitimacy since it was held under the auspices of the UN. As a result of controversy and the evident bias of the Conference, which led the US to leave it especially because of the proposed final declaration of Durban I, a second Conference was delayed for eight years. This Durban II meeting was prepared by a committee whose chairs were representatives from Libya and Cuba. Some highly critical and disparaging remarks about Israel written in the Preparatory Committee Report for Durban II were eliminated in the final Outcome Document of the Conference. Also, nine countries, starting with Canada and including the US, declined to attend, and twenty-three other countries sent only low-level representatives to Durban II. The Ford Foundation which had helped to finance Durban I did not do so for its successor.

The first paragraph of the Document of Durban II in April 2009 affirms the statement of the earlier Durban I Conference. That statement, in Article 72, while not specifically naming Israel, is clearly directed at it. The Document reaffirms that a foreign occupation founded on settlements, its laws based on racial discrimination with the aim of continuing domination of the occupied territory, as well as its practices, which consist of reinforcing a total military blockade, isolating towns, cities and villages under occupation from each other, totally contradicts the purposes and principles of the Charter of the United Nations. Such an occupation constitutes a serious violation of international human rights and humanitarian law, a new kind of apartheid, a crime against humanity, a form of genocide and a serious threat to international peace and security. At Durban I, terms such as genocide, ethnic cleansing, and Holocaust were used against Israel. Moreover, paragraph 63, mentioning only one group in the world, states that, "We are concerned about the plight of the Palestinian people under foreign occupation," and paragraph 65, again implicitly confining itself to one group, says, "We recognize the right of refugees to return voluntarily to their homes and properties in dignity and safety." No other group is mentioned specifically, nor is any country other than Israel charged with occupation, racism and with being an apartheid state. China's occupation of Tibet, and Russia's occupation of Japanese islands remain unmentioned.

If the Durban II meeting was more moderate than its predecessor, it did also provide an official platform for a speech by Iranian President Mahmoud Ahmadinejad, the only head of government to attend the meeting, who, in his customary manner and rhetorical restraint, declared that Israel was a racist state masquerading as a religious one and that it was the most cruel and repressive racist regime. He accused the West of using the Holocaust as a pretext for aggression against the Palestinians. He referred to the Holocaust as "an ambiguous and dubious position," and advocated the end of the State of Israel. His raucous declamation may not have received universal admiration, but the political thunder has not ceased. In December 2010 the UNGA, by a vote of 104-22-33, adopted a resolution that Durban III, a special UNGA session, be held in New York in September 2011 to commemorate the tenth anniversary of Durban I. Among the 14 countries refusing to attend Durban III were the United States, Canada, the Netherlands, Israel, Italy, Austria, Australia, and the Czech Republic. The stated purpose of the one-day meeting was to focus on "victims of racism, racial discrimination, xenophobia, and related intolerances." No one needed reminding that the only alleged victims of racism named by the delegates were the Palestinians.

Chapter 6

The Charge of Colonialism

Like the words racism and imperialism, "colonialism" has become a loaded word in the lexicon of politics, particularly in relation to Israel. Certainly throughout history strong or dominant powers such as Rome, Greece, Arab dynasties, the Moors, Britain, France, Spain, the Netherlands, Belgium, Portugal, the Ottoman Empire, Russia, China, Japan, and the United States, have sought colonial possessions for political or economic reasons. Though "colonialism" and also "imperialism" can be defined in different ways, essentially the terms imply a system of occupation and domination by a country or people of a foreign land, and of a dissimilar people from the inhabitants. Such occupation may be based on the belief that the mores of the colonizing power are superior to those of the colonized. The colonial power exercises central functions of the state, levying taxes, administering justice, controlling police and military forces, and responsibility for diplomatic relations.[82] Fundamental decisions affecting the life of a colonized people are made and implemented by the colonial rulers.

Less strong forms of direct colonialism are "informal colonialism," in which a country is able to function, but is sovereign only to a certain degree while a dominant power obtains political, economic, and social privileges from it; the relations between the United States and Cuba for the first fifty years of the 20th century can illustrate this case . Colonialism could also be interpreted as an asymmetrical relationship, largely economic and military in character, in which a stronger power could influence a weaker one.

Throughout history different factors account for the existence of colonialism, such as the Russian expansion to the Caucasus and the Far East, the Moorish conquest of Spain, the French control in Indo-China, Tunisia, and Senegal, the struggle over Jerusalem by the Crusaders and the Arabs, or the competition of five European powers in the scramble for Africa. These factors would include the desire and search for wealth, spices, and gold; love of adventure; religious zeal; demographic pressure; desire for revenge by conquest; expansion of markets; economic benefits; desire to be and to be considered a great power; and motivation by a "superior" people to civilize or modernize an "inferior" one, by carrying the "white man's burden" or *mission civilisatrice*. In light of these factors, can Israel rightfully be termed a "colonialist" state or haunted by the ghost of Western imperialism?

THE JEWISH HISTORICAL PRESENCE

Unlike the peoples of recognized colonial powers, Jews were historically in exile, and for the most part were a persecuted minority. It would be a travesty or a fallacious historical narrative to argue that Israel fell into the pattern of an outside power eager to impose its will on, or to conquer, an indigenous population. Israel has not sought conquest, or domination, or economic or financial control, or searched for markets to dump surplus goods, or sought to spread a religious faith. Allegations of this kind have arisen as a result of deliberate distortions of historical events and of statistics concerning the differences between Israelis and Arabs over existence and casualty figures, which have often been deliberately exaggerated by Palestinians, as well as over territory. Granted, there are differences of opinion about the control and destiny of the West Bank or disputed territories. Yet it is somewhat incongruous that Israel is accused of colonialism as the result of Jews returning to the Jewish ancestral home, or of having a colonial heritage because of the Balfour Declaration and the British Mandate. Both favored the creation of a Jewish national home which would lead to Jewish immigration to Palestine.

The fact is usually left unmentioned that most of the present day Arab states have not existed since time immemorial, but owe their existence to decisions by European powers, Britain and France, who semi-secretly cut deals over the remains of the Ottoman Empire and created new countries which became sovereign states after World War I and World War II. The French League of Nations Mandate led to the creation of Syria, and Lebanon. Syria, as seen by T.E. Lawrence in his *Seven Pillars of Wisdom*, was a vividly colored racial and religious mosaic. Libya, containing about 150 tribal units, was created in 1931 by Italy, by joining together three regions of the Ottoman vilayat (Cyrenaica, Tripolitania, and Fezzan), nominally under the control of the Ottomans for 400 years. Mussolini in 1937 had in Tripoli declared himself "Protector of Islam." With the defeat of Italy in World War II in 1943, the country came under British and French control. It was recognized by the United Nations as an independent country in 1949 and became a united kingdom under Idris Sanusi I, a member of the Sanusiyya Islamic sect, in 1951. The monarchy was overthrown by a military coup led by the twenty seven year old Colonel Gadhafi, a member of a minor tribe, in 1969. The tribes with their family ties, have differed in their support of, or opposition to, the regime of Gadhafi. That regime was renamed by Gadhafi as the Great Socialist People's Libyan Arab Jamahiriyah (the State of the Masses). Gadhafi also renamed himself as the Revolution's Guide, giving up his own official governmental position. Power, however, remained with him, with his family, which controlled much of the economy, and with trusted members of his tribe until his murder by Libyan insurgents on October 20, 2011.

Bahrain, for long a British protectorate, became an independent state in 1971, at first an emirate and then a kingdom in 2002. In both of these regimes the Al Khalifa family, Sunni Muslims, has ruled over a Shiite majority population. Saudi Arabia became a unified kingdom in 1932 and is ruled by a royal family which now has 7,000 princes. Interestingly, perhaps because the country was the fount of Wahhabism, the extreme Islamic movement, Osama bin Laden referred to it not by its political name, but as the "Land of the Two Mosques." Yemen, with hundreds of tribes led by sheiks, became a united country in 1990.

The gibe has some merit in referring to these states set up by colonial powers as "tribes with flags," artificial states mainly composed of and divided by tribes, ethnic groups, and sects, but without citizens in the modern sense, or commitment to a national community. The only Arab exception is Egypt, with its long history, witnessed strikingly by the Pyramids of Giza, symbolizing autocratic rule of the Pharaohs with an empire stretching from Syria to the Sudan. Egypt became a unified state around 3100 B.C., but for most of its history it was under the control of foreign empires: Libyan, Nubian, Assyrian, Persian, Roman, Britain. Greek was the administrative language under the rule of the Ptolemies (330-305 B.C.). The transformation to modern Egyptian independence resulted from the break with the Ottoman Empire during and after World War I, a separation recognized by the 1923 Treaty of Lausanne, and the end of British colonial rule by a unilateral declaration in 1922, and the creation of a monarchy. The monarchy, incompetent and corrupt, was overthrown by a group of army officers, in which Gamal Abdel Nasser was prominent, and a republic was declared in 1953. The overall security framework in the area was at first largely controlled by Britain and, after its withdrawal from the region by the 1970s, by the US, with a virtual protectorate over the Persian Gulf. Autocratic monarchies co-existed with regimes created by military officers.

By contrast to this relatively recent creation of Arab states, Jews can trace their presence in the area of Palestine back to about 1400 B.C., after their exodus from Egypt. The Hebrew tribes later were united and formed a political kingdom under Saul, then under David who around 1006 B.C. established Jerusalem as his capital, and then under Solomon who built the First Temple around 967 B.C. These rulers acted with full national sovereignty at a moment of a temporary decline in the power of surrounding empires.[83] The united Jewish kingdom split circa 930 B.C. into two units. The kingdom of Israel in the north of the area was ended by the Assyrian Empire around 720 B.C, and the Israelite tribes (the Lost Tribes) were exiled. The kingdom of Judea in the south was conquered by the Babylonian Empire under Nebuchadnezzar, who destroyed the First Temple in 586 B.C. The Jews were deported to Babylon, the first Diaspora. After the Persian king Cyrus allowed the return of Jews to Jerusalem in 539 B.C., the Second Temple was built. The Jewish population had limited autonomy in religion and administration. Between 140-37 B.C. an independent Jewish kingdom existed under the Hasmonean Dynasty.

Even after the Roman conquest of Palestine and their administration of Judea and Samaria in the first century A.D., the destruction by Titus of the Second Temple in 70 A.D., and the unsuccessful revolt against their rule by Bar Kokhba in 132 A.D., small Jewish communities remained in the area, primarily in Jerusalem, Safed, Tiberias, and Hebron. However, most of the Jewish population was dispersed throughout the world, constituting the Diaspora and exile for the Jewish people. For almost five hundred years Jews were not allowed to reside in Jerusalem. The repeated prayer for nearly two thousand years, performed toward the direction of Jerusalem, and the dream for many, was to return from exile to the city. For more than the last 150 years Jews have been the majority group in Jerusalem. A poignant statement of this yearning, and of the concept of a Jewish people linked by religion, is that in George Eliot's *Daniel Deronda,* written in 1876, where the Jewish hero in England tells his lady friend that "The idea that I am possessed with is that of restoring a political existence to my people, making them a nation again, giving them a national center such as the English have, though they are scattered over the face of the globe...I am resolved to devote my life to it."[84]

This idea of a Jewish nation has not been acceptable to some people, even those who are otherwise sympathetic to Jewish individual rights. This reluctance was shown in the celebrated speech of Count Stanislas de Clermont-Tonnerre in the debate on the emancipation of Jews, in the French Constituent Assembly on December 23, 1789. It is in essence an early illustration of the supposed tension between universalistic ideals of liberalism and humanitarianism, and a particularistic view of Jewish history and destiny as a nation with a state of its own. Clermont-Tonnerre, while approving of the emancipation of Jews asserted, "To the Jews as a Nation, nothing; to the Jews as individuals, everything... They must not form a political corps or an Order in the state; they must be citizens individually."

However, what is apparent today is that the supposed tension can be overcome and that the State of Israel, emanating from the particularistic view of Jews as a nation and the unique link between religion and nationality, can also embody universal principles of liberty, civic equality, and religious tolerance. Two conclusions follow. One is that the Jewish nation, the result of the self-determination of a people in the creation of Israel, collectively embodies the rights of individual Jews as described in the French emancipation. The other is that there is no inherent logical contradiction between Zionist ideals and the policies of a changing, diverse Israeli society which, while addressing issues of material needs and security concerns, also has a commitment to universalist-humanist principles, of freedom, equality, and human rights.

The entity known as "Palestine" has no clear geographical boundaries other than the Mediterranean coast. Any boundaries have to a large extent depended on the outcome of clashes of warring powers over the area. Until the League of Nations Mandate of 1922, the contours of Palestine had never been defined in any precise legal fashion. It was not a distinctive area with a political or cultural life different from those in the surrounding areas. Nor, except for a short period when the Crusaders established the Latin Kingdom of Jerusalem (1099-1187), has the area been ruled by an independent sovereign state since the Hebrew Kingdom of Judea was crushed by the Romans, who continued to put down Jewish revolts, such as the Bar Kokhba revolt between 132 and 135 A.D., against them. The Romans captured Jerusalem in 70 A.D. and destroyed the Second Temple of the Jews on the Temple Mount, and built a temple to honor Jupiter. Later, Jerusalem was renamed as Aelia Capitolina. The area became a Roman province administered by the governor of Syria. In the fifth century B.C. the Greek historian Herodotus wrote of a district of Syria called "Palaistine." The Romans adopted this term and renamed Judea and Samaria, the area of the former Jewish principality, as Syria Palaestina, after the Philistines, an Aegean people who were driven out of the Greek islands and Phoenicia and settled in the southern part of "Palestine." The land, as James Parkes suggested, was named Palaestina or Palestine by the Romans to eradicate all traces of more than a thousand years of Jewish history.[85]

It is rarely mentioned that the only historic political sovereign state in Palestine was the Jewish one of Saul, David, and Solomon. From that date, with the exception of the short interlude of the Crusader kingdom, the area of Palestine, which was called by different names, was never a country with frontiers, but only one with administrative boundaries and changing provisional subdivisions. It was with the British Mandate in 1922 that the area called "Palestine" had the contours of what is today Israel, the West Bank, and Gaza. Palestine was never an independent state, nor a single administrative or cultural unit, nor historically was there a Palestinian people different in any way from other Arabs in the Middle East area. The non-Jewish population of the area, largely coming from invaders and those seeking economic improvement, was divided along religious, denominational, regional, economic, and clannish lines.[86] After Emperor Constantine's conversion to Christianity in 330 A.D., that religion became for a time the official religion of the area. Yet from the seventh century on, the area for most of the next 1,300 years was ruled by Islamic Empires. Though successive rulers persecuted Jews and tried to eliminate them, a Jewish presence of varying numbers remained in the area which was controlled through the centuries by the different empires; the Romans and Byzantium (136-636 A.D.), the Muslim dynasties (the Umayyads, the Abbasid caliphate and the Fatimid dynasty), the Crusaders who established the Latin kingdom, Saladin, the Mongols briefly, the Mamluks, and the Ottoman Turks until 1918.

Jerusalem has historically been a place of conflict between different peoples who have besieged and captured it on many occasions and even destroyed it twice. The city, then with a population of about 16,000 people, was captured by the Ottoman Turks from the Mamluks in 1516. It was, and remains, divided into four quarters—Jewish, Muslim, Christian, and Armenian. It was, and remains, a Holy City or an important religious center for the different religions. For Jews the Holy Place is the Western Wall of the Old Temple, for Christians the Church of the Holy Sepulchre, for Muslims the Haram al-Sharif, or Temple Mount, with the Dome of the Rock, built between 685 and 715, and the Al-Aqsa Mosque.

The city has different degrees of symbolic reference for the different religions. Since King David in 1004 B.C. declared it was the capital of the Jewish state and Solomon, according to the Bible, built the First Temple, *Beit Hamikdash*, Jerusalem has been the most important and the most holy city for Jews who recognize the city in ritual practice and prayers and festival celebrations. This was passionately and most famously expressed by Psalm 137; "If I forget thee, O Jerusalem, let my right hand forget her cunning. If I do not remember thee, let my tongue cleave to the roof of my mouth."

When Jews, then termed Israelites, returned from exile in Babylon they reclaimed Jerusalem as their capital and built there the Second Temple. Coins made during the revolt, 68-70 A.D., against the Romans during which almost 1 million Jews were killed, bear in Hebrew the phrase "Freedom of Zion." During the Jewish revolt, 132-135, led by Bar-Kokhba against the Romans, a coin was struck with the words, *Herut Yerushalayim* (the freedom of Jerusalem), symbolizing the temporary capture of the city by the Jews. In Jewish consciousness the yearning for Jerusalem has been enticing for some and nostalgic for others, expressed in religious prayer, ritual practice and holiday celebrations. Centuries before the existence of London, Paris, Washington, or Moscow, it was the capital of a Jewish state. It was proclaimed the capital of Israel in 1949, and declared the capital by a law on July 30, 1980. Other peoples have passed through or been present in the city, Assyrians, Babylonians, Jebusites, Thracians, Romans, Crusaders, Persians, Arabs, Ottomans, British, but it was the Jewish ancestral city. The significance of Jerusalem was indicated by Amos Elon: "Among the many vanquished capital cities of the ancient world, only Jerusalem survived in the imagination of her exiles and in that of their descendants from generation to generation."[87]

By comparison with this unique importance of Jerusalem in the Jewish consciousness, the city has less resonance, historically, politically and religiously, for Muslims. Jerusalem is mentioned over 600 times in the Bible. Though sometimes Muslims have come to refer to Jerusalem as Al-Quds (The Holy), the city is never mentioned in the Koran. It is less a place of veneration than are Mecca, the place of Muhammad's birth, and Medina where the Prophet ruled, established as the first Muslim state and where he is buried. The significance of these two places is shown by the fact that Saudi King Abdullah prefers to refer to himself as the "Custodian of the Two Holy Places," rather than as the monarch of his country. While Jerusalem is mentioned in Jewish prayers including the Passover Service which entreats "Next Year in Jerusalem," it is not mentioned in Muslim prayers. For Muslims, the pilgrimage to Mecca, the (*Hajj*), in which over two million a year participate, remains one of the Five Pillars of Islam. Muhammad lived all his life in Arabia. Though the prophet Muhammad is said to have ascended from Jerusalem to heaven on his "Night Journey" for a meeting with Allah, the mosque, the al-Aqsa mosque, with which this event is associated was not constructed until fifty years after his death in 632. Though Jerusalem was governed for over 1,300 years by Islamic dynasties, no Muslim state made Jerusalem its capital. Indeed, for centuries they had little interest in the city. This was shown in 1229 when, following an agreement among the Muslim ruler, the Egyptian Sultan, and the Crusaders, Jerusalem was ceded to the Christian Holy Roman Emperor Frederick II, who crowned himself "King of Jerusalem;" however, Christian rule lasted only fifteen years.[88]

No Palestinian state has ever been established. Israel was not established on the ashes of any such state. The last generally recognized sovereign power in the area was the Ottoman Empire. Under that Empire, from 1516 until World War I, the area of Palestine was a district, not a political entity. Officially, it was part of the *vilayet* (province) of Damascus-Syria and then part of the *vilayet* of Saida (Sidon), and then split again into three administrative units, the *vilayet* of Beirut, the district of Jerusalem, and the *vilayet* of Hijaz. Foreigners had certain privileges as a result of a number of Capitulation Agreements made between the Ottoman Empire and Western Powers, which had their own courts, schools, and religious institutions.

The inhabitants of the general Palestine area were subjects of that Turkish Empire, not of an Arab nation. The Christian and Jewish communities enjoyed a certain degree of communal autonomy in religious, economic, and personal matters. After the defeat in 1918 of the Ottoman Empire, which sided with Germany in World War I, the Empire by the Treaty of Sèvres surrendered its Middle East territories which were then divided. It is salutary to recall that out of the districts of the Ottoman Empire new states, Iraq, Syria, Lebanon, Jordan, were created by decisions of the European powers, not by self-determination of the different populations. Political problems, still acute, have stemmed from the division of that Empire into states, some of them having little meaning for their inhabitants. For example one such state, Iraq, was artificially created by Britain out of the three Ottoman *vilayets* of Basra, Baghdad, and Mosul. Lebanon, a state resulting from French influence, is still troubled by a dysfunctional system in which power is divided among hostile confessional religious communities and personalities, leading to weak central government and making a notion of citizenship questionable. The fractionalized Lebanese society includes Maronite Catholics, Greek Orthodox, Armenian Apostolic and Melkite Greek Catholics, Sh'ia Muslims, Sunni Muslims, and Druze, the largely secret religion that is an offshoot of Ismali Islam. Jordan is a country whose king is supported by the Bedouins of the Zubeidi clan, only part of the population. The question of Israeli citizenship is discussed later.

Chapter 7

On the Road to a State

Zionism is a national, not a colonial, movement. Its aim was colonization, a diverse and complex phenomenon in the return of Jews to an ancient homeland, and one that is quite different from colonialism.[89] Zionists did not go to the territory to dominate the Arab inhabitants of Palestine or improperly expropriate their land.[90] Nor did they fulfill the Arab expectation that Jews would eventually depart from the area. Zionist settlement and place in Palestine is not comparable to that of the British settlers in Rhodesia, who left the country, or to the French settlers, *pieds noirs*, in Algeria, who departed after Algeria gained its independence.

Jewish return to Palestine, from 1517 under Ottoman control, began in larger number from the sixteenth century, at first by those escaping the Spanish Inquisition. By the 1840s Jews constituted a majority in Jerusalem. Much larger waves of immigration started in the 1880s, the First Aliyah (1881-1903), as Jews began escaping from persecution and the savage pogroms, during which over 30,000 Jews were murdered, and the antisemitism in Tsarist Russia, Eastern Europe and Yemen. An important intellectual expression of this movement was the pamphlet, *Auto-Emancipation*, written in 1882 by Leo Pinsker, a medical doctor in Odessa, who argued that Jews were guests everywhere and never at home. He urged the Jewish people to work for independence and implementation of national consciousness. Interestingly, the physician Pinsker, instead of using the word "antisemitism," preferred the term "Judeophobia" to indicate the psychological disorder of hatred, a variety of demonology, of those who hated Jews. Immigration of pioneers into Palestine was diverse. Yet, Jews wanting to live a religious life in the Holy Land, those who wanted to escape persecution in Eastern Europe, and those who were political Zionists, all returned to their ancient homeland, ruled then by the Ottoman Empire.

The latter group of political Zionists was influenced by and centered round Theodor Herzl, the cosmopolitan journalist for the liberal Viennese paper, the *Neue Freie Presse,* who was conscious of antisemitism in his own country, Austria, and who was crucially affected by the animosity against Jews in the Dreyfus Affair, while he was in Paris. The cosmopolitan writer and playwright essentially founded the political movement of Zionism, starting with his book, in essence a manifesto, *Der Judenstaat* (The Jewish State), published in 1896. He and his followers held that Jews should be regarded not as an ethnic or religious minority, but as a nation. Herzl's Zionism was a national movement, the aim to create a state through political and diplomatic means. His group challenged the solution of assimilation in the countries in which Jews lived, a process heralded by the emancipation of Jews during the French Revolution, but made questionable by the prejudice shown by the Dreyfus Affair; instead a territorial state for Jews should be created. Herzl's fundamental arguments were that Jews are "a people, one people," that the Jewish people needed a state, and that the international community should recognize and support the creation of such a state since the "Jewish Question" could only be solved by making it a "political world-question" in which the civilized nations of the world would be involved.

To implement these views Herzl developed the Zionist movement. The declaration of the First Zionist Congress, which met in the Municipal Casino in Basel in August 1897, and which he organized, was that "the aim of Zionism is to create for the Jewish people a publicly legally assured home (*Heimstätte*) in Palestine." That home would be given international approval.[91] The two elements, the concept of a national home and the recognition of the existence of a Jewish people which had a historical connection with Palestine, were to be recognized in the 1917 British Balfour Declaration and then in the League of Nations

Mandate. When fulfilled, the national home would put an end to the gibe that Jews have too much history and too little geography.[92]

Zionism was never a monolithic ideology. Besides Herzl, who died on July 3, 1904, at the age of 44, other thinkers and activists in the Zionist movement stressed other issues. Max Nordau, anxious to overcome what he regarded as the "degeneration" of Jewish life in the Diaspora, spoke of the need for "muscular" Jewry which would be developed in a Jewish state. Those who were socialists spoke of the desirability of creating a new kind of society. An alternative path to that of Herzl was proposed by Ahad Ha'am, an intellectual from Odessa concerned about Jewish assimilation, who advocated a concept of cultural Zionism, stressing the moral values of Judaism, and believing that the creation of a state would solve not only the Jewish problem, but also the problem of Judaism by implementing those moral values. He envisaged the land of Israel as the spiritual center, the *merkaz ruhani*, of Jews.

ZIONISM IN ACTION

The First Congress in 1897 was attended by over two hundred Zionists, including five from the area of Palestine, advocating their different positions; parenthetically, the first Arab Congress in 1913 in Paris was attended by only thirteen Arabs. In his speech to the Congress, which established the World Zionist Organization, Herzl claimed to have founded the Jewish State. If this claim was somewhat immodest, and though Herzl was sometimes disparaged as an adventurer whose command of Jewish knowledge was minimal—he spoke neither Yiddish nor Hebrew and was devoted to Viennese culture—his enthusiasm, organizational and diplomatic efforts in the nine years left to him were a major influence on the Jewish nationalist movement. The 1897 Congress created the World Zionist Organization (WZO). This movement was rich and diverse with competing points of view incorporating widely different policies, though underlying it was the basic thesis of a community of destiny for all Jews and Jewish political sovereignty in Palestine for the Jewish people. Zionism saw the Jewish people as a historical entity, a nation made up of diverse anthropological elements; like other nations it was not a racial entity.

In his book Herzl rejected Jean-Jacques Rousseau's idea of a state founded by a social contract. He explained the source of sovereignty by using the concept of Roman law, *negotiorum gestio;* when the property of an oppressed person is in danger a person, the *gestor*, an agent, may step forward to save it, working for the good of the people. The *gestor* of the Jews must be a corporate body, the "Society of Jews," led by a Jewish Company, in effect the Zionist movement. This movement would be the vanguard of the Jewish people everywhere.[93] A state, for Herzl a Jewish state, would be formed by people united under sovereign rule. That sovereign state would, Herzl hoped, lead to the ending of antisemitism in the world.

In his book, *Der Judenstaat,* and his novel *Altneuland,* Herzl imagined a multi-cultural normalized Jewish people living in its old homeland. That imagination was to become reality beyond Herzl's dreams, with Operation Moses in 1984-1985 and Operation Solomon in 1991, when Israel took in over 20,000 Beta Israel, East African Ethiopian Jews and Falash Mura of whom there is now over 100,000, and absorbed Christians fleeing Sudan, as well as integrating the Jews from Arab and Islamic countries. Israel in one weekend in May 1991 used thirty-four El Al planes to transport the Ethiopians to Israel.

Herzl is generally regarded as a national hero and his name has been honored in many ways in Israel. Curiously however in a book, *The History and Politics of Street Names in Israel*, author Maoz Azaryahu calculates that though in Israel Herzl has fifty-two streets named after him, as well as the city of Herzliya, his political rival Jabotinsky has been honored by fifty-five streets.[94] Comparing the two rivals is instructive. The charming Herzl hoped to achieve his goal by meetings, with Pope Pius X, the King of Bulgaria, twice with the German Kaiser Wilhelm, then in 1901 with the Ottoman Sultan, from whom he tried to obtain a "charter" for Palestine, and in 1903 with V.K.Plehve, the Russian Minister for the Interior, who was suspected of playing a role in the pogrom in 1903 in the city of Kishinev in Bessarabia where forty-nine Jews were killed, 500 wounded, and 2,000 left homeless. The meetings were not successful. It was Jabotinsky, who in an essay first published in Russian in 1923, perceived that Arabs would never accept Jewish settlement in Palestine and therefore Jews had to settle "behind an iron wall which the native population cannot breach." He conceived the iron wall as protection by a Jewish battalion in the British army, a somewhat improbable occurrence, and an idea that was rejected by the Zionist leaders. Yet in retrospect, his disciples have argued that the iron wall, or the use of strong defense by Israel, has led to negotiations and peace with Egypt and Jordan. President Sadat of Egypt, in particular, recognized the political reality of the state of Israel and made peace.

Zionism connected the People of the Book with the Land of the Bible.[95] The Jews coming into the land in the First Aliyah did not displace Arabs by conquest; they bought the land from willing sellers. Jews, returning to the ancient homeland, for various reasons, began settling and establishing agricultural villages in an area, which Sir Herbert Samuel, appointed the first British High Commissioner for Palestine in 1920 after the League of Nations Mandate for Palestine was granted to Britain, called "a desolation" and largely uninhabited. Similar remarks on the condition of the land were made by many other observers; probably the most well-known example is Mark Twain who wrote after his visit to the Holy Land in 1867: "Palestine sits in sackcloth and ashes... the stateliest name in history, has lost all its ancient grandeur and is become a pauper village...Palestine is desolate and unlovely."[96] Another famous writer, Pierre Loti, commented on his visit in 1895 to the area that "everywhere in Palestine cities and palaces have returned to the dust; this melancholy of abandonment weighs on all the Holy Land."[97] A similar view was expressed by the Swiss clergyman, Felix Bovet, who was disappointed on his visit to the Holy Land in the 1860s that the Arabs had turned the Land "into a wilderness where they do not dare step without fear. The Arabs...cannot be considered but temporary residents...They created nothing in the Land."[98]

Those opposed to the creation of the state of Israel, or who are unwilling to accept it, sometimes decry as fallacious the phrase used about Palestine by early Zionists, "a land without a people for a people without a land," and usually attribute it to the Jewish British writer Israel Zangwill. In fact, the first use of the phrase, or one in almost identical language, was by Alexander Keith, a Scottish evangelical clergyman, in 1843.[99] He argued that Christians should help fulfill the biblical prophecy of Jews returning to Palestine. More familiar is the statement in 1853 by Lord Shaftesbury to Lord Palmerston, the British foreign minister, that Greater Syria was a country without a nation in need of a nation without a country. That nation was the Jews. By the late nineteenth century the phrase, in varying language supporting the return of Jews to Palestine, was used by Christians in both Britain and the United States.

Israel Zangwill's frequently quoted statement, "Palestine is a country without a people; the Jews are a people without a country" was not made until 1901.[100] Herzl himself never used the phrase, which was rarely mentioned by the Zionist movement. Ben-Gurion, replying to a later article by Zangwill, wrote in 1918 that Eretz Israel was not an empty country, but the home of three quarter of a million people. The case for the recreation of a Jewish national home in Palestine did not rest on the phrase, or on the belief that Arabs were not present in the area. It rested on Jewish desire to return to the old homeland, and on the right of Jews to choose to do so after the state was established. Herzl did say that "Palestine is our ever-memorable historic home. The very name of Palestine would attract our people with a force of marvelous potency." Herzl's assertion was legally endorsed on July 24, 1922, by the League of Nations, which spoke of the fact that "recognition has been given to the historical connection of the Jewish people with Palestine and to the grounds for reconstituting their national home in that country."

It is simplistic to argue that Israel was approved by international agreement after World War II, solely as a result of Western guilt about the Holocaust or as a refuge against antisemitism, rather than to speak of the historical and religious connection and emotional ties of the Jewish people to the land, and its right to self-determination, a principle of international law.[101] Undeniably, international opinion and decision makers in 1947 were affected by the horrors of the Holocaust and this made the argument for a Jewish state more cogent and urgent. It was indeed a result of his awareness of the increasing number of Jews murdered by the Nazis that led Ben-Gurion, then chairman of the executive of the Jewish Agency, at the Extraordinary Zionist Conference at the Biltmore Hotel in New York on May 9, 1942, to call for "a clear and unequivocal reaffirmation of the original intention of the Balfour Declaration and the Mandate to re-establish Palestine as a Jewish Commonwealth" and to champion the adopted resolution on those lines. It also called for the opening of Jewish immigration into Palestine. His call, in New York and again before the Jewish National Assembly in Palestine on November 30, 1942, was not merely a response to the Nazi horrors, but also a declaration that the self-determination of the Jewish people in Palestine meant a reconstituting rather than a completely new establishment of a political entity.

The Zionist organization tactically took advantage of opportunities encountered and initiated other options. The call for a National Home had metamorphosed into the goal of a Jewish state. A tantalizing memory of this connection of people and land was the advocacy in 1844 for the return of Jews to the Holy Land and a rank of honor for them among the nations by Professor George Bush of New York University, ancestor of two future presidents. In addition, the State of Israel, as Julius Stone argued, rests, as do many other states in the world, "on assertion of independence by its people and government, on the vindication of that independence by arms...and on the establishment of orderly government within territory under its stable control."[102]

The manner by which this was to be achieved was subjected to controversial, even contentious, discussion among the different Zionist ideologues and political parties. The chaos of diverse, sometimes antagonistic, opinions, starting with Moses Hess' *Rome and Jerusalem: the Last National Question,* published in 1862; embraced Theodor Herzl's practical, political and diplomatic Zionism; Ahad Ha'am's cultural Zionism; Nahum Syrkin's socialist Zionism; Ben-Gurion's practical Zionism, which stressed the creation of an infrastructure of Jewish life and settlements; Martin Buber's spiritual and ethical Zionism; Ber Borochov's Marxist Zionism; Joseph Trumpeldor's militant Zionism; A. D. Gordon's romantic and spiritual form of nationalism focused on a philosophy of work; Jabotinsky's political and diplomatic Revisionist Zionism, which emphasized state power; Chaim Weizmann's General Zionism; the pacific religious Zionism of Rabbis Avraham Yitzhak Kook and Yitzhak Ya'acov Reines; and later the more militant religious Zionism of Kook's son, Rabbi Zvi Yehuda.

To these Jewish theorists and active figures must be added the non-Jewish advocates and activists on behalf of Zionism in the 19th and 20th centuries. Protestant support was important for the success of Zionist political aspirations. In his book, *Zeal for Zion*, Shalom Goldman has provided a valuable account of gentile sympathizers and supporters of the Zionist project.[103] Those gentiles included the 19th century British diplomats and clergy, such as Laurence Oliphant, Lord Shaftesbury, Lord Palmerston, and William Hechler, the 19th century American Professor George Bush, and in the 20th century a diverse group including Vladimir Nabokov, Jorge Luis Borges, Robert Graves, Jacques Maritain, Reinhold Niebuhr, and Orde Wingate.

Probably the most important early advocate of Christian Zionism was William Blackstone, an Evangelical missionary Chicago businessman, who was affected by the pogroms in Russia in the late 1880s. He organized a petition, usually referred to as the Blackstone Memorial, which was presented to President Benjamin Harrison on March 5, 1891. Significantly, it was signed by over 400 Christians coming from different backgrounds; the clergy, business, politics, and journalism, and among whom were J. P. Morgan, John D. Rockefeller, William McKinley, future President of the US, and the then owner of the New York Times. The thrust of the Memorial was that Palestine should be given back to the Jews. It propounded that according to God's distribution of nations, Palestine was the home of Jews; it was an inalienable possession from which they were expelled by force. During World War I, Blackstone joined with American Zionist leaders, including Louis Brandeis and leaders of mainstream Protestants, to present another petition to President Woodrow Wilson, calling for a Jewish state to be established in Palestine. Blackstone's role was acknowledged. In May 1916, Nathan Straus, acting on behalf of Brandeis, wrote to Blackstone that "he agrees with me that you are the Father of Zionism as your work anticipates Herzl."

The different formulations of Zionism had their adherents, but the development of the area of Palestine proceeded. A second Aliyah took place between 1904 and 1914; about 40,000 entered and founded communal agricultural settlements. The first new Jewish city, Tel Aviv, was founded in 1909. In the same year, the first Degania was established and previously uncultivated land began to be transformed. The language used by the settlers gradually changed, from that of the country from which they came, or from Yiddish, to Hebrew, the ancient language and the only one which Jews in prayer had in common, and which was revived as a native language partly through the efforts of Eliezer Ben-Yehuda, who came to Palestine in 1881. A Committee of Hebrew Language was started in 1890, and the first high school, the Gymnasia Ivrit, in which Hebrew was the official language of instruction, opened in Jaffa in 1906. One of the more unusual ways in which the language was used was the translation by Jabotinsky of the Sherlock Holmes stories into Hebrew. Under British administration in Palestine from 1922 on, Hebrew was recognized, together with English and Arabic, as an official language.

The Zionist pioneers and, later, founders of the state were colonizers, not colonialists seeking imperial domination of another people. They had been anticipated three hundred years earlier, in the middle of the sixteenth century, when the wealthy Portuguese Marrano woman, Dona Gracia (Gracia Mendes Nasi) sent Jews to live in Tiberias and paid for the city to be rebuilt. In the mid-nineteenth century small scale pioneering activities were assisted by support from Sir Moses Montefiore in London and Adolphe Crémieux in Paris. Montefiore, who visited Palestine seven times, the last time when he was ninety-one, funded charitable bodies, schools, the first Jewish settlement outside the walls of the Old City of Jerusalem, and the windmill that has become a symbol in the state of Israel.[104] The Alliance Israélite Universelle, in 1870, set up the first agricultural training center near Jaffa. The end of the century witnessed the entrance of more immigrants, many of whom had fled Eastern Europe after the pogroms starting in 1881 in the Russian Pale of Settlement, who began creating a new society in a relatively undeveloped and impoverished land, though one in which Arabs lived.

The early settlements of the first aliyah were aided by funds from Baron Edmund de Rothschild of France and Baron Maurice de Hirsch of Hungary, who financed the Jewish Colonization Association founded in 1891. The objective was to make the settlements self-sustaining. An objective, if unattractive, portrait of the land at that time was painted by the historian David Landes: "...centuries of Turkish neglect and misrule, the land given over to sand, marsh, the Anopheles mosquito, clan feuds, and Bedouin marauders."[105] A similar picture was drawn by Walter Clay Lowdermilk, the American soil conservationist, who wrote in his 1944 book, *Palestine, Land of Promise,* of the poor environmental conditions, the erosion debris, the pestilential marshes infested with dreaded malaria, the doleful ruins, the denuded slopes, and the sandy wadis.

A biography of Yigal Allon, the left-wing politician and military leader, documents the struggle starting in 1908, of Allon's father, a tenant farmer, to make the land fertile.[106] Lowdermilk praised the Jews in Palestine, who had accomplished so much in a short time, in draining the swamps, conquering malaria, planting millions of trees, digging wells and canals, irrigating thousands of acres, developing agriculture and citriculture, and building industries. Lowdermilk was optimistic: "if the forces of reclamation and progress Jewish settlers have introduced are permitted to continue, Palestine may well be the leaven that will transform the other lands of the Near East."

This development brought benefits for the Arabs in the area. Because of this, thousands came from surrounding areas to join the Arabs already there. They were aware that the wage paid to Arab workers was considerably higher than that in those surrounding areas, and services in general were better. The 1936 British Peel Commission reported that "The whole range of public services (in Palestine) has steadily developed to the benefit of the fellaheen (Arab workers)...the revenue for those services having been largely provided by the Jews."

Nevertheless, Arabs often attacked the Jewish settlers, both by individual acts and by larger assaults, growing in intensity in 1947-48. Arab attacks, such as the massacre of Jews in Tiberias in 1938, were met with Jewish reprisals against Arab villages. The Arab leaders called for an end to Jewish immigration, for Arabs to stop selling land to Jews, and above all rejected all proposals in the 1920s and 1930s, and in 1947, for sharing the territory of Palestine between the two sides. For them the Zionist movement was not a national liberation movement, but rather a colonial intrusion, a modern version of the Crusaders fighting to recover the Holy Land. Indeed, for the Arabs the Jewish immigration was more challenging than were the Crusaders, because it was a reminder of the historical connection of Jews with the land of Israel.

The Zionists acquired land by legal purchase; most Arabs were compensated with other land, were relocated within Palestine, or became wage earners. The Labor Zionists ideologically wanted a Jewish working class to emerge in Palestine, thus avoiding exploitation of Arab labor. Even if jobs were therefore filled by Jewish immigrants, the Arab population greatly benefited, both by its increased standard of living resulting from the Zionist economic development of the country, and by the Kupat Holim health care extended to them. Lawrence of Arabia was aware of the likely impact of what he called "the Jewish experiment" in Palestine, which would be beneficial to the Arabs. In an article, *The Changing East*, he wrote that the success of that Zionist experiment "will involve inevitably the raising of the present Arab population to their own material level, only a little after themselves in point of time, and the consequences might be of the highest importance for the future of the Arab world."[107] The Arab population, about 565,000 in 1922, expanded to 1,200,000 in 1947, resulting not only from natural increase, but also from immigration from other Arab countries, largely because of the attraction for Arabs of the better quality of life resulting from the Jewish development of the area.

For Arab critics, the original sin of Zionism was the call for Jewish settlement in the area called Palestine by immigrants to establish a national home, and the injunction not to depend for survival on Arab labor. For those critics, such a settlement and the injunction meant displacing non-Jewish Palestinians. Yet, this was not the original intention of the Zionist pioneers. Nor was any displacement the objective of Jewish/Israeli military actions in 1947-48 in response to attacks on the settlers, before and immediately following the establishment of the State of Israel on May 14, 1948.

Palestinian leaders tried to prevent Jewish settlement by calling on Britain as the Mandatory power to limit immigration, and calling on Arabs to refuse to sell land to Jews, as well as engaging in constant violence against those settlements. The violence in turn led to Jewish pre-occupation with self-defense and institution building. During the Mandate period Britain did hold that immigration of Jews into Palestine had to be related to "the economic absorptive capacity of the area." The British were reluctant to acknowledge that the entrance of Jews had led not only to economic development of the area, but also to an increase in the standard of living for Arabs. Yet the Peel Report of 1937 clearly made this point: it spoke of the "general beneficent effect of Jewish immigration on Arab welfare," though it also said that "though the Arabs have benefited by the development of the country owing to Jewish immigration, this has had no conciliatory effect." The Report also mentioned that, contrary to other Arab nationalist movements, Palestinian Arab nationalism was "inextricably interwoven with antagonism to the Jews."

When Israel was created, it did not establish any legal system of territorial segregation, though for understandable security purposes it did control the movements of Israeli Arabs through a military administration, which ended in 1966. Yet, with the conflict between Israel and Palestinians still unresolved, a cogent reply to the criticism of this control was given by Professor Ruth Gavison, who argued that the "contiguity of Arab settlement both within Israel and with the Arab states across the border...invites irredentism and secessionist claims, and neutralizing the threat of secession is a legitimate goal."[108] From its inception, Israel has been in a state of emergency which requires limits on normal behavior, restraints similar to those imposed by many states, including France, Germany, Italy, and Spain, in order to counter violence or threats of terrorist attacks. In fact, Israel in 1948, maintained many of the emergency regulations introduced by Britain in the Mandate period.

Though the historian Salo Baron, in a number of his writings, was critical of the "lachrymose" version of the Jewish past, the view that it was solely one of persecution and suffering, it is still true that Jews have lived with differing degrees of insecurity and have been obliged to defend themselves against enemies and aggression. Memories of heroic struggles against that aggression and also of inability to act have been part of the Jewish ethos. To a certain degree, the emergence of a national Jewish consciousness springs from the commemoration of wars and the battle over the memory and relevance of them, not from the wars themselves.[109] The story of the Masada Zealots, fighting against the Romans and committing suicide rather than surrender, was in the early years of the state of Israel seen as an echo of heroism in defense of the state and a reminder that in the present, as in the past, Israel has been surrounded by enemies. Similar heroism in the first years of Israel was displayed on many occasions, especially by the young men from the kibbutzim who, in addition to their pioneering activities, became a major part of the country's combat elite.

No Compromise

Why does Israel control any Palestinian areas outside of the Green Line? And why is there a refugee problem? The answer to both is really simple. These circumstances are the consequence of the 1948-49 and 1967 wars between Israel and Arab, including Palestinian, forces, who had launched the wars or threatened Israel. Palestinians and other Arabs were not prepared to accept the existence of the state of Israel, were unwilling to negotiate any compromise arrangement, and had tried to destroy the state and believed they would emerge victorious; thus, they had caused their own fate. For them, the "original sin" of Israel was its creation. Besides desire for the destruction of the state of Israel, the invading Arab armies in 1948 had little interest in the Palestinians as such, but mainly in the division of the captured territory if they had won the war. Even more injudicious was the statement of the commander of the Arab forces in Jaffa in February 1948, that "I do not mind the destruction of Jaffa if we secure the destruction of Tel Aviv."

The Palestinian refugee problem does not require a complicated explanation. If the Arab states had not initiated the war in 1948, the Palestinians would not have left their villages and homes, nor would the new State of Israel have had to deal with this issue. The objective of the Zionist movement was to establish a state for the Jewish people, and to that end had been building in the Yishuv (the Jewish community in Palestine) political and social institutions, and a trained militia, the Hagana, (defense). The Hagana, set up in 1920 as a para-military force to protect Jewish farms and kibbutzim, developed into an underground army. It was given military advice in training and strategy starting in the late 1930s by Orde Wingate, a member of British Army Intelligence in Palestine, who unexpectedly had become a passionate Zionist, among other reasons because of his Biblical education, and his study of the Jews in Palestine.[110] The political institutions of the Yishuv included elected representative bodies; this was the basis for the Constituent Assembly, elected in 1949 after the establishment of Israel to draft a constitution, but which never did so and instead declared itself the first Knesset (Parliament) of the new state.

Arab Palestinians, and the general Arab world, for the most part, had refused to accept division of the land and a two state solution, one Jewish and the other Arab. Violence continued from the 1920s on, escalating in 1928-29 with riots and attacks in Jerusalem, including some at the Western Wall, and massacres of Jews in Safad and Hebron. As a result, the British Colonial Office in September 1929 appointed a Commission of Inquiry (Commission on the Palestine Disturbances of August 1929) to investigate the causes of the violence and to suggest possible remedies to prevent further violence. It consisted of three members of the British Parliament and was chaired by Sir Walter Shaw. The Commission reported in March 1930 that the fundamental cause of the violence resulted from the "Arab feeling of animosity and hostility to the Jews consequent on the disappointment of their political and national aspirations and fear for their economic future." It stated that the violence in Jerusalem on August 23, 1929, "was from the beginning an attack by Arabs on Jews for which no excuse in the form of earlier murders by Jews has been established." For the most part the disturbances were "a vicious attack by Arabs on Jews accompanied by wanton destruction of Jewish property." By a 2-1 majority, the Commission recommended limitation of both immigration and land purchases by Jews. The dissenter, Harry Snell, a Labour Party Member of Parliament, argued for the continuation of Jewish immigration and purchases which had improved the standard of living of Arab workers in Palestine. He also argued the need for a "change in mind on the part of the Arab population who have been encouraged to believe that they have suffered a great wrong."

Another British Commission, led by Sir John Hope-Simpson, reported on the recommendation of the Shaw Commission. It also concluded that Jewish immigration and land purchases should be restricted. In addition it reported, what in hindsight is somewhat surprising, that there was "no margin of land available for agricultural settlement by new immigrants." The recommendations of Hope-Simpson were essentially incorporated in the British government White Paper of October 1930, issued by the then Colonial Secretary, Lord Passfield, formerly Sidney Webb; it accepted the proposed limits on Jews. After Zionist criticism of the White Paper, Prime Minister Ramsay MacDonald wrote in February 1931 to Chaim Weizmann, who had resigned as head of the World Zionist Organization and the Jewish Agency, that "the obligation to facilitate Jewish immigration and to encourage close settlement by Jews in the land remains a positive obligation of the Mandate, and that it can be fulfilled without prejudice to the rights and position of other sections of the population of Palestine."

Renewed Arab violence starting in 1936 in Jaffa and spreading elsewhere, caused hundreds of casualties. The Arab Higher Committee, led by the Mufti of Jerusalem, called for a general strike throughout Palestine in spring 1936. The violence, which lasted until 1939 and is generally referred to as the Arab Revolt, led to the establishment of a British Royal Commission, a six member group under the chair of Lord Peel, former British secretary of state for India. The leading and influential figure in it was Reginald Coupland, professor of colonial history at Oxford. It is surprising that there are few, if any, streets in Israel carrying the name of Coupland, who was the real author of the Commission's report and can fairly claim to be the main British advocate influencing the argument for partition of Palestine and the creation of a Jewish state. The report issued in July 1937 was that the Mandate was not workable and that an "irrepressible conflict" existed between Arabs and Jews in the area. It spoke of the general beneficent effect of Jewish immigration on Arab welfare, illustrated by the fact that the increase in the Arab population was most marked in urban areas affected by Jewish development. It indicated the paradox that though the Arabs had benefited by the development of the country owing to

Jewish immigration, this had no conciliatory effect; on the contrary, improvement in the economic situation had meant the deterioration of the political situation. The Commission rejected Arab allegations about Jewish land purchases. Much of the land carrying orange groves had been sand dunes or swamp and was uncultivated before it was bought and developed by Jews. The land shortage that Arabs spoke about was due less to the amount of land acquired by Jews, than to the increase in the Arab population.

The idea of two states was first officially and clearly proposed by most of the British Peel Commission in 1937, which went beyond its given task of examining and reporting on the causes of the 1936 Arab Revolt and then proposing methods for removing the causes of Arab and Jewish grievances. The Commission, which reported on June 22, 1937, rejected the possibility of dividing the country into cantons, an idea modeled after the Swiss system that had been discussed by the British Colonial Office for a number of years, and even mentioned once by Chaim Weizmann in 1919. Instead, it recommended a Jewish state in about twenty per cent of Palestine, about 5,000 square kilometers, but without exact details, while most of the rest, some eighty per cent, was to be under Arab sovereignty as the best palliative for "the disease from which Palestine is suffering." The Report continued with its medical metaphor by asserting that the only hope of a cure for the disease was "a surgical operation." The Jewish state would be a small one, extending only about forty kilometers to the south of Tel Aviv, excluding Jaffa. The Arab state would be joined with Transjordan. The Report suggested a transfer of land and an exchange of population between the two states. Jerusalem and Bethlehem would remain under the British Mandate. It suggested the transfer to neighboring countries of 225,000 Palestinian Arabs living in the area that was to become Israel. King Abdullah of Transjordan was the only Arab leader to approve partition. The Arab Higher Committee had boycotted the Peel Commission.[111]

The Peel Commission report was accepted in principle by the Jewish Agency, though some of the Jewish leadership was disappointed by the small proportion of the land allotted to a Jewish state. It was totally rejected by the Arab Higher Committee, which called for a single Arab state in all of Palestine. The British Foreign Office and the India office were less enthusiastic than the Colonial Office about the partition solution, largely in the belief that Arab opposition to it would destabilize Britain's position in the Middle East and India.[112] A new British High Commissioner in Palestine, Sir Harold MacMichael, an official regarded as favorable to the Arab side, was appointed in March 1938. Another British Commission headed by Sir John Woodhead of the Indian Civil Service was set up in 1938 to make recommendations about partition, but its members were divided on the issue and, by a split vote, decided that it was not feasible. Following this failure the British Colonial Secretary Malcolm MacDonald organized a Round Table Conference in London in February 1939 to discuss a possible agreement. The Conference suffered from the fact that the representatives of the five Arab states and the Arabs in Mandatory Palestine refused any direct contact or discussion with the Jewish representatives or even to sit in the same room with them. They rejected the Balfour Declaration and demanded that Jewish immigration and land purchases be stopped. Not surprisingly the Conference, which ended on March 27, 1939, was a failure, with no agreement on any crucial issue.

Conscious not only of this lack of agreement, but also of the threatening international situation and possibility of war in the near future against Nazi Germany, the British government, interested in placating the Arabs, was anxious for a settlement. On May 17, 1939, the Colonial Secretary issued a White Paper. It held that the framers of the Mandate did not intend that Palestine should be a Jewish state against the will of the Arab population. It imposed a limitation on Jewish immigration to 75,000 during the next five years, a quota from which the number of illegal Jewish immigrants would be deducted. After five years Jewish immigration would depend on the majority of the population, in fact the Arabs. The High Commissioner could prohibit land purchases. There would be a transitional period of ten years before the establishment of an independent state in the whole of Palestine; in effect, a bi-national state in which the Jews would be no more than a third of the population. Favorable though this White Paper presented by MacDonald was for Arabs, nevertheless the Arab Higher Committee rejected it because it did not stop Jewish immigration completely. The

Jewish Agency, mindful of the existing and increasing Nazi persecution of Jews in Europe, was saddened that "It is in the darkest hour of Jewish history that the British Government proposes to deprive the Jews of their last hope and to close the road back to the Homeland."

With one exception, British policy statements and reports recommended limits on Jewish immigration and settlement in the face of intransigent Arab hostility. Ironically, the Mufti of Jerusalem, who caused so many Jewish casualties in Mandatory Palestine, fled during World War II, first to Iraq, and then to Nazi Germany. In contrast, the Jewish Agency supported Britain in the war, though the small Stern gang was hostile. In addition to the 26,000 individual Jews who volunteered to join the British armed forces, the Jewish Agency called for the creation of a specifically Jewish military force, which was belatedly done in 1944 with the setting up of a brigade. It is rather enticing to find that Hannah Arendt took a similar view. As a refugee in New York she called for a Jewish army "to join the battle against Hitler as Jews, in Jewish battle formations under a Jewish flag."[113] The British also used a group of about 1,500 specially trained Jewish guerrillas to fight the Axis powers in the Libyan desert; this became known as the Palmach, the elite force of the Hagana. The British in 1944 also used thirty-seven Palestinian Jews, wearing British uniforms, to parachute into areas from which these men and women had originated, such as Hungary, Romania, and Slovakia, to contact resistance groups against the Nazis. Of these, seven were killed or murdered in concentration camps. One of them, Hannah Szenes, executed in Budapest as a British spy, became a symbol of heroism in the early years of Israel.

At the end of World War II hundreds of thousand displaced Jews, including survivors of the concentration camps, were in Europe, some in relocation centers. The Jewish Agency was anxious for them to reach Palestine. The report presented on August 24, 1945, of the Intergovernmental Committee on Refugees, headed by Earl G. Harrison, Dean of the University of Pennsylvania Law School, on the conditions in the Displaced Persons (DPs) camps referred to the refugees as "being in concentration camps in large numbers under our military guard instead of SS troops...except we do not exterminate them." The report recommended "the quick evacuation of all nonrepatriable Jews in Germany and Austria, who wish it, to Palestine." The US State Department under George C Marshall, and the Defense Department under James V. Forrestal, were not happy about the report; for them it conjured up the danger of an aroused Arab world and might lead to developments in the Arab world from which the Soviet Union could take advantage. The State Department had already displayed this concern when in 1945 it recommended to President Truman the development of the Dhahran airport in Saudi Arabia; this was approved and War Department funds were used for the project.[114] However, in spite of State Department opposition, President Truman who was moved by the plight of the Jews as conveyed in the Harrison report, set up, together with British Prime Minister Clement Attlee, the Anglo-American Committee of Inquiry on Palestine, consisting of six British and six American individuals, to find a resolution of the post-war Jewish refugee problem within the wider issue of Jewish immigration into Palestine.

One of the American members of the Committee was Bartley Crum, a San Francisco corporation lawyer, best known as Rita Hayworth's lawyer, and a campaign manager for Wendell L. Wilkie during the presidential election in 1940. Crum was previously unversed in the complexities of the Palestine issue, but quickly became a shrewd observer of Middle Eastern politics and personalities, and contrasted Jewish and Arab culture.[115] He saw Jews in Palestine as representing a progressive force in the Middle East, and held that support for a Jewish national home was the first and logical step to advance democracy in the area. By contrast, Arab leaders were forces of reaction: they regarded Zionism with its social and technological innovations as a threat to maintaining the Arab population in a condition of ignorance and serfdom, and called for a boycott of Jewish products. Crum was aware of two pertinent aspects of the Arab-Jewish issue: the intransigent, monolithic, negative view of Arab spokesmen about Jews, and the lack of sympathy of American and British officials for the creation of a Jewish independent state.

Crum's assessment of American and British policy, with its concerns over Soviet encroachment in the Middle East, ensuring the flow of oil, maintaining links with Arab leaders, and belief in the strategic importance of the Arabs, was reflected in the Committee's report. Crum argued for a Jewish state, but the report was a compromise, with some mutually incompatible items, deferring the national claims of Jews and Arabs for future resolution. The Committee expressed the view that "any attempt to establish either an independent Palestinian state or independent Palestinian states would result in civil strife such as might threaten the peace of the world." It recommended the continuation of the authority of Britain, the Mandatory Authority, pending the execution of a trusteeship agreement under the newly formed United Nations. Implicitly, it recommended a bi-national state by suggesting that in its constitutional future Palestine should be "neither a Jewish state nor an Arab state." It also recommended that Britain immediately admit into Palestine 100,000 Jewish refugees languishing in the DP camps in Europe. At the same time it called for restrictions on land purchases. Prime Minister Attlee declared that the report could not be implemented without US support, nor until the "illegal armies" in Palestine had been disbanded. President Truman, whether out of genuine belief, humanitarian concern, desire to pre-empt a statement favoring Jewish immigration by Thomas Dewey, Governor of New York and his political rival for the Presidency, or political pressure and response to lobbying, publicly agreed to the immediate admitting of 100,000 Jews into Palestine.

Since the Anglo-American Committee (AAC) report was an unsatisfactory compromise another attempt was made to find a solution of the Palestinian problem by the Grady-Morrison plan of July 1946. Henry F. Grady was an American career diplomat, a former Assistant Secretary of State, and Herbert Morrison was a prominent member of the British Labour Party and then a member of the Cabinet. The new plan proposed the division of Palestine for administrative purposes, though not as boundaries, into four areas, each with a degree of autonomy and with the executive and legislative functions initially under the British High Commissioner for Palestine. It endorsed the AAC recommendation that 100,000 Jews be admitted immediately into Palestine, but also that steps should be taken to resettle Jews in Europe. At first Truman was inclined to accept the AAC plan, but, after it had been criticized by both Jews and Arabs, he abandoned that approval.

A significant part of the Arab opposition to any proposed settlement of the conflict in Palestine was voiced by the Mufti of Jerusalem Grand Mufti of Palestine, Haj Amin Husseini, who not only opposed any compromise with the Zionists, but also reiterated on many occasions the call for expulsion of the Jews. His story should be told in more detail.

Chapter 9

The Mufti of Jerusalem and the Nazis

The passion for expulsion of Jews from Palestine had been first voiced by Arab leaders as early as 1919 to the King-Crane Commission, which was appointed by President Woodrow Wilson, to inquire whether people in the Middle East lands wanted independence. It was to be reiterated many times by the Mufti of Jerusalem (Grand Mufti of Palestine) Haj Amin Husseini, the influential and formidable personality who became regarded as the leading spokesperson of the Palestinians. He was a member of the notable Husseini clan of wealthy landowners around the district of Jerusalem, which had long competed with the rival Nashashibi clan for power. Surprisingly, and probably because the rival clan held the post of mayor of Jerusalem, he had been appointed to the position after it became vacant in March 1921 by Sir Herbert Samuel, the British High Commissioner who also bestowed on him the title, *Grand Mufti*. The appointment also surprised many in the area because Husseini was more prominent as a political figure and as an activist, than as a religious dignitary. Husseini, who had been an officer in the Ottoman army in World War I, by his inflammatory speech helped to incite the riots in Jerusalem in April 1920, which resulted in the death of five Jews and 234 injured. As a result, he was sentenced by a military court to ten years imprisonment, but never served the sentence since he fled the area and then was pardoned a few months later.

For the next twenty-five years Husseini was a crucial player in the Arab-Israeli conflict,

which he helped inflame. At first Husseini was a Pan-Arabist, believing in a Greater Syria of which Palestine would be a part, but he soon concentrated on an Islamic solution for Palestine, and the removal of Jews from Palestine. His Islamic solution, based on Islamic political ideology, would entail imposition of sharia law to be enforced as the state's legal system, and would require Muslims to be active in pursuing the creation of an Islamic state as a religious duty. The pursuit would thus foster and legitimate the violent action to achieve this rejection of the Western system of democratic values. A relentless opponent of Zionism, and a virulent antisemite, Husseini declared there was no room in Palestine for two peoples; Jews should go to other parts of the world where there were vacant places. Husseini exemplified the aphorism of Montesquieu (*Persian Letters,* no. 85); "religious wars are not produced by the fact that there is more than one religion, but by the spirit of intolerance, urging on the one which believed itself to be dominant."

Husseini, in 1922, was also made head of the Supreme Muslim Council, which controlled the Waqf funds, the religious Islamic courts, and the naming of heads of mosques. He used this position to disseminate passages from *The Protocols of the Elders of Zion* through newsletters, pamphlets, and indoctrination of students in schools.[116] It was Husseini who emphasized the importance of Jerusalem for the Muslim world. He called in the 1930s for an all-Arab congress that would make the Palestinian question a common political cause, by alleging that Jews were seeking to control the Muslim Holy Places in Jerusalem. Already in 1929, he had called the mosque in Jerusalem "sacred." In his role as head of the Supreme Muslim Council, he instigated anti-Jewish riots and led the Palestinian resistance in August 1929 in Jerusalem; in the same week, sixty-seven were massacred in Hebron. The violence included the beheading of babies and the castration of old rabbis.[117] Further killings occurred in Safed, Motza, and Haifa. In all, 133 Jews were killed and hundreds more were injured. A British committee of inquiry stated that the Mufti had a share in the responsibility for the disturbances. He further organized in 1931 a General Islamic Congress in Jerusalem, which set up a Permanent Secretariat that would seek to raise funds for Islamic shrines in Palestine. He also called for a band of jihad fighters who would use violence to deter Jewish immigrants from settling in Palestine.[118]

The Mufti thus had made the Palestine issue one that would involve both the wider Arab and the Islamic world. That involvement became more manifest with the Arab Revolt in Palestine, that began in April 1936. As head of the Arab Higher Committee, which represented the different Arab political groups in Palestine and to which he was appointed in 1936, Husseini was largely responsible for this Arab Revolt, beginning with mob attacks in Jaffa and then a strike by the Arabs, which called for an end to Jewish immigration.

During the 1936 Revolt, the Mufti ruthlessly killed his Arab opponents, such as the members of the Nashashibi family, within the Palestinian camp; not only those who were willing to negotiate with the Jewish leaders, but also those who did not accept his anti-Western dress code or strictly obey the Sharia law.[119] Between 1936 and 1939, his supporters were responsible for the killing of about 1,000 Arabs by fellow Arabs; sometimes money was paid for the killing of "traitors," defined as both moderate Arabs, who Husseini regarded as "collaborators," and those who had sold land to Jews. For personal, as well as religious, reasons he made the Palestinian national cause one of holy jihad. At this time the Mufti was being supplied with both funds and weapons from Nazi Germany. He resisted arrest for his activity in the Revolt by fleeing to the Al-Aksa Mosque in Jerusalem and then to Syria in 1937. During World War II, he lived first in Lebanon and then in Iraq, where he participated in the overthrow of the regime and the British supported monarchy, and in the taking of power by the pro-Nazi Rashid Ali in April 1941. At this point he called, in May 1941, for a holy war against Britain who among other things, he claimed, had profaned the Al-Aqsa Mosque, ironically the very place in which he had hidden. Rashid Ali's coup only lasted a few months, but during it he declared an alliance with Nazi Germany and was responsible for a massacre of over 170 Jews, the wounding of several hundred other Jews, and the destruction of Jewish property and religious institutions, in Baghdad. The Mufti, aided by 400 Palestinians there at the time, was an accessory to the anti-Jewish crimes of June

1941. So was General Khairallah Talfah, the uncle, father-in-law, and mentor of Saddam Hussein.[120] One later consequence of this pogrom, the *Farhud,* was its contribution to exodus of 124,000 Jews from Iraq after World War II.

THE LINK WITH NAZI GERMANY

After the Iraqi Rashid Ali regime was quickly overthrown by British forces in May-June 1941, Husseini fled for a short time to Persia, Turkey, and Italy, where he met Mussolini, and then to Germany where he lived for the most part between 1941 and 1945. These were years of interaction between the Nazis and the Palestinian leader, who on the advent of Hitler's appointment as Chancellor in 1933, contacted the Nazis to welcome the new regime and expressed his hope that fascist and anti-democratic forms of government would spread to other countries. It was the Mufti, a man with blond hair and blue eyes, who took the initiative in making the contact; the Nazis were at first cool towards the Mufti because they still hoped to reach an understanding with Britain by which they might expand in Eastern Europe, while agreeing that Britain remain in control of Palestine. In Germany, he met in Berlin with Adolf Hitler in November 1941, stating, as the self-appointed spokesman of the "Arab nation" that "the Arabs were Germany's natural friends because they had the same enemies as had Germany, namely the English, the Jews, and the Communists." The Arabs would therefore collaborate with Germany in the war both by acts of sabotage and instigating revolutions, and by an Arab Legion. He would produce a great number of volunteers eager to fight for Germany.

In reply the Nazi leader assured the Mufti that the real German aim in the Orient was "the destruction of the Jewish element residing in the Arab sphere under the protection of British power." The Mufti would be given the task for Arab operations to accomplish this.[121] Hitler assured him that the struggle against the Jewish homeland in Palestine formed part of the uncompromising struggle against the Jews and "Anglo-Jewish capitalism." The Arabs and other "non-European peoples" would, at the right time, "solve the Jewish problem just as the European nations had done." In a study, "Hitler's Shadow: Nazi War Criminals, US Intelligence, and the Cold War," released in 2010 by the US National Archives, it was revealed that for a time the Mufti was paid a salary of 50,000 marks a month by the Nazis, and 80,000 marks living expenses, and was given a luxurious house with servants and chauffeurs in Berlin.

Husseini, who had been greeted at his meeting with Hitler with a guard of honor of 200 German soldiers, met more frequently with fellow antisemites, including SS leader Heinrich Himmler, who invited him to his East Prussian estate, Adolf Eichmann, Herman Goering, and German Foreign Minister Joachim von Ribbentrop. The objective was to discuss solving the "Jewish problem" or, less euphemistically, obtaining details and helping plan the Holocaust. Husseini stressed that Arab interests were completely identical with those of the Germans, and that the Arabs felt a very close bond of solidarity with Germany in the struggle against international Jewry and the elimination of the Jewish National Home in Palestine.[122] He praised Germany as the only country that had finally decided to put an end to the Jewish question. On his broadcasts on Germany's Arab language radio service, he called for a *jihad* against the Allies and the Jews, specifically for the Jews to be annihilated.

The Mufti became the honorary chair of the Islamic Central Institute in Berlin, which was initiated on December 18, 1942. On that occasion, he hoped that thousands of Muslims in the world would cooperate with Germany against common enemies, Jews, Bolsheviks, and Anglo-Saxons. He went further in his acerbic antisemitism. The Jews and their accomplices were to be counted among the bitterest enemies of the Muslims; they would always remain a divisive element in the world, devising schemes, provoking wars, and playing peoples off against one another. In his ominous remarks in November 1943 he said that German Nazism knew how to save itself from the evil done by Jews.[123] The Mufti's own words make clear that he knew the Holocaust was occurring and supported it. Germany, he said in 1943, ironically on November 2, the anniversary of the Balfour Declaration, was fighting against the common enemy which oppressed the Arabs and Muslims in their differently lands. Germany "recognized the Jews exactly and decided to find a final solution to the danger that came from the Jews which will end their mischief in this world."[124]

Husseini demanded of the Nazis, and of the leaders of Hungary, Bulgaria and Rumania who still had a degree of independence, that they not send any Jews in their countries to Palestine. He wrote letters to all of them demanding they withdraw their authorization of Jewish emigration. In this, he was even more extreme than the Nazi leaders, who were prepared in 1943 to allow some Jews to emigrate, for a price. Himmler had been prepared to trade 5,000 Jewish children in the Balkans for the release of 20,000 German POWs, but Husseini demanded, with considerable success, that these and all the Jews be sent to Poland where "they are under active control," about to be exterminated.[125] As a result 400,000 Jews from Hungary, 4,500 from Bulgaria, and 80,000 from Rumania lost their lives. The Mufti was aware of the fate of individuals sent to Nazi concentration camps, since one of his assistants had visited the camp of Sachsenhausen and reported on it.

The Mufti wrote to Hitler on January 20, 1941, stating he would use the Palestine question "to coalesce (with the Nazis) all Arab countries in a common hatred against the British and the Jews." He would join forces with the Axis powers to defeat the Anglo-Jewish coalition. The Jews, he wrote Hitler, were dangerous enemies with weapons of finance, corruption, and intrigue, who had joined with the "British bayonets." In his memoirs, published in Damascus in 1999, the Mufti recounts his frequent meetings with Himmler, who informed him at one meeting on July 4, 1943, that by that time about three million Jews had been liquidated. Himmler later told the Mufti that since its inception, the National Socialists had inscribed the struggle against world Jewry on its banners. Himmler wrote a telegram to the Mufti on November 2, 1943, saying he was following with particular sympathy the struggle of the freedom-loving Arabs, especially in Palestine, against the Jewish invaders. He also wrote of the natural alliance between National Socialist Germany and freedom-loving Muslims in the entire world. Indeed, Himmler in this collaboration with the Mufti tried to persuade Muslims that the Koran predicted and assigned to the Fuhrer the mission of completing the work of the Prophet.

In addition to these meetings, Husseini recruited Muslims for the Nazi war effort, raising an SS unit of Muslims, the 13th Waffen Division (Handschar) of the SS of 20,000 men, who were trained in Germany and officered by Germans, in the Balkans to fight with the Nazis. Himmler had established a special military school in Dresden to train Husseini's Bosnian Muslim recruits. This unit was responsible for the death of about ninety per cent of the Jews in Bosnia. The Mufti denied knowing Adolf Eichmann; but, at the Nuremberg trials in July 1946, S.S. Hauptsturmführer Dieter Wisliczeny, a close associate of Eichmann in the Jewish Affairs Division of the Reich Central Security Office, said that "the Mufti was one of the initiators of the systematic extermination of European Jewry...He was one of Eichmann's best friends and had constantly incited him to accelerate the extermination measures. I heard him say that, accompanied by Eichmann, he had visited incognito the gas chambers of Auschwitz." One Nazi proposal during the war was that the Mufti would head a post-war government in Palestine, in which only those Jews who had lived there before 1914 would be allowed to stay.[126]

Wisliczeny, in 1946, also stated that the Mufti had asked Himmler to help him, after the presumed German victory in the war, "solve the Jewish question in the Middle East." The defeat of the Nazis did not give the Mufti this opportunity, but instead after the war he called on Palestinian Arabs and all Muslims to slaughter the Jews in Palestine. Following a similar path, the Mufti of Egypt, Sheikh Muhammad Mahawif, proclaimed in April 1948 that a jihad, a holy war, was the duty of all Muslims in Palestine, because the Jews intended to take over all the lands of Islam. Husseini escaped any punishment for his wartime activities, and began organizing opposition through the Arab League to the 1947 UN Partition Plan.

German interest in using Islamic concepts for political ends was already apparent in World War I when Kaiser Wilhelm II called for a jihad by the entire Muslim world against the British Empire, "a hateful, lying, and unscrupulous nation," and set up a jihad bureau in Berlin.[127] But collaboration between German Nazis and Muslim Arabs at first appeared improbable. Hitler, in *Mein Kampf,* had written of the racial inferiority of the Arabs and found the idea of a Holy War unacceptable.

However, political events and proposals, particularly the 1936 British Peel Commission's proposal for a Jewish state, led Germany to see the desirability of a relationship against their common enemy, world Jewry. The career of Husseini is one illustration of the close connection starting in the 1930s between German Nazi leaders and Muslim extremists, which included the Muslim Brotherhood in Egypt, as well as the Mufti.

An interesting intellectual debate has focused on this issue; was antisemitism and the concept of "Jewish world conspiracy" imported into the Muslim world from Nazi Germany, or did it stem primarily from Islamic and Arab sources? Some statements made by Arab writers are relevant to the debate. One is the statement by Sami al-Jundi, an early member of the Syrian Ba'th party, writing in the 1960s of the early influences on his group; "We were racialists admiring Nazism, reading its books and the sources of its thought…Anyone who had lived through this period in Damascus can assess the inclination of the Arab people towards Nazism. Nazism was the force that took revenge for them." Another study in 2000, by Mas'ud Dahir, offers a different perspective about Beirut in the 1930s: "Beirut provided the stage for crucial intellectual competitions between the calls of Mediterraneanism, Phoenicianism, Pharaonism, Fascism, Nazism, and Zionism."[128]

Even accepting the influence in the Arab world of different intellectual traditions and trends, the Nazi option was significant for Arab spokesmen. Nazi antisemitism was interwoven with virulent passages from the Koran hostile to Jews in their Muslim ideology. Arab leaflets in 1936 contained the sign of the swastika, and the youth attached to the Mufti paraded as "Nazi-scouts." The Mufti had invented a "new form of Jew-hatred by recasting it in an Islamic mold." He outlined a number of values that Islam and the Nazis had in common. What is most important in this debate is that the essential shared value was that Islam and National Socialism had the same view of Jews against whom the struggle must be fought. At a meeting between Hitler and the special envoy of Saudi King Abdul-Aziz in June 1939, Hitler "entertained warm sympathies for the Arabs for two reasons: because we have no territorial aspirations in Arabia, and because we have the same enemies…we are jointly fighting the Jews."[129]

On this issue of a war to destroy the Jews, Husseini and Hitler became collaborators, and laid the foundation for later Islamist attitudes to Israel. After the defeat of Germany, the antisemitic elements of Nazism found a positive reception in the utterances of radical Islam and in the Arab world.[130] It influenced both the language of al-Qaeda, Hamas, and Hezbollah, and the nature of the Israeli-Arab conflict. It also helps explain the hospitality accorded German military officers, Nazi party officials, SS personnel, scientists, propagandists, and Hitler's commando leader Otto Skorzeny, after World War II, in Middle East countries, especially Egypt and Syria, where they aided the intelligence and military activities of those countries.

A crucial figure in this alliance of Nazis and Arab leaders was the shadowy Swiss financier François Genoud, an admirer of Hitler after he first met him in Germany in 1932, at the age of seventeen. Genoud was an associate and financial adviser of the Mufti, whom he first met in Palestine, then later in Berlin and even later in Beirut, and also the financial supporter of Nazi and Arab causes during the War. After the War he helped Nazis escape from Germany, remained a banker of neo-Nazis or made investments for them, as in the case of Hjalmar Schacht, the former Nazi minister of finance, and helped manage the Nazi assets and gold stolen from Holocaust victims and held in Swiss banks. He founded in 1958 the Arab Commercial Bank in Geneva which, among other things, managed the assets of the Algerian National Liberation Front (FLN). In addition he established AraboAfrika, an import-export company that really disseminated anti-Jewish and anti-Israeli propaganda, and delivered weapons to the FLN. Genoud financed terrorist groups, funneled considerable money and provided legal counsel to the Palestinians, and paid for, or is said to have helped pay, the legal costs for the defense of Adolf Eichmann, Klaus Barbie (the Gestapo " butcher of Lyon"), and the terrorist Carlos, the Jackal. He assisted the accused at the trial of the members of the Popular Front for the Liberation of Palestine, who in 1969 were responsible for the destruction of an EL Al Israeli jet in Zurich, as well as assisting the Palestinian hijackers of a Lufthansa plane in 1972.[131]

THE MUFTI AND VIOLENCE

The 1936 Arab revolt was the first large-scale attack on the Zionists in Palestine and was the real start of the major conflict, military, political, economic, and cultural, between Jews/Israel and Arabs. As a consequence, Britain invited Arab leaders from six countries to the London Conference in 1939 to discuss a solution to the Palestine conflict. Not surprisingly, those leaders supported the Palestinian demands for an end to Jewish immigration and sale of land to Jews, and for the creation of an Arab state in Palestine. They thought the British compromises were insufficient and publicly condemned the British White Paper on Palestine proposed by Colonial Secretary Malcolm MacDonald on November 9, 1938, the day of Kristallnacht in Germany, and approved by the British Parliament in May 1939.[132]

The White Paper had suggested a one state solution, an independent state with a large Arab majority, instead of partition; limitation of Jewish immigration to 75,000 over the next five year period, after which further immigration would depend on agreement of the Arab majority; and restrictions on the sale of land by Arabs to Jews. In effect, this implied the future creation of an Arab state in all of the Palestine Mandate area. At that time the anti-Zionist British Foreign Office feared severe violence would occur in Palestine if Jewish immigration was unlimited. Consequently, Britain, in July 1939, had suspended all Jewish immigration, beginning in October. Interestingly, Harry Truman, then Senator from Missouri, was immediately critical of the British action; "it made a scrap of paper out of Balfour's promise to the Jews." It was clear that Britain did not support partition or the establishment of a Jewish state. For its perceived strategic and national interests, Britain had sided with the Arabs on the eve of World War II.

After the war, British agencies, particularly the Secret Intelligence Service between 1946 and early 1948, staged operations to deter Holocaust survivors from reaching Palestine. Among the methods used were the bombing of five ships in Italian ports to prevent immigration, intimidation, and the creation of a fake group called Defenders of Arab Palestine, which could be blamed for the actions.[133] Some Arab gangs had already gone further than simple opposition to political proposals and began assassinating fellow Arabs prepared to talk to or reach a compromise with the Jews in Palestine. At least several hundred, perhaps more, were killed in this way, including the acting mayor of Hebron and other prominent Arab politicians. Fakhri Nashashibi, the rival of the Mufti, narrowly escaped assassination in June 1937, though he was to be murdered by Palestinian Arabs in November 1941. The British Government now understood the disruptive role of Husseini. In May 1938 it issued a statement that the Mufti was not only the head of the organization responsible for the campaign of terrorism and the assassination of British soldiers and Jews, but also the head of a faction which had pursued a similar campaign against large numbers of Arabs. Britain became even more conscious of the problem of the Mufti as a result of his activities in Berlin during World War II and his linkage of Islam and Nazism. He could not return to the area of Palestine after the War. In 1945 he was in French custody, but no country would indict him for his participation in Nazi crimes for fear of offending the Arab world.

THE EXTREME REJECTIONIST

About the collaboration of Husseini with Nazi Germany and his endless fulminations of antisemitism, two assumptions can be made. One is that this leader of Palestinian Arabs did play a role in assisting the German activity of the Holocaust. Palestinians were not completely innocent of helping the Nazi genocide. The other is that his call for Arabs to attack Jews collectively may have contributed to the 1948 Arab attack on the new state of Israel.

The League of Arab States, formed in Cairo in March 1945, was actively involved in the Palestinian conflict. In June 1946, in an effort to reconcile conflicting Palestinian groups, it reconvened the Arab Higher Committee with the Mufti Husseini as President; since he was in refuge in Cairo, that city became the locus of the Arab League, which generally accepted the extreme proposals of the Mufti as common policy. That policy included the imposition of an economic boycott on Jewish companies, industry and trade in Palestine. Though this boycott was only partially successful, it did lead to a boycott on all Jewish trade, as well as increased antisemitism in Arab countries. The Arab League in 1948 formally organized a boycott, which had begun more informally three years earlier and had preceded the establishment of Israel, not only of Israeli companies and products, but also of those from other countries maintaining economic relations with or who are perceived to be supporting Israel. The boycott activity, widening in scope in the 1950s, was and is administered by a Central Boycott Office in Damascus. The boycott consists of three tiers. The primary boycott forbids the importation of Israeli goods and services into the Arab League countries. The secondary boycott forbids individuals, firms and organizations from dealing with anyone doing business in Israel. Most major Japanese and Korean car manufacturers, except Subaru, complied with this secondary boycott. A boycott was launched against Burger King and Benneton because they had franchises in Israeli settlements. The tertiary boycott prohibits business with anyone who has dealings with firms on the Arab League blacklist. Theoretically, the boycott is still in existence, though it is not forcefully implemented. Yet, the boycotts cost Israel considerable amounts of finance in terms of lost markets and economic problems.

At the London Conference, September 1946-February 1947, the last attempt by Britain to reconcile the conflicting points of view, the Arab League, which had emerged as a result of consultations among Arab states during World War II, strongly rejected any plan for partition of Palestine or for any Jewish state. The Arab League Charter declared that Palestine had become an independent country since its separation from the Ottoman Empire.[134] The League, in May 1948, repeated the view it had expressed at the London Conference and elsewhere that the only fair and just solution to the problem of Palestine was the creation of the United State of Palestine. In October 1947, the League had set up a Military Committee with representatives of five countries. Two months later the Committee was given weapons, money, and authority to dispatch a force of 3,000 volunteers to Palestine, who then crossed into the area and began attacking Jewish settlements. Thus, the Arabs countries did invade Palestine, but their leaders, limited by personal rivalries and conflicting ambitions, were divided among themselves on the character and tactics of that invasion.

In March 1948, Husseini, who had been elected president of the National Palestinian Council, advocated an extreme, uncompromising position and refused to negotiate with the Zionists. Instead, he urged Arabs to attack the Jews collectively and destroy them. He stated that the Arabs would continue fighting until the Zionists were annihilated by a holy war and the whole of Palestine became a purely Arab state. He said that, at best, this might include Jews who had lived in Palestine before 1914 or 1917. The latter date refers indirectly to the Balfour Declaration of November 2, 1917. In this crucial document Lord Balfour, then British Foreign Secretary, stated in a letter to Lord Rothschild that "His Majesty's Government views with favour the establishment in Palestine of a national home for the Jewish people, and will use their best endeavors to facilitate the achievement of this object."

ISLAMISM AND FASCISM

Not coincidentally, this was the time when the basis was laid for the emergence of what has been termed "Islamofascism" with Muslim Arab groups emulating Nazi and Fascist movements. The great French poet and diplomat, Paul Claudel, on May 21, 1935, had been prescient about the reverse relationship: commenting on a speech by Hitler he wrote in his journal that "a kind of Islamism is being created at the center of Europe." Nazis joined with Arabs and Muslims in attacking Zionism, both as the product of Western imperialism and as the continuation of the hostility of Jews towards Islam; this was the classic case of what Herf has called the convergence of antisemitism and anti-Zionism.[135]

One group, later in 1947 to be termed the Ba'th Party, adapted Nazi ideas and methods to the Arab world, especially Syria and Iraq. Already in 1928 in Egypt Hasan al-Banna, a schoolteacher in the Suez Canal town of Ismailiyya who became an admirer of Mussolini, and was later to become an even greater admirer of Hitler, had founded the fundamentalist Muslim Brotherhood, whose objective was to weaken the secular Arab nationalist parties that had appeared after World War I, to replace existing Arab regimes with fundamentalist Islamic ones, and to implement sharia worldwide and establish a global Islamic state (caliphate), imperial Islamic rule. Al-Banna's message was clear: Andalusia (Spain), the Balkans, south Italy, and the Roman sea islands were all Islamic lands that had to be restored to the homeland of Islam.

The Brotherhood's objective was to instill sharia law as the basis for ordering the life of the Muslim family, individual, country, and state. This entails imposing its strict views on morality, religion, social life, and the working of the economy. It means that women's participation in society and in political life is limited. The Brotherhood creed is "Allah is our objective; the Koran is our law; the Prophet is our leader; jihad is our way; and dying for the sake of Allah is the highest of our aspirations." The overall strategy is the call for jihad and the use of violence to reach the desired objective, but the tactics could vary at different times and places. Rather than insisting on immediate jihad, the Brotherhood spread its Islamist views and interpretation of Islam in stages, to prepare for the creation of the desirable society. It reached out to all sectors of the community, socially and politically. This meant not only the creation of some health clinics, social aid, and charity welfare, but also moderating its rhetoric, attempting to form coalitions with political parties, participating in parliamentary elections, especially in Egypt where in 2005 it won 88 out of 454 seats, and from time to time condemning terrorist attacks, not for humane reasons, but because they were counterproductive. It did not win seats in the 2010 election, which was rigged against it. The Brotherhood also controls non-governmental organizations such as professional and student associations. In a somewhat unusual fashion the Brotherhood has been officially banned, yet the organization is tolerated and allowed to nominate candidates for election as independents. The exact nature of the Brotherhood remains puzzling; does it embrace different points of view, hardliners and pragmatists? Does it genuinely believe in peaceable and moderate, step by step progress, or is it still committed to the doctrine that government must be based exclusively on the law of Allah, and to the policy of refusing to recognize the existence of Israel as legitimate?

Though the question is still open, the rhetoric of two prominent individuals close to the Brotherhood suggests the answer is not ambiguous. One of them, Sheik Yusuf al-Qaradawi, the controversial and influential Sunni preacher linked to the Brotherhood, was imprisoned three times in Egypt, fled to Qatar in 1961, and returned to Egypt in 2011. In February 2006 he had called for a day of rage against the cartoons published in the Danish newspaper, *Jyllands-Posten* in September 2005; riots against Western targets soon followed. Though he sometimes argued in his sermons that Islamic law supports concepts of pluralism and multiparty democracy, which gives Muslims space in which to maneuver and compromise, he also called for a global caliphate. Islam, he declared, would return to Europe not by conquest by the sword, but by preaching and spreading Islamic ideology. Islam would then spread until it conquered the entire world. More immediately, he called for the destruction of Israel and the conquest of Jerusalem. He issued fatwas between 2001 and 2003 approving suicide bombings against Israel, even by women, and the killing of American forces and civilians in Iraq. Moreover, in a sermon in 2009 Qaradawi explained that throughout history "Allah imposed on Jews people who would punish them for their corruption," and that the last divine punishment so far was carried out by Hitler. The next punishment would be inflicted by Muslims. The Sheikh implored Allah "to kill Jews down to the very last one." This would be done in the "land of jihad," Israel.

The second person is Mustafa Mashhur, who was head of the Brotherhood 1996-2002. In his book *Jihad is the Way*, he wrote that the Islamic nation must regain its power and be the most exalted nation. Jihad must continue until all the land of Islam is liberated and the state of Islam is established. Israel must end, and honor must be given to those who achieved martyrdom on the soil of beloved Palestine in their jihad against the criminal gangs of Zion. This indeed has been done in some Palestinian areas where streets and squares have been named after the "martyrs" who killed Israeli civilians. One square in Al-Bireh near Ramallah was named after Dalal Mughrabi, the person who in March 1978 had directed the hijacking of two buses on the coastal road between Haifa and Tel Aviv, which led to the murder of thirty-seven Israelis, including thirteen children. Sport has also been used for political propaganda; one football tournament of the Palestinians was dedicated to Wafa Idris, the first female suicide terrorist, and another to the terrorist Abu Jihad.

The Muslim Brotherhood does not have a religious leadership in the same way as the Islamic state of Iran since 1979, but has a "general guide;" since January 2010, this has been Mohammed Badie. His guidance has asserted that the Koran should be the constitution of the Egyptian state, and included a call for a holy war against Israel, and also against Zionist and American "arrogance and tyranny," and thus to "carry out the command of Allah to wage war for his sake;" urged the closing of the Suez Canal; the stopping of Egyptian natural gas exports to Israel; and all forms of resistance to liberate every occupied piece of land in Palestine. On the website of the Brotherhood in September 2010, Badi wrote of the United States that it did not champion moral and human values, cannot lead humanity, and that its "wealth will not avail it once Allah has had His say...The struggle against Israel was a priority. The Arab and Muslim regimes have forgotten, or are pretending to have forgotten, that the real enemy is the Zionist entity." His stark message was that the improvement and change sought by the Muslim nation could only be attained by raising a jihadi generation that pursued death, just as the enemies pursued life.

Realistically, the Brotherhood has sought to influence and to penetrate government, legislative, intelligence agencies, the media, and military and academic institutions. Since 1940 it has had a military wing, the "Special Chapter." In the 1940s, its forces targeted Egyptian officials and British soldiers, and in 1948 assassinated Mahmud Nokrashi, the Egyptian prime minister. It helped Gamal Abdel Nasser and the group of young military officers to overthrow King Farouk in 1952; two years later Nasser banned it and imprisoned thousands of its members. The Egyptian Islamic Jihad, an offshoot of the Brotherhood, assassinated President Anwar Sadat in 1981, and tried to kill President Hosni Mubarak in 1995. The Brotherhood also founded Al-Gama'a al-Islamiyya, which has been classified as a terrorist group by the US. That group has been responsible for scores of murders and attempted murders, the victims of which have been not only policemen, soldiers and prominent Egyptian writers, but also tourists and foreigners in the massacres in Cairo in 1996 and in Luxor in Egypt in 1997. Outside Egypt it was responsible for terrorist attacks in Islamabad, Pakistan and in Croatia in 1995. Its spiritual leader, Omar Abdel-Rahman, was accused of participating in the New York World Trade Center bombing conspiracy in 1993. It has numerous connections in other countries. In Jordan, the Islamic Action Front, the only opposition group in the country, is the Brotherhood's political wing. In Europe, the Cordoba Foundation based in London is regarded as a front for the Brotherhood and the Muslim Association of Britain as its representative.

The Brotherhood has had an impact, internally and externally, both on individuals and on political groups. This is strikingly shown by the fact that currently most Egyptian women wear the hijab. The former general guide, Muhammad Akef, in July 2007 opposed the "corrupt American democracy" partly because of its attempt to stop female circumcision in Africa, a practice he said which was current in thirty-six countries and which had been prevalent since the time of the Pharaohs. Nevertheless, the Brotherhood was involved with the US CIA, as well as with former German Nazis, and anti-Soviet Muslim central Asians in the curious story of the use of the Islamic Center, the mosque, in Munich for anti-Soviet broadcasts in the post-war period.[136] It may be excessive to argue there is an ideological convergence between Nazis and the Muslim Brotherhood in Egypt. What is more certain is that from this association in Munich, the Brotherhood emerged in control of the mosque which has been the hub of radical Islam in Europe, and has been associated with individuals responsible for terrorist acts in the West, including the attacks on the World Trade Center in New York.

Antisemitism, as well as anti-Zionism and anti-Americanism, has flourished in the rhetoric of the Brotherhood, as it did in the utterances of other important figures such as Rashid Rida (1865-1935), a major founder of modern Islamic fundamentalism, though in his early life he had condemned the European antisemism of the Dreyfus Affair, Shakib Arslan, the Lebanese Druze leader, Saudi King Ibn Saud, and, of course, the Grand Mufti of Jerusalem.[137] Some of the individuals who were influenced in their early years by this rhetoric of the Brotherhood have become notorious. The most well known is the Al Qaeda leader, Osama bin Laden, who was taught by Abdullah Azzam, a Palestinian member of the Brotherhood whose ambition was to reunite all lands that had once been under Islamic rule, under a restored Caliphate. Among others who were members of the Brotherhood are Ayman al-Zawahiri , formerly head of Islamic Jihad; Omar Abdel Rahman, the blind Sheikh, head of Gamaat (Islamic Group) whose followers were responsible for the 1993 World Trade Center in New York bombings; and Khalid Sheikh Mohammed, alleged to be the mastermind behind the September 11, 2001, bombings. As mentioned earlier, the Brotherhood gave rise to the Palestinian Hamas group. It also claims branches in over eighty countries; these include the Al-Nahda movement in Tunisia, the AKP in Turkey, the Islamic Action Front in Jordan, and the Islamic Party in Iraq.

Sayyid Qutb, to be executed for treason and participation in a planned armed insurgency, by President Gamal Abdel Nasser in 1966, was the main influential ideologue, intellectual and theological, of the Brotherhood. Qutb had taken an ideological route from secular nationalism, when he was briefly involved with the Egyptian Free Officers who overthrew the monarchy, to Islamic socialism and then to Islamic Radicalism.[138] His essay "Our Struggle with the Jews," published in 1951 and republished by Saudi Arabia in 1970, was a harshly antisemitic text, written only a few years after the Holocaust. He listed some of the Jews he found troublesome: Marx with his atheistic materialism, Durkheim with his shattering of sacred relationships, Freud with his animalistic sexuality. In his book *Milestones,* Qutb attacked Muslim governments and societies which had forsaken Islam and been corrupted by Western values and secularism. His animus was not confined to Jews. He viewed the enemy of Islam as the alliance of "Crusaders and Jews." His writings show him as racist, despising blacks, anti-feminist, anti-Western and particularly anti-American, in spite of, or because of, his visit to the US in 1949-50. One of the people who acknowledged his influence is Ayman al-Zawahiri, the deputy to Osama bin Laden and the man considered to be the main ideologue of al-Qaeda.

Hasan al-Banna was assassinated in 1949, probably by an Egyptian intelligence unit, for participation in a planned armed insurgency. The mind-set of this Muslim Brotherhood group exemplified Winston Churchill's conclusion in an early book of 1899, *The River War*, that "Mohammedanism is a militant and proselytizing faith." Al-Banna was not simply attracted by Nazism, sharing the belief in a Jewish international conspiracy, but also participated in the translations into Arabic of Hitler's *Mein Kampf* and also the infamous antisemitic forgery, *The Protocols of the Elders of Zion*. He argued that hatred of Jews was an important part of Islamic history. The Brotherhood received subsidies from Nazi organizations; the transfer of the funds seems to have been coordinated by the Mufti, Husseini.[139] It also cooperated with the German army, General Erwin Rommel's Afrika Korps, in North Africa during the war. The defeat of Rommel by the British Army under General Montgomery at El Alamein in October-November 1942 meant that the German forces never reached Egypt. This prevented the extermination of the Jewish population in Palestine, because a special SS commando unit, *Einsatzgruppe*, of seven SS officers and a number of non-commissioned soldiers, already in Athens had made plans to liquidate its Jewish population when the Germans captured Cairo. One of the SS officers was Husseini's security chief. To his credit Rommel, was disgusted with the idea and would have nothing to do with it.

Some of the members of the Brotherhood, said to number 200,000 in 1938 and which claimed a million members in 1946, joined in the attack on the new State of Israel in 1948. Egyptian army officers, including Nasser, were associated with the Brotherhood. They were attempting to fulfill the version of jihad presented by Al-Banna: "To a nation that perfects the industry of death and which knows how to die nobly, God gives proud life in this world and eternal grace in the life to come."[140] The Brotherhood called, as did the Nazis, for a boycott of Jewish goods and Jewish shops, and indicated the nature of the "Jewish menace." It also evoked the Koran in considering Jews as "the worst enemy." In a speech in 1946, Al-Banna not only praised Husseini profusely as a hero, but also declared that he had a divine spark in his heart and that "God entrusted him with a mission and he must succeed. There must be a divine purpose behind the preservation of the life of this man, namely the defeat of Zionism."[141] In recent years the Brotherhood has discouraged attempts at a peaceful negotiation of the Israeli-Palestinian problem, and has refused to recognize the legitimacy of the State of Israel. Disparaging remarks about Israelis and Jews by the Brotherhood have continued into the present. Kamal El-Helbaury, the founder of the Muslim Arab Association of Britain in 1997, stated in a BBC broadcast in January 2009, at a time when he was a spokesman for the Brotherhood, that all Israeli children were "future soldiers" and were raised in the belief that the Arabs are contemptible sheep.

This statement was relatively mild compared with the saying from the Koran, Sura 5:82, which closely resembles the remarks of Hitler. The Koran passage says "Truly you will find that the most implacable of men in their enmity to the faithful are the Jews and the pagans;" Hitler in *Mein Kampf* wrote, "By resisting the Jews everywhere, I am fighting for the Lord's work." After World War I the Weimar Republic of Germany, seeking to promote its influence in the Middle East, supported a Jewish National Home in Palestine and rejected Arab demands for independence.[142] The Nazi regime, for different reasons, maintained this policy until 1938, and did not support Arab nationalist movements. During World War II the improbable relationship between Nazi Germany and the Muslim world began. In public statements Islam and National Socialism were said to share the same goals and ideals. Jeffrey Herf analyzed the thousands of hours of shortwave radio broadcasts from Zeesen, near Berlin, in Arabic, which had been transcribed by the American Embassy in Cairo under Ambassadors Alexander Kirk and S.Pinkney Tuck.[143] These Nazi broadcasts, as well as millions of pamphlets, during the war not only attacked, in inflammatory language, the common demons, Zionism, Jewish power, and the Jewish intentions to conquer the Arab countries, but also praised Islam as an ally and assured Muslims of the Nazi respect both for the Koran, which was frequently quoted, and for the Prophet. The broadcasts were targeted at and gained a mass audience, especially because radio was more potent than print in light of the limited rate of literacy in the Arab world at that time.

The broadcasts compared the Prophet's struggle against the Jews in ancient times to that of Hitler in the present. Herf, reviewing in the broadcasts the uniting of Nazi and Islamic themes, the values of piety, obedience, and community, suggests that from the Nazis the Arabs took some of the points of antisemitic thinking, while the Nazis learned to focus on Palestine. The result was the significant Islamist and Arab nationalist collaboration with Nazi Germany, with its Foreign Ministry,

Ministry for Public Enlightenment and Propaganda, and the SS. For Husseini, Muslims and Nazis were allies, both pursuing jihad against Jews; he argued that "in the struggle against Jewry, Islam and National Socialism are very close."

What is important in this partnership is the fact that the Mufti and like-minded Muslims used the Koran and Islamic authorities to reach this conclusion, to share the Nazi fantasy of a Jewish conspiracy to establish a state from the Nile to the Euphrates, and to promote the dogma that the world would never be at peace until the Jewish people were exterminated. The Mufti proclaimed that the Jews were conspiring against Islam and against Arabs. In Berlin, the German liaison with the Mufti was Fritz Grobba, former Ambassador to Iraq and to Saudi Arabia, who in July 1942 accused the Jews of pulling the Americans' strings.[144] In the latter part of World War II, about three quarters of the broadcasts on Radio Zeesen were attacks on Jews. Paul Berman, as well as Klaus Gensicke, concludes that the Mufti and Muslim associates based their hatred of Jews on theological precepts within Islam, not on biology and pseudo-science or on versions of the medieval superstitions of Christian Europe. In his speech in Berlin on December 18, 1942, the Mufti said the Koran judged the Jews to be "the most irreconcilable enemies of the Muslims...the Holy Koran and the story of the Prophet's life is full of evidence of Jewish lack of character and of their insidious, lying and deceitful conduct."[145] The Mufti, in a well-known broadcast on March 1, 1944, called on Arabs to "Kill the Jews wherever you find them. This pleases God, history, and religion. This serves your honor. God is with you."[146] The Mufti and the Nazis agreed on the extermination of Jews, in Palestine as elsewhere. Anti-Zionism, meaning opposition to the State of Israel, had merged with antisemitism. The very word "Zionist" had become debased and used as a derogatory description of organized Jewish activity.

Official estimates by the US and Britain make clear the success of the propaganda; over three quarters of the Middle East Muslim world was in favor of the Nazis. In that world most people who had radios listened to Berlin. The success of this Nazi anti-Zionist and antisemitic propaganda on the Muslim world had a significant impact on the behavior of the Allies during the war. It is striking that the Allies refrained in any declarations from mentioning the persecution, murder, and genocide of European Jews. The British and American leaders thought doing so would allow the charge of an alleged relationship between them and world Jewry to appear valid. Nor did they specifically counter the allegation that Jewish power dominated the Allies.

Political Islamism today is not identical with Nazism or Fascism. Yet there is obvious continuity and lineages between the Nazi war-time propaganda in Arabic, and the messages of radical Islamists, after the Nazi regime was destroyed in the war. Both share a hatred of Jews and of Zionist aspirations, a belief in conspiracy theories, and a rejection of liberal democracy.[147] This is apparent in the Hamas Covenant of 1988, the declaration by Osama bin Laden of war against the "Zionist-Crusader alliance," and in the continuing Muslim calls to eliminate the state of Israel. That covenant is conformation of the proposition by the German political scientist Matthias Kuntzel, in his book *Jihad and Jew-Hatred*, that Arab antisemitism is not simply part of modern day jihadism, but is its core thesis.

THE ANTI-WESTERN THREAT

With the relentless rhetoric and activity of the Mufti Husseini, the antagonism of Arabs and Palestinians against the Jews in Palestine before the establishment of the State of Israel became a complex mixture of religious, territorial and national objectives. Benny Morris, examining the rabid Muslim rhetoric of the time in public broadcasts and in mosques, has argued that the struggle in fact became a Muslim holy war against infidels.[148] The 1948 War, he argues, was a war of religion as much as, if not more than, a nationalist war over territory. Morris also argues that historians have tended to "belittle the importance of the religious rhetoric during the war" and the central role of religious motivation. The threat of elimination of "infidels" was present. The rector of Al-Azhar University in Cairo, Muhammad Mamun Shinawi, told the Egyptian invading army that "The hour of Jihad has struck." On the day after the declaration of the establishment of the State of Israel, the secretary of the Arab League, Abdul Rahman

Hassan Azzam, who in September 1947 had said it was too late for a peaceful settlement, proclaimed that the war starting that day would be one of annihilation in which the Jews would be swept into the sea and the story of the slaughter would be told like the Mongolian massacre and the Crusades.[149] Similarly, Husseini stated, "I declare a holy war, my Moslem brothers! Kill the Jews! Murder them all." In view of this rhetoric the Jews at first simply fought for survival, as at Nirim and Degania in May 1948, as well as for the effort to establish a state. Later, as they gained victories in 1948-49, they were eager to hold the newly captured land. Consequently, about 2,000 square miles were added to the original 6,000 square miles of Israel.

Another aspect of Husseini's rhetoric was to have a wider influence through his participation in the Third World movement that essentially started at the meeting in 1955 in Bandung, Indonesia, of twenty-nine African and Asian countries aiming to create a new international co-operative order. In this anti-colonialist gathering, at which an anti-Israeli resolution was agreed, the Mufti, who appeared as the representative from Yemen, informed the delegates from the twenty-nine countries attending, that Israel was preparing to annex the entire Middle East. The Mufti, for different reasons, but to the same effect as the Soviet Union, had spurred the Third World into opposition to the State of Israel and to Zionism.

This opposition became apparent with Ayotollah Ruhollah Khomeini, who had listened to the Arabic broadcasts from the Nazi Radio Zeesen during the war. His book, *The Islamic State* published in 1971, is replete with antisemitism: "It is the Jews who were the first to begin with anti-Islamic propaganda and ideological conspiracies. And that continues until the present day." In 1967 he was calling on all Muslims to "annihilate unbelieving and inhuman Zionism…The duty of the Palestinian people is the duty of every Muslim even in the most distant lands." Israel must be boycotted. The most recent reincarnation of this point of view in the Islamic world is the Iranian president Mahmoud Ahmadinejad with his frequent calls that "The Zionist regime" be wiped out and thus humanity will be liberated.

The State of Israel Established

With the termination of the Indian Empire and the Declaration of Indian Independence, British concerns in the Middle East changed from those of an imperial power to practical issues, such as protection of the Suez Canal and oil concessions from Arab countries. Britain, the Mandate Authority for Palestine since 1922, announced that because of the difficulties, both political and military, in resolving the conflict between Jews and Arabs, it would terminate the Mandate and withdraw its administration and military forces from the area by May 1948. It would transfer the Palestine question to the United Nations for resolution and called on the UN Secretary General to place it before the UN General Assembly.

In April 1947, the UN Secretary General, Trygve Lie, called a special meeting of the General Assembly, which decided to set up the UN Special Committee on Palestine (UNSCOP) of eleven members to make recommendations. By chance, some of the members were on a fact-finding mission in Palestine when the ship *Exodus from Europe -1947* with over 4500 Jewish refugees was intercepted by British naval vessels and not allowed to dock in Haifa. The refugees were eventually taken, in another ship, *Empire Rival*, by British forces to Germany, where they were put for a time in a Displaced Persons Camp in Poppendorf, a former SS camp near Hamburg. This incident, with its symbolic implications of survivors of the Holocaust being sent to a Nazi camp, may have influenced the decision of UNSCOP in August 1947 to issue a majority recommendation for the termination of the Mandate and the partition of Western Palestine into two states, one Jewish and one Arab.

The recommendation of UNSCOP was adopted on November 29, 1947, by the UN General Assembly Partition Resolution 181(II) by 33 in favor, 13 against, 9 of which were Muslim countries, and 10 abstentions. Britain was one of the abstainers. Faced with the intransigent Arab attitude the Jewish leaders, though divided on the issue, accepted as a practical compromise the Resolution which called for separate Jewish and Arab states and an internationalized Jerusalem (a *corpus separatum*), the municipality and surrounding villages and towns, to be administered under a trusteeship system by the United Nations. The Zionists, anxious to create their state, were prepared to allow Jerusalem to be administered in this unusual manner. The special regime for Jerusalem was to be limited in time, after which the residents of the city were to express their views by a referendum.

The Resolution was rejected by the Palestinian Arabs and by six of the seven member-states of the Arab League which had replaced the League of Arab States, which was focused on anti-colonialism; only Jordan abstained. The Soviet Union supported the Resolution, arguing that because of World War II the Jewish people had suffered more than any other. The consequence of the Arab rejection was three wars and countless combative activity. The Arab League not only opposed the partition proposal, it pledged to launch a relentless war to prevent its implementation. The constant Arab position from the 1930s was insistence on the whole of Mandatory Palestine as an Arab state, not on any two-state solution or even a binational state.

The Resolution proposed the boundaries of the new Jewish state (which six months later on May 14, 1948, was established and named Israel) within part of Mandatory Palestine. The Jewish state would have about fifty-five per cent of Western Palestine, which at that time included about 555,000 Jews and about 450,000 Arabs. It would not obtain the historic areas of Judea and Samaria, nor the area east of the Jordan River, for which Zionists had once hoped. The Jewish leaders accepted this decision because of the urgent need to establish a safe haven for the Jewish people in part of Palestine after the experience of the European extermination of Jews in World War II. The consequence of the Resolution also meant that a considerable Arab minority would reside in the Jewish state.

Four facts are crucial in this narrative about a Jewish state. One is that a majority of states in the international community at that moment recognized the right of the Jewish people to political self-determination in part of Palestine. This recognition was reaffirmed when Israel was admitted to membership of the United Nations in May 1949, after the UN Security Council decided that "Israel is a peace-loving country and is able and willing to carry out the obligations contained in the (UN) Charter." A second is that the UNSCOP intended that the new state would be the national home of the Jewish people, rather than merely the inhabitants of Palestine. A third is that Resolution 181(II) referred over thirty times to the new state as the "Jewish state."

The fourth fact is that the Palestinians refused to establish their own state or to "draft a democratic constitution for its state," actions which the Resolution called for. The Arabs made it clear to the British Mandatory Government that they would not cooperate with the UN Commission in implementing the Partition Plan; indeed they proposed to attack and impede its work. On February 16, 1948, the representative of the Arab Higher Committee stated that the Committee did not accept the validity of the partition recommendations or the authority of the United Nations to make them. The Arabs of Palestine regarded the creation of a Jewish state as an act of aggression and they "would never submit or yield to any power going to Palestine to enforce partition."

This intention was put into practice when the Palestinians and fellow Arabs immediately waged war against the new Jewish state. Though they publicly engaged in "military bluster," the Arab states did not act in a consistent, unified military way against the highly motivated and more disciplined Israeli Haganah, who were fighting for survival.[150] Israel prevailed over the Arab attack, but the Arabs refused to accept the establishment of a Jewish state in any part of Palestine. The 1948-49 war ended with separate armistice agreements signed between

Israel and the states that had attacked it, Egypt (February 24), Lebanon (March 23), Jordan (April 3), and Syria (July 20), but apart from agreement on the *de jure* internationally accepted border with Lebanon the other agreements, on Arab insistence, accepted the Armistice Demarcation lines only as cease fire lines. The Arabs explicitly rejected "frontiers," or "borders." Those cease fire lines became in practice *de facto* boundaries, but they were provisional boundaries; the lines were where the fighting stopped. The cease fire lines are not "secure and recognized boundaries," which Security Council Resolution 242 recognized as necessary. Iraq refused to sign an armistice, but in practice has acted in accordance with the agreements signed by the other Arab countries.

According to the 1949 Armistice Agreements, the Demarcation Line between Israel and the different Arab states was "not to be construed in any sense as a political or territorial boundary." Resolution of the political and territorial boundaries was to wait until the permanent peace settlement, but this as yet has not materialized. The resolution was supposed to come through negotiations between the parties, not by unilateral actions. Similarly, other issues, such as control of water and the shore of Galilee, remain to be resolved. In the absence of that ultimate settlement, the Arabs engaged in discriminatory actions. Jordan, then in control of the Old City of Jerusalem and the West Bank, allowed Israeli Christians into Jerusalem only once a year, on Christmas Day. It refused to allow Jews from any country to enter the area. Access to the Jewish holy sites in East Jerusalem was not allowed. Syria never recognized an international border with Palestine, and claimed the water line dividing the Jordan River and Lake Kinneret. Moreover, Syria sponsored raids of Palestinian guerrillas against Israel and tried to divert the waters of the Jordan River.[151]

The armistice arrangements did not lead to peace. The UN Palestine Conciliation Commission in April-May 1949 launched a "peace conference" in Lausanne, but it failed largely because the Arab participants refused to meet publicly and unconditionally with Israelis, insisting that this would be tantamount to recognition of Israel without concessions from Israeli on withdrawal from certain territory and repatriation of refugees, concessions with which Israel would not agree without negotiation.[152] Instead of peace, the conflict continued, with Arab refusal to recognize Israel, blockage of traffic and goods, economic boycott, propaganda warfare both anti-Israeli and antisemitic in tone, continuing attacks on Israeli civilians and soldiers and Arab infiltration into Israeli territory.

In his 1775 speech in the British House of Commons on "Conciliation with America," Edmund Burke said that "every prudent act is founded on compromise and barter." His assertion is germane to any settlement of the Palestine question. Appropriate boundaries, acceptable to all parties, will only be decided in the context of peace negotiations and the recognition by all parties of the existence and legitimacy of the State of Israel. Hitherto boundaries, lines dividing the area, have been set by outside powers, by the Ottomans in 1906 when they separated Sinai from the provinces of Jerusalem and Hejaz, by Britain and France in 1922-23 in setting the lines between Palestine and Lebanon and Syria, and by Britain in separating Transjordan from the rest of Palestine in 1922, and thus essentially creating the area of 27,000 square kilometers it called "Palestine," an area acknowledged by the League of Nations and then by the United Nations.

In 1949, as a result of the war, Israel consisted of an area of 8,000 square miles between the western edge of the West Bank and the Mediterranean Sea, which at its narrowest point was less than ten miles wide, and at its widest point about fifteen miles. The extension of Israeli control over additional territory, and over 600,000 Arabs in the West Bank, resulted from the 1967 war. After 1967, Israel controlled not only the whole of Mandatory Palestine, west of the Jordan River, but also the Golan Heights taken from Syria, and the Sinai Peninsula, formerly ruled by Egypt. As a result of the peace treaty with Egypt in March 1979, which included mutual recognition between the two countries, Israel returned the Sinai, withdrawing to the old armistice line, withdrew all Israeli settlers from the area and agreed to Egyptian possession of the Taba resort area. Jordan, which had at first thought of a partnership with the Palestine Liberation Organization in the West Bank, decided after the first *intifada*, the spontaneous uprising of mostly young Palestinians, that began in December 1987, that this was undesirable and in 1988 waived any claim to the West Bank.

A second peace treaty, between Israel and Jordan in October 1994, did not change the boundaries or control of territory between them. The treaty reaffirmed the co-ordinates of the boundaries stated in the provisions of the 1922 British Mandate as the international boundary between the two states. Tacitly, the treaty allowed Israel to maintain control over territory captured in the 1967 war. Israel after 1967, formulated different procedures to deal with the captured territory. The West Bank was put under Israeli military administration. The Golan Heights was also put under military rule until 1981, when Israeli civilian administration and law was extended to it. East Jerusalem, which had been ruled by Jordan since 1949, was put under civilian administration as well. On July 30, 1980, the Knesset passed a law that a "complete and united Jerusalem," eternal and indivisible, was the capital of Israel. A border crossing at Kuneitra allows Arabs, mainly Druze residents of the Golan, to travel from one side to the other. After the 1973 war the UN established the UN Disengagement Observer Force (UNDOF), which enforces the cease fire between the two countries, imposed by the UN Security Council, through more than forty outposts.

In the discussion of possible resolution of the Israel-Palestinian dispute, it is worth remembering that no document has ever called on Israel to withdraw to the pre-1967 lines. The UN Security Council Resolution 242 of November 22, 1967, specifically did not call for Israel to withdraw unilaterally from all captured territory, nor did it condemn Israel. The deliberate omission of the word "all" is important; the Resolution calls for "Withdrawal of Israeli armed forces from territories occupied in the recent conflict." That the omission of "all" was intentional is clear from the statement of Lord Caradon, then British Ambassador to the UN, who introduced the Resolution, and who said, "It would have been wrong to demand that Israel return to its position of June 4, 1967, because those positions were undesirable and artificial,...they were just armistice lines." The Resolution does not define the extent of withdrawal, and its language implies less than complete withdrawal of Israeli forces from "territories occupied in the recent conflict." The extent of withdrawal was left open. It does not speak of "occupied territories," but called for a negotiated settlement of the conflict, and a just settlement of the refugee problem. It also does not state a priority between Israeli withdrawal, and the end of belligerency and the recognition of Israel.

The extent of acceptance of Resolution 242 and its interpretation have been disputed. The Resolution was fully accepted by Israel, but, except for Egypt and Jordan, the Arab states did not, and even Egypt and Jordan accepted it only with qualification. It was interpreted differently by the contending parties: the Arabs insisting on withdrawal from "all" territories, and Israel arguing the opposite. Israel also insists that any withdrawal was to be part of, and to be associated with, successful peace negotiations, recognition by the Arabs of the legitimacy of the state, and the existence of secure and recognized boundaries.

In spite of what seems clear from Resolution 242, international declarations since the passage of 242 have reinforced the Arab, rather than the Israel position on the question of territory. For example, UN Security Council Resolution 465 of March 1, 1980, determined that "all measures taken by Israel to change the physical character, demographic composition, institutional structure or status of the Palestinian and other Arab territories occupied since 1967, including Jerusalem, or any part thereof, have no legal validity." It said that Israel's policy and practice of settling parts of its population and new immigrants in those areas was a flagrant violation of the Fourth Geneva Convention. Since the Convention was adopted as a *post facto* condemnation of Nazi Germany, ironically Israel became the first country to be found guilty in an international document of behaving as the Nazi regime had done. Similarly, UN Security Council Resolution 478 of August 28, 1980, affirmed that the "enactment of the 'Basic Law' (the July 30, 1980 law unifying Jerusalem) was a violation of international law."

TWO STATES OR ONE?

Arguments still range about the nature of the political entity or entities that should control the area between the Mediterranean Sea and the Jordan River. The existence of a separate state of Israel, whether it be regarded as Jewish or not, is approved by the majority of Israelis. Palestinians, Arab countries and many in the international community, however, are divided on whether the political structure should consist of two states or one, which would essentially be a bi-national state of Jews and Arabs. The latter solution was at one point supported by a small, though influential, part of the Jewish Yishuv: Brit Shalom (the covenant of peace) founded in 1929, Hashomer Hatzair, the left wing party some of whose members were admirers of Stalin, by scholars like Martin Buber and Judah Magnes, who was with the small Ihud group. Magnes was one of the founders and became the first president of the Hebrew University in Jerusalem, serving for twenty-three years, during which he continued to be an advocate for a binational state, but never finding an Arab partner who shared his view. At the end of his life, a few months after the establishment of the State of Israel, he was proposing a confederation, the United States of Palestine, with a Palestinian state.

For a short time the idea of binationalism was supported in 1922 by Jabotinsky, leader of the militant New Zionist Organization (later Revisionists), and in the early 1930s by David Ben-Gurion, then chairman of the Jewish Agency Executive and leader of Mapai, the Social Democratic party.[153] Politically, the main argument for binationalism came from the left wing faction of Mapam, most notably Simha Flapan. For a brief period, before the bloody riots of 1936-39, Ben-Gurion thought of two possibilities: one would be for Palestine to become an Arab-Jewish federation, the other was Zionist acknowledgement of the national aspirations, and even the right of self-determination of the Arabs. Yet the idea of a binational state was not accepted at that time by the Arabs, nor was the idea of a federation. At his appearance before the Ad Hoc Committee of the UN General Assembly on September 23, 1947, the delegate of the Arab Higher Committee declared that, "The Arabs of Palestine are, therefore, solidly determined to oppose, with all means at their disposal, any scheme that provides for the dissection, segregation or partition of their country."[154]

One of the early responses to the argument for a binational state was made by Reinhold Niebuhr, who indicated that the United Nations had rejected this possibility "primarily because the Arabs were unwilling to grant the Jews any freedom of immigration in such a binational state."[155] In recent years however, this concept of binationalism has been favored by some Palestinians and some Israeli post-Zionists, individuals who differ on various issues, but who believe that traditional Zionism is no longer appropriate to deal with current issues, especially the occupation of territory since 1967. They hold that Palestinian Arabs have experienced injustice and argue that the Jewish State should be transformed into "a state of its citizens," that Jewish nationality and the State should be separated, and that the national flag and anthem should be "dejudaised" in the interest of Jewish universal humanism. However, in view of the realistic demographic changing numbers of Jews and Arabs this would probably soon result in Jews becoming a minority group, and a possible, even probable, return to pre-state problems of antisemitism and persecution. Moreover, looking at the failure of former binational or multi-national states, such as the Soviet Union, Yugoslavia, and Czechoslovakia, and the political difficulties of Belgium divided between Flemish and Walloons, and Bosnia, the creation of a binational state is not a guarantee of success. Nor is it acceptable to most Israelis; both secular and mainstream religious Zionists today agree on the existence of a secure Israeli state coexisting peacefully with an Arab state.

Chapter 11

Original Sin

I n the Palestinian Arab lexicon, the founding of Israel and the war of 1948-49, which Israel terms "the War of Independence," is labeled the *Nakba* (catastrophe). The term reflects not merely the Arab distress about defeat in the war, but even more the belief that the creation and very existence of Israel in 1948 is the "original sin." Indeed, the term was first used by the Syrian intellectual Qustantin Zurayq in his 1945 book *Ma'na al-Nakbah* (The Meaning of Catastrophe), as a warning of the consequences of a Jewish victory in Palestine.[156] The emphasis in the Palestinian narrative, and by some extreme Israeli critics, on the 1948 war and the *Nakba* raised the question of how the creation of Israel was to be perceived. In the formulation of Benny Morris, was Israel to be seen as born pure and innocent, and therefore worthy of assistance and support, or was it born tarnished, besmirched by original sin and therefore not worthy of grace and assistance? The odd thing about this controversy is that the Christian concept of original sin has been brandished by Muslims.

The Palestinian narrative of catastrophe has even led some Palestinians to equate the *Nakba* with the Holocaust. In this narrative Zionism is seen as a colonial and expansionist ideology, and the war, then and later, is claimed to be the result of unprovoked Israeli aggression. Martha Gellhorn in an article, "Casualties and Propaganda," in the Manchester Guardian, July 24, 1967, was more perceptive: she wrote of the Arabs before 1967 "intoxicated by propaganda drug, expected to wipe out Israel." The Palestinian narrative is not made more credible by actions such as the issuance by the deputy minister of information of the Palestinian Authority of a supposedly scientific report that the Western Wall in Jerusalem was never a Jewish historic site. Rashid Khalidi rationalizes the Arab failures and defeats by pointing out that the Palestinians had a divided leadership, exceedingly limited finances, no centrally organized military forces, and no reliable allies; they faced a Zionist movement and a Jewish society in Palestine which, although small, was politically unified, had centralized institutions, and was exceedingly well led and extremely highly motivated.[157]

A more generally accepted objective view is that the Israelis did not seek the war in 1948 in which they suffered severe casualties of about 6,000, which was one per cent of the Jewish population, though it should be noted the Arabs lost over 20,000. It was the Arab campaign to end any Jewish right to national self-determination in Palestine that led to the hostilities. The Palestinian narrative, that Jews were the cause of the 1948 War and consequently of the refugee problem, contrasts with both the perception of contemporary officials of the United Nations and the statements of Arab leaders. Trygve Lie, then Secretary-General of the UN, called the Arab invasion "armed defiance of the United Nations," the first armed aggression since the end of World War II.[158] Emile Ghoury, Secretary-General of the Arab Higher Committee, stated in the *Beirut Telegraph*, September 6, 1948, that "the fact there are refugees is a direct consequence of the act of the Arab states in opposing partition and the Jewish State."

THE 1948-49 WAR AND THE EMERGENCE OF THE REFUGEE PROBLEM

The 1948-49 war resulted from the Arab rejection of any compromise on the partition of Palestine, a rejection that was expressed by the Palestinians and Arab countries. The onset of hostilities was the so-called "civil war," from late 1947 to May 1948, between the Jews and Arabs in Palestine starting with the Arab attack on a Jewish passenger bus in which five passengers were killed on the way to Jerusalem on November 30, 1947, the day after the UN General Assembly Partition

Resolution.[159] Two weeks later the Arab League called on its member-states to send "volunteers" to fight in Palestine. Units of the Arab Liberation Army (ALA) in January 1948, under command of a former captain of the Iraqi army, crossed the Syrian border into Northern Palestine, and other units followed.[160] Arab countries infiltrated irregular fighters into Palestine, who engaged in ambushes, bombings, and violence; the most dramatic was the ambush on March 27, 1948, of a Hagana convoy from Gush Etzion in which thirty-six Jews were killed. The Arab Liberation Army tried to close off routes to Jewish settlements and to block the supply road to Jerusalem.

The second phase of hostilities, the international conflict, began on May 15, 1948, one day after the Israeli Declaration of Independence, when the armies of Egypt, Syria, Lebanon and Iraq, and the Arab Legion of Transjordan, said to be the best trained army in the Middle East and led by the British General Sir John Bagot Glubb and forty, soon to be seventy, other British officers, and contingents from Saudi Arabia and Yemen, attacked the new state. Britain had supplied military and financial assistance, which was supposed to end in May 1948, to the Arab Legion.[161] The ensuing war, both guerrilla and conventional warfare, which essentially ended in January 1949, but continued for another few months, cost Israel over 6,000 killed, one percent of the Jewish population, and 12,500 wounded, out of a population of 600,000. A comparable figure of casualties in American terms would be over two million killed and four million injured.

Ben-Gurion's call to resolve the Palestine issue by non-violence and his promise to do the utmost to maintain, strengthen, and deepen friendly relations with Arab neighbors were not heeded. At the same time, if he stressed the peaceful intentions of Zionism, he also made clear that the new state would response to a challenge to its existence. The most disputed part of that response was the attack on April 9, 1948, on the Arab village of Deir Yasin, where over 100 people were killed. This raid was carried out not by the official Hagana, but by the two militant groups, the Irgun Zvai Leumi (IZL), a paramilitary organization founded in 1931 and loosely connected with the Revisionist Party of Jabotinsky, and the Fighters for the Freedom of Israel (Lehi), usually known as the Stern Gang, which had seceded from the IZL. Deplorable as it was, however, the Deir Yasin episode was an exceptional event, not an act of official Zionist/Israeli policy. It was in fact condemned by the leadership of the Yishuv. The Arabs replied, to what they considered a massacre, was the killing of seventy-seven Jewish doctors and nurses on their way to the Hadassah hospital on Mount Scopus.

Particularly important for the Arab cause, was the propaganda value of Deir Yasin, which has been endlessly symbolized as an example of Jewish aggression. Rarely mentioned are the Arab attacks on the Jewish kibbutzim, especially Mishmar Haemek in the western Galilee, led by Fawzi Qawuqji, who had lived in Nazi Germany for most of World War II. In unintended consequence the very emphasis on Deir Yasin by Arab leaders may have contributed to the flight of some Palestinians who feared a similar fate at the hands of Israelis during the 1948 war.

The Arab states, more concerned with their own territorial interests than in the fortune of the Palestinians, were divided on the future of the territory of Palestine. Egypt was thought to have had designs on some of the land in the south, the Negev. Syria, as a minimum, was interested in the northern area and claimed some of the land near Lake Galilee, including the town of Al-Hamma which was seen as part of Syria. More ambitious Syrians claimed the whole of Palestine as a part of Syria. Some of the Mediterranean coastal area near Acre, they thought, could be added to Lebanon. The ambition of Abdullah, the Emir of Transjordan who became king of the Hashemite Kingdom (later renamed Jordan) in 1946, was to annex Palestine or parts of it to create a "Greater Syria."[162] Interestingly, it was the Israeli leaders, Ben-Gurion and Foreign Minister Moshe Shertok (Sharett) particularly, who favored a separate Palestinian state in the area, rather than have the territory broken into fragments as the Arab states desired.[163]

Not only the most virulent, but also the general Arab rhetoric suggested that the Arab attacks were aimed at driving Jews into the sea. During the 1948 war, Arab forces did expel Jews from the Gush Etzion area and from the Jewish Quarter in the Old City of Jerusalem, and from areas they captured such as Neveh Ya'akov and Atarot, north of Jerusalem, settlements which were demolished.[164] Indeed, after the war no live Jews were allowed to remain in or return to territory captured by the Arabs who also desecrated and destroyed a number of cemeteries, notably the ancient one in Jerusalem, where Jews were buried. Interestingly, in symbolic memory of this, Kfar Etzion, close to the scene of the May 1948 massacre when almost all the Jews were murdered by Arabs after the battle, was the first Jewish settlement re-established in the areas captured by Israel in the 1967 War. Similarly, another settlement was established in 1968 in Hebron, a town with a long Jewish history going back over 3000 years, where sixty-seven Jews had been massacred by Arabs in 1929.

The refugee problem was not created by the decision of the 1947 United Nations General Assembly Resolution 181(II) to partition Mandatory Palestine, and therefore to favor the establishment of a Jewish state. It was created because Arab governments refused to accept that Resolution which also called for the establishment of an Arab state in Palestine. Rather than agree to the creation of such a state, they were more motivated to use force to destroy the Jewish state. The refugee problem remains unresolved because most of the Arab leaders have for over sixty years rejected proposals for a compromise solution, starting with that put forward by UN General Assembly Resolution 194(III) of December 11, 1948. This called for the creation of a Conciliation Commission, to seek agreement by negotiation for a final settlement of all questions outstanding, for return of those refugees wishing "to return to their homes and live at peace with their neighbors," and for compensation paid for the property of those choosing not to return.

Paragraph 11 addressed the refugee question, and Arab leaders have claimed that it endorsed the Palestinian right of return, but this is questionable. First is that this part of the Resolution is a conditional desire, not a categorical statement. Secondly, it does not specifically mention Arab refugees, thereby implicitly including the even larger number of Jewish refugees from Arab countries. It speaks of individuals and does not guarantee any collective right of return. It refers to those prepared to "live at peace with their neighbors," thereby excluding those who have no such desire but have "irredentist" intentions. It is noticeable that the Arab states, Egypt, Syria, Lebanon, Iraq, Saudi Arabia, and Yemen, voted against the Resolution.

There will probably never be complete agreement on the issue of responsibility for the flight of Palestinians from their homes or for their expulsion during the 1948-49 war. Historians have reached widely different conclusions, sometimes for partisan purposes, evoking passionate dispute. For instance there are conflicting views about the strategy, Plan D of March 1948, formulated by Yigael Yadin, the Hagana commander, but which in fact was never carried out. On one hand it is seen by Israelis as a way of governing the land allotted by the UN to the Jewish state and as Jewish defense against the expected Arab invasion; on the other hand Palestinians view it as intended to expel Arabs.

From its inception the Zionist movement never in any official or unofficial fashion proposed the transfer or expulsion of the Arab population, though some leaders such as Ben-Gurion, occasionally thought this was desirable, when confronted with Arab belligerence and riots against Jews. It was the British Peel Commission Report that stated Arabs should be transferred, a transfer that would be carried out by agreement or by British forces. It is interesting to note that a similar idea had been endorsed earlier by the League of Nations concerning Turkey and Greece. Ben-Gurion, the Zionist leader since 1933, continually rejected transfer of population as a solution to the conflict. Indeed, in a meeting of the Jewish Agency Executive on June 7, 1938, Ben-Gurion had said, "the Arab policy of the Jewish State must be aimed not only at full equality for the Arabs, but at their cultural, social, and economic equalization, namely, at raising their standard of living to that of the Jews."[165] Similarly, in a speech of December 13, 1947, Ben-Gurion spoke of non-Jews in a Jewish state as "equal citizens, equal in everything without any exception...the state will be their state as well." On many occasions Ben-Gurion vowed that Arabs would enjoy full civic and political equality, and access to public services on the same terms as Jews.

The Arab refugee problem, and indeed that of the exodus of Jews from Arab countries, was created by the events leading to the establishment of Israel and by the consequent 1948-49 war. The Arab problem was born out of war and fear of war, not out of design.[166] If Israel cannot claim complete moral purity, it is still true that Arabs bear the major responsibility for their war to prevent a Jewish state. Despite partisan advocacy to the contrary on the issue, no evidence exists of any systematic Israeli policy of "ethnic cleansing" of Palestinian Arabs.[167] On the contrary, some Arab rhetoric focused on throwing the Jews into the sea if the Arabs were victorious.

It is likely that most Arabs fled, expecting they would return with the anticipated Arab victory. No doubt Israeli military actions in the heat of battle account for some of the Arab flight and expulsion, but this was not a planned maneuver. More relevant is the forthright acknowledgement of Khalid al Azm, Syrian prime minister 1948-49, in his *Memoirs* that "we (Arabs) doomed a million Arab refugees, by calling on them and insisting that they abandon their land, their homes, their work and their occupations, and we made them unemployed and homeless."[168] His forthright statement was that "Since 1948 we have been demanding the return of the refugees...but we ourselves encouraged them to leave." They were to take refuge in the neighboring Arab countries.[169]

From the Israeli archives of the period now available, it appears that the departure of thousands of Arabs, first about 6,000 from Tiberias, occurred as a result of the advice of the Nazareth National Committee. This was followed by similar departure of Palestinians, about a third of the Arab population in Haifa, from their homes. The early departures took place before the outbreak of major hostilities, and in some cases even before the November 29, 1947, UN General Assembly Resolution on partition. The major departure from Haifa, starting with wealthy, educated, and professional Arabs began in December 1947, and was followed by the political leadership of the area, and then by most of the Arab workers, in spite of pleas by both the British Commander, General Hugh Stockwell and the Jewish mayor, Shabtai Levy, for them to remain. General Stockwell was astonished at the announcement by the Arab dignitaries that the Arabs would leave for Lebanon, rather than remain and live under Jewish control. Another 75,000 Arabs left their homes in February and March 1948. In April 1948, A.J. Bridmead, the British Chief of Police in Haifa, reported that "Every effort is being made by the Jews to persuade the Arab populace to stay and carry on with their normal lives." He also reported that the Arab leaders in Haifa had reiterated their determination to evacuate the entire Arab population.

Only 3,000 Arab residents remained in the city. This departure, which later influenced the flight of Arabs elsewhere, was largely due to fear, lack of efficient Arab administrative structures, dislocation as a result of the fighting in the "civil war," poor military organization and desertion of military leaders, either due to cowardice or miscalculation, and disillusion of Arabs with their leader and social elites.[170]

In view of the controversy and fierce light focused on the refugee issue, it is worth repeating that Palestinians fled largely because the Arab leaders themselves fled or urged hundreds of thousands of Palestinians to leave their homes. Paradoxically some of this occurred during the early period of the war, when the Arabs were gaining victories. During the months of April and May, over twenty Arab villages were wholly or largely evacuated because of orders by local Arab commanders, Arab governments, or the Arab Higher Committee (AHC). Later, these orders were applied to Jaffa, the largest Arab city, whose municipality organized the flight, and Jerusalem, where the AHC ordered women and children to leave. Palestinian Arabs thus became refugees, if generally unwelcome, in neighboring Arab countries. They were betrayed, not by the British, nor by the Zionists, but by the Arab leaders, some of whom had ambitions to create an Arab empire in the area formerly ruled by the Ottoman Empire.

On a number of occasions the British High Commissioner for Palestine, General Alan Cunningham, commented on the departures. In a telegram of April 26, 1948, he wrote that "the collapsing Arab morale in Palestine is in some measure due to the increasing tendency of those who should be leading them to leave the country...in all parts of the country the effendi class has been evacuating in large numbers over a considerable period."[171] Cunningham reported on May 5, 1948, that nearly all the city Councilors and members of the National Committee in Jaffa had fled. Morale there had collapsed as fear increased. Sir Henry Gurney, the last British Chief Secretary of the Palestine Mandate Government (October 1946-May 1948) was no friend to the Jewish population; he wrote that Zionism was built "on a foundation of lies, chauvinism, suspicion, and deception."[172] Nevertheless he wrote in his dairy of May 5, 1948, that ninety per cent of the population of Jaffa had run away; the mayor had gone without saying goodbye. Within a few days only a few thousand Arabs remained in the city. A week earlier, on April 28, 1948, Gurney had written that it was "pathetic to see how the Arabs have been deserted by their leaders, and how the firebrands all seek refuge in Damascus, Amman and elsewhere when the real trouble starts."[173] Gurney also wrote in his diary that the Jewish offensive in Haifa was staged as a direct consequence of four days of continuous Arab attacks. He documented the fact that Arab leaders, and the Arab Higher Committee and the Emergency Committee in Haifa were responsible in March 1948, for ordering women, children, and the elderly to leave the city.

By the end of April nearly 300,000 Palestinians had fled. During the fighting in 1947 the Commander of British forces in Northern Palestine, Major-General Hugh Stockwell, who tried to mediate unsuccessfully a truce in Haifa commented, "You (the Arabs) have made a foolish decision...it was you who began the fighting, and the Jews have won." Among those who fled were Ghaleb Khalidi, chairman of the National Committee, who went to Egypt, and Hussein Khalidi, a senior member of the Arab Higher Committee and once mayor of Jerusalem. Many Arab villages were partly or wholly depopulated to accommodate local gangs, the arrival of contingents of the Arab Liberation Army and of the Arab Legion of Transjordan. As a result of the fighting in Safad on May 9, 1948, the whole Arab population fled the city. Arabs also fled from many villages and from cities such as Acre, Lydda, and Ramle. Karsh argues that the Lydda and Ramle operation, largely under Yigal Allon, and in which Yitzhak Rabin was involved, was the only instance where a substantial urban population was driven out by the Jewish forces.[174] In other cases, in the heat of battle and for military reasons, Arabs were told to leave their villages. These cases apart, the general policy of Israel was to prevent flight; one example was that during the fighting in Nazareth, Prime Minister Ben-Gurion specifically ordered that no people were to be moved from the city.

On August 16, 1948, the Arab flight was explained by Msgr. George Hakini, the Greek Catholic Archbishop of Galilee who said, "The refugees had been confident that their absence from Palestine would not last long; that they would return within a few days or within a week or two; their leaders had promised them that the Arab armies would crush the 'Zionist gangs' very quickly and that there would be no need for panic or fear of a long exile." Emile Ghoury, secretary of the Arab Higher Committee in his statement on September 15, 1948, already quoted above, reached a similar conclusion. In an unusual, if belated, statement the Palestinian Authority Chairman Mahmoud Abbas, in a TV broadcast on July 6, 2009, made a frank admission that his own middle class family was not expelled or driven out of their town Safad in 1948, but left out of fear that the Jews might take revenge for the Arab slaughter of twenty Jews in the city in 1929.

The new State of Israel did not seek to evict Palestinians from their homes, but it did decide that almost all those who had fled, probably about 600,000, would not be allowed to return. About 140,000 Arabs remained in Israel and another 50,000 returned soon after the end of the war. Of the others, about two-thirds went to the West Bank and Gaza, and the rest to Jordan, Lebanon, and Syria. Most stayed within about twenty-five miles from their previous homes, moving from one part of Palestine to another.

In addition, and often forgotten, is the fact that, after the series of cease-fires and then the armistice agreements signed in 1949 between Israel and four of the five Arab countries (Egypt, Lebanon, Jordan, and Syria) that had attacked it, it was Egypt and Jordan that ruled Palestinians in the areas known as the Gaza Strip and the West Bank. The fate of the Palestinians in those areas was in the hands of fellow Arabs, not of Jews. Equally forgotten is the fact that no Arab country, except Jordan and Lebanon in part, has been willing to grant citizenship or political rights to Palestinian refugees, even those locally born descendants in their midst, nor absorb or resettle them in their own Arab societies. The Arab League, now consisting of twenty-one countries with 350 million people, and occupying about five and a quarter million square miles, though divided on other matters, argues that this denial avoids dissolution of Palestinian identity and protects the right of Palestinians to return to their homeland. In 1949, no Palestinian official body existed with which Israel could reach any agreement, and no Arab state was prepared to tackle the issue of a Palestinian political structure of its own.

Chapter 12

The United Nations Relief and Works Agency

The Arab states refused to absorb the Palestinians and integrate them into their own societies, in spite of lip service about their concern for the refugees. Syria has refused to provide citizenship or full property rights for the Palestinians within their borders. Lebanon has about 400,000 Palestinians, most of whom cannot own land and do not have the benefits of education, health care, and welfare. Jordan has been the most generous, but even there the relationship between Palestinians and other citizens has been uneven. The Arab states rejected any solution that proposed resettling or integrating Palestinians outside of Palestine. Therefore, sixty years later, large numbers of the refugees are still housed in camps run by the United Nations Relief and Works Agency (UNRWA) and are financed by international aid.[175] Ironically, the sixtieth anniversary of the agency, whose function should have ended many years earlier, was celebrated in 2008, with a lavish display. Its annual budget has been over half a billion dollars; in 2010-2011 it rose to $1.23 billion. Together the US and the EU provide half of the funding of UNWRA. The US in 2009 provided about $268 million, twenty-seven percent of the budget, and the European Union gave $232 million. The funds given by the EU supplements its help to Palestinians by financing the PEGASE mechanism, designed to support Palestinian development, and it provides significant direct financial assistance to the Palestinian Authority. Arab countries have contributed less than two per cent to the budget. In 2009, only two

Arab countries provided funds; Kuwait gave $35.5 million and Saudi Arabia $27.6 million. Turkey gave $1 million, of which half was for the Gaza Emergency Appeal; between 2000 and 2009, Turkey provided a total of $7 million. In addition to the large sums it has received and spent, UNRWA has considerable amounts deposited in pension funds.

Refugee status was supposed to be a temporary condition, as was the existence of UNRWA, but because Arab states refused to admit Palestinians on a permanent basis as citizens of their countries it has been an ongoing process. Those states argued that to grant citizenship to Palestinians would be to accept Israel explicitly, and the consequences of 1948 and 1967. Even the creation of the Palestinian Authority (PA) in 1993 did not reduce the role of UNRWA in providing civil services for the refugees. UNRWA therefore became a long-term social welfare agency, rather than a resettlement or a temporary humanitarian aid agency. This "moral hazard", as Fred Gottheil calls it, discouraged many Palestinians from pursuing viable options to resolve their long-term refugee status, and also encouraged many non-refugees in the region to attempt to register for refugee status, or at least to take advantage of the entitlements UNRWA offered.

Part of the problem stems from the fact that no official document defines who is a "Palestinian refugee." In the Geneva Convention relating to the Status of Refugees of July 1951, Article IA(2), a refugee is defined as one who, for various reasons, "is outside the country of his nationality and is unable to avail himself of the protection of that country...or is unwilling to return to it." As of 2011, 147 states are parties to the Convention. But according to Article I (D) of the Convention, that definition does not apply to Palestinian refugees because they are given protection and assistance by UNRWA.

By broadening the definition of "refugee," UNRWA has perpetuated the problem in a number of ways. It counted as a refugee anyone whose normal place of residence between June 1946 and May 1948 was in the part of Palestine territory allotted by the United Nations to the State of Israel. Secondly, this count includes not only Arabs who fled and lost their homes, but also people who stayed and lost their means of livelihood because of the war. Logically, only first-generation refugees, those resulting from the 1948 and 1967 wars, should be so considered. Yet, the UNRWA definition also includes children and grandchildren who are fourth generation descendants of 1948 Palestinian refugees. These descendants are the only group in the world ever to be granted refugee status on the basis of descent. A reasonable conclusion is that Arab nations are not interested in solving the refugee problem, but want to use it as a weapon against Israel. It is a striking fact that the Arab states have not contributed any significant amount to the operation of UNRWA; most of the funding comes from the United States and member-states of the European Union. For those Arab states the refugees have been, as Martha Gellhorn earlier wrote in the Manchester Guardian on July 26, 1967, both a vested interest, as far as goods and services were concerned, and a propaganda weapon against Israel.

UNRWA does not govern the refugee camps; it only provides services to them. UNRWA provides free health care largely through 122 clinics based in or near the camps; since birth rates there are among the highest in the world, a priority in the program is maternal and child healthcare. UNRWA has provided education, jobs, and welfare, functions that the United Nations High Commissioner for Refugees (UNHCR) usually leaves to countries where refugees have obtained asylum. It has also created a relatively large bureaucracy, now about 25,000, almost all of whom are Palestinians, who pursue political agendas which have tended to increase the number of those counted as "refugees." In every refugee case in the world, except one, the numbers go down over the years; by contrast the number of Palestinian refugees has vastly increased. The number, about 711,000 in 1950, is now said to be over 4.6 million, about 1.5 million of whom live in or near one of fifty-nine camps in five geographical areas.

It is also striking that the Palestinian Authority (PA), the ruler of the West Bank and, for a time, Gaza since 1994, has made no or little effort to remove the refugees from camps into permanent housing. Not a single Palestinian has ever lost his refugee status.[176] Even those given citizenship in Jordan are regarded as refugees by UNRWA. This international body has perpetuated the Israeli-Palestinian problem, and become a vehicle for Arab propaganda. Its existence has allowed the

PA to disclaim responsibility for the refugees, even to oppose housing programs proposed by Israel, and at the same time to use the refugees as a symbol of Palestinian nationalism.

In addition, in recent years members of the anti-Israeli Hamas organization have been employed by UNRWA, a fact that was admitted in 2004 by Peter Hansen, then head of UNRWA, who said, "I don't see that as a crime." Some of the UNRWA staff has been associated with radical causes; some of their operations are said to have aided terrorist activity. Bias was clear from the beginning. In 1968-69 reports on the UNRWA school system, with 684 schools, 17,000 teachers and staff, and over 500,000 students, found that teachers appointed by the UN were inculcating antisemitism. The UNESCO commission of three eminent scholars, from Turkey, France, and the United States, all distinguished professors of Arabic, appointed to examine the issue found that textbooks used in the schools described the Jewish community as the eternal and irreconcilable enemy of the Muslim community. They concluded that the textbooks were preoccupied with indoctrination against Jews, rather than strictly educational aims.[177] Schoolbooks at first contained antisemitic passages, which are said to have been removed and the treatment of Israel is said to be less hostile, though the Jewish connection to the region in general and to the Holy Land in particular is understated or missing. It is startling that these schools were and are maintained, operated, and financed by an international organization. This critical report presented to the 82nd Session of UNESCO on April 4, 1969, was never published. In 2011, UNRWA planned to teach the 200,000 children in the 228 schools in Gaza about the Holocaust; Hamas attempted to stop this. The subject of the Holocaust has not been taught in UNRWA schools for Palestinians in other areas.

Another strongly critical report in 2009, by James G. Lindsay, former UNRWA general-counsel, bluntly states that "UNRWA has taken very few steps to detect and eliminate terrorists from the ranks of its staff or its beneficiaries, and no steps at all to prevent members of terrorist organizations such as Hamas from joining its staff."[178] Lindsay's statement is all the more persuasive because he acknowledges the real accomplishment of UNRWA in education, health, welfare, microfinancing, and housing services. He then, however, stated that UNRWA had adopted a distinctive political viewpoint that favors the Palestinian and Arab narrative of events in the Middle East. This has counteracted humanitarian assistance, encouraged Palestinians to continue fighting long-lost wars, and discouraged those who favor moving toward peace.

In dramatic contrast to the stateless condition of Palestinians, and the unwillingness of Arab states to extend hospitality to fellow Arabs, the 600,000-700,000 Jews who fled or were expelled from Arab countries in the Middle East and North Africa, where their families had lived for hundreds of years, because of the war in 1948 or because of Arab violence and discrimination, have mostly been absorbed and resettled in Israel and in Western countries. Arriving mostly penniless, because their property had often been confiscated, and despite the fact that they were almost all Sephardim, they were immediately given citizenship in Israel by the Ashkenazi majority who had come from Western countries. This approximately equal number of Jewish and Palestinian refugees can be seen as an exchange of populations, and one in which the Jews from Arab countries had lost most of their property.

Wherefore is the Palestinian refugee problem different from all other refugee problems? In many areas of the world millions became refugees as the result of conflicts and civil wars, or moved through exchange of religious or ethnic populations. An important example was the exchange of some nearly two million Greeks and Turks across boundaries in the 1920s. Refugees have been resettled through agreement of the parties or through the activity at first of the International Refugee Organization (IRO), to facilitate the resettlement of Europeans removed from their homes in World War II, or through the Office of the UNHCR, set up to protect and assist refugees in December 1950 which replaced the United Nations Relief and Rehabilitation Administration, and which continues to have the function of resettlement, voluntary repatriation or rehabilitation of the refugees. These organizations have dealt with over 25 million people with the aim of finding long term solutions to refugee problems, despite the tensions between ethnic and religious groups.

Perhaps the most important of the voluntary resettlements were those between India and the new state of Pakistan in 1947, when about 15 million Hindus/Sikhs and Muslims were transferred from one country to the other. Thousands of Turks were admitted into Turkey from Bulgaria. Less voluntary, but successfully accomplished, was the post World War II exchange of East Germans, Sudeten Germans and Poles when the Soviet Union changed the borders in Eastern Europe. Germany gave up all claims against Poland, including the right of its refugees to return. West Germany, after World War II, absorbed and rehabilitated about 10 million displaced persons. Other countries have experienced the absorption of refugees. France has admitted several million people of French background, *pieds-noirs*, from North Africa. Italy provided asylum for over half a million Italians displaced from areas given to Yugoslavia after World War II. Austria admitted nearly 200,000 Hungarians who fled their country after the 1956 events. Resolution of refugee problems in other areas of the world, the Balkans, Vietnam, and some African countries, has been undertaken. The Palestinian one remains unique because of the refusal of Arab states, except Jordan, to help absorb their fellow Arabs, as well as Palestinian intransigence.

A crucial difference, and indeed a further irony, is that the Palestinians are receiving preferential treatment. The UNHCR was established to deal with all the world refugees in general. UNRWA was set up by UN General Assembly Resolution 302(IV) of December 8, 1949, to deal with only one refugee problem, the Palestinian one. Taking account of the money spent on refugees throughout the world one can fairly conclude that Palestinian refugees receive more funding and are better treated than other refugees. The function of UNRWA remains to provide "direct relief and works programs" for Palestinian Arab refugees only. But by employing terrorists and allowing schools to be centers for indoctrination and training camps against Israel it is perpetuating, not solving the Palestinian refugee issue.

It is interesting to compare the constant criticism of Israeli policy with the reality regarding people and property in Arab countries. Jordan, which occupied and "annexed" the West Bank between 1949 and 1967, granted citizenship by laws of 1950 and 1954 to any Arab born in Jordan or the "usurped" part of Palestine and left there, and also to children of those people wherever they were born. However, this did not apply to Jews, who not only were denied citizenship, but also were forbidden to live there under pain of death. In 1973, a Jordanian law prevented the sale of immovable property to the enemy who was defined as "any man or judicial body of Israeli citizenship living in Israel or acting on its behalf." The law was repealed after the peace treaty between Israel and Jordan, but some statutes still prevent Israelis from buying or leasing land in Jordan. Parenthetically, Jordan revoked the citizenship of West Bank Palestinian Arabs in 1988, except for those in UNRWA camps. Justifying this discriminatory action, which left about three quarter of a million people stateless, King Hussein of Jordan, who had cut off his country's administrative and legal ties with the West Bank, said it was done with "the aim of enhancing the Palestinian national orientation, and highlighting the Palestinian identity."

King Hussein already had faced assassination attempts on his life and aggressiveness on the part of the militant Palestine Liberation Organization, founded in Cairo in 1964, which in the late 1960s and early 1970s had been hijacking planes. The PLO leader Yasser Arafat was virtually establishing a state within the state of Jordan. As a response Hussein declared martial law and ordered an attack on the headquarters of the PLO and Palestinians in the refugee camps in his kingdom killing thousands, perhaps as many as 25,000, in what has become known as Black September 1970. Palestinians expelled from Jordan to Lebanon propelled the civil war in that country, in which over 100,000 were killed. Jordanian authorities have gone further in recent years in this disengagement policy by revoking the citizenship of thousands of Palestinians living in Jordan so that they may not be regarded as resettled permanently in the country, in which about seventy per cent of the population is of Palestinian descent.

Jordan now has a complex system under which some Palestinians have yellow cards, which allow full residency for those who left the West Bank, and others have green cards which are valid for two years, and renewable, but do not provide a right of residence. In recent years, Jordan has been revoking the Jordanian citizenship that thousands of those of Palestinian descent had been granted. Jordan has provided Palestinians with passports, but made clear that on the establishment of a Palestinian state the refugees would have to choose whether to be Jordanian citizens or return to Palestine. Syria and Lebanon have made it equally clear that the refugee camps in their territory are temporary and that the refugees must return to Palestine. Human rights organizations have been unusually silent about this Arab discriminatory behavior, not only in Jordan, but also in Lebanon and in Syria, where the movement of Palestinians in refugee camps in those countries is controlled.

Yasser Arafat and his PLO supporters, forced to leave Jordan, went to Lebanon where they did manage to create a state within a state (Fatahland), attacking Lebanese Shi'a and Christians and setting up military training camps, which led to civil war in that country. Little mention has been made by the international community that is concerned with human rights, about the killing and wounding of Palestinians in the Lebanese refugee camp, and of the bombing by the Lebanese Army of the Nahr-al-Bared refugee camp in north Lebanon. Over 400,000 Palestinians still live in twelve refugee camps in Lebanon; they are regarded as "foreigners," have experienced inadequate conditions in health care, medical treatment, social services, education, and lack opportunities to obtain employment in many services and institutions. The ban imposed in 1946 in Lebanon, preventing Palestinians from taking anything but menial jobs, was only amended in 2010. Kuwait had expelled in 1991 about 400,000 Palestinians working in the country because of Yasser Arafat's support for Saddam Hussein's invasion of Kuwait in the first Gulf War of 1990-91. Libya had expelled 30,000 Palestinians after the PA was set up, and Iraq similarly expelled thousands of Palestinians. Observing this record, it is apparent that Palestinians have been more used by Arab countries as propaganda weapons against Israel, than treated with generosity.

The Right of Return

The refusal of the Arab countries to help resolve the refugee problem has given rise to a demand, increasingly asserted, for Palestinian refugees, who now include grandchildren and great-grandchildren of the original inhabitants of the area to return to it. Irrespective of their differences about the responsibility for the flight of Palestinians and their disagreement on political strategic objectives, Palestinian leaders and supporters unite in the call for "the right of return," the right of Arab refugees who fled their homes in what is now Israel, during the fighting between Jews and Arabs. The resolute conviction of Palestinian leaders is that the principle of repatriation must be accepted. The first proposal on the subject appears to have come not from Arabs, but from Count Folke Bernadotte, former president of the Swedish Red Cross and the person appointed by the UN in May 1948 as mediator of the Arab-Israeli conflict. He wrote on June 27, 1948, that refugees should have the "right to return home without restriction and to regain possession of their property." However, he amended his own proposal, in light of the political and military situation, to state "the right of return to their home at the earliest practical date should be established." Israeli leaders, who did not regard Bernadotte sympathetically because of his controversial negotiations with Heinrich Himmler during the war on behalf of the Swedish Red Cross, countered that return of refugees would constitute a threat to the security of the new country.

After the assassination of Bernadotte on September 17, 1948, by the Stern Gang, the UN acted. The UN General Assembly Resolution 194(III) of December 11, 1948, established a Conciliation Commission which was instructed to help achieve a final settlement of all questions in Palestine, including the refugee one. The essential provision on this issue, as stated above, was that refugees wishing to return be willing to "live in peace with their neighbors." It also issued the instruction that the Conciliation Commission "facilitate the repatriation, resettlement and economic and social rehabilitation of the refugees and the payment of compensation." The Arab states originally rejected the Resolution.[179] This was a non-binding Resolution; under the UN Charter the General Assembly is not authorized to adopt binding resolutions. It did not make the right of return a principle of international law. In any case, the Resolution was superseded by UN Security Council Resolution 242 of November 22, 1967, which called for "a just settlement of the refugee problem," although it did not call for any particular solution. This Resolution was also rejected by the Arabs; Egypt, Saudi Arabia, Iraq, Syria, Lebanon, Yemen voted no. The Resolution did not mention the "Palestinians." Nor, in what was a deliberate decision, did it mention Jerusalem. Moreover, the Resolution did not state there was an unconditional right for Palestinians to return to the area that is now Israel. As discussed earlier, though the numbers remain disputed it is probable that between 600,000 and 700,000 Palestinians fled. The Palestinian demand for the right of return has been a political maneuver, rather than one based on genuine humanitarian concern.

In the 1970s the refugee question became linked with the advocacy of a Palestinian right of self-determination.[180] The UN General Assembly, Resolution 3376, in 1975, set up the Committee on the Inalienable Rights of the Palestinian People which proclaimed that "the exercise of the individual right of the Palestinian to return to his homeland was a *conditio sine qua non* for the exercise by this people of its rights to self-determination, national independence and sovereignty." The following year it recommended "full implementation of the inalienable rights of the Palestinian people." Recently, more emphasis has been put on the "private right," sanctioned by international law, of all the refugees to return, irrespective of the attitude or compromises by the

PA or international bodies. In addition, the Palestinian leadership has remained adamant that Palestinians have never waived their right and will never forego it. In 2010 both the Palestinian National Council and the PLO Executive Committee published statements on the issue. The former stated, "we will not accept any solution whatsoever that will derogate from the right of the Palestinian people to return to the homes from which they were expelled." The latter declared it was behind the "right of the Palestinian people to return to the dwelling places from which they were expelled by the Zionist gangs 62 years ago."

The Arab continual emphasis on "the right of return" has occasioned understandable sympathy on the part of well meaning outsiders. However, this sympathy does not take account of or minimizes four relevant factors. One is the combined import of the peace arrangements between Egypt and Jordan and the Camp David Accords of September 1978, between Egyptian President Anwar El Sadat and Israeli Prime Minister Menachem Begin, when there was recognition of the need to resolve "the Palestinian problem in all its aspects," and to take account of the "legitimate rights" of the Palestinians. The Camp David Accords constituted a milestone along the problematic path of peace between Israel and Arabs, showing that differences could be resolved peacefully and by political bargaining. Israel agreed to withdraw by a gradual process from the whole area of Sinai, an area three times larger than the state of Israel, giving up three airfields, settlements, early warning stations, and control over oil fields, in return for peace and normalization of relations with Egypt. Israel also gave up strategic depth by its withdrawal, especially air space for training and operating its air force. Egypt, if imperfectly, implemented the process of normalization, with full diplomatic exchanges at ambassadorial level, ending all boycotts against Israeli trade, and opening its ports to Israeli shipping. Cultural and academic exchanges started.

Following Camp David came the Israeli offer of negotiations and autonomy, the establishment of the Palestinian Authority in 1994, the Israel-Jordan peace treaty in 1994, the Oslo Accord of September 1993, the series of interim agreements between Israel and the Palestinians from 1993 to 1995, in which it is understood that the refugee issue must be solved in conjunction with permanent status negotiations between Israel and the Palestinians, and the agreement in October 1999 on safe passage between the West Bank and Gaza.[181] Those interim agreements, cover a number of issues, not only settlements but also security, elections, human rights, and jurisdiction, remain legally valid. The 1995 Interim Agreement between Israel and the Palestinians divides jurisdiction in the West Bank into three areas, two under the Palestinians and one under Israel; it defines respective powers and responsibilities in the areas they control. The international community has been slow to recognize that these powers are in place until the outcome of permanent status negotiations.

A second factor is the continuing cynical perpetuation of the human tragedy of the Palestinian refugees by Arabs, who have rejected the concept of resettlement in different parts of the Middle East, first proposed in 1949 and again by Dag Hammarskjold, UN Secretary-General, in 1959, when he introduced a plan for Palestinians to be integrated into their host countries. The UNGA Resolution 413 of January 26, 1952, urged countries to assist in carrying out Hammarskjold's plan. Instead, Arab countries continued to use the issue as a political weapon against Israel.[182]

The third factor is a series of obstacles self-imposed by the Palestinians that prevent them from taking advantage of opportunities to establish a state, especially after UN Security Council Resolution 1397 of March 2002 explicitly called for one. After the end of World War I, the Palestinians failed to create any genuine institutions of self-government, national militia, or real competitive democratic political parties. They did not mobilize or organize the economic, social, and political potential in their societies, as the Jewish Yishuv had done. Only in recent years has there been a slow development of a political and economic infrastructure and security arrangements in the West Bank that might lay the groundwork for a future state. No clear picture has yet emerged of the geography of such a state, whether it will be limited to the West Bank and Gaza and part of Jerusalem or will include the whole of Palestine and sovereignty over the whole of Jerusalem, particularly the Temple Mount. Nor is it known whether the nature of a Palestinian state will be secular, or fundamentalist Islamic based on sharia law.

Walter Bagehot once wrote that the role of the British monarch was "well considered inaction." To this point Palestinians, unlike Dickens' Mr. Micawber, seem to be always waiting for something to turn down. They have been reluctant to deal with practical arrangements. Instead, they are rendered incapable of positive action by their ideological fixation on rejection of the state of Israel, especially because it is a "Jewish state." Palestinian spokespeople anticipate that history will be on their side as they envisage the problems that will increase for Israel as a result of demography, the larger birthrate of Arabs (in 2011 in Gaza it is 3.3% and in the West Bank 2.13% compared with the Jewish rate of 1.7%), the growing wealth and increasing salience of the Arab and Islamic worlds, and the passivity of European countries.[183]

The Palestinians did try to move history on three occasions. The first, curiously during the 1948-49 war, occurred on October 1, 1948, when the Arabs announced the creation of a state. A second was that while in Algiers on November 15, 1988, the Palestinian National Council in its 19th session declared the statehood of Palestine. Yasser Arafat immediately assumed the title of "President of Palestine." This Declaration of Independence, written by the Palestinian poet Mahmoud Darwish, defined Palestine as the "land of the three monotheistic faiths, (is) where the Palestinian people was born, on which it grew, developed, and excelled. The Palestinian people was never separated from or diminished in its integral bonds with Palestine. Thus the Palestinian Arab people ensured for itself an everlasting Union, between the people, its land and its history." In a way it echoed the Israeli Declaration of Independence. It referred to the Palestinian people's "inalienable rights in the land of its patrimony." Thus, the Palestinian people "ensured for itself an everlasting union between the people, its land, and its history."

Whatever the merits of this historical narrative, the declaration of a Palestinian identity was accompanied by a rejection of the historic Jewish link with Palestine. Among other parts of this rejection, King Herod (37-4 B.C.) is described as "the Arab Edomite," and Jesus as an Palestinian Aramaic Arab. Yet interestingly, the Declaration, implicitly acknowledged if it did not exactly recognize, the legitimacy of Israel by referring to UNGA Resolution 181 (1947), which "partitioned Palestine into two states, one Arab, one Jewish." This acceptance of Resolution 181 was a reversal of the PLO's own Covenant which rejected the partition of Palestine in 1947 as entirely illegal. Now, the Declaration stated that Resolution 181 "still provides those conditions of international legitimacy that ensure the right of the Palestinian people to sovereignty on their homeland."[184] It argued that because of the authority bestowed by international legitimacy and in accordance with the rights to self-determination of the Palestinian Arab people, a state of Palestine was established on "our Palestinian territory with its capital Jerusalem (Al-Quds Ash-Sharif)." Some Palestinian leaders still call for a unilateral declaration of independence, claiming this would be based on precedents such as the American Continental Congress declaring America's independence unilaterally, and a similar action by Kosovo in 2008.

The third development was at the UNGA meeting on December 15, 1988, when Resolution 43/177 was approved, 104-2 (Israel and the United States)-36, stating that the Palestinian people have a right to declare a state; in addition the PLO "observer" could now be termed "Palestine," which among other things now had the right to submit communications directly to the UN Secretary-General for official UN publications. This "state" was immediately recognized by eighty-nine states. Recognition of this kind does not in itself create a state, and has no definitive significance. It is essentially an indication of sympathy and of the political opinions of the "recognizers." They paid no attention to what is held as the most authoritative description of "statehood," the 1933 Montevideo Convention on the Rights and Duties of States.[185] That description includes four main factors: the ability to govern, a permanent population, a defined territory, and an ability to enter into relations with other states.

Divisions among the Palestinians, especially between the Fatah (PLO) and the more militant Hamas which won the January 2006 election and since 2007 has ruled Gaza and imposed aspects of sharia law on its population, have been a major handicap to the acceptance of a central authority that controls the use of force and a system of law and order, essential requirements for a state. Since 1968, the Fatah faction has dominated the PLO, which in October 1974 was recognized as "the sole legitimate representative of the Palestinian people" by the Arab League Summit Conference of 20 Arab states and PLO representatives held in Rabat. Jordan accepted the PLO in this capacity, as did the European Union in its 1980 Venice Declaration. Jordan's interest in, and claims to, the West Bank had lasted forty years. At the Jericho Conference in December 1948, West Bank delegates had declared the West Bank to be an integral part of the Hashemite Kingdom of Jordan. In July 1988 King Hussein renounced claims to the West Bank and East Jerusalem, saying he respected the expressed wish of the PLO that Palestinians not be part of the state of Jordan, but instead would create their own independent Palestinian state. However, Hamas has never accepted the legitimacy of the PLO.

A fourth factor is the realistic impact of the implementation of a Palestinian "right of return" on Israel. The return of Arabs claiming to be refugees or the return of their descendants to the area which is now the State of Israel, would dramatically change the demographic composition of the country and would thus challenge the nature of Israel as a Jewish state and would destabilize and endanger, even end, the state. That issue remains a crucial one, both in assessing the domestic differences about territory and religion facing Israel and in addressing the problem of a compromise solution in the peace process between the contending parties. The creation of Israel left open the question of its "Jewish" nature. The Declaration of the Establishment of the State of Israel by thirty-eight members of the provisional Jewish government in Tel Aviv on May 14, 1948, defined the new State as a Jewish State in *Eretz Israel* and used the term "Jewish State" six times, as well as "Jewish people" twenty times. The Declaration defined the land of Israel as "the birthplace of the Jewish People" where their spiritual, religious and national nature was shaped, and where they first attained statehood, and created cultural values of national and universal significance. Explicit in this definition is the affirmation that Jews had never ceased being a nation and had once lived in sovereign independence. In his last public speech in the Knesset, a few days before he was assassinated, Yitzhak Rabin on October 5, 1995, reiterated this. He said, "The land of the prophets, which bequeathed to the world the values of morality, law and justice, was, after two thousand years, restored to its lawful owners, the members of the Jewish people."

Chapter 14

The Captured Territories

At the foundation of Israel in 1948, its size was 5,500 square miles. After the 1948-49 war, it increased to 8,000 square miles, and as a result of the 1967 war Israel controlled 10,500 square miles. The controversy over occupation of territory by Israel is inherently related to the controversy over responsibility for the June 1967 Six Day War, a war that initially no country or group wanted or expected.[186] Intent to destroy Israel was in the air. The Arab League in a meeting in Cairo in 1964, called for the diversion of the waters of the Jordan River, water that is vital for Israel. The Palestine Liberation Organization (PLO), proclaiming its objective to destroy Israel, was founded in the same year. Though Israel has sometimes been accused of aggression, it was reacting against the threat to its security and use of force against it.

President Gamal Abdel Nasser, a charismatic, revolutionary leader, both authoritarian and populist, had emerged as the most powerful figure in the Arab world with his pan-Arab policy, challenging the Western world, as well as Israel. He persuaded the African and Asian representatives at the Bandung Conference in April 1955 to offer support to the rebellion against France. As a result, France became at least temporarily an ally with Israel against Egypt, the common threat. The arms deal of September 1955 between Egypt and nominally with Czechoslovakia, but in essence with the Soviet Union, indicated to the world the increasing Soviet influence in the Middle East, and for Israel the quantitative and qualitative military advantage Egypt was presumed to have over Israel. Israel was not able to obtain arms from the US, which had put an embargo in December 1947 on arms sales to the Middle East, an embargo that was reinforced by the Tripartite Declaration, of the United States, Britain, and France of December 1950, to the same effect. In spite of a number of requests by Israel for arms supplies, the Eisenhower Administration rejected almost all of them in 1953 and 1954.

Israel, therefore, turned to France with which, at that time, it shared common enemies and common strategic interests. France felt resentful about British policy in the Middle East. It was concerned about the fall in Syria of the leader Colonel Adib al-Shishakli, thus opening the door to Soviet penetration of Syria, and it was unhappy about the 1955 Baghdad Pact, signed by the United States, Britain, Turkey, Pakistan, Iran, and Iraq, but from which France was excluded. France, between 1954 and 1956, supplied Israel with important, high-level arms supplies, including Sherman tanks and Mystères (Mark IV) jets. This virtual alliance between the two countries led to discussion of joint action against Nasser, and after the secret talks in Sèvres in October 1956 between the two and Britain, to the Sinai campaign. In the war Israel captured the Sinai Peninsula, but was forced to withdraw because of the threats from both Soviet Prime Minister Nikolai Bulganin and President Eisenhower.[187] Israel had entered into the 1956 war after consultation and coordination with France and Britain. However, in the Six-Day War of 1967, it acted alone, and indeed rejected President de Gaulle's advice not to attack. One of the consequences was the ending of the virtual alliance with France, when de Gaulle at his press conference on November 27, 1967, in somewhat sibylline language made his famous reference to Jews as "an elite people, self-assured, and domineering (*un peuple d'élite, sûr de lui-même et dominateur*)." For him, one of the fundamental bases of French foreign policy was resumption of "that same policy of friendship and cooperation with the Arab peoples of the Orient that France had pursued for centuries," now that the Algerian War had ended.

For sixteen years Egypt had blocked Israeli navigation through the Suez Canal, which Nasser had nationalized on July 26 1956. It had also encouraged terrorist activity, carried out by fedayeen units organized by Colonel Mustafa Hafiz, Egyptian intelligence head in Gaza. Israel responded to this activity during 1954-56 by attacking Egyptian military and police facilities. Nasser began reorganizing the Egyptian army in 1957 and, with the help of German Nazi scientists who had been in Egypt after World War II, had begun a rocket and jet program. He had become the leading figure in the Non-Aligned Movement. He was able to convince Syria to form a "United Arab Republic," though it was short-lived, and set up a "Supreme Planning Committee" to define policy on the Palestinian question. He advocated the creation of the United Arab Command. He also became embroiled from 1962 to 1967 with an invasion of Yemen, sending about one-third of the Egyptian army to fight a hopeless war.

In the present intellectual climate of revisionist history or willful obfuscation of the true nature of the Arab-Israel conflict, it is illuminating to read the speeches of Nasser at the time, full of verbal extremism and refusal to accept the legitimacy of Israel, though the extremism was sometimes tempered by empirical prudence.[188] At various times in May 1967, Nasser said that his basic objective was the destruction of Israel, and that he would not accept any coexistence with Israel. Nasser was able to acquire arms from the Soviet Union, and material goods from the United States. In April 1956 the US State Department already believed that Nasser was aspiring to overthrow some Arab leaders friendly to the US.

In addition, the Soviet Union continuously supported the Arab states, especially Egypt, and the Palestinians politically and diplomatically in international forums, as well as with arms. It was supplying Syria with economic and military assistance, and had stationed considerable numbers of "advisers" in the country. It still remains unaccountable why the Soviet Union disseminated false information on May 12, 1967, to Egypt and Syria that Israel was massing troops, eighteen brigades, "huge armed forces," on the border with Syria and was preparing to invade the country. The Soviet Ambassador to Israel was invited by the government to travel to the Syrian border to check the accuracy of the reports of troop movements, but refused to do so. That the information was obviously false is apparent in the memoirs of General Muhammad Fawzi, the chief of staff of the Egyptian army, who went to Syria on May 14. He reported he did not find any concrete evidence to support the received Soviet information. There was no Israeli troop concentration and no mobilization, but nevertheless Nasser on May 14-15, 1967, immediately sent armored divisions into Sinai, which had been demilitarized since 1956. Equally mysterious was the Soviet assertion on the last day of the 1967 Six Day War that Israeli troops were advancing on Damascus, when the IDF had stopped at the town of Kuneitra in the Golan Heights of its own volition.

There is no mystery, however, about the partial responsibility of the Soviet Union for the outbreak of the Six-Day War. One possible explanation is that the real intention of the Soviet Union was to cause a war in order to provide an opportunity to destroy Israel's nuclear facilities in Dimona.[189] Nasser's policy and actions were not the only factors leading to war, but Israel responded to what appeared to be his increasing determination to engage Israel militarily: the naval blockade in the Gulf of Aqaba and the closure of the Straits of Tiran on May 22, 1967, to all Israeli shipping and ships bound for the Israeli port of Eilat. This closure was both a violation of President Eisenhower's assurance to Israel in 1957, guaranteeing freedom of navigation in the Straits and a contravention of the Geneva Conference of 1958 on free navigation through straits used for international navigation. Nasser began the build up of forces in Sinai after the surprising and speedy compliance by U Thant, Secretary-General of the United Nations, within two days of the demand by Nasser that the United Nations Emergency Force in the Sinai (UNEF) be withdrawn. U Thant did this without the approval of the General Assembly, which was required. The umbrella, as Abba Eban remarked, was taken away when it started to rain. UNEF had provided Israel with freedom of navigation in the Strait of Tiran. Nasser had now provided Israel with a *casus belli* though, after all the hostile activity, it did not need one.[190] Besides Nasser, the president of Iraq, Abdel-Rahman Aref, was equally belligerent in 1967, as is shown by his utterance that "The existence of Israel is an error that must be rectified...Our goal is clear...to wipe Israel off the map."

Israel also responded to the attack by Jordan on the Israeli held part of Jerusalem. This attack was surprising, since Israel had explicitly conveyed to King Hussein of Jordan the message that Israel would not attack his country if Jordan did not attack Israel. By his attack and defeat Hussein, lost the whole western bank of the Jordan River, including the eastern part of Jerusalem. Israel's speedy victory, beginning on June 5, 1967, and ending on June 11, led to control of the Sinai Peninsula up to the Suez Canal, the Gaza Strip, most of the Golan Heights, and the whole of Jerusalem. Israel had lost 759 soldiers, with 2,500 wounded in a war that cost $750 million. Egypt lost about 11,500 men and over eighty per cent of its military equipment. Jordan's casualties were 6,100 dead, and Syria lost 7,000. By its victory Israel had reduced its tentative border lines with the Arab countries; the total land boundaries had been shortened from 985 to 603 km. Syria had lost the topographical advantage of the Golan Heights.

The Golan Heights had been joined to Syria after World War I in accordance with the Sykes-Picot Agreement.[191] The area, about 1,250 square kilometers (500 square miles) with its borders resembling almost exactly the old Ottoman district of Kuneitra, was captured from Syria in 1967 and placed under Israeli military control. The Israeli offer on June 19, 1967, to withdraw completely from the Golan Heights, as well as from the Sinai Peninsula, in return for peace and demilitarization was rejected. By the May 31, 1974, Separation of Forces Agreement about forty square miles was returned to Syria, and the United Nations agreed to guard the demilitarized areas between the two sides. On December 14, 1981, an Israel law applied Israeli judicial authority and administration to the territory, though it did not use the word "annexation." The United Nations Security Council, in the non-binding Resolution 497, Deploring Annexation of the Golan Heights of December 17, 1981, rejected the Israeli decision and decided that it "is null and void and without international legal effect." It demanded that "Israel, the occupying Power should rescind forthwith its decision." This rejection is a typical example of the continuing attitude of a majority in the UN Security Council, to reject Israeli decisions. In a number of other Resolutions (446 of March 22, 1979, 465 of March 1, 1980, and 484 of December 19, 1980) the Council described the areas captured by Israel as "occupied Arab territories" or as "all the Arab territories occupied by Israel since 1967." Today, the Golan Heights, with a population of about

40,000, half Israeli and half Druze, is a land of vineyards, fruit orchards, ski slopes, and artist colonies.

The UN General Assembly on December 13, 1983, adopted Resolution 38/58, On the Question of Palestine, which spoke of the need "to put an end to Israel's occupation of the Arab territories" and "the need to secure Israeli withdrawal from the territories occupied since 1967, including Jerusalem." In December 1988, in its Resolution 43/176, the UNGA spoke of (Palestinian) "territory occupied since 1967." The International Committee of the Red Cross and the International Court of Justice both made similar pronouncements. Though this term, occupied territory, has now become familiar in political discussion of Israel's policies, its use has been challenged. In view of the history of the area it may be appropriate to talk of the territories in the Palestine area as "disputed," rather than as "occupied." To use the latter term is likely to prejudge the outcome of any negotiations over them. The territories have not been under the legitimate sovereignty of any state since the end of the Ottoman Empire, and therefore no nation has any clear automatic legal right to them. Nor were the West Bank and East Jerusalem ever legally recognized by international agreement as the sovereign territory of any state, either Jordanian or Palestinian, before they were captured by Israel in 1967.

The annexation in April 1950 by Jordan, of the West Bank and East Jerusalem, was recognized only by Britain and Pakistan, though even then Britain recognized only *de facto* Jordanian annexation of East Jerusalem. Three issues are pertinent to this action. The first is that for over a century and a half Jews had constituted a majority in the city of Jerusalem. Secondly, from 1950 until 1967 the whole area west of the Jordan River was ruled from Amman, declared by the Jordanian parliament as the capital of the whole kingdom of Jordan, not from Jerusalem. Discontent over Jordanian rule over the West Bank led not only to considerable tension and violence, but also to the assassination of the Jordanian King Abdullah in Jerusalem in July 1951. Thirdly, most revealingly, no Arab country accepted the Jordanian declaration of annexation.

At Arab insistence, the Armistice Agreements of 1949 did not establish permanent borders; they were to be decided by negotiations. The changing dividing lines and power relationships between the contending parties have resulted from the outcome of various military actions and numerous diplomatic agreements. Starting with those laid down in the 1947 United Nations Partition Plan, the lines have changed in 1949 and 1967 after wars, in 1979 after the Israeli-Egyptian Peace Treaty, and in 1993 after the Oslo Accord (the Declaration of Principles on Interim Self-Government Arrangements). This Accord, signed at the White House on September 13, 1993, established the self-governing Palestinian Authority and led to the election of a Palestinian Legislative Council in 1996, and was supposed to result within five years in a negotiated permanent status agreement. Israel recognized the West Bank and the Gaza Strip as a single territorial unit. Israel offered withdrawal from Gaza and almost all of the West Bank in return for peace. Power over the Gaza Strip and Jericho was transferred to the PLO by an agreement in May 1994. Power over parts of the West Bank was transferred by a number of agreements starting with "Oslo II," the Israel-PLO Interim Agreement of September 1995. Israel retained control over external security and supervision of Israeli settlements and citizens during the transitional period.

Final withdrawal of Israeli forces from Lebanese territory took place in 2000 after the controversial Israeli military Operation Peace for Galilee. Other withdrawals and agreements were proposed by the Israeli government in the Hebron pact of May 1998 and the Wye River Memorandum of October 1998. In 2005, Israeli disengagement from Gaza was carried out by the government of Ariel Sharon through forcible removal of the Israeli settlers who lived there, partly by Israeli police and partly by the military. The career of Sharon illustrates the insight of Oliver Wendell Holmes, "general propositions do not decide concrete cases." Sharon had also withdrawn settlements from the Sinai in 1982, after the Egyptian-Israeli peace treaty, even though he had been the one who originally proposed them. During the six years, 1994-2000, of the Oslo Peace Process over 200,000 Palestinians were admitted to the West Bank and the Gaza Strip. It is arguable that Sharon, had he not suffered a debilitating stroke while prime minister, might have envisioned a withdrawal from the West Bank, in a manner parallel to that of President Charles de Gaulle who withdrew France from Algeria by 1962, in spite of his declaration "vive l'Algérie française" in 1958.

It is worth remembering that between 1949 and 1967 international organizations did not refer to the rule of Egypt over Gaza and of Jordan over the West Bank, as rule over "occupied" territories. Moreover, Israel controls disputed territories not because of any interest to "occupy" them, but because they resulted from victory in a war initiated by Arab forces. It is sometimes forgotten that, when in 1967 Israel captured the West Bank, former Prime Minister David Ben-Gurion suggested that all territory, except Jerusalem, be returned to Jordan. Ben-Gurion, though a strong defender of the country, was never an advocate of a Greater Israel. In any case, Israel unilaterally withdrew all forces from Sinai in 1979, which was then demilitarized; from southern Lebanon in 2000; from some towns in the West Bank; and from Gaza in 2006.

These Israeli actions did not lead to a more harmonious Arab response. Withdrawal from the West Bank towns led to suicide bombings and consequent Israeli return to the area with Operation Defensive Shield in 2002. Israeli withdrawal from Lebanon, in 1983 and 1985, was greeted by over 4000 Katyusha rockets shot from Lebanon into northern Israel. Attempting to halt these attacks, Israel responded by the Second Lebanon War in July 2006. Similarly, Israel withdrawal from Gaza led to thousands of rockets and mortars being fired from there between 2005 and 2009 at territories in southern Israel; the attacks led to Operation Cast Lead in January 2009 as Israel sought to end them. What is disconcerting in all these cases is that the international criticisms of the actions, and charges of "war crimes" focused on the Israeli responses, not on the terrorist attacks that caused them. Colonel Kemp commenting on the criticism of Israel in that Operation spoke of "the frenzies in the media and human rights groups to expose faults among (Israeli) military forces fighting in the toughest conditions."[192]

Chapter 15

The Charge of Occupation

I t was self-defeating for the Arab leaders meeting at a summit conference on September 1, 1967, in Khartoum to declare, in response to the Israeli proposal for a compromise solution, that the basic principles to which the Arab states adhered were "no peace with Israel, no recognition of Israel, no negotiation with Israel, and adherence to the rights of the Palestinian people in their own country," thus preventing any compromise agreement on territory after the Six-Day War.[193] There must be few, if any, cases in history where a defeated party, after hostilities, refused to negotiate about territory it wanted to regain, even demanding unconditional surrender by the victors. Relating the story of lost opportunities by Arab leaders to negotiate a peaceful settlement of the Arab-Israeli conflict is a minor cottage industry. The Arab leadership, in its refusal of any chance for compromise, seemed, as Abba Eban remarked, to "have written failure into its birth certificate." Israel was thus left with control over the captured territory. That control has been described in different ways; one characterization is that it is "belligerent occupation," a status defined by the Hague Regulations of 1899 and 1907 which outline what constitutes "occupation;" the Regulations are supplemented by the Fourth Geneva Convention.

In a famous opinion in 1970 Stephen Schwebel, former State Department legal advisor and later judge, and then head of the International Court of Justice in The Hague (1981-2000), wrote that, "Where the prior holder of territory had seized that territory unlawfully (implicitly Jordan), the state which subsequently takes that territory in the lawful exercise of self-defense (implicitly Israel) has, against that prior holder, better title."[194] Schwebel distinguished between territories taken as a result of "aggressive conquest," such as that of Japan and Nazi Germany, and those resulting from a war of self-defense, as in the case of Israel. The authority of Israel over the territories is based on the international law of "belligerent occupation," especially the Hague Conventions (Israel Supreme Court 2004, 2005). Schwebel's argument that "a state may seize and occupy foreign territory as long as such seizure and occupation are necessary to its self-defense" was similar to that of Rosalyn Higgins. She argued that "there is nothing in either the UN Charter or general international law which leads one to suppose that military occupation, pending a peace treaty, is illegal."[195] Israeli law does not apply in the territories which have not been annexed. Instead, international law applies to them. (HCJ1661/05 Gaza Coast Regional Council v.The Knesset et al.). The international law precept *ex injuria non orbitur jus* also holds that an occupant is entitled to remain in control of territory, pending conclusion of a peace treaty.

The law of belligerent occupation allows the occupant to take measures to ensure that it is protected from hostile acts. The relevant Hague Regulations are Articles 42 and 43. The first Article states, "Territory is considered occupied when it is actually placed under the authority of the hostile army. The occupation extends only to the territory where such authority has been established and can be exercised." Regulation 43 states that "The authority of the legitimate power having in fact passed into the hands of the occupant, the latter shall take all the measures in his power to restore, and ensure, as far as possible, public order and safety, while respecting, unless absolutely prevented, the laws in force in the country." The problem is that these Regulations are subject to legitimate differences in interpretation. Also pertinent in interpretation of the complex law on the subject is the definition in a Nuremberg trial in 1949 that "an occupation indicates the exercise of governmental authority to the exclusion of the established government."[196]

The Israeli Court, in a June 2005 ruling, gave its own interpretation: "The Judea and Samaria areas are held by the State of Israel in belligerent occupation...the military commander is not the sovereign in the territory held in belligerent occupation...Israeli law does not apply in these areas. They have not been "annexed" to Israel. The legal regime which applies in these areas is determined by public international law." The Court also held that its judgment on the specific case before it rested on a factual basis, "facts lie at the foundation of the law, and the law arises from the facts (*ex facto jus oritur*)."

International law properly distinguishes expectations about the exercise of human rights in normal and abnormal situations. Provision is made for some qualification of the human rights outlined in the universal of Human Rights of 1966, and the International Covenant on Civil and Political Rights (1966). This is the case concerning internments and administrative detentions regarded necessary for security purposes in times of war. Article 78 of Geneva 4 provides for safety measures, which may subject individuals to assigned residence or to internment. In the 1961 case of *Lawless v. Ireland,* the European Court of Human Rights ruled that international law permitted the use of administrative detentions in times of emergency. (1961 Y.B. Eur.Ct.Hum.Rts, 430-32). The practice of administrative detentions is permitted by article 64 of Geneva 4. Israel has applied in practice the Convention to the territories.

Can Israel's actions relating to the territories secured in 1967 be regarded on any impartial assessment as "occupation," particularly now that substantial control of them is in the hands of Palestinians? Since the 1967 Six-Day War, Israel has used different procedures in governing the territories. Many of the Israeli procedures were concerned with security and defense against terrorist attacks as well as responsibility for the life of Palestinians. Israeli civilian law was employed for all Jerusalem and, after a while, in the Golan Heights, previously ruled by Syria between 1948 and 1967. The Golan Heights only became part of the new state of Syria after the French Mandate of the area ended in 1944.

In assessing whether the territories should be regarded as occupied or disputed, some legal issues are relevant. There are no "1967 borders"; there are only 1949 armistice lines. No borders have been established or recognized by the contending parties; the *de facto* lines are the armistice lines resulting from the wars. Secondly, the language of the Fourth Geneva Convention refers to "occupation of the territory of a High Contracting Party," but the territories have never been legally held by a High Contracting Party. Most important, no state has any clear right to the territories since no state had legitimate or recognized sovereignty over the West Bank, the Gaza Strip or East Jerusalem. Those territories did not have recognized legitimate rulers with whom Israel could deal. Since a "prior legitimate sovereign" was lacking in those two areas, Israel did not regard its control over them as constituting "occupation," as defined in customary law. For security reasons, from the end of the 1967 war until 1993 most people in the West Bank were subject to Israeli military administration, which ruled at first on the basis of the system of government inherited from Jordan. In the exchange of letters in September 1993, after Yasser Arafat said he recognized "the right of the state of Israel to exist in peace and security," Yitzhak Rabin, prime minister of Israel, replied that the government of Israel had "decided to recognize the PLO as the representative of the Palestinian people."

Moreover, since the Oslo Accords and the Interim Agreement in September 1995 between Israel and the Palestinian leadership, Israel no longer exercises the functions of government in the West Bank and Gaza. The areas from which Israel withdrew its military forces have been under the jurisdiction of the Palestinian Authority (PA). Since June 2007, when Fatah was ousted by Hamas from control of Gaza, the PA has received generous outside assistance. The Bush administration ended its embargo of the PA and Israel released over $500 million of tax revenues. The US Congress began appropriating funds for assistance to the Palestinian security services in July 2007, and the amounts have increased each year. In addition to US funding, the United States State Security Coordinator has been helping to train the National Security Force of the PA in deploying its forces in the West Bank, to ensure security. In 2010 the PA got $1.8 billion in foreign aid of which $550 million came from the US, which also gave the PA another $268 million by assisting UNRWA.

During his first term as prime minister (1996-1999), Benjamin Netanyahu transferred control over Hebron to the PA. Since then, the PA has controlled most of Palestinian life: schools, medical facilities, civic and political organizations, government ministries, legislative assembly, courts, police force, diplomatic representatives, passports, an international airport, and a flag. Almost the whole Palestinian population in the West Bank is ruled by the PA. Following the Israeli unilateral disengagement, the total withdrawal of all Israeli troops from Gaza in 2005 and the abandonment of twenty-one settlements there, and the subsequent success by Hamas over Fatah, the population of Gaza has been ruled by Hamas, since June 2007. Edmund Burke, in a famous remark, wrote that "magnanimity in politics is not seldom the truest wisdom." The Israeli withdrawal may have been wise, but the magnanimity was not reciprocated.

By the 1995 Interim Agreement, Israeli military forces can be deployed to specified military locations, but Israel does not govern the areas. These troops are not an occupying force, since the area is under Palestinian control. Israel did not annex the West Bank, nor does Israeli law apply in it. Israel has also applied the humanitarian aspects of the Fourth Geneva Convention, rules of substantive and procedural fairness and rules of proportionality, to the West Bank. (The Jami'at Ascan Case, HCJ 393/82). One pertinent, if somewhat puzzling, factor concerning the future of the West Bank stems from the 1994 Peace Treaty between Israel and Jordan. Acknowledging that the Treaty establishes the international boundary between the two countries, Article 3(2) states that "The boundary is the permanent, secure and recognized international boundary between Israel and Jordan, without prejudice to the status of any territories that came under Israeli military government control in 1967." By implication, the Green Line is not necessarily the boundary between Israel and a future Palestinian state.

In 2005, Israel implemented a unilateral withdrawal from Gaza of all military personnel, civilian authority, and settlements in which 9,000 Israelis were living; it also withdrew from the Philadelphia Route, the narrow strip adjacent to the Gaza border with Egypt. It does not exercise effective control or authority over the land or institutions in the Gaza Strip. Nevertheless, some in the international community, not acknowledging the security problem for Israel, still refer to the "occupation" of Gaza, because Israel controls the Gaza airspace and territorial waters, and movements of people in and out of the area. That security problem became more pronounced when, in 2007, Hamas took control of the Gaza Strip, and began rocket attacks on Israel. Because of this belligerence, Israel imposed a blockade on Gaza.

Regarding all this, two matters are relevant. The first is that Gaza does not legally belong to any sovereign state. The other is that the concept of occupation, according to international law, is defined as full control of an area. (Hague Regulations, 1907). Since 1994, the Palestinian Authority has been responsible for setting and collecting all taxes in Gaza; since 2007, this has been done by Hamas. Israel does collect customs duties for cross-border transactions on behalf of the PA, but to term this function as "occupation" would appear unreasonable, since no Israeli hostile army exercises the function of governmental authority. Moreover, the argument that Israel remains in control of Gaza's borders and of Gaza's airspace and territorial waters, ignores the reality that Egypt can at any time open its border with Gaza, to the free flow of people and goods.

Chapter 16

The Issue of Settlements

When Britain withdrew as Trustee of the Mandate for Palestine in May 1948, the Trust was transferred to the United Nations without change. After the 1967 war, Cyrus Vance, then US Secretary of State, on July 29, 1967, asserted "it is an open question as to who has legal right to the West Bank." Israeli settlements, originally military and agricultural outposts before 1967, began to be built by groups of Israelis in different parts of the captured areas after 1967. Not surprisingly, they were condemned in the UN Security Council. The eighteen in Sinai were withdrawn by 1982 to comply with the peace treaty with Egypt. Those in Gaza, containing 9,000 people, were unilaterally withdrawn in 2005, and some others were removed from the West Bank and the Golan Heights, as a result of the disengagement plan of the then prime minister Ariel Sharon. Ironically, Gaza, now for the first time in two thousand years, does not have any Jewish presence.

Settlements remain elsewhere in the West Bank, areas beyond the Green Line, and in East Jerusalem. They have been the subject of considerable controversy, with different arguments being made for their continuance or removal. The initial problem is the fact that the areas now known as Israel and the West Bank were only provinces of the Ottoman Empire, rather than states, either Israeli or Palestinian, with their own sovereignty.

At the core of the issue are five factors: the question of who can claim sovereignty over the West Bank; the requirements of Israeli national security; the right of Jews to settle in what has been characterized as disputed territory; the confiscation of private property; and the use of international law by opponents of Israel to delegitimize the settlements.

On the controversial question of Jewish settlements, no clear answer is available in international law. The Hague Regulations do not apply to the question of civilian settlements in the disputed territories. Article 49 of the Fourth Geneva Convention does forbid "individual or mass forcible transfers" and the "transfer of parts of (the occupant's) civilian population." This may apply to government movement of population, but Israeli governments have not aimed at displacement of the existing population as a prelude to future annexation. The Article does not appear to be applicable to the establishment of voluntary settlements on an individual basis, nor on their location, if the underlying purpose is security, public order, or safety, and as long as the settlements do not involve taking private property. The Israeli Supreme Court has rendered different decisions on the settlements issue, approving them on security grounds (Beth-El case, March 1979), and denying them where it held they did not contribute to security (Elon Moreh, 1979).

After the 1967 war, Yigal Allon proposed a plan for settlement activity, especially in the Jordan Valley, based on security and defensible borders. Since the Peace of Westphalia of 1648, the doctrine of defensible borders has been an acceptable concept in international relations. In a country where the 1967 lines separating the adversaries are only eleven miles from Tel Aviv, twenty-one from Haifa, and a few yards from Jerusalem, security and militarily defensible borders are a predominate concern. In the West Bank the mountain ridge runs north-south, and rises over the coastal plain to the West, and the Jordan Valley to the east. It does not take a military strategist to appreciate that the 3,000 feet high ridge line which overlooks the coastal plain and Ben-Gurion airport would, in enemy hands, endanger all Israeli cities. The Allon Plan was to control the Jordan Rift Valley, which runs from Syria to the Red Sea. It entailed ceding most of the West Bank to Jordan, then ruling the area, while Israel would retain a twelve mile security belt, including the Valley and the ridge above it.

The settlements built in the Sinai, which ended after peace with Egypt in 1982, and in the Golan Heights were established primarily for security reasons. In the 1970s, the orthodox Gush Emunim (Bloc of the Faithful) claimed title to all the historic land of Israel, and therefore, the right to establish settlements in the West Bank. Some settlements have been authorized by the government while others, especially outposts, have not. They have been created outside of the Israeli legal framework. Although unofficial and unauthorized "wildcat" outposts, they have usually been given government services and provisions, such as electricity and roads, after they have been established. Some were begun for economic reasons by secular individuals wanting cheap housing, mostly in the suburbs of Jerusalem.

The city and suburbs now contain thriving areas, that might be considered as early settlements, such as French Hill, Pisgat Ze'ev, and Ramat Eshkol started in 1969, Neveh Ya'acov, reestablished in 1973, Gilo, founded in 1971, Har Homa begun in 1997, and Ramat Shlomo begun in 1995. Some were built for military protection, such as the Nahal camps, which later became civilian settlements. Some were established by the ultra-Orthodox religious groups around the Jerusalem area, primarily to obtain affordable housing not available in Jerusalem or Tel-Aviv. Some were built by national-religious persons fulfilling what they perceive as biblical claims to Judea and Samaria. Those individuals and the groups supporting them constitute a formidable political group. Some outposts are essentially satellites of existing settlements. In the Golan Heights, settlements were first built for security reasons. Some were reestablished after 1967, on sites that had been settled before 1948; they include the Silvan area in Jerusalem, Gush Etzion, Hebron, Kalia and Beit HaArava.

Most of the settlements are small, but some, such as Ma'ale Adumin, about 4.5 kilometers from the Green Line, and Modi'in Illit, and Beitar Illit, both less than a kilometer from the Green Line and both with an ultra-Orthodox population, are virtually self-contained cities, with a considerable population of over 30,000 each. From them, many residents commute to Jerusalem to work. Some settlements, such as Alfei Menashe and Elkana, are towns with local Councils. Others are villages, such as Kfar Adumim and Neve Daniel, which are run by local elected committees. The small sized places, such as Argaman and Gilgal, are collective entities in the tradition of kibbutzim and moshavim. Settlement blocs, such as Gush Etzion, the reestablishment in 1967 of four communities destroyed by Jordan in 1949, and the vicinity of Ariel, contain a number of groups close together. Frontier villages parallel the Jordan River. Though the figures of residents in settlements, now numbering about 130, are disputed in the vociferous debate surrounding them, it is likely that they number about 300,000 in the West Bank, 20,000 in the Golan Heights, and the 190,000 in East Jerusalem, who Palestinians argue should be regarded as settlers. The area used by settlements in the West Bank is less than two per cent of the total area of the West Bank. In the complex existing situation, Israeli civil law does not officially apply to settlers in the West Bank. Theoretically they are subject to military law; but nevertheless, cases in which they are involved are generally tried in Israeli civil courts.

THE FOURTH GENEVA CONVENTION

Can the settlements be regarded as colonialism, occupation, or violations of international law? International organizations have increasingly made the charge that Israeli settlements violate Article 49(6) of the Fourth Geneva Convention, quoted earlier, but worth repeating in this connection, which provides that "The Occupying Power shall not deport or transfer parts of its own civilian population into the territory it occupies." The Convention was formulated because of the activities during World War II of the Nazi regime, and by inference the Soviet Union, in transferring some of their population into occupied territory for political or racial reasons or for colonization. Millions, perhaps as many as 40 million, of Germans, Russians, Poles, Ukrainians, Hungarians and Jews, were subjected to forced migration, expulsion, slave labor, and extermination.

Israel ratified the Convention in July 1951, and abides by its humanitarian provisions. It does not, however, agree that the Convention applies to the legal status of Israeli settlers. It appears absurd to suggest that the State of Israel "deported" or "transferred" its own citizens anywhere.

The Geneva Convention speaks of prohibiting "Individual or mass forcible transfers," but this is irrelevant to the voluntary movement of Israelis. The international lawyer, Julius Stone, pointed out the irony in this issue: "Article 49(6), designed to prevent repetition of Nazi-type genocidal policies of rendering Nazi territories *judenrein*, has now come to mean that the West Bank must be made *judenrein*."[197] Another prominent legal authority, Eugene Rostow, former Dean of the Yale Law School, argued that the West Bank and the Gaza Strip were unallocated parts of the Palestine Mandate, that the right of the Jewish people to settle in the West Bank under the Mandate had never been terminated, and that Jewish settlement in the West Bank was not an intrusion into alien territory held as a result of war, nor a violation of the Geneva Convention.[198] Whether one agrees or not with this legal argument, it is incontestable that Jewish settlers in the West Bank have not been deported or transferred to the area by the Government of Israel, nor have they been used for purposes of extermination, slave labor, or colonization, which is forbidden by the Fourth Geneva Convention. It is equally unquestionable that Jews lived in the area of East Jerusalem, in Hebron, and in the Etzion Bloc, before being driven out by Jordan, which occupied the areas in 1949. Moreover, settlement was at first approved by international authority. The League of Nations Mandate for Palestine, Article 6, stated that the Administration of Palestine "shall encourage... close settlement by Jews on the land, including State lands."

Furthermore, according to the legal argument, the Fourth Geneva Convention is not applicable to the parties involved in the issue. The Convention applies, as explained above, only to territory belonging to "another High Contracting Party." Jordan, the former occupier as a result of the 1948-49 War, had no legal title to the West Bank and thus cannot formally be considered such a party. In February 1981, President Reagan held that the settlements might be ill advised, but that they were not illegal.

From a practical point of view, are they unilateral, ill-advised actions that make negotiations for a peace settlement more difficult? It was the latter argument that led Senator George Mitchell in his May 2001 report to recommend that Israel should freeze all settlement activity, including the 'natural growth' of existing settlements, in order to restore "calm and the resumption of negotiations." This recommendation was endorsed by President George W. Bush and by President Obama. President Bush, however, in 2004 had agreed that Israel could retain "existing major Israeli population centers" in the West Bank. It should also be noted that Israeli construction in Jerusalem and elsewhere did not prevent the 300 negotiation sessions that took place between Israel and the PA between the November 2007 Annapolis Conference talks and 2008.

The twenty-one Israeli settlements with 9,000 residents in the Gaza Strip, and Israeli troops there, were withdrawn by Israeli unilateral decision in 2005, but the settlements in the West Bank, in East Jerusalem, and in the Golan Heights remain as a source of friction. The Israeli Supreme Court has dealt with the complicated issue of settlements in various ways. Two cases in 1979 illustrate the nature of the complication. In *Ayyub v. Minister of Defense*, the Court held that private property could be requisitioned for a civilian settlement if military security was involved. However, in the Elon Moreh case (*Dwaikat v. Israel*), the Court held that the State could not seize private land for the purpose of allowing a civilian settlement to be built, unless it were for a specific and concrete security reason. The general position is that those settlements which have been legally authorized have been built on "state-owned" or "public" land or on land bought by Jews from Arabs after 1967.[199] The disputed settlements thus exist on state or public land, the possession of which is still undecided by negotiations. The problem becomes more complex since, according to critics, the state or public lands amount to a considerable part, perhaps forty per cent, of the West Bank.

The existence of the settlements, in the West Bank and in East Jerusalem, is a source of bitter controversy, which has included calls for all construction there to be frozen. This is connected with charge of occupation discussed above. Israel argues that the provisions of Article 49 of the 1949 Fourth Geneva Convention prohibiting " individual or mass forcible transfers, as well as deportations of protected persons from occupied territories to the territory of the occupying power or to that of any other country" and stating that the "occupying power shall not deport or transfer parts of its own civilian population into the territory it occupies" are not applicable to their case, because Israelis were not forcibly transferred. Nor were settlements intended to displace Arab residents of the territories. The settlements have been established for a combination of economic, religious, and military reasons, not for purposes of colonialism or even colonization. It is a reasonable conclusion that the Geneva provisions, written with legislative intent to refer to Nazi atrocities of forcibly sending people from occupied territories to death and work camps, are not applicable to the existence of Israeli settlements.

JERUSALEM

The city of Jerusalem is a separate problem, though it is connected with the general settlement issue. Since the middle of the nineteenth century the city had contained a Jewish majority, but it was also the center of the Arab elite in the area.[200] As a result of the 1948-9 war Israel captured the west part of the city, while Jordan captured East Jerusalem and the Old City and declared them annexed in 1950. The Mandelbaum Gate, from 1949 to 1967, was both the barrier and the symbol of partition. Jews were barred from entering the Old City and East Jerusalem. During the period between 1949 and 1967, in Arab controlled areas of Palestine, Jewish sanctuaries, including over fifty synagogues and cemeteries, were desecrated. Jordan paved roads and even latrines with Jewish tombstones, some going back 2,000 years. The area of the Mount of Olives was closed to Jewish visitors. The Intercontinental Hotel and Jericho Road were built over Jewish graves. Jordan also destroyed the Jewish villages of Atarot and Neve Yaakov, slightly north of Jerusalem. Only in March 2010, was the Hurva Synagogue in Jerusalem, which had been destroyed by the Jordanians in 1948, rebuilt and rededicated. During the nineteen years of Jordanian rule, Jews were denied access to visit or to pray at the Jewish Holy Places, to the Mount of Olives, and the Western Wall. That denial of access was also a violation of Article VII of the 1949 Armistice Agreement. Nor were Jews allowed to live in or to visit the West Bank and Jerusalem. During Jordanian rule, Christian Arabs also suffered discrimination. They were largely denied access to churches in the Old City of Jerusalem and in Bethlehem; the number of Christians in Jerusalem declined by more than a half. The UN disregarded this Jordanian discriminatory behavior.

In the 1967 war, Israel captured eastern Jerusalem, the area that had been ruled by Jordan, and subsequently applied its "laws, jurisdiction and administration" to it. The municipal borders of Jerusalem were thus extended. Under Israeli administration, Muslims enjoy the religious freedom that had been denied to Jews under Jordanian occupation. The holy places of the three religions, Jewish, Muslim, and Christian, were placed under the administration of their respective clergy. Christians control the Ten Stations of the Cross. Muslim authorities, first Jordanian and then Palestinian, control and are responsible for the Dome of the Rock. Israel went even further; it took account of Muslim sensitivities by preventing Jews from praying on the Temple Mount. The Jewish Quarter in the Old City, which had been destroyed in 1948, was rebuilt.

By the Basic Law of July 1980 Jerusalem "complete and united " though no boundaries were specified, was proclaimed as the eternal and indivisible capital of Israel, thus making East Jerusalem part of the city by official decree. It would be given "special priority in the activities of the State." Not unexpectedly, the UN Security Council, by Resolution 478, declared the action "null and void" and a violation of international law, and called for it to be rescinded. It also called on countries with diplomatic representatives in Jerusalem to move them elsewhere; most countries complied. No country presently has an embassy in Jerusalem. Some may be surprised to learn that Jerusalem, not Tel Aviv, is the capital of Israel. Nevertheless, the United States Congress in 1995, implicitly accepting that a country has the right to choose its capital, passed a law stating that Jerusalem should be recognized as the capital of Israel, and that the US embassy should be moved there. This ruling has not yet been fulfilled. By the Israeli-Palestinian agreement of September 13, 1993, settlement of the status of Jerusalem was deferred until the final stages of negotiations between Israel and the Palestinians. In the meantime, since 1998, the 28th of the Jewish month of Iyar, the day in 1967 when the Western Wall in Jerusalem was liberated, has been known in Israel as "Jerusalem Day."

Chapter 17

The Charge of Discrimination

Even if one accepts the argument that the Israeli system prefers the interests of Jews over others in deciding interests and preferences, this does not entail that the minorities, the Arab population including Bedouins and Druze within Israel who now make up about one-fifth of the population, experience discrimination. Certainly inequalities in the social and economic system and restrictions have existed, and to some extent persist in the Israeli multicultural society. Israel is a society with a diverse national, religious, ideological, ethnic population, including not only Western Jews, but also a considerable Arab minority, secular Jews and religious orthodox (*haredim,* or those who tremble before God) Jews from Arab countries, immigrants from the former Soviet Union, many of whom are non-Zionists, and black African Jews. Languages, dress styles, and cuisines jostle each other in the multicultural mosaic. Occupational changes have transformed its economy from an agrarian one, with its supposed idealistic relationship between Jews and the land, into one based on knowledge and high technology. In the contemporary world of globalization, it is private property, market economy, and material culture that have been more emphasized, if not replacing a central welfare state. The diversity is also illustrated in the very language in the country; the Sephardic pronunciation of Hebrew has been preferred to the Western Ashkenazi version.

Distinction between people is not necessarily discrimination. A fair and objective assessment would be that many of the past and present restrictions result from the need to provide security and protection not only from wars instigated by Arab countries, but also from relentless attacks by belligerent Palestinians, especially by suicide bombers, on civilians. It is certainly understandable that Israeli Arabs are not employed in industries connected with military affairs. But Israel has also taken actions to ensure rights for minorities. The Israeli Supreme Court has issued decisions upholding the rights of Arabs, and the Israeli government established seven Bedouin towns in the Negev to encourage settlement of these traditionally nomadic tribes. Land was made available at deliberately low prices for Bedouins, and non-Bedouins are not allowed to lease any of that land. This government action followed the Israeli Supreme Court (*Eliezer Avitan v. The Israel Land Administration et al.*, HCJ 528/88) decision that there was a public interest in assisting Bedouins to settle permanently in urban communities, thus justifying a policy of preferential treatment for a minority group. Of the 155,000 Bedouins who live in the Negev, about sixty per cent now live in the seven towns built between 1979 and 1982.

The concern for minority points of view can be seen in other court decisions as well. The Israeli Supreme Court, sitting as the High Court of Justice, in January 2009 overturned the disqualification by the Central Elections Committee of two Arab parties, Balad and United States Arab List, running candidates for parliament, when they were accused of supporting terrorist activity against Israel and refusing to recognize the legitimacy of the state. Though no independent Arab party has of yet been part of any Israeli coalition government, Arabs have been not only members of parliament (the Knesset), but also members of national and local governments, parliamentary officials, ambassadors and diplomatic representatives, and there are many Arab judges through the country, including a judge on the Supreme Court. The first Muslim Arab appointed to a full ministerial position was Raleb Majadele of the Labor Party, who was made Minister of Science and Culture in 2007. This appointment followed that of Salah Tarif, a Druze, who was made Minister without Portfolio in 2001.

Israeli Jews are obligated to serve a three year term in the IDF (the Israeli Defense Forces), and, under a law of January 2010, can be summoned to the reserves for a total of fifty-four days in three years. On the other hand, Israeli Arabs are exempt from military service, though they may volunteer. Since 2007, Arabs can volunteer for civilian national service. They participate in almost every sector of Israeli life, including the Israeli soccer team in international games and the "Miss Israel" pageants. The Arab writer Emile Habibi was honored with the major Israeli literary prize in 1986.

Interestingly, members of the 122,000 Arabic speaking Druze people, about 1.5 per cent of the total population, who are recognized as a distinct religious group separate from Muslims, do serve in the military; after the establishment of the State of Israel they declared that as Israeli citizens with full rights, they would also accept full duties. No member of the Druze fled or was expelled from home as a result of the 1948-49 war. Moreover, members of the Druze, which changed sides during the war in 1948, volunteered for the Israeli army, along with Circassians and Bedouins. The Druze are subject to conscription, but the Bedouins who enter the military are volunteers. The Druze have their own religious courts dealing with marriage and divorce, a Religious Council, and a school system of their own. They are members of different political parties; they have members in the Knesset and some hold executive positions in government. The Circassians, a small number of people, have their own schools in which the language used is Arabic, and are able to make their own rules on marriage and divorce.

Arabic is one of the two official languages in the country, and most official signs are in Arabic as well as Hebrew, as are food labels and messages published by the government. A High Court decision in 2002 ruled that Tel Aviv, and some other cities, must post official information in Arabic as well as in Hebrew. Since 2007, an Arabic language academy, centered in Haifa, parallels the Academy of the Hebrew Language. Arab students may be taught in Arabic language schools. They attend universities in Israel in increasing numbers, for both undergraduate and graduate degrees. In Haifa University in 2009, the proportion of Arab students was about forty per cent of the total number of students. Arab professors have tenure positions in Israeli universities. Arabs, of whom eighty-five per cent are Muslim and about eight per cent are Christian, can practice their religion without constraint. Palestinians in the West

Bank, as well as Israeli Arabs, can petition the Supreme Court about Israeli actions in the areas in which they reside. Also, Arabs, not only those who are Israeli citizens, but also those in the West Bank and Gaza, have access to Israeli social and medical services. About forty per cent of the patients in the pediatric oncology department of Tel Hashomer hospital in Tel Aviv come from the West Bank and Gaza. Arabs also get professional advice to assist with housing permits.

Whatever differences may be expressed on the issue of the nature and degree of inequities in Israel, there is virtual unanimity on the existence of full political and legal rights for the Israeli Arabs who constitute about twenty per cent of the population of the country. They have legal protection for their property rights, and have free access to the courts and to due process procedures. Their educational system, cultural institutions using Arabic, an official language, religious institutions and religious courts are financed by the State of Israel in full or in part. All public facilities are open to them. Arabs participate in political activity, not only in voting, but as members and advocates of various political parties, including three specifically Arab ones. In 2010, eleven Arabs were members of the Knesset; three of them were deputy speakers. Non-Jews have held seats in every Knesset since Israel was established. Indeed, Israel Arabs have a free press in Arabic and they, including the Arab members of parliament, some of whom have been women, are free to express their views, including criticism of the existing government and what they perceive as mistakes or injustice, in uncensored fashion in parliament and on television. The fundamental reality is that Arabs in Israel are not only better off in education, health, and personal security, but are also freer, including freedom to leave the state, than are the majority of Arabs in any Arab country.

Israel faces not only the problems perplexing all societies, but also the existential one. As an open, self-critical society, it is constantly aware of the demands of Israeli Arabs, for both full civic equality and also acceptance as a cultural minority, some members of which are reluctant to acknowledge civic allegiance to the state or feel they do not belong to it. It is also aware not only that equality does not mean sameness, but also of the disparities in economic, social, and educational conditions of Jews and Arabs, though those gaps have been lessening since 1948. Three observations are pertinent. First, the economic gap between Israeli Christian Arabs and the average level of Jews is considerably less than that between the Palestinian Muslims and the Jewish majority, even though according to OECD surveys, about half of Israeli Arabs and some sixty per cent of Haredim, or ultra-Orthodox Jews, have disposable income that is less than half the national median, the OECD measure of poverty. A second is that in 1998 the Knesset passed legislation on state corporations and on appointment to the civil service that is tantamount to measures of affirmative action for minorities.

A third factor is that the Israeli High Court, in a number of decisions, has been active in safeguarding the rights of the Arab minority. In 1999 it held that "Discrimination on the basis of religion or national affiliation in the allocation of the country's resources is forbidden even if it is done indirectly, and, *a fortiori*, if it is done directly." HC 1113/99(Adallah et al. v. Minister of Religious Affairs). It even allows a voice for non-Israeli residents of the territories, who can bring a case against the government and its military and civilian agencies. The Court has heard petitions from Palestinians asking for remedies for alleged arbitrary or illegal acts. Military commanders are subject to the jurisdiction of the Court. In exercising this jurisdiction the Court has relied not only on principles of Israeli administrative law, but also on customary international law.

Empathy of the majority towards the minority, and concessions made as a result of demands by the minority, is not always reciprocated with the loyalty of that minority or its acceptance of majority decisions. Indeed, for Israel a formidable problem remains if it cannot count on Israeli Arab shared territorial loyalty, which can transcend existing or imagined loyalties to family, religion, or clan. To attend to this problem the Israel Parliament proposed in 2011 that naturalized citizens swear an oath to Israel as "a Jewish and democratic state," words taken from the Israeli Declaration of Independence. This proposal was controversial, though oaths of allegiance are normal in democratic countries. Another controversial proposal by Arab members of the Knesset was that "Nakba Day" (referring to the founding of Israel in 1948) be commemorated. A potential problem, if an independent Palestinian state is established, may be the question of the primary loyalty of self-described "Palestinian citizens of Israel." Some define Israeli Arabs as "internal refugees." A related aspect of this problem is the denial of the Holocaust by a part of the Israeli Arab community.

Particularly troubling was the behavior of the Arab political party, Rakah (New Communist List), which labeled the 1967 Six-Day War an act of Israeli aggression and which sided with Egypt and Syria in the Yom Kippur War of 1973. As a result of the second *intifada* in September 2000, some Israeli Arabs endorsed the validity of armed struggle against Israel. Some Israeli Arabs view themselves as part of the Arab Middle East majority, rather than as a minority within a general Israeli culture. During the 2006 war in Lebanon, Azmi Bishara, a prominent Arab and former member of the Knesset, publicly supported Hezbollah, against which Israel was fighting at the time. Bishara fled Israel in 2007, when he was being investigated for spying for Hezbollah during the war with Lebanon. As a result, the Knesset passed the Bishara Law, which forbids individuals who illegally visited an enemy country from being a candidate for a seat in the Knesset. Two things are pertinent about these Israeli Arab incidents. One is the fact that Israeli Arabs enjoy a greater freedom of expression than is the case in any Arab country. Secondly, Israel is more tolerant of potential enemies within it, than is true in other democratic countries. For example, during World War II the US imprisoned Japanese Americans and Britain imprisoned, at least for a time, German and Italian refugees. Israel has not imprisoned or curtailed the freedom of expression of Israeli Arabs.

It is understandable that the Arab minority may have a sense of anger and injustice, and may feel a certain antipathy towards the Israeli national anthem *Hatikva,* which speaks of the hope for 2,000 years for the Jewish people in exile to be a free people in their own land of Zion and the city of Jerusalem. That minority also criticizes the Law of Return for offering preferential treatment to Jews in the Diaspora to enter Israel. At the same time, that minority ignores or minimizes the reality of the historical connection of the Jewish people with Palestine. Considering the needs of security and public order, it is not realistic under present conditions to expect absolute freedom of movement. It is also discouraging, as mentioned above, that Palestinians and Arab states have been unwilling to deal with the refugee problem. Indeed, the Arab League has instructed its members to deny citizenship to the Palestinian refugees and their descendants, so that they would maintain a separate identity. In contrast, the Israeli Supreme Court has sought in a number of cases to limit or overcome discrimination against non-Jews, particularly in the marketing and allocation of land.

In this recounting of the position of Arabs in Israel it ought to be made clear that Arabs living in the West Bank, in Gaza, and in East Jerusalem, which is a geographical not a political appellation, who before 1967 had Jordanian passports, are not Israeli citizens. They carry Palestinian identity cards issued by the Palestinian Authority. Doubtless, the existence of a considerable minority of Israeli Arabs remains a difficult and not wholly resolved issue. It is difficult for Israel to agree on official recognition of Arabs as a national, cultural group when the concept of a "Jewish" state is being disputed. Moreover, identification by some Israeli Arabs with the national aspirations of the Palestinian people, and their refusal to accept the legitimacy of Jewish statehood and sovereignty and right of self-determination, appears incompatible with their status as citizens with duties and obligations while the Israeli-Palestinian conflict is unresolved.[201] This incompatibility is sometimes unpleasantly displayed as when Israeli Arab members of the Knesset openly gloated over Israeli military problems in battle. It was particularly exhibited when Hannen Zoabi, the first woman to be elected to the Knesset on an Arab party line, and an individual who rejects the idea of Israel as a Jewish state, participated in 2010 in the Gaza-bound flotilla on board the *Mavi Marmara*; she described the Israeli action against the ship as a pirate military operation.

Chapter 18

Palestine and the Mandate

The question of competing claims over the land of Palestine goes back to the Mandate for Palestine, which the Principal Allied and Associated Powers (Britain, France, Italy, and Japan, with the United States as observer) participating in the San Remo Conference on April 24, 1920, negotiated in disposing of the territories formerly ruled by the Ottoman Empire for almost 500 years. The Mandate system was legitimized by Article 22 of the Covenant of the League of Nations, which had been drafted by the Paris Peace Conference in April 1919 and embedded in the Treaty of Versailles of June 1919. France was to be given a Mandate for the areas which were to become Syria and Lebanon, while Britain was accorded a Mandate over Mesopotamia (which was to become Iraq) and Palestine. By agreement in 1923, between Britain and France, the borders between the two Mandates were established; the Golan Heights went to France, and the northern Jordan Valley to Britain.

It is important to note that originally "Palestine," about 43,000 square miles, included the areas both east and west of the Jordan River and the Sea of Galilee. The definition of "Palestine" would soon change, when the area east of the Jordan, which was three times larger than the area west of it, was separated and became the emirate of Transjordan (about 32,500 square miles). From that moment "Palestine" (10,500 square miles) became limited to the area west of the Jordan. By decision of the League of Nations in 1921, Transjordan was still included in the British Mandate, but it would not be part of the Jewish National Home.

The total area of Palestine, as originally defined, was to be entrusted to a Mandatory Power which was charged to put into effect the Balfour Declaration "in favor of the establishment in Palestine of a national home for the Jewish people." The Resolutions on Palestine, agreed upon in San Remo, were reaffirmed in the Treaty of Sèvres between the Allied Powers and the government of Turkey on August 10, 1920, and unanimously approved on July 24, 1922, by the Council of the League of Nations. That declaration included the sentence: "Whereas recognition has been given to the historical connection of the Jewish people with Palestine and to the grounds for reconstituting their national home in that country." By Article 6 of the Mandate, Jewish immigration into Palestine under suitable conditions was to be encouraged, as was close settlement by Jews on the land, while "ensuring that the rights and position of other sections of the population are not prejudiced." The Mandate became operative in September 1923.

The Mandate was also approved by a joint resolution of both Houses of the United States Congress on June 30, 1922; it favored "the establishment in Palestine of a national home for the Jewish people." Despite this Congressional approval, the US State Department did not favor such an establishment; its contrary view continued at least into the 1940s. After World War II, when the League of Nations was dissolved in April 1946, its assets and duties were allocated to the newly created United Nations which, therefore, by Article 80 of its Charter, implicitly accepted the validity of the Mandate, and would soon take responsibility for the legal implementation of its objective.

Britain was entrusted in 1922 to administer the area of the Mandate. Sir Herbert Samuel, the first British High Commissioner, signed a piece of paper, "Received from Major General Sir Louis J. Bols K.C.B. (the Chief Administrator of Palestine from June 1919 to June 1920) One Palestine complete." As the Mandatory Power Britain was given full powers of legislation and administration though the degree of authority, control, or administration was to be explicitly defined by the Council of the League of Nations and the objectives that had been approved in the Mandate. Under Article 2 of the Mandate, Britain was given responsibility for securing the establishment of the Jewish National Home, the development of self-governing institutions, and for safeguarding the civil and religious rights of all the inhabitants of Palestine, but there were no explicit provisions regarding legal rights. Under the Mandate, the Jewish Agency was established to deal with the Jewish population and to help in the establishment of a Jewish National Home. In 1929, at the 16th Zionist Congress, Chairman Chaim Weizmann was able to get some prominent non-Zionists, such as Albert Einstein, Léon Blum, and Louis Marshall, to join the Agency. The chair of the Executive Committee of the Jewish Agency from 1935 to 1948 was David Ben-Gurion.

In contrast, the Arabs from 1921 on refused to establish a parallel Arab Agency or to participate in any plan or joint legislature with the Jews. In 1921, at the London Conference, they turned down the idea of an elective assembly for Palestine in which they would have been the majority. The next year the proposal for a Palestinian Constitution, with a Legislative Council having a majority, and therefore controlled by Arabs, of non-official members was accepted by the Jews, but rejected by the Arabs, who also boycotted the election for the Council. The Arabs were strongly critical of both the Balfour Declaration and the terms of the Mandate which were based on it. Arab leaders had earlier, at the General Syrian Congress, declared their opposition to Jewish immigration into any part of Syria, which for them included Palestine.[202] They also argued, though others disagreed, that the correspondence between Sir Henry McMahon and Sherif Hussein of Mecca, 1915-1916, included Palestine to be part of the area which Britain had agreed would become independent Arab states.

As a result of the violence against the Jews in different areas of Palestine that occurred in 1920 and 1921, and then the passage of a motion in June 1922 in the British House of Lords that the Mandate was inconsistent with pledges made during World War I to Arab inhabitants of the area of Palestine, Winston Churchill, then Secretary of State for the Colonies, issued a White Paper, an official government statement, stating that the Jews were in Palestine "as of right and not on sufferance" and that the British government would not depart from the policy embodied in the Balfour Declaration. The White Paper also made other decisions. Jewish immigration should continue, but should not exceed "whatever may be the economic capacity of the country at the time to absorb new arrivals." Though no objective assessment of the "absorptive capacity" was ever made, certificates were then issued to allow Jewish entry into Palestine. From 1920 until 1937, about 250,000 Jews were officially admitted. Jews, however, were not able to enter the area east of the Jordan River. The crucial decision was made that this area would be ruled under a separate British Mandate, with the name of the Emirate of Transjordan, later to become the Kingdom of Jordan in March 1946. By this decision Britain sharply reduced the land available for the promised Jewish national home in Palestine.

The Palestinian Arabs boycotted the elections of 1923 in Palestine and refused to accept the British plan at the time, because they argued that participating in these would imply accepting the terms of the Mandate and the creation of a Jewish national home.[203] Instead, Palestinian Arab leaders began the campaign to stop or limit the "Jewish national revival" in Palestine. This scenario of Jewish willingness to compromise and Arab leadership intransigence and hostility was to become familiar and to continue throughout the Mandate period and after, with only some exceptions. Genuine dialogue, devoid of hate and ignorance, between the adversary parties over "the site of contested memory" has rarely occurred.[204] Over the decades, there has been some collaboration in work, social life, some personal friendship, some help given to the Zionists, and above all land sales by Palestinian landlords to the Zionist movement. The degree of collaboration depended on the choices made by the different groups in Palestinian Arab society; farmers, merchants, professionals, rural or urban, clan or villagers, nationalists or moderates. However, those Arabs who did seek to maintain contact or collaborate with the Jews, for material, political or personal reasons, such as Fakhri al-Nashashibi, head of the "Peace units," the Zaynati family who sold land, and the Abu Ghosh family, were often punished by fellow Palestinian Arabs.[205]

The boundary lines in the two Mandates were not set by the League of Nations, but by Britain and France. A new and essentially artificial dividing line was created. The French Mandate in the north part was divided into two areas, Syria and Lebanon, and France established the boundary between the two countries. The south part became the British Mandate. Britain was given responsibility for putting into effect the goal of the Balfour Declaration of November 2, 1917, the creation of a Jewish National Home in which it was understood that nothing would be done which might prejudice the civil and religious rights of existing non-Jewish communities in Palestine. Interestingly in the Mandate, Jews were the only group in Palestine labeled "national" as well as a religious community; all remaining groups were "other inhabitants of Palestine."[206] The civil and religious rights of all the inhabitants of Palestine, irrespective of race or religion, were to be safeguarded. (Article 2). Britain was to encourage "close settlement of Jews on the land, including State lands and waste land not required for public purposes," and was to facilitate Jewish immigration "under suitable conditions." (Article 6). Curiously, Jerusalem, as such, was not mentioned in the Mandate, but the Holy Places were, in Articles 13 and 14 which deal with responsibility for them. The two issues were and remain separated: the governing of the city, and the issue of the Holy Places.

As a result of complex Arab pressures and political rivalries, Britain soon changed the nature of the Mandate. Winston Churchill, as British Colonial Secretary, accepted in March 1921 the advice of T. E. Lawrence (Lawrence of Arabia) to remove the eastern part of the area from the objective of the Palestine Mandate. Lawrence, well known for his sympathy for Arab nationalism, during World War I had cultivated the Hashemite Emir Feisal ibn Hussein of the Hejaz who, in return for substantial subvention, had promised to lead an "Arab revolt," which in fact was more fanciful than realistic. Philip Graves, the correspondent of the *Times of London* punctured the myth of Arab help for the British, as he was to expose the forgery of the *Protocols of Zion* in three articles in the paper in August 1921. He was annoyed at the pretensions of the Arabs in Palestine, who had deserted in large numbers from the Ottomans to the British who fed and clothed them, and then tried to claim "credit for helping the British to bolster their claim for Palestine."[207]

Despite his sympathy for Arab ambitions, Lawrence had been instrumental in bringing together in London in December 1918 and again in 1919, the Emir Feisal, a direct descendant of Muhammad, and Chaim Weizmann, the Zionist leader, then president of the World

Zionist Organization. On January 3, 1919, an Agreement was signed in London between Feisal, acting on behalf of the Arab Kingdom of Hedjaz, and Weizmann, acting on behalf of the Zionist Organization. The important Article III said that all measures adopted in the administration of Palestine "will afford the fullest guarantees for carrying into effect" the Balfour Declaration of November 2, 1917.

Also interesting and rarely mentioned is that this Feisal-Weizmann Agreement of January 3, 1919, spoke of the racial kinship and ancient bonds between the Arabs and the Jewish people and urged "the closest possible collaboration in the development of the Arab State and Palestine," explicitly referring to the future Jewish political entity as "Palestine." Article IV of that Agreement said that "All necessary measures shall be taken to encourage and stimulate immigration of Jews into Palestine on a large scale, and as quickly as possible to settle Jewish immigrants on the land through closer settlement and intensive cultivation of the soil. In taking such measures, the Arab peasant and tenant farmers shall be protected in their rights and shall be assisted in forwarding their economic development." Feisal said in a letter of March 3, 1919, to Felix Frankfurter that he felt "that the Arabs and Jews are cousins in race, having suffered similar oppressions at the hands of powers stronger than themselves" and that "We Arabs, especially the educated among us, look with the deepest sympathy on the Zionist movement." In the light of future Arab negative actions and international opinions about Israel, it is saddening to read the positive comments in Feisal's letter and realize the lost opportunities in solving the conflict, if other Arab leaders had followed his lead. Feisal commented that "The Jewish movement is national and not imperialist. Our movement is national and not imperialist, and there is room in Syria for both of us."

As a result of machinations in the complicated politics of the Middle East by Britain, the main influential country there after World War I, Feisal was chosen to be king of Syria in 1920. After he was driven out of Damascus by the French, he became king of Iraq. Feisal was the son of Sherif Hussein of Mecca, king of the Arabian Hedjaz, who had hoped to rule over the whole Arab Middle East, but was expelled from Arabia by the Saudis who gained power in 1924. Hussein's other son, the brother of Feisal, was Abdullah who was to become the emir of the territory east of the Jordan River. In March 1921, Lawrence was able to persuade him to limit his ambition to that east side of the River and to refrain from any action against the provisions for a Jewish National Home in the Palestine Mandate west of the Jordan.[208] The east part in September 1922 thus became not part of Palestine, but a separate unit, an area of 70,000 square kilometers which was about seventy-seven per cent of Palestine. The Council of the League of Nations on September 16, 1922, endorsed the creation of Transjordan, thus giving international approval to the change, and Britain defined its boundaries. Abdullah agreed to relinquish any authority in, and to refrain from any action against, the area of Jewish habitation west of the Jordan River. The consequences of this arrangement were that the eastern boundary of Palestine was set, and therefore the National Home for the Jewish people would not include the area called Transjordan (and later Jordan). By agreement with Britain, France as the Mandatory power for Lebanon and Syria, established the Palestine-Lebanon boundary and also a line, a kind of international boundary between Palestine and Syria.

As a result of these decisions, the west part of the Mandate area was therefore limited to an area of 27,000 square kilometers, ruled directly by Britain until May 1948. This designation of the area was of historic importance since it was the first official naming of "Palestine" as a country, and one with a defined territorial area, a definition that still remains today. All people living there were regarded as "Palestinians," without any ethnic connotation, though the name was used only by the Jews. The main Jewish newspaper, founded in 1932, was *The Palestine Post*; only in 1950 was its name changed to *The Jerusalem Post*. The blue and white collection boxes of the Jewish National Fund bore the words "Fight for a Free Palestine." A major Jewish bank, Bank Leumi L'Israel, was named the Anglo-Palestine Company. The main Jewish musical orchestra, now the Israel Philharmonic Orchestra, was the Palestine Symphony. The Jewish brigade that fought with the British in World War II was known as the Palestine regiment. At the 1939 New York World's Fair, the Palestinian Pavilion was a Zionist enterprise. It was only after the establishment of the State of Israel in 1948 that the word "Palestinian" was used in widespread fashion to refer exclusively to Arabs, rather than to Jews as well. Yet Palestinians did not at that point constitute a cohesive national group. As Bernard Lewis has suggested "it was not as a Palestinian nation that the Arabs of Ottoman Palestine objected to what they saw as the encroachments of the Zionist immigrants and settlers."[209] This view is borne out by the declaration of the first Congress of Muslim-Christian Associations in February 1919, that "We consider Palestine as part of Arab Syria, as it has never been separated from it at any time. We are connected with it by national, religious, linguistic, moral, economic, and geographical bonds."[210]

Indeed, the Syrian delegate to the UNGA, on a number of occasions in 1947, declared that Palestine "used to be a Syrian province...There is no distinction whatever between the Palestinians and the Syrians and, had it not been for the Balfour Declaration and the terms of the mandate, Palestine would now be a Syrian province, as it used to be." The celebrated scholar Philip Hitti, testifying before the Anglo-American Committee in 1946, stated there was "no such thing as Palestine in history, absolutely not." On this question of the distinctiveness of a "Palestinian people" the objective report of September 3, 1947, of the UN Special Committee on Palestine (UNSCOP), made a pertinent remark, "Palestinian nationalism, as distinct from Arab nationalism, is itself a relatively new phenomenon, which appeared only after the division of the 'Arab rectangle' by the settlement of the First World War." Indeed, official documents before 1947 generally spoke of "Arabs in Palestine," not of a "Palestinian people."[211] A "Palestinian identity" was not immediately obvious. It was only one part of a "rich tapestry of identities, mostly predicated on Arab and Islamic solidarity."[212]

It was George Antonius, the Lebanese-born Christian Palestinian historian and spokesman, who wrote that the Palestinian Arab national movement stemmed from literary societies and Christian missionary schools in the late 19th century and the impact of the Arab Revolt 1916-1918 in the Hijazi desert in Arabia.[213] Arabs had to develop a distinct Palestinian political ideology, while their Arab and Islamic identities remained important for them.[214] Some part of that identity stemmed from the influence of Muslim Arabs, who had called for Arab autonomy and independence in response to the Young Turks, who, in 1908, had seized power in the Ottoman Empire. Though historians disagree on the issue the beginning of some form of Palestinian Arab nationalism started in the 1920s, after the downfall of the Ottoman Empire and with the increasing importance of Zionist nationalism, and the British Mandate of a territory named "Palestine." But that nationalism was limited to the more educated and upper class families and did not have mass support. It was not opponents of liberation or self-determination of Arabs who regarded the concept of a "Palestinian people" as a figment of unhistorical imagination, but the Palestinian leaders themselves. The head of the PLO Military Operations Department, Zuhair Muhsin, said on March 31, 1977, that "there are no differences between Jordanians, Palestinians, Syrians, and Lebanese...Only for political reasons do we carefully underline our Palestinian identity... the existence of a separate Palestinian identity is there only for tactical reasons."

In the post-World War 1 period various local Arab nationalist identities had developed and Palestinian nationalism emerged largely, if not wholly, as a result of the opposition to Zionism during the years of the British Mandate. Only decades later, however, did the political dynamic resulting from assertion of the self-determination of the Jewish people and the creation of Israel lead to a similar claim for the self-determination of the Arabs of Palestine.[215] The evidence for this is that as late as 1956, the Palestinian Ahmad Shuqairy said to the UN Security Council that Palestine was nothing more than southern Syria.[216] Even later, on March 18, 2003, the PLO in its new version of its Charter or Amended Basic Law defines the "Palestinian nation." Article 1 says that Palestine is part of the large Arab World, and the Palestinian people are part of the Arab nation. The Palestinian People will work to achieve Arab unity. In other Articles, Jerusalem is declared the capital of Palestine. Islam is "the official religion in Palestine," and Islamic Sharia is to be the main source of legislation. It may well be argued that the single most important factor leading to the development of a Palestinian nationalism is the Arab defeat of 1949, after the creation of Israel. A Palestinian national identity largely arose out of the conflict with Israel. The emergence of that nationalism was formally asserted with the formation of the Palestine Liberation Organization in 1964. The *Nakba* was officially commemorated for the first time in 1998, in public meetings and exhibits in the main towns of the West Bank and the Gaza Strip.[217] This fixation on a past traumatic event, regarded as a disaster because of defeat, the loss of territory, and the shock to Arab Palestinian society, has become a unifying Palestinian national factor.

It is also enlightening to observe the changing political control over adjoining Arab areas, Gaza and the territory that has become known as the "West Bank." After the first Israeli-Arab 1948-49 war the area that was generally called the "Gaza Strip," an area of about 360 square kilometers, was ruled by Egypt between 1949 and 1967. It was not annexed by Egypt, but was held as "a military occupied area." By the March 26, 1979, peace treaty between Egypt and Israel, which established the Mandatory boundary line as the accepted boundary between the two countries, Egypt also renounced any claim to the Gaza Strip. A future solution was envisaged. In a joint letter to President Carter written by President Sadat and Prime Minister Begin on the same day as the peace treaty, the two leaders agreed to continue negotiations, the objective of which was the "establishment of the self-governing authority in the West Bank and Gaza in order to provide full autonomy to the inhabitants."

The historic Judea and Samaria (the area just west of the Jordan) was ruled from 1949 to 1967 by Jordan, which termed this area, about the size of Delaware, "the West Bank," and annexed it in 1950, an annexation that broke the 1949 Israel-Jordan Armistice Agreement, and which was not recognized internationally, except by Britain and Pakistan. No attempt was made, either by Arab countries or the international community, to establish the West Bank as an independent Palestinian state. Even Britain only gave *de facto*, not full legal, recognition to this Jordanian annexation of East Jerusalem. Jordan, therefore, was not the recognized and legitimate ruler of that area, nor did it have any legal title in Palestine. Under Jordanian rule, Jews were barred from living or buying property in that territory.

Even from this brief historical account of the changing political picture of the Middle East territories, it is manifest that the boundaries and control of "Palestine" and the decision about the exercise of sovereign power within it remain to be determined in an overall peace settlement.

What is important in this regard, though international organizations have ignored this, is that the land captured in 1967 by Israel was not the accepted legal territories of any particular people or country. In the interim period some small adjustments of territory have been made. An area in the Arava Valley, of about 320 square kilometers, had been occupied by Israel between 1955 and 1993; after the Israel-Jordan peace treaty of 1994, it was transferred to Jordan. Somewhat symbolically, this was the area where the peace treaty between the two countries was signed.

Chapter 19

Land Ownership

Another complex issue regarding Israel and the West Bank is that of land ownership, since current land laws are grounded on the Ottoman Land Code, starting with the Land Law of 1858, with its complications of private, absolute ownership (*mulk*) and conditional usufruct tenure, a form of leasehold (*miri*) to which modifications were made by Britain and Jordan. Individual cultivators could register their land and gain secure tenure to it. The state controlled land that was uncultivated or unused. Under both Ottoman rule from the sixteenth century and British rule from 1918 to 1948, most of the land in the area of Palestine was government owned. Not surprisingly, different opinions exist about the ownership of non-governmental land. A major problem is that Palestinians who are required to produce title to their land they claim, frequently lack documentation. During the Mandate period, a considerable amount of land was sold to the Zionists not only by Arab large landowners with large estates but by small Arab landowners, as well.[218] The more moderate Palestinian clan, the Nashashibis, were among those who secretly sold land to Jews, as well as collaborating with Zionists in other ways. In 1917, the Jews in Palestine owned about 100,000 acres; by 1930 this had increased to 300,000 acres, of which 170,000 came from large estates, and 140,000 from small holders.

The most useful starting point for examining this complex issue is the British 1946 Survey of Palestine. According to that Survey, Jews owned 8.6 per cent of the land, and Arabs owned 28.6 per cent, but this latter figure included Bedouin grazing land (8.4 per cent), and waste land, (13.4 per cent). The true calculation for Arab ownership was probably 6.8 per cent. No matter which statistic is accepted, the reasonable conclusion is that the majority of the land was not owned by Palestinians, nor, since there was not a Palestinian Arab state, was it owned by any Palestinian authority. Today within the contours of Israel as defined by the Green Line, about ninety-three per cent of land is now managed as public property. About eighty per cent of this land is owned by the Israeli government, through the Israel Lands Administration (ILA). Some thirteen per cent is administered by the *Keren Kayemet*, the Jewish National Fund (JNF), which was set up in 1901 by Theodor Herzl at the fifth Zionist Congress and financed through voluntary contributions by Jews throughout the world, and by a small tax, the shekel, paid by Zionists, to buy land in Palestine for the Jewish people. Herzl declared that "the JNF shall be the eternal possession of the Jewish people;" the Jewish people would be its owners. It would buy land from local landowners for Jewish settlement and develop it.

The JNF is still a private company and an independent body, with a separate administration from that of the State of Israel. Its independence was recognized by a Covenant signed in 1961 between the State of Israel and the JNF. By this agreement the Israel Lands Administration was to administer the lands of the JNF, which still retained title to them, in accordance with the directives that establish their use by Jews, and was pledged to preserve "the basic principle of the JNF that the land will remain under the ownership of the people." The JNF is not an official state body. Its essential function was, and remains, buying and leasing land for the purpose of settling Jews on lands and properties. Those settlements in the past have included the kibbutz and the moshav (celebrated communal settlements), and modern farming units, as well as private dwellings. It is regarded as the caretaker of the land of Israel on behalf of its owners, Jewish people everywhere. The policy of the JNF from the start was that it would not sell the land it bought, only lease it. Important differences exist. The Israel Lands Administration land is available for lease by Arabs, as well as Jews, but the JNF land has not until recently been legally available for lease by Arabs; though in practice provisions have been made for such leasing by an informal arrangement between the two bodies. Accordingly, JNF land has been leased to Bedouins who have benefited through highly subsidized land programs.

Arrangements of this kind, when land is leased by a non-Governmental entity to individuals but retains ownership of it, are not limited to the JNF. Religious bodies owning land in Israel, such as the Muslim *wakf,* or the Christian Churches, especially the Holyland Christian Ecumenical Foundation, also have rules forbidding the leasing or selling of their property to anyone who is not a member of their religious faith. The Foundation, in fact, buys land exclusively for Christian settlement. In contrast, the Palestinian land law states that Palestinians who sell land to Jews can be executed.

However, in recent years, mostly as a result of legal challenges by Adalah (The Legal Center for Arab Minority Rights in Israel), an organization set up in 1996 to serve Arab citizens which is concerned with human rights, some modifications to the basic principle of the JNF have been discussed and made. In 1995, Adel Kaadan, an Israeli Arab, applied for and was refused permission to build a home in Katzir, a communal settlement planned as a Jewish residential area on state land leased from the ILA to the Jewish Agency. He appealed to the Israeli Supreme Court, which decided in his favor. The Court, in March 2000, arguing that equality was one of the fundamental principles of the State of Israel, and that this applied to the allocation of State land, held (A. Kaadan et al.v. The Israel Lands Administration et al., HCJ 6698/95) that it was discriminatory to prohibit Arabs from leasing land in certain areas. It pointedly referred to and borrowed from the US Supreme Court's decision in *Brown v. Board of Education* that a policy of "separate but equal" was inherently unequal. The Court held that the values of the State of Israel as a Jewish and a democratic State did not justify state discrimination between its citizens on the basis of religion or nationality. Indeed, those values themselves proscribe discrimination and require equality between religions and nationalities. Chief Justice Aaron Barak concluded, "there is no contradiction between the values of the state of Israel as a Jewish and democratic state and full equality for all its citizens."

In October 2004, Adalah petitioned the Israeli Supreme Court (Adalah v. The ILA et al., HC 9205/04) to cancel the ILA marketing and allocation of JNF lands through bids open only to Jews. It claimed that these land allocation policies constituted racial discrimination and were incompatible with the principle of equality. As a result Israeli authorities began discussing possibilities of a "land swap" between the ILA and the JNF. This would mean, as first stated by the Gadish Committee set up in 2004, that if the JNF leased land to a non-Jew it would be compensated by an equal value of state-owned land in the country, probably undeveloped land in the Negev and Galilee. In two further decisions (Fuad Abu Riyya, HCJ 7452/04 and Fatna Abrik-Zbeidat HCJ 8036/07), the Court held that JNF lands should be marketed in an equitable manner.

Chapter 20

Nationality and Citizenship

Following its victory in the 1967 war, accusations against Israel of discrimination, racism, and colonialism escalated. The argument that discrimination exists is based on a number of policies, particularly on the complex one of defining an Israeli. By law, "Jewish nationality" is different from "Israeli citizenship." The 1952 Citizenship Law provides that all immigrants under the Law of Return are entitled to citizenship. The July 5, 1950 Law of Return, adopted by unanimous vote of the Knesset, is not racist or discriminatory against anyone for ethnic or religious reasons, but is directed only towards Jews. It entitles Jews from any country to enter *Eretz Israel* and be given nationality and legal and political rights. In this policy Israel is not unique. Many other countries have similar provisions granting certain privileges to particular groups. Thus, Israeli law provides for preferential treatment for Jews, yet it does not discriminate against any specific group. To take only two examples of similar rules elsewhere: Germany provides for automatic citizenship for those of "German origin" who were expelled from their homes in the former Soviet Union, and Italy confers citizenship on all Italians exiled from areas that were under Austrian rule before 1920.[219] The Israeli Law of Return applies to Jews throughout the world, individuals with a Jewish mother or grandmother, those with a Jewish father or grandfather, and even converts to Judaism. In essence it is a unique example of a state being founded on a combination of nationality, ethnicity, and religion.[220]

Thus, Jewish nationality is extra-territorial and embraces Jewish citizens of other countries. Understandably, Jews who are considered to be engaged in an activity directed against the Jewish people or are likely to endanger public health or the security of the State, can be excluded from citizenship. In the amendment of the law in 1954 those persons "with a criminal past likely to endanger public welfare" can also be excluded. Another 1970 amendment of the Law of Return resulted from two difficult Supreme Court cases, those of Oswald Rufeisen and Benjamin Shalit. By this, a Jew was defined as "a person who was born of a Jewish mother or has become converted to Judaism and who is not a member of another religion." The amendment also granted the right to immigrate to family members and descendants of Jews. While still favoring Jews, the law is not discriminatory against non-Jews. Individuals who are not Jewish can become citizens by birth, naturalization, by residence, or by marrying an Israeli citizen; Israeli laws relating to these issues are consonant with those in other democratic countries. It is noticeable that Israel was one of the few countries to give shelter, and then citizenship, to a number of Vietnamese boat people who sought political asylum in the late 1970s. It also gave refuge to thousands of Sudanese, especially from Darfur, fleeing their country and who came to Israel, knowing they would be allowed to stay.

The concept of Jewish nationality stems from the belief in the existence of a Jewish people which shared some commonalities for over 3,000 years. This existence has been challenged by some who doubt there is an ethnic continuity between the ancient Israelites and contemporary Jews. An argument of this kind, more rhetorical and pseudo-historical than scholarly, was put forward more than a generation ago by some Tel Aviv intellectuals, known as the Canaanites, or New Hebrews, led by the poet Yonatan Ratosh and by Aharon Amir, who tried to differentiate the idea of an Israeli nationality, based on territory, Hebrew language, and Canaanite ancestry, from one based on a conception of the bonds of a historical Jewish people, a religious and ethnic group which they argued consisted of Jews whose ancestry did not originate in Palestine, but rather in Eastern Europe. That nationality and identity was, they suggested, linked only to those who were descendants of forbears who lived in the area of the Fertile Crescent.[221] Though the

Canaanites differed on some issues, two general political objectives could be drawn from their arguments; one is that the New Hebrews would be integrated into the Middle East rather than into world Jewry; the other is to assert the place and at least equal rights of Palestinian Arabs in contemporary Israel.

Sometimes a similar argument is made in a milder form. The French intellectual Raymond Aron, a self-described "de-Judaised Jew," while not addressing the historical argument, argued there is no teleology in Jewish history leading to Zionism. More extreme assertions came from those who deny the historical existence of a Jewish people and question what they call the "myth" of supposed links between different Jewish communities in the world. Writers of this point of view reject the idea of a "Jewish people" who went into exile, or of a bond between those Jews and the land of Israel. This argument is most familiar from the book by Arthur Koestler, which argued that Ashkenazi Jews are a "pseudo-nation," mostly stemming from conversions in the eighth century in the Khazar Kingdom in south Russia, in the Caucasus, and therefore Jews are the descendants of the Khazars, rather than of the Jews of the Bible.[222]

Almost no serious scholar believes that an argument of this kind has any basis in fact. Studies of DNA of Jews tend to confirm that the Middle East strain is the dominant one. Those studies of the Y-chromosome and mtDNA do not support the view that Jews are descended in any great numbers from the Khazars or some Slavic group. Most Jews do share a common ancient ancestry, and are connected to each other and to biblical Israel.[223] Nevertheless, some critics, with a political agenda, make at least five highly controversial arguments of the following kind. There never was a "Jewish people," a group with a common background. The claim there is such a people is based on an "invented" entity or "implanted memory" with no connection to the land of Israel; the "people" were only Jewish religious communities which have sprung from mass conversions throughout history. The exile from the Holy Land never happened and thus there was no return. In this view a myth of exile was promoted by early Christians to recruit Jews to their faith. Therefore, the creation of a national identity told in the Bible is also a myth. The familiar portrait of the Jewish people today as the descendants of those in biblical times stems from important Jewish historians of the late 19th and 20th centuries, such as Heinrich Graetz, Simon Dubnow, and Ben-Zion Dinur, all of whom indicated the descent of the Jewish people from biblical ancestors. The political point of all these arguments is to assert that the Zionist movement, starting in the late nineteenth century, deliberately formulated the idea of a common Jewish ethnicity and a historical continuity that is unwarranted. That point has become a significant one in the polemics of the anti-Israeli rhetoric.

It is a truism that not all contemporary Jews descend from biblical Israelites and that some Jews descend from different nations, which converted to Judaism at different times. An early example was Adiabene, a district in Mesopotamia, whose rulers converted to Judaism in the first century, and whose Queen lived for a time in Jerusalem. Clearly, converted Jews, such as Marilyn Monroe, Elizabeth Taylor, or Sammy Davis Jr., cannot claim ancestry from biblical Jews. It is also true that Jews in the Diaspora did not share the same spoken language. But this does not lead to the conclusion that Palestine is not the homeland of the Jewish people. Whatever the merits of the historical argument, one which has been considerably disputed by knowledgeable authorities, it is evident that the selection of historical facts and themes has been informed by a political agenda, a large part of which is criticism of Israel's "outdated religion and its literal corpus." Arguments of this kind denying the bond between the Jewish people, historical Judaism and the land of Israel may well be correlated with the denial by their proponents of the right of the Jewish people to a state of its own, a Jewish state.[224] Those arguments certainly deny or, at best, minimize, the existence of Jews as an independent people with an important history and civilization of its own, and a common biological origin.

The Israeli laws on nationality and citizenship have not gone without criticism, especially the Citizenship and Entry into Israel Law, putting temporary limits on granting citizenship to residents of the Palestinian Authority. This was passed on July 31, 2003, as a result of the terrorist attacks against Israelis in June 2001, when a suicide bombing in a discotheque in Tel-Aviv killed 21 and injured 132, and in March 2002 with the second *intifada,* which broke out after the failure of the Camp David talks in 2000. Some of the perpetrators were persons who had taken advantage of Israeli identity cards to pass through checkpoints. The most serious of the attacks at that time, on March 27, 2002, was that at a Passover Seder at Netanya where 30 Israeli civilians were killed and 140 others were injured by a Palestinian terrorist. The 2003 law places age restrictions for the automatic granting of Israeli citizenship and residency permits to spouses of Israeli citizens. This law, which critics argue is discriminatory because it disproportionately affects Israeli Arabs, whose spouses might immigrate into Israel from the West Bank, was upheld 6-5 by the Israeli High Court in 2006. The majority held that Israel was "entitled to prevent the immigration of enemy nationals into it, even if they are spouses of Israeli citizens, while it is waging an armed conflict with that same enemy."

The laws on citizenship appear to be justified by international law. The International Convention on the Elimination of all forms of Racial Discrimination, (ICERD), adopted by the UN General Assembly on December 21, 1965, which came into force on January 4, 1969, allows states to make provisions "concerning nationality, citizenship, or naturalization, provided that such provisions do not discriminate against any particular nationality." It also allows states to exercise preferences in granting citizenship to remedy the effects of past discrimination. International law recognizes that a nation-state can maintain official ties with its "kin" outside its borders and treat them preferentially in certain areas, including immigration and naturalization.[225]

All nations prescribe conditions for citizenship and do not accept those who do not assent to their fundamental values. Similar provisions to those of Israel, with privileged entry or granting of citizenship for people of the same ethnic or cultural group living outside the borders of a country, exist in a number of countries; Germany, Britain, Greece, Turkey, Poland, Slovakia, Hungary, Spain, Japan, Bulgaria, Finland, and Ireland are among them.[226] None of these have been challenged in the European Court of Human Rights. A striking, and for Israel an ironic, example of the provisions are those in Germany which extended the right of automatic citizenship to include any person of "ethnic German origin" residing in the Soviet Union or Eastern European (then Communist) countries, as well as refugees and displaced persons. Similarly, Poland in 2000 enacted a Repatriation Law granting citizenship to people of Polish origin living in the former Soviet Union and who wanted to return to Poland. Bulgaria grants the right of citizenship to any person of Bulgarian origin. At the October 2001 meeting of the European Commission for Democracy through Law (Venice Commission), 48th Plenary Meeting, the policy of preferential treatment of national minorities by their kin-state was adopted. Countries can provide benefits for a given people, provided they do not discriminate against another given people.[227] In general, countries have a right to impose conditions for entry; the United States has a referred visa program for certain foreigners.

Differentiation among religious, ethnic, gender, and linguistic groups is present in a number of countries which give special recognition to one particular group, and its language, culture and religion, even while minorities from other groups are resident in them. In Greece, the 1975 Constitution gives priority to the Eastern Orthodox Church as the prevailing religion. A number of European countries include Christian crosses in their flags. In Britain, for over five centuries, the head of state, the monarch, has also been head of the established Anglican Church. In Spain, Castilian is the official language of the state, though millions speak Catalan and Basque. In the province of Quebec, French is the sole official language, though almost a quarter of the population consists of primarily English speakers. The Turkish constitution defines a citizen as a Turk, though a third of its population is Kurdish. Since 1971, Egypt is officially "The Arab Republic of Egypt," though the country contains Coptic, Nubian, and Berber minorities. Syria, though it contains Kurds, defines itself as an "Arab Republic." The Syrian Constitution of 1973 states that Islamic jurisprudence is the main source of legislation. Similarly, Algeria, with many Berbers, and Morocco are "Arab" countries. Even the PLO, in a statement made in Algiers in 1988, proclaimed that its future state would be "an Arab state, an integral and indivisible part of the Arab nation, at one with that nation in heritage and civilization."[228] In it, Islam would be the official religion of the state, and Islamic sharia law would be a major source for legislation.

Provisions and regulations of behavior in Israel can be compared with the discrimination in policies and rules in Arab countries and Islamic organizations. In a majority of Arab countries women are subject to harsher penalties than men charged with the same crime. Those countries have often had an "obedience" clause in their law, which requires a woman's obedience to her husband; women thus may not be able to open a bank account or travel on their own.[229] In Lebanon, Palestinians are denied the right to own property or to register real estate under their own names or bequeath it to their children; they do not receive social security benefits or health care at hospitals, and they are banned from certain occupations. In Syria, Palestinians are subjected to a nightly curfew and are restricted in their movements in daytime. Emancipation of women in Islamic countries has been limited by political pressure, legal action, threats and intimidation, and physical violence. Where sharia has been established as the basis of society, women suffer from forced marriages, honor killings, and female genital mutilation. In the Islamic Republic of Iran the constitution, among other things, bans women from becoming president or a judge in most courts. Women in Saudi Arabia cannot vote, drive a car, or hold a passport, and are subject to a dress code. Its legal code sanctions public beheadings for homosexuality, apostasy, armed robbery, and sodomy. Non-Muslims in that country cannot become citizens nor can they openly practice their religion. In Arab countries, non-Muslims are second class citizens, and may not only be denied citizenship, but also denied visas to enter the country on the basis of religion. The Organization of the Islamic Conference (OIC), which describes itself as "the collective voice of the Muslim people," and as safeguarding the true values of Islam and the Muslims and its fifty-seven members, in January 2009 opposed the establishment of a Special *Rapporteur*, on behalf of the Human Rights Council, to monitor laws that discriminate against women. The OIC has been active in condemning public criticism of Islam, as in the case of the Danish cartoons, since these were contrary "to the principles of the sharia," which it had declared in its Cairo Declaration of Human Rights in Islam in 1990. Up to this time no Organizations of the Christian or Jewish Conference have been established.

Chapter 21

The Importance of Peoplehood

The acceptance of Jewish peoplehood is crucial for any attempt to resolve the Israeli-Palestinian conflict. The essential problem is that the Palestine Liberation Organization, in its National Charter of 1964, amended in 1968, denies this. Article 20 of the Charter, supposedly *nullified in December 2009, but never formally changed*, which argues that the Balfour Declaration and the Mandate for Palestine, and everything based on them is null and void, states, "Claims of historical or religious ties of Jews with Palestine are incompatible with the facts of history and the true conception of what constitutes statehood. Judaism, being a religion is not an independent nationality. Nor do Jews constitute a single nation with an identity of its own; they are citizens of the states to which they belong."

Modern genetic research has thrown some light on the question of the bonds within and among Jewish communities around the world and their links to the Middle East, but it is wise to be cautious about characterizing Jewish people, as coreligionists or as genetic isolates that may be related. Two recent studies help in this regard, with both essentially concluding that Jews today, both Ashkenazim and Sephardim, are genetically similar and share many genes inherited from the Jews of 3,000 years ago. One research project published in June 2010, found that regarding the people originating from the seven different Jewish communities it studied, the genetic linkage between Jews in each community was much greater than to non-Jews in the same area, and that there was significant linkages between Jews of different communities.[230] It concluded that the "studied Jewish populations represent a series of geographical isolates or clusters with genetic threads that weave them together." It therefore supports the concept of Jewish peoplehood. A second study examining fourteen Jewish communities and comparing them with sixty-nine non-Jewish populations suggested a shared regional Middle East origin of these Jewish communities.[231] There was also a close relationship between Jews and non-Jewish populations from the Levant. This was consistent with an historical formulation of the Jewish people as descending from ancient Hebrew and Israelite residents of the Levant.

Though there may be legitimate differences of opinion among scholars about the accuracy of the portraits of Biblical figures, and the exact extent of the kingdom of David and Solomon, most objective historians have never denied the ancient link between Jews and *Eretz Israel*, or that the connection can be traced back thousands of years; in Babylon Jews "sat down and cried as we remembered Zion." That link was shown by the finding, as recently as 2011, of an underground aqueduct dating from the time of Herod in the Second Temple Period (515 B.C. to 70 A.D.), linking the Temple Mount to the city of David and providing drainage for the western part of the city. Archeological digs have found not only pottery, coins, ritual baths, stonework, and artifacts of the ancient past, but also writings and inscriptions which appear to confirm the existence of a Kingdom of David, the use of the Hebrew language, and the contributions of scribes who wrote literary texts such as the books of Samuel and Judges. Clear evidence exists of an underground tunnel cut around 702 B.C., on orders of King Hezekiah, to bring water into Jerusalem from the spring outside the city walls. For archeological scholars, it was unfortunate that Arab riots in 1988 and 1996 prevented the opening of other ancient tunnels by Israel. Archeology has become a part of Palestinian lawfare. It was unfortunate that the Palestinian Authority in November 2010 published a study, more germane for its political agenda than helpful for objective scholarship, that the Western Wall of the Temple Mount was not a Jewish holy site, but really part of the Al-Aqsa mosque. In contrast, Israeli archeologists and the Israel Antiquities Authority have studied and preserved Islamic sites.

The Romans did end the sovereign Jewish state, did destroy the Second Temple, did change the name of the land to Syria Palestina, and did banish Jews from Jerusalem, but did not end all of the Jewish presence in the area of the old kingdom. Nor did the end of that Jewish state end the consciousness of Jews in the Diaspora of "the historical connection of the Jewish people with Palestine," a connection that was acknowledged in the League of Nations Mandate.

No doubt Jewish nationalism has used legends of figures such as Abraham, Moses, and David, as common ancestors and founders of the Jewish people, as other nations have used myths about their origin; Vercingetorix and Clovis, or "our ancestors the Gauls" in France, Arminius in Germany, and Romulus and Remus in Italy. Similarly, Jewish nationalism, like that of other countries, may include traditions which seem to be ancient, but which may be quite recent and sometimes invented.[232] It has long been generally accepted, though some have disagreed, that the Jewish people consists of individuals linked not only by a common religion of Judaism in its different forms, but also as a common ethnic community with memories of a shared past, ceremonies and culture, a certain solidarity, legal codes, social behavior, myths and symbols, a bond felt by descendants of those dispersed from Judea and Samaria to their ancient homeland, a subjective belief in their common descent, and a desire to continue their partnership.

THE COMPLEX MIXTURE OF JEWISH IDENTITY

The question of identity has never been easy to answer, as is seen in the story of a Homeric hero in the Iliad (7.123), who when asked who he is responds by giving a list of his ancestors. The answer to the question may vary over time and be subject to continual changes.[233] Attempting to define "Jewish identity," whether seen as religious, communal, or cultural in character, is as difficult as describing the proverbial elephant. In the complex mixture of identity one can comprehend a variety of elements: a way of life regulated by *Halakhah* and ethical norms; adherence to some basic ideas and values; commitment to essential principles of justice and humanitarianism; belief in a vision of national redemption; acknowledgement of historical pedigree; membership of a collective entity; attachment to synagogues; common folkways and lifestyle; fear of antisemitism; commitment to Israel; or simply a feeling of Jewishness. Identity may today be more celebratory in a festive or domestic fashion, than in a devout or even public sense.

Among Jews, in a fashion similar to that of some other Middle Eastern peoples "genealogical filiation is interwoven with fervent territorial attachments in myth, memory and symbolism."[234] Past, present, and future are linked, in a manner that echoes President Lincoln's words, "the mystic chords of memory, stretching…to every living heart and hearthstone." Jews retained their distinctive identity, even when scattered. The strong bond of ethnic solidarity was fed through various other factors such as a common name, common myths of origin and descent, a whole canon of memories centered on charismatic heroes, a common liturgical language and script, an attachment to *Eretz Israel* and particularly to Jerusalem. That solidarity was renewed by reaction against outside hostility.[235]

The ancestral homeland is closely associated with the characteristics of Jewish historic culture, sense of communal identity, religion, and expected destiny. For some the Bible, with its commentaries on Jewish life in Judea and Samaria, together with archeology, provides the guidelines for definition of the contours of the national homeland. For more secular Jews, the homeland would be based on settlement and a progressive social order. In the Diaspora there was, in addition to the language of the host country, usually a vernacular spoken by Jews; Yiddish, Judeo-Arab, Judeo-Persian, Judeo-Espagnol, but the sacred and common language of the scriptures and the synagogue was Hebrew. Although the genetic research described above suggests that Ashkenazim, most of whom lived in Eastern Europe and Russia, and Sephardim Jews, descendants of Jews who had lived in Spain and were exiled at the end of the fifteenth century, have common genes, race is not the definition of Jewish identity. Nor does it imply that the origins of Jews are totally ethnically and biologically pure.[236]

The indication of the interrelationship of nation and religion is first found in the Bible when Abraham is instructed by God to leave for the land of

Israel. Abraham is told that Israel would become a great nation through which all the families of the earth would be blessed. By a covenant, Abraham would instruct his Jewish descendants to keep the way of the Lord by acting with compassionate righteousness and moral integrity. The Jewish people and nation were thus interrelated with ethical monotheism.

Some notable Jews have addressed the subject of the interrelationship of national and religious elements, and the connection of the Jewish people, the land of Israel, and the Torah. In a great speech on April 25, 1915, to the conference of the Eastern Council of Reform Rabbis, "The Jewish Problem: How to Solve it," Louis Brandeis, while admitting that the Jews were not an absolutely pure race, remarked that a "common race is only one of the elements which determine nationality. Conscious community of sentiments, common experiences and qualities are equally, perhaps more, important. Religion, traditions, and customs bound us together, though scattered throughout the world." Among those experiences was common suffering. Martin Buber in similar fashion held that the Jewish people eluded classification and was like no other. because from its earliest beginning it has been both a nation and a religious community. Sigmund Freud held that the bond was not faith, but consciousness of an inner identity, the intimacy that comes from the same psychic structure. Ahad Ha'am felt the spirit of Jewish nationality in his heart. Albert Einstein saw Jewish nationality as a fact, and held that "the Jewish nation is a living fact in Palestine as well as in the Diaspora."[237] Another illustration of the complexity of the issue is the statement by Isaiah Berlin in his answer on January 23, 1959, to Prime Minister David Ben-Gurion, who had asked his opinion about the relationship of religion and nationalism in the formulation of Jewish identity. Berlin wrote, among other matters, that "historically, the Jewish religion, the Jewish race, and all the factors which combine into Jewish culture, have combined into a single, persistent entity, incapable of being neatly fitted into the political pattern of a modern State of a Western type."[238]

An indication of the complex and unique nature of this question of "peoplehood" is illustrated by the decision of Beth Hatefutsoth, in Tel Aviv, to change its English name from the Museum of the Jewish

Diaspora to Museum of the Jewish People. It intends to be more inclusive of the diverse Jewish populations in the world, thus indicating the bonds between those people and the State of Israel, by linking Jews living in Israel with those living anywhere else in the world. The view of critics "that the State of Israel should be 'a state of all its citizens'" (ironically, a term apparently coined by Azmi Bishara, a former Arab member of the Knesset) rather than a Jewish state may be intellectually arguable, but this ideological political position does not require doing violence to the true history of the Jewish people. Nor should it ignore the achievement of Israel as a democracy, imperfect thought it may be as are all other systems, in a setting where it has for over sixty years faced war and violence.

Israel, Jews
and the Diaspora

The establishment of the State of Israel has not ended the debate over the essence of Jewish identity in the Diaspora or the nature of the relationship between Israel and Jews living elsewhere. Are Jews to be defined as a people because of descent and common ancestry, bound by ties of solidarity, or as a religious group because of their faith and practice, or a combination of both? Jewish identity has been and remains difficult to define, because of its multi-faceted character at different times and different places. A major aim of the Jewish Agency, led in recent years by Natan Sharansky, in Israel has been to strengthen the secular identity of Diaspora Jews.

In a lecture in 1969, Gerson Scholem confessed he had not previously spoken on the relationship between Israel and the Diaspora, partly because of the difficulty of saying anything new on the subject, and partly because of his own contradictory thoughts about it. The relationship, a troubled, complicated, and historically unique one, is more likely to raise questions, which can be presented with clarity, than to lead to definitive answers. An early indication of the tension in the relationship between Israel and the Diaspora came in 1950, and again in 1961, in the correspondence between David Ben-Gurion, prime minister at the time, and Jacob Blaustein, then president of the American Jewish Committee in New York. At the core of the controversy was the question of whether Israel represented all Jews in the world, or whether American Jews were at home in the United States and not in exile, as Blaustein maintained. The pragmatic Ben-Gurion, in spite of his fundamental concept of "statism" and his stress on the need for Jews to immigrate into Israel, finally agreed in April 1961, that it was "perfectly natural for differences of view on the essence and meaning of Judaism and Jewishness" to exist between Israel and Jews living in other countries.

The compromise was that on one hand, American Jews owed no political allegiance to Israel though they could support the development of the country by philanthropy and in various political ways, while Israel would not interfere in the internal affairs of Jews elsewhere. Since then, the relationship has varied, depending on political and religious issues, and on the attitudes of different generations. Israel and the Diaspora can both be regarded as viable expressions of Jewish life. Jews who freely choose to live in the Diaspora, and do not consider it as exile, and hold that the Diaspora consists of vibrant, creative group of people, may still tend to acknowledge some spiritual and cultural ties to the Holy Land as the ancestral homeland and show concern for the survival of Israel, even if they differ on the wisdom of particular Israeli policies.

A report in July 2010 by the Institute for Jewish Policy Research of the attitudes of British Jews towards Israel showed that about ninety percent of the respondents to its inquiry believed that Israel was the "ancestral homeland" of the Jewish people, that eighty-two percent said that Israel played a central or important role in their Jewish identities, and that seventy-seven percent thought that Jews had a special responsibility to support Israel. However, this strong personal attachment to Israel did not prevent respondents from criticism of Israeli society. One major source of difference is over the question of conversions to Judaism. Many in the Diaspora, with its various religious denominations and secular individuals, have been troubled by attempts in Israel to grant a monopoly over conversions to the Orthodox establishment, instead of allowing an ambiguity on the issue present for some time to remain.

In recent years, a working consensus has been reached on the relationship between Jews in the Diaspora and the State of Israel. It is accepted that it cannot be based on the "negation of the Diaspora" (*shlilat hagolah*), since vibrant Jewish communities exist, especially that of the United States, which has achieved a significant place in mainstream American society. The Diaspora is now voluntarily chosen; it is not 19th century Minsk. The danger to Jewish identity today is assimilation, not oppression. Yet at the same time those communities recognize the meaningfulness of Israel, even if it is not always central to their life, and/or if they think that it is not a necessary condition for Jewish survival. The question of the centrality of Israel in Jewish life therefore remains open, as does the significance of Ahad Ha'Am's belief in a *merkaz ruhani*, Israel as a spiritual center that would be an inspiration for all Jews. Moreover, to suggest there is a contrast between "abnormality" of Jewish life in the Diaspora and "normal" life in Israel now seems inappropriate. The relationship may more properly be described in terms of bipolarity and mutuality, than in centrality and subordination. Still, the relationship is unique because of the Israeli Law of Return and the automatic citizenship granted to Jews immigrating into Israel.

Chapter 23

The Need for Security and Defense

Geographically, Israel is a long, narrow country with little strategic depth. The whole country is within artillery and rocket range of the West Bank, Gaza Strip, and Lebanon.[239] A fighter jet can travel between the Jordan River and the Mediterranean in four minutes and between the Jordan and Jerusalem in two minutes. A considerable part of the history of Israel, and indeed that of the Jews in the Yishuv, stems from the need for security and defense against violence. In Israel's seventh decade that need is still present, as was shown with the second Palestinian *Intifada* (uprising), which started in September 2000, the day before the Jewish New Year. At that time, rocks were thrown from the Temple Mount by Palestinians on to Jewish worshipers at the Western Wall in Jerusalem.

Ironically, it happened as the Palestinian economy was improving, with a decline in unemployment, with about 100,000 Palestinians coming into Israel to work, and with Palestinian business people also entering Israel. However, Yasser Arafat rejected the Israeli offer for the Palestinians to establish their own state in Gaza and in most of the West Bank, and instigated the uprising. By mid 2005, almost 1,000 attacks, in restaurants, hotels, schools, and buses, had occurred within Israel and about 9,000 in the West Bank, mostly against civilians. Israeli Jews were murdered on the highways. Israel combat operations had not been able to end all the activity, suicide attacks, bombings, mortar

256

fire, and rocket fire against its communities, which had cost over 1,000 Israeli lives.

To prevent or minimize Arab attacks, such as that in Netanya on March 27, 2002, and to deter additional acts of terrorism, especially suicide bombing attacks launched from Jenin and other places in the West Bank, Prime Minister Ariel Sharon decided in June 2002, simply for reasons of self-defense, to build a multi-layered separation fence system, which Arabs, using different vocabulary, see as a wall, between Israel proper and some settlements on one side, and the West Bank on the other. No doubt this has caused inconveniences for some Palestinians and restricted their mobility to some degree, and led to some disputes over the loss of land. Recognizing this, the Israeli government did try to minimize the affect on the daily lives of Palestinians. The fence has greatly improved security, been an effective defensive deterrent, and has successfully reduced the threats to Israeli citizens and the loss of life. The results are evident. For three years after the start of the September 2000 *intifada,* there were 93 suicide attacks resulting in 447 Israeli deaths and over 4,300 wounded; since the building of the fence there have been only five attacks a year and an average of ten Israelis killed a year. In 2010, there were five Israeli casualties.

European countries have been constant in their opposition to the fence. The European Council on November 18, 2003, called on Israel "to stop and reverse the construction of the so-called security fence inside the occupied Palestinian territories, including in and around East Jerusalem which is in departure of the armistice line of 1949." At the prompting of the Palestinians and Arab states, the UN General Assembly by Resolution ES-10/14 of December 8, 2003 requested an advisory opinion from the International Court of Justice (ICJ) on the legal consequence of the security fence being built by Israel. In effect, it was pretending to seek guidance on an issue it had already decided, and on which it had already stated its political opinion in a previous resolution. As a result, the ICJ, by a majority of 14-1, gave its advisory opinion in July 2004 that the building of the fence or barrier or wall was "contrary to international law." The opinion held that the International Covenant on Civil and Political Rights, adopted in December 1966 and entered into force in March 1976, was "applicable to acts by a state in the exercise of its jurisdiction outside its own territory" (Advisory Opinion, para, 111). The ICJ called on Israel "to terminate its breach of international law" and to stop "the works of construction of the wall in the Occupied Palestinian Territory, including in and around East Jerusalem." It argued that Israel could not "rely on a right of self-defense or on a state of necessity in order to preclude the wrongfulness of the construction of the wall." Only the American judge, Thomas Buergenthal, dissented from the opinion. The court, he said, was issuing an advisory opinion without having or seeking "all relevant facts bearing directly on issues of Israel's legitimate right of self-defense, military necessity and security needs, given the repeated deadly terrorist attacks in and upon Israel."

The UNGA Resolution ES-10 of July 20, 2004, by majority of 150-6-10, condemned the fence and voted that Israel comply with the opinion of the ICJ. No similar opinion was ever issued about the wall that divided Germany, or the physical barriers between the United States and Mexico, or the barrier, about 460 miles, started in 1990 by India in disputed Kashmir to separate Indian and Pakistani forces, or the metallic border fences established by Ceuta and Melilla, autonomous cities of Spain, to stop illegal emigration from Morocco into Europe, or the barrier built by South Africa to stop illegal immigration from Zimbabwe and Lesotho. All members of the European Union voted for the UNGA Resolution and condemned the fence, as did the World Council of Churches. The European Council, on December 8, 2009, declared the "separation barrier where built on occupied land" was illegal under international law. The Europeans tried to influence and change American policy on the fence by funding a Palestinian team, the Negotiation Support unit of the PLO, which periodically lobbies Washington policy makers.[240]

In response, the Israel Supreme Court (in Beit Sourik Council v. The Government of Israel, HCJ 2056/04, and later in High Court Ruling Docket HCJ 7957/04 of September 2005) ruled that indeed there was no authorization for Israel to build a fence if the goal was a political one of annexing territory or drawing political borders. But the state is entitled to defend itself and its citizens, even in territories defined as under "belligerent occupation." In this case, the Israeli military commander did have proper authorization, since it was not a matter of annexation, but it was one of military necessity to erect the fence. The fence was a measure motivated by security concerns for the protection of Israeli citizens from Palestinian terror, and "did not express a political border, or any other border." Moreover, the fence was not a permanent one, but was erected temporarily for security needs to provide a solution to existing and future threats of terrorism.

Nevertheless, the Court, in Docket HCJ 7957/04, also held that some segments of the fence route violated the Palestinian residents' rights disproportionately, and that the needs of the local population must be considered. As a result Israel altered some segments of the existing route and changed some of the plans for the extension of the fence. In a second case in 2005, the Court again determined that the government must change the route of the fence to lessen the impact on the rights of the resident Palestinian residents. The cases are remarkable in that the Israeli judiciary enforced the rule of law, in spite of military considerations.

However, the problem remained; was the separation fence legal? This was examined in Israel High Court Ruling Docket HCJ 7957/04, and a decision rendered on September 15, 2005. The Court outlined the attempts that Israel had made to counter the attacks against civilians since the start of the *intifada*. The Court criticized the ICJ for disregarding the facts on the ground, the reality that the Israeli actions were based on military exigencies, national security, or public order, and that they were applicable to the fence as a whole or to individual parts of it. The ICJ, it argued, had almost totally ignored the security problems facing Israel, and that perhaps its opinion was colored by a political hue. The Court pointed out that construction of the fence was unrelated to expropriation, confiscation or transfer of ownership of land, and that Israeli possession for the construction was accompanied by payment of compensation for the damage caused. The rationale for the construction of a fence to defend the lives and safety of Israeli settlers in the area is derived from the need, made clear in The Hague Regulations, 43, to preserve public order and safety. The fence went beyond the Green Line and into the West Bank because the topography of the area, mountain ridge, riverbeds, thick vegetation, which did not allow for defense of the Israeli soldiers patrolling the area if it was confined to construction within Israel.

On a number of occasions, the Israeli Supreme Court has subsequently grappled with the two conflicting considerations for the military command: legitimate security interests and safety of Israeli citizens, and the rights, needs and interests of the local Arab population. It has called for a proper balance between the two. (Hess Case, pp. 455-6; HCJ 953/83 Levy v. The Commander of the Southern District of the Israeli Police, 38(2) P.D. 393). In a later case, Alfei Menashe, HCJ 7957/04, September 2005, the Court upheld the legality of a fence if it minimized the difficulties of the local population in its attempt to protect Israeli settlers in the West Bank. In a third case,(The Public Committee against Torture in Israel v. The Government of Israel, HCJ 769/02, December 11, 2005), the Summary Judgment of the Court held that targeted killing, within certain rules, was a legitimate form of self-defense against terrorists.

In another case brought by the Association for Civil Rights in Israel, an Israeli human rights group, the Court in December 2009 had to balance security and Palestinian rights. It ordered that a road, a major commuter highway 443, a short cut around the outskirts of Jerusalem that had been closed in 2002 to Palestinians from the West Bank because Israeli motorists had been killed there by snipers during the second *intifada*, should be reopened to Palestinian motorists. The chief justice, Dorit Beinisch, the first woman appointed to the position, delivered the ruling that the IDF had no legal basis for forbidding permanently the use of highway 443 by Palestinians, who had been forced to travel on alternative roads. She also made an interesting broader statement: "The comparison made by the petitioners between the use of separate roads for security reasons and the Apartheid policy carried out in the past in South Africa, as well as the actions that accompanied it, is improper. Apartheid is a most serious crime...it is the policy of racial segregation and discrimination, based on legal practices which are meant to make certain races superior, while keeping other races oppressed." She concluded that the difference between the security measures taken by Israel to defend itself from terror attacks and the policies of Apartheid "should forbid us from making any comparisons or use this term."

The Israeli Supreme Court in rendering its decisions, has been conscious not only of the specific problems involved, but also of the general legal problem in reaching a balance between security, the need for Israel to defend itself and to counter terrorism, and the basic principles of liberty. The balance had to be found by observing general principles of law, including reasonableness and good faith. The Court recognized the difficulties in weighing the merits of the two concepts and understood that no simple answer was available to the question of how the balance should be resolved. It did hold that the starting point for its consideration should the principle of proportionality. According to this principle the liberty of individuals or of local inhabitants could be limited if the restriction was proportionate. The Court had earlier pronounced that "proportionality is recognized today as a general principle of international law." (Beit Sourik Village Council v. The Government of Israel, HCJ 2056/04 (June 30, 2004). That general principle is indeed inherent in Additional Protocol 1 of the Geneva Convention and in the Rome Statute, which aim to protect civilians from excessive harm or damage in relation to anticipated military advantage, but it is not a mathematical concept.[241] The Israeli Court obviously could not formulate in any precise form how Israel should respond in proportionate military means to the extent of destruction by the enemy. It did rule that the decision of a military commander had to be in the "zone of reasonableness." (HCJ 1005/89 Aga v. Commander of the IDF Forces in the Gaza Strip Area). The Court has also challenged Israeli Administration rules on the use of torture on persons suspected of terrorism. (H.C. 390/79 Dawikat v. The State of Israel, 34 (1) P.D. 1.

A difficult legal problem is the applicability of the 1949 Geneva Conventions and human rights principles to present day terrorist activity. The Conventions, responding to the issues arising from World War II, assumed that armed conflicts were between states, that the main combat forces were national armies, that there was a clear distinction between combatants (who wore uniforms) and non-combatants, that combatants fought under a command responsible for the conduct and discipline of its subordinates, and that military operations were not conducted in civilian areas, which should not be targeted unless they directly participate in hostilities. Article 48 of the Additional Protocol 1 of the Geneva Convention clearly states "the parties to the conflict shall at all times distinguish between the civilian population and combatants and between civilian objects and military objectives and accordingly shall direct their operations only against military objectives." Its purpose was to protect innocent civilians from attack; Article 51 (2) says "The civilian population as such, as well as individual citizens, shall not be the object of attack."

Today, in many cases and particularly regarding Israel, the nature of war has changed, with the activity of fighters in civilian clothing and helped by civilians, and terrorist groups who do not abide by these Geneva Convention assumptions. Recent years have witnessed asymmetric warfare in the different capacities of the contending parties. The weaker party attempts to blur the distinction between its forces and the civilian population. This scenario has become familiar in the fighting in Iraq and Afghanistan, as well as in the Israeli-Palestinian conflict. Democratic countries, especially Israel, are handicapped in their response to insurgents. Civilians aid the fighters by storing weapons, producing propaganda, provide food and shelter, and may even agree to be civilian shields.[242]

A major problem therefore, is how to apply the standard of proportionality to respond to terrorists who deliberately merge with and use civilians in their activity. Their members do not wear military uniforms and are not technically soldiers, often operate in and make use of civilian areas, attack sporadically and unexpectedly, try to hit civilian areas of the other side, and if captured do not qualify as prisoners of war.[243] Even more, Hamas in Gaza has deliberately attempted in inhumane fashion to provoke Israel into firing on areas where civilians are located to gain an advantage in public relations. The Israeli Supreme Court has been faced with this problem of deciding about terrorists who are not official combatants according to Geneva 4. In two cases, the Court regarded terrorists as unlawful combatants according to international law. (HCJ 769/02 The Public Committee against Torture in Israel v. The Government of Israel, December 13, 2006, and Cr. App. 6659/06 A v. The State of Israel, June 11, 2008). In upholding the policy of "targeted killing" of terrorists operating against Israel outside its territory, the Court held that the terrorists were civilians engaged in hostilities against the state.[244] The Court followed Article 51 (3) of the 1977 Additional Protocol to the Geneva Convention, stating that "civilians shall enjoy the protection afforded by this section, unless and for such time as they take a direct part in hostilities."

The Court observed that the fight against terror is subject to the rule of law and that Israel must act according to the rules of international law. Faced with this problem of the military response to terrorism, the Court has on occasions ruled against the army and the government. It agreed to exercise legal oversight over military authorities in the West Bank, it banned the use of human shields by the military to protect Israeli soldiers, it stopped the IDF from forcing a neighbor of a suspected terrorist to cooperate, it ruled against certain parts of the security fence that Israel was building, and took a qualified position on "targeted killings," the death of those planning or committing terrorists attacks in Israel.[245] Aharon Barak, president of the Court, concluded that in a democracy such as Israel, not all means were permitted, including the methods used by her enemies. (HCJ 5100/94 The Public Committee against Torture in Israel v. The State of Israel, 53(4) PD 817, 845).

TERRORISM

Terrorism can be defined as the deliberate and systematic murdering, injuring, and frightening of people to achieve political ends. Individuals, groups, and states through the years have all been complicit in this activity. In recent years this activity has been directed against the Western social and political order, and democratic systems and institutions. Groups and states have supplied terrorists with arms, financial assistance, training, logistical support, and safe havens. Three canards are here relevant for examination. One canard, attempting to defend terrorists, is to equate them with guerillas. This is a misnomer since "guerrillas," a term first used in Spain in 1810, are fighters who war on regular military forces, not on civilians. Terrorists attack defenseless and innocent civilians and avoid facing soldiers, if possible.

By their actions they blur any distinction between combatants and civilians. A second canard is to identify a terrorist as someone else's "freedom fighter." Again, this is faulty linguistic equivalence. Freedom fighters oppose oppressive governments; terrorists deliberately murder innocent people, are allies of repressive regimes, and embody anti-democratic and often inhumane attitudes towards their own people. A third canard is that national liberation movements are entitled to use violence and terrorism as part of that movement. The argument is faulty because terrorism is a deliberate choice, not necessitated as a response to perceived grievances or required to advance the cause of liberation.

Political terrorism in the Arab world is not new; it goes back to the assassinations of the Caliph 'Umar in 644, Uthman in 656, and Ali, the fourth caliph in 661, and to the Assassins, a twelfth-century group.[246] Since the establishment of the State of Israel, Palestinian and Islamic groups, with some assistance from outside states and groups, have conducted terrorist activities against it and against Jews in other countries. All of the groups, including the most well-known, such as the Popular Front for the Liberation of Palestine-General Command led by Ahmad Jibril, the Revolutionary Command of Sabri al-Banna, the Popular Front led by George Habash, the Palestinian Islamic Jihad, the Algerian Groupe Islamique Armée, the World Islamic Front against the Jews and the Crusaders led by Osama bin Ladin, the Army of Muhammad, the Muslim Brotherhood, Hezbollah and Hamas, have engaged in attacks on Jewish schools, synagogues, shops, banks, and restaurants in different countries.

Incitement against Israel has come into two forms: continuing acts of terrorist violence, and anti-Israel and antisemitic indoctrination. An increasingly troubling feature of the terrorist violence is not only the continuing attacks themselves, but also the glorification of terrorism and its perpetrators, who are seen as role models for Palestinian and Arab youth, thus reinforcing hatred towards Israel. That hatred has been reinforced by the Palestinian educational system, literature, songs, theater, and cinema, in youth movements, schools and universities, in all of which anti-Israeli indoctrination sometimes degenerates into antisemitism.[247] Antisemitism has been given intellectual legitimacy. A popular song in East Jerusalem and in Arab capitals was "I hate Israel." The threat to Israeli and Jewish persons and property, repeated in endless Arab text-books, media, mosque sermons, political rhetoric, and most recently the electronic media, has caused Israel to impose controls. That threat became more overt after Hamas, which is committed to the destruction of the State of Israel and the "liberation" of cities such as Haifa, Beersheba, and Acre, was the virtual winner in the Palestinian election in January 2006, and since 2007 has controlled Gaza. Hamas appears to have forgotten that Beersheba, over 4,000 years old, was the city of Abraham, the founding place for three of the world's great religions.

All these can be considered acts of bad faith. The 1995 Israeli-Palestinian Agreement stipulated that the two sides shall abstain from incitement, including hostile propaganda, against each other, and shall take legal measures to prevent such incitement by any organizations, groups, or individuals within their jurisdiction. They agreed to refrain from the introduction of any motifs that could adversely affect the process of reconciliation. Further, by the Wye River Memorandum of October 23, 1998, the Palestinians agreed to issue a decree prohibiting all forms of incitement to violence or terror, and to establish mechanisms for acting systematically against all expressions or threats of violence or terror. However, this is an agreement more honored in the breach than in the observance. No peace process is likely to succeed while the policy of incitement and indoctrination, of hatred and mistrust, continues.

An almost equally troubling problem for Israel is that Israeli Arabs may not welcome their Israeli citizenship, and may see Arab identity as a higher priority. It is true that travel to and from the West Bank has been controlled to some degree, that freedom of movement has been restricted, including on main roads, and that a modified permit system was introduced. It is equally true that the fence and physical obstacles have been built to prevent infiltration and unlawful entry, and to forestall terrorist attacks. Clearly, all this is based on the need for security for a country constantly being attacked by Palestinians, some of them based in neighboring Arab countries. Apart from Egypt and Jordan, those countries, as well as the Palestinian leadership, have refused to accept in any formal manner Israel's existence and legitimacy. Even after the peace treaties, relations have been cool between Israel and those two countries, with little agreement on joint projects such as water reclamation, energy, and tourism.

For nearly a century it has been abundantly clear to all but the most credulous that Palestinian Arab spokespeople have been unwilling to recognize Israel's right to exist as the national home of the Jewish people and reject a Jewish state of any size in the area, as they publicly did in 1937, 1947, and 1978. Indeed, Palestinian representatives only first appeared to accept Israel's existence, with recognition of "mutual legitimate and political rights," in September 1993 by the Oslo Accords, which was intended to be a framework for future discussions of outstanding problems between the two sides, and even that acceptance seems indeterminate. The hope was that the opportunity had arrived for a negotiated resolution of the conflict. Both sides agreed in 1995 that "neither side shall initiate or take any step that will change the status of the West Bank and the Gaza Strip pending the outcome of the permanent status negotiations."

For Israel, the consequences after Oslo have been disappointing, in spite of its attempts at negotiations, general acceptance of the idea of the establishment of a Palestinian state, unilateral withdrawals, possible compromises on Jerusalem, and even proposals for Muslim control over Islamic holy sites in Jerusalem. Ceding territory did not stop violence against Israel. Nor has it lead to Arab public recognition of the legitimacy of the State of Israel, or acknowledgment of the historical connection with the land, or the withdrawal of Palestinian and Arab maps on which the name of the State of Israel does not appear. On the contrary, Yasser Arafat on a number of occasions compared the Oslo Accords with the peace Treaty of Hudaibiya, which was signed by the Prophet Muhammad in 628 with the infidels, the people of Mecca, and which was ended two years later. Both were a device to buy time in the struggle against the enemy.[248] Arafat put the symbolism into practice: instead of compromise, the ostensible Oslo peace process was followed by suicide bombings against Israeli civilians, the *intifada*, the coup by Hamas in Gaza, and rocket attacks against the Israeli south.

The Israeli withdrawal from territory and its political proposals for compromise did not lead to rhetorical or political moderation by Palestinian groups, either by the Hamas movement or by the more moderate PLO one. The National Charter of the PLO, created in May 1964, still defines Israel as "the Zionist entity" and as "racial, colonial, and aggressive in ideology, goals, organization and method." (Article 7). It also calls for "the complete liberation of Palestine, and eradication of Zionist economic, political, military and cultural existence." (Article 12). Other articles in the constitution speak of the continuing struggle until the Zionist state is demolished and Palestine is completely liberated. Moreover, the PLO Charter is a threat, perhaps ambiguous, to two countries, since its Article 2 states "Palestine, with the boundaries it had during the British Mandate is an indivisible territorial unit." It thus may pose a challenge to Jordan as well as to Israel.

The more Islamic oriented Hamas Charter of 1988 states in Article 7, that Hamas is one of the links in the chain of jihad in the confrontation with the Zionist invasion, which must be obliterated. It says that Hamas links up with those who fought the Holy War in 1936, 1948, and 1968, and thereafter. It dismisses the "so-called peaceful solutions and the international conferences to resolve the Palestinian problem," which it regards as contrary to the beliefs of the Islamic Resistance Movement. The Charter calls on all Arab countries, Islamic peoples and associations everywhere to act on behalf of Islam, to face the "despicable Nazi-Tartar invasion" and make possible the next round with the Jews, the merchants of war. It makes extreme statements, some of which can be characterized as astonishing, if not asinine, such as that Zionist scheming has no end and covets expansion from the Nile to the Euphrates. That scheming is said to have been laid out in the *Protocols of the Elders of Zion*. To disguise this, the cunning Zionist organizations take on all sorts of names and shapes, such as the Freemasons, Rotary Clubs, and gangs of spies; Muslims must confront them. Most importantly, jihad for the liberation of Palestine is a duty binding on all Muslims.

It is a disconcerting experience, when Israel is accused of various forms of discrimination, to discern the popularity in Arab countries of animosity displayed in many ways towards Jews in general, and the

State of Israel in particular. One particularly disturbing example is the continuing use and reiteration in those countries of the antisemitic forgery and hoax, the discredited *Protocols of the Elders of Zion,* assembled from an essay of 1864, *A Dialogue in Hell,* written by a French lawyer, Maurice Joly, in which he imagined a fictional discussion between Machiavelli and Montesquieu, in intent a satirical criticism of Napoleon III. The *Protocols,* which was originally written in French by the Parisian circles of the Russian Secret Police, was published in a newspaper in St. Petersburg in installments in August and September 1903, for Russian internal political reasons. The editor-in-chief of the newspaper, Paul Krushevan, was also partly responsible for organizing the pogrom in Kishinev, on Easter Sunday in 1903. The fiction of the *Protocols* became even more imaginary in 1917, with the charge that it was a plan presented to Herzl at the first Zionist Congress in Basel in 1897. It is telling that more editions of translations of the forgery have been published in Arabic than in any other language. The racist *Protocols* have become a significant part of Arab antisemitic propaganda, in publications, television broadcasts and school text books in Middle Eastern countries. In the widest popular form, the *Protocols* was featured in a forty-one part television series in Egypt in 2002.

Perhaps most acutely troubling for Israel is Article 32 in the *Hamas Charter* that states, "The Zionist plan is limitless…Their plan is embodied in the "Protocols of the Elders of Zion," and their present conduct is the best proof of what we are saying." Article 20 speaks of "The Nazism of the Jews (that) does not skip women and children, it scares everyone." For Hamas, the power of Jews appears unlimited; they control and are responsible for the world media, news agencies, publishing houses, broadcasting stations (article 22). No war broke out without Jewish fingerprints on it. Jews were behind many events: the French Revolution, the Communist Revolution, World War I, which was waged to destroy the Islamic Caliphate (the Ottoman Empire), World War II, from which Jews benefited immensely from trading in war materials, the establishment of the United Nations, in order to rule through their intermediaries, and the creation of the State of Israel. Antisemitism and hatred of Jews, the motif common to Nazis and Arab extremists, was linked with refusal to accept the Jewish state and with

Holocaust denial. People who spout that hatred and denial in the post World War II world have been termed "Assassins of Memory" by the French historian Pierre Vidal-Naquet. Some of them allege that Zionists exaggerated the number of Jewish victims of the Holocaust, and even that some Zionists cooperated with the Nazis. This latter argument is found in the book *The Other Face: The Secret Connection between the Nazis and the Zionist Movement,* written by Mahmoud Abbas, co-founder of Fatah and president of the Palestinian Authority; it was based on his doctoral dissertation of 1982, at the Moscow Institute of Oriental Studies.

POLITICAL REALITY

Even well meaning, or "even handed," intervention by outside powers, such as the United States and Britain, to forward a "peace process" by suggesting territorial and other changes, sometimes misunderstood the reality of the attitudes of the two parties. Some examples in the 1950s illustrate these failed attempts. The effort of Eric Johnston, the US businessman sent by President Eisenhower to arrange an agreement on the use of water from the Jordan River, failed because the Arabs rejected his proposals.[249] The secretive Project Alpha, first proposed by the US and Britain in October 1954 and then elaborated in different ways in 1955, notably in the speeches by Prime Minister Anthony Eden at the Guildhall in November 1955 and by John Foster Dulles, US Secretary of State, to link Egypt and Jordan by giving them two areas in the Negev to create a land bridge which would not pass through non-Arab territory, failed.[250]

The reality was that Arab leaders continued to give financial aid for Palestinian resistance to the State of Israel and continually opposed the idea of the partition of western Palestine since it was first officially proposed in 1937 by the British Royal Commission headed by Lord Peel. Arab opposition to this and to a compromise settlement continued throughout the twentieth century, before and after the establishment of Israel, as Arab leaders devised obstacles to block the peace process until the signing of treaties between Israel and Egypt and Jordan.

In 2000, Yasser Arafat, the PLO leader, rejected the Israeli offer of a Palestinian state which would have been located in Gaza and in almost the whole, about ninety-five per cent, of the West Bank. Instead, he inaugurated an *intifada*, (literally "shaking off") violence against Israeli civilian facilities. An agreement in 2003, by which the Palestinians were to engage in final status negotiations, was never fulfilled.

Israeli disengagement from Lebanon and Gaza, with its implicit inference of "territory for peace," has not led to desired results. The unilateral withdrawal from Lebanon in 2000 led to the seizure and control of land there by Hezbollah and the launching of rocket attacks against Israeli civilians, not to a peace agreement. Parenthetically, the Israeli withdrawal took place before UN Security Council Resolution 1559 of September 2004, which called for withdrawal of all foreign troops from Lebanon; Syrian troops which have been there for over thirty years, however still remain in place. The presence of those Syrian troops has been regarded by Israel in two ways: they constitute a constant threat, but they have also restrained Palestinian forces in Lebanon from time to time.

In the dysfunctional Lebanese system Hezbollah, the followers or soldiers of God, the Shi'a militia organization formed in 1982 and announced publicly in an Open Letter in February 1985, has become a powerful force in the country. In addition to its religious fervor, its pronounced aim was to drive all Israeli forces out of Lebanon and conduct guerilla warfare against Israel; the ultimate aim was "Israel's final obliteration from existence." It is calculated that in 2011, Hezbollah possesses about 50,000 rockets, including Zelzal II missiles which it obtained from Syria and Iran and which have a range of 200 km. It has graduated from being a group once responsible for kidnappings, suicide bombings and coordinating terrorist attacks, as in September 1984 when it was associated with the bombing of the United States Embassy and marine barracks in Beirut which killed nearly 300 people, the skyjacking of an American airliner in June 1985, the bombing of the US and French embassies in Kuwait in December 1985, the kidnapping of Western hostages in Lebanon between 1984 and 1991, the attacks on the Jewish Community Center and on the Israeli embassy in Buenos Aires in 1994, the bombing of the Khobar Towers in Saudi Arabia in

1995, to being both an important military presence, conducting military campaigns against the Israel Defense Forces, firing Katyusha rockets into Israeli towns, and fighting a war against Israel in July and August 2006, and also a key political actor in Lebanese affairs.

Among those affairs is the economic activity of Hezbollah, which includes its production and distribution of narcotics, a trade that helps finance the war against Israel and the Western world. By its control over the Bekaa valley, it has converted much of the once arable land there to producing cannabis and poppies, from which marijuana and heroin are derived. The drugs are smuggled to the rest of the world. Hezbollah has also been involved in the tri-border area of Argentina, Brazil, and Paraguay, where it has engaged in joint operations with the narcotic drug lords of the region.[251]

Chapter 24

A Jewish State

D efining a "nation" with accuracy has always been a challenging task. Ernst Renan wrote of two necessary conditions: possession in common of a rich heritage of memories; and agreement and desire of people to live together. In his most famous sentence, Renan wrote that "the existence of a nation is a daily plebiscite." (*Qu'est-ce qu'une nation*) John Stuart Mill, in his *Representative Government*, defined a nationality as consisting of people united by common sympathies which do not exist between them, and others and who have a desire to govern themselves. One recent example of this complex issue of nationality and self-determination concerned Kosovo, whose population is mainly ethnic Albanian and which unilaterally declared its independence from Serbia and its statehood in February 2008. The International Court of Justice in July 2010, in a non-binding advisory opinion, decided that Kosovo's declaration of independence was legal and did not violate international law. Similar problems remain in northern Cyprus, Somaliland (separating from Somalia), Nagorno-Karabakh and South Ossetia (separating from Georgia), Abkhazia (separating from Azerbaijan), and Transnistria (separating from Moldova).

John Stuart Mill suggested that in general, it was "a necessary condition of free institutions that the boundaries of governments should coincide in the main with those of nationalities."[252] Following the argument of Mill, all these peoples mentioned above assert their distinctive nationalities, identity, culture, and heritage, and thus their right to self-determination. The intensity of the assertions by these peoples, and by Israel, for separate national institutions refutes the argument made by some that in the present age of globalization, universal cultural expressions, and international legal organizations, the creation of individual states, or one particular one, Israel, can be considered anachronistic.[253] In the contemporary era, a more relevant argument is that the nation-state is "peculiarly well adapted to the modern need for civic responsibility and active and effective political participation."[254] If the creation of the European Union was meant to indicate the decline of the importance of the nation-state and of nationalistic sentiments, it did not invalidate the desire of peoples in the world for self-determination. The problem facing Israel is the denial by its opponents of the right of the Jewish people to self-determination, and even denial that Jews constitute a people, as well as the calls for the destruction of the Jewish state. No such problem posed by the international community confronts the fourteen separate states created in areas occupied by the Soviet Union after its downfall.

The argument made in the Declaration of the State of Israel about *Eretz-Israel* being "the birthplace of the Jewish people" stems from Jewish experience with its common historical memories enshrined ritual and recital, common descent, beliefs, values, religious experience, ways of life, language, and association with a particular territory.[255] The political and national units are congruent.[256] Israel illustrates the coincidence of a nation and the territory of a state, of an organic people with national sovereignty. Chains of memory, myth and symbol are linked with the enduring Jewish community, the *ethnie* (the French equivalent of the Greek *ethnos*).[257] The Jewish people, while in exile, had kept faith with their land in all centers of their dispersion.

One unresolved problem facing Israel is the imprecise contours of *Eretz Israel,* the land which according to the Bible, was promised by God to the descendants of Abraham, Jacob, and the Israelites. The Biblical definitions do not automatically correspond to present day Israel, or even to the Israeli kingdoms of the past. David Ben-Gurion, aware of the problem, stated that the creation of Israel by no means derogated from the scope of historic *Eretz Israel.* Other Zionists, Berl Katznelson, Joseph Brenner, and A. D. Gordon, explained the bond between the Jewish people and the land of Israel rested less on the Bible, than on the ability of the people to cultivate the land.[258] Israel would be a nation "like all other nations." A different point of view, by Ahad Ha'am (Asher Ginsberg), based on the uniqueness of the Jewish people, held that the "chosen people" would exemplify moral excellence in the land of Israel. He believed that the Jewish prophets had taught respect for spiritual, rather than for material power, and in spiritual power "we are not inferior to other nations and we have no reason to efface ourselves."[259] This point of view led some to the conclusion that a Jewish State would lead to a "new Jewish person," different from the stereotype of the weak, unmanly, powerless Jew, or of the neurotic Jew more recently made popular by Woody Allen, in the Diaspora. The Jewish physical character would change.

Some saw the creation of such a sovereign State in *Eretz Israel* as the "negation of the Diaspora." It would break the sequence of Jewish history, detach the state from the metaphor of the *shetl* for the Jewish condition in exile, and would end the use of Yiddish.[260] While religion has a place in Israeli public life, the Declaration did not and still does not mean that religious institutions have any official function. There is no one official state religion; fourteen religious denominations are officially recognized by the state. This contrasts sharply with the provisions in Arab constitutions that "Islam is the religion of the state." However one defines Israel, as a Jewish state it is not a theocracy, because "it is not religion that orders the lives of its citizens but the law." (Supreme Court Decision 72/62, Oswald Rufeisen v. Minister of the Interior(1962) 15 P.D. 2428). The state does not impose any specific religious concept of Jewish identity on its citizens.[261] The "Jewish" state refers to national identity and to Jewish values and culture, rather than to religion.

About those values, compromise has been inevitable. Orthodox Jews in Israel accept the reality that laws are made by parliament, not by rabbis, though the latter do make rules over matters of personal status of marriage and divorce, and run separate religious schools. The secular Prime Minister Ben-Gurion compromised on this issue by agreeing that state institutions would observe religious dietary laws. However, unlike the case in some other religions, no religious hierarchy provides authoritative interpretations of Jewish faith. There is no strictly religious or Halachic definition of who is a Jew. Much of the original Zionist writings stem from the heritage of Haskalah, the Jewish Enlightenment after the French Revolution, but the influence of the Jewish religion remained. Neither the secular nor the religious element is wholly dominant. Deep divisions exist within Israeli society over the extent of Jewish religious law in society; issues such as observance of the Sabbath, kosher or non-kosher food, dietary laws on public occasions, the right to civil marriage, and different views over conversion to Judaism.

The issue that has caused most tension regarding the ultra-Orthodox (haredim), about ten per cent and increasing in proportion to the whole Jewish population, is the exemption of this most theologically conservative group, from conscription into the military.[262] The issue results from the compromise made by Ben-Gurion in 1948, when he excused about 400 yeshiva students from serving in the army in order to study the Torah, and provided state finances for their yeshiva study. Since then, thousands of yeshiva students, now numbering about 60,000, have been given draft exemptions; they are enrolled in full time study, and many do not work. However, some haredim have served in a combat battalion set up in the late 1990s, and in Shahar, a special army program for training in the military.

The Declaration of Establishment does not suggest that a Jewish state and a democratic one with equal rights for all are incompatible, though the balance between complete equality and majority decision making is not always easy to reach. Nor did it mean any discrimination against or between citizens in the state; non-Jews could obtain citizenship by birth, residence, naturalization, or by marrying an Israeli citizen. Arabs, Muslim and Christian, can practice the religion of their choice and have the same kind of equal rights as Jewish citizens, except that Israeli Arabs have received exemption from the mandatory military service required for almost all other citizens of Israel.

Indeed, the Declaration of Establishment states that "the State of Israel...will ensure complete equality of social and political rights to all its inhabitants, irrespective of religion, race, or sex." On this last issue a large difference exists between the practice in Israel and Arab countries. Israeli laws of 1988 and 1992 prohibit discrimination against homosexuals, who receive civil rights protection and can openly serve in the military, and the laws provide for same sex partners to receive benefits in both the public and private sectors. Israel has annual gay-pride parades in both Tel Aviv and Jerusalem. In contrast, in some Arab countries homosexuality is outlawed and sodomy is a capital crime. In Kuwait, Lebanon, Oman, Qatar and Syria, homosexual conduct may be punished by imprisonment or by flogging. In Iran, Saudi Arabia, and Yemen, the penalty may be death.

The Declaration of Establishment proclaims freedom of religion and conscience. It also appealed to the Arab inhabitants of the State "to preserve peace and partnership in the building of the State on the basis of full and equal citizenship and due representation in all its provisional and permanent institutions." What the Declaration does mean, as was made statutory in the Law of Return of 1950, which was to be amended in 1954 and 1970, was that Jews and their spouses had the right to settle in Israel and would be regarded as having nationality. In explaining the Law of Return, Ben-Gurion in 1950 said that "no other law better expresses the uniqueness of the State of Israel. This law fuses history, culture and religion; past, present, and future; aspirations, dreams and realities." By this law every Jew has the right to enter Israel as an *oleh*, (immigrant) and to become an Israeli national. By the Nationality Law of 1952, anyone having the certificate of an *oleh* would automatically become a citizen if that person desired it. Jewish nationality is thus extra-territorial.

The Law of Return was expanded in 1970 to include children, grandchildren and spouses of a Jew, and they too, would be eligible for a certificate as an *oleh,* provided they did not practice a religion other than Judaism. This law defined a "Jew" as someone born to a Jewish mother or who converted and had no other religion. The Israeli High Court has been confronted by a number of cases in which the Israeli and Jewish mixture of religious and national factors has to be considered. One, mentioned above, was the case in 1962 of Oswald Rufeisen, a Jew who had become a Carmelite monk, but who declared he was still connected to the Jewish people. His request for Israeli citizenship was rejected. A more recent case in 2010 involved a woman born in Israel in 1950, who had married a Catholic in Jaffa and emigrated with her husband to Germany, and had declared she had been baptized in the Christian faith. The decision of the High Court illustrated the complex factors relevant to Israeli and Jewish identity. It held that the woman could not regain her Israeli citizenship under the Law of Return, but that she could regain citizenship if she could prove her commitment to the Jewish people. It was left unclear how the "commitment" could be manifested.

Already the view of Israel as a Jewish state had been proclaimed in international documents. The UN Special Committee on Palestine report of September 3, 1947, which recommended partition of Palestine into two states, held (para 127) that "the issues of the Jewish State and unrestricted immigration are inextricably interwoven." The report recognized that such a state was urgently needed to assure a refuge for Jewish immigrants who wanted to come from the displaced persons camps and other places at the time in Europe. Moreover, the report (para 128), in explaining the Jewish case and the right of Jews to "return" to Palestine, said, "Aside from contentions based on biblical and historical sources as to this right, the Jewish case also rests on the Balfour Declaration of November 2, 1917, and on the Mandate for Palestine which incorporated the Declaration in its preamble and recognized the historic connection of the Jewish people with Palestine and the grounds for reconstituting the Jewish National Home there." Interestingly, one of the British individuals who collaborated in the negotiations leading to the brief, sixty-seven words long, Balfour Declaration was Sir Mark Sykes, best known as the joint author of the Sykes-Picot Agreement of May 16, 1916 (between Sykes, assistant secretary of the British War Cabinet and François Georges-Picot of the French Foreign Office), which defined the anticipated future British and French spheres of influence in the Middle East and would have restricted Zionist ambitions.

The reasons for the Balfour Declaration, a letter of November 2, 1917 to Lord Rothschild from Arthur Balfour, British foreign minister, have been much debated. If the primary reason was genuine sympathy and admiration felt by Christian Zionists and by many, if not all, British leading political figures, including Prime Minister David Lloyd George, for Zionist aspirations, at the same time personal, practical and tactical concerns were also evident. The personal factor was the possible gratitude to Chaim Weizmann, the Russian born Zionist resident in Britain since 1906, and a man close to British leaders and newspaper editors, who as a research chemist had devised a fermentation method for manufacturing acetone useful for explosives, essential for the British military at a moment when Germany had the largest access to calcium acetate. A tactical concern was British interest in safeguarding the Suez Canal and thus the route to India, which would be facilitated by a Jewish presence in the eastern Mediterranean. A Jewish home was viewed as a possible outpost of British influence in the area. More important, resulting from the belief in the myth of the international importance of the power and unity of world Jewry, a myth that Weizmann to some extent encouraged, was the conviction that Jews in the United States and especially in Eastern Europe and Russia in 1917, would influence their countries to support the Allies, Britain and France. The British hoped that Russia would remain in the war, rather than be neutral or support Germany. Balfour himself thought that "from a purely diplomatic and political point of view it was desirable that some declaration favorable to the aspirations of the Jewish nationalists should now be made."[263] Among those who believed that world Jewry would be helpful to Britain in the war, was a small, but influential group of British Catholics, which included Hugh James O'Brierne, a diplomat, and Sir Mark Sykes.

The Balfour Declaration was the outcome of prolonged discussion within the British cabinet, and between it and Zionist leaders; in addition President Wilson was among those consulted. The Declaration, now regarded as an essential factor legitimizing the creation of the State of Israel, read that the British Government "viewed with favor the establishment in Palestine of a national home for the Jewish people." As indicated above, the Declaration also said "it being clearly understood that nothing shall be done which may prejudice the civil and religious rights of existing non-Jewish communities in Palestine." Both of these statements were significant in three ways, for further political deliberations. The letter spoke of "a national home" rather than a "state." It recognized the existence of a "Jewish people." And it spoke of "civil and religious" rights of non-Jews, referring to Palestinian

Arabs, not to national or political rights. Lord Rothschild, the recipient of the letter that was the Declaration, understood the momentous statement. In a speech in London on December 2, 1917, he thanked the Government for the Declaration "which marked an epoch; for the first time since the dispersion, the Jewish people have received their proper status by the declaration of one of the great powers."

Paradoxically it was Edwin Montagu, a Jewish member of the British Cabinet, who was a main opponent of the Balfour Declaration, arguing that Jews were not a nation and therefore had no claim to a national homeland. However, both France and Italy endorsed the Declaration in 1918, and it was further endorsed in 1919 by two statements. One was in the Agreement, Article III, of January 3, 1919, reached in London between Emir Feisal and Chaim Weizmann. Feisal, in the letter of March 3, 1919, already mentioned, to Felix Frankfurter wrote that, "we Arabs, especially the educated among us, look with the deepest sympathy on the Zionist movement." The second was by President Wilson who wrote in 1919 that, "I am persuaded that the Allied Nations, with the fullest concurrence of our own government and people, are agreed that in Palestine shall be laid the foundations of a Jewish Commonwealth." He spoke of the historical claims of the Jewish people in regard to Palestine.

The Balfour Declaration, however, was not the only statement about the geographical area. In the context of World War I, the war against Germany and the Turks, and the rivalry with France, Britain was anxious to get aid from both Jews and Arabs. Other statements were made, some of them vague, and contradictory promises given to the Arabs, resulting from the complicated political maneuvering and the machinations of Britain and France during World War I to get Arabs to revolt against their rulers, the Ottoman Empire, which had sided with Germany. That decision of the Ottomans led both to their defeat and the ending of the Empire, and to the creation of new states in the area and accompanying geo-political problems. In return for their help provided in the war against Turkey, the Arab leaders wanted the creation of post-war Arab states. Accordingly, an agreement, the Sykes-Picot Agreement of May 1916, had been secretly negotiated by the two countries for the post-war division of the Ottoman possessions. This understanding called for the whole Fertile Crescent to be divided into two zones, one under British or French rule, and the other under Arab states. Palestine was to be part of the British sphere of influence.

Another attempt to assuage Arabs was the exchange of letters in July 1915 between the Hussein ibn Ali, Sheriff of Mecca, and Sir Henry McMahon, British High Commissioner of Egypt. That vague exchange and the supposed promises have been subjected to various interpretations. The crucial statement in the correspondence about the Ottoman area was that "the districts of Messina and Alexandretta and portions of Syria lying to the west of the districts of Damascus, Hama, Homs, and Aleppo cannot be said to be purely Arab and should be excluded from the proposed limits and boundaries." No exact maps were ever published illustrating the boundary description. McMahon himself, in a letter to *The Times* of London on July 23, 1937, explained his position "definitely and emphatically." He wrote that he had not intended to give any pledge to "King Hussein to include Palestine in the area in which Arab independence was promised," and that he had every reason to believe at the time that the fact that the "portion of Syria now known as Palestine" was not included in the pledge was well understood by King Hussein.

Hussein was ambitious and wanted a large future Arab kingdom, which included the area of Palestine, but no final agreement was reached. After General Sir Edmund Allenby, leader of the British army captured Jerusalem on December 9, 1917, and then the whole of the Levant, the British government sent a message to Hussein on January 4, 1918, that the Balfour Declaration, which in contrast to the McMahon-Hussein correspondence was clear, did not conflict with earlier promises made to the Arabs. Part of the statement read that the government was "determined that insofar as is compatible with the freedom of the existing population, both economic and political, no obstacle should be put in the way of the realization of this ideal (a return of Jews to Palestine)." A reasonable conclusion about British policy at the time, and after, is that it emanated from muddle and confusion rather than from deliberate deception. In the Mandate period, the tension between the Colonial Office, responsible for administering Palestine and fulfilling the terms of the Balfour Declaration, and the Foreign Office, unwilling to alienate Arabs, was notorious.

The League of Nations Mandate, which was allotted to Britain, incorporated the Balfour Declaration in its preamble and recognized the "historic connection of the Jewish people with Palestine and the grounds for reconstituting the Jewish National Home there." In a sense, this was recognition of Jewish pre-existing rights in Palestine. Ben-Gurion, in his presentation to the 1937 British Peel Commission had made this point, "I say on behalf of the Jews that the Bible is our Mandate, the Bible which was written by us, in our own language, in Hebrew, in this very country. That is our Mandate. It was only recognition of this right which was expressed in the Balfour Declaration." The assertion was reiterated in the Israeli Declaration of Independence which spoke of "our natural and historic right" in establishing "a Jewish State in *Eretz-Israel.*" The Declaration also stated that the "recognition by the United Nations (on November 29, 1947) of the right of the Jewish people to establish their State is irrevocable." It continued by stating that "This right is the natural right of the Jewish people to be masters of their own fate, like other nations, in their own sovereign state." The brief Declaration referred to the experience of the Jewish people; exile, return to the ancient homeland, Herzl's role, the importance of the Balfour Declaration, the Holocaust, and Jewish homelessness. It mentioned the term "Jewish state" five times.

The case for the right of the Jewish people to have a sovereign state of its own was enunciated by Supreme Court Justice Moshe Landau, who was the presiding judge at the trial, when he defended Israel's right to prosecute Adolf Eichmann in Israel in 1961. After the guilty verdict Eichmann was executed on May 31, 1962; this has been the only judicial execution ever carried out in Israel. Some people held that Israel did not have the legal right to capture and to try him for crimes committed before the state was established. Arguing that the connection between the Jewish people and the State of Israel was an integral part of the law of nations, Landau justified the Israeli actions and declared that the State of Israel is the sovereign state of the Jewish people. Israel had acted on behalf of Jews who had been murdered. Was the sovereign state a "Jewish state?" Chief Justice Aharon Barak held that "the content of the phrase 'Jewish state' will be determined by the level of abstraction which shall be given it…The values of the state of Israel as a Jewish state are those universal values common to members of a democratic society." The difficulty in dealing with the issue was shown by the decision regarding a Knesset law of 1985. This forbade political parties opposed to the recognition of Israel as a Jewish state, from participating in national elections. However, in 1996 representatives in the Knesset of Arab parties advocating that Israel become a non-Jewish "state of its citizens" were allowed to take their seats.

Chapter 25

A Jewish and Democratic State

The nature of society and politics in Israel has, for "post-Zionists" in Israel and some individuals in the international community, raised the question of possible incompatibility between a state which can be considered Jewish and one that is democratic. This would be problematic if Israel had an official state religion, and Orthodox religion was the only criterion to be considered, but this is not the case and the state's Jewishness is also based on national and cultural factors. A number of problems then arise. Is Zionist particularism compatible with concepts of universal justice? Is the State of Israel intended to be a state for the whole Jewish population of the world, a state "which would open the gates of the homeland to every Jew?" Does a "Jewish" state inevitably entail unequal treatment for the Arab minority? Herzl was aware of the issue from the beginning. In thinking about a future state he said that, "Zionism includes not only the yearning for a plot of Promised Land legally acquired for our weary people, but also the yearning for ethical and spiritual fulfillment." His concern was not simply a new social system, but also a righteous one. That concern was to inspire the early Zionists entering Palestine, who were anxious to create a system based on political self-determination, an internationally acknowledged moral principle.

The problem of nation building absorbed the energies of Jews who immigrated into Palestine. Ben-Gurion had been disappointed that the Balfour Declaration had not mentioned the word "state," but nevertheless praised the British magnificent gesture. However, he wrote that "only the Jewish people can transform this right into tangible fact: only they, with body and soul, with their strength and capital, must build their national home, and bring about their national redemption." The immigrants created the essential infrastructure of a state before it was established; municipal councils, central executive and elected parliamentary bodies, a multi-party system, institutional creativity, kibbutzim, a strong trade union, the Histadrut, organization for the control of schools, an elected Chief Rabbinate and Rabbinical Council, a banking system, a central electricity grid, and the KKL in 1901 to buy land. David Ben-Gurion was the first General Secretary of the Histadrut. The immigrants were aided by the Women's International Zionist Organization (WIZO), founded in 1920, and which helped the status of women in Palestine by establishing children's clinics, neighborhood based medical care, day care centers, and training women for jobs. Its first president, Rebecca Sieff, was a suffragette in Britain. The economy had been grounded on the use of Jewish labor, the outcome of the ideology of the Zionist Left. In the early years of the Yishuv and of Israel, the kibbutz represented a culturally significant and elite group, pioneers living in their agricultural setting and also participating in traditional aristocratic occupations: politics, diplomacy, and war. Over sixty years however, social and economic changes in Israel have included the decline both in the ideal of the kibbutz, and in their number, especially the collective kibbutzim, where all received equal compensation. Their members have in recent years played a less prominent role than earlier in governmental and parliamentary affairs.

Throughout history, Hebrew had been the language of the rabbinical culture, but not the vernacular of most Jews. With Hebrew in Palestine as the exclusive language, used in prose and poetry, the Zionists established cultural, academic and scientific institutions and professions, an animated press and literature, the Herzlia Gymnasium, Hebrew kindergarten in Jerusalem, the Hebrew University on Mount Scopus in 1925, the Technion in 1924, and Bezalel art group in 1906.[264]

The Israeli Declaration of Independence stated that "The Constitution which shall be adopted by the Elected Constituent Assembly no later than October 1, 1948." But Israel does not have a written constitution, largely because of an absence of a national consensus on identity and fundamental values of the society, differences between the religious and secular views of the state, and the existence of a considerable number of cultural and ideological sub groups.[265] Instead, it has a number of Basic Laws, which amounted to eleven by 2010, which the Court has, on occasion, subjected to its own interpretation, especially when Aharon Barak was chief justice of the Court. The initial decision in 1950 to avoid enacting a formal constitution helped prevent a direct clash over the Jewish identity of the state.[266] Controversial constitutional decisions have been deferred. Instead, a gradual, incremental approach, one of pragmatic politics, has been used to deal with fundamental issues.

Two Basic Laws of 1992, dealing with the preservation of human dignity and liberty, and with freedom of occupation, define Israel as "Jewish and democratic."[267] This description of the State of Israel, while implied, was not formally enunciated in the Declaration of Independence. Inevitably, some tension exists between the two values of democracy and Jewishness, in the same way that there is between the two desirable values of individual liberty and equality, but this does not invalidate the right of the Jewish people to self-determination, or suggest a lack of democracy in the state. The two Basic Laws restrict the authority of the legislature to violate the rights stated except in certain circumstances. The stated purpose is to "protect human dignity and liberty, in order to establish in a Basic Law the values of the State of Israel as a Jewish and democratic state."

A PLURALISTIC SOCIETY

Israel is a country embodying differences between Jewish religious and secular personnel, and between the Jewish majority and the Arab minority. In the Jewish society and in the State of Israel Jewish religious law co-exists with secular law, which was always dominant. Do these differences amount to a *Kulturkampf* ? Religious law courts can adjudicate marriage and divorce issues, but the Orthodox accept the validity of law made by the Knesset as authoritative. The existence of a chief rabbinate, state symbols (such as the national flag and the Star of David, the seven-pronged lamp, and *Hatikva* [the hope], which became the official national anthem in 2004, about 120 years after it was written), the political role played by religious parties, the state education system which, among other things, inculcated the values of Jewish culture, the creation of Yad Vashem, the celebration of the Holocaust Martyrs' Remembrance Day, observance of the Sabbath as the official day of rest, the requirement that all government institutions obey religious dietary laws, and the fact that Jewish Holy Days have become national holidays, are reminders of the Jewish nature of the state, a kind of civil religion. However, in the pluralistic Israel, with its diversity of beliefs and life-styles, differences exist about orthodox control over marriage, problems over transport and shopping on the Sabbath, and the question of religious conversion.

The adoption of symbols of a Jewish state, however, is similar to regulations in other countries; in France, for example the national holidays are Catholic in an officially laic Republic. Scandinavian countries have established Lutheran churches, and Britain has an established Anglican church. Laws in India on issues of personal status are related to the various religious communities in the country. The official ban in Israel on public transport on the Sabbath and protests by the ultra Orthodox (Haredim) over Sabbath parking near the Jaffa Gate in Jerusalem, do not today prevent individuals driving to play or witness games at the same time on the beach of Tel Aviv. Being Jewish has no simple definition. For secular individuals, religious sensibility may be confined to some ethical maxims and traditional celebrations of holy days. In the early years of the state, Israel virtually shut down on the Sabbath; now shopping and attending entertainment events is possible on Saturdays in many areas.

Pluralism in Israel extends into ethnic-religious, political, economic, and population areas. Freedom of religion is a central element of that pluralism. Within Israel is a variety of communities: Muslim, Druze, Circassian, Armenian, and Greek Orthodox. The Jewish population is split among a number of religious affiliations: civil, religious Zionist, ultra-Orthodox of various sects, and traditional. It is also split between the mainstream Ashkenazis (European Jews), who at the beginning constituted the elite group in society and in the military, and the Sephardim (Oriental Jews), many of whom came from Arab countries. Public and private, free market, enterprises share the economic space in a society that is now largely urban. Kibbutz collective farms are less significant than high technology. Politically, the country is divided into different camps, each with nuances: social democratic, nationalist, religious, Arab. The population, still speaking a variety of native languages, has origins in every part of the world.

With such diversity, policy making has been difficult and national unity has been manifested only on rare occasions of immediate crisis or sense of danger. A consensus has been developing about an Israeli identity that stems from success in building a state and defending itself, which belies the traditional antisemitic stereotype of the Jew being rootless, physically weak, and unwilling to engage in manual or agricultural labor. At the same time, the country is divided over the nature of a comprehensive peace with the Palestinians and the price to be paid for that peace. The country increasingly faces issues such as ethnicity, class, identity, cultural dominance, and the consequences of globalization, the emergence of non-governmental organizations, and communication technology; some of these have had the effect of wider dissemination of defamation, hate language against Israel, Holocaust denial, and even calls for genocide, by those hostile to Israel. In this regard hate speech is particularly troubling, not only because it violates the principles on which free speech rests, but also because that its utterances, such as that of a member of the Palestinian Legislative Council to "vanquish the Jews, and their supporters...kill them all down to the very last one," and calling Jews "apes and pigs," are reminders of the Holocaust.

Israel in a sense retains, as did the British Mandatory authorities, the Ottoman millet system, providing for autonomy of religious communities in personal law and allowing minority communities— Muslim, Christian, and Druze—to adjudicate family affairs according to their religious and legal traditions. Marriage, divorce, and inheritance issues are settled in this way by both Jewish and non-Jewish courts. Like other democratic countries, Israel has to cope with the simultaneous presence of belief in religion and unbelief among its citizens. Nearly two hundred years ago Alexis de Tocqueville wrote of the attitude to religion, "guard against shaking it, but rather preserve it carefully as the most precious inheritance from aristocratic centuries." On this maxim Israelis differ, with no consensus on priority of religious beliefs or a national cultural identity.[268]

A "Jewish state," however defined, is not incompatible with a democratic one, nor is Zionism incompatible with universal and democratic values. Israel, like other states, can maintain the national ethnic identity of the majority of its citizens and still respect the political and civic rights of its minority citizens. It is not surprising that Israeli Arabs, like minorities in other countries, often regard themselves as experiencing unequal treatment. Yet Israeli Arab citizens receive the same benefits as Jews in areas such as health insurance, child allowances, and social security. If discrimination and actual inequalities against Arabs exists, because of discretionary administrative action, to some degree in certain areas, such as housing, schools, job opportunities, and infrastructure in their cities, the country has been attempting to reduce or eliminate them. One noticeable feature about the Arab minority is that Christian Arabs, about ten per cent of Israeli Arabs, have a higher standard and are better educated than their Muslim counterparts. In any case, the existing inequities do not justify any call for the dismantling of the Zionist enterprise or providing aid to those groups and states advocating the elimination of Israel.

It is worth exploring one of the inequities in the context of the complex reality of life in the area, that of alleged discriminatory water allocation policy. It is true that the average Israeli per capita water consumption (300 liters a day) is nearly four and a half times larger than that of Palestinians in the West Bank and Gaza (70 liters). A number of factors are pertinent. Access to piped water has dramatically improved and continues to do so, while the Palestinian population has tripled. Almost half of the water used by Palestinians is provided by Mekorot, the Israeli national water carrier, from sources inside Israel. No doubt the amount of water available to Palestinians is less than desirable, but the Palestinian Authority has been negligent and invested little in improving water delivery as well as being corrupt both in general and in its charging of exorbitant rates for bottled or tanker water. About a third of Palestinian water leaks out of poorly maintained pipes. The PA has dug wells that threaten to contaminate major aquifers. An objective report of the World Bank in April 2009 noted that Israel was responsible for a fifty per cent increase in the number of West Bank Palestinians who have access to networked water supply.[269] One can conclude that this record, if insufficient, is a dramatic improvement in a developing economy.

One can appreciate that Palestinians entertain strong perceptions of their dispossession, displacement, or expulsion, and about what they see as Israeli occupation of territory. This argument about the ignoring of Palestinian suffering has been forcibly made by Rashid Khalidi in the reissue of his book on Palestinian identity.[270] Admitting the Israeli fears, rooted in the searing experiences of 20th century Jewish history culminating in the Holocaust, about threats to the continued existence of the Jews as a people and therefore of Israel, he contends nevertheless, that such fears seem to blind people to "the fact that the Palestinians are tormented by their own profound existential crisis as a people, one born largely of their traumatic historical experience suffered at the hands of Zionism and Israel over the last century."

Zionists from the beginning were not unaware of the presence of Arabs in Palestine and realized the consequent political and moral problems. In spite of contacts and attempts at agreement, the conflict between Jews and Arabs was unavoidable. Two national movements are present in the same territory. Yet, for an Israeli nation established after the horrors of the Holocaust, postulating a moral equivalence between the Holocaust and such Palestinian perceptions, or between Palestinian refugee camps and Nazi concentration camps, or between the Nazi Wehrmacht and the Israeli Defense Forces, or between Gaza and the Warsaw Ghetto, or between Jewish victims of the Holocaust and "victims of Zionist aggression," would appear to be unconscionable. Demonstrations by the British Muslim Initiative in London bear the slogan "Stop the Holocaust in Gaza." The suggestion of such equivalence appears even more immoral because of the refusal, up to the present at any rate, of a general Arab Muslim acceptance of a Jewish state. Instead, a war, now virtually one hundred years long with intermittent truces, has been waged with strong passion against a sovereign Jewish entity. It is the Arab opposition on the existential issue and the desire to see Israel disappear, not the settlements, that prevents an end to the conflict. Indeed, Israel is still threatened with annihilation not only by extreme Palestinian groups, but also by Islamists and by Iran, a country intent on achieving nuclear weapons. The key to peace in the Middle East does not rest on ending Israeli settlements beyond the Green Line. The highly emotional issue of settlements is only resolvable with an overall negotiated agreement between Israel and its neighbors. In that settlement, it is improbable that Israel will return to the precise 1967 lines or agree to the general idea, except in a token fashion, of the right of return of Palestinians to Israel. More probable is an agreement as has happened in other cases, which combines financial compensation and the housing of refugees in agreeable host countries.

Chapter 26

Conclusion

In recent years non-democratic countries have come to an end when their citizens and many in the international community no longer accept their legitimacy or their ability to govern in accordance with acceptable norms of law. This has been exemplified by the fate of East Germany in 1990, the Soviet Union in 1991, and apartheid South Africa in 1994.[271] Some critics of Israel are waging a campaign of political warfare and constant propaganda in the political international arena and in the intellectual world, seeking to achieve the same fate for this democratic country. However, an objective assessment of Israel's nature and behavior would conclude that Israel is different from those failed states.

In contrast to these failed non-democratic countries, Israel is the only full democracy in the Middle East and Zionism has been a successful liberation movement. In the Freedom in the World Survey of 2011, Israel is the only country in the Middle East to be classified as free and having a meaningful electoral democracy. Its electoral system, one of proportional representation in which voters cast ballots for a national party rather than individuals, has always resulted in a number of political parties gaining seats in the Knesset according to the proportion obtained of the total vote. All governments have been coalitions, many including members of religious parties; the government led by Prime Minister Benjamin Netanyahu in 2010 contained members of six parties, some of whom have conflicting opinions on political and other issues, which has made compromise inevitable. Nevertheless, despite the problem of governmental decision-making, the democratic nature of the country has survived in a society of vibrant non-governmental organizations and civic groups.

The country has also prospered economically in spite of the heavy burden of defense, the threats to its security and the attempts to boycott it in various ways. Those ways, involving primary, secondary, and tertiary boycotts, have included embargoes on weapons and strategic materials, not buying Israeli products or investing in Israel, divesting Israeli securities, preventing appearances by Israeli performers, sportspeople and academics.[272] Among those who have engaged in a boycott of some kind are Shell Oil, British Petroleum, Standard Oil, Socony Mobil, and Texaco. During the Arab boycott in the 1960s and 1970s, Western companies that complied with the Arab League demands to stop commerce with Israel usually made their decision on economic grounds. Today, the call by Western organizations for a boycott of Israel and the response to it is more a moral and political decision than an economic one.

Troubling though these challenges have been, Israel, essentially changing in the mid 1980s from a quasi-socialist society, with flourishing kibbutzim and cooperatives, and a powerful trade union movement, the Histadrut, to a market economy, has in spite of the lack of local markets in the surrounding area, the scarcity of physical resources, and the boycotts against it, registered remarkable successes. This has been shown by its entrepreneurial culture in attracting venture capital and in the number of start-up enterprises per capita, and by its general efforts in shaping technological change through innovation, improvisation and willingness to take risks.[273] Israel has registered 7,600 patents in its history; the twenty-one Arab states have registered 700 in the same period. Recently, Israel has had the second largest number of start-up companies in the world, after the US, and the largest number of Nasdaq-listed companies outside North America. The Hebrew University in Jerusalem is ranked no. 21 among world universities in computer science, outranking Cambridge University which is no. 30, and Yale University no. 31. Israel has devised the world's first nationwide battery-switching and vehicle-charging network, allowing drivers to switch depleted batteries for full ones in a short time. Israel has been prominent in, and concentrated on, developing software, computer, and telecommunication components, all enterprises that can overcome the boycotts and restrictions put on its exports, especially those of large manufactured goods. One unusual success is that of a major Chinese web site, which is actually an Israeli start-up company.

The UN Human Development Report of 2010, assessing 169 countries in terms of life expectancy, gross national income per capita, and education, ranked Israel fifteenth. Since its establishment this culturally diverse, politically divided, and complex, technologically advanced, economically competitive society, partly private and partly public, with no homogeneous elite, but a mosaic of minorities speaking multiple languages, this society engaged in nation building and development has embodied Western values, civic and political rights, freedom of speech and of religion, regular and free elections, free parliament, peaceful political change, rule of law, rights of women and gays, independent and impartial judiciary, autonomous and liberal universities, scientific research and achievements, and openness to the outside world. Paradoxically, that very openness and free flow of information in its multi-ethnic society has invited the characteristically critical reporting by media and scholarship on actions inside the country.

INTERNAL CRITICS

In spite of its political and economic record, Israel faces intellectual, internal and external, as well as diplomatic and military challenges. Critical statements, as well as activity by organizations such as the Israeli Committee against House Demolitions (ICAHD) and Israeli-Arab groups such as Adalah and Mossawa, concerning the nature and existence of the state of Israel in its present form, as well as its specific policies, have come not only from hostile outsiders, but also from Israelis concerned about the policies and the political direction of their country. Particularly pointed criticisms have emerged from the group of writers and academics who have been termed "New Historians," and "Critical Sociologists." They advocate what they conceive as a true historiography of the factors leading to the establishment and the history of Israel. They offer a counter "narrative" of the reality and consequences of Zionism, of the political personnel connected with it, and of the "founding myths" of the State of Israel, which some consider illegitimate and unjust, and a form of Western imperialism.

Most of these arguments are familiar from Soviet propaganda in the past and Arab polemics in the present. Some internal Israeli critics can more properly and accurately be regarded as "anti-Zionists," than "post-Zionists," challenging the very validity of Israel as a "Jewish" nation-state. Even when voiced in a temperate, if partisan fashion, these critics, with some influence in university faculties and in the media, argue for Israel to be a state of "all its citizens" rather than a "Jewish" state. More extreme forms of this point of view are that Israel is a colonial state, that its existence is fundamentally immoral, that Zionism is a form of imperialism or identified with European imperialism, that Arabs are innocent victims of that imperialism, that there is no connection between Jews and the land of Israel, even that the "Jewish people" is an invention of late nineteenth century Zionism, and that the Zionist movement has used moral blackmail in making use of the Holocaust for its own political purposes, to provide a basis for Jewish unity, and support of the State of Israel.

The last argument, about the Holocaust, is particularly troubling and insensitive. Clearly, especially after the Eichmann trial in 1961, the nature and extent of the Holocaust became well known in the world in general, and became a significant factor in the psyche, collective memory, and outlook of Israelis as for Jews everywhere. Knowledge of the Holocaust provided an opportunity for the world to consider the past persecution of Jews, and undoubtedly helped shape a mood to support the creation and existence of Israel. One can acknowledge the use made of the Holocaust narrative to provide one rationale for the establishment of the state. But some critics have gone far beyond this position in arguing that Israel has also made use of the Holocaust for military and political purposes.[274] Others, even while admitting the significance of the Holocaust, argue that the establishment of the State of Israel meant "a massive injustice to the Palestinians."[275] The remedy, in their perspective, is that Israel has "to arrive at the reckoning of its own sins against the Palestinians." For these critics the significance of the Holocaust is not as prominent in their agenda as the condemnation of Israel for its past and present moral failings. On this point, perhaps the dictum of the English historian, Herbert Butterfield, is pertinent: misinterpreting historical developments and historical figures brings the effort of understanding to a halt, and prejudices, accompanied by generalizations and vague philosophizing, hinder true understanding of events.

Internal criticism of Israel is not new. For over a century Jewish intellectuals inside Palestine have voiced criticism of the direction of Zionism. Among them in early years were prominent people such as the philosopher Martin Buber, a key figure at the Hebrew University in Jerusalem, Joshua Prawer, Gershom Scholem, and members of the Brit Shalom movement, who were concerned about any injustice perpetrated against the Arab population. Somewhat later, after the 1967 war, another professor at Hebrew University, Yeshayahu Leibovitch, in extreme language, spoke of Israel's "Judeo-Nazi" character because of its treatment of the Palestinians. More moderate criticism of the Zionist ideology that had dominated Israeli political culture increased after the Yom Kippur War of 1973, with the questioning of the validity of historical, social, and cultural "truths" and "myths." These critics, claiming that this questioning was based on values and principles of universalism and humanism rather than on Jewishness, emphasized the need for and the resulting consequences of peace with Arabs.[276] Part of the explanation for the continued internal criticism within Israel in recent years may be the influence of the teaching and research of these former prominent intellectuals on their students.[277]

The impact of this negative image of Israel and its people has been to induce a more pessimistic mood within the country, as well as to affect international opinion. Less stressed are the once influential and accepted portraits of an optimistic new country with "hard and powerful heroes" and tough sabras, asserting ethnic pride and, fighting for their homeland as depicted in Leon Uris's 1958 novel *Exodus* and the 1960 film directed by Otto Preminger. These depictions jettisoned the negative images of Jews as defenseless victims. Such optimism was expressed, for example, by Bartley Crum, the non-Jewish San Francisco lawyer who wrote, in his introduction in 1948 to I.F. Stone's book, *This is Israel,* of the "miracles (the Israelis) have performed in peace and war...They have set up a government which is a model of democracy... (they are) a free people who made a two thousand year dream come true in their own free land."[278] At that point in his career, Stone himself was enthusiastic about Israel; later he became a critic of Zionist "moral myopia." It is revealing to read, in his 1948 book, the fulsome praise of the heroic Israelis, "a tiny bridgehead" with precarious borders fighting against 30 million Arabs and 300 million Muslims who made no secret of their intentions. He pointed out the remark of Abdul Rahman Azzam, head of the Arab League, who threatened that the 1948 War against the new Israel "will be spoken of like the Mongol massacres and the Crusades."

Younger critics who came to adulthood a generation after 1948, have also challenged the meaningfulness of heroic symbols and individuals heralded by the Zionist movement: the mass suicide of the Zealots at Masada, the plateau in the Judean desert, fighting the Romans in 73 A.D., the devastating defeat of the rebellion by Shimon Bar Kokhba in 133-135 A.D., and the defense led by Joseph Trumpeldor, who was killed in the fighting, in 1920 around Tel Hai, a small Jewish settlement in the Galilee, which had been attacked by Arabs. Were these self-defeating actions? The former head of Israeli military intelligence, Yehoshafat Harkabi, not himself a "post-Zionist," was particularly critical of Bar Kokhba for a pointless revolt which led to the death of thousands of Jews and the destruction of their community.[279] The parallel with contemporary Israel was clear: Israeli policy had to be prudent and realistic, not based on hubris or desire for temporal power, and not reckless action doomed to failure. Cultural changes were occurring; the tough macho Israeli was falling from glory.[280] Israeli military problems, especially in the 1973 Yom Kippur War, contributed to this more critical attitude of the actions and policies of the elite group symbolized by Moshe Dayan.

While poignant and well-meaning anguish, feelings of guilt, ambivalence, critical irony, and internal complexities about identity are not unfamiliar to some Jews living in Palestine and later Israel, that anguish has not reached the stage of undermining the national spirit of Israel, but it has been aggravated by a number of factors, dealt with below.[281]

THE NEW ANTISEMITISM

Antisemitism, historically persistent and widespread, the baffling obsession, has taken a new form because of the complex association of Jews and Judaism with Israel. Antisemitism was based in the past on religious and racial grounds; now it is linked with anti-Zionism and Israel. Antisemitism and "anti-Zionism," the term popularized by the Soviet Union and made familiar in the writings there of Trofim Kitchko, and then accentuated by the European left, have converged and are thus difficult to distinguish. In theory, the two concepts are distinct, but in practice they are intertwined and not mutually exclusive. The triple test of antisemitism suggested by Natan Sharansky—demonization, double standards, and delegitimization regarding Jews—is now equally applicable to the condemnations of Israel. One result of the impact of those condemnations has been an increase in the Western world of antisemitic manifestations and violence towards both Israel and Jews elsewhere. Islamists use passages from the Koran to justify this violence and hatred. This interaction of old and new antisemitism, coming from different wings of the political spectrum, has resulted in a contemporary ideological configuration described by the French author Pierre-André Taguieff as "Judeophobia," a term originally used by Leon Pinsker.[282] What is new is that the new antisemitism, or Judeophobia, is not confined to any particular political group, but is present in the radical left, in Arab and Muslim propaganda, and in extreme right wing groups such as that of Jean-Marie Le Pen, founder and first leader of Front National in France, who though fearful of the number and behavior of Muslims in France, nevertheless has formed a working alliance with Muslim leaders to denounce the international Jewish lobby.

THE IDEOLOGY OF THIRD WORLDISM

The ideology of Third Worldism, coming mainly from the political left, has permeated both individual activists and prestigious American and European universities, where it is espoused by many faculty members, the speeches of activists, and the writings of public intellectuals. This ideology postulates a hypocritical and violent West, eternally to be judged guilty for its colonial empires and activity that have been destructive of indigenous cultures. Paradoxically, proponents of this ideology often do not pay attention to the important differences among the individual indigenous cultures, but rather lump them all together in one vast "Third World." Their attack on the "West" is often accompanied by a vicarious mental rapture for or idealistic fantasy of a universal better world. In this fantasy, the Arab world became part of the progressive forces for freedom and progress.

Few today are likely to echo the extravagant rhetoric of H.G. Wells that "The Soviet Union upholds the tattered banner of world collectivity and remains something splendid and hopeful in the spectacle of mankind."[283] Now that the Soviet Union has collapsed and the bloodbaths of the Stalinist era have become known, and the Communist god and the noble dream of the sublime Soviet Union has failed or gone astray and with it the promised better future, and now that the supposed revolutionary hero Mao Zedong has been revealed as the Chinese brutal murderer of 70 million people, the disappointment suffered over these developments by the pessimistic critics of Western culture has been redirected to enthusiasm for revolutionary insurgencies and violent energy in non-West countries, irrespective of the human cost. Even if they may still be nostalgic about that noble leftist dream of Communist societies that has gone astray, the Third World for them appears to be the desirable resolution of the endless search for new saviors of humanity who will overcome the imagined evils of Western civilization.

The irony in the criticism of Israel and the United States is that the non-West is lauded not for positive reasons, but because it is not Western and does not adhere to Western practices, such as liberal democracy, an open capitalist economy, rule of law, free elections, personal autonomy, individual freedom, constitutional rights, emancipation of women, and sexual freedom. It is not disconcerting for these critics of Israel that rogue regimes, dictatorships such as North Korea and Venezuela, ostensibly revolutionary, can form an unnatural alliance with Islamic fundamentalists. Critics of Western values posture as idealists with high moral standards, but their actions or non-actions reveal a lack of consistency about those standards. For instance, just to give two examples. Radical leftists in general have shown more compassion for Arab dictators than for democratic Israel. Feminists, gay and lesbian groups have been curiously silent about the place and treatment of women and homosexuals in Muslim Arab countries. No woman in an Arab country has been elected to a prominent position, as was Golda Meir in Israel, the first woman prime minister elected anywhere who was not the wife or daughter of a previous head of government.

THE TWO SATANS

The chief enemies demonized in this scenario of demons and evils are the United States and Israel, seen as oppressive, powerful, entities committing crimes of imperialism, and whose liberal values are soulless and morally inferior to the non-West. The relationship between the two countries has been an unusual one; beneficial to both sides, in spite of occasional differences. Both share a commitment to freedom, personal liberty, democratic values, and the rule of law. Israel has obtained from the United States military, economic and financial aid, and support in international organizations. It has received $3 billion in military assistance. About this assistance, two factors are relevant. The first is that three-quarters of this aid must be spent in the US. The other is that, with impartial generosity, the US also provides military aid to Egypt ($2 billion) and to Jordan and Lebanon, thus increasing their military capacities and necessitating more investment and military expenditure by Israel.

Israel is generally viewed by American foreign policy makers and military officials as a reliable ally; the relationship involves, among other things, sharing intelligence and missile technology, joint weapons projects and partnerships in producing military equipment, allowing US Air Force planes to refuel at Israeli bases, providing the American Sixth Fleet access to the port of Haifa, Israel serving as a testing ground for American weaponry in combat conditions, experience later useful in the fighting in Iraq and Afghanistan, such as the detection and neutralization of improvised explosive devices (IEDs), as well as in the hundreds of modifications of the F-16, bilateral military training in aerial combat and special operations, law enforcement, and cooperation in the common war on terrorism. One interesting contribution was the coagulating bandage, the product of a Jerusalem company, which was supplied not only to US forces, but also to the SWAT team which helped save the life of Congresswoman Gabrielle Giffords, when she was shot near Tucson on January 8, 2011.

One can argue that the American objectives in the Middle East comprise a number of factors: political commitment to Israel; preservation of a balance of power in the area; prevention of Russian domination there; friendly relations with Arab states; ensuring supply of oil; and fostering a peaceful settlement of the conflict between Israel and Arabs. Between the US and Israel there is agreement on many issues. Both countries share a commitment to freedom, personal liberty, democratic values, and the rule of law. Both face the threat of terrorism by the enemies of freedom. Both find it useful to cooperate in a number of ways, including military research, intelligence gathering, bilateral military training, counter-terrorism practices and law enforcement.

The qualities that Israel possesses and the contribution it makes to a progressive world order and to democratic values are more intangible than the manifest assets of oil, markets, and wealth of Arab countries, but nevertheless they are appreciated. At the same time it is understandable that the global interests of the United States may make the American concept of a desirable settlement of the Arab-Israeli conflict differ from that of Israel with its regional concerns.

It is interesting to look briefly at the history of American and Zionist and Israeli relationships. Differences between the two, before and after the creation of Israel, on policy issues are not unknown. In 1917, contrary to the opinion of President Wilson, the US State Department opposed endorsing the Balfour Declaration. Robert Lansing, then Secretary of State, was concerned about the Christian reaction to "turning the Holy Land over to the absolute control of the race credited with the death of Christ." Another serious problem arose in 1948. The US State Department under George Marshall opposed recognition of the new state. In this he was supported by a formidable group of individuals, including under Secretary of State Robert A. Lovett, Dean Acheson, John McCloy, Paul Nitze, Charles Bohlen, George F. Kennan, then head of Policy Planning, Dean Rusk, and Loy Henderson, director of the Near Eastern and African Affairs Division of the State Department. All argued that support for Zionism was not helpful for vital US interests, including the need for oil supplies, in the Middle East. They held that the Arab states would be alienated by support for partition. In addition, the Central Intelligence Agency, the newly created Department of Defense headed by James V. Forrestal, and the Joint Chiefs of Staff all opposed partition and suggested that a Jewish state might become an ally or at least friendly to the Soviet Union.

Representative of this point of view was the Policy Planning Staff Report (PPS/19) issued by its director, George F. Kennan, on January 19, 1948. In recommending that the US take no further initiative in implementing or aiding partition, Kennan wrote that to do otherwise would suggest that "in supporting a Jewish state in Palestine we were in fact supporting the extreme objectives of political Zionism, to the detriment of overall U.S. security interests."[284] Kennan was disappointed by the creation of Israel and predicted a forbidding aftermath. In his message to Secretary George Marshall of May 21, 1948, he wrote that the US support could bring it into conflict with Britain, threaten American national interests in the Middle East and the Mediterranean, disrupt the unity of the Western world, undermine the entire US policy towards the Soviet Union, and might even lead to the disintegration of the United Nations.[285]

In spite of this intense opposition by US officials, about eleven minutes after the Israeli Declaration of Independence and formation of a government in Tel Aviv the new state was approved by President Harry Truman, who had been given support by White House advisers,

David Niles and Clark Clifford. On behalf of the United States, Truman wrote that "This Government has been informed that a Jewish state has been proclaimed in Palestine, and recognition has been requested by the Provisional Government there. The United States recognizes the Provisional Government as the *de facto* authority of the State of Israel." However, Truman did not remove the US embargo on arms to Palestine, which had been suggested by Loy Henderson and which the US State Department had instituted on December 5, 1947. Moreover Truman's recognition was *de facto*; the Soviet Union had gone further and immediately recognized the State of Israel *de jure*. Britain not only did not recognize Israel for nine months, contending that Israel had not fulfilled the "basic criteria" of an independent state, but also opposed its admission into the United Nations.

The State Department had attempted to prevent the implementation of the partition resolution and thought that Truman had been too partial towards Israel. The Eisenhower Administration, especially Secretary of State John Foster Dulles, was less favorable towards Israel in its attempt to improve relations with Arab countries. It did not approve of Israel's hydroelectric project, it blocked Israel's interest in joining NATO, and it did not allow American Jewish servicemen to serve at the military base at Dhahran because of the objections of Saudi Arabia. The US Administration forced Israel to withdraw from Sinai after the 1956 Suez War, signaling that otherwise it would end aid to Israel, and suspend the tax-exempt status of the United Jewish Appeal.

A further crisis began in 1960 and continued on from there, when first President Eisenhower, then Presidents John F Kennedy, Lyndon Johnson, and Richard Nixon were all concerned about Israel's nuclear deterrent program. Other crises involved the Jackson-Vanik Amendment of 1973, legislation that would help Soviet Jews by allowing them to emigrate, Menachem Begin's rejection of Jimmy Carter's demand in 1978 for a freeze on building settlements, the selling of AWACS to Saudi Arabia in 1981, and differences over the massacre by Lebanese militias of Palestinians in Sabra and Shatila in 1982. In 1991 President George H. W. Bush refused to supply a $100 million loan promised to Israel for immigrant housing, in effect for settlements in the West Bank. Other differences included Ariel Sharon's refusal in 2002 to end operations against terrorists as President George W. Bush had requested, and President Obama's disagreement in 2010 with Israel over the issue of settlements, and a building freeze.

Yet, the thrust of US policy has been to recognize the importance of the common values and democratic nature of society shared with Israel, and to maintain a commitment to Israel's right to exist within secure and recognized boundaries achieved through direct negotiations. US Administrations have assisted the various peace and disengagements agreements between Israel and Egypt and Syria, the Camp David Accords (1978), and the Madrid Conference (1991). The US became the main arms supplier of Israel, with the sale, by President Lyndon Johnson in 1968, of Phantom jets, providing a qualitative edge for Israel in the region. One surprising act was that by President Richard Nixon who, in spite of his well-known animosity towards Jews, ordered, although his own advisers suggested otherwise, the deployment of hundreds of jumbo US military aircraft delivering over 22,000 tons of armaments to Israel during the Yom Kippur War in 1973. He did this not only when the State Department and Defense Departments were reluctant, but also when no European country was helpful to Israel. President Ronald Reagan saw Israel as important in helping "thwart Moscow's designs on territories and resources vital to US security and national well-being."[286] Strategic ties and joint security arrangements have developed, as well as free trade economic agreements. American leaders have tried to end or limit the boycott of Israel, and have aided Israel's confrontation with terrorists. Whether the relationship between the two countries can be construed as "special" is arguable, but it is significant that for the most part the US has supported Israel in international forums.

THE ARAB LOBBY

Even without going to the extreme of positing a Jewish conspiracy, which some do, or engaging in antisemitism, critics of Israel sometimes argue that pro-Israeli organizations constitute a "lobby" that has exerted too much influence on United States policy in the Middle East and that controls American media, finance, and politics.

Three things are pertinent about this criticism. The first is that lobbying on behalf of another country is a familiar activity in American politics; for many years Greek, Irish, Armenian, Cuban, Latvian, and other groups have been prominent in that activity. A second fallacy in the argument, both explicit and implicit, is that the national interest of the United States has suffered from the relationship. The third factor is that these critics leave unmentioned or pay little heed to the existence of an Arab lobby and groups friendly to Arab interests, in the United States as well as in Western Europe. That lobby, active in both national and local politics, is focused on criticism or detraction of Israel and Zionism, on advocating trade arrangements with Arab countries, and on support for the Palestinian cause, rather than on calls for observance of human rights or democratic values in Arab countries. It has called for the reduction or end of US aid to Israel, for stopping loan guarantees and ending the purchases by states in the US of Israeli bonds. The lobby, not necessarily receiving material rewards, in the United States is extensive; it includes the Arab American Institute, founded in 1985, the National Association of Arab Americans, founded in 1972, the Middle East Policy Council (formerly the American-Arab Affairs Council), established in 1981 and headed by George McGovern, the American-Arab Anti-Discrimination Committee, founded in 1980 by former senator James Abourezk, the Council on American Islamic Relations (CAIR) founded in 1994, the Council of Presidents of Arab-American Organizations, the American Muslim Council founded in 1990, the Palestinian American Congress, founded in 1995, the National Arab American Businessmen's Association, and the Muslim Public Affairs Committee, founded in 1988. Groups generally supporting the Arab position in the Arab-Israeli conflict include the American Educational Trust and the Council for the National Interest, both founded by foreign service officers, Andrew Killgore and Richard Curtiss; the group publishes *The Washington Report on Middle East Affairs*.

Those attempting to convince American policy makers to be concerned about Arab interests include advocates and public relations consultants such as International Consultants Inc., defense contractors, corporations with commercial interests, oil industry officials from time to time, such as those of Gulf Oil, Mobil, Texaco, and SoCal (Chevron), and especially the ARAMCO (Arabian American Oil Co) group, non-evangelical Christians, the National Council of Churches, and some former US diplomats, Senators, public figures, and State Department Arabists. Notable examples of the latter groups were ex-Senator J. William Fulbright, former chair of the Senate Relations Committee, who had a position funded by Saudi Arabia and the United States Arab Emirates, Clark Clifford, and Fred Dutton, former Assistant Secretary for Legislative Affairs in the Kennedy Administration, who lobbied for major arms sales to Saudi Arabia. They have less love for Palestinians, less interest in supporting a peace process or in helping develop sustainable Palestinian political or economic structures than in establishing self-interested cordial relationships with Arab states, especially with Saudi Arabia. Above all, for many of them, their most evident public activity, directly and indirectly, is a negative one, strong condemnation of Israel for any of its actions.[287] Even President Jimmy Carter at one point in 1977 complained of the Arab lobby pressure on him.

The impact of this Arab lobby and friends is visible in disparate ways. One effect is the willingness of American, and some European, academic institutions and centers interested in Middle Eastern affairs to accept Arab funding. Most of this has been the investment by Saudi Arabia and other Arab countries in university classrooms through providing subventions for academic programs, friendly appropriate centers for Middle Eastern and Arab Islamic studies in the United States and Western Europe, and for financing named professorial chairs. A few prominent examples suffice. One was the gift to Georgetown University in 2005 of $20 million by Saudi Prince Alwaleed bin Talal, for the Center for Muslim-Christian understanding, which has been given his name. Another was the gift of $4.5 million by Kuwait to the Institute for Middle East Studies at Georgetown. Georgetown had given an honorary doctorate of law to the Emir of Kuwait in 2005 for his "great contributions" to public service. Interestingly, the University established a chair to conduct research in the region of the "Arabian Gulf," a term that has been deliberately used by Arab nationalists to replace the words "Persian Gulf," the term traditionally used for the region and which in 1917 was adopted by the US as the official name. Harvard University was given $20 million by Prince Talal, mainly for the study of Islam and Islamic history and jurisprudence. Among other American universities receiving donations from Middle Eastern countries are Princeton, Columbia, and Cornell.[288] It is also worth noting that the Carter Center in Atlanta has received considerable funding from Arab sources, $5 million from King Fahd and another $5 million from Prince Talal, $500,000 from the United States Arab Emirates, and funds from Oman and from the brothers of Osama bin Laden, providing a substantial part of its annual budget, and that Jimmy Carter himself received in 2001 the $500,000 Zayed International Prize for the Environment. This Prize is connected with the Zayed Center in Abu Dhabi, funded by Sheikh Zayed. That Center has aided terrorist groups, has declared there is an international Jewish/Zionist conspiracy for world domination, and even that a Jewish/American conspiracy carried out the atrocities of 9/11.[289] In contrast to the behavior of those accepting gifts from Arab sources, Rudolf Giuliani, then Mayor of New York, returned $10 million for the Twin Tower Fund given by Prince Talal, because the Prince had linked the 9/11, 2001 attacks on New York to US policy.

British universities also have welcomed gifts from Saudi and other Islamic sources. Between 1995 and 2008, eight universities—Oxford, Cambridge, Durham, University College London, Exeter, Dundee, City, and the London School of Economics (LSE)—accepted more than £233.5 million from Muslim rulers or associates. The European Muslim Research Centre at Exeter University accepted funds from the Cordoba Foundation, Islam/Expo, and the Al-Jazeera Satellite Network. Since 2008 the scale of funding to British universities has increased. The director of LSE resigned, confessing a personal error of judgment, after the revelation that the college had agreed to accept £1.5 million from the son of Colonel Gadhafi of Libya, and a further £2.2 million for a contract with Libya's Economic Development Board, and that he had been to Libya to provide advice on economic matters. In return, Gadhafi himself provided what he considered advice to LSE students via a video conference. Much of the money given to these British colleges went to found or support Islamic study centers. It is still an open question whether these centers exist to promote understanding of Islam or to be a propaganda vehicle for an extremist strain of Islam. It was noticeable that in the very week in February 2011 of the revelation of the gifts by Libya to the LSE, the college's Center for Middle East Studies voted to support a boycott of Israel.[290]

IDEALISM PERVERTED

George Orwell offered the pertinent remark that "even an idealistic politics, perhaps especially an idealistic politics, can pervert itself." He was addressing the perversion of those supporting the Stalinist regime in the Soviet Union. Contemporary idealism, in addition to similar intellectual perversion, has also become fantasy; armchair revolutionaries in San Francisco, New York, and Paris saw Yasser Arafat as the embodiment of anti-colonial heroism. In their common hostility to Israel, some European and American intellectuals are allied with Muslim organizations. Both the left and Muslims tend to see Israel as a formidable, and even sometimes as the greatest, threat to world peace.

With the end of the demon regime of apartheid in South Africa the image of the demonic state in the eyes of some, particularly those radicals in the academic world and in the media, has shifted from South Africa to Israel. Ironically, academics of the radical left in universities in the US and in Western Europe have registered more support for Hamas in Gaza, than has the Palestinian population in the West Bank. Even more, other believers in this fantasy world have not only suggested that the actions of Islamic suicide bombers in New York and elsewhere result from the alleged control over the US government and media by Jewish interests, but also argue that Israel provoked the US wars against terrorism in Iraq and Afghanistan. The shared belief about Israel on the part of normally opposed groups, the Western radical left, the Islamic fundamentalists, Arab nationalists, Christian humanitarians, anti-globalists, and environmentalists, "the red-brown-green" coalition, is one of the more bizarre manifestations in contemporary politics. The common motif is dislike, even hatred, of Israel, which is depicted as a criminal state and the accomplice or lackey of the United States.

Even the most well meaning idealist and radical leftist can find little comfort about the present, as well as the past, behavior of the twenty-one countries of the Arab League, divided as they are by civil wars and religious tensions in Egypt, Iraq, Iran, Saudi Arabia and Lebanon. During the regime of Nasser in Egypt in the 1950s and 1960s, all political parties were banned and civic organizations, including trade unions, were strictly controlled. Though President Sadat introduced a limited form of political pluralism, his successor, Hosni Mubarak, reintroduced controls over political parties and organizations, and manipulated the conduct of elections. The Arab League countries are beset with Islamist insurgencies, enmity between Sunni and Shiite Muslims, and discord between mainstream and extremist Sunnis. Most of the Arab regimes in 2011, some of which came to an end, were autocracies, or based on military dictatorships, or presidencies for life as in Tunisia, or tribal elders as in Yemen, or hereditary family dictatorships, or Islamic clerics in Iran, and seemingly immutable for life. Before being deposed in 2011, Hosni Mubarak had ruled in Egypt for twenty-nine years. Zine el-Abidine Ben Ali governed in Tunisia for twenty-three years, during which his family acquired control of over one-third of the $44 billion economy. Muammar al-Gadhafi ruled Libya for forty-one years. Omar Al Bashir, though wanted on charges of war crimes, had controlled Sudan for twenty-one years, Qaboos bin Said, Sultan of Oman, who deposed his father, had reigned for forty years. Ali Abdullah Saleh ruled in Yemen for thirty-two years, after he seized power after the assassination of the existing president; his family members occupied the key government positions, and tribal leaders were bribed to support him. Bashar Assad ruled in Syria for ten years, Abdelaziz Bouteflika in Algeria for eleven years, and the Saudi royal family, in parts or most of Arabia, for over 250 years. The Syrian Ba'ath Party, led by General Hafez al Assad, former air force commander and Defense Minister, who ruled for thirty years, and then by his son who has ruled since 2000, has governed under emergency laws and banned all opposition groups. The country's security services are immune from prosecution under a 2008 law. In Syria the minority Alawites, once second-class citizens of the country who are a sect with a controversial faith that is frequently categorized, if inaccurately, as an offshoot of Shiite Islam, dominate the Sunni Muslim majority and hold most of the top positions in the government and military. About three-quarters of the 200,000 career soldiers in the Syrian army are Alawites. The most elite military division, the Fourth Division, and the Republican Guard, which is an all-Alawite unit, is led by the President's brother, Maher. By contrast, until recently many Syrian Kurds were not considered citizens and did not have equal access to education and health services. The overthrow of the Shah in Iran in 1979 led to an even worse regime, a theocratic regime which has lasted for over thirty years. Islamic militants in other countries threaten the existing regimes, all of which have strong security forces for protection. Though some of the states are fabulously wealthy because of their oil and natural gas reserves, all suffer from a deficit of freedom and political rights.

POST-COLONIAL IDEOLOGY

Overlapping with Third Worldism, another factor that may explain the unwarranted hostility towards Israel is the impact of fashionable postcolonial theory—a mixture of post structuralism, post modernism, cultural relativism, and multiculturalism. In addition to anticolonialism, postcolonial theory is also characterized by or generally accompanied by anti-capitalist, anti-American, and anti-Israel views. Postmodern theory emphasizes the positing of alternative historical "narratives," tends to deny that texts have any fixed meaning, and makes the distinction between fact and fiction sometimes difficult to discern. Writers who espouse this theory state that history is "what the historian chooses to make it."[291] To accept the argument of Hayden White, that the grounds for preferring one version of history over another are "moral and aesthetic ones," might mean taking the perverse arguments of Holocaust denial or the belief in a world wide Jewish conspiracy seriously. Are the writings of David Irving, the British Holocaust denier whose writings have been discredited in court, to be given equal weight to those of Primo Levi, himself a survivor of the death camps? To debate Holocaust deniers would be asinine. Disinterested historical scholarship or examination of complex political issues is not served by the assertion, made by Claude Lévi-Strauss, that historical fact has no objective reality at all, but only exists as retrospective reconstruction.

CULTURAL AND MORAL RELATIVISM

Similar problems arise with cultural relativism, which may regard all cultures as having acceptable moral value, or more strongly that Western culture is inherently imperfect. Relativism, the recognition of the diversity of societies and the plurality of systems, has a long intellectual pedigree and is useful for understanding various cultures. The concept may be traced back to well known anthropologists, particularly Franz Boas, who, in his study of tribes and cultures, *The Mind of Primitive Man*, held that all peoples had contributed to cultural progress in one way or another, and would be capable of advancing the interests of human beings if given a fair opportunity. Others, Bronislaw Malinowski, Ruth Benedict, Margaret Mead, and Claude Levi-Strauss, all in their different ways were concerned with cultural autonomy and the significance of the diverse cultures they studied. Praiseworthy though this may be, this relativist view tends to reject or minimize universal and ethical judgments. The dilemma is that cultural relativism in practice, instead of being used for dispassionate and unprejudiced analysis, has been used ideologically to put forward the claims of non-Western societies as being equal, or even superior, morally and socially with Western democratic nations such as the United States and Israel.

At its extreme, moral relativism regards all societies and systems as equally acceptable. An ideology of this kind might imply that non-Westerners not be judged by Western standards and, for those mistrusting the use of power, appease illiberal aggressors confronting democratic countries. Defenders of nations or groups perpetrating terrorist acts like Hamas, or claiming victimhood like the Palestinians, rationalize their actions by asserting the validity of "alternative narratives." They question whether Westerners have the right to comment on the appropriateness of forced marriages or bullying of young girls in Arab Islamic countries. Raymond Aron, the French political writer, in 1979 pointedly asked his colleague, Claude Lévi-Strauss a question which the great anthropologist refused to answer: "Are universal moral judgments on behavior or conduct compatible or incompatible with cultural relativism?"[292]

A multiculturalist view, next discussed, may well regard all cultures as valid expressions of identity which ought to be recognized, or consider cultural differences as largely superficial, with no one culture being superior to any other. Influential philosophers, such as Martin Heidegger, Hans-Georg Gadamer and Jacques Derrida, argue that the evils of the contemporary world stem from what they regard as the excesses of the heritage of the European Enlightenment. In this view the emancipation from the tradition and authority heralded by the 18th century Enlightenment leads to a rejection of the idea of absolute truth, to a belief in the equal dignity of cultures, and to tolerance for national, ethnic, racial, and ethnic groups even when those groups are intolerant or unwilling to grant equal rights to others. In this post-modernist view the Enlightenment is seen as cultural imperialism masquerading as a higher form of rationality.[293]

Allan Bloom, in his *The Closing of the American Mind*, commented that his incoming students believed, or said they believed, that truth is relative. The concept of moral relativism, meaning that objective moral values do not transcend individual or group convictions, results in the analysis of disputes in terms of the moral equivalence of the contending parties. For many, it is now for many the starting point of political decision-making. The problem with this philosophical point of view is that those professing a belief in moral equivalence may misjudge appropriate standards in particular and even disregard reality and the presence of evil. In practice it has led to harsh judgments on Israeli actions in response to terrorist attacks against its citizens. Israel is often measured by absolute standards that do not take into account the context of the actions. Its social practices are judged by "utopian standards of political values."[294]

The argument for relativism and moral equivalence has a somewhat patronizing air about it; it implies that Israel has to be judged by a higher standard because Arab countries and the Palestinians are unlikely to reach the standard of achievement and civilization that Israel, a more advanced country, has attained. On that basis it excuses the Arabs and Palestinians for the lack of freedom of expression in political and public life, the absence of personal liberty of life style, the existence of inequalities based on religion, race, and gender, and particularly the inferiority of women to Muslim men. It implies that the Arab and Muslim countries in the Middle East are to be protected from criticism of their societies, while Israel is to be subjected to the strictest judgment.

British colonial experience in India is an interesting historical example of how decisions and judgment will differ if made on the basis of moral equivalency, or on the moral values that emerged from the period of Western Enlightenment. Sir William Jones, British Supreme Court Judge in Calcutta, argued that the British judiciary there in the 1780s should ensure that the Indian natives there should "be indulged in their own prejudices, civil and religious, and suffered to enjoy their own customs unmolested." This meant preserving the caste system, among other matters.[295] On the other hand, Governor-General Lord William Bentinck in 1829 dispensed with the concept of moral relativism by formally banning the practice of sati, by which a widowed Hindu woman was forced to immolate herself on her husband's funeral pyre.[296]

Similarly, the belief that a particular culture cannot be judged by the ethos of another culture, has led to a reluctance to criticize actions and convictions that are different and unpalatable. George Orwell, in his essay "Looking back on the Spanish War," was aware of the problem; what impressed him was that the atrocities committed in the war were believed or disbelieved "solely on grounds of political predilection."[297] Western style cultural relativism, maintaining there is no dominant or guiding culture, has led to a disinclination to criticize non-Western societies and their actions. This is particularly noticeable in the comments in the international community on the physical attacks on Israel. Some of these relativists resemble what Ernest Gellner called "anthropological Hamlets," tortured by doubts about how one culture could ever grasp the categories of another, reluctant to rebuke intolerant and unjust ideas and societies, and more specifically hesitant to criticize actions of Islamicists. Some of this stems from a positive welcoming of diversity and its supposed broadminded benevolence. Claude Lévi-Strauss was a major figure in raising awareness of the existence and value of indigenous cultures and social arrangements. Yet he also wrote of the destructive aspects of Western civilization on humans.[298] In negative fashion, the adherence of some Western intellectuals to relativism is more likely to derive from disenchantment with the values of their own culture, and the view of everything in it as contemptible. Hatred of those values may be more potent than love of others.

MULTICULTURALISM

That the concept of multiculturalism has drawbacks as well as benefits, has long been recognized. The British historian R. H. Tawney, in his 1931 book *Equality*, wrote that a community requires "a common culture because without it, it is not a community at all." The great 14th century Arab historian, Ibn Khaldun, wrote that civilization arises only where there is solidarity. Today this idea of solidarity, and commitment to the basic structures and values of a country, is challenged by identity politics, by the advocacy of diversity and the presence of competing groups. Multiculturalism aims at accommodating different religions, cultural and ethnic traditions within a society. At the same time it also confers benefits on ethnic or racial minorities and may lead to separation and friction. As Brian Barry, strongly defending the universalism of the Enlightenment, argued in his book, *Culture and Equality*, that multiculturalism, by proposing and defending group rights, may be a threat to liberal egalitarianism because it disparages individual rights, fragments society, supports the politicization of group identities, does not focus on socio-economic and legal inequalities, and undermines a politics of redistribution.

Multiculturalism presents both intellectual and political problems. In effect, it has in recent practice led to restriction rather than protection of free speech, to laws making it a criminal offense with penalties for making critical remarks about some religious, ethnic, or national groups. The European Court of Human Rights decided that hate speech was not protected by the 1950 European Convention on Human Rights. Multiculturalism in practice has led to tolerating intolerant minorities in Western countries and Israel. In practice it may mean excusing or minimizing crimes perpetrated by non-Westerners. The French writer, Pascal Bruckner, has defined multiculturalism as racism of the antiracists; it chains people to their roots, and they are imprisoned in an ethnic or racial definition. It may undermine individuality and self-reliance. People are thus prevented from liberating themselves from their own traditions. The British writer, Andrew Anthony, has similarly argued that, like all faiths, multiculturalism has constructed its own theology of irrational ideas, a theology that has spread without informed debate. It imprisons individuals in group identities, and in celebrating differences between people has become a means of enforcing group conformity.[299]

Contemporary politicians have understood the political problem. German Chancellor Angela Merkel on October 16, 2010, declared that multiculturalism "has failed totally." Multiculturalism, at least in Germany, was not in fact a humane formula to respect other cultures, but a concept through which immigrant workers could remain committed to the culture of their homeland, not to Germany. In this declaration, she reflected the fact that the state had not always imposed rules on or promoted German values to newcomers and had even accommodated the demands of immigrants. In a study in 1998, the German-Syrian scholar, Bassam Tibi, contended that, though differences may exist, European countries needed a *leitkultur*, a core or guiding culture, which was necessary for a democratic community, concerned with modernity, secularism, and human rights.[300]

Similarly, David Cameron, the British Prime Minister on February 5, 2011, said that "under the doctrine of state multiculturalism we have encouraged different cultures to live separate lives, apart from each other and apart from the mainstream...We have even tolerated these segregated communities behaving in ways that run completely counter to our values." Equally important, Cameron drew attention to the problem of double standards: "when a white person holds objectionable views, racist for example, we rightfully condemn them. But when equally unacceptable views or practices come from someone who isn't white, we've been too cautious to stand up to them."

The contemporary belief that all cultural groups and religions should be tolerated and have a right to self-determination or autonomy may be salutary as a general proposition, but the degree of that tolerance should be relevant both to democratic values and principles of human rights being applied to the behavior of those groups and religions, and to the momentum of demographic changes. The British Liberal Democrat lawyer, Lord Carlisle, warned in February 2011, that rulings by the European Court of Human Rights in Strasbourg had undermined British efforts to deport dangerous individuals. The human rights of these suspected terrorists carried more weight than the risk of harm to British citizens. There is today no easy balance for nations between protecting their cultural values and protecting minority rights.[301]

MODERN THOUGHT AND ISRAEL

How does modern style of thought affect Israel? From its beginning, Israel was confronted with the problems of a society that would incorporate religious and secular strains of thought, social cultures, class differences, Askenazim and Sephardim, and the Arab minority. To consolidate the system, in a sense to try to emulate the American melting pot experience, the attempt was made to speed up the integration of citizens into one Hebrew culture. Ben-Gurion formulated his concept of *mamlachtiyut,* the ideology that the state is supreme in exercise of statehood or sovereignty, including creating a state educational system, and absorbing into the bureaucracy of the state important organizations such as the military Palmach unit, the Histadrut school network, and the various youth movements. This concept, and the Zionist enterprise, have been challenged by the argument for multiculturalism and the criticism that the Israeli system treats various sectors of the pluralistic society unjustly. For Israel, the dilemma of how to coordinate the political agendas of differing religious and ethnic groups makes national political decisions and the acceptance of a national agenda more difficult to reach. The underlying problem is that groups in Israel want to continue their own traditional culture and identity, rather than assimilate or adapt to the cultural values and identity of the national majority. This problem was made clear by Aristotle (1303a): "A state cannot be constituted from any chance body of persons...Most of the states which have admitted persons of another stock, either at the time of their foundation or later, have been troubled by sedition."

LINGUISTIC BIAS

Philosophical pragmatism, originally formulated by William James and John Dewey, and revived in recent years by Richard Rorty and others, purports to reject absolutes and "embrace uncertainty and provisionality," but in reality may advocate certain partisan goals.[302] That reality, on the campuses of the United States, Canada, and in some European countries has been exhibited by abuse of academic freedom through constant antisemitic and anti-Zionist verbal attacks, discriminatory activities which prevent genuine scholarly discussion of relevant issues. Far from the pluralistic opinions that might be expected, a substantial section of the media, as well as many in academia, follow a similar ideological discourse hostile to Israel. Pierre-André Taguieff has described the process by which Israel and Jews are defamed, while the crimes of the supposed deprived, especially the Palestinians, are condoned. Language has been corrupted. The Palestinians are spoken of as the most dominated and oppressed people in the world. Those using violence against Israel are described by the media as victims. Hobbes, in his passage in the *Leviathan* on abuses of speech, warned that words used metaphorically may deceive others.

Linguistic bias and semantic falsification regarding Israel is apparent in terminology used or not used in the media. Critics of Israel, when referring to hostile Arab actions, may use impersonal language; thus "war happened in 1948," or "armed conflict broke out," or "missiles rained down on Israel," or "Palestinian warriors defended." By contrast, in stark and prejudiced language, Israel "aggressively attacked" whatever was the target, or "militants," not "terrorists," who were the perpetrators of attacks against Israel.

POST-ZIONISM

The politically dominant Zionist group, from early years in the Yishuv, the Jewish settlement in Palestine, was socialist and nationalist. It saw the creation of a Jewish state as part of the historical movement to fulfill the leftist dream of a socialist international world or a new world order. It did not subscribe to the biblical injunction (Numbers 23.9) that "the people shall dwell alone and shall not be reckoned among the nations." For a time in the newly created Israel, the ideology of the Zionist Left fostered an alliance of Jewish and Arab workers against the supposed common class enemy. However, the political reality of Arab hostility forced Israel to place more emphasis on Jewish nationalism, rather than adhere to a socialist agenda. Post-Zionists have criticized Israel as too nationalistic, and called for what they consider a more liberal, secular, and open society.[303] In their desire for the state to exhibit these values they have raised the questions of Israeli identity and of a Jewish state.

In addition to this post-Zionist criticism of present day Israel, postmodernist theorists view Israel as a colonial oppressor and a racist opponent of the Palestinian liberation movement. The Palestinians are seen as victims, as "The Other" in modern terminology, as helpless, oppressed people, who should benefit from the contemporary fashionable stress on entitlement or what Robert Hughes called a "culture of complaint."[304] If some minimal compassion was ever shown for Jews when they were weak and persecuted, little approval is evinced for an Israel, strong and victorious in the wars it has fought, and a flourishing nation-state in an era when European countries have formed a union limiting their sovereign power.

Admittedly, the victory in 1967 led some Israelis to high expectations about the future of the captured territories, though the Israel government and mainstream Israelis awaited a phone call which never came from the Arab governments to negotiate a peace settlement. Thus, little David was now seen to have become Giant Goliath; forgotten was the reality that Israel, surrounded geographically and demographically by the large Arab and Muslim world, was still little David. The historically defenseless and powerless Jews, who had suffered defeat and exile, the eternal, vulnerable victims everywhere, were now the tough individuals making their own destiny and exercising power over others. That change in power relationships has had a dramatic, perhaps traumatic, effect on Arab sensibility. Since the battle of Khaibar in 629, when the forces of Muhammad defeated the Jews in the area, the condition of Jews in Muslim countries was one of *dhimmi* status, a subordinate position imposing obligations and the *jizya*, poll tax.[305] The persecuted Jew was now in 1967 the arrogant Israeli colonialist. The Israeli state of 8,000 square miles was confronting the Arab world of 8.6 million square miles, stretching from the Atlantic to the Persian Gulf. Only on rare occasions have the actions of Israel been welcomed, if surreptitiously and for self-interested motives, by the surrounding Arab countries for an action that benefited them. Such hypocritical approval was accorded to the action in 1981, when Israel in defiance of international law destroyed Osirak, the nuclear bomb installation in Iraq, that Saddam Hussein was planning and which other Arab nations feared. Arab nations said little about Israeli violation of international law at the time, when they were saved from a nuclear Iraq. Israel had acted in its own self-defense and also, it turned out, in the interests of all countries opposing nuclear proliferation.

THE PALESTINIAN NARRATIVE

Postmodern thought tends to interpret events and history by designing a "narrative," since it suggests the full truth is unknowable. Radical critics of Israel tend to accept the Palestinian narrative of the Arab relationship with Israel and with Jews as more appropriate than the accepted and acknowledged historical account. To this date, no "new historians" have appeared among Palestinians to challenge that narrative. Elements of that narrative have been discussed in previous chapters, regarding the creation of Israel, the responsibility for violence and the various wars, the reason for refugees, and the supposed injustice done to Palestinians who are portrayed as victims of Israeli aggression. The narrative of victimhood is sometimes formulated in extreme fashion. Some Palestinians regard themselves as the "new Jews," even to the extent of suffering a "new Holocaust." In this linguistic reversal, Jews are the new Nazis.[306] A Spanish cartoon depicted Ariel Sharon with a Hitler mustache. Such excessive rhetoric, stemming from the Palestinian narrative, is rarely applied to truly reactionary regimes and groups that violate human rights in the world, or engage in terrorist acts. Radical critics accepting that Palestinian narrative even refuse to recognize Israel's need to defend itself against threats to its very existence.

This refusal is an illustration of a more general issue to the analysis of which the case of the political canary of Israel is pertinent. The moral imperative of the Western critics who accept the Palestinian narrative of Israel has been transmuted into relativism and a stance of appeasement, a mindset that has as its outcome an inability or refusal to defend the West against threats to its culture and way of life. Europe, it has been argued, is turning away from power.[307] That mindset was surprisingly exhibited by Baroness Eliza Manningham-Buller, former head of Britain's secret service MI5, who said, after her retirement, that the "war on terror" was unwinnable and that the British government should "reach out" to al-Qaida.

The problem of misplaced idealism, or naïve acceptance of a "narrative," is a familiar one. In his critical writings on the Soviet Union, Robert Conquest wrote about the Western acceptance of the Soviet narrative of its affairs and its version of totalitarian concepts. "Many in the West gave their full allegiance to these alien (totalitarian) beliefs. Many others were at any rate not ill disposed towards them. And beyond that there was a sort of secondary infection of the mental atmosphere which still to some degree persists, distorting thought in countries that escaped the more wholesale disasters of our time."[308] His views of the "mental aberrations" of Western intellectuals are pertinent to the attitudes of some critics and public opinion view towards Jews and Israel. His argument is borne out in the egregious example of the German philosopher Martin Heidegger, who believed that Hitler and Nazism were morally and aesthetically preferable to apolitical liberalism.[309]

This remembrance of things in the Soviet past, the willingness of millions of people to respond to the call for support of distasteful totalitarian regimes, a support intensified by propaganda, teaching in schools, universities, and youth organizations, and justified by some well-meaning people, the kind that Lenin once called "political idiots," resembles the behavior of those accepting the Palestinian narrative. Some contemporary intellectuals are prone to dismiss the threat of radical Islamists, of Hamas and Hezbollah, against Israel as a deliberate exaggerated scare, an attitude reminiscent of the similar dismissal by an earlier generation of intellectuals of any criticism of the Soviet Union or even of the dangers of German Nazism. Symbolically, they may wear the Palestinian headdress, the keffiyeh. Politically, the present generation may accept Palestinian narratives both of their general "victimhood" and of individuals seen as heroic figures. They may also accept the false statements that Israel had bombed Red Cross ambulances during the fighting in Lebanon, indicating Israeli brutality.

Aware of the power of myth and symbol, the Palestinian narrative has used the fate of two particular individuals as illustrative of the brutality of Israel. One was Mohammed al-Durra, the twelve year old boy allegedly killed by the IDF; the allegation turned out to be false. The other was Rachel Corrie, who had worked with the International Solidarity Movement and was accidentally killed in Gaza in 2003 by an Israeli bulldozer, that she deliberately tried to block. She became a symbol of defiance of Israel. The narrative has made its way into the theater as well as in public activity. In London, the 2009 production of an eight minute play, "Seven Jewish Children" by Caryl Churchill, at best an exhibition of radical chic, has echoes of the historic blood libel charge against Jews, and implications that Israelis have no pity for the Palestinian babies they are accused of killing. Opponents of Israel expressed outrage and accepted the false statement that Israel had bombed Red Cross ambulances during the fighting in Lebanon. More extremely, they have engaged in pro-Palestinian rallies, promoted the call for boycotts, divestments, and sanctions against Israel, and used social networks over the internet to spread their passion for delegitimization of the state. The impact of innovation in communication has become familiar since the success of video cassettes, in 1978-79, of Ayatollah Ruhollah Khomeini while in exile in Paris, in mobilizing Iranians to demonstrate against and to overthrow the Shah of Iran in 1979.

Some changes have taken place. An increasing number of states, including the republics of the former Soviet Union, and many African and Asian countries, have established or upgraded diplomatic relations with Israel over the last twenty years. Israel has not only the peace treaties with Egypt and Jordan, cold though they may be, but also unheralded informal and trading relations with other Arab countries in the Gulf and the Maghreb, and with Muslim countries in Asia.[310] Relations with Europe are more uncertain. The leaders of some European countries, France, Germany, Italy, have been supporters of Israel, but individuals and groups in other countries, including the Scandinavian countries, Ireland, Spain, and Belgium, have exhibited antisemitic, as well as anti-Israeli, feelings. Governments in those countries have been constant critics of Israeli actions. Similarly, most international organizations, which are dominated by non-democratic and Islamic nations, have been hostile to Israel, though the country was admitted in 2010 into the OECD, the organization of the thirty-three most developed countries in the world that are democratic.

However, the impact of the Palestinian narrative remains. In one of his *Unpopular Essays*, Bertrand Russell wrote of the delusion held by some since the French Revolution of the superior virtue of the oppressed, and the misconception that some sections of the human race are morally better or worse that others. Since World War II, the radical left in the contemporary world, often obsessed with the heritage of that Revolution, has painted a fanciful, romantic picture of less developed countries and their superior virtue, regardless of their actual behavior. Realistic assessment has given way to clichés of "Third Worldism," anti-capitalism, and anti-imperialism. The radical left has joined with Islamist extremists in condemnations of Western civilization, particularly of the United States and Israel. Two of the numerous examples of this alliance are sufficient. One is the reported utterance of Karlheinz Stockhausen, the well known German avant-garde composer, who said the attack on the World Trade Center on 9/11 was "the greatest work of art for the whole cosmos."[311] The other is the series of statements by the French philosopher, Michel Foucault, who had met the Ayatollah Khomeini in Paris in 1978, and not only thought he was a saint, but also that his taking of power in Iran in 1979 would mean a new Muslim style of politics that could signal the beginning of a new form of "political spirituality" not only for the Middle East, but also for Europe. Foucault, expressing the need for "authenticity" and new forms of creativity, found this spirituality in militant Islam. He argued that the demand for the "legitimate rights of the Palestinian people" hardly stirred the Arab peoples. This cause would become acceptable with "the dynamism of an Islamic movement," something much stronger than the Marxist, Leninist, or Maoist one.[312]

Conscious now that the Western proletariat is not about to become revolutionary, post-Marxist theorists manifest solidarity with or pity for Third World countries, the "wretched of the earth" in the words of Franz Fanon, and also view non-Western liberation movements as the instruments for desirable change. The danger is of a "transfer of loyalties to a far worse and thoroughly inimical culture, or at least to a largely uncritical favoring of such a culture."[313] Are Palestinians to be regarded as among "the wretched of the earth?" The Palestinian movement has benefited in terms of military assistance and training, and diplomatic and propaganda support, from being associated with the radical left and the Third World, with their calls for human rights, economic justice, and world wide national liberation. It took the strategic advice of General Nguyen Giap, the Vietnamese military commander of the People's Army, who told Yasser Arafat to "stop talking about annihilating Israel, and instead turn your terror war into a struggle for human rights. Then you will have the American people eating out of your hand."[314] Help on how to apply this advice was given to Arafat by the Communist leaders of Romania, Nicolai Ceausescu, the President, and Ion Mihai Pacepa, head of intelligence.

It is Israel's misfortune that the Palestinians have been selected by the radical chic critics or haters of the West as the exemplar of desirable change and as the symbol of the oppressed and the Muslim disinherited. Indeed, for the Western radical left, the Palestinians are the ultimate victims. Traditional antisemitism has often used Jews as scapegoats, responsible for all or most of the problems of the world. By tortuous logic and with pathological intensity the State of Israel has now become the convenient scapegoat for expressions of Western guilt over the past behavior of Western countries in wars, in colonial acquisitions, and in economic exploitation. In contrast, the Palestinians have been regarded by the anti-imperialist left as part of the Third World. With rhetorical overkill, that hypercriticism, that self-denunciation, even self-hatred or what Alain Finkielkraut once termed "penitential narcissism," along with an accompanying posture of anti-colonialism, expressed by radicals in Western democratic systems has concentrated on the State of Israel. Forgotten is the complexity of Western historical experience and the fact that the West has had heroes, as well as villains. Ignored is the reality that anti-colonial movements in practice have often been more preoccupied with self-determination than with human rights, ostensibly the concern of the radical left. Disregarded is the nature of the Arab countries surrounding Israel, countries that lack genuine democratic institutions, pluralism, willingness to challenge their own convictions, and which impose strict limits on free expression. Instead, Palestinian and Arab nationalism, the nationalism of "the oppressed," is admired and justified, while Jewish nationalism is identified as imperialist and racist. The national struggle of Jews in the Yishuv, the Zionist liberation movement, against British rule is disregarded.

Some of the more notable, and well-publicized, figures among the relentless critics of Israel and its policies, are Jewish or of Jewish origin, or non-Jewish Jews in the words of Isaac Deutscher, such as Noam Chomsky, Harold Pinter, and Avi Shlaim.

To suggest that they are self-hating Jews may be excessive, but their continuous animus and unique concentration on the imperfections of Israel suggests a problem with their Jewish identity. Moreover their claim to be heroic dissenters fighting against an entrenched Jewish mainstream, keen to censure their utterances, is belied by the ease to which they have access to prestigious outlets such as the BBC, American television networks, Time Magazine, the New York Review of Books, the London Review of Books, the Guardian and the Independent newspapers, and many other publications.

The obsession with Israel, the focus on the crimes and sins it has supposedly committed, and the extent and degree of hostility defies rational explanation. For Arab rulers, attacks on the Jewish state are a welcome distraction from attention to the problems of their own societies or their political culture. For the West, it may be an attempt to acquit itself of guilt for persecution of Jews. Some, cynically or otherwise, see the "victimhood" of the allegedly oppressed Palestinians, with its overtones of noble melodrama, anger, and despair as equivalent in moral abhorrence to Auschwitz. For some the obsession may be due to an antisemitism, which can be disguised as an anti-Zionist or anti-Israel attitude, or as a pretense for equity for the Palestinians.

Any analysis of the media in the Western world, let alone elsewhere, would show an inherent bias in the reporting. Israel is generally viewed as primarily responsible for the continuation of the Palestinian-Israeli conflict. Israeli settlements in the West Bank are deemed to be the main obstacle to any peace settlement. The Arab world and the Palestinians, specifically, are viewed as having made a substantial effort to achieve peace. The reports and analyses, and the acceptance of the Palestinian narrative by these media critics may reflect their genuine convictions or their support for the cause of those they regard as "the oppressed," or it may be the result of intimidation by Arab threats and occasional violence. Israeli leaders are described as "hawkish" or "irredentist" or "ultra-nationalist." Little commentary is focused on terrorism directed against Israelis or on the Arab refusal to accept Israel as a Jewish state. Israel's use of force in its own defense is often characterized as "disproportionate." With all these factors in mind, and remembering that it has been two thousands years since Jews last exercised sovereign political power, perhaps the beginning of wisdom in discussion of Israeli politics and society is to avoid what Raymond Aron called "abstract moralism."

Notes

1 Michael Oakeshott, *Rationalism in Politics and Other Essays*, new ed.,(Indianapolis: Liberty Press, 1991), 95.

2 Elie Wiesel. "The Perils of Indifference," Speech in Washington, D.C., April 12, 1999.

3 Julien Benda, *The Treason of the Intellectuals* (New York: Morrow, 1928).

4 Hermann Rauschning, *Hitler Speaks* (London: Butterworth, 1939), 233-234.

5 Adolf Hitler, *Mein Kampf*, trans. Ralph Manheim (Boston: Houghton Mifflin, 1943), 231.

6 Reinhold Niebuhr, "David and Goliath," *Christianity and Crisis* 27 (June 22, 1967):141.

7 Justice Dorit Beinish, "Protecting Democracy and Human Rights in Tense Times: the Israeli Supreme Court," *Israel 21c Newsletter*, December 6, 2002.

8 David Ben-Gurion, quoted in Eli Sha'altiel,"David Ben-Gurion on Partition 1937," *Jerusalem Quarterly* no. 10 (Winter 1979): 42.

9 George Gilder, *The Israel Test* (New York: Vigilante Books, 2009), 4.

10 David Mamet, "If I forget thee, Jerusalem: the Power of blunt Nostalgia," *Forward*, February 2002.

11 Murray Edelman, *Politics as Symbolic Action*, (Chicago: Markham, 1971) 83.

12 Barry Rubin, *The Tragedy of the Middle East* (Cambridge, UK: Cambridge University Press, 2002).

13 Caroline B. Glick, "Lara Logan and Media Rules," *The International Jerusalem Post*, February 25-March 3, 2011.

14 Arthur Schlesinger, Jr., "Foreign Policy and the American Character," *Foreign Affairs* 62 (1983-84): 8.

15 Natan Sharansky, *Defending Identity: its indispensable role in protecting democracy* (New York: Public Affairs, 2008).

16 Allan Gerson, *The Kirkpatrick Mission: Diplomacy Without Apology: America at the United Nations, 1981-85* (New York: Free Press, 1991).

17 Walter Lippmann, *Public Opinion* (New York: Harcourt, Brace, 1922).

18 Irving Janis, *Groupthink: Psychological studies of policy decisions and fiascoes* (Boston: Houghton Mifflin, 1982).

19 Aharon Megged quoted in *Introduction*, Edward Alexander and Paul Bogdanor, eds., *The Jewish Divide over Israel: aggressors and defenders* (New Brunswick: Transaction, 2006), xviii).

20 Ruth Wisse, *Jews and Power* (New York: Schocken, 2007).

[21] Michael Oren, "Jews and the Challenge of Sovereignty," *Azure*, no. 23 (Winter 2006).

[22] Ben-Gurion, "In Defense of Messianism," *Midstream*, 12, (March 1966):68).

[23] Assaf Sagiv, "The Sad State of Israeli Radicalism," *Azure*, no. 40 (Spring 2010).

[24] Michel Foucault, *Security, Territory, Population*, lectures at the Collège de France, 1977-78 (New York: Palgrave, Macmillan, 2007), 390.

[25] Jean-Paul Sartre, preface in Frantz Fanon, *The Wretched of the Earth* (New York: Grove, 1961), 22).

[26] Norman Cohn, *Warrant for Genocide: the Myth of the Jewish World-Conspiracy and the Protocols of the Elders of Zion* (Chico,CA: Scholars Press, 1981); George Mosse, *Towards the Final Solution: a History of European Racism* (New York: Howard Fertig, 1978), 20-22; Saul Friedlander, *Nazi Germany and the Jews: the years of persecution, 1933-39* (New York: HarperCollins, 1997), 94-95.

[27] John Bolton, *Surrender is not an Option* (New York: Threshold Editions, 2007), 451.

[28] Timur Kuran, *The Long Divergence: How Islamic Law Held Back the Middle East* (Princeton: Princeton University Press. 2011), 5, 279-302.

[29] Adam Roberts, "Prolonged Military Occupation: The Israeli-Occupied Territories since 1967," 84 *American Journal of International Law* 44-45(1990).

[30] Edmund Burke, *Reflections on the Revolution in France.*

[31] Steven J. Rosen, "Obama's Moment of Truth at the UN," *Commentary* (January 6, 2011).

[32] Michael R. Fischbach, *Jewish Property Claims Against Arab Countries* (New York: Columbia University Press, 2008).

[33] Ya'akov Meron,"Why Jews Fled the Arab Countries," *Middle East Quarterly* (September 1995):47-55).

[34] Anne Bayefsky, *Eye on the UN*, February 11, 2010).

[35] Hillel Neuer, "Ziegler's Follies," *Azure*, no.32 (Spring 2008).

[36] Stephen M. Walt, "A Visit to Libya: First Impressions," *Foreign Policy*, January 19, 2010.

[37] Meir Litvak and Esther Webman, *From Empathy to Denial: Arab Responses to the Holocaust* (New York: Columbia University Press, 2009).

[38] Ian Brownlie, "The Politics of Human Rights in relation to the Rule of Law," in Miodrag A. Jovanovic & Ivana Krstic, eds., *Human Rights Today-60 Years of the universal Declaration* (Utrecht: Eleven International Publishing, 2010), 21-28.

[39] Chatham House Report on the Goldstone Report, November 27, 2009.

[40] Laurie R. Blank, "The Application of IHL in the Goldstone Report: a Critical Commentary," 12 *YIHL* 347-402 (2009).

[41] Henry Kissinger, "The Pitfalls of Universal Jurisdiction," *Foreign Affairs* (July/August, 2001).

[42] Jon Carlson and Neville Yeomans, "Whither goes the Law: Humanity or Barbarity" in *The Way Out* (Melbourne: Landsdowne, 1975).

[43] Colonel Charles J. Dunlap, Jr., "Law and Military Interventions: Preserving Humanitarian Values in 21st Conflicts," *Harvard University*, November 29, 2001; Dunlap, "Lawfare: a Decisive Element of 21st Century Conflicts?", 54, *Joint Force Quarterly* 34 (2009); Michael A. Newton, "Illustrating Illegimate Lawfare," *Case Western Reserve Journal of International Law*, vol.23 (2011).

[44] Véronique Zanetti, "Global Justice: is Interventionism Desirable?", *Metaphilosophy*, vol. 32, issue 1-2 (January 2001): 196-211.

[45] Anne-Marie Slaughter, "A Liberal Theory of International Law," 94, *American Society International Law Proceedings* 240, (2000): 246.

[46] Tony Blair, "Confronting Gadhafi is Not Enough," *Wall Street Journal*, March 19-20, 2011.

[47] Greg Rose, "Lawfare," *Austalian/Israel Review*, March 2011.

[48] Richard K. Betts, "Compromised Command," *Foreign Affairs* (July/August, 2001): 130.

[49] David Rivken and Lee Casey, "The Rocky Shoals of International Law," *The National Interest* (Winter 2000/2001): 35.

[50] Brooke Goldstein, "Countering Lawfare," *Aviation Week,* January 3, 2011.

[51] Pascal Bruckner, *The Tyranny of Guilt: an Essay on Western Masochism* (Princeton: Princeton University Press, 2010).

[52] Robert Cryer, *Prosecuting International Crimes: selectivity and the International Criminal Law Regime* (New York: Cambridge Press, 2005), 39).

[53] Dan Plesch, *America, Hitler and the UN: How the Allies Won World War II and Forged a Peace* (London: Tauris, 2011).

[54] Mark Mazower, "The Strange Triumph of Human Rights, 1933-1950," *The Historical Journal*, 47,2 (2004):397.

[55] Roger Normand and Sarah Zaidi, *Human Rights at the UN: the Political History of Universal Justice* (Bloomington: IN, University Press, 2008), 9.

[56] Ruti G. Teitel, *Transitional Justice* (New York: Oxford University Press, 2000).

[57] Anne Herzberg, "NGO Lawfare, Exploitation of Courts in the Arab Israeli Conflict," NGO Monitor, September 2008, p.6; Luc Reydams, *Universal Jurisdiction: International and Municipal Legal Perspectives* (New York: Oxford University Press, 2003), 5.

[58] Quoted in Anne Herzberg, op. cit., p. 11.

[59] Steven Emerson, "Combatting Lawfare," *Jewish World Review* (March 16, 2010).

[60] Maurice Olender, *Race and Erudition* (Cambridge,MA: Harvard University Press, 2009).

[61] François Jacob, quoted in Olender, 2.

[62] Maurice Olender, *The Languages of Paradise* (Cambridge,MA: Harvard University Press, 1992).

[63] François Jacob, *Le Jeu des possibles* (Paris: Fayard, 1981), 12.

[64] Ashley Montagu , "Man's Myth: the Fallacy of Race," reprinted in Ellis Cashmore and James Jennings, eds., *Racism:Essential Readings* (London: Sage, 2001).

[65] Norman and Zaidi, p.261.

[66] Mark Gardner, "One 'blood libel' but what about the others?" *Community Security Trust* (January, 14, 2011).

[67] Walter Laqueur, *A History of Zionism* (New York: Holt, Rinehart and Winston, 1972), 578-79.

[68] Timothy Snyder, *Bloodlands:Europe between Hitler and Stalin* (New York: Basic Books, 2010).

[69] Robert O. Freedman, ed., *Soviet Jewry in the 1980s* (Durham,NC: Duke University Press, 1989), 35.

[70] Yevgeny Primakov, *Russia and the Arabs* (New York: Basic Books, 2009).

[71] Goronwy Rees, "Columny," 46, *Encounter* (1976): 29-30; Daniel P. Moynihan, *A Dangerous Place* (Boston: Little, Brown, 1978).

[72] Paul Johnson, *A History of the Modern World* (London: Weidenfeld and Nicolson, 1983), 690.

[73] Joel Fishman, "The Message of the BDS," *SPME,* January 4, 2011.

[74] Alexander Yakobson and Amnon Rubinstein, *Israel and the Family of Nations: the Jewish Nation-state and Human Rights* (New York: Routledge, 2009), 93.

[75] Lippmann, *Public Opinion,* 14.

[76] Michael Curtis and Susan Gitelson, *Israel in the Third World* (New Brunswick: Transaction, 1976).

[77] Moshe Decter, *To Serve, To Teach, To Leave* (New York: American Jewish Congress, 1977).

[78] Elizabeth Samson, "Warfare through Misuse of International Law," *BESA Center Perspectives Papers No. 73* (March 23, 2009)

[79] Matthias Hartwig, "Human Rights in Times of War," in Miodrag A. Jovanovic & Ivana Krstic, *Human Rights Today-60 Years of the Universal Declaration* (Utrecht: Eleven International Publishing, 2010), 173.

[80] Jonathan Fox, "Muslim Hypocrisy: On the Violation of Religious Freedoms," BESA Center Perspectives Paper, no. 120 (November 14, 2010).

[81] Martin Kramer, "Islam vs. Democracy," *Commentary* (January 1993) : 38.

[82] Juergen Osterhammel, *Colonialism: a Theoretical Overview* (Princeton: Marcus Wiener, 1997); Marc Ferro, *Colonization: a Global History* (New York: Routledge, 1997).

[83] David Biale, *Power and Powerless in Jewish History* (New York: Schocken Books,1986), 12-13.

[84] George Eliot, *Daniel Deronda* (New York:Knopf, 1999) p. 890.

[85] James Parkes, *Whose Land?* (Harmondworth: Penguin, 1970), pp. 17,31

[86] Meir Litvak, ed., *Palestinian Collective Memory and National Identity* (New York: Palgrave Macmillan, 2009), 2

[87] Amos Elon, *Jerusalem, City of Mirrors*, (Boston: Little, Brown, 1989), 33.

[88] Bernard Lewis, *Faith and Power: Religion and Politics in the Middle East* (New York: Oxford University Press, 2010), 7.

[89] Bruckner , *The Tyranny*, 30.

[90] Bernard Avishai, *A New Israel: Democracy in Crisis, 1973-1988, essays* (New York: Ticknor & Fields, 1990), 186.

[91] Yakobson and Rubinstein, 87.

[92] Isaiah Berlin, *The Power of Ideas*, ed., Henry Hardy (Princeton: Princeton University Press, 2000), 143.

[93] Biale, *Power,* 136, 147.

[94] Quoted in *Haaretz* , October 22, 2010.

[95] Chaim Herzog , (UN 1975).

[96] Mark Twain *The Innocents Abroad* (New York: Library of America, 1984), 485-86.

[97] Pierre Loti, *La Galilée,* cited in Landes, pp 48-49.

[98] Felix Bouvet, *Voyage en Terre-Sainte*, 8th ed. (Paris, Lévy, 1895).

[99] Diana Muir, "A Land without a People for a People without a Land," *Middle East Quarterly* (Spring 2008): 55.

[100] Israel Zangwill, "The Return to Palestine,' *New Liberal Review* (December 1901) : 615

[101] Rosalyn Higgins, *Problems and Process: International Law and how we use it* (Oxford: Oxford University Press, 1995).

[102] Julius Stone, Israel the United Nations, and International Law, Memorandum of Law, June 1980, S/14045/Annex,UN Doc. A/35/316 (1980).

[103] Shalom Goldman, *Zeal for Zion: Christians, Jews and the Idea of the Promised Land* (Chapel Hill, University of North Carolina Press, 2010).

[104] Abigail Green, "Rethinking Sir Moses Montefiore." *AHR*, vol. 110, no.3 (June 2005): 631-658.

[105] David Landes, "Palestine before the Zionists," *Commentary* (February 1976): 49.

[106] Anita Shapira, *Yigal Allon, Native Son:a Biography* (Philadelphia: University of Pennsylvania Press, 2008).

[107] Quoted in Martin Gilbert, "Lawrence of Arabia," *Azure*, no. 38 (Autumn 2009).

[108] Ruth Gavison, "The Jews' Right to Statehood: a Defense," *Azure* 15 (Summer 2003): 96.

[109] Anthony D. Smith, *Chosen Peoples* (New York: Oxford University Press, 2003), 218-253; Yosef Yerushalmi, *Zakhor: Jewish History and Jewish Memory* (Seattle: University of Washington Press,1982), 9-12.

[110] Michael Oren, "Orde Wingate: Friend under Fire," *Azure,* no. 10 (Winter 2001): 38.

[111] Gilbert Achcar, *The Arabs and the Holocaust: the Arab-Israeli war of narratives* (New York: Holt, 2010), 127.

[112] Penny Sinanoglu, "British Plans for the Partition of Palestine, 1929-1938," *The Historical Journal,* 52,1 (2009): 151.

[113] Hannah Arendt, *The Jewish Writings,* eds. Jerome Kohn and Ron Feldman (New York: Schocken, 2007).

[114] Parker T. Hart, *Saudi Arabia and the United States: Birth of a Security Partnership* (Bloomington: IN, University Press, 1998), 20.

[115] Bartley Crum, *Behind the Silken Curtain: a Personal Account of Anglo-American Diplomacy in Palestine and the Middle East* (Port Washington, NY: Kennikat Press, 1947).

[116] Efraim Karsh, *Palestine Betrayed,* 18-19.

[117] Benny Morris, *Righteous Victims* (New York: Knopf, 1994),111-120.

[118] Yitzhak Gil-Har, "Political Developments and Intelligence in Palestine in Palestine, 1930-40," *Middle East Studies,* vol.44, no.3 (May 2008): 419-434.

[119] Yehoshua Porath, *The Emergence of the Palestinian-Arab Movement, 1918-1929* (London: Cass, 1974), 250.

[120] Sean McMeekin, *The Berlin-Baghdad Express: the Ottoman Empire and Germany's Bid for World Power* (Cambridge, Mass: Harvard University Press, 2010), 361.

[121] Klaus-Michael Mallmann and Martin Cüppers,"'Elimination of the Jewish National Home in Palestine': The Einsatzkommando of the Panzer Army Africa, 1942" *Yad Vashem Studies* (Jerusalem, 2004): 26; Martin Cüppers and Klaus-Michael Mallman, *Croissant fertile et croix gammée, le Troisième Reich, les Arabes et la Palestine* (Paris: Lagrasse, 2009); *Documents on German Foreign Policy 1918-1945,* no. 515); David G. Dalin and John F. Rothmann, *Icon of Evil: Hitler's Mufti and the rise of radical Islam* (New York: Random House, 2008); Jennie Lebel, *The Mufti of Jerusalem and National-Socialism* (Belgrade: Cigoya Stampa, 2007).

[122] Karl Laske, *Le Banquier noir: François Genoud* (Paris: Editions du Seuil, 1996), 83.

[123] Klaus Gensicke, *Der Mufti von Jerusalem und die Nationalsozialisten* (Darmstadt: Wissenschaftliche Buchgesellschaft, 2007).

[124] Quoted in Gerhard Hoepp, *Mufti-Papiere; Briefe, Memoranden, Reden und Aufrufe Amin al-Husainis aus dem Exil. 1940-1945* (Berlin: Klaus Scwarz Verlag, 2004), 197.

[125] Bernard Lewis, *Semites and Anti-Semites* (New York: Norton, 1986),156.

[126] Wolfgang G. Schwanitz, "Germany's Middle East Policy," *The Middle East Review of International Affairs,"* Vo. 11, no.3 (September 2007): 31.

[127] McMeekin, op.cit.

[128] Both quoted in Götz Nordbruch, "'Cultural Fusion' of Thought and Ambitions? Memory, Politics, and the History of Arab-Nazi Encounters," *Middle East Studies,* vol. 47, no.1, (January 2011): 189-190.

[129] Documents on German Foreign Policy, 1918-1945, Series D, vol. 6 (London: Stationery Office, 1956), 743.

[130] Jeffrey Herf, foreword to Matthias Küntzel, *Jihad and Jew-Hatred: Islamism, Nazism, and the Roots of 9/11*.

[131] Pierre Péan, *L'Extremiste: François Genoud, de Hitler à Carlos*(Paris: Fayard, 1996); Karl Laske, *Le Banquier noir:François Genoud* (Paris: Seuil, 1996).

[132] Thomas Mayer, "Arab unity of Action and the Palestine Question, 1945-48," *Middle East Studies*, vol. 22, Issue 3 (1986): 331-349.

[133] Keith Jeffery, *The History of the Secret Intelligence Service, 1909-1949* (London: Bloomsbury, 2010).

[134] Cablegram from the Secretary-General of the League of Arab States to the Secretary-General of the United Nations, May 15, 1948.

[135] Jeffrey Herf, ed., *Convergence and Divergence: Antisemitism and Antisemitism in Historical Perspective* (London: Routledge, 2007).

[136] Ian Johnson, *A Mosque in Munich: Nazis, the CIA and the Rise of the Muslim Brotherhood in the West* (New York: Houghton Mifflin Harcourt, 2010).

[137] Achcar, op. cit.,114.

[138] John Calvert, *Sayyid Qutb and the Origins of Radical Islamism* (New York: Columbia University Press, 2010).

[139] Brynjar Lia, *Architect of Global Jihad: the life of al-Qaida strategist Abu Mus'ab al-Suri* (New York: Columbia University Press, 2008), 175.

[140] Mattias Küntzel, "Hitler's Legacy: Islamic Antisemitism in the Middle East," paper presented at Yale University, November 30, 2006.

[141] Paul Berman, *The Flight of the Intellectuals* (Brooklyn, NY: Melville House, 2010), 105-106.

[142] Francis R. Nicosia, "Fritz Groba and the Middle East Policy of the Third Reich," in Edward Ingram, ed. *National and International Politics in the Middle East* (London: Cass, 1986), 207).

[143] Jeffrey Herf, *Nazi Propaganda for the Arab World* (New Haven, Yale University Press, 2009); Herf, *The Jewish Enemy: Nazi Propaganda during World War II and the Holocaust* (Cambridge, MA: Harvard University Press, 2006).

[144] Matthias Küntzel, "Iranian Antisemitism:Stepchild of German National Socialism," *The Israel Journal of Foreign Affairs*, vol. 4, no.1 (2010): 47.

[145] Quoted in Klaus Gensicke, *The Mufti of Jerusalem and the Nazis: the Berlin Years* (London: Valentine, Mitchell, 2011), 108.

[146] Paul Berman, *The Flight of the Intellectuals*, 92.

[147] Herf, p.266.

[148] Benny Morris, *1948: A History of the First Arab-Israeli War* (New Haven: Yale University Press, 2008), p. 393.

[149] Karsh , *Palestine Betrayed*, 209.

[150] Benny Morris, *1948: the First Arab-Israeli War* (New Haven: Yale University Press, 2008),181.

[151] Mordechai Bar-On, ed., *A Never-Ending Conflict: a Guide to Israeli Military History* (Westport: Praeger, 2004), 6.

[152] Benny Morris, *Israel's Border Wars*, 1949-1956 (Oxford: Clarendon Press, 1993), 9.

[153] Susan Lee-Hattis, "Vladimir (Zeev) Jabotinsky's Parity Plan for Palestine," *Middle East Studies*, vol. 13, no.1 (1977): 93-94.

[154] Yakobson and Rubinstein, p. 30.

[155] Reinhold Niebuhr, *Christianity and Crisis* 8 (March 15, 1948): 30.

[156] Itamar Rabinovich, "Palestine Portrayed," *Jewish Review of Books* (Fall, 2010).

[157] Rashid Khalidi, *Palestinian Identity: the construction of modern national consciousness* (New York: Columbia University Press, 1997), 190; Walid Khalidi, ed., *From Haven to Conquest* (Beirut: The Institute for Palestinian Studies, 1971).

[158] Trygve Lie, *In the Cause of Peace: Seven Years with the United Nations* (London: Macmillan, 1954), 174).

[159] Jonathan Fine, "Establishing a new Governmental System: the Israeli Emergency Committee, October 1947-April 1948," *Middle East Studies*, vol. 44, no.6 (November, 2008) : 986.

[160] Shabtai Teveth, "The Palestine Arab Refugee Problem and its Origins," *Middle East Studies*, vol. 26, no.2, (April 1990) : 221.

[161] Meir Zamir, *Lebanon's Quest: the Road to Statehood, 1926-39* (London:Tauris, 1997), 35.

[162] Avraham Sela, "Transjordan, Israel and the 1948 War," *Middle East Studies*, vol. 28, No.4 (October 1992: p.631.

[163] Efraim Karsh, *Palestine Betrayed* (New Haven: Yale University Press, 2010), 234).

[164] Anita Shapira, "The Past is not a Foreign Country," *The New Republic*, November 11, 1999: 26-37.

[165] Efraim Karsh, *Fabricating Israeli History: the New Historians* (London:Cass, 1997), pp. 45,67.

[166] Benny Morris, *The Birth of the Palestinian Refugee Problem, 1947-1949* (New York: Cambridge University Press, 1989), 286.

[167] Benny Morris, *One State, Two States* (New Haven: Yale University Press, 2009).

[168] Bernard Lewis, *Semites and Anti-Semites* (New York: Norton, 1986), 270.

[169] Shabtai Teveth, p.223.

[170] Karsh , *Palestine Betrayed*, 134.

[171] Karsh, 27.

172 Motti Golani, ed., *The End of the British Mandate for Palestine, 1948: the Diary of Sir Henry Gurney* (New York: Palgrave, Macmillan, 2009), 61.

173 Karsh, 242.

174 Karsh ,216.

175 Fred Gottheil,"UNRWA and Moral Hazard," *Middle East Studies*, vol.42, no. 3(May 2006) :413.

176 Barry Rubin, et al.. "UNRWA:Refuge of Rejectionism," *Global Politician* June 19, 2009; Benjamin N. Schieff, *Refugees unto the Third Generation:UN Aid to the Palestinians* (Syracuse: Syracuse University Press, 1995).

177 Bernard Lewis, *Semites and Anti-Semites*, 220

178 James G. Lindsay, *Fixing UNRWA: Repairing the UN's Troubled System of Aid to Palestinian Refugees,* Washington Institute for Near East Policy (January 2009).

179 Ruth Lapidoth, "Legal Aspects of the Palestinian Refugee Question," *Jerusalem Letter,Viewpoints* (September 2002) : 4.

180 Howard Adelman, "Refugee Return: by right or by law," in Dan Avnon and Yotammm Benziman, eds., *Plurality and Citizenship in Israel: moving beyond the Jewish/ Palestinian Civil Divide* (New York: Routledge, 2010), 43.

181 Lapidoth, p.5; Rotem M.Giladi,"The Practice and Case Law of Israel in Matters Related to International Law," *Israel Law Review*, 29 (1995): 506-534.

182 Avi Beker, "The Forgotten Narrative: Jewish Refugees from Arab Countries," *Jewish Political Studies Review*, vol. 17, nos.3-4(Fall 2005) : 5-6.

183 Benny Morris, "Bleak House," *Tablet,* (December 2, 2010).

184 John Quigley, *Palestine and Israel: A challenge to Justice* (Durham: Duke University Press, 1990), 231.

185 David Raic, *Statehood and the Law of Self-Determination* (The Hague: Kluwer Law International, 2002), 24.

186 Michael Oren "The Six-Day War," in Bar-On, pp134-135.

187 Guy Ziv, "Shimon Peres and the French-Israeli Alliance, 1954-9," *Journal of Contemporary History*, vol. 45, no.2 (April 2010): 406-429.

188 Abba Eban, *Personal Witness: Israel through my Eyes* (New York: Putnam, 1992).

189 Isabella Ginor and Gideon Remez, *Foxbats over Dimona: the Soviets' Nuclear Gamble in the Six-Day War* (New Haven: Yale University Press, 2007).

190 Oren, p.135.

191 Elisha Efrat, *The Golan Heights: Occupation, Annexation, Negotiation* (Jerusalem: ABC Publishers, 2009), 47.

192 Colonel Richard Kemp, address to *Jerusalem Center for Public Affairs*, June 18, 2009.

[193] Henry Kissinger, *The White House Years* (Boston,: Little Brown, 1979), p. 344; William Quandt, *Decade of Decision* (Berkeley: University of California Press, 1977), p.65.

[194] Stephen Schwebel, "What Weight to Conquest?", *American Journal of International Law,* 64(1970): 344-7.

[195] Rosalyn Higgins, "The Place of International law in the Settlement of Disputes by the Security Council," 64, *American Journal of International Law* 1, 8 (1970).

[196] United Nations War Crimes Commission, Law Reports of Trials of War Criminals, vol. VIII, 1949.

[197] Julius Stone, *International Law and the Arab-Israeli conflict* (Bellevue Hill, Australia: Jirlac Pty, 2003), 15.

[198] Eugene Rostow, "Historical Approach to the issue of the Jewish settlement activity," *The New Republic* (April, 23, 1990).

[199] David M. Phillips, "The Illegal-Settlements Myth," *Commentary*, December 2009.

[200] Yoav Gelber, "The Israeli-Arab War of 1948: History versus Narrative," in Bar-On, p. 66.

[201] Ruth Gavison, "The Jews' Right to Statehood: a Defense," *Azure,* no.15 (Summer 2003).

[202] Sir Reader Bullard, *Britain and the Middle East: from the earliest times to 1950* (London: Hutchinson, 1951), 95.

[203] Mary C. Wilson, "A Passage to Independence," in Edward Ingram, ed., *National and International Politics in the Middle East* (London: Cass, 1986), 199.

[204] Pierre Nora, *Realms of Memory* (New York: Columbia University Press, 1998), 3; Pierre Vidal-Naquet, *Assassins of Memory*, trans. Jeffrey Mehlman (New York: Columbia University Press, 1992), xxiv.

[205] Hillel Cohen, *Army of Shadows: Palestinian Collaboration with Zionism, 1917-48* (Berkeley: University of California, 2008).

[206] Penny Sinanoglou, "British Plans for the Partition of Palestine, 1929-1938," *The Historical Journal,*52,1 (2009) : 131.

[207] Philip Graves, *Palestine: The Land of Three Faiths* (London: Cape, 1923), 112-113.

[208] Martin Gilbert, "Lawrence of Judea," *Azure* no. 38 (Autumn 2009): 6.

[209] Lewis, Semites, 169.

[210] Yehoshua Porath, *The Emergence of the Palestinian-Arab National Movement, 1918-1929,* vol.2, (London :Cass,1974) , 81-82.

[211] Julius Stone, *No peace—No War in the Middle East* (Sydney: Maitland,1969), 14-15.

[212] Ephraim Vavie, "The Palestinians-Competing Group Identities in the Absence of a State," in Asher Susser, ed., *Challenges to the Cohesion of the Arab State* (Tel Aviv: Dayan Center, 2008), 123.

[213] George Antonius, *The Arab Awakening: the Story of the Arab National Movement* (Philadelphia: Lippincott, 1939).

[214] Yehoshua Porath, 56-99.

[215] Pierre Manent, *La Raison des Nations: Democracy without Nations? The Fate of Self-government in Europe* (Wilmington, DE: ISI Books, 2007).

[216] Harris O. Schoenberg, *A Mandate for Terror* (New York: Shapolsky, 1989), 59.

[217] Esther Webman, "The Evolution of a Founding Myth:the Nakba and its fluctuating Meaning," in Meir Litvak and Esther Webman, p. 27.

[218] Hillel Cohen, 32-33.

[219] Amnon Rubinstein, "The Problem is How to Become an Israeli," *Ha'aretz*, January 4, 2000.

[220] Ruth Gavison, "Jewish and Democratic? A Rejoinder to the 'Ethnic Democracy' Debate," *Israel Studies*, vol. 4, no.1 (Spring 1999):53.

[221] Anita Shapira, "The Jewish-people Deniers," *The Journal of Israeli History*, vol.28, no 1 (March 2009): 63.

[222] Arthur Koestler, *The Thirteenth Tribe: the Khazar Empire and its Heritage* (London:Hutchinson, 1976).

[223] Jon Entine, *Abraham's Children: Race, Identity, and the DNA of the Chosen People* (New York: Grand Central Publishing, 2007), 219-20, 221.

[224] Anita Shapira, "The Jewish-people Deniers," *The Journal of Jewish History*, 71.

[225] Alexander Yakobson and Amnon Rubinstein, *Israel and the Family of Nations: the Jewish Nation-State and Human Rights,* (London: Routledge, 2009), 126.

[226] Christian Joppke, *Immigration and the Nation-state* (New York: Oxford University Press, 1999), 110.

[227] Amnon Rubinstein, "The Problem is How to Become an Israeli," *Ha'aretz,* January 4, 2000: 1-2.

[228] Yakobson and Rubinstein, p. 45.

[229] Sameena Nazir and Leigh Tomppert, *Women's Rights in the Middle East and North Africa-Citizenship and Justice* (Nw York: Rowman and Littlefield, 2005).

[230] Gil Atzmon, et al., "Abraham's Children in the Genome Era: Major Jewish Diaspora Populations Comprise Distinct Genetic Clusters with Shared Middle Eastern Ancestry," *American Journal of Human Genetics*, vol.86, Issue 6 (June 3, 2010): 850-859.

[231] Doron Behar et al., "The Genome-wide Structure of the Jewish People," *Nature* 466 (July 8, 2010): 238-242.

[232] Eric Hobsbawn, *The Invention of Tradition* (Cambridge,UK: Cambridge University Press, 1992), 1-2.

[233] Angelos Chaniotis, "European Identity:Learning from the Past," in Angelos Chaniotis , et al., eds., *Applied Classics: Comparisons, Constructs, Controversies* (Stuttgart: Steiner, 2009).

[234] Anthony D. Smith, *The Ethnic Origins of Nations* (Oxford: Blackwell, 1987), 34.

[235] Anthony D.Smith, "The Origins of Nations," *Ethnic and Racial Studies*, vol. 12, no. 3 (July 1989):345.

[236] Israel Bartal, "Inventing an Invention", *Haaretz*, July 6, 2008.

[237] Albert Einstein, *Collected Papers,* vol. 7 (Princeton: Princeton University Press, 1987), 236.

[238] Isaiah Berlin, Memorandum of January 23, 1959 to David Ben-Gurion, *Israel Studies*, vol. 13, no.3, (Fall 2008) :170-77.

[239] Meron Medzini, "Israel's Evolving Security Concept," *MERIA Journal*, vol. 14, no.,4 (December 2010).

[240] Steven J. Rosen, "The Arab Lobby: the European Component," *Middle East Quarterly* (Fall 2010): 17-32.

[241] Laurie R. Blank, op.cit, 366.

[242] Michael L. Gross, *Moral Dilemmas of Modern War:Torture, Assassination, and Blackmail in an Age of Asymmetric Conflict* (New York: Cambridge University Press, 2009).

[243] Daphne Barak-Erez, "Terrorism and Human Rights: Challenges to the FoUNdations of the Legal Order," in Jovanovic and Krstic, 188-189.

[244] Ibid, p. 191.

[245] Samy Cohen, *Israel's Asymmetric Wars* (New York: Palgrave Macmillan, 2010),130-132.

[246] Bernard Lewis, *The Assassins: a Radical Sect in Islam* (New York: Octagon Books, 1980).

[247] Alan Baker, "Are the Palestinians Ready for Peace," *Jerusalem Center for Public Affairs*, March 2011.

[248] Karsh, *Arafat,* 60-61.

[249] Benny Morris, *Israel's Border Wars: 1949-1956* (Oxford: Clarendon Press, 1993), 300.

[250] Neil Caplan, *Futile Diplomacy* (Totowa, NJ: Cass, 1983).

[251] Geoffrey Clarfield, "What does Hezbollah do for a Living," *New English Review*, December 2010.

[252] John Stuart Mill, *Considerations on Representative Government* (Chicago: Regnery, 1962), 312.

[253] Tony Judt, "Israel: the Alternative," *New York Review of Books* (October 2003).

[254] Tony Judt, *A Grand Illusion: an Essay on Europe* (Hill and Wang: New York, 1996), 121.

[255] Isaiah Berlin, *The Proper Study of Mankind: an Anthology of Essays,* eds., Henry Hardy and Roger Hausheer (New York: Farrar, Straus, Giroux, 1998), 590.

[256] Ernest Gellner, *Nations and Nationalism* (Ithaca: Cornell University Press,1983), 43.

[257] Anthony D. Smith, *Nations and Nationalism in a Global Era (*Cambridge, Mass.:Polity Press, 1995), p.159.

[258] Anita Shapira , "The Bible and Israeli Identity," *AJS* vol. 28, no.1 (November 2004): 11-42.

[259] Ahad Ha'am, *The Jewish State and the Jewish Problem* (New York: Jewish Publication Society, 1912).

[260] Anita Shapira, "Whatever became of 'Negating Exile?'," in Anita Shapira, ed., *Israeli Identity in Transition* (Westport: Praeger, 2004): 78.

[261] Ruth Gavison, "The Jews' Right", *Azure, no. 15* (Summer 2003).

[262] Guy Ben-Porat, "Israeli Society: Diversity, Tensions, and Governance," in Guy Ben-Porat et al., eds. *Israel Since 1980* (New York: Cambridge University Press, 2008), 30.

[263] Arthur Balfour on October 31, 1917, quoted in Alex Grobman, *The Palestinian Right to Israel* (Noble,OK: Icon Publishing Group, 2010), 63.

[264] Arich Bruce Saposnik, *Becoming Hebrew: the Creation of a Jewish National Culture in Ottoman Palestine* (New York: Oxford University Press, 2008).

[265] Mordechai Bar-On, in Shapira, *Israeli Identity*, p.7.

[266] Hanna Lerner, "Constitution-writing in deeply divided societies," in Benny Morris, ed., *Making Israel*, (Ann Arbor: University of Michigan Press, 2007), 75.

[267] Amnon Rubinstein, "The Curious Case of Jewish Democracy," *Azure*, no.41 (Summer 2010).

[268] Ruth Garrison, "The Shalit Case" in Michael Walzer et al., eds., *The Jewish Political Tradition*, vol. 2 (New Haven: Yale University Press, 2003), 305-339.

[269] Alon Tal, "Thirsting for Pragmatism; a constructive alternative to Amnesty's International Report on Palestinian Access to Water," *Israel Journal of Foreign Affairs*, vol. 4, no. 2 (2010): 59-71.

[270] Rashid Khalidi, *Palestinian Identity: the Construction of Modern National Consciousness* (New York: Columbia University Press, 2010), xxvi.

[271] Robert Rotberg, *When States Fail* (Princeton: Princeton University Press, 2004).

[272] Manfred Gerstenfeld, ed., *Academics against Israel and the Jews* (Jerusalem: Jerusalem Center for Public Affairs,2007), 23).

[273] Dan Senior and Saul Singer, "What's next for the Start-Up Nation?", *Wilson Quarterly* (Summer 2010):

[274] Idith Zertal, *Death and the Nation: History, Memory, Politics* (Or Yehuda:Dvir, 2002).

[275] Avi Shlaim, *The Iron Wall* (New York: Norton, 2000).

[276] Charles Liebman and Yaacov Yadgar, "Israeli Identity: the Jewish Component," in Anita Shapira, *Israeli Identity*,168-169.

[277] Yoram Hazony, *The Jewish State: the Struggle for Israel's Soul* (New York: Basic Books, 2000), 298.

[278] I.F.Stone, *This is Israel* (New York: Boni and Gaer, 1948).

[279] Yehoshafat Harkabi, *The Bar Kokhba Syndrome: Risk and Realism in International Politics* (Chappaqua, NY: Rossel Books, 1983).

280 Anita Shapira, "Whatever Became of 'Negating Exile?'," in Shapira, *Israeli Identity*: 99.

281 Eliezer Schweid, "The Construction and Deconstruction of Jewish Zionist Identity," in *Ideology and Jewish Identity in Israeli and American Literature*, ed. Emily M. Budick (Albany: State University of New York, 2001), 40.

282 Pierre-André Taguieff, *La Nouvelle Judéophobie* (Paris: Mille et Une Nuits, 2002); Taguieff, *La Nouvelle Propagande antijuive* (Paris: Presses Universitaires de France, 2010).

283 H.G. Wells, *The Work, Wealth, and Happiness of Mankind*, 505-6

284 Shlomo Slonim, "The 1948 American Embargo on Arms to Palestine," *Political Science Quarterly*, vol. 94 (Fall 1979): 503.

285 William D. Miscamble, *George Kennan and the Making of American Foreign Policy, 1947-1950* (Princeton: Princeton University Press, 1992), 101; John Lukacs: *George Kennan: a Study in Character* (New Haven: Yale University Press, 2007).

286 Quoted in Mitchell G. Bard and Dan Pipes, "How Special is the U.S.-Israel Relationship?", *Middle East Quarterly* (June 1997).

287 Mitchell Bard, *The Arab Lobby: the Invisible Alliance that Undermines America's Interest in the Middle East* (New York: Harper, 2010).

288 Franck Salameh, "Arab Gulf and Other Fairytales," *Hudson Institute, March 22, 2011*.

289 Lloyd Grief, New York Daily News, April 26, 2008.

290 Stephen Pollard, "Libya and the LSE: large Arab gifts to universities lead to 'hostile' teaching," *The Telegraph* (March 3, 2011).

291 Gertrude Himmelfarb, *On Looking into the Abyss: Untimely thoughts on Culture and Society* (New York: Knopf, 1994), 190.

292 Dominique Schnapper, "Relativism," *Society* 46 (2009):177.

293 Robert Darnton, "George Washington's False Teeth," *New York Review of Books*, 27 (March 1997): 34-38.

294 Jeanne Kirkpatrick, "The Myth of Moral Equivalence," *Imprimis*, January 1986, vol. 15, no 1.

295 Jonathan Israel, *A Revolution of the Mind: Radical Enlightenment and the Intellectual origins of Modern Democracy* (Princeton: Princeton University Press, 2010), 46.

296 Ibn Warraq, "In Defense of Ayaan Hirsi Ali and Afshin Ellian," *New English Review* (February 2011); Jonathan Israel, *A Revolution of the Mind. Radical Enlightenment and the Intellectual Origins of Modern Democracy* (Princeton: Princeton University Press, 2010), 46.

297 George Orwell, *A Collection of Essays* (Garden City: Doubleday, 1953), 191.

298 Bernadette Bucher, Obituary of Claude Lévi-Strauss, *American Anthropologist*, vol. 112, no.4 (2010).

299 Andrew Anthony, *The Fallout* (London: Cape, 2007), 139.

300 Bassam Tibi, *Europa ohne Identitat* (Munich: Bertelsmann, 1998), 154.

[301] Tzvetan Todorov, La Peur des Barbares: au-delà du choc des civilizations (Paris: Laffont, 2008).

[302] James T. Kloppenberg, *Reading Obama: dreams, hopes, and the American Political Tradition* (Princeton: Princeton University Press, 2011).

[303] Zeev Sternhell, *The Founding Myths of Israel: Nationalism, Socialism, and the Making of the Jewish State*, trans. David Maisel (Princeton: Princeton University Press, 1998), 4.

[304] Robert Hughes *Culture of Complaint: the Fraying of America* (New York: Oxford University Press, 1993).

[305] Martin Gilbert, *In Ishmael's House: a History of Jews in Muslim Lands* (New Haven: Yale University Press. 2010).

[306] Christopher Caldwell, *Reflections on the Revolution in Europe: Immigration, Islam, and the West* (New York: Doubleday, 2006), 266.

[307] Robert Kagan, *Of Paradise and Power: America and Europe in the New World Order* (New York: Knopf, 2003).

[308] Robert Conquest, *Reflections on a Ravaged Century* (New York: Norton, 2000), 16.

[309] Frederic Jameson, *Postmodernism, or the Cultural Logic of Late Capitalis*m (Durham: Duke University Press, 1991), 257.

[310] Efraim Inbar, "Is Israel more isolated than ever?", *BESA Center Perspectives Paper*, No. 114, September 14, 2010.

[311] *The Guardian*, September 29, 2001.

[312] Janet Afray and Kevin B. Anderson, *Foucault and the Iranian Revolution: Gender and the Seductions of Islamism* (Chicago: University of Chicago Press, 2005), 241.

[313] Robert Conquest, *Reflections*, p.117.

[314] Quoted in David Meir-Levy, *History Upside Down* (New York: Encounter, 2007), 28-29.

Index

A

Abbas, Mahmoud, 179, 269

Academics, 8, 17, 27, 29, 73, 292-293, 307, 338

Abdullah, King of Saudi Arabia, 230

Abdullah, Emir of Transjordan, 173

Adalah, 238-239, 293

Ahmadinejad, Mahmoud, 87, 105, 160

Al-Aksa Mosque, 45, 140

Al-Assad, Hafez, 86

Al Azm, Khalid, Syrian Prime Minister, 176

Al-Banna, Hasan, 150, 155

Ali, Rashid, 140-141

Aliyah, immigration, 116

Allenby, General Sir Edmund, 280

Allon, Yigal, 125, 178, 211, 330

Allon plan, 211

American objectives in the Middle East, 300

American universities, 306

Anglo-American Committee Report, 136

Annan, Kofi, 14

Annapolis Conference, 215

Anti-Americanism, 154

Antisemitism, 8, 10, 12, 19, 23, 76-77, 79-82, 84, 86-87, 116-117, 119, 121, 142, 145, 148-150, 154, 158-160, 169, 183, 250, 264, 268, 297, 303, 322, 324, 332

Anti-Zionism, 8, 79-80, 82, 150, 154, 158, 297

Anti-Zionist Committee of Soviet Public Opinion, 81

Antonius, George, 232, 335

Apartheid, 6, 8, 17, 24, 40, 77, 83, 88-90, 92, 94-95, 97-98, 102, 104-105, 260-261, 291, 307

Arab collaboration with the Nazis, 157

Arab flight, 176, 178

Arab-Israeli wars, 129

Arab Higher Committee, 78, 131-133, 140, 148, 163, 168, 171, 177-179

Arab Human Development Report, 32

Arab League, 86, 144, 148-149, 159, 162, 172, 179, 194, 196, 224, 292, 296, 308

Arab Legion, 141, 172, 178

Arab Liberation Army, 172, 178

Arab lobby, 303-305, 337, 339

Arab minority in Israel, 238, 285

Arab parties, 86, 219, 282

Arab revolt 1936, 131-132, 140, 147

Arab societies, 22, 179

Arava Valley, 235

Arabic, 32, 39, 77, 124, 156-157, 159-160, 183, 220-221, 268

Arafat, Yasser, 34, 45, 186-187, 192, 207, 256, 266, 270, 307, 322

Archeology, 248, 250

Aristotle, 93, 315

Aron, Raymond, 242, 310, 324

Ashkenazim, 247, 250

Ashton, Catherine, 20-21

Association for Civil Rights, 260

Attlee, Clement, 135

Ayatollah, 320-321

Azzam, Abdul Rahhman Hassan, 159, 296

B

Bahrain, 21, 108

Balfour Declaration, 107, 117, 122, 133, 142, 150, 226-227, 229-230, 232, 247, 277-281, 284, 301

Battle of Khaibar, 629, 318

Bandung Conference 1955, 196

Barak, Aharon, 263, 281, 285

Barak, Ehud, 72

Bar Kokhba Revolt, 85, 111

Barbie, Klaus, 146

Basic Law, Israel, 285

Bedouins, 115, 218-220, 238

Benda, Julien, 11, 326

Benedict XVI, Pope, 101

Ben-Gurion, David, 16, 33, 93, 168, 203, 227, 251, 253, 273, 284, 326, 337

Bernadotte, Count Folke, 188

Bethlehem, 10, 44, 132, 217

Birnbaum, Nathan, 18

Black September 1970, 31, 186

Blaustein, Jacob, 253

Blockade, 45, 47, 52, 55-59, 62, 104, 199, 209

Bloom, Allan, 311

Bosnian Muslim Nazi recruits, 144

Boycott, 11, 26-27, 61, 88-89, 99, 104, 135, 148-149, 156, 165, 292, 303, 307

Brandeis, Louis, 123, 251

Brit Shalom, 168, 295

British Mandate, 13, 107, 112, 132, 166, 225, 228, 233, 267, 334

British universities, 306

Browne-Wilkinson, Lord, 68

Bruckner, Pascal, 101, 313, 328

Buber, Martin, 122, 168, 251, 295

Bulganin, Nikolai, 81, 197

Burke, Edmund, 34, 165, 208, 327

Bush, President George W., 35, 72, 87, 215, 302-303

C

Cairo, 20, 37, 103, 148, 153, 156-157, 159, 186, 196, 246

Cairo Declaration on Human Rights, 103

Cameron, David, 314

Camp David Accords, 37, 190, 303

Canaanites, 241-242

Captured territories, 6, 196, 317

Caradon, Lord, 166

Carter, Jimmy, 35, 97, 302, 305-306

Central Boycott Office, Damascus, 149

Churches, 17, 28, 88-89, 102, 112, 217, 238, 245, 258, 286, 305

Churchill, Winston, 155, 227, 229

Citizenship, 7, 11, 20, 30, 89, 91, 93, 115, 179-182, 184-186, 224, 240-241, 243-246, 255, 265, 275-277, 334

Civilians, use of, 25, 30-31, 40, 47-55, 57-58, 61-62, 69-70, 73-74, 152, 165, 219, 244, 256, 259, 261-264, 266, 270

Clermont-Tonnerre, Count Stanislas de, 110

Cold War, 78, 81, 95, 142

Colonialism, 6, 17, 81, 83, 88, 90, 96, 106-107, 116, 213, 216, 240, 329

Commission on Human Rights, 38, 49, 76

Congress of Muslim-Christian Associations, 232

Control of water, 164

Conquest, Robert, 319, 340

Coupland, Professor Reginald, 131

Council of Europe, 33, 99

Crum, Bartley, 135, 295, 331

Crusaders, 107, 111-114, 126, 155, 264

Cultural relativism, 11, 309-310, 312

Cunningham, General Alan, 177

"Cycle of violence", 29

Czechoslovakia, 78, 169, 196

D

David, King, 113

Dayan, Moshe, 82, 296

De Gaulle, Charles, 203

Deir Yasin, 172-173

Demarcation line, 164

Democratic countries, 12-13, 61, 63, 222-223, 241, 262, 287, 310

Dhimmi status, 318

Diaspora, 7, 86, 109-110, 118, 223, 243, 249-255, 274, 336

Discrimination, 6, 17, 28, 30-31, 75-76, 78, 81-83, 88-90, 92-94, 98, 100-101, 103-105, 184, 217-218, 222, 224, 238-240, 244, 246, 260, 267, 275, 288

Displaced Jews, 134

Disproportionate response, 47

DNA, 242, 336

Dreyfus Case, 10, 117, 154

Druze, 115, 154, 166, 201, 218-220, 286-287

Dugard, John, 41, 90

Dulles, John Foster, 269, 302

Durban Conferences, 104

E

East Jerusalem, 46, 72, 93, 164, 166, 194, 201, 207, 210, 213-217, 224, 234, 257-258, 265

Eban, Abba, 199, 204, 334

Eden, Anthony, 269

Egypt, 13, 19, 21, 31, 37, 48, 58-59, 74, 81, 86, 102, 109, 120, 144-146, 150-154, 156, 164-165, 167, 172-174, 178-179, 189-190, 196-198, 200, 203, 208-210, 212, 223, 234, 245, 265, 268-269, 280, 299, 303, 308, 321

Eichmann, Adolf, 142, 144, 146, 281

Eisenhower, President Dwight D., 197, 199, 269, 302

Eliot, George, 110, 329

Elon Moreh case, 215

Emancipation of Jews, 110, 117

Emancipation of Women, 246, 299

Enlightenment, 158, 275, 311-313, 339

Eretz Israel, 11, 121, 194, 240, 248, 250, 273-274

Eshkol, Levi, 83

Ethnic cleansing, 17, 28, 74, 105, 176

European Court of Human Rights, 206, 244, 313, 315

European Union, 20, 28, 64, 180, 182, 194, 258, 273

F

Fanon, Franz, 322

Fatah, 58, 193, 207-208, 269

Fatahland, 187

Fawzi, General Muhammad, 198

Feisal, Emir, 229, 279

Fence, 28, 62, 72, 89, 257-260, 263, 265

Fertile Crescent, 241, 280

Flotilla, 47-48, 55-58, 224

Foucault, Michel, 25, 321, 327

France, 27, 59, 100, 106, 108, 124, 127, 165, 183, 185, 196-197, 203, 225, 228, 231, 249, 278-279, 286, 297, 321, 327, 339

Frankfurter, Felix, 230, 279

G

Galilee, 164, 173, 178, 202, 225, 239, 296

Gaza, 13, 18, 26, 30, 39, 45, 47-58, 62-64, 68-72, 92, 112, 179, 181-183, 191-193, 198, 200, 202-203, 205, 207-210, 214-215, 221, 224, 234, 256, 261-262, 265-266, 270, 288-289, 307, 320

Gellner, Ernest, 312, 337

General Syrian Congress, 227

Geneva Conventions, 61, 73, 261

Genocide, 17, 39, 47, 65-67, 71, 82, 105, 148, 159, 287, 327

Genoud, François, 146, 331-332

Ghoury, Emile, 171, 179

Glubb, Sir John Bagot, 172

Golan Heights, 37, 92, 165-166, 199-200, 206, 210, 212-213, 215, 225, 334

Goldstone, Richard, 48, 90

Goliath, 8, 317, 326

Graves, Philip, 229, 335

Greater Syria, 121, 139, 173

Green Line, 92, 129, 208, 210, 212, 237, 259, 290

Grobba, Fritz, 158

Gromyko, Andrei, 78

Grossman, David, 14, 17

Group think, 24

Gulf War, 72, 87, 187

Gurney, Sir Henry, 177, 334

Gush Emunim, 212

Gush Etzion, 172-173, 212-213

H

Ha'am, Ahad, 118, 122, 251, 255, 274, 338

Hagana, 129, 134, 172, 175

Hague Regulations, 48, 204-205, 209, 211, 259

Haifa, 139, 152, 161, 176, 178, 211, 220, 265, 300

Hama, 30, 280

Hamas, 26, 47-49, 51-55, 57-58, 64, 68-69, 71-72, 146, 155, 159, 183, 193-194, 207-209, 262, 264-268, 307, 310, 320

Hamas Covenant 1988, 159

Hammarskjold, Dag, 191

Haredim, 218, 222, 275, 286

Harkabi, Yehoshafat, 296, 338

Harrison, Dean Earl G., 134

Haskalah, 275

Hatikva, 223, 286

Hebrew, 18, 92, 109, 111, 113, 118, 124, 168, 218, 220, 241, 248, 250, 281, 284, 292, 295, 315, 338

Hebrew University, 168, 284, 292, 295

Hebron, 10, 44-45, 110, 130, 139, 148, 174, 202, 207, 212, 214

Hebron Pact, 202

Herf, Jeffrey, 157, 332

Herzl, Theodor, 93, 117, 122, 237

Hezbollah, 58, 146, 223, 264, 270-271, 320, 337

Higgins, Rosalyn, 205, 330, 335

Hijacking, 152, 186

Himmler, Heinrich, 142, 188

Histadrut, 284, 292, 315

Hitler, Adolf, 141, 326

Hitti, Philip, 232

Hobbes, Thomas, 316

Holocaust, 18, 22, 40, 47, 75-76, 105, 121, 142, 146-148, 155, 161, 170, 183, 223, 269, 281, 286-287, 289, 294-295, 309, 318, 327, 331-332

Holocaust denial, 47, 269, 287, 309

Holy Places, 18, 114, 139, 216-217, 229

Hope-Simpson Report, 1930, 131

Human Development Report, UN, 32, 293

Human Rights, 8-9, 11-12, 16-17, 20-21, 23, 28-30, 32-33, 36, 38-44, 46, 48-55, 60-61, 64-68, 72-73, 76, 81, 90, 98-99, 101, 103, 105, 111, 187, 191, 203, 206, 238, 244, 246, 260-261, 304, 313-315, 319, 322-323, 326-329, 336-337

Humanitarian law, 41, 48, 50-51, 53, 65, 71, 105

Hussein, King of Jordan, 86, 186, 194, 199

Hussein, Saddam, 40, 141, 187, 318

Hussein, Sherif of Mecca, 227, 230

Husseini, Haj Amin, Mufti of Jerusalem, 137-138

Husseini clan, 138

I

Idealism perverted, 307

Ideology, 10, 26, 62, 79, 84, 92-93, 103, 118, 139, 145, 152, 170, 232, 267, 284, 295, 298, 309-310, 315, 317, 339

Imperialism, 64, 78-79, 81-83, 93, 106-107, 150, 294, 299, 311

Internal critics, 293

International community, 3, 13, 16, 19-20, 31, 33, 37-38, 42, 56, 61, 65, 67, 87, 103, 117, 163, 167, 187, 191, 208, 234, 273, 283, 291, 312

International Convention on the Elimination of all forms of Racial Discrimination, 76, 81, 244

International Court of Justice, 72, 201, 204, 257, 272

International Covenant on Civil and Political Rights, 69, 100, 206, 257

International Criminal Court (ICC), 52, 54, 64-65, 67, 71-72, 90, 97

International Criminal Tribunal, 39, 67

International law, 9, 11-12, 23, 33, 39, 41, 45, 50, 52, 54, 56-57, 59, 61-64, 66-67, 69-70, 77, 85, 89-90, 98-99, 121, 167, 189, 205-206, 209, 211, 213, 217, 222, 244, 257-258, 261-263, 272, 318, 327-330, 334-335

International politics, 23, 60, 66, 95, 332, 335, 338

Intifada, 64, 74, 165, 223, 244, 256-257, 259-260, 266, 270

Iran, 14, 21-22, 30, 43, 52, 87, 102, 153, 197, 246, 270, 276, 290, 308-309, 320-321

Iraq, 21, 30, 37, 73, 115, 134, 140-141, 150, 152, 155, 158, 164, 172, 174, 187, 189, 197, 199, 225, 230, 262, 300, 307-308, 318

Irgun Zvai Leumi (IZL), 172

Islam, 10, 22, 26, 32, 40, 63, 98-103, 108, 114-115, 144-146, 148, 150-152, 154-155, 157-158, 233, 245-246, 267, 274, 306-308, 322, 329, 331, 337, 340

Islamic Conference, 43, 85, 98, 246

Islamic extremists, 8

Islamic jihad, 153, 155, 264

Islamofascism, 150

Israel: criticism of, 8-9, 11, 16, 23, 25, 28, 35-36, 42, 49, 61, 77, 89, 96, 203, 213, 235, 243, 295, 298-299, 321

Israeli Declaration of Independence, 94, 172, 192, 222, 281, 284, 301

Israel: Defense Forces (IDF), 51, 54, 63, 68-72, 74, 199, 219, 260-261, 263, 271, 289, 320

Israel: Jewish State, 7-8, 11, 18, 25, 78, 93, 113, 117-119, 121-123, 131-133, 136, 145, 147, 149, 162-163, 169, 171, 174-176, 192, 194, 224, 243, 249, 252, 266, 268, 272-275, 277, 281-283, 286, 288-289, 294, 301-302, 317, 323-324, 338, 340

Israel : Lands Administration, 214, 237-238

Israel: society, 15-17, 19, 24, 46, 85, 89, 111, 218, 221, 254, 275, 282-283, 285, 292-293, 303, 315, 317, 324, 337-338

Israel: Supreme Court (also High Court), 205, 258-259, 326

Israel: ultra-orthodox, 25, 212, 222, 275, 286

Israeli Arabs, 92-93, 127, 219-224, 244, 265, 275, 288

Israeli-Egyptian Peace Treaty 1979, 202

Israeli-Jordan Peace Treaty 1994, 166, 186, 208, 235

Israeli-Palestinian conflict, 10, 64, 72, 224, 247, 262

J

Jabotinsky, Vladimir (Zeev), 93, 333, 340

Jacob, François, 75, 328-329

Jaffa, 124, 129, 131-132, 140, 177, 276, 286

Jericho, 74, 194, 202, 216

Jerusalem, 6, 15, 18, 29, 44-46, 72, 74, 77, 93, 107, 109-114, 116, 122, 124, 130-132, 134, 137-140, 152, 154, 162, 164-168, 171-174, 177-178, 189, 191, 193-194, 199-201, 203, 206-207, 210-217, 223-224, 229, 231, 233-234, 243, 248-250, 256-258, 260, 265-266, 276, 280, 284, 286, 292, 295, 300, 326, 330-332, 334, 337-338

Jewish Agency, 122, 131-132, 134, 168, 175, 227, 238, 253

Jewish conspiracy, 26, 158, 303, 309

Jewish identity, 249-251, 253, 255, 274, 277, 285, 323, 339

Jewish National Fund (JNF), 231, 237-239

Jewish National Home, 107, 121, 135, 142, 157, 225-229, 231, 277, 281, 331

Jewish nationality, 169, 240-241, 251, 276

Jewish Quarter in the Old City, 173, 217

Jewish refugees, 37, 136, 161, 174, 334

Jewish state, 7-8, 11, 18, 25, 78, 93, 113, 117-119, 121-123, 131-133, 136, 145, 147, 149, 162-163, 169, 171, 174-176, 192, 194, 224, 243, 249, 252, 266, 268, 272-275, 277, 281-283, 286, 288-289, 294, 301-302, 317, 323-324, 338, 340

Jews, 7-9, 16, 22, 25-26, 34, 37-39, 45, 57, 64-65, 74, 77-85, 87-88, 90, 93, 102, 107, 109-113, 116-127, 130-148, 150, 152, 155-164, 168-169, 171-176, 178-179, 183-184, 186, 188, 194, 197, 201, 211, 213-219, 221-223, 226-231, 234, 236-243, 247-256, 264, 267-268, 273-274, 276-281, 283-284, 287-289, 294-297, 302-303, 316-320, 322-324, 326-327, 330, 335, 338, 340

Johnson, President Lyndon, 302-303

Johnson, Paul, 85, 329

Jordan, 13, 31, 57, 86, 92, 102, 115, 120, 154-155, 162, 164-167, 173, 179-180, 182, 185-187, 190, 194, 196, 199-201, 203, 205, 207-208, 211, 213-214, 216-217, 225, 228, 231, 234-236, 256, 265, 267, 269, 299, 321

Jordan annexes West Bank, 185, 201, 234

Jordan Valley, 211, 225

Judaism, 45, 118, 240-241, 243, 247, 249, 254, 275-276, 297

Judea and Samaria, 110-111, 162, 205, 212, 234, 249-250

K

Kahan Commission of Inquiry, 71

Karsh, Efraim, 331, 333

Kemp, Colonel Richard, 70, 334

Kennan, George F., 301, 339

Kfar Etzion, 174

Khaldun, Ibn, 313

Khalidi, Rashid, 171, 289, 333, 338

Ki-moon, Ban, 49, 58

Kibbutzim, 128, 130, 173, 213, 284, 292

Kissinger, Henry, 60, 327, 335

Knesset, 15, 84, 130, 166, 194, 205, 219-224, 240, 252, 282, 286, 291

Koran, 100, 103, 113, 143, 145, 151, 153, 156-158, 297

Kuntzel, Matthias, 159

Kurds, 30, 40, 245, 309

Kuwait, 31, 181, 187, 270, 276, 305

L

Land ownership, 7, 11, 236

Landes, David, 125, 330

Language, use of, 9, 11, 17, 28, 32-33, 38, 42, 47, 49, 75, 84, 86, 94, 104, 109, 121, 124, 142, 146, 157, 166, 197, 207, 218, 220-221, 241, 243, 245, 248, 250, 268, 273, 281, 284, 287, 295, 316

Law of Return, 223, 240-241, 255, 276-277

Lawrence, T.E., 108, 229

Lawfare, 6, 60-63, 68, 248, 328

League of Arab States, 20, 148, 162, 332

League of Nations, 13, 108, 111, 117, 120-121, 165, 175, 214, 225-226, 228, 231, 249, 281

League of Nations Mandates, 228

Lebanon, 13, 21, 31, 37, 41, 63, 67, 108, 115, 140, 164-165, 172-174, 176, 179-180, 186-187, 189, 203, 223, 225, 228, 231, 246, 256, 270, 276, 299, 308, 320, 333

Lehi (Fighters for the Freedom of Israel), 172

Le Pen, Jean-Marie, 297

Lévi-Strauss, Claude, 309-310, 312, 339

Lewis, Bernard, 232, 330-331, 333-334, 337

Libya, 21, 39-43, 104, 108, 187, 306-308, 327, 339

Lie, Trygve, 161, 171, 333

Lincoln, President Abraham, 250

Linguistic bias, 316

Livni, Tzipi, 71

Lloyd George, David, 277

Lobbying, 136, 304

London Conference 1939, 133, 147

M

MacDonald, Malcolm, 133, 147

Madison, James, 14

Madrid Conference, 303

Magnes, Judah, 168

Mamet, David, 17, 326

Mamlachtiyut, 25, 315

Mandatory Palestine, 133-134, 162, 165, 174

Mao Zedong, 298

Masada, 128, 296

McMahon, Sir Henry, 227, 280

McMahon-Hussein correspondence, 280

Meir, Golda, 81, 96, 299

Merkel, Angela, 314

Middle East, 8-10, 12-15, 19-21, 29-30, 32, 35, 38, 55, 61, 81, 87, 112, 114, 133, 135, 138, 144, 146, 157-158, 160-161, 172, 184, 191, 196-197, 223, 230, 234, 242, 247-248, 277, 290-291, 300-301, 304-305, 307, 312, 322, 326-327, 330-337, 339

Mill, John Stuart, 103, 272, 337

Millet system, 287

Mitchell, Senator George, 214

Modernization, 32, 62, 96

Montagu, Edwin, 279

Montefiore, Sir Moses, 124, 330

Moral equivalence, 9, 29, 51, 289, 311, 339

Morris, Benny, 159, 170, 331-334, 337-338

Morrison, Herbert, 136

Mount of Olives, 216

Moynihan, Daniel Patrick, 87

Mufti of Jerusalem (see Husseini, Haj Amin), 6, 131, 134, 137-138, 154, 331-332

Muhammad, 63, 74, 99-102, 113-114, 144, 154, 159, 198, 229, 264, 266, 318

Multiculturalism, 11, 309, 313-315

Muslim antisemitism, 145, 322

Muslim Brotherhood, 21, 57-58, 145, 150, 153-155, 264, 332

Muslim countries, 47, 101, 162, 312, 318, 321

Muslims in France, 100, 297

N

Nakba, 170, 222, 233, 336

Nashashibi clan, 138

Nasser, Gamal Abdel, 109, 153, 155, 196

National self-determination, 11, 62, 78, 171

National interest, 23, 304, 328

Nazi Germany, 18, 33, 64, 66, 73, 75-76, 133-134, 140-141, 145, 148, 157, 167, 173, 205, 327

Nazi broadcasts, 157

Nazis, 6, 18, 66, 73, 82-83, 121, 134, 138, 141-146, 150, 154, 156-158, 268-269, 319, 332

Negation of the Diaspora, 255, 274

Negev, 173, 219, 239, 269

New antisemitism, 297

New historians, 86, 293, 318, 333

News bureaus, 17

Niebuhr, Reinhold, 12, 123, 168, 326, 333

Nixon, President Richard, 35, 302-303

Non-Aligned Movement, 82, 85, 198

Non-Governmental Organizations (NGOs), 8, 17, 24, 28, 64, 104, 151, 287, 292

Nuremberg trials, 33, 144

Norway, 29

O

Obsession with Israel, 6, 13, 323

Occupation, 6, 17, 20, 27-28, 33, 36, 44, 61, 65, 73, 83, 88-90, 92, 96, 104-106, 169, 196, 201, 204-209, 213, 215, 217, 259, 285, 289, 327, 334

Oil, 10, 96, 135, 161, 190, 292, 300-301, 305, 309

Oil companies, 292

Operation Cast Lead, 13, 47, 50-52, 63, 69-70, 203

Operation Defensive Shield, 74, 203

Operation Peace for Galilee, 202

Organization for Economic Co-operation and Development (OECD), 46, 222, 321

Organization of African Unity, 83, 96

Organization of the Islamic Conference (OIC), 43, 98, 101, 103, 246

Orwell, George, 307, 312, 339

Oslo Accords, 207, 266

Ottoman Empire, 59, 106, 108-109, 114-115, 117, 149, 177, 201, 210, 225, 232-233, 268, 279, 331

Ottoman Land Code, 236

Ottoman vilayets, 115

P

Palestine, 6, 11, 13, 18, 21, 28, 34, 43, 47, 52, 57, 73, 77-78, 81, 83-84, 97, 107, 109-112, 114, 116-127, 129-144, 146-150, 152-153, 156-159, 161-165, 168, 170-174, 177-181, 185-187, 189, 191-193, 196, 201, 210, 214, 216, 223, 225-234, 236-237, 241, 243, 247, 249, 251, 267, 269, 277-281, 283-284, 289, 295-296, 301-302, 317, 330-335, 338-339

Palestine Liberation Organization (PLO), 34, 57, 77, 81, 165, 186-187, 190, 193-194, 196, 202, 207, 233, 245, 247, 258, 267, 270

Palestinian Authority, 41, 98, 171, 179-182, 190, 202, 207, 209, 224, 237, 243, 248, 269, 288

Palestinian narrative, 170-171, 318-321, 324

Palestinian National Council, 190, 192

Palestinian State, 114, 136, 168, 173, 187, 191, 194, 208, 222, 234, 266, 270

Palestinians, 9, 13-14, 17, 20-22, 30-31, 49, 56, 58, 61-62, 64, 71, 73-74, 77, 81, 88-90, 92-93, 95, 104-105, 107, 126-127, 129-130, 138, 140, 146, 148, 152, 159, 163, 165, 167, 169-171, 173, 175-194, 198, 202, 206, 213, 217, 219-220, 222-223, 231-233, 236-238, 246, 256-257, 260, 265, 270, 287-290, 294-295, 302, 305, 310-311, 316-318, 322-324, 334, 337

Passfield White Paper, 1930, 131

Peace treaties, 266, 321

Peel Commission Report, 1937, 132, 175

PEGASE, 180

Peoplehood, 7, 247-248, 251

Pillay, Navanethem, 39

Pinsker, Leo, 116

Plan D of March 1948, 175

Pluralism in Israel, 286, 323

Pogroms, 116, 123-124

Political left, 19, 21, 73, 95, 298

Post-colonial ideology, 309

Post-Zionism, 317

Power, 11, 20, 25-26, 29, 34, 44, 48, 50, 58, 61-62, 65, 72, 77, 82, 97, 106-109, 114-115, 122, 127, 138, 140-141, 152, 157, 159, 161, 163, 200, 202, 205, 213, 215, 226, 230-232, 234, 268, 274, 278, 296, 300, 308, 310, 317-321, 324, 326, 329-331, 340

Power, use of, 25, 61, 310

Postmodernism, 11, 340

Pragmatism, 316, 338

Project Alpha, 269

Protocols of the Elders of Zion, 26, 79-80, 139, 156, 267-268, 327

Purity of arms, 69

Q

Qutb, Sayyid, 155, 332

R

Rabin, Yitzhak, 14, 84, 178, 194, 207

Race, 38, 75-76, 80, 86, 89-90, 93-94, 101, 229-230, 250-251, 275, 301, 311, 321, 328-329, 336

Rachel's Tomb, 10, 44

Racial discrimination, 76, 81, 83, 101, 103-105, 239, 244

Racism, 6, 17, 35, 42, 52, 64, 74-77, 79-83, 85, 87-89, 96, 102-106, 240, 313, 327, 329

Reagan, President Ronald, 35, 303

Red Cross, 46, 188, 201, 320

Refugee camps, 31, 182, 186-187, 289

Relativism, 11, 309-313, 319, 339

Renan, Ernst, 272

Revisionists (New Zionist Organization), 168

Right of Return, 6, 28, 174, 188-190, 194, 290

Roberts, Adam, 33, 327

Rocket attacks, 48-49, 209, 266, 270

Romans, 74, 85, 111-113, 128, 249, 296

Rome Statute, 64-65, 90, 97, 261

Rommel, Erwin, 156

Roosevelt, Franklin, 34

Rose, Flemming, 100

Rostow, Eugene, 214, 335

Rothschild, Lord, 150, 277, 279

Rule of law, 15, 38, 44, 61-62, 68-70, 259, 263, 293, 298-300, 327

Russell, Bertrand, 321

S

Sadat, Anwar, 153

Samuel, Herbert, 120, 138, 226

San Remo Conference, 225

Sartre, Jean-Paul, 26, 327

Saudi Arabia, 31, 43, 58, 74, 76, 98-99, 102, 108, 135, 155, 158, 172, 174, 181, 189, 246, 270, 276, 302, 305, 308, 331

Scholem, Gerson, 253

Schwebel, Stephen, 204, 335

Semitic language, 75

Sephardim, 184, 247, 250, 287, 315

Settlements, 6, 20-21, 92, 97, 104, 122, 124-125, 127, 149, 172-173, 190-191, 202, 208, 210-216, 237, 257, 290, 302-303, 324

Sharansky, Natan, 23, 253, 297, 326

Sharett (Shertok), Moshe, 173

Sharia law, 139-140, 151, 191, 193, 245

Sharon, Ariel, 71, 73, 202, 210, 257, 302, 319

Shaw Commission, 1930, 130

Shuqairy, Ahmad, 233

Sieff, Rebecca, 284

Six-Day War, 25, 82, 197, 199, 204, 206, 223, 334

Solomon, King, 109, 112-113, 119, 248

South Africa, 27-28, 83, 89-91, 93, 96-98, 258, 260, 291, 307

Soviet Union, 36, 65, 77-82, 84, 86-87, 95, 101, 135, 160, 162, 169, 185, 196, 198-199, 213, 218, 240, 244-245, 273, 291, 297-298, 301-302, 307, 319-321

Stalin, Josef, 79, 81, 168, 329

Stockwell, General Hugh, 176, 178

Stone I.F., 295, 338

Stone, Julius, 122, 214, 330, 335

Suez Canal, 81, 150, 153, 161, 197, 200, 278

Supreme Muslim Council, 139

Sykes-Picot Agreement, 200, 277, 279

Syria, 21, 30-31, 39, 52, 86, 102, 108-109, 111, 115, 121, 139-140, 146, 150, 164-165, 172-174, 179-180, 187, 189, 197-200, 206, 211, 223, 225, 227-228, 230-233, 245-246, 249, 270, 276, 280, 303, 308

T

Taguieff, Pierre-André, 297, 316, 339

Talmon, Jacob, 25

Tel Aviv, 13, 15, 28, 124, 129, 132, 152, 194, 211, 217, 220-221, 241, 251, 276, 286, 301, 335

Temple Mount, 18, 45, 77, 111-112, 191, 217, 248, 256

Temples, 18, 45, 77, 109-113, 191, 217, 248-249, 256

Terrorism, 18, 21, 38, 62-63, 68, 72, 74, 98, 148, 257, 259, 261, 263-264, 300, 307, 324, 337

Thant, Secretary General U., 199

Third Worldism, 11, 298, 309, 321

Tiberias, 110, 124-125, 176

Tomb of the Patriarchs, 10, 44-45

Traditional antisemitism, 19, 23, 82, 322

Transjordan, 132, 165, 172-173, 178, 225, 228, 231, 333

Treaty of Hudaibiya, 628, 266

Treaty of Sèvres, 114, 226

Trimble, Lord, 56

Tripartite Declaration 1950, 197

Truman, Harry, 147, 301

Truro Synagogue, 14

Tunisia, 21, 107, 155, 308

Turkel Commission, 53, 56

Turkey, 30, 36, 57, 141, 155, 175, 181, 183, 185, 197, 226, 244, 279

Tutu, Desmond, 28, 88

Twain, Mark, 120, 330

U

United Arab Republic, 198

United Nations, 6, 9-10, 14, 16, 23, 32, 34-36, 38, 44, 46, 48, 52, 64-66, 69, 79, 82-83, 90, 101, 105, 108, 136, 161-163, 165, 168, 171, 174, 180-182, 184, 199-200, 202, 210, 226, 268, 281, 301-302, 326, 330, 332-333, 335

United Nations Charter, 105, 226

United Nations Committee on the Exercise of the Inalienable Rights of the Palestinian People, 46, 189

United Nations Disengagement Observer Force (UNDOF), 166

United Nations Educational, Scientific, and Cultural Organization (UNESCO), 10, 44-46, 87, 183

United Nations Emergency Force in the Sinai (UNEF), 199

United Nations General Assembly (UNGA), 34, 36-38, 40, 47, 52-53, 64, 76, 78-79, 83-84, 86-87, 89, 96, 98-100, 104-105, 174, 191-193, 201, 232, 258

United Nations General Assembly Resolution 194 (III), December 11, 1948, 174, 189

United Nations High Commission for Refugees (UNHCR), 182, 184-185

United Nations Human Rights Council (UNHRC), 9, 36, 38-40, 42-43, 48-50, 52, 54, 70, 98, 104

United Nations Palestine Conciliation Commission, 164

United Nations Partition Resolution, 181 (II), November 29, 1947, 174

United Nations Relief and Works Agency (UNRWA), 6, 10, 180-186, 207, 334

United Nations Security Council, 14, 200

United Nations Security Council Resolution 242, November 22, 1967, 164, 166-167, 189

United Nations Special Committee on Palestine (UNSCOP), 161-163, 232

United Nations War Crimes Commission (UNWCC), 66, 335

United States, 4, 12, 15, 27-28, 33, 35-36, 38, 40, 42, 57, 59, 63, 65, 68, 70, 76, 84, 87, 100, 105-106, 121, 153, 168, 182-183, 193, 197-198, 207, 217, 219, 225-226, 245, 254-255, 258, 269-270, 278, 298-300, 302, 304-307, 310, 316, 321, 331

United States Congress, 217, 226

United States, State Department, 198

Universal jurisdiction, 6, 52, 60, 65-68, 70-71, 73, 327-328

V

Vance, Cyrus, 210

Venice Declaration, 28, 194

Victimhood, 22, 310, 318, 320, 324

Vidal-Naquet, Pierre, 269, 335

W

Wakf, 238

Waldheim, Kurt, 34

Washington, George, 14, 339

War, 1948-49, 79, 129, 159, 170-171, 173, 184, 220, 267, 296, 316, 333, 335

Weizmann, Chaim, 122, 131-132, 227, 229, 278-279

West Bank, 21, 30, 34, 45, 52, 62, 70, 72, 74, 89, 92, 107, 112, 164-166, 179, 182, 185-186, 191-192, 194, 201-203, 207-208, 210-216, 220-221, 224, 234, 236, 244, 256-257, 259-260, 263, 265-266, 270, 288-289, 302, 307, 324

Western Wall, 18, 45, 77, 112, 130, 171, 216-217, 248, 256

Wilders, Geert, 100

Wilson, President Woodrow, 123, 138

Wingate, Orde, 123, 130, 331

Winograd Commission, 53

Wisliczeny, Dieter, 144

Withdrawals, 202, 266

Women's Year Conference, 83

World Conference on Women, 87

World War II, 23, 31, 35, 38, 61, 78-79, 83, 86, 108, 121, 134, 140-141, 146-149, 157-158, 162-163, 171, 173, 184-185, 198, 213, 223, 226, 231, 261, 268-269, 321, 328, 332

Wye River Memorandum, 202, 265

Y

Yadin, Yigael, 175

Yemen, 21, 31, 37, 108, 116, 160, 172, 174, 189, 198, 276, 308

Yishuv, 129-130, 168, 173, 191, 256, 284, 317, 323

Z

Zangwill, Israel, 120-121, 330

Zionism, 18, 35, 45, 52, 76-77, 79-87, 96, 104, 116-118, 120, 122-123, 126, 135, 139, 145, 150, 156-157, 160, 169-170, 172, 177, 233, 242, 283, 288-289, 291, 294-295, 301, 304, 329, 335

Zionist Congress (WZO), 16, 117-118, 227, 237, 268

Zionism is racism resolution, 52

Zionist theories, 159

Zionists, 12, 78-80, 94, 116-118, 120, 126, 137, 147, 150, 162, 169, 177, 228, 236-237, 269, 273, 277, 283-284, 289, 330

Zola, Emile, 10

Please visit our website for other great titles:

www.balfourstore.com

DEATH
OF A
HOLLOW
MAN

ALSO BY CAROLINE GRAHAM

THE KILLINGS AT BADGER'S DRIFT

DEATH
OF A
HOLLOW
MAN

A CHIEF
INSPECTOR
BARNABY
MYSTERY

CAROLINE
GRAHAM

WILLIAM MORROW
AND COMPANY, INC.
NEW YORK

c.1
M

Library of Congress Cataloging-in-Publication Data

Graham, Caroline, 1931–
Death of a hollow man: a Chief Inspector Barnaby mystery /
Caroline Graham.
p.   cm.
ISBN 0-688-09116-4
I. Title.
PR6057.R232D4 1990
823′.914 — dc20

89-35571
CIP

Printed in the United States of America

First U.S. Edition

1   2   3   4   5   6   7   8   9   10

BOOK DESIGN BY WILLIAM McCARTHY

TO BERYL ARNOLD
WITH LOVE

CONTENTS

CURTAIN RAISER   11

DRAMATIS PERSONAE   21

REHEARSALS   51

ENTR'ACTE: 79
(CAUSTON HIGH STREET, SATURDAY MORNING)

FIRST NIGHT   101

ENTER THE BROKER'S MEN   127

EXIT, *PURSUED BY A BEAR*   169

ANOTHER OPENING,
ANOTHER SHOW   259

Curtain Raiser

"You can't cut your throat without any blood."

"Absolutely. People expect it."

"I disagree. There wasn't any blood in the West End production."

"Oh, Scofield," Esslyn murmured dismissively. "So mannered."

The Causton Amateur Dramatic Society (CADS) were taking a break during a rehearsal of *Amadeus*. The production was fairly well advanced. The Venticelli were finally picking up their cues, the fireplace for the palace at Schönbrunn was promised for the weekend, and Constanze seemed at long last to be almost on the point of starting to learn at least one or two of her lines, while remaining rather hazy as to the order in which they came. But the sticky question as to how Salieri should most effectively cut his throat had yet to be solved. Tim Young, the only member of the company to shave the old-fashioned way, had promised to bring his razor along that very evening. So far, there was no sign of him.

"You ... um ... you can get things, can't you? That make blood? I remember at the Royal Shakespeare Company—"

"Well, of course you can get things, Deidre," snapped Harold Winstanley. (He always reacted very abrasively to any mention of the RSC.) "I don't think there are many people present who are unaware of the fact that you can *get* things. It's just that I do try to be a tiny bit inventive ... move away from the usual hackneyed routine. *Comprenez?*" He gazed at the assembled company, inviting them to admire his superhuman patience in the face of such a witless suggestion. "And talking of routine—isn't it time we had our coffee?"

"Oh, yes, sorry." Deidre Tibbs, who had been sitting on the stage hugging her corduroyed knees in a rather girlish way, scrambled to her feet.

"Chop-chop, then."

"If you think Scofield was mannered," said Donald Everard, picking up Esslyn's put down, "how about Simon Callow?"

"How *about* Simon Callow?" shrilled his twin.

Deidre left them happily trashing their betters and made her way up the aisle toward the clubroom. Deidre was the assistant director. She had been general dogsbody on dozens of productions until a few weeks ago, when, fortified by a couple of sweet martinis, she had shyly asked the committee to consider her promotion. To her delight they had voted, not quite unanimously, in her favor. But the delight was short-lived, for it seemed that her role vis-à-vis the present state of play at the Latimer was to be no different from that at any time previously. For Harold would brook no discussion (his own phrase) on points of production, and her few tentative suggestions had either been ignored or shot down in flames. In the clubroom she took the mugs from their hooks and placed them very carefully on the tray to avoid clinkage, then turned on a thin thread of water and filled the kettle. Harold, quick to describe himself as a one-man think tank, found the slightest sound disturbing to his creative flow.

Of course, as a director, Deidre admitted sadly to herself, he had the edge. Twenty years earlier, before settling down in the little market town of Causton, he had acted at Filey, produced a summer season at Minehead, and appeared in a Number One Tour (Original West End Cast!) of *Spider's Web*. You couldn't argue with that sort of experience. One or two of them tried, of course. Especially newcomers, who still had opinions of their own and hadn't divined the pecking order. Not that there were many of these. The CADS were extremely selective. And Nicholas, who was playing Mozart while darkly awaiting the results of an audition from the Central School of Speech and Drama. He argued sometimes. Esslyn didn't argue. Just listened attentively to everything Harold said, then went his own unsparkling way. Harold consoled himself for this intransigence by directing everyone else to within an inch of their lives.

Deidre spooned cheap powdered coffee and dried milk into the mugs and poured on boiling water. One or two little white beads bobbed to the surface, and she pushed them down nervously with the back of a spoon, at the same time trying to remember who took sugar and who was sweet enough. Best take the packet and ask. She went cautiously back down the aisle, balancing her heavy tray. Esslyn had got onto Ian McKellen.

"So—quite against my better judgment—I allowed myself to be dragged along to this one-man effort. Nothing but showing off from start to finish."

"But," said Nicholas, his gray eyes innocently wide, "I thought that's what acting was."

The Everards, poisonous brown-nosers to the company's leading man, cried, "I know exactly what Esslyn means!"

"So do I. McKellen has always left me stone cold." Deidre slipped in her question about the sugar.

"Heavens, you should know that by now, poppet," said Rosa Crawley. "Just a *morceau* for me." She dragged the words out huskily. She was playing Mrs. Salieri, and had never had such a modest role, but in *Amadeus* it was the only mature feminine role available. Obviously servants and senior citizens were beneath her notice. "You've been keeping us sustained through so many rehearsals," she continued. "I don't know how you do it." There was a spatter of mechanical agreement in Deidre's direction, and Rosa trapped a small sigh. She knew that to be gracious to bit players and stage management was the sign of a real star. She just wished Deidre would be a bit more responsive. She accepted her chipped mug with a radiant smile. "Thank you, darling."

Deidre parted her lips slightly in response. Really, she was thinking, with a waistline like a Baleen whale, even one *morceau* was one too many. To add to her annoyance, Rosa was wearing the long fur coat she (Deidre) had bought from Oxfam for *The Cherry Orchard*. It had disappeared after the closing-night party, and wardrobe had never been able to lay hands on it again.

"Oh, my God!" Harold glared into his mug, blue glazed with H.W. (DIR) on the side in red nail polish. "Not those bloody awful ferret droppings again. Can't somebody produce some real milk? *Please?* Is that too much to ask?"

Deidre handed out the rest of the mugs, following up with the sugar bag, avoiding Harold's eye. If real milk was wanted, let someone with a car bring it. She had enough stuff to lug to rehearsals as it was.

"I'm a bit worried about the idea of a razor at all," said Mozart's Constanze, returning to the point at issue, "I don't want a fatherless child." She made a face into her mug before leaning back against her husband's knee. Esslyn smiled and glanced around at the others as if asking them to excuse his wife's foolishness. Then he drew the nail of his index finger delicately across her throat, murmuring, "A biological impossibility surely?"

"One of the problems about a lot of blood," said Joyce Barnaby, wardrobe mistress/keeper of the cakes/singing noises off, "is getting Esslyn's shirt washed and ironed for the next night. I hope we're going to have more than one."

"*Molto costoso,* my darling," cried Harold. "You all seem to think I'm made of money. The principals' costumes cost a bomb to hire as it is. All very well for Peter Shaffer to ask for ten servants all in eighteenth-century costume..."

Joyce sat back placidly in her seat, picked up Katherina Cavalieri's braided skirt, and continued turning up the hem. At least once during the rehearsals of any production, Harold railed about how much they were spending, but somehow, when things were urgently needed, the money was always there. Joyce had wondered more than once if it came out of his own pocket. He did not seem to be a wealthy man (he ran a modest import-export business), but threw himself so completely into the theater, heart, body, mind, and spirit, that none of them would have been surprised, if he had thrown his profits in as well.

"I don't envy Sarah the weight of that skirt," Rosa clucked across at Joyce. "I remember when I was playing Ranevskaya—"

"Will my padding be ready soon, Joyce?" asked the second Mrs. Carmichael, collecting many a grateful glance by this intercession. When Rosa started on her Ranevskaya, everyone ran for cover. Or her Mrs. Alving. Or even, come to that, her Fairy Carabosse.

"And the music?" asked Nicholas. "When are we having the music?"

"When I get a forty-eight-hour day," came back Harold, whippet quick. "Unless"—he positively twinkled at the absurdity of the idea—"you want to do it yourself."

"Okay."

"What?"

"I don't mind. I know all the pieces. It's just a question of—"

"It's not 'just a question of' anything, Nicholas. The stamp of any director worth his salt must be on every single aspect of his production. Once you start handing over bits here and pieces there for any Tom, Dick, and Harry to do as they like with, you might as well abdicate." It was an indication of Harold's standing within the company that the verb struck no one present as inappropriate. "And rather than worry about your padding, Kitty, I should start worrying about your lines. I want them spot on by Tuesday. Dead-Letter Perfect. Got that?"

"I'll try, Harold." Kitty's voice just hinted at a lisp. Her *d's* were nearly *t's*. This pretty affectation plus her tumble of fair curls, smooth, peachy complexion, and exaggerated Cupid's bow mouth created an air of childlike charm so appealing that people hardly noticed how at variance it was with the sharp gleam in her azure eyes. As she spoke, her delicious bosom rose and fell a shade more rapidly, as if indicating an increased willingness to please.

Harold regarded her sternly. It was always a complete mystery to him when anyone connected with the CADS declined to commit his every waking moment to whatever happened to be the current production, in deed while at the theater and in thought while absent. Avery had once said that had it been within his power, Harold would have ordered them to dream about the Latimer. And Kitty, of all people, Harold was now thinking, had enough time on her hands. He wondered what she found to do all day, then realized he had wondered aloud. Kitty demurely lowered her glance, as if the question had been faintly naughty.

Deidre started to reclaim the mugs. Several still held coffee, but no one insisted on a divine right to full rations. She looked elsewhere when collecting Kitty's, for Esslyn had now stopped caressing his wife's throat and had slipped his fingers into the neck of her drawstring blouse, where they dabbled almost absentmindedly. Rosa Crawley also looked elsewhere at this evidence of her onetime husband's insensitivity, and blushed an ugly crimson. Harold, oblivious as always to offstage dramas, called across to his designer, "Where on earth *is* Tim?"

"I don't know."

"Well, you should know. You live with him."

"Living with someone," riposted Avery, "doesn't give you psychic powers. I left him filling in the Faber order, and he said he'd only be half an hour. So your guess is as good as mine." Although he spoke stoutly, Avery was, in fact, consumed with anxious fears. He couldn't bear not to know where Tim was and what he was doing and whom he was doing it with. Each second spent in ignorance of this vital information seemed like a year to him. "And don't expect me to stay late," he added. "I've got a *daube* in the oven."

"*Daubes* pay for a long simmer," suggested wardrobe. Fortunately her husband was not present, or he might well have choked to hear the casual way in which Joyce, whose culinary disasters went from strength to strength, claimed kinship with a man whose cooking was legendary. Every member of the CADS had angled and wangled and hinted and nudged their way toward a possible invitation to dine chez Avery. Those who succeeded ate at humbler tables for weeks afterward, recreating their triumphs and doling out gastronomic recollections a crumb at a time to make them last. Tom Barnaby, a Detective Inspector in the Causton CID, would listen with increasing wistfulness as his wife regaled him with such tales of *haute cuisine*.

Now, Avery replied crisply, "Long simmers, Joycey darling, must stop at precisely the right moment. The line between a wonderful, cohesive stew with every single item still quite separate yet relating perfectly to the whole and a great sloppy mess is a very narrow one indeed."

"Bit like a theatrical production, really," murmured Nicholas, lobbing a subversively winning smile across at his director. Catching the smile but quite missing the subversion, Harold nodded pompously back.

"Well . . ." Colin Smy got to his feet and struck a no-nonsense pose as if to emphasize both his importance to and difference from the surrounding actors. "Some of us have got work to do." Having thrown his dart, he gave it a moment to sink in, standing chunkily on slightly bowed legs. He wore jeans and a tartan shirt and had rough, wiry hair cut very short. Tufts of it stuck up here and there, and this, combined with a great deal of snapping energy, made it, someone had once said, like having a rather ferocious fox terrier charging around the place. Now, he disappeared into the wings, calling pointedly over his shoulder, "If I'm wanted, you'll find me in the scene dock. There's plenty going on down there, if anyone's interested."

No one seemed to be, and the hammering that shortly reached their ears remained aggrievedly solitary. Over their heads Deidre turned on hot water and scrubbed at the mugs, clattering them crossly and adding yet more chips. Not a single person ever came up to give her a hand, with the exception of David Smy, who was often waiting around to drive his father home. She knew this was her own fault for not putting her foot down long ago, and this made her crosser than ever.

"Well, I think we should give Tim five more minutes," Emperor Joseph was saying back in the stalls, "and then get on."

"No doubt you do," replied Esslyn, "but I have no intention of 'getting on' until we have this practical problem solved. It's all very well to say these things can be left till the last second..."

"Hardly the last second," murmured Rosa.

"...but I'm the one whose going to be out there facing the serried ranks." (Anyone'd think, observed Nicholas to himself, that we were going on at the Barbican.) "It's horrendous enough, God knows, a part that size." (What did you take it on for, then?) "But after all, Salieri's attempted suicide is the high point of the play. We've got to get it not only right but brilliantly right."

Nicholas, who had always regarded *Mozart's* death as the high point of the play, said, "Why don't you use an electric razor?"

"For Christ's sake! If this is the sort of—"

"All right, Esslyn. Simmer down." Harold soothed his fractious star. "Honestly, Nicholas—"

"Sorry." Nicholas grinned. "Sorry, Esslyn. Just a joke."

"Stillborn, Nico," said Esslyn loftily, "like all your jokes. Not to mention your..." He buried his lips in the golden fronds tenderly curling on Kitty's neck, and the rest of the sentence was lost. But everyone knew what it might have been.

Nicholas went very white. He said nothing for a few moments, then spoke overcalmly, picking his words with care. "It might not seem like it, but I am concerned about this problem. After all, if Esslyn doesn't have enough time to get used to handling what's going to be a very vital prop, the whole business is going to look completely amateurish." There was a crescendoed hum, and breaths were held. Harold got to his feet and fixed his Mozart with a rabid eye.

"Don't you ever so much as breathe that word in my presence, Nicholas—Okay? There is *never* anything amateurish about my productions."

In so boldly refuting the adjective, Harold was being a mite economical with the truth. The whole company was proud of what it fondly regarded as its professional standards, but let a breath of adverse criticism be heard, and suddenly they were only amateurs, mostly with full-time jobs, and really, it was a miracle any of them found time to learn their lines at all, let alone get a show on the road. Now, Nicholas, having drawn blood all around, appeared mortified at his clumsiness. But before he could open his mouth to make amends, the auditorium doors swung open, and Tim Young appeared. He walked quickly toward them, a tall man in a dark Crombie overcoat and Borsalino hat carrying a small parcel.

"Sorry I'm late."

"Where have you been?"

"The paper work seemed to take forever...then the phone started. You know how it is." Tim spread his answer around the group rather than replying directly to Avery, who then said, "Who? Who phoned?"

Tim slipped off his overcoat and started to undo his parcel. Everyone gathered around. It was very carefully wrapped. Two layers of shiny brown paper, then two of soft cloth. Finally the razor was revealed. Tim opened it and laid it across his palm.

It was a beautiful thing. The handle, an elegant curve of ebony, was engraved in gold: E.V. BAYARS. MASTER CUTLER. (C.A.P.S.) Around this imprint was a wreath of acanthus leaves and tiny flowers inlaid in mother-of-pearl. The reverse side was plain except for three tiny rivets. The blade, its edge honed to a lethal certainty, winked and gleamed. Esslyn, mindful of its reason for being there, said, "Looks bloody sharp."

"As it must!" cried Harold. "Theatrical verisimilitude is vital."

"Absolutely," seconded Rosa—rather quickly, some thought.

"I don't give a fairy's fart for theatrical verisimilitude," enjoined Esslyn, holding out his hand and gingerly taking the razor. "If you think I'm putting this thing within six inches of my throat, you can think again."

"Haven't you ever heard of mime?" inquired Harold.

"Yes, I've heard of mime," replied Esslyn. "I've also heard of Jack the Ripper, Sweeney Todd, and death by misadventure."

"I'll work something out by the next rehearsal," Harold said reassuringly. "Don't worry. Wrap it up again for now, Tim. I want to get on with Act Two, Deidre?" Pause. "Where is she now?"

"Still washing up, I think," said Rosa.

"Good grief. I could wash up the crockery from a four-course banquet for twenty in the time she takes to do half a dozen cups. Well... to our muttons. Phoebe—you'd better go on the book." Everyone dispersed to the wings and dressing rooms with the exception of Esslyn, who remained, still studying the razor thoughtfully. Harold crossed to his side. *"Pas de problème,"* he said. "You have to get used to handling it, that's all. Look—let me show you."

He took the beautiful object and carefully eased the blade back toward the handle. Suddenly it sprang to forcefully, with a sharp click. Harold gave a little hiss of alarm, and Esslyn a longer one of satisfaction. "You don't seem to have trained this very well, Tim," called Harold, giving Esslyn a smile of rather strained jocularity. Then he put the razor down and took the other man's arm companionably. "Now, when have you ever known me with a production headache I couldn't put right? Mm? In all our years together?" Esslyn responded with a wary look, rife with disenchantment. "Believe me," said Harold, spacing out his words and weighting them equally to emphasize the power of his conviction, "you are in safe hands. There is nothing whatsoever to worry about."

DRAMATIS
PERSONAE

 In his room over the Blackbird bookshop Nicholas lay on the floor doing his Cicely Berry voice exercises. He did them night and morning without fail, however late he was getting up or getting in. He had reached the lip and tongue movements, and rat-a-tat sounds filled the room. Fortunately the neighbors on both sides (Browns, the funeral parlor, and a butcher's) were past caring about noise.

Nicholas had been born nineteen years ago and brought up in a village midway between Causton and Slough. At school he had been regarded as just above average. Moderately good at games, moderately good at lessons, and, as he was also blessed with an amiable disposition, moderately good at making friends. He had been in the upper sixth and thinking vaguely of some sort of future in a bank or on the management side of industry when something happened that forever changed his life.

One of the texts for his English "A" level was *A Midsummer Night's Dream.* (Or, as he had since learned to call it, simply *The Dream.)* A performance of the play by the Royal Shakespeare Company was booked to take place in the vast gymnasium of Nicholas's comprehensive school. Within two days of the announcement, the performance was sold out. Several of the sixth form went, Nicholas more for the novelty of the thing than anything else. He was intrigued by the site the company had chosen for their performance. He had always believed that theaters, like cinemas, had a stage at one end, curtains, and rows of seats, and was curious as to how the RSC was going to cope in the gym, which had none of these.

When he arrived, there seemed to be hundreds of people

milling about, and the place was transformed. There were rostrums and flights of steps, trestle tables, artificial green grass, and a metal tree with golden apples on it. Scattered about the floor were huge cushions made of carpet material. Five musicians were sitting on the vaulting horse.

Overhead was an elaborate grid of metal with dozens of lights attached. Two of the gym ropes had been released, and swung gently to and fro. Then Nicholas noticed, at the other end of the hall on a dais, a stocky man in evening clothes with a broad red ribbon across his breast pinned with a jeweled star and medals. He was chatting to a woman in a dark green bustled dress wearing diamonds in her ears and a tiny crown. Suddenly he held out his arm, she rested her gloved hand on his wrist, and they stepped down from the platform. The lights blazed white and hard, and the play began.

Immediately Nicholas was enthralled. The vigor and attack and intense proximity of the actors took his breath away. The brilliant costumes, their colors blurred by the quickness of the players' movement and dance, dazzled him. He was caught up in the sweep and power of emotions that defied analysis. And they changed so quickly. He no sooner felt the most intense sympathy for Helena than he was compelled to laugh at her incoherent rage. The mechanicals, good for a snigger in his English class, moved him almost to tears as he saw how passionately, how urgently, they longed for their play to be performed. The scenes between Titania and Bottom were so sensual he felt his face burn.

He had to move lots of times. Red ropes were set up at one point and, standing just behind them, he was a part of Theseus's court. Then he got bundled onto the dais to watch Bottom carried shoulder high by a shouting, cheering mob to his nuptials. The ass's head turned, and the yellow eyes glared at him as the man went by braying and raising one brawny arm in unmistakable sexual salute. And in the midst of this seemingly unstoppable splendid flux of dance and movement and energy and rhythm were remarkable points of stillness. Oberon and Titania, each spinning casually on a climbing rope, silk robes fluttering, swinging nearer and nearer to each other, exchanging glances of passionate hatred, unexpectedly stopped and shared a chaste ironic kiss. Pyramus's grief at Thisbe's death expressed simply but with such pain that all the court and audience too became universally silent.

And then the wedding feast. After a great fanfare the court

and servants threw plastic glasses into the audience, then ran around with flagons to fill them. Everyone toasted Theseus and Hippolyta. Balloons and streamers descended from the grid. Faery and human danced together, and the hall became a great swirling mass of color and light and melodious sounds. Nicholas climbed a flight of steps and stood watching, his throat closed and dry with excitement; then, as if on the stroke of midnight, all movement ceased, and Nicholas realized that Puck was standing next to him. So close their arms were touching. The actor spoke: "'If we shadows have offended...'"

Then Nicholas realized that it was coming to an end. That the whole glorious golden vision was going to fade away and die..."no more yielding but a dream." And he thought his heart would break. Puck spoke on. Nicholas studied his profile. He could feel the dynamic tension in the man, see it in the pugnacious tightness of his jaw and the rippling muscles of his throat. He spoke with tremendous force, emitting a small silver spray of saliva as he declaimed the closing lines. And then, on "Give me your hand, if we be friends," he stretched out his left arm to the audience in a gesture that was all benevolence and, with his right, reached out to Nicholas and seized his hand. For the space of one more line they stood, the actor and the boy whose life would never be the same again. Then it was over.

Nicholas sat down as the applause went on and on. When the company finally dispersed and the audience drifted away, he remained, clutching his glass, in a daze of passionate emotion. Then one of the stagehands took the steps away. Nicholas emptied his glass of the last spot of black currant, then spotted a red streamer and a pink paper rose on the floor. He picked them up and put them carefully in his pocket. The lighting grid was being lowered and he felt in the way, so he took himself off with the deepest reluctance.

Outside in the road were two large vans. Someone was loading the metal tree with golden apples. Several of the actors emerged. They set off down the road and Nicholas followed, knowing that tamely going home was out of the question. The group went into the pub. He hesitated for a while by the door, then slipped in and stood, a rapt observer, just behind the cigarette machine.

The actors stood in a circle a few feet away. They were not dressed stylishly at all. They wore jeans, shabby afghans, sweaters. They were drinking beer; not talking or laughing loudly or showing off, and yet there was something about them. . . . They were simply different from anyone else there. Marked in some subtle way that Nicholas could not define. He saw Puck, a middle-aged man in an old black leather jacket wearing a peaked denim cap, smoking, waving the smoke away, smiling.

Nicholas watched them with a degree of longing so violent it made his head ache. He wanted desperately to overhear their conversation, and was on the point of edging nearer when the door behind him opened and two teachers came in. Immediately he dodged behind their backs and into the street. Apart from feeling that he could not bear to be exposed so soon to the banalities of everyday conversation, Nicholas felt sure that the enthralling experience through which he had just passed must have marked him physically in some way. And he dreaded what he felt would be clumsy and insensitive questioning.

Fortunately, when he got home, everyone had gone to bed. He looked at himself in the kitchen mirror, surprised and a little disappointed at the modesty of his transformation. His face was pale and his eyes shone, but apart from that he looked pretty much the same.

But he was not the same. He sat down at the table and produced the glass, the flower, the streamer, and his free cast list. He smoothed the paper out and ran down the column of actors. Puck had been played by Roy Smith. Nicholas drew a careful ring around the name, washed and dried his glass carefully, put the rose and the paper and the streamer inside, then went to his room. He lay on his bed reliving every moment of the evening till daylight broke. The next day he went to the library, asked if there was a local drama group, and was given details of the Latimer. He went to the theater that same evening, told them he wanted to be an actor, and was immediately co-opted to help with the props for *French Without Tears*.

Nicholas quickly discovered that there was theater and theater, and adapted philosophically. He had a lot (everything) to learn and had to start somewhere. He was sorry that none of the CADS, with the exception of Deidre, had been to see *The Dream*, but sensed very quickly that to attempt to describe it, let alone mention its effect on him, would be a mistake. So he made and borrowed props and ran about and made himself so useful that he was co-opted permanently. For the next play, *Once in a Lifetime*, he went on the book. He made a mess of prompting at first, bringing down on himself Esslyn's scorn and Harold's weary disdain, but he took the play home and read it over and over, absorbing the quick-fire rhythms, getting to sense the pauses, making himself familiar with exits and entrances, and became much better. He helped build the set for *Teahouse of the August Moon,* and Tim taught him basic lighting, letting him share the box and patting his bottom absentmindedly from time to time. He did the sound effects and music for *The Snow Queen,* and in *The Crucible,* he got a speaking part.

Nicholas learned his few lines quickly, and was always the first actor at rehearsals and the last to leave. He bought a cheap tape recorder and worked on an American accent, ignoring the amused glances between certain members of the cast. He made up an entire history for his character and listened and reacted with intense concentration to everything that went on around him onstage. Long before the first night he could think of nothing else. When it arrived and he was incompetently putting on too much makeup in the packed dressing room, he realized he had forgotten his lines. Frantically he sought a script, wrote them down on a piece of paper, and tucked it into the waistband of his homespun trousers. Waiting in the wings, he was overcome with a wave of nausea and was sick in the firebucket.

As he stepped onto the stage, terror struck him with hurricane force. Rows of faces swam into his line of vision. He looked once and looked away. He spoke his first line. The lights burned down, but he felt cold with exhilaration and excitement as, one after the other, the rest of his lines sprang to the forefront of his mind when needed and he experienced for the first time that strange dual grip that an actor must always keep on reality. Part of him believed in the Proctors' kitchen in Salem with its iron pots and pans and crude furnishings and frightened people, and part of him was aware that a stool was in the wrong place and that John Proctor was still masking his wife and Mary Warren had forgotten her cap. Afterward in the clubroom he experienced a warm, close camaraderie ("Give me your hands, if we be friends") that seemed fleetingly to surmount any actual likes and dislikes within the group.

In the pantomime he played the back legs of a horse, and then was offered the part of Danny in *Night Must Fall.* Rehearsals started six weeks before his "A" levels, and he knew he had failed the lot. The endless grumblings that had been going on at home for months about all the time he was spending at the Latimer erupted into a blazing row, and he walked out. Almost immediately Avery offered him the tiny room over the Blackbird bookshop. It was rent-free in exchange for dusting the shop every morning and cleaning Avery's house once a week.

He had lived there now for nearly a year and subsisted, sometimes superbly (on Avery's leftovers), but mainly on baked beans purloined from the supermarket where he worked. Nearly all his wages went on voice and movement classes—he had discovered an excellent teacher in Slough—and on theater tickets. Once a month he hitched up to London to see a show, determined to keep his batteries recharged by frequent injections of what he thought of as "the real thing." (It was after an exhilarating performance of *The Merry Wives of Windsor* at the Barbican that he had chosen Ford's Epicurean speech for his Central audition.)

He still didn't know if he was any good. Brenda Leggat, first cousin to the Smys, reviewed the CADS productions in the local rag, and her perceptions were about as original as her prose. Every comedy was sparkling, every tragedy wrenched the heart. Performances, if not to the manner born, were all we have come to expect from this actor/actress/soubrette/ingenue/cocktail cabinet. And Nicholas soon understood the group well enough to know that any direct questions regarding his performance would receive anodyne if not gushing reassurances. Plenty was said in the clubroom about absent friends, but it was almost impossible for an actor to get an honest opinion to his face. Everyone except Esslyn and the Everards (and Harold, of course) told Nicholas that he was marvelous. Harold rarely praised (he liked to keep them on their toes), except at first nights, when he behaved like a Broadway impresario, surging about hysterically, kissing everyone, distributing flowers, and even squeezing out a histrionic tear.

Nicholas finished his exercises, did a series of stretches and some more deep breathing, undressed, brushed his teeth, climbed into bed, and promptly fell into a deep sleep.

He dreamed it was the first night of *Amadeus*, and he stood in the wings dressed all in black with wrinkled tights and a skull under his arm, having learned the part of *Hamlet*.

Rosa Crawley's husband was waiting up, having spent the evening in the Cap and Bells with some fellow Rotarians and their polyestered spouses. He always tried to get home before his wife, not only because she hated finding the house empty but because he looked forward to hearing the continuing saga of theatrical folk that started almost the minute she came through the door. She never accompanied him to the pub, of course, and Earnest basked a little in her absence, knowing that his companions were aware that his wife had much more interesting fish to fry. Tonight he was home only minutes before her, and had just made his cocoa when she arrived. Earnest plumped up the sofa cushions, poured a double scotch on the rocks so that his wife could unwind, and sat back with his own drink, his face bright with anticipation.

Rosa sipped her whisky and watched Earnest pushing aside the wrinkled skin of his steaming cocoa a little enviously. Sometimes, especially on a night like this, she quite fancied a cup of cocoa but felt that it was surely (Slippery Elm Food apart) the least sophisticated drink in the entire world. Starting to take it of an evening could well be the first step on the sliding slope to coziness and a public admittance of middle age. Next thing she'd be padding around in a warm dressing gown and wearing thermal underwear. She slipped off her high-heeled shoes and massaged her feet. The shoes lay, vamp down, spiky four-inch heels stabbing the air.

She was a tiny woman, just over five feet tall with a Gypsyish appearance that she nurtured to an extreme degree. The black of her dark hair was regularly intensified, her fine dark eyes ringed with kohl and decorated with a double fringe of false lashes, while her coppery complexion spoke of the wind on the heath and a star to steer by. Her nose was larger than she would have liked, but she capitalized on this by hinting at a rather tragic immigrant Jewish background, a suggestion that would have horrified her grandparents, sturdy Anglo-Saxon farm workers from Lincolnshire. She nourished this vaguely Semitic Romany ancestry by wearing dark clothes with accessories that were so dazzling they seemed to be going off like fireworks rather than making a fashion point.

Looking over at Earnest placidly sipping his nightcap, she wondered anew at the strange fact of their marriage. It had been out of the question, of course, that she remain single after her divorce from Esslyn. Apart from the matter of pride, she couldn't bear to be alone for more than five minutes. She had assumed that, with her looks and personality, men would come flocking out of the woodwork once word got around that she was available, but this had not been the case. Earnest Crawley, local builder, widower, and comfortable had been the only serious suitor.

He was a sweet man who knew his place, and she accepted him the first time he proposed. He was shy of and a little alarmed by the CADS, and apart from going to Rosa's first nights and the closing night party, kept well away, perhaps sensing that this would please her best. Occasionally Rosa gave the leading lights in the company lunch, and then Earnest played mine host barricaded behind a trestle table and pouring out the Frascati. They all drank like whales, it seemed to him, and he was glad when it was all over and the hothouse atmosphere damped down to normal again. Now, he asked how it had gone tonight.

"Ach," Rosa said exhaustedly, resting the back of her hand against her forehead, "quite horrendous. Joyce still hasn't done a thing about my costume, David Smy is like an elephant loose on the stage, and the Everards—who play the Venticelli—are hopeless."

Earnest finished his cocoa, picked up his pipe, and tamped it in contented anticipation. He had his own dramas at work, of course. Complaints from the foreman, rows in the hut, occasionally a serious accident. But there was something about the activities at the theater. Rosa relayed them with such panache that they rose far above the ordinary pettinesses of his working day.

"Harold says he's going to strangle them." (Rosa always opened her monologues with a flourishing bit of hyperbole.) "One at a time and very slowly, if they don't pick up their cues."

"Does he now?" Earnest made his response deliberately noncommittal. Rosa's attitude to her director was variable. Sometimes her loathing and jeers at his affectations knew no bounds: At others—usually when Harold had a clash with some supporting actress—he had all her sympathy. Then they were coevals, talent burnished bright, swimming in harness in a sea of mediocrity. This was clearly going to be one of those nights.

"The Venticelli open the show, right? Just the two of them . . . quick fire . . . nonstop. Like Ros and Gil in that Stoppard play."

"The Venti . . . what?"

"Venticelli. Italian for 'little winds.' They carry the news around."

Earnest nodded sagely and waited for further juicy details about the Everards, whoever they might be. The poor buggers had obviously better get their skates on if they wanted to survive the course. But his wife had now moved on to Boris, who, she said, had painted his face up to the hilt and was playing the emperor Joseph as a mad Bavarian hausfrau.

The fact was that Rosa, like almost everyone else in the company, detested the Everards. Her tongue had no sooner alighted on their names than it winced and shrank away, as if tasting some noxious substance. They were well cast in *Amadeus*, for gossip was what they thrived on. They had been with the company six months, during which time they had dripped venom into more than one ear and mouthed spiteful tittle-tattle into many others. Esslyn alone escaped their rancor. They would slither and slide around him, their unforgiving eyes bright with admiration, like a pair of doting serpents.

"And Boris moves like a camel!" Rosa cried, flinging her hands in the air. "Dragging himself all over the place. He seems to think that being stately is the same thing as being practically immobile."

Earnest nodded again and did a bit more tamping. And if it occurred to him to think it odd that never in the past two years, during which twelve plays had been produced, had Rosa's tongue, so sharply dismembering performance after performance, ever once alighted on the name of her first husband, he wisely kept this observation to himself.

"Ruined, ruined!" Avery ran through the carpeted hall, pulling off his cashmere scarf and dropping it as he went. Gloves fell on the Aubusson, his coat on the raspberry satin sofa. Tim strolled along in the wake of all this turbulence, picking up Avery's things and murmuring "Bad luck for some" when he came to the gloves. He stuffed one into each pocket of the coat and hung it up in the tiny hall next to his own, amused by the contrast between the Tattersall check with its garland of turquoise cashmere and little chestnut fingers sticking beseechingly up in the air, and his own somber dark gray herringbone and navy muffler.

Avery, already wrapped in his *tablier* and wearing his frog oven mitts, was pulling the le Creuset out of the oven. He put it down on a wooden trivet and eased the lid off a fraction of an inch at a time. While hurrying home, he had made a bargain with the Fates. He would not question Tim about the source and content of the previously mentioned phone calls if they would keep an eye on the *daube*. Avery, knowing the superhuman restraint that would be necessary to stick to his side of the agreement, had felt an almost magical certainty that the least the other party could do was to honor theirs. But running up the garden path, sure that he smelled a whiff of carbon on the cold night air, his certainties evaporated. And as he ran with quailing anticipation through the sitting room, he became firmly convinced that the bastards had let him down again. And so it proved to be.

"It's got a crust on!"

"That's all right." Tim sauntered into the kitchen and picked up a bottle opener. "Aren't you supposed to break that and mix it in?"

"That's a cassoulet. Oh, God . . ."

"For heaven's sake, stop wringing your hands. It's only a stew."

"A stew! *A stew.*"

"At least we won't be able to say there's not a crust in the house."

"That's all it means to you, isn't it? A joke."

"Far from it. I'm extremely hungry. And if you were that worried, you could have come home earlier."

"And you could have come to the theater earlier."

"I was doing the Faber order." Tim smiled and smoothed the irritation from his voice. With Avery in this state, it could be midnight before a morsel crossed his lips. "And the phone calls were from Camelot Antiques about your footstool, and Derek Barfoot rang asking us for Sunday lunch."

"Oh." Avery looked sheepish, relieved, grateful, and encouraged. "Thank you."

"Look. Why don't we use this spoon with the holes in—"

"No! You'll never get it all!" Avery stood in front of his casserole like a mother protecting her child from a ravening beast. "I've got a better idea." He produced a box of tissues and lowered half a dozen with slow and exquisite care into the crumbling top layer. "These will absorb all the bits, then I can lift the whole thing off with a fish slice."

"I thought it was in the topsoil where all the goodness lay," murmured Tim, going to the larder to get the wine.

The larder was really Avery's domain, but it had a deep, quarry-tiled recess with a grilled window onto the outside wall that made it beautifully cool and the perfect place for a wine rack. The tiny room was brilliantly lit and crammed with provisions. Walnut and hazelnut and sesame oils. Olives, herbs, and pralines from Provence. Anchovies and provolone; truffles in little jars. Tins of clams and Szechuan peppercorns. Potato flour and many mustards. Prosciutto, water chestnuts, and a ham with a wrinkled, leathery skin the color of licorice hanging from the ceiling next to an odoriferous salami. Tiny Amaretti and snails. Tomato paste and marron paste, cured fish and lumpfish, gull's eggs and plover's eggs, and a chili sauce so hot it could blast the stones from a horse's hoof. Tim moved a crock of peaches in brandy, took a bottle from the rack, and returned to the kitchen.

"What are you opening?"

"The Château d'Issan."

Chewing his full marshmallow lip (the tiny drop of reassurance re: the phone calls having already vanished into a vast lake of more generalized anxiety), Avery watched Tim twist the corkscrew, press down the chrome wings, and, with a soft pop, pull the cork. Avery thought it the second most beautiful sound in the world (following hard on the easing of a zipper), while having a terrible suspicion that for Tim it might be the first. Now, looking at the flat dark silky hairs on the back of his lover's wrist glinting in the light from the spot lamps, noticing his elegant hands as they tilted the bottle and poured the fragrant wine, Avery's stomach lurched with a familiar mixture of terror and delight. Tim took off his suit jacket, revealing an olive-green doeskin vest and snowy shirt, the sleeves hitched up by old-fashioned elasticized armbands. Then he lowered his narrow, ascetic nose into the glass and sniffed.

Avery could never understand how anyone who cared so passionately about what he drank was not equally fastidious when it came to what he ate. Tim would consume anything that was what he called "tasty," and his range was catholic to say the least. Once, stranded for an hour in Rugby station, he had demolished cheeseburger and chips, several squares of white, spongelike bread, a lurid pastry with three circles of traffic-light-colored jam, two Kit-Kats, and a cup of pungent, rust-colored tea with every appearance of satisfaction. And he did not even, Avery had reflected while toying miserably with an orange and a glass of lukewarm Liebfraumilch, have the excuse of a working-class background. (Tim had declined the wine on the grounds that it was not only likely to be the produce of more than one country, but liberally laced with antifreeze to boot.)

So why, Avery sometimes asked himself, as he leafed through his vast collection of cookbooks, did he labor so long and ardently in the kitchen? The answer was immediate and never changing. Avery prepared his wood pigeon *à la paysanne, truite à la crème,* and *fraises Romanof* out of simple gratitude. He would place them before Tim in a spirit of excitable humility, because they were his supreme attainment, the very best his loving heart could offer. In the same manner he ironed Tim's shirts, chose fresh flowers for his room, planned little treats. Almost unconsciously, when he went shopping, his eye was alert for something, anything, that would make a surprise gift.

He never ceased to marvel at the fact that he and Tim had been together for seven years, especially when he discovered the truth about his friend's background. Avery had always been homosexual, and had innocently supposed that Tim's experience had been the same. Then he discovered that Tim's understanding of his true nature had come painfully and gradually. That he had regarded himself as heterosexual as a teenager, and bisexual for several years after that. (He had even been engaged for eighteen months while in his early twenties.)

The acquisition of this knowledge had thrown Avery into a turmoil of fear. Tim's assurances and his reminder that this had all happened twelve years ago had done little to calm a temperament that was volatile by nature. Even now, Avery would watch Tim without seeming to, looking furtively for signs that these earlier inclinations were reasserting themselves, just as a showily colored plant occasionally reverts to its more pallid origins.

Avery reasoned thus because he could never, ever, in a trillion zillion years understand what Tim saw in him. For a start there was the physical contrast. Tim was tall and lean with hollow cheeks and a mouth so stern in repose that his sudden smile seemed almost shocking in its sweetness. Avery thought he was like a figure in a Caravaggio painting. Or perhaps (his profile at the moment looked alarmingly austere) a medieval monk. Nicholas had said he thought that Tim, although emotionally lean, was spiritually opulent. This was not what Avery wanted to hear. He didn't give a fig for spiritual opulence. Give him, he had replied, a nice filet mignon and a fond caress any old day of the week.

Avery knew he cut a ridiculous figure when compared to Tim. He was tubby, and his features, like his personality, were sloppy and spread all over the place. His lips were squashy and overfull, his eyes a washed-out blue and slightly protuberant, with almost colorless lashes, and his nose, just to be different, was neat and small and seemed quite lost in the pale pink expanse of his face. His head was very round, with a fringe of curls, butter yellow and softly fluffy like duckling down. He had always been agonizingly conscious of his baldness, and until he met Tim, had worn a wig. The morning after their first night together he had found it in the wastebasket. It had never been mentioned between them again, and Avery bravely continued to live without it, treating himself and his scalp to a weekly going-over with a sun lamp instead.

Then there was the difference in their dispositions. Tim was nearly always calm, while Avery veered excitedly between elation and despair, touching all the psychological stations of the cross on the way. And he reacted so dramatically to things. This had always seemed to amuse Tim, but once or twice lately Avery had noticed a twitch or two of impatience, a spot of lip-tightening. Now, draining his glass of Bordeaux, he framed in his mind the latest of many small vows. He would learn to take things more calmly. He would think before speaking. Take several deep breaths. Perhaps even count to ten. He turned his attention back to the le Creuset. All the tissues had sunk without trace. Avery let out a scream that could have been heard halfway down the street.

"Bloody hell!" Tim banged his glass down on the countertop. "What's the matter now?"

"The Kleenex have sunk to the bottom."

"Is that all? I thought at the very least you were being castrated."

"I meant them to soak up all the bits," sobbed Avery.

"Well, now you've discovered that they won't. Knowledge is never wasted. We'll just give it to Nicholas."

"You can't do that—it's full of tissue."

"Riley, then." Riley was the CADS feline mascot.

"Riley! There's half a bottle of Beaune in there."

"So he'll think it's Christmas."

"Anyway, Riley's a fish man, not a meat man. What are you doing?"

"Toast." Tim was slicing bread on the marble pastry slab. Now, he reached across Avery and switched on the grill. Then he refilled both their glasses. "Drink up, sweetheart. And stop flowing all over the furniture."

"Sorry..." Avery sniffled and snuffled and drank up. "You're... you're not angry with me, are you, Tim?"

"No, Avery, I'm not angry with you. I'm just bloody starving to death."

"Yes. So—"

"Don't keep saying you're sorry. Get off your backside and give me a hand. There's some duck pâté left over. And we could finish the mango ice cream."

"All right." Still mopping and mowing, Avery crossed to the fridge. "I don't know why you put up with me."

"Stop being ingratiating. It doesn't suit you."

"Sor—"

"And if I didn't, who else would?"

This question, so casually posed, seemed to Avery no more than the simple truth. Awash with sorrow, he hung his head and pondered, looking down at his round tummy and chubby little feet. Then he looked up and met Tim's sudden brilliant smile. O frabjous day! thought Avery, beaming widely in his turn. And then, to make things absolutely perfect and he and Tim equal in carelessness, the toast caught fire.

"We can pretend they're charcoal biscuits," said Avery, draining the rest of his wine. Then, quite forgetting the earlier strictures about him being ingratiating: "I wish I were more like you. More calm."

"Good grief, I don't. I'd hate to live with someone like me. I'd be bored to death in a week."

"Would you, Tim?" Magically the dolorous beat of Avery's heart quickened. "Would you really?"

"A drama a day keeps the doldrums away."

"Mm." Avery helped himself to some more wine. "That's true, I suppose."

"But we've had our ration for tonight. Now, we must get on."

"Yes, Tim." Avery bustled happily about finding unsalted butter, celery, the pâté, and a white china bowl of tomatoes. Tim was quite right, of course. Everyone knew about the attraction of opposites. That's why it all worked so well on the whole. Why they were so happy together. It was just foolishness for him to struggle to destroy the very characteristics that his partner found attractive.

Avery took the hand-operated coffee grinder and put some beans in the little wooden drawer. Tim put more bread under the grill. He refused to use an electric contrivance, believing that the uncontrollably high speed overheated the beans, sent by mail by the Algerian Coffee Company, and impaired their flavor. The fragrance of the beans met and mingled with the succulent scent of the wine, and the very ordinary but always to Avery deeply satisfying smell of fresh toast. He sat down at the scrubbed deal table full of anticipation. This was the time he loved best of all. (Well, nearly.) When there was food and wine and gossip and jokes.

Even if all they had done during the day was sell books and get on with the paper work, there was always at least one customer who was ripe for exaggerated mimicry or grotesquely imaginative suggestions as to how he got his jollies. But of course the nights that sparkled, the nights that offered the most superlative entertainment, were the nights when they had been to the Latimer. Then performances could be put through the mincer, relationships scrutinized and surmises made and opinions mooted as to Harold's precise degree of sanity (always open to question and anybody's guess).

But occasionally, if there had been "a drama" in the home, Tim might withdraw a little and affect a lack of interest in the theatrical proceedings. These were anguished times for Avery, who gossiped as easily as he drew breath, and with almost the same urgent necessity. Now, as he slathered butter all over his toast, he looked across at Tim spreading neatly, with a small degree of perturbation. But it was all right. Tim looked across at Avery, and his slatey eyes, which could look so cold, were warm with a sudden flare of malice.

"But apart from that, Mrs. Lincoln," he said, reaching for the celery, "how did you enjoy the play?"

When Joyce Barnaby entered the sitting room, her husband was dozing in front of the fire. He had been drawing a sprig of *Hammamelis mollis,* and his pencil was still cradled in his hand, although the sketch pad had fallen to the floor. He woke when his wife, standing behind his chair, folded her arms across his chest and gave him a hug. Then she picked up the pad.

"You haven't finished."

"I dropped off."

"Did you eat your lasagne?"

Tom Barnaby gave a noncommittal grunt. When Joyce had come home from the casting evening of *Amadeus* and told him she was playing cook to Salieri, only the fact that a raging heartburn was running amok in his breast at the time had stopped him laughing aloud. He could never get over the fact that she ate her own cooking if not with relish at least with no evidence of distaste. He wondered sometimes if his genuine expressions of dismay at mealtimes had, over the years, assumed a ritualistic or even a fossilized stamp, and that Joyce had decided they were some sort of running gag. He watched her bend over the sprig of yellow flowers and inhale appreciatively.

"How did it go, my lovely?"

"Like an evening with the Marx Brothers. I've never known so many things go wrong. Fortunately Tim arrived in the break with his razor, which cheered Harold up. Until then he'd been grousing all night. *Molto disastro,* my darlings!"

"What's the razor for, anyway?"

"You wait and see. If I tell you now, it'll spoil the first night."

"Nothing could be spoiled for me that has you in it." He took her hand. "What's that big bag for?"

"Wardrobe. Trousers to be let out. Broken zips. Some braid to replace."

"You do too much."

"Oh, Tom"—she nudged his feet off a low stool and sat on it herself, holding her other cold hand out to the fire—"don't say that. You know how I love it."

He did know. Earlier he had been listening to a tape she had made of the arias sung by Katherina Cavalieri. Joyce had a beautiful voice, a rich, soaring soprano. A little blurred now in the higher register, but still thickly laced with plangent sweetness. The aria *"Marten Aller Arten"* had moved him to tears.

His wife had been a student at the Guildhall School of Music when they had met and fallen in love. He had been a constable on the beat. When he had first heard her sing at a public performance in her final year, he sat there listening to the marvelous sounds, stunned and afraid. For a long while after that he had been unable to believe that she could really love the ordinary man he knew himself to be. Or that she would ever be safely his.

But they had married, and for four years she had continued to sing, at first giving small, ill-attended recitals, then joining the chorus at the Royal National Opera House. Barnaby, learning fast, had reached the rank of detective sergeant when Cully was born. Alternately bogged down in the office by administrative work or exhilaratingly abroad hunting an elusive prey, he worked long hours and used his time at home to eat and sleep. And as the months went by, to play with his increasingly delightful baby daughter. The fact that Joyce's career had virtually come to a halt almost (as he admitted with shame much later) escaped his notice.

Progress in the force had been slow—he had remained a sergeant for many years—and money tight, so when Cully was three, Joyce had got a job understudying in *Godspell*. But her husband was frequently on night duty, which meant engaging babysitters, and one or two unsettling experiences left her so full of guilt and anxiety that when she did get to the theater, she was quite unable to concentrate. So, *pro tem,* she joined the Causton Light Operatic Society to keep her voice supple; then, when that folded, the CADS. Not what she'd been used to, of course, but better than nothing. And she and Tom agreed it was only until Cully was old enough to be left by herself.

But when that time came, Joyce found that the musical world had moved on and was full of bright, gifted, tough, and pushy young singers. And the years of more or less contented domesticity had blunted the knife edge of her ambition. She found she didn't want to drag herself up to London and stand in a vast dim theater and sing to a faceless trio somewhere out there in the dark. Especially with a crowd of twenty-year-olds watching from the wings sharp as tacks with determination and buoyant with energy and hope. And so, gradually and without any fuss or visible signs of dismay, Joyce relinquished her plans for a musical career.

But her husband never saw her playing with such perceptive truthfulness the modest parts that were her lot, or heard her lovely voice in the Christmas pantomime gloriously leading all the rest, without a terrible pang of sorrow and remorse. The pang had become muted over the years, given their continuing happiness, but now, *"Marten Aller Arten"* fresh in his ears and the great bag of alterations seen out of the corner of his eye, a sudden shaft of sadness, of pity at the waste, went through him like a knife.

"Tom..." Joyce seized his other hand and stared intently into his face. "Don't. It doesn't matter. All that. *It doesn't matter.* It's you and me. And now there's Cully. Darling...?" She held his gaze forcefully, lovingly. "All right?"

Barnaby nodded and allowed his face to lighten. What else could he do? Things were as they were. And it was true that now there was Cully.

Their daughter had been obsessed with the theater since the age of four, when she had been taken to her first pantomime. She had been quickly on-stage when the dame had asked for children to watch for the naughty wolf and had had to be forcibly removed, kicking and screaming, when the scene was over. She had performed at her primary school with great aplomb (oak leaf/young rabbit), and had never looked back. Now in her final year reading English at New Hall, her performances in the ADC were formidable to behold.

"I thought you knew all that," continued Joyce. "Silly old bear."

Barnaby smiled. "Been a long while since anyone called me that."

"Do you remember when Cully used to? There was that program she loved on television..." Joyce sang, "'Barnaby the bear's my name....' I forget the rest."

"Ah, yes. She was a little cracker when she was seven."

"She's a little cracker now." The conversation rested for a moment, then Joyce continued, "A message from Colin." Barnaby groaned. "Could you paint the fireplace? Please?"

"Joycey—I'm on holiday." He always demurred when asked to help out with the set, and he always, work permitting, gave a bit of a hand.

"I wouldn't ask if you weren't on holiday," Joyce lied brazenly. "We can all chuck a bit of paint on flats, but this fireplace Colin's made. It's so beautiful, Tom—a work of art. We can't let any old slap-happy Charlie loose on it. And you're marvelous at that sort of thing."

"Soft soap and flannel."

"It's true. You're an artist. Do you remember that statue you did? For *Round and Round the Garden?*"

"Only too well. And the letters to the local press."

"You could do it Saturday afternoon. Take a flask and some sandwiches." She paused. "I wouldn't ask if it were gardening weather."

"I wouldn't do it if it were gardening weather."

"Oh, thank you, Tom." She rubbed his hand against her cheek. "You are sweet."

Detective Chief Inspector Barnaby sighed, seeing the last few precious days of his annual vacation filling up with bustling activity. "Try telling them that at the station," he said.

Harold aimed his Morgan at the space between the gateposts topped with polystyrene lions at seventeen Madingley Close and bombed up to the garage. He encouraged the engine to give a final great, full-throated roar, then switched off and braced himself for the awkward business to follow. Getting in and out of the Morgan was not easy. On the other hand, driving along in it, handling it, being seen in it, was tremendous. Heads were turned as the scarlet hood flashed past, slaking temporarily Harold's ultimately un-quenchable thirst for admiration. The fact that his wife disliked the car added to his pleasure. He withdrew his keys and patted the dashboard appreciatively. One instinctively knew when something was right, mused Harold, having long ago taken this cunning adman's lie to his heart.

On the leather bucket seat next to him lay a sheaf of posters that Mrs. Winstanley would dish out to fellow members of the Townswomen's Guild, her flower-arranging class, and the local shops. Apart from racking his brains promotionwise and being interviewed whenever he could create the opportunity, Harold had no truck with publicity. After all, he would tell any jibbers, you didn't see Trevor Nunn popping in and out of his local newsagent's with footage on the latest extravaganza. Briefly reflecting on that famous name, Harold swallowed hard on the bile of dissatisfaction. He had long been aware that if it had not been for his careless early marriage and the birth of three numbingly dull children now, thankfully, boring themselves and their consorts to death miles away, he would currently be one of the top directors in the country. If not (Harold had never been one to shirk hard truths) in the world.

All you needed was luck, talent, and the right wife. Harold believed you made your own luck, talent was no problem. He had that, God knew, burgeoning from every pore. But the right wife

. . . ah, there was the rub. Doris was a simple bourgeoise. A philistine. When they were first married (she had been a slim, shy, pretty girl), the children had kept her occupied, and she had had no spare time to take an interest in the Latimer. Later, when the young Winstanleys were growing up and following their own pursuits, her attempts to comment on the productions had been so inept that Harold had forbidden her to come to the theater except on first nights.

He had briefly considered trading her in when Rosa had come on the market, seeing the latter as a far more suitable mate for a producer. (Sometimes he wondered if Doris was really grateful for, or even aware of, the status that his position as the town's only theatrical impresario conferred.) However, after exposing this fleeting fancy to the cold light of reason, Harold had to admit that it was gravely flawed. Rosa was used to, nay, reveled in, her role as leading lady, and he could not see her deliberately lowering her wattage to show him to best advantage. Whereas Doris, in spite of her peculiar absorptions—pickling eggs, drying flowers, and stuffing innocent knitted creatures with chunks of variegated foam—did have the supreme virtue of dimness. Indeed, Harold was pleasureably aware that when he entered a room, she practically vanished into the woodwork like the moth *Melanchra persicariae*. And perhaps most important of all, she was not grasping. He had provided modestly for his wife and children, far more modestly, in fact, than he might have done. Over half the profits he made from his business went into his productions, so that whatever snipers might find to criticize in any other direction, they could never say the play was not well dressed.

An amber rectangle of light fell across the windshield. "Harold?"

Harold sighed, gave the mileage dial a final quick polish with his hankie, and called, "Give me a chance."

He struggled out of the cockpit. This was the cutoff point for him. The moment when he turned away from the full-blooded rumbustious razzle-dazzle rainbow ring of circus and stepped into the shady gray half-formed and quite unreal world of bread.

"Your supper's getting cold."

"Dinner, Doris." Already consumed with irritation, he pushed past her into the kitchen. "How many times do I have to tell you?"

*   *   *

"How has he been, Mrs. Higgins?" Deidre entered the kitchen quietly through the back door, and the elderly woman dozing by the fire jumped. "I'm sorry. I didn't mean to startle you."

"He's been ever so good," replied Mrs. Higgins. "Considering."

Deidre thought the "considering" uncalled for. They both knew that Mr. Tibbs wasn't always ever so good and why. Deidre glanced at the mantelpiece. Mrs. Higgins's envelope had gone, and Deidre spied it sticking out of the woman's grubby apron pocket as she heaved herself to her feet. "Upsadaisy."

"Is he still asleep?"

"No. Just chatting away to hisself. I made him a lovely plate of soup."

Deidre spotted the tin in the sink, said, "You're so kind," and helped Mrs. Higgins on with her coat. The thankfulness and gratitude in her voice were not feigned. If it were not for Mrs. Higgins, Deidre would have no life at all. No life, that is, apart from home and the Gas Board. Because where else would she find someone to sit with a befuddled old man for a couple of pounds? Not that the money was ever mentioned. The first time Mrs. Higgins came, Deidre had offered, only to be told "Don't you worry dear, I'd only be sitting next door on me tod watching the goggle box." But the coins Deidre had left under the teapot disappeared, and so, always since then, had the manila envelope.

When Mrs. Higgins had gone, Deidre locked and bolted the door, put some milk for her Horlicks on a very low heat, and climbed the stairs. Her father was sitting up ramrod straight in crisp pajamas under a large, dimmish print of "The Light of the World." His gray, still faintly gingery mustache was soaked with tears of joy, and his eyes shone. "He is coming," he cried as Deidre entered the room. "The Lord is coming."

"Yes, daddy." She sat on the bed and took his hand. It was like holding a few slippery bones in a bag of skin. "Would you like another drink?"

"He will take us away. Into the light."

She knew it was no good trying to settle him. He always slept upright, his back bolted into a perpendicular line against a cumulus of pillows. She patted his arm and kissed his damp cheek. He had been a little bit disturbed for several months now. The first indication that all was not well had occurred when she arrived home from the theater one night after set-building to find him in the street going from house to house, rapping on doors and offering the startled occupants a shovelful of live coals.

Horrified and amazed, she had led him back home, replaced the coals on the kitchen fire, and questioned him gently, trying to find a rational explanation. Of course there had been none. Since then he had frequently been befuddled or confused. (Deidre always used these unemphatic terms, avoiding the terrible official definition. When one of the workers at the center where Mr. Tibbs spent his days had used the word, Deidre had screamed at her in fear and anger.)

He still had lengthy periods of marvelous clarity. There was just no way of knowing when they would arise or for how long they would last. The previous Sunday had been a lovely day. They had gone for a walk in the afternoon, and she had been able to tell him all about *Amadeus,* exaggerating her role in the production as she always did to make him proud of her. In the evening they had had a glass of port and some lumpy home-made cake, and he had sung songs that he remembered from his childhood. He had been over forty when Deidre was born, so the songs were very old ones. "Red Sails in the Sunset," "Valencia," and "Oh, Oh, Antonio." He had put on his bowler hat and tapped and twirled his stick, shuffling in a sad, transmogrified echo of the routines he had leaped through when, years before, he had so delighted Deidre and her mother. His hair had been reddish gold then, and his mustache had gleamed like a ripe chestnut. They both wept before going to sleep last Sunday.

Deidre crossed to the window to draw the curtains, and stood for a moment looking up at the sky. There was a brilliant moon and a cavalcade of scudding clouds. Gabriel, her guardian angel, lived up there. As well as on the earth walking, bright and shining, just an immortal breath away, keeping a loving eye on the Tibbses' worldly concerns. When she was a little girl, Deidre would whip around quickly sometimes, as she did in a game of statues, hoping to catch sight of his twelve-foot wings before he put on his invisible cloak. Once, she was convinced she had found the outline of a golden footprint before hearing, over her head, a rushing, beating swoosh of sound, like the passing of a thousand swans.

As well as the archangel, everyone had a star to watch over them. When she had asked her father which was hers, he had said, "It's always the star that shines the brightest." They all looked the same tonight, thought Deidre, letting the curtain fall, and rather cold. She remembered the milk and hurried down to the kitchen just too late to stop it boiling over.

She refilled and replaced the pan, then took her script for the next production, *Uncle Vanya,* from the dresser. It had been dissected and reassembled, interleaved with blank pages, as had all the copies of plays on which she had been assistant stage manager. Deidre worked long and ardently on every one before the first rehearsal. She would read and reread the play, getting to know the characters as well as if she had lived with them. She struggled to realize the subtext and sense the tempo. Her head buzzed with ideas on staging, and she used long rolls of thin cardboard to design her sets. She was as enthralled by *Uncle Vanya* as she had been by *The Cherry Orchard,* intoxicated by Checkhov's particular ability to produce a seemingly natural world full of precisely observed, psychologically real human beings, then reconcile this world with the urgencies of dramatic necessity.

Now, becoming aware that she was hungry, she closed *Uncle Vanya* and put the book aside. She hardly ever managed to eat on theater evenings, not if she wanted to be on time. She found a bit of salad dressing in the fridge together with a small, hard piece of leftover beef and two slices of beetroot, and while spreading margarine on the stretchy white bread that was all her father's gums could tackle, she slipped into a frequent and favorite reverie in which she reviewed edited lowlights from the latest rehearsal, rewriting the scenario as she went along.

DEIDRE: I think the Venticelli are far too close to Salieri in the opening scene. They wouldn't huddle in that intimate way. And they certainly wouldn't be touching him.

ESSLYN: She's quite right, Harold. They've been getting more and more familiar. I thought if someone didn't say something soon, I'd have to myself.

HAROLD: Right. Stop nudging the star, you two. And thanks, Deidre. Wish I'd taken you aboard years ago.

             OR

HAROLD: Coffee all around, I think, Deidre.

DEIDRE: Do you mind? Assistant directors don't make coffee.
        (GENIAL LAUGHTER)

HAROLD: Sorry. We're so used to you looking after us.

ROSA: We've been taking you too much for granted, darling.

ESSLYN: And all the time you've been hiding all these dazzling ideas under your little bushel.

HAROLD: Careful—I'm turning green.
(MORE GENIAL LAUGHTER. KITTY GETS UP TO MAKE THE COFFEE.)
                    OR

HAROLD: (SLUMPED IN A CHAIR IN THE CLUBROOM) Now the others have gone, I don't mind telling you, Deidre, I just don't know what I'd have done without you on this production. Everything you say is so fresh and original. (HEAVY SIGH). I'm getting stale.

DEIDRE: Oh, no, Harold. You mustn't think—

HAROLD: Hear me out, please. What I'm working around to is our summer production. There's such a lot of work involved in *Uncle Vanya*...

DEIDRE: I'll be happy to help.

HAROLD: No, Deidre, *I'll* help. What I'd like—what we'd all like—is for you to direct the play.

Even Deidre's feverishly yearning soul found this final dialogue a bit hard to credit. As she scraped out the last bit of solid, shiny yellow salad dressing and distributed it patchily on the spongy bread, she reverted to simpler fantasies. Harold crashing his car. Or Harold having a heart attack. The latter was the most likely, she thought, recalling his stout tummy under its popping brocade vest. She surveyed her completed sandwich. The beetroot was falling out. she caught it, stuffed it back in, and took a bite. It wasn't very good. The milk boiled over again.

"How do you think it went then, Constanze?"

Kitty was sitting by the dressing table. She had peeled off her tights and propped up her milk-white legs on an embroidered footstool. Although she had announced her pregnancy barely three months ago, she was already inclined to hold the small of her back and smile brave, aching smiles. She winced sometimes, too, in the manner of one reacting to tiny blows. Now, she carefully dotted cleansing cream over her face before giving the expected response.

"Well, darling, I thought you were wonderful. It's coming along brilliantly."

"Almost there, wouldn't you say?"

"Oh, I would. And with so much against you."

"Absolutely. Christ knows what Nicholas thinks he's doing. I'm amazed Harold lets him get away with it."

"I know. Donald and Clive are the only ones who say anything. And then only because they know how you feel."

"Mm. They're useful creatures in many respects."

Esslyn had brushed his teeth, put on his midcalf-length pajamas with the judo-style top, and was sitting up in bed tautening his facial muscles. Mouth dropped open, head tilted back, mouth closed, aiming bottom lip at the tip of his nose. He had the jawline of a man of twenty-five, which, on a man of forty-five, couldn't be bad. He blew out his cheeks and let them collapse slowly. (Nose-to-mouth lines.) Then studied his pretty wife as she finished taking off her makeup.

He always fell slightly in love with the most attractive female member of the cast (they expected it), and in *Rookery Nook* had got really carried away in the props room with the frisky young ingenue who was now Mrs. Carmichael. She had been playing Poppy Dickie at the time. Unfortunately, when the pregnancy was discovered, he was unmarried, so had felt it incumbent upon him to propose to Kitty. He did this rather ruefully. He had been looking forward to several years of louche living before finding someone to care for him in his old age. But she was a biddable little piece, and he couldn't deny that this latish fatherhood had upped his status potentwise in the office. And of course it had been the most tremendous sock in the eye for Rosa.

He felt he owed her one for the way she had behaved when he had asked for a divorce. She had screamed and wailed and wept. And bellowed that he had had the best years of her life. Esslyn—reasonably enough, he felt—pointed out that if he hadn't had them, someone else would have. She could hardly have kept them, pristinely unlived, in a safe-deposit box. Then she had sobbed that she had always wanted children, and now it was too late and it was all his fault. This seemed to Esslyn just plain ridiculous.

They had sometimes discussed starting a family, usually when cast as parents in the current production, but Esslyn always felt it only right to point out that while their stage children would disappear after the final performance, real ones would be around for a whole lot longer. And that although his own life might not be much affected, Rosa's, since he would definitely not be shelling out for a nanny, would never be quite the same again. He'd thought she'd appreciated the logic of this, but she brought it all up when the question of moving out of *White Wings* was broached, refusing to budge until she had had some compensation for her "lost babies." Quite a hefty sum they had cost him, too. He had got his own back, though. When Kitty had become pregnant, he had announced it and their forthcoming nuptials at the end of a rehearsal of *Shop at Sly Corner*. Tenderly holding Kitty's hand, his eyes on Rosa's face, Esslyn had more than got his money's worth.

Of course, by then she had married that boring little builder. To be fair, though, Esslyn admitted to himself, finishing his cheek exercises and starting on some head rolling to reduce the tension in his neck, there were people who thought accountancy just as dreary a job as putting up houses. Perhaps even drearier. Esslyn could not agree. To him, the sorting and winnowing of claim and counterclaim, the reduction of stacks of wild expense-account imaginings to a column of sober, acceptable figures, and the hunting down of obscure wrinkles and loopholes in the law enabling him to reduce his clients' tax bill was a daily challenge that he would not have felt it too imprecise to call creative.

Esslyn preferred to handle the accounts of individuals. His partner, a specialist in company law, dealt with larger concerns, with the single exception of the charitable trust that supported the Latimer. As an insider with an intimate knowledge of the company's affairs, Esslyn had automatically taken this on, together with the accounts for Harold's import-export business, which was a modest one but not without interest. He never charged Harold quite as much as he would a nonacquaintance, and often wondered if his producer-director really appreciated this.

Having come to the end of his reminiscences and rolling his head about, Esslyn returned his attention to Kitty. Becoming aware of his regard, she tossed her highlighted curls in a coquettish gesture, which a less complacent husband might have thought a touch calculated. Then she admired her neck in the mirror. Esslyn admired her neck as well. Not a ring or a blur or a fold in sight. She had a charming little face. Too pointed to be called heart-shaped, it obtained more to a neat foxiness that, combined with the narrow tilt of her sparkling eyes, was very appealing. Now, she stood up, smoothing the rosy fabric of her nightdress close against her belly, as yet no rounder than when they had wrestled in the props room, and smiled into the glass.

Esslyn did not smile back, but contented himself with a simple nod. He was very sparing with his smiles, bringing them out only on special occasions. He had long been aware that, while they lit up and transformed his face, they also deepened and reinforced the nose-to-mouth lines somewhat. Now, he called, "Darling," in a manner that spoke more of instruction than endearment.

Obediently Kitty crossed to the four-poster and stood by his side. Esslyn made a "going up" gesture with his hand, plam held flat, and his wife lifted her nightdress over her head and let it fall, a cool raspberry ripple of satin, into a pool around her feet. Esslyn let his gaze slide over her lean, almost boyish flanks and hips, and small, appley breasts, and his lips tightened with satisfaction. (Rosa had allowed herself to become quite grotesquely fat during the last years of their marriage.) Esslyn tugged at the cord of his pajamas with one hand while patting his wife's pillow with the other.

"Come along, kitten."

She felt really nice. Firm and young and strong. She smelled of honeysuckle and the iffy white wine they sold in the clubhouse. She was sweetly compliant rather than saucily active, which, it seemed to Esslyn, was just how things should be. And to round off her character to perfection, she couldn't act for beans.

This last reflection recalled the rehearsals for *Amadeus,* and as Esslyn started to move briskly inside his wife, he mulled over his latest role at the Latimer. Quite a challenge (Salieri was never off-stage), but he was starting to feel that acting was no longer quite enough. It had been suggested that he might try a spot of direct-ing, and the truth was that Esslyn was rather drawn to this idea. He had once read a biography of Henry Irving, and quite fancied himself in a long dark coat with an astrakhan collar and a tallish hat. He might even grow sideburns—

"How was that for you, darling?"

"How was what? Oh—" He gazed down at Kitty's face, her lips shinily parted, her eyes closed in soft eclipse. "Sorry. Miles away as per usual. Fine...fine." He gave her a postcoital peck on the cheek in the manner of one putting the finishing touch to an iced cake and rolled over to his own side of the bed. "Do try and get your lines down for Tuesday, Kitty. At least for the scenes when we're together. I can't stand being held up." Unconsciously he echoed Harold. "I don't know what you find to do all day."

"Why"—Kitty got up on one elbow and beamed a shining, blue glance in his direction—"I think of my pettipoos, of course."

"And I think of you too, puss-wuss," rejoined Esslyn, really believing at that moment that he did. Then he said, "Don't forget —by Tuesday," plumped up his pillows, and, two minutes later, was fast asleep.

The Everards, toadies to the company's leading man, lived in unspeakable disarray in the crumbling terraced house down by the railway lines.

They were objects of curiosity to the rest of the street, who could not make them out. They did not seem to have jobs (the curtains were still sometimes drawn at midday), and would often not come flitting out with their expandable string shopping bags until well past teatime.

That they had little money seemed obvious. They never gave at the door and could occasionally be seen at five o'clock on market day scavenging behind the stalls with dainty precision, picking over the thrown-out fruits and vegetables. Various subtle and not-so-subtle attempts by the neighbors to get into the house had failed. They had not even managed to set foot on the tacky linoleum in the hall. And the windows were so thickly coated with grime that even when the tattered curtains were pulled aside, the mildewed interior of the house remained a mystery.

The sour patch of ground that passed for a back garden was overgrown with nettles and thistles and tall grass that occasionally swayed and rustled, disturbed by the passing of rodents. On the asphalt beneath the front bay window, their car slumped. This was a fifteen-year-old Volkswagen held together by spot welding and willpower, with a Guinness label where the tax disc should have been. Mrs. Griggs at the corner newsagent's had reported them to the police over this, and the label had disappeared for a while but was now back again. The Everards, Mrs. Griggs was fond of saying, gave her the creeps. She couldn't stand Clive's front teeth, which looked very sharp and protruded slightly, or Donald's blinking and squinting. She called them Ratty and Moley, although never in their presence.

They were rarely seen apart, and if they were, a certain dimness about the single Everard was noticeable. It was as if only by close physical proximity could the spark be struck that enabled them to shine with their full malevolent wattage. They seemed to feed off each other; wax fat on spiteful prediction and exchange. Nothing gave the brothers more happiness than the intense discomfiture of their fellow men, although they would never have been honest enough to say so. For hypocrisy was their middle name. Nobody could have been more surprised than they when someone took a remark amiss. Or when a plot or a plan resulted in the collapse of frail parties and distress all around. Who would have thought it? they would cry, and would retire to their appalling kitchen to plot and plan some more.

Passers by number 13 Axon Street would stare at the gray windows and mutter and raise their eyebrows. Or tap their foreheads. The question "What are they up to?" was not infrequently posed. Answers ranged pleasurably over a wide spectrum of subversive activities, from the stealthy printing of underground literature to the making of bombs for the IRA. They were all quite wide of the mark. The beam of the Everards' malice, though powerful, was a narrow one, and if they could make just a little mayhem within the immediate circle of their acquaintances, they were quite content.

REHEARSALS

The theater was perfectly situated in the very center of Causton, at the corner of the main thoroughfare. Actually it turned the corner, having originally been the last shop (a baker's) on the High Street and the first, (haberdashery and sewing-machine repairs) on Carradine Road. Both shops went back a long way (the bread had been baked on the premises), and they each had several poky rooms above. Having the strong support of the then-mayor Latimer, the Causton Amateur Dramatic Society leased the two buildings and, with the aid of a grant from the council, the proceeds from various fund-raising activities, and a modest amount of professional help had gutted them both and transformed the shell.

They had built a stage with a plain proscenium arch, fitted a hundred dark gray plastic seats to a raked floor, and installed a simple lighting grid. There was a stage door and two large plate-glass doors that fronted the tiny foyer. This doubled as an office and had in it a desk, a chair, a telephone, an old filing cabinet, and a pay phone. There was also a board showing colorful photographs of the current production. A huge cellar running between both shops became the scene dock and dressing rooms. These were more than adequate except at Panto time or during the run of a play with an exceptionally large cast, such as *Amadeus*. Toilets for the actors were halfway along a corridor connecting the wings to the foyer.

Three quarters of the top floor was taken up by the club-room, which was open to the public at performance times, when coffee and glasses of wine were available. Plastic tables and chairs were scattered about, and there were a couple of settees, which, imperfectly disguised, performed onstage as often as some of the actors and, it must be said, frequently with more conviction. The rest of the upstairs space was taken up by two rest rooms for the audience and Tim's lighting box, which had a notice on the door: PRIVATE. KEEP OUT. The Latimer was carpeted throughout in charcoal haircord, and the walls were roughcast white.

Many of the CADS now looked back wistfully to those early days fifteen years past when, surrounded by rubble and timber and cables, and choking on brick dust, they had wrought out of chaos their very own theater. Things had been different then. Harold, for example. Beardless and slim in old corduroys, he had mucked in, getting filthy in the process, cheering them on when they were tired, holding the dream before their flagging spirits and their gritty, dust-filled eyes.

They had all seemed equal then, in those glorious early days. Each with his part to play, and no part more valuable than any other. But after the theater was officially opened and Mayor Latimer had made his long-winded speech, imbibed hugely, and vanished under the drinks table, things started to change, and it soon became plain that some were very much more equal than others. For gradually, sinuously, Harold had eased his way to the top, stepping firmly on the necks of those too timid, too dim, or just too lazy to complain until (no one could quite put their finger on the point of no return) a czar was born. And now, occasionally people joined the company who knew nothing of those grand pioneering times when each member could have his say and be treated with respect. Renegade newcomers who couldn't care less about the past.

Like Nicholas, for instance, now approaching the Latimer stage door. As far as Nicholas was concerned, the Causton Amateur Dramatic Society came into existence during the rehearsals of *French Without Tears* and would die the death if his audition at Central was successful (as it must be, *it must*) with *Amadeus*. He fumbled in his pocket for the key. He had been given his own as soon as Colin became aware of his willingness to appear early, stay late, run about, fetch and carry, and generally make himself useful. Even now, in his illustrious position as what Esslyn grudgingly admitted to be second lead, Nicholas had arrived a good half hour before the stage management.

In fact, it was barely six o'clock when he entered the building, so he was not surprised to find himself immediately swal-

lowed up by silence. He stood for a moment inhaling voluptuously, and although the air smelled of nothing more exotic than
the peel of an orange left in a tin wastebasket, it became transmuted in his apprentice's nostrils to something rare and ambrosial.
Nicholas padded silently, happily down the stone stairs to the
dressing rooms.

He flung his anorak down, slipped on Mozart's brocade coat,
and picked up his sword. Nicholas was a short man, barely five
feet six, a fact that caused him considerable anguish—Ian Holm,
Antony Sher, and Bob Hoskins notwithstanding. Even on a good
day when the wind was southerly, the sword caused him problems, especially when getting up and down at the pianoforte. He
had planned to take it home and practice wearing it about the
place, but had foolishly asked Harold's permission, which had
promptly been refused. "You'll only lose it, and then where shall
we be?"

Now, Nicholas buckled it on and made his way toward the
stage muttering the lines leading up to his move, anticipating the
first night when he tripped over the thing and fell flat on his face,
firmly putting this anticipation aside. A moment later, sneakers
muffling his footsteps, he was on the set. He stood for a moment
excitedly aware of that frisson—half terror, half delight—that
seized him whenever he walked onto a stage, even when the theater was empty.

But in fact it wasn't. There was a sound. Startled, he looked
about him. All the seats were unoccupied. He turned, facing the
way he had come, but there was no one in the wings. Then he
crouched and looked along the raked floor of the auditorium, expecting to see Riley mauling some disgusting tidbit. But no cat.
Then it came again. Squeaky. Almost rubbery-sounding in its effect. Such as might be made if you dragged your finger over a
windowpane. What could it be? And where was it coming from?
Having checked the stage, the wings, and the auditorium, Nicholas was quite baffled. Until he lifted up his head.

The sight that met his eyes was so surprising that it took him
a couple of seconds to realize precisely what he was staring at.
Someone was in Tim's box. A girl. Nicholas swallowed hard. A
naked girl. At least naked as far as he could see, which was to just
below her waist. Below this the glass panel changed to solid
wood. The girl had tumbling fair hair and narrow shoulders, and
her back was pressed against the glass. When she arched it, as she

now did, her skin imprinted uneven misty circles, like pearly flowers. Her arms were outstretched, and it was her fingers, clenching and unclenching against the glass, that had made the strange sound. He knew who it was. Even before she wrenched her body suddenly sideways, revealing one small pointed breast and a swooning profile. Her eyes (thank God) were closed. Cemented to the floor, he stared and stared, unable to drag his eyes away, and Kitty smiled, an intense, private smile gluttonous with satisfaction.

Whoever else was in the box must be either kneeling or crouching in front of her. Vivid pictures of what the lucky devil might be doing crowded Nicholas's brain, and he was swept by a wave of lust so powerful that it left him with a bone-dry throat and gasping for air. When the wave had receded somewhat, he took several deep breaths and ruminated on the extreme awkwardness of his position. Not, he felt, since Oedipus had found himself at the crossroads had a chap been so severely in the wrong place at the wrong time. Then the sound started again, and he watched Kitty slowly slide down the glass, her shoulder blades leaving two damp, equidistant tracks. She turned her head away again as she disappeared and laughed, a raucous, throaty chuckle quite unlike her usual tinkling carillon.

Released, Nicholas exhaled very carefully, even though common sense told him the sound must be barely audible, (he was amazed they had not heard the beating of his heart), then he tiptoed off stage and bore his bulging groin off to the john. Once there, he stayed longer than was absolutely necessary, mulling over the best course of action and praying that Kitty's playmate didn't decide to come in for a pee. He had just decided to creep out to the street and make a great noise coming back in when he heard beneath him the slam of a door. He waited for another five minutes, then made his way back to the basement.

As he passed the ladies' dressing room, he heard a clatter, as if someone was moving a bottle or jar. Nicholas opened the door. Kitty, demurely buttoned up in an apricot blouse and securely—nay, chastely—swathed in a long matching skirt chirruped with alarm, then said, "You made me jump."

"Sorry . . . hello."

"Hello yourself." Kitty frowned at him. "What's the matter?"

"Mm?"

"You're not getting a sore throat, are you?"

"Don't think so."

"You're croaking."

"Ah. Just the proverbial frog." He cleared his throat once or twice. Then did a mock gargle. But the dryness at the sight of her remained. "That's better."

"It doesn't sound better. You look a bit peaky actually, Nico . . . quite drained." She narrowed her eyes at her reflection. "*Now* what's the matter?"

"Nothing." Nicholas turned his sudden laugh into a cough. "You first here, then? You and Esslyn?"

He linked the names automatically; then, finding ignorance established and Kitty misled, congratulated himself on his cleverness. But no sooner had he done this than a further thought developed. What if Kitty had actually been with Esslyn in the box? Stranger things had happened. Married couples were supposed to sometimes need peculiar settings or bizarre games to turn them on. Look at that Pinter play. Him coming home "unexpectedly" in the afternoons; her in five-inch heels. But surely that was only after decades of marital boredom? The Carmichaels hadn't been together five minutes. Kitty was speaking again.

"Oh, Esslyn's working till half six. So I came on early in my little Suzuki. I need lots of time to get ready. In fact—" she smiled, her lovely lips parting like the petals of a rose—"I thought I'd find you here when I arrived."

". . . Er . . . no . . ." stammered Nicholas. "Tried to get away, but it was one of the manager's keen-eyed days."

"Oh, what a shame." Another smile, warmly sympathetic. "We could have gone over our lines together."

Nicholas absorbed the impact of the smile, (a soft, featherlight punch to the solar plexus), and his knees buckled. He hung grimly on to the door handle. For the first time in his life he cursed the enthusiasm that had brought him to the Latimer long before anyone else could reasonably have been expected to be present. Then he wondered how the hell, feeling like this, he was going to be able to concentrate onstage. Forcefully he reminded himself that this was only Kitty. Pretty, silly, ordinary Kitty. Her very silliness and the fact that she was an indifferent actress would normally have been enough to ensure his complete lack of interest. And if his mind could reason thus, reasoned Nicholas, why then should his viscera, still churning rhapsodically, not be brought under equally firm control? As he continued to argue against this onrush of carnality, Kitty picked up a wire brush and started to rearrange her hair. She brushed it up and away from her face, which looked even more piquant without the surrounding auerole of golden curls.

Nicholas told himself it was more pointed than heart-shaped. Sharp. A bit ferrety, really. Then she opened her mouth, filled the damp, rosy cavity with bobby pins, and started to pile the hair on top of her head. This movement pushed her bosom out. It strained against her blouse. Then, as Nicholas watched, every button burst its moorings. The fabric fell apart, and her small, exquisite breasts were revealed, doubly dazzling by being reflected in the mirror. She stood up and, with a light, thrillingly lascivious shrug, magically shed the rest of her garments except for silky, lace-topped stockings and thigh-high boots. Then she turned, placed one foot firmly on the seat of her chair, and beckoned to him.

"Nico . . . ?" Kitty removed the bobby pins. "What on *earth's* the matter with you tonight?"

"Ohhh. Nerves, I guess."

"Right. You and me both. Oh, drat—" Kitty's hair collapsed. "It's going to be one of those days when it just won't stay up."

Nicholas, whose problem could hardly have been further removed from his companion's, was temporarily distracted by something being shifted around in the adjacent scene dock. "Ah," he murmured, "seems we're not the only ones here early."

"I'd like to have it cut"—Kitty reskewered the pins forcefully—"but Esslyn'd go mad. He doesn't think a woman's truly feminine unless she's got long hair."

"I wonder who it is."

"Who what is?"

"In the workshop."

"Colin, I suppose. He was moaning the other night about how much he had to do."

"Par for the course."

"Mmm. Nico . . ." Kitty put down her brush and turned to face him. "You won't . . . well . . . go to pieces on the first night, will you, darling? I should be absolutely frantic."

"Of course I won't," Nicholas cried indignantly. This insult managed to damp his ardor in a way that all the earlier rationalizations had failed to do. Silly cow. "You should know me better than that."

"Only you've so many lines—"

"No more than in *Night Must Fall.*"

"—and Esslyn said... with your inexperience... you'd probably just dry up and leave me stranded...."

"Esslyn can get stuffed."

"Oohh!" Neat foxiness beamed. Then she cocked her head on one side conspiratorially. "Don't worry. I shan't pass it on."

"You can pass it on as much as you like, as far as I'm concerned."

Nicholas went out slamming the door. Patronizing bastard. "It won't be me who goes to pieces on the first night, mate," he muttered. In the men's dressing room he slung his coat and sword, glanced at his watch, and discovered that, incredibly, barely twenty minutes had passed since he had entered the theater. He decided to pop along and have a look at the scene dock.

A man was there putting the finishing touches to a small gilt chair. He stood back as Nicholas entered, studying the tight hoop of the chairback, his brush dripping glittering gold tears onto an already multicolored floor. It was not the man Nicholas expected to see, but he experienced an immediate warmth, almost a feeling of kinship, toward the figure who was regarding his handiwork so seriously. Anyone who could make a cuckold out of Carmichael, thought Nicholas, was a man after his own heart.

"Hullo," he said. "The boss not in yet?"

David Smy turned, his handsome, bovine face breaking into a slow smile. "No, just me. And you, of course. Oh"—his brush described a wide arc, and Nicholas, not wishing to be gilded, jumped briskly aside—"and the furniture."

"R-i-g-h-t." Nicholas nodded. "Got it." Then he performed the classic roguish gesture seen frequently in bad costume dramas but rarely in real life. He laid his finger to the side of his nose, tapped it, and winked. "Just you and me and the furniture it is then, Dave," he replied, and went back to the stage for some more practice.

After fifteen minutes or so sitting down at and getting up from the piano and striding about getting used to his sword, Nicholas went up to the clubroom to see who else had arrived. Tim and Avery sat at a table, their heads close. They stopped talking the moment Nicholas entered, and Tim smiled. "Don't worry," he said. "We weren't talking about you."

"I didn't expect you were."

"Didn't you really?" asked Avery, who always thought that everyone was talking about him the second his back was turned, and never very kindly. "I would have."

"Oh, not your childhood insecurities, Avery," said Tim. "Not on an empty stomach."

"And whose fault's that? If you hadn't been so long at the post office—"

"Nico..." Tim indicated a slender bottle on the table. "Some De Bortoli?"

"Afterwards, thanks."

"There won't be any afterwards, dear boy."

"What *were* you whispering about, anyway?"

"We were having a row," said Avery.

"In *whispers*?"

"One has one's pride."

"More of a discussion," said Tim. "I'm sorry I can't tell you what it's about."

"We're burning our boats."

"Avery!"

"Well, if we can't tell Nico, who can we tell?"

"No one."

"After all, he's our closest friend."

Nicholas tactfully concealed his surprise at this revelation, and the silence lengthened. Avery was biting his bottom lip as he always did when excited. He kept darting beseeching little glances at Tim, and his fists opened and closed in purgatorial anguish. He looked like a child on Christmas morning denied permission to open its presents. Even his circle of curls danced with the thrill of it all.

Nicholas bent close to Avery's ear. "I've got a secret as well. We could do a swap."

"Ohhh... could we, Tim?"

"Honestly. You're like a two-year-old." Tim looked coolly at Nicholas. "What sort of secret?"

"An *amazing* secret."

"Hm. And no one else knows?"

"Only two other people."

"Well, it's not a secret then, is it?"

"It's the two other people that the secret's about."

"Ah."

"Oh, go on, Tim," urged Nicholas. "Fair exchange is no robbery."

"Where do you find these ghastly little homilies?"

"*Please . . .*"

Tim hesitated. "You must promise not to breathe a word before the first night."

"Promise."

"He said that rather quickly. If you break it," continued Avery, "you won't get into Central."

"Oh, God."

"He's gone quite pale."

"That was a stupid thing to say. Since when have you had crystal balls?"

"Why the first night?" asked Nicholas, recovering his equilibrium.

"Because after then everyone will know. Do you promise?"

"Cut my throat and hope to die."

"You've got to go first."

Nicholas told them his secret, looking from face to face as he spoke. Avery's mouth opened like a starfish in an *ooo* of astonishment and pleasure. Tim went scarlet, then white, then red again. He was the first to speak.

"*In my box.*" Nicholas nodded affirmation. "Of all the fucking cheek."

"Ever the *mot juste,*" chuckled Avery, practically rocking on his seat with satisfaction. Nicholas thought he was like one of those weighted Daruma dolls that, no matter how hard you pushed them down, sprang straight back up again. "But . . . if you couldn't see the man, how do you know it was David?"

"There was no one else in the place. Just me, Kitty—who surfaced in the dressing room about ten minutes later—and David in the scene dock. I know he and his dad are often early. But they're never *that* early."

"I thought you always kept your box locked," said Avery.

"I do. But there's a spare key on the board in the prompt corner," said Tim, adding, "I shall take it home with me in future. I must say," he continued, "he's a bit . . . lumpen . . . David. For Kitty, I mean."

"Constanze's bit of rough." Avery giggled. "Must have given you quite a thrill, Nico. If you like that sort of thing."

"Oh," Nicholas said pinkly, "not really."

"Still, he's a nice lad," continued Tim, "and I should think almost anyone'd be a relief after Esslyn. It must be like going to bed with the Albert Memorial." He pulled back his cuff. "Nearly the quarter. Better go and check the board."

He picked up his bottle and moved quickly to the door, Avery scuttling after. Nicholas, in hot pursuit, cried, "But what about your secret?"

"Have to wait."

"I've got time. I'm not on for twenty minutes."

"And I'm not on," echoed Avery, "at all. I can tell him."

"We tell him together." Tim tried the door of his box, then got out his key. "At least David locked up after himself."

He opened the door, and just for a moment the three of them stood on the threshold, Avery quivering like the questing beast. His button nose pointed (as well as it was able), and he sniffed as if hoping to detect some faint residual flavor of wickedness in the stuffy air.

"For heaven's sake, Avery."

"Sorry."

The image of Kitty rushed back to Nicholas so vividly that it seemed impossible that the tiny place could have remained unmarked by her presence. Then he saw faintly on the glass the now barely visible tracks made by her dragging shoulder blades.

Avery said, "I wonder what made them choose here?"

"Sheer perversity, I should think. Well...see you later, Nicholas."

Dismissed, Nicholas was just turning away when a thought struck him. "Oh, Avery... you won't repeat what I've told you to anyone?"

"*Me?*" Avery was outraged. "I like the way you ask me. What about him?"

Nicholas grinned. "Thanks."

Downstairs he collided with Harold, who arrived as he did everything else, Napoleonically. He started shouting as he entered the foyer, and didn't stop until he had seen some flurry of movement, however unnecessary, in every corner of the auditorium. He called it keeping them on their toes. "So who's ahead of the game?" he cried, subsiding into row C, lighting a Davidoff, and removing his hat. Harold had quite a collection of fur hats. This one was black and cream and yellowish-gray, and definitely the product of more than one animal. It had a short tail, squatted on his head like a ring-tailed lemur, and was known throughout the company as Harold's succubus.

"Come on, Deidre!" he roared. "Chop-chop!"

The play began. The Venticelli loped down to the footlights and stood, secretively entwined, like a pair of gossipy grasshoppers. They were an unattractive pair, with pasty, open-pored complexions and most peculiar hair. Flossy and flyaway, it was that strange color—dirty blond with a pinkish tinge—that hairdressers call champagne. Their eyelids drooped in the lizardlike manner of the old, although they were barely thirty. They invariably seemed to be on the verge of imparting some distasteful revelation, and spoke in a sort of sniggering whisper. Harold was always having to tell them to project. Seemingly secure under Esslyn's patronage, they discussed anyone and everyone vindictively, and their breath smelled dank and malodorous, like a newly opened grave. Now, having finished their opening dialogue and wrapped their cloaks tightly about them, they pranced off.

Esslyn took the floor and Nicholas in the wings watched the tall figure with a certain degree of envy. For there was no denying that his rival cut a splendid figure onstage. Take his face, for a start. High cheekbones, rather thick but beautifully shaped lips, and that rare feature, truly black eyes. Hard and bright, the pupils glittered like tar chippings. His jowls were always a faint steely blue, like those of the villains in gangster cartoons.

Nicholas's own face could not be more ordinary. It was an "ish" face. Brownish hair, grayish eyes, straightish nose. Only the fact that his even features were unevenly distributed gave it any distinction at all. Rather a lot of space between the tip of the nose and the top lip, which he thought made him look a trifle monkeyish, although Hazel at the checkout had pronounced it "very sexy." A wide space also between his eyes, and a very wide one indeed after the eyebrows and before the hairline. So apart from being dwarfish and clumsy, with nondescript features, Nicholas reflected sourly, he would probably be completely bald before the age of twenty-one. He stared, aggrieved, at Esslyn's crisp sloe-black hair. Not even a flake of dandruff.

"Cheer up," whispered David Smy, arriving ready for his first entrance. "It might never happen."

Nicholas barely had time to smile back before his companion went on. Poor old David, thought Nicholas, watching Salieri's valet sidling across the boards with that constipated cringe that afflicts people who loathe acting and are coaxed onto a stage. Fortunately the valet was a nonspeaking part. The only time David had been given a line to say containing seven words, he had managed to deliver them in a different order every night of the run without repeating himself once.

"*David . . .*" Nicholas heard from the stalls. "Try not to walk as if you've got a duck up your knickers. Get off and come on again."

Blushing, the boy complied. On reentering, he strode manfully to his position only to hear the Venticelli sniggering behind his back.

"My God—it's the frog footman."

"No, it's not. It's Dandini."

"You're both wrong," mouthed Esslyn in a Restoration aside. "It's the fairy Quasimodo."

"For heaven's sake, get on with it!" cried Harold. "I'm putting on a play here, not running a bear garden." He sat back in his seat, and the rehearsals rolled on. *Amadeus* was not an easy play, but Harold had never been one to shirk a challenge to his directorial skills, and the fact that it had a large cast and thirty-one scenes did not deter him. Six keen fifth-formers from the local comprehensive had been recruited to help onstage management, and Harold watched them now drifting vaguely on and off the set with an exasperated expression on his face. It was all very well for Peter Shaffer to suggest that their constant coming and going should by a pleasant paradox of theater be rendered invisible. *He* wasn't lumbered with a crew of sleepwalking zombies who didn't know their stage right from a 97 bus. And Esslyn, who was onstage throughout and could have been a great help, was worse than useless. Years ago, Harold had made the mistake of saying that when he was in the business, no actor of any standing would demean himself by touching either stick or stone during a performance. All that was strictly stage management. Since then their leading man had steadfastly refused to handle anything but personal props.

"Deidre" shouted Harold. "Speed this lot up. The set changes are taking twice as long as the bloody play."

"If he'd read the author's notes," murmured Nicholas to Deidre, who had been testing a pile of newly stacked furniture in the wings for rockability and was now back in the prompt corner, "he'd know you're supposed to carry on acting through the changes."

"Oh, you won't find Harold bothering with boring old things like author's notes," said Deidre, as near to malice as Nicholas had ever heard her. "He has his own ideas. I hate this scene, don't you?"

Nicholas, poised for his entrance, nodded briefly. The reason they both disliked *The Abduction from the Seraglio* was the lighting. Futilely, when Harold had asked for crimson gels, Tim had attempted one of his rare arguments. In reply, speaking very slowly as if to an idiot child, Harold explained his motivation.

"It's all about a seraglio. Right?"

"So far."

"Which is another word for a brothel—right?"

Tim murmured, "Wrong," but could have saved his breath.

"Which is another word for a red-light house. Ergo... surely I don't have to further spell it out? I know it's theatrical, Tim, but that's the kind of producer I am. Bold effects are my forte. If what you want is wishy-washy naturalism, you should stay at home and watch the telly."

Nicholas was always glad when the scene was finished. He felt as if he were swimming in blood. He came offstage dissatisfied with his performance and irritated with himself. Avery's secret was nagging at his mind. He wondered what on earth it could be. Probably some piddling thing. Nowhere near as scandalously interesting as Nicholas's own secret. He wished they'd either told him at once or not mentioned it at all. Perhaps he could persuade them to cough it up at the intermission.

Pausing only to give David Smy a very insinuating moue and a nudge in the ribs, Nicholas returned to the dressing room. Next time Colin came up from the paint shop, David approached his father and asked him if he thought Nicholas could possibly be gay.

Three rehearsals later, the difficulties with the razor had still not been sorted out. When the moment arrived to wield it and David stood deferentially by holding his tray with the water, wooden bowl of shaving soap, and towel, the action ground to a halt. Esslyn moved downstage and stared challengingly at row C. The Everards, lizard lids aflicker, capered behind. Tim and Avery, sensing a possible fracas, left the lighting box, and the stage staff gathered round. Harold rose and, with an air of quite awesome capability, took the stage.

"Well, my darlings," he cried as he mounted the steps, "we have a wide-open situation here, and I'm offering it to the floor before I sound off with any of my own suggestions, which, I need hardly say, are myriad." Silence. "Never let it be said that I'm not open to new ideas from whatever direction they may arise." The silence took on an incredulous, slightly stunned quality, as if someone had thwacked it with a baseball bat. "Nicholas? You seem to be on the verge of suggestive thought."

"He always is," said Avery.

"Well..." said Nicholas, "I was wondering if it might not look very exciting done with Salieri's back to the audience. An expansive movement"—he leaped to his feet to demonstrate—"like so—"

"I don't believe this," retorted Esslyn. "Is there nothing you wouldn't do to sabotage my performance? Do you really think you could persuade me to play the most exciting moment of my entire career facing upstage?"

"What career?"

"Of course, everyone knows you're jealous—"

"Me? Jealous? Of you?" The smidgen of truth in this assertion caused Nicholas to splutter like fat in a pan. "Hah!"

"I should climb back into your swamp, Nicholas," snickered a Venticelli. "Before you have yet another brilliant wheeze."

"Yes," agreed his twin. "Back to the Grimpen Mire with you."

"It'll be a funny old day," snapped Nicholas, "when I take any notice of a pair of bloody bookends."

"Now, now," beamed Harold. He adored displays of temperament by his actors, fatuously believing them to be sign of genuine talent. "Actually, Esslyn, you know it might look quite effective—"

"Forget it, Harold."

Everyone sat up. Confrontation between the CADS director and his leading man was unheard of. Harold directed Esslyn. Esslyn went his own way. Harold ignored this intransigence. It had been ever thus. Now, every eye was on Harold to see what he would do. And he was worth watching. Various emotions chased over his rubicund features. Amazement, disgust, rage, then finally (after a great struggle), compliance.

"Obviously," he said, presaging the frankly incredible, "I would never force an actor to do something that was totally alien to his way of working. It would simply look wooden and unconvincing." Then, quickly: "Does anyone else have any ideas?"

"What happened about those bag things," asked Rosa, "that we talked about earlier on?"

"They didn't work. Or rather," continued Harold, evening the score, "Esslyn couldn't make them work."

"You don't pull off a trick like that the first time," retorted Esslyn. "You have to practice, which I could hardly do with you yelling '*Molto costoso*' in my face every time I asked for another."

"Then you'll have to mime streaming with blood," said Rosa, smiling sweetly. "I'm sure if anyone can do it, you can."

"Ouch!" said Kitty, exchanging a rueful, collusive glance with her husband. It was a complicated glance, and managed to suggest not only that Rosa was jealous of her husband's present happiness but also that she was not quite right in the head. The assistant director cleared her throat.

"Whoops," whispered Clive Everard. "Page the oracle."

"The problem's as good as solved."

"Perhaps," Deidre began hesitantly, "we could cover the blade with Scotch tape. I'm sure it wouldn't show from the front."

There was a pause, then a deep sigh from Harold. "At last." He nodded, a wry, reproachful nod. "I was wondering who would be the first to think of that. Got some here, I trust, Deidre?"

"Oh, yes . . ." She took the razor from David's tray, holding it carefully by the handle, and bore it off to her table. There she tipped her carrier bag onto its side. The tape rolled out, closely followed by a grudgingly provided bottle of milk. She saved the milk just in time, sat down beneath the anglepoise lamp, picked up the tape, and started scratching at it to find the ends. Then she cut off a strip and laid it lengthwise against the cutting edge. It was too short (she should have measured before she started) as well as being too narrow to wrap over the steel completely. She hesitated, wondering if it was necessary to take the first piece off before trying again, and decided she wouldn't dare come so close to that gleaming steel. Even at the thought, her hands started to sweat. She felt all hot and bothered, as if everyone was watching her, then glanced up and discovered she was right.

"Shan't be a sec," she called cheerily. The tail of the tape had vanished, and she started scratching again. "More haste, less speed."

"I always find," Rosa returned the call, "that folding the end bit over every time is a great help."

"Oh, what a good idea," Deidre ground out, "I must remember that." Holding the razor firmly, she attached the tape to the handle end and wound the reel round and round, up and down the blade until it was well and truly covered. Then she cut off the tape. The result was dreadful. Very uneven and bumpy, with half a dozen thicknesses in one place and two or three in others, all of which would be clearly visible from the stalls in that intimate theater. Oh, God, thought Deidre, what on earth am I going to do? The thought of trying to remove the tape again terrified her. Even supposing she could find the tag end.

"What's the problem, Deidre?" David Smy put his valet's tray down and pulled up one of the little gold chairs.

"It's all gone wrong." Deidre blinked hard behind her lenses thick as bottle glass. "I had a terrible job getting it on. Now, I'm frightened to try and take it off in case I cut myself."

"Let's have a look."

"Be careful." Deidre handed the razor over.

"Got some scissors? No...smaller than those." When Deidre shook her head, David produced a Victorinox Swiss army knife and eased out a tiny pair of clippers. Deidre watched his brown fingers tipped with clean, short nails, which had dazzlingly white half-moons. He handled things so precisely, almost gracefully, and without any floundering or wasted movements. Snip, snip, and the tape was off. Deidre unrolled more. David measured the blade against it, cut off two lengths, and, with Deidre holding the handle, folded them very carefully over the length of the blade, first one side, then the other. Then he ran the razor hard down the prompt copy. It fell apart. "That should do it."

"*David*. You mustn't say that. Not even in fun. We'll have to put some more on."

"If you insist." His slow smile was reassuring. "I was only pulling your leg."

"I should hope so." After a few moments she smiled rather nervously in return. David recovered the blade, and this time produced no more than a faint indentation when he pressed the page.

"Come *on*, Deidre—chop-chop. We could all have cut our throats ten times over by now."

"Sorry, Harold."

"You go when you're ready," said David. "You don't want to let that lot run you about. Load of wankers." Then he added hastily, "Pardon my French."

"Oh, if it's French," Deidre murmured apologetically, "it's right over my head, I'm afraid. Well...let's see how this goes down." She handed the razor to Esslyn, who received it warily. "You could try it out on your thumb first."

"I shall certainly try it out on someone's thumb," Esslyn replied crisply, handing it straight back. Obligingly Deidre illustrated its newly rendered bitelessness. Esslyn said, "Hm," and sawed tentatively, then more firmly, back and forth across his knuckles. "Seems okay. Right...Harold?"

Esslyn waited until everyone's attention was on him, then stood, center stage, in a martyr's pose, hands across his breast, eyes on a glorious horizon, looking for all the world, as Tim said later, like Edith Cavell in drag. He spoke loudly, in a doom-laden voice: "...and in the depth of your downcastness you can pray to me...And I will forgive you. *Vi saluto!*" Then, throwing his head back and holding the razor in his right hand, he drew it quickly across his throat. One sweeping dramatic movement from ear to ear. There was a terrible silence, then someone murmured, 'My God.'

"Works, does it?"

"You could practically see the blood," squawked Don Everard.

"They'll be carrying people out."

Esslyn smirked. He liked the idea of people being carried out. Harold swung around, letting his satisfied smile embrace them all. "I knew that would work," he said, "as soon as I thought of it."

"I really believe that's the secret of our success," chipped in Nicholas, "an ideas man at the helm."

"Well, of course that's not for me to say," demurred Harold, who never stopped saying it.

"Wasn't it Deidre," David Smy said loudly, "who thought of it?"

"David," whispered Deidre across the table, "don't. It doesn't matter."

"It was Deidre," said Harold, "who *vocalized* it. I thought of it weeks ago, when the production was in the planning stage. She simply caught my idea on the ether, as it were, and vocalized it. Now, if the stage management have stopped showing off, we really must get on..."

But the rehearsal was further delayed by Kitty, who, white-faced, was now clinging to her husband, her arms around his waist, her head buried in his chest. "...it looked so real..." she mewed, "I was fwightened..."

"There, there, kitten." Esslyn patted her as if soothing a fretful animal. "There's absolutely nothing to be frightened about. I'm quite safe. As you can see." He let loose a smug, apologetic look over her head.

Now if she could act like that, thought Nicholas, when she's onstage with me, I'd be a happy man. He glanced across at Kitty's lover to see how he was reacting to this little display, but David was continuing his conversation with Deidre and affecting not to notice. Nicholas observed the rest of the company. Most were looking indifferent, one or two embarrassed, Boris ironical, Harold impatient. The Venticelli, to Nicholas's surprise, appeared jealous. He was sure this was not romantic resentment. In spite of their affectations and flouncings and toadily awful obsequiousness, Nicholas did not believe they were sexually interested in Esslyn. In fact, they both struck him as almost asexual. Dry and detached and probably more interested in making mischief than in making love. No, Nicholas guessed they were simply peeved that the object of their sycophancy was being so crass and ungrateful as to show public affection for another.

Then, eyes traveling on, Nicholas received a shock. Sitting a little behind the others and surely believing herself to be unobserved, Rosa was staring at Esslyn and his wife. Her face showed pure hatred. Not a muscle moved, and the emotion was so concentrated, so extreme, that she might have been wearing a mask. Then she noticed Nicholas's gaze, dropped her rancorous eyes, and immediately became herself again. So much so that by the time, half an hour later, she made her usual flurried departure (trailing her scarf, dropping her script, whirling her Madame Ranevskaya coat about, and crying "Night-night, my angels"), he was almost convinced that he had imagined it.

*   *   *

The book arrived about a week before the dress rehearsal. Deidre found a small parcel neatly wrapped in brown paper on the floor in the foyer. It was directly beneath the mail slot set in the wooden surround of the plate-glass doors. She turned the parcel over, frowning. On the front, hand-printed in small capital letters, were the words HAROLD WINSTANLEY. She laid it on top of her basket and made her way to the clubroom to unload her two bottles of milk and tea and sugar replenishments. As she entered, Riley hurried forward to greet her. She put the milk bottles in a pan of cold water, then bent down and rubbed his ears. He permitted this for as long as it took him to realize that she was not bearing gifts, then stuck his tail in the air and wandered off. Deidre watched him go sadly, wishing he were not so stingy with his affections. Only Avery got the full treatment—purring, rubbing round the legs, little *mrrs* of satisfaction—but then, only Avery dished up the dinner. He bought fish trimmings or "cheeks" for the cat, which Riley would remove from his dish to consume at his leisure. Deidre was always coming across the bluish-white pearly wings of bone that remained.

He was a handsome animal. White bib and socks, mixed whiskers, and a white tip to his tail. The rest of his coat, once black and gleaming like newly mined coal, now had a rusty tinge, which made him look a bit seedy. He was a full-blooded tom and had a hairless patch above one eye that was no sooner grown over than some bold adversary clawed it back to its original glabrous state. He had brilliant emerald-green eyes, and when the theater was dark, you could see them walking about on their own between the lines of seats.

No one knew how old he was. He had appeared two years ago, suddenly strolling across the set during a run-through of *French Without Tears.* The immense, almost magical theatricality of this appearance had at once appealed to everyone. He had got a round of applause, a piece of haddock, (Deidre having been sent to Adelaide's), and had been adopted on the spot. This, although he had not been able to say so in so many words, had not been his intention. For Riley was looking for a more orthodox establishment. He had been vastly deceived in the sitting room of *French Without Tears,* which had disappeared shortly after he had made its acquaintance, only to reappear in a totally different guise several weeks later. This was really not his scene. He wanted an ordinary, even humdrum, home, where the furniture was fairly stable with at least one human being more or less constantly in worshipful attendance. He often tried to follow Avery when he left the theater, but had always been firmly brought back. Deidre, who had always longed for a pet, would have loved to have taken him home, but her father was allergic to both fur and feather.

Now, having unpacked the tea and sugar and set out the cups, Deidre made her way to the auditorium to chalk up the stage for Act I. As Nicholas was already there going over his "opera" speech, she slipped silently into the back row to listen. It was a complicated piece, and Nicholas was making a mess of it. It started on a high point of anger, broke in the middle into giggling almost frenzied effusiveness, and ended on a note so elated as to be practically manic.

He had been going over it at home every night the previous week, and was agonizingly conscious that it wasn't working. Now, he pumped amazement into his voice: "Astonishing device. A Vocal Quartet!" Following up with forced excitement: "On and on, wider and wider—all sounds multiplying and rising together..." He plowed on, ending with an empty rhetorical shout: "...and turn the audience into God!"

Despair filled him. Nothing but ranting. But what was he to do? If emotion wasn't there, it couldn't be turned on like a faucet. A dreadful thought lurking always in the back of his mind leaped to the fore. What if he felt dry and stale like this on the first night? Without technique, he would be left clinging desperately to the text like an ill-equipped mountaineer on a rock face. He almost envied Esslyn his years of experience; his grasp of acting mechanics. It was all very well for Avery to describe their leading man's performance as "just like an Easter egg, darling. All ribbons and bows and little candied bits and pieces with a bloody great hollow at the center." Nicholas was not comforted, being only too aware that when his emotions let him down, he could offer neither ribbon nor bow, never mind anything as fancy as a candied trimming. Deidre came down the aisle.

"Hi," said Nicholas morosely. "Did you hear all that?"

"Mm," said Deidre, putting her basket on the edge of the stage and climbing up.

"I just can't seem to get it right."

"No. Well—you haven't got the feeling, have you? And

you're just not experienced enough to put it over without."

Nicholas, who had expected some anodyne reassurance, stared at Deidre, who crossed to the prompt corner and started to unpack her things. "If I could make a suggestion...?"

"Of course." He followed her around the stage as she crouched to re-mark the entrances and exits smudged or quite erased at the previous rehearsal.

"Well... first you mustn't take the others into account so much when you're speaking. Salieri... Van Swieten... they matter in Mozart's life only so far as they affect his income. They mean nothing to him as people. Mozart's a genius—a law unto himself. You seem to be trying to relate to them in this speech, which is fatal. They are there to listen, to absorb. Perhaps to be a little afraid...."

"Yes... yes, I see... I think you're right. And God—how do you think he sees God?"

"Mozart?" He doesn't 'see' God as something separate, like Salieri does. Music and God are all the same to him. As for the delivery, you're working the wrong way round. That's why it sounds stale before you've even half got it right—"

"I know!" Nicholas smote his forehead. *"I know."*

"If you stop thinking about the words and start listening to the music—"

"There isn't any music."

"—in your head, silly. If you're making a passionate speech about music, you have to *hear* music. Most of the other set pieces either have music underneath them or just before. This is very... dry. So you must listen to all the tapes and see what evokes the emotion you need, then marry it in your mind to the lines. I don't mean 'must,' of course"—Deidre blushed suddenly—"only if you like."

"Oh, but I do! I'm sure that would... it's a terrific idea."

"You're in the way."

"Sorry."

Nicholas looked down at Deidre's bent head and chalky jeans. He had not, unlike most of the rest of the company, underestimated her proficiency behind the scenes. But he had never talked to her about play production, and although he was aware of her ambitions in that direction, had thought (also like the rest of the company) that she would be no better at it than Harold was.

Now, he gazed at her rather as men gazed at girls in Hollywood films after they had taken off their glasses and let their hair down. He said, "It's a wonderful play, don't you think?"

"Very exciting. I saw it in London. I'll be glad when it's over, though. I don't like the way things are going."

"What do you mean?"

"Oh, nothing specific. But there's not a nice feeling. And I'm dying to get on to *Vanya*. I do love Chekhov, don't you, Nicholas?" She regarded him with shining eyes. "Even *The Cherry Orchard*, after all Harold managed to do to it . . . there was still so much left."

"Deidre." Nicholas followed her around in the wings, where, clipboard in hand, she started to check the props for Act I. "Why on earth . . . I mean . . . you should be with another company. Where you can really do things."

"There isn't one. The nearest is Slough."

"That's not far."

"You need your own transport. At night, anyway. And I can't afford to run a car. My father's— He can't be left alone. I have to pay someone to sit with him on theater evenings. . . ."

"Oh, I see." What he did see—a sudden yawning abyss of loneliness, creative imagination starved of expression, and stifled, unrealized dreams—made him deeply, ashamedly embarrassed. He felt as if he were with one of those awful people who, uninvited, hitch up their clothes and show you their operation scar. Aware of the unfairness of this comparison and the banality of his next remark, Nicholas mumbled, "Bad luck, Deidre," and retreated to the stage. Here, more for the sake of bridging an awkward moment than anything else, he picked up the parcel. "Someone sending Harold a bomb?"

"Heavily disguised as a book." Nicholas eased the brown paper lightly Scotch-taped folds and attempted to peer inside. "Don't do that," called Deidre. "He'll say someone's been trying to open it. And he's bound to blame me."

But Harold seemed to notice nothing untoward about his parcel. He arrived rather later than usual and was changing into his monogrammed directing slippers when Deidre gave him the book. There had been a time when Harold had always removed his footwear during rehearsals, explaining that only by doing so could he arrive at the true spirit of the play. Then he had seen a television interview with a famous American director during which the great man had stated that people who took off their shoes to direct were pretentious pseuds. Harold, naturally, did not agree, but just in case other members of the same company had also been viewing, he covered up his feet forthwith. As he took the parcel, Rosa, noticing, called out, "Oohh, look . . . Harold's got a prezzie." And everyone gathered around.

The "prezzie" proved to be a bit of a letdown. Nothing unusual or exciting. Nothing to do with Harold's only real passion in life. It was a cookbook. *Floyd on Fish.* Harold gazed at it blankly. Someone asked who it was from. He spun the pages, turned the book upside down, and shook it. No card.

"Isn't there something written inside?" nudged an Everard. Harold turned the first few pages and shook his head. "How extraordinary."

"Why on earth should anyone send you a recipe book?" asked Rosa. "You're not interested in cooking, are you?" Harold shook his head.

"Well, if you're going to start," said Avery, "I shouldn't start with that. The man's basically unsound."

"Gosh, you are a snob," said Nicholas.

"Right, young Bradley. That's the last time you sit down at my table."

"Oh! I didn't mean it, Avery—honestly." Half-frantic, half-laughing, Nicholas continued, "*Please.* I'm sorry . . ."

"I shall think of it," said Harold, "as a gift from an unknown admirer. And now we must get on. Chop-chop, everyone . . ."

He put the parcel inside his hat. The momentary warmth that its appearance had engendered (it had been years since anyone had given him a present) had vanished. In its place was a faint unease. What a peculiar thing for anyone to do. Spend all that money on a book, then send it anonymously to someone for whom it could be of no interest whatever. Ah, well, thought Harold, he certainly didn't have time to ponder on the mystery at the moment. The mystery of the theater—that was his business. That was what he had to kindle. And plays did not produce themselves.

"Right, my darlings," he cried, "from the top. And please . . . lots and lots of verismo. Nicholas, you remember— Where *is* Nicholas?"

Mozart stepped out from the wings, "Here I am, Harold."

"Don't forget the note I gave you on Monday. *Resonances.* Okay? That's what I want—plenty of resonances. You're looking blank."

"Sorry, Harold?"

"You know the meaning of the word 'resonances,' I assume?"

"... um ... Don Quixote's horse, wasn't it?"

"Oh, God!" cried Harold. "I'm surrounded by idiots."

A week passed. None of the rehearsals went well, and the first couple of run-throughs were absolutely dreadful. But it was at the dress rehearsal (so everyone later told Barnaby) that things really came to a head.

As Esslyn strode around the stage with his spring-heeled tango dancer's walk in his blue-and-silver coat, so his performance grew in glossy fraudulence. He had stopped acting with—indeed, he hardly even looked at—his fellow players and strutted and posed in splendid isolation. Backed up by his myrmidons, he continued to snipe at David and Nicholas.

Nicholas was coping with all this very well. His earlier talk with Deidre had been the first of several, and he was now groping his way toward what he believed would be a truthful, intelligent, and lively rendering of the part of Mozart. He was halfway through the opening scene and playing to the back of Salieri's neck when Esslyn suddenly stopped what he was saying and strolled down to the footlights.

"Harold?" Harold, his face marked with surprise, climbed out of his seat and walked forward. "Any particular stress on *che gioia?*"

"What?"

"Sorry. To be frank, my problem is ... I'm not quite sure what it means." Silence. "Perhaps you could enlighten me?" Long pause. "I'd be most grateful."

"Now who's being *cattivo,*" murmured Clive.

"Don't you know?" said Harold.

"I'm afraid not."

"Do you mean to tell me that you've been saying those lines over and over again for the last six weeks and you don't know what they mean?"

"So it appears."

"And you call yourself an actor?"

"I certainly call myself as much of an actor as you are a director."

An even longer pause. Then, softly on the air, it seemed to everyone present, came a faint reverberation, like the roll of distant drums. Harold said, very quietly, "Are you trying to wind me up?"

"Didn't think it was necessary," muttered Donald.

"Thought he ran on hot air."

"Of course not, Harold. But I do think—"

"I'm not going to translate it for you. Do your own homework."

"Well, that seems a bit—"

"All right, everyone. Carry on. And no interval. We've wasted enough time as it is."

Esslyn shrugged and sauntered back to his previous position, and the reverberations rippled away into a silence shot with disappointment. The second confrontation, you could almost see everyone thinking, and it's over before it really gets going. But their frustration was short-lived, for a few minutes later Esslyn stopped again, saying, "Do you think it's true he's never really laid a finger on Katherina?"

"Of course it's true!" shouted back Harold. "Why on earth should he tell himself lies?"

Then there was a query on court etiquette, on the timing of the Adagio in the library scene, and on the position of the pianoforte. Harold once more made his way to the footlights, this time with a savage tic in one eyelid.

"If you've noticed all these hiccups before," he said icily, "may I ask why you have left it till this late stage to say so?"

"Because I'm not in charge. I was waiting for you to pick them up. As you're obviously not going to, I feel, for the good of the play and the benefit of the company, I have to say something."

"The day you have any concern for the rest of the company, Esslyn, will be the day pigs take to the skies."

After this, as if the earlier interruptions had been just appetizers, the merest titillations, things started to go more splendidly wrong. Kitty's padding would not stay up. The more it slid about, the more she grabbed at it. The more she grabbed at it, the more she giggled, until Harold stood up and yelled at her when she promptly burst into tears.

"It's not so easy," she wept, "when you're already pregnant in the first place."

"How many places are there, for godsake?" retorted Harold. "Wardrobe!" He stood tapping his foot and sucking his teeth until Joyce had secured Baby Mozart. Then the manuscript paper was not in its place on the props table. Or the quill pen. Or Kitty's shawl. Deidre apologized and swore they had been there at the start of rehearsal. Salieri's wheelchair jammed, and gold railings, not quite dry, imprinted themselves on the emperor Joseph's white satin suit.

But the most dramatic, alarming, and ultimately hilarious *contretemps* was that the trestle table holding the bulk of the audience for the first night of *The Magic Flute* collapsed. It was piled high with sausage-chewing, pipe-smoking Viennese rabble. Belching, joshing, pushing each other about, and generally over-acting, all this to the loud accompaniment of rustic accents. These were mainly "Zummerset," but one conscientious burgher who had really done his homework kept shouting, *"Gott in Himmel!"*

Then, as the glorious *"Heil sei euch Geweihten"* soared above their heads, the trestle creaked, groaned, and gave way, tumbling the by now hysterical peasantry into a large heap in the center of the stage. Everyone except Harold thought this wondrously droll. Even Esslyn jeered with cold delicacy into his lace cuff. Harold rose from his seat and smoldered at them all.

"I suppose you think that's funny?"

"Funniest thing since the Black Death," replied Boris.

"Right," said his director. *"Colin."* A helpful soul repeated the cry, as did someone in the wings followed by someone in the dressing rooms, then finally a faint echo was heard under the boards of the stage.

"Good grief," grumbled Harold as he stomped down yet again, "it's like waiting for the star witness at the Old Bailey."

Colin arrived with a woodshaving curl on his shoulder as if to designate rank, a hammer in his hand, and his usual air of a man dragged away from serious work to attend to the whims of playful children.

"You knew how many people this table had to hold. I thought you said you were going to reinforce it."

"I did reinforce it. I nailed a wooden block in each corner where the struts go in. I'll show you." Colin picked his way over the still-supine actors, lifted the table, then said, "Stone me. Some silly sod's taken them out again."

"Ohhh, God!" Harold glared at his actors, one or two of whom were still weeping quietly. "You have no right to be in a theater, any of you. You're not fit to sweep the stage. Better make some more, Colin. Now, *please,* let us get on."

He was walking back to his seat when Clive Everard, hardly bothering to lower his voice, said, "That man couldn't direct his piss down an open manhole."

Harold stopped, turned, and replied forcefully into the shocked silence, "I hope you don't see yourself appearing in my next production, Clive."

"Well... I did rather fancy Telyegin...."

"Well," repeated Harold, "I suggest you start fancying yourself in an entirely different company. Preferably on an entirely different planet. Now, I want to get to the end of the play with—no—more—interruptions."

And they just about did. But by this time nerves were in shreds. Umbrage had been given and taken and returned again with interest. More props had erred and strayed in their ways like lost sheep. The scenery had learned the wisdom of insecurity, and at least one door left the set almost as smartly as the actor who had just pulled it to behind him. As the final great funeral chords of music died away, actors gathered onstage, drifting into despondent clumps. Harold, after making one grand gesture of despair, flinging his arms above his head like an imperial bookmaker, joined them.

"There's no point in giving notes," he said. "I wouldn't know where to start." This admission, the first such that had ever passed his lips, seemed to shake Harold as much as his companions. "You're all as bad as one another, and a disgrace to the business." Then he left, striding out into the winter night in his embroidered directing slippers, not even waiting to put on his coat.

No sooner had he left than the atmosphere lightened. And as tension was released, laughter broke out, and some healthy moaning on the lines of who did Harold think he was, and it was only a bit of fun, for heaven's sake, it's not as if we're getting paid.

"Personally," said Boris, "I'm sick of saying 'Heil, Harold.'"

"No one can do a thing right it seems to me," said Rosa. "We might as well be in the Kremlin."

"I wouldn't mind if he were competent," whispered a Venticelli.

"Quite," agreed the other. Then, aside to Esslyn: "The peasants are revolting."

There was a bit more Bolshevik rumbling, then Riley strolled down the aisle and jumped onto the stage. Several of the fifth-formers who didn't know his nasty little ways, and Avery, who did, said, "Aahhh..."

The cat took a crouching position. His haunches quivered, his shoulders contracted, then started to jerk. He made several loud gulping noises and a strangulated cough, then deposited a small glistening heap of skin and bones and fur and blood on the boards and walked off. There was a long pause broken by Tim.

"A critic," he said. "That's all we need."

"Ah, well," said Van Swieten, "let's look on the bright side. Everyone knows a bad dress rehearsal means a good first night."

ENTR'ACTE:

(SATURDAY MORNING, CAUSTON HIGH STREET)

 Causton was a nice little town, but small. People who could not adequately function without their Sainsburys or Marks and Spencers had to travel to Slough or Uxbridge. But those who stayed at home were capably if unadventurously served. In the main street were a supermarket and a fishmonger's, a dairy, a bakery, and a very basic greengrocer. Two butchers (one first class who hung his meat properly and could prepare it the French way), McAndrew's Pharmacy, which also sold perfumes and cosmetics, two banks, and a hairdresser's, Charming Creations by Doreece. There were two funeral parlors, a bookshop, the wine merchant's and post office, and a small branch library.

Causton also had three eating places: Adelaide's, which produced every combination of fried food known to man from behind a phalanx of hissing tea urns, and the Soft Shoe Cafe, which served home-made cakes, cream teas, dainty triangular sandwiches with the crusts cut off, and morning coffee. There was also a pub, the Jolly Cavalier (née the Gay Cavalier), which sold shepherd's pie and goujons in a basket. And, of course, there was the theater.

Saturday, November 17, was a brilliant day. The pavement sparkled crystalline with frost, and people strode briskly about, visibly preceded by the white exhalations of their breath. Carol singers held forth. Deidre and her father stood, arm in arm, outside the fishmonger's. She was worried about the cold air on his chest, but he had so wanted to come out and had seemed very calm and collected, so she wrapped him up in two scarves and a balaclava, and here they were. Mr. Tibbs held tightly onto the empty shopping basket and gazed at his daughter with the same mixture of pride in achievement, anxiety in case he might be found wanting, and simple love that might have been found on the face of a Labrador in a similar position. Together they studied the display.

Red mullet and a huge turbot flanked by two crabs rested on a swell of pale gray ice. Humbler creatures lay, nose to tail, on white trays, plastic parsley flowering in their mouths. Mr. Tibbs regarded this piscatorial cornucopia with deep interest. He was very fond of fish. Deidre opened her purse, guiltily aware that if it wasn't for her involvement with the Latimer, her father could dine on fish every day of his life.

"D'you think . . . the herrings look nice, Daddy?"

"I like herrings."

"I could do them in oatmeal." Deidre smiled gratefully and squeezed his arm. "Would that be all right? With brown bread and butter?"

"I like brown bread and butter."

They joined the queue. Deidre was so used to people ignoring her father, even when she knew those same people to be his former pupils, that she was quite overwhelmed when a woman next to them turned and said how nice it was to see him up and about and how well he was looking.

And he did look well, agreed Deidre, taking a sidelong glance. His eyes were clear and shining, and he was nodding in reply to the greeting and offering his hand. He evinced some concern when the plump, glittering herrings disappeared inside sheets of the *Daily Telegraph,* but relaxed again once they were safely in his basket. Then he shook hands with the rest of the queue, and he and his daughter left and made their way to the church.

After listening to the carols for a few minutes and putting something in the vicar's box, they went to the bakery, where Deidre bought a large, sliced loaf of white bread, and a cheap sponge cake oozing scarlet confectioner's jelly and mock cream, then they went home. Mr. Tibbs took to his bed, saying he was tired after his walk, and Deidre made some tea.

She made her own bed while waiting for the kettle to boil and, smoothing the coverlet, caught sight of herself in the wardrobe mirror. She avoided mirrors usually, except for the briefest of toilets in the morning. What was the use? There was no one special to make an effort for. This had not always been the case. Ten years ago, when she was eighteen and a boy at the office seemed to be interested, she had studied the magazines for a while and tried to do things with her dark curly hair that stuck out in all directions and her overly rosy complexion, but then her mother had died and she had got so involved with domestic affairs that the boy had, understandably, drifted off, and was now happily married with three children.

It wasn't that she was a bad shape, thought Deidre, removing her glasses so that her image became a reassuring blur. She was quite tall and quite slim, although her bottom was a bit droopy. And she had nice eyes if only she didn't have to wear the hideous glasses. Joyce had suggested contact lenses at one point, but the expense made them out of the question, and in any case Deidre feared her prescription was too strong. She had worn the glasses since she was three. At school a Catholic friend, knowing her loathing for the wretched things, had offered to petition Lucia, patron saint of the nearsighted, on her behalf. But although she assured Deidre a few days later that this had been done, the results were negligible. Either the deity had not been in the giving vein that day or, more likely, had sniffed out a heretical supplicant and resolutely withheld the influence. Deidre gave a brief sigh, put the glasses back on and, hearing the kettle whistle, hurried downstairs.

She took some tea and a piece of cake upstairs, waiting to make sure her father drank the warm brew. Suddenly he said, "How's it all coming along, dear? *Amadeus*?"

"Oh . . ." Deidre looked at him, surprised and pleased. It had been so long since he had shown any interest in the drama group. She always talked to him about the current production, playing down her subservient role, telling him only about her ideas for the play, but not for months had he been responsive. "Well, we had the most appalling dress rehearsal yesterday. In fact, it was so bad, it was funny." She retailed some of the highlights, and when she came to the collapsing table, her father laughed so much he almost spilled his tea. Then he said, "D'you know, I think I might come to your first night. That is," he added, "if I don't have one of my off days."

Deidre picked up his cup and turned away. She felt the quick sting of tears, yet at the same time a flood of hope. This was the first time he had referred directly to his illness. And what a brave, lighthearted way to speak of it. "One of my off days." What a calm, rational, intelligent, *sane* way to describe things. Surely if he could talk about his other self in this detached manner, he must be getting better. Going to the theater, mingling with other people, above all, listening to the glorious music, could surely do him nothing but good. She turned back, smiling happily.

"Yes, Daddy," she said. "I think that's a lovely idea."

The Blackbird bookshop was, briefly, empty of customers. Avery sat at his beautiful *escritoire* near the door. The ship was on two levels connected by an ankle-snapping stone step glossy with use. There was a convex mirror over the step, revealing the only hidden corner, so that Avery had a comprehensive view. People still managed to pinch things, of course, especially during the Christmas rush. Avery got up, deciding to put away some of the volumes that browsers had left out any old way on the two round tables. The Blackbird's stock was displayed under general headings, and customers occasionally replaced books themselves, often with hilarious results. Tutting loudly, Avery pulled *The Loved One* from the Romance shelf and *A Room with a View* from Interior Design.

"Look at this," he called a moment later to Tim, who was stirring something on the hot plate, in the cubbyhole at the rear of the shop. "*Forever Amber* in Collecting for Connoisseurs."

"I should leave it there, if I were you."

"And *A Severed Head* under Martial Arts."

"That's nothing," said Tim, lifting the spoon to his lips. "I found *A Fatal Inversion* under Pure Mathematics. In any case"—he sipped again—"I'm not sure that Martial Arts is an entirely inappropriate designation for Murdoch."

"I don't know why you're stirring and tasting in that affected manner," cried Avery, moving to the cubbyhole, "we all know what a cunning way Mr. Heinz has with a tomato."

"You said I could have what I liked for lunch."

"I must have been mad. Even a bay leaf would add a smidgen of veracity."

"All right, all right."

"Or a little yogurt."

"Don't make a meal of it."

"No danger of that, duckie." They both laughed. "What's in the rolls?"

"Watercress and Bresse Bleu. And there are some walnuts. You can open the Chablis if you like."

"Which one?" Avery started pulling bottles out of the wine rack under the sink.

"The Grossot. And give Nico a shout."

"Isn't he at work, then?" Avery opened the bottle, then pulled aside the thick chenille curtain and bawled upstairs.

"Says he couldn't concentrate with the first night so close."

"All those empty shelves. The housewives of Britain will be in a tizz. *Nico...*"

"Who were you waving to just now?"

"When?" Avery frowned. "Oh, then. Poor old Deidre and her papa."

"God, what a life. Will you promise to shoot me if I ever get like that?"

Dazed with joy at this casual assumption that they would be together when Tim was old and gray, Avery took a deep breath, then replied crisply, "I shall shoot you long before you get like that if you bring any more muck into my kitchen."

There was a clattering of footsteps on the uncarpeted stairs, and Nicholas appeared. "What's for lunch?"

"Cheese and whine," said Tim. "You'd be better off upstairs, believe me."

"I thought I smelled something nice."

"There you are," said Tim. "Someone else with a nose for a bargain."

"Like Dostoevsky's for a dead cert."

"Clever dick."

"Famous for it."

"Be quiet," said Tim. "You're embarrassing Nicholas."

"No, you're not," Nicholas replied truthfully, "but I am jolly hungry."

"Oh, Lord..." A woman wearing a squashed felt hat was staring urgently in at the window. "Nico—run and put the catch down, there's a love. And turn the sign. I know her of old. Once she's in, you'll never get her out." When Nicholas returned, Avery added, "She's very religious."

"Obviously. What other reason would anyone have for wearing a hat like that?"

"D'you know," said Avery approvingly, "I think we shall

make something of this boy yet. Would you like a little wine, Nico?"

"If it's not too much trouble."

"Oh, don't be so *silly*," retorted Avery, splashing the Chablis into three large tumblers. "I hate people who say things like that. They're always the sort who never mind how much trouble they give you. She came in the other day prosing on—"

"Who did?"

"Her out there. Came rushing up and asked me what I knew of the Wars of the Spanish Succession. I said absolutely nothing. I hadn't stirred from the shop all day." Avery looked at his companions. "Laugh, I thought they'd never stop."

"Start."

"Start what?"

"The joke is," Nicholas explained patiently, "laugh, I thought they'd never start."

"You're making it up." Nicholas reached out for a second roll and got his fingers slapped. "And don't be such a pig."

"Don't mention pigs to me. Or meat of any kind."

"Oh, God—he's turned vegetarian." Avery blanched. "I knew all those beans would go to his head."

"That would make a change," said Tim. "What's up, Nicholas?"

"The first-night frantics, I'll be bound," said Avery. "If you're worried about your lines, I'll hear them after we close."

Nicholas shook his head. He knew his lines and no longer feared (as he had in *The Crucible*) that they would vanish once and for all the moment he stepped onstage. What was disturbing him were his pre–first night dreams. Or rather dream. He was now quite used to having some sort of nightmare before the opening of a play, and had discovered most of his fellow actors had similar experiences. They dreamed they had learned the wrong part or their costume had vanished or they stepped onstage into a completely strange drama or (very common) they were in a bus or car that went past the theater again and again and refused to stop. Nicholas's dream fell into this last category, except that he was traveling under his own steam to the Latimer. On roller skates. He was late and flying along, down Causton High Street, knowing he would only just make it, when his feet turned into the butcher's shop. No matter how hard he fought to carry straight on, that is where they would go.

Inside the shop everything had changed. It was no longer small and tiled with colorful posters, but vast and cavernous; a great warehouse with row after row of hanging carcasses. As Nicholas skated frantically up and down the aisles trying to find a way out, he passed hundreds of slung-up hares with their heads in stained paper bags, lambs with frills around newly beheaded necks, and huge sides of bright red marbled meat rammed with steel hooks. Sweating with fear, he would wake, the reek of blood and sawdust seemingly in his nostrils. He had had this dream now every night for a week. He just hoped to God once the first night was over, he never had it again.

He described it lightheartedly to his companions, but Tim picked up the underlying unease. "Well," he said, "there's only two more to go. And don't worry about Monday, Nico. You're going to be excellent." Nicholas looked slightly less wan. "Avery was in my box last night, and he cried at your death scene."

"Ohhh." Nicholas's face was ecstatic. "Did you really, Avery?"

"That was mostly the music," said Avery, "so there's no need to get above yourself. Although I do think, one day, if you work very hard, you are going to be quite good. Of course, appearing opposite Esslyn, anyone would look like the new Laurence Olivier. Or even the old one, come to that."

"He's so prodigiously over the top," said Tim. "Especially in the *Don Giovanni* scene."

"Absolutely," cried Nicholas, and Tim watched with approval as some color returned to his cheeks. "That's my favorite. "Makea this one agood in my ears. Justa theesa one..." His voice throbbed with exaggerated Italianate fervor. "Granta thees to me."

"Oh! Can I play God?" begged Avery. *"Please."*

"Why not?" said Tim. "What's different about today?"

Avery climbed onto a stool and pointed a chubby Blakean finger at Nicholas. "No...I do not need you, Salieri. I have... *Mozart!"* Demon-king laughter rang out, and he climbed down holding his sides. "I've missed my vocation—no doubt about it."

"Didn't you think," said Nicholas, "that there was something funny about the whole dress rehearsal?"

"Give that man the Barbara Cartland prize for understatement."

"I mean funny peculiar. I can't believe all those upsets were accidental, for a start."

"Oh, I don't know. One sometimes has glorious evenings like that," said Tim. "Remember the first night of *Gaslight*?"

"And the Everards. They're getting more and more contemptuous," continued Nicholas. "That remark about the manhole cover. I don't know how they dare."

"They dare because they're under Esslyn's protection. Though what he sees in them is an absolute mystery."

"Don't talk to me," said Nicholas, sulkily sidetracked, "about mysteries."

"You're not going to start on that again," said Avery.

"I'm sorry, but I don't see why I should let it drop. You promised if I told you my secret, you'd tell me yours."

"And I will," said Tim. "Before the first night."

"It's before the first night *now*."

"We'll tell you on the half, honeybun," said Avery. "And that's a promise. Just in case you tell someone else."

"That's ridiculous. I trusted you, and you haven't told anyone else... have you?"

"Naturally not." Tim was immediately reassuring, but Avery said nothing. Nicholas looked at him, eyebrows raised interrogatively. Avery's watery pale blue eyes wavered and slid around, alighting on the remaining crumbs of cheese, the walnuts, anything, it seemed, but Nicholas's direct gaze.

"Avery?"

"Well..." Avery gave a shamefaced little smile, "I haven't really *told* anyone. As such."

"Oh, Christ—what do you mean, 'as such'?"

"I did sort of hint a bit... only to Boris. He's the soul of discretion, as you know."

"Boris? You might as well have had leaflets printed and handed them out in the High Street!"

"There's no need to take that tone," Avery shouted, equally loudly. "If people don't want to be found out, they shouldn't be unfaithful. And anyway, you're a fine one to talk. If you hadn't passed it on in the first place, no one else would know at all."

This was so obviously true that Nicholas could think of nothing to say in reply. Furiously he pushed back his chair and, without even thanking them for the lunch, clattered back upstairs.

"Some people," said Avery, and looked nervously across the table. But Tim was already stacking the glasses and plates and taking them over to the sink. And there was something about the scornful set of his shoulders and his stiff, repudiating spine that warned against further overtures.

Poor Avery, cursing his careless tongue, tidied and bustled and kept his distance for the rest of the afternoon.

Colin Smy was replacing the blocks of wood in the trestle table, and Tom Barnaby was painting the fireplace. It was a splendid edifice, which Colin had made from a fragile frame of wooden struts covered with thick paper. It had then been decorated with whorls and loops and arabesques and swags made from heavily sized cloth. It now looked, even without the benefit of lighting, superb. Tom had mixed long and patiently to find exactly the right faded brickish red, which, together with swirls of cream and pale gray, gave a beautiful marbled effect. (In the Penguin *Amadeus* the fireplace had been described as golden, but Harold hoped he had a bit more about him than to slavishly copy other people's ideas, thank you very much.)

Although Barnaby ritually grumbled, there had been very few productions over the past fifteen years that he hadn't spent at least an hour or two on, sometimes even tearing himself away from his beloved garden. Now, looking around the scene dock, he remembered with special pleasure a cutout garden hedge, all silver and green, which had represented the forest in *A Midsummer Night's Dream,* and how it had shimmered in the false moonshine.

Barnaby derived great nourishment from his twin leisure activities. He was not greatly given to self-analysis, believing the end result, given man's built-in capacity for self-deception, to be messy and imprecise, but he could not but observe, and draw conclusions from, the contrast between the fruitfulness of his off-duty time and the aridity of much of his working life. Not that there was no call for imagination in his job: The best policemen always had some (not too much) and knew how to use it. But the results when it was applied were hardly comparable to those of his present occupation.

If he failed, the case would be left as a mass of data awaiting a lucky cross-reference from some future keen-eyed constable eager for promotion. If he succeeded, the felon would end up incarcerated in some institution or other, while Barnaby would experience a fleeting satisfaction before facing once more, for the umpteenth thousandth time, the worst humanity had to offer, which, if you caught it on a bad day, could be terrible indeed.

So was it any wonder, he now reflected, that in what little spare time he had, he painted pictures or stage scenery or worked in his garden? There, at least, things grew in beauty, flowered, withered, and died all in their proper season. And if freakish Nature cut them down before their allotted span, at least it was without malice aforethought.

"You've done a grand job there, Tom."

"Think so?"

"Our *Führer* will be pleased."

Barnaby laughed. "I don't do it for him."

"Which of us does?"

They worked on in a companionable silence surrounded by fragments from alien worlds. There was the bosky world (spotted toadstools from *The Babes in the Wood)*, the chintzy (fumed oak from *Murder at the Vicarage),* and the world of pallid chinoiserie *(Teahouse of the August Moon*—paper screens). Barnaby glanced up and caught the shy eye of a mangy goose peering through the frame of a french window *(Hay Fever).*

Colin finished hammering four new blocks into the trestle, then upended it, saying, "That'll do it. They can dance on that with hobnail boots and it should hold."

"Who do you think took the others out?" said Tom, Joyce having described the scene to him.

"Oh, some silly bugger. I shall be glad when this play's over and done with. Every rehearsal something goes wrong. Then it's Colin do this, Colin fix that...."

Barnaby selected an especially fine brush for one of the curlicues and stroked the paint on carefully. Colin's automatic grumbling flowed peacefully around his ears. The two men had worked together, on and off, for so long that they had now reached the stage of feeling that really they'd said all they had to say and, apart from certain ritualistic remarks, kept a silence as comfortable as a pair of old slippers.

Barnaby knew all about his companion. He knew that Colin had brought up his son, motherless since the age of eight. And that he was a gifted craftsman who carved delicate, high-stepping animals full of lively charm. (Barnaby had bought a delightful gazelle for his daughter's sixteenth birthday.) And that Colin loved David with a protective devotion that had not grown less as the boy developed into a young man more than capable of taking care of himself. The only time Barnaby had seen Colin lose his temper was on David's behalf. He thought how fortunate it was that Colin was rarely in the wings at rehearsal and so missed most of the sniping that David was having to put up with. Now, knowing of the younger Smy's reluctance to perform, Barnaby said, "I expect David'll be glad when next Saturday comes."

Colin did not reply. Thinking he had not heard, Barnaby repeated his remark, adding, "At least he hasn't got any lines this time." Silence. Barnaby took a sideways look at his companion. At Colin's stocky frame and tufty hair, black when they had first met, now brindled silver like his own. Colin's usual expression of sturdy self-containment was slightly awry, and a second, much less familiar, lurked beneath. Barnaby said, "What's up?"

"I'm worried about him." Colin looked sharply at Barnaby. "This is just between us, Tom."

"Naturally."

"He's got involved with some girl. And she's married. He hasn't been himself for some time. A bit . . . quiet . . . you know?" Barnaby nodded, thinking that David was so quiet anyway, it would take a father to spot the silence deepening. "I thought it might be that," continued Colin. "I'd be really delighted to see him settled—after all, he's nearly twenty-seven. So I said, 'Bring her home then and let's have a look at her,' and he said she wasn't free. He obviously didn't want to talk about it."

"Well . . . I suppose there isn't a lot of point."

"Not what you hope for them though, is it, Tom?"

"Oh," said Barnaby, "I shouldn't worry too much. Things might still work out." He smiled. "They don't mate for life these days, you know."

"I pictured him going out with some nice local girl. A bit younger than himself, perhaps courting in the front room on the settee like me and Glenda used to. And grandchildren. What man our age hasn't pictured his grandchildren?" Colin sighed. "They never turn out like you think, do they, Tom?"

Barnaby pictured his little girl, now nineteen. Tall, clever, malicious, stunningly attractive, with a heart of purest platinum. He could not help being proud of her achievements, but he knew what Colin meant.

"That they don't," he said. "Nothing at all like you think."

Earnest Crawley was carving the joint. He worked like a surgeon, unemotionally but with great precision and a certain amount of éclat, wielding the long, shining knife like a scimitar and laying the slices of meat tenderly on the hot plates.

Rosa browned the potatoes on top of the stove. She wore a loose, flowing garment, the cuffs of which sailed dangerously close to the fragrant, spitting fat.

"How are them fellas getting on with their part then, love?"

"What fellows?"

"The ones that sound like an Italian dinner."

"Oh—the Venticelli. Awful—in more ways than one."

As Rosa retailed one or two of the more amusing incidents from the dress rehearsal, she could not help comparing Earnest's innocent and rather touching curiosity with Esslyn's grandiose self-absorption, always present but intensified to an incredibly high degree on the eve of a new production. The whole house had fizzed then with prima-donnaish emotion. In fact, all their married lives had been conducted with as much noise and flourish as a carnival procession. A fanfaronade of first nights, last nights, rehearsals, parties, and nonstop dramas both on and off the set.

Caught off guard and drawn carelessly into bitter recollection, Rosa corrected herself. All *her* married life. Esslyn, fortunate man, had inhabited another world for a large part of the working week. He went to the office, dined with clients, had drinks with acquaintances (never friends) who were not of the theater. Rosa had lost, through neglect and narrowing interests, the few women friends she had ever had. And so intertwined had her role as Mrs. Carmichael become with her many performances at the Latimer that it had grown to seem equally chimerical until the crunch came.

She had become aware quite early in the marriage that Esslyn was playing around. He'd said that sort of behavior was expected of a leading man in a theatrical company, and he would always come safely home. Rosa, furious, had yelled back that if all she'd wanted was something that would come safely home, she would have linked her future to a racing pigeon. However, as the years flew by and he always did come safely home, she became not just resigned to his philandering but also in a strange way rather proud of what she saw as his continuing popularity, like a mother whose child consistently brings home all the prizes. There was also a positive side to all this unfaithfulness, namely that he had less sexual energy to spare for his wife. Like many people who live in a cloud of high-flown romanticism, Rosa didn't care for a lot of heavy activity in the bedroom. (Here again, as in so many other ways, dear Earnest was ideal, seeming quite happy to bounce about, gently and rather apologetically, in the missionary position, usually after Sunday lunch.) So, as far as Rosa was concerned, Esslyn's announcement that he wanted a divorce had come out of the blue. He said he had fallen in love with the seventeen-year-old playing Princess Carissima in *Mother Goose,* and although within a few weeks the girl had found a boyfriend of her own age, passed her "A" levels, and sensibly taken herself off to university, Esslyn, having tasted the heady wine of freedom, had still pressed ahead.

Rosa's reaction to his defection had frightened and amazed her. At first, so accustomed was she to living in a state of almost perpetual mimesis, she hardly recognized that a great core of real pain lay behind her shoutings and ravings and great sweeps of dramatic movement. Then, after she had been bought off and left White Wings, she had spent long, terrible weeks in her new flat picking over her emotions, struggling to separate the false regrets from the true, attempting to follow the wretched thread of her anguish to its source. During this time she would prowl about, her arms locked across her chest as if she were literally holding herself together; as if her whole body were an open wound. Gradually she started to understand her true feelings. To be able to examine them, test them, give them a name. The bleak, regretful sorrow that persistently invaded her mind she now recognized as a state of mourning for the child she'd never had. (Had not even realized she'd really wanted.) She carried this bereavement continually, like a small, cold stone, in her breast.

During this period she had forced herself, buttressed by natural pride and tremendous efforts of self-control, to continue her activities at the Latimer, and the second emotion was named for her the moment Esslyn announced Kitty's pregnancy. Although Rosa was looking fixedly elsewhere, she could tell by the sideways stretch to his voice that he was smiling broadly. Hatred had rampaged then so furiously and with such power through her body that she felt had she opened her mouth she must have roared. She had been terrified, fearing this hot malevolence would control her. That she might simply go out one dark night and savage them both. Now, she no longer thought that. But the bruising embers still slumbered, and sometimes she would open the furnace door to peep and poke at them a little, and the burning would scorch her cheeks.

"Are you all right, dear?"

"Oh." Rosa turned her attention to the potatoes. "Yes, love. I'm fine."

"Don't let them catch."

"I won't."

The potatoes looked and smelled wonderful; buttery deep brown with little crisp bits around the edges. Rosa gave them another minute, more to regain her equilibrium than because they needed it, then decanted them into a Pyrex dish and flung over some chopped parsley. They sat down. Earnest helped himself to the vegetables, then passed them to Rosa, who did the same.

"Only three potatoes?"

"Well, you know..." She patted the folds of her tummy, concealed beneath the billowy robe.

"What nonsense," cried Earnest. "If Allah had meant women to be thin, he'd never have invented the djellaba."

Rosa laughed. He had surprised her more than once, had Earnest, with his witticisms. She helped herself to several more potatoes while Earnest congratulated himself, not for the first time, on his foresight in placing a regular order for the *Reader's Digest*.

Esslyn sat at the breakfast table with *The Times* and squares of Oxford marmalade–coated toast, patronizing his wife. "You'll be perfectly all right. After all, you're not actually overloaded with lines. Hardly any more than with Poppy Dickie."

"I feel sick."

"Of course you feel sick, my angel. You're pregnant." Esslyn folded back the business section before reverting to the matter in hand. "How on earth would you cope if you were tackling Salieri? I'm never off."

"But you love it!"

"That's hardly the point." Esslyn abandoned his attempt to follow the fortunes of Rio Tinto Zinc and looked at his wife severely. "Apart from the satisfaction of knowing that one has given a great deal of pleasure to a great many people, if one has a talent, it is one's duty to exercise it to the full. I hate waste."

Kitty followed his glance, picked up her remaining square of toast—now a bit clammy and congealed—and chewed on it morosely. "I'd hardly call our audiences a great many people."

"I was speaking figuratively."

"Huh?"

"Try not to look so vacant, kitten." Esslyn scraped back his chair. "What have you done with my briefcase?"

"I had it with some mushrooms and bacon before you came down."

"Ah." Esslyn crossed to the old deal dresser holding pretty blue-and-white jugs and plates, picked up his case, and put *The Times* into it. Then he returned to the table and brushed her cheek with his cool lips. "Back soon."

"Where are you going?"

"Work. I have to call in"—he moistened his finger and pressed a crumb to it that had strayed from his plate—"something at the office."

"But you never go in on Saturday," exclaimed Kitty, turning down her pretty lips.

"Don't whine, my precious. It doesn't become you." Esslyn deposited the crumb in the breadbasket. "I shan't be long. Come and help me on with my coat."

After she had wound Esslyn's silk Paisley muffler perhaps a trifle too snugly around his neck and buttoned his coat on the wrong side, Kitty insisted on feathering her husband's lips with many little kisses. Then she clip-clopped back to the kitchen and watched him back the BMW out of the double garage and down the drive. She opened the window, flinching a little in the sharp air, and waved. She listened, loving the machine-gun spatter of tires on gravel. There was something about that sound. Why it should give her such intense satisfaction she could never understand. Perhaps it was simply a matter of luxurious association—all those wealthy cardboard cutouts in American soaps crunching grandly around pillared porticoes in their stretch limos. Or maybe it was because the sound reminded her of happy childhood holidays in Dorset with the cold waves dragging the pebbles to and fro. Or perhaps it was simply that the rattling gravel meant her husband had finally left the house.

Kitty gave a last wave for luck and went upstairs to their bedchamber, scene of mutual delights, where Salieri's blue-and-silver coat, lace-ruffled shirt, and cream trousers were laid over a chair back. While everyone else had been happy to leave their costumes in the dressing room (which was, after all, securely locked), Esslyn had ostentatiously brought his back to White Wings, insisting that after such a dress rehearsal, he wouldn't trust the stage management to look after a pair of worn-out jock straps.

He had tried the costume on before getting properly dressed this morning, strutting his stuff in front of the cheval glass, anticipating aloud the moment when he would stand up from his wheelchair, fling off his tattered old dressing gown, and take the audience's collective breath away. Kitty only half listened. He had paraded a bit more, then said something in garbled French before changing into his business suit and properly subduing the day. Now Kitty scrunched the coat into a tight ball, threw it in the air, and kicked it as far as she could before tripping into the connecting bathroom.

She turned the necks of two golden swans and tipped some Floris Stephanotis bath oil into the steaming water. Then she poured a generous amount of the sweet-scented stuff into her cupped hand. She massaged her calves and thighs, then her stomach, and, last of all, her breasts. She closed her eyes, swaying with pleasure. Reflected in the dark glass wall tiles, four glittering bronzy Kittys swayed, too. Then, fully anointed, she turned off the taps and slid into the sunken circular bath.

Around the rim, carpeted in ivory velour, were creams and unguents, several bottles of nail polish, her copy of *Amadeus,* and a telephone covered with mock ermine. She picked up the receiver, dialed, and a male voice said, "Hullo."

"Hullo yourself, scrumptious. Guess what? He's gone to work." The voice rumbled, and Kitty said, "I couldn't let you know. I didn't know myself till he was halfway through his boiled egg and soldiers. I thought you'd be pleased...Oh.... can't you?" She pouted prettily. "Well, I haven't. In fact, I've got nothing on at all at the moment. Listen." She splashed the water with her hand. A chuckle came down the line, and Kitty laughed, too. The same raunchy, harsh sound that Nicholas had heard in the lighting box. "I shall just have to settle for the Jacuzzi then, darling. Or a go on the exercise bike." Another snort. "But it won't be the same. See you Monday, then."

Kitty hung up, and as she did so, the flexible cord caught on her script and it fell into the bath. Kitty sighed, and her lovely coral lower lip pushed forward delightfully, half covering the twin lascivious peaks of the upper. Sometimes, she thought, life was just too too much. Paul Scofield, clutching his shabby shawl, glared up at her from beneath the blue water like some astonishing new specimen of marine life. She poked him crossly with her toe, leaned back, closed her eyes, rested her head on the herb-filled pillow, and thought of love.

Harold was meeting the press. The real press, not just the regular, potbellied, beer-swilling hack from the *Causton Echo* who had interviewed Harold during the run of *The Cherry Orchard,* then described the play as "an epic agricultural drama by Checkoff." Although, to be fair to the man, this might have been due to Harold referring to the play simply as *The Orchard.* He always tried to shorten titles, believing this made him appear more *au fait* with theatrical parlance. He had spoken of *Rookers (Rookery Nook), Once (in a Lifetime), Night (Must Fall),* and *Mother (Goose).* "This *Mother*'s going to be quite a show," he had confided to the local inkslinger, who had, perhaps fortunately, replaced the missing noun before submitting his copy.

But today, aahh, today Harold was meeting with Ramona Plume from the features page of the *South East Bucks Observer.* Naturally he had always let them know about his work, but the response until now had been, to say the least, tepid. However, two letters, followed by a diligence of phone calls extolling the dazzlingly inventive nature of the current production, had finally produced a response. Anticipating a photographer, Harold had dressed accordingly in a longish gray overcoat with an astrakhan collar, shining black knee boots, and a Persian lamb hat. The weather was bitterly cold, and hailstones like transparent marbles were bouncing about on the pavement. A pigeon, its wing feathers stiff with ice, regarded him glumly from the Latimer doorway.

They were late. Harold had rather ostentatiously looked at his watch, shaken it, lifted one of his earflaps, and listened, then started to pace tubbily up and down, looking like a cross between Diaghilev and Winnie the Pooh. The pigeon, perhaps thinking a spot of exercise might warm up the feathers, left the doorway and joined him. Harold was very much aware that people were noticing him, and favored the occasional passerby with a gracious nod. Most of them would know who he was—he had, after all, been the town's theater director for many years—the others, as became plain from their glances and whispered comments, recognized his quality. For Harold walked in an aura of barnstorming splendor.

In him the strenuous creative struggle of rehearsal, the glamor of first nights, and the glittering aftermath of post-performance soirées were made manifest.

Sometimes, to underline the extraordinary superiority of his position, Harold would torture himself, just a little, with one of his most magnetic and alarming daydreams and, to pass the time, he slipped into it now. In this dream he would fantasize, rather like Marie Antoinette milkmaiding about at the Trianon, that he was living in Causton as a nonentity. Just another middle-aged dullard. He saw himself at the Rotarians with other drearies, pompously discussing local fund-raising or, worse, serving on the parish council, where an entire evening could be frittered away delving into the state of the drains. Activities generating a self-righteous glow while filling in an abyss of boredom. On Sunday he would clean the car (a Fiesta), and in the evening there would be television with programs of interest noted well in advance. After this would come the writing of a why-oh-why letter to the *Radio Times,* pointing out some faulty pronunciation or error in period costume or setting, and a temporary leg up, statuswise, in the community if it was actually printed.

It was usually at this point that Harold, his face sheened with the cold sweat of terror, stopped the panorama, leaped down from the tumbril, and hotfooted it back to reality. Now, he was helped on his way by the sight of a shabby Citroen 2CV parking at the corner of Carradine Street on a double yellow line. He collected himself and hurried forward.

"You can't stop there."

"Mr. Winstanley?"

"Oh." Harold adjusted his hat and facial expression. He said, disbelievingly, "Are you from the *Observer*?" She hardly looked old enough to be in charge of a paper route, let alone a feature column.

"That's right." Ramona Plume pointed at the windshield as she scrambled out. A large disc was stamped PRESS. "I'm okay for a few minutes, surely?"

"A few . . ." Harold led the way to the Latimer's glass doors. "The story I have to tell, my dear, will take a lot longer than a few minutes."

As the girl followed him into the foyer, she laughed and said, "Is he with you?" jerking her head at the pigeon. Harold tightened his lips. Ms. Plume opened a small leather case slung on a thin strap across her chest. Harold, who had assumed this to be a handbag, watched disconcertedly as she undid a flap, pressed a button, and started a tape. He leaped into speech. "I first thought of producing *Ama*—"

"Hang on. Just rewinding."

"Oh." Miffed, Harold strolled over to the photograph board and stood in a proprietorial stance, one arm draped across the top. "I thought—when your colleague turns up—the first set of photographs might be here?"

"No piccies."

"What!"

"It's Saturday. Nobody free." She tossed back a long fall of blond hair. "Weddings. Dog Shows. Pudding and Pie. Scouts' Xmas Fair."

"I see." Harold bit back a sharp rejoinder. It never did to antagonize the press. And he had plenty of stills, including a recent one of himself wreathed in a Davidoffian haze directing Nicholas in *Night Must Fall*.

Ms. Plume poked a microphone not much bigger than a toothbrush at him, saying, "I understand from your letter that this is the Latimer's ninetieth production?"

Harold smiled and shook his head. There was an awful lot of ground to be covered before they discussed the precise place of *Amadeus* in the Winstanley pantheon. He took a deep breath. "I always knew," he began, "that I was destined for—"

"Just a sec." She dashed into the street, looked up and down, and dashed back. "They're getting very sniffy at the office about paying fines."

"As I was saying—"

"Are the programs done yet?"

"What for?"

"*Amadeus,* of course."

"I should hope so. It's the first night on Monday."

"Could I have one?"

"What . . . now?"

"In case I have to zip off. Get the names right—that's the main bit, isn't it? With Amdram."

Amdram! Harold went to the filing cabinet, feeling sourly that the way things were going it might be a good idea to skip his formative years. He took two first night tickets from the cash box and slipped them into a program, saying, "I don't know if you're familiar with the play at all?"

"I'll say. Saw it at the National. That Simon Callow. Am*aa*yzing."

"Well, of course Peter Hall and I do approach the text from an entirely different—"

"Did you see *Chance in a Million?*"

"What?"

"On the telly. Simon Callow. *And* Faust. Totally in the nudies at one point."

"I'm afraid I—"

"Am*aa*yzing."

"You seem very young," said Harold acerbically, "to be a reporter."

"I'm their cub." The cuddliness of the noun did not mollify, especially when she added, "I always get the short straw."

"Look. If we could go on to my next—"

A black and yellow shape peered through the doors. The girl gave a piercing squeal and flew across the carpet. "*I'm coming . . . Don't book me . . . please . . .* Press. Press!" She waved her microphone at the phlegmatic profile and disappeared into the street. Harold hurried after and caught up with her as she climbed back into the car. She wound the window down. "Sorry it was a bit rushed."

"There's some tickets inside the program." He dropped it into her lap as she took first gear. "Front row. Do try to come. . . ."

On the way back to Slough the *Observer's* cub drew into a rest area, changed her tape of Bros for the Wedding Present, and checked her appointments list. In half an hour Honey Rampant, the TV personality, was opening a garden center. There'd probably be snacks and munchies, so Ms. Plume decided to drive straight there instead of stopping for a sandwich. Before driving off again, she tore up the front-row tickets for *Amadeus* and threw the fragments out of the car window.

AMADEUS
by
PETER SHAFFER

THE VENTICELLI:
CLIVE EVERARD
DONALD EVERARD
DAVID SMY

VALET TO SALIERI: JOYCE BARNABY
COOK TO SALIERI: ESSLYN CARMICHAEL
ANTONIO SALIERI: ROSA CRAWLEY
TERESA SALIERI,
JOHANN KILIAN
VON STRACK: VICTOR LACEY
COUNT ORSINI-
ROSENBERG: JAMES BAKER
BARON VAN
SWIETEN: BILL LAST
CONSTANZE
WEBER: KITTY CARMICHAEL
WOLFGANG
AMADEUS NICHOLAS BRADLEY
MOZART: ANTHONY CHALLIS
MAJOR-DOMO:
JOSEPH II,
EMPEROR OF BORIS KENT
AUSTRIA:
KATHERINA SARAH PITT-KEIGHLEY
CAVALIERI:
CITIZENS OF KENNY BADEL, DAVID SMY,
VIENNA: SARAH PITT-KEIGHLEY, JOYCE
BARNABY, KEVIN LATIMER,
NOEL ARMSTRONG, ALAN
HUGHES, LUCY MITCHELL,
GUY CATCHPOLE, PHOEBE
GLOVER

AVERY PHILLIPS
TIM YOUNG
JOYCE BARNABY
COLIN SMY

DESIGN:
LIGHTING:
WARDROBE:
STAGE MANAGER:
ASSISTANT STAGE
MANAGER: DEIDRE TIBBS

DIRECTED BY HAROLD WINSTANLEY

FIRST
NIGHT

Everything was ready. Checked and counter-checked. Deidre sent her young assistants up to the clubroom for some orangeade or a cup of coffee, leaving Colin to set the pianoforte. It was already past the half, and a buzz of excited conversation came up from the dressing rooms.

"I shall come in on a wing and a prayer," Boris was informing everyone.

"I thought you were an atheist."

"No one's an atheist on first nights, darling."

"Where's Nicholas?"

"He's always here *hours* before anyone else."

"Someone's pinched my eyebrow pencil."

"I've forgotten every line. You'll all have to cover for me."

"Has anyone seen my stockings?"

"I hear Joyce's daughter's coming."

"Oh, God. Well, I hope she keeps her opinions to herself. I can still remember what she said about *Shop at Sly Corner*."

"I thought Harold was going to go into orbit."

"I mean—no one minds *constructive* criticism."

"*You've* got my stockings."

"No, I haven't. They're mine!"

"If any of the furniture collapses tonight, I shall dry up completely."

"They are *not* yours. Look—here's the stain where I upset my wet-white."

"We've got an almost full house."

"Oh, the master will be pleased. 'A bum on every seat, my loveys.'"

"'And mass genuflection.'"

"It's nearly the quarter. Where on earth can Nicholas *be?*"

Nicholas was late for the most thrilling of reasons. Tim and Avery had just told him their secret, and he had been so excited and alarmed that he had stayed in the lighting box questioning them until the very last minute. The facts were these. Tim always designed his own lighting for each production, working at home with a model of the set. He was especially pleased with his plan for *Amadeus,* amber and rose for Schönbrunn, grays behind the whispering Venticelli, crepuscular violet when Mozart died. Harold, as always, would have none of it. ("Just who is directing this epic? No—I'm serious. I really want to know.") That same night Tim carried out Harold's lighting plot for the first time, and when he and Avery got home, Avery burst into tears, saying his beautiful set looked as if it were part of a sewer after its star product hit the fan.

It was then that Tim decided that he had had enough and put forward his proposition. It was simply that, on the first night, he would light the play from his own original plan. Once the curtain was up, there would be nothing Harold or anyone else could do about it, and he would hardly wish to make a scene during intermission. Of course, it would mean the end of their time at the Latimer, but both were prepared to face that and had already put out feelers toward a group in Uxbridge. They had sneaked into the theater on Sunday afternoon to reset everything and run through the new plot.

Now, Nicholas entered the dressing room bursting with suppressed information and squeezed into the only remaining space. Around him actors were nearly all in costume. Von Strack was pulling on white stockings, David Smy struggled with his cravat, the Venticelli—caped and masked and looking more like bats than grasshoppers—whirled about with seedily sinister affection. The air smelled of powder, after-shave, and hair spray. Nicholas got into his lace-trimmed shirt, picked up a tube of Kamera Klear, and rubbed some in, watching his pallid complexion turn a warm apricot. He wore very little makeup now, and looked back to his debut in *The Crucible,* where he sported heavy lake wrinkles and wisps of crinkly snow-white hair with not a little condescension.

On the other side of the room Esslyn was shaking powder onto his wig, and Nicholas, seeing in his mirror the other man's reflection, was uncomfortably reminded of his own loose-lipped-ness. Behind Nicholas, the emperor Joseph, heavy in white satin and jeweled decorations, paced slowly up and down like a great glittering slug. Nicholas imagined the small rouged lips pushed forward and whispering what had once been his own secret into the collective company ear.

Esslyn, apparently unaware of his invisible horns, was look-ing especially pleased with himself, like a cat that has swallowed a particularly succulent canary. He lifted his hands and adjusted his wig, and Nicholas saw his rings sparkle. He wore six. Most were encrusted with stones, and one had short, savage spines and perched on his finger like an embattled baby porcupine. Now, he pushed a tin of Cremine that had had the temerity to stray onto his turf smartly aside and began to speak.

Even as he tuned in, Nicholas knew he would not like what the other man was going to say. There was relish in his voice; it curled with spite. He was talking about Deidre. Relaying some-thing that she had told him in confidence but that he felt was too delightful not to pass on. Apparently she had received a telephone call at work last week from the police. It seemed her father had wandered off from the day center in the rain without a coat or even a jacket, and had been found half an hour later attempting to direct the traffic at the junction of Casey Street and Hillside.

"So I said," continued Esslyn, "trying to keep a straight face at the thought of that senile old fool out in the pouring rain, 'How dreadful.' And she said, 'I know'—he paused then, giving them the benefit of his immaculate timing—'he doesn't know that area at all.'"

Spontaneously they nearly all roared, Nicholas included. True, he laughed less long and heartily than the others, but still, he did laugh. A moment later Deidre appeared in the doorway.

"A quarter of an hour, everyone."

There was an immediate chorus of overloud and falsely grateful thank you's. Only Esslyn, carefully applying lip liner, said nothing. It was hard to tell, thought Nicholas, whether she had overheard or not. Her high color would conceal a blush, and as her expression was always riddled with anxiety, this gave no clue, either. She stood poised in the doorway for all the world, as the Everards said the second she'd disappeared, as if she was about to break into a gallop. To do the dressing room credit, there was no laughter this time.

Someone got up and followed her out, and Nicholas nearly got up and followed *him*, he was so sick of them all. He felt he should try to make amends, and pictured himself approaching Deidre in the wings. But what could he say? I wasn't one of those who laughed? Deeply embarrassing as well as untrue. I'm sorry, Deidre, I didn't mean to be hurtful and I'm really sad about your father? Even stickier, and what if she hadn't overheard at all? In that case, putting her so firmly in the picture would simply cause unnecessary pain. Then, to make himself feel better, he started to feel irritated with her. Honestly, he thought, for someone always dependent on the kindness of strangers, she could certainly pick her confidants. A callous sod like Esslyn was the last person she should be opening her heart to. What else did she expect? But shifting a fair proportion of his guilt onto Deidre's already bowed shoulders made him feel even worse. He became aware that he was furious with Esslyn for catapulting him into this emotional distraction when all his thoughts should be channeled toward Act I, scene 1. Almost before he knew he meant to, he spoke.

"You know your trouble, Esslyn?" Esslyn's hands were still. He looked inquiringly into his glass. "You're too full of the milk of human kindness."

There was an immediate hush. Blanched faces turned exaggeratedly to each other. Boris stopped pacing and stared aghast at the back of Nicholas's head. Van Swieten said, "You fool." Nicholas stared back at them all defiantly. This respect for Esslyn could be taken too far. He may have been the company's leading man for fifteen years, but that didn't make him God Almighty.

"Do you know what you've done?" asked Boris.

"I've spoken my mind," said Nicholas. "Anyone'd think it was a hanging matter."

"*You've quoted from* The Scottish Play.*"

"What?"

"'Yet I do fear thy nature,'" quavered Boris. "'It is too full of the milk of human kindness—'"

"Shut up!" yelled Orsini-Rosenberg. "You'll make it worse."

"That's right," said Clive Everard. "Nicholas did it unknowingly."

"It's Boris who'll bring trouble on our heads."

"You must both go out and turn round three times and come back in," said Von Strack.

"I'll do nothing of the sort," said Nicholas, but hesitantly.

After all, if he was going to enter the profession, he should (longed to) embrace all its myths and mysteries. "It's not as if I did it on purpose."

"Come *on*." Boris was already in the doorway. Nicholas hovered half out of his seat. "It's the only way to avert disaster."

"That's true, Nicholas. There are terrible stories about what happens if you quote *The Scottish Play* and don't put it right."

"Oh...if you say so." Nicholas joined Boris at the door. "Which way do we turn? Clockwise or anti-clockwise?"

"How should I know?"

"I don't suppose it matters."

"It matters terribly," called Van Swieten.

"In that case, we'll turn three times each way."

"But"—Boris had almost chewed off all his carmine lip rouge in his anxiety—"won't that mean they cancel each other out?"

Colin had finished setting the pianoforte, and now disappeared behind his superb fireplace to check that the struts and weights that held it secure were firmly in position. Crouching down, he heard footsteps and, looking through the huge space beneath the mantel, saw Deidre almost run through the wings opposite. A second person followed and disappeared into the toilet, coming out again almost immediately. Colin was about to stand up and call across the stage when he was struck by something intensively furtive about the figure. It stood very still looking round the deserted wings, then it moved to the dark area at the back of the props table and bent down. A minute later it straightened up, glanced around once more, and hurried back into the bathroom. Colin crossed the stage and approached the table, but he had no time for more than a quick check (it all looked perfectly in order) when Deidre returned from the clubroom shepherding her giggling gaggle of assistants. She crossed to him and said, "Oh, Colin, would you call the five please? My father's taxi's due in a minute, and I have to get him to his seat."

The foyer was packed. Tom Barnaby, accompanied by a tall girl, darkly beautiful, pushed his way toward the Winstanleys. He held a drink in one hand and a program in the other. Strings played over the P.A. system.

"What awful music. It simpers."

"Salieri."

"Ahhh . . ." said Cully, adding, "can you see the divine afflatus?"

"You behave yourself, my girl. Or I'll take you home."

"Dad," Cully laughed delightedly—"you are a hoot. Look —there he is."

Harold was in evening dress. A large yellow silk hanky peeped out of one jacket pocket. He also wore a maroon cummerbund and a dress shirt so stiffly starched you could have sliced tomatoes with the ruffles. He was welcoming the audience graciously. Harold adored first nights. They came closer to satisfying his longing for recognition than any other occasion. Mrs. Harold, in a black button-up cardigan unevenly spattered with pearls teamed with a tartan skirt of uncertain length drifted dimly in his glorious wake echoing the greetings, getting the names wrong, and wishing she were at her flower-arranging class.

"Hello, Doris."

"Oh, Tom." Relieved at the sight of a friendly face, Mrs. Winstanley thrust out her hand, and blushed when her companion was unable to take it. "Harold tells me you've done a wonderful job on the set." Knowing it would never occur to Harold to do anything of the kind, Barnaby just smiled and nodded. "And I understand," continued Doris, "that Joyce is singing better than ever." She didn't add, as she had been wont to do when they first met, "You must come and have a meal with us soon." Harold had really torn into her as soon as they were alone, saying that when he wanted a great clod-hopping philistine of a policeman cluttering up his lounge, she would be the first to know.

Barnaby was aware of this attitude, which caused him not a little quiet amusement. Now, he talked to Doris about horticulture, having long ago recognized a passion as great as his own. In fact, all the shrubs in the Winstanleys' garden were grown from cuttings from Arbury Crescent, and he kept some of his seeds back for Doris every year. Although she loyally pretended these gifts were unnecessary, Barnaby guessed that Harold's dashing lifestyle left little money to spare for what he would regard as inessentials. Now, Harold's wife turned on Barnaby's companion a look of polite, slightly dazed inquiry.

"You remember my daughter?"

"Cully?" Last time Doris had met Barnaby's daughter, the child had sported a green and silver crest of hair, was covered in black leather, and hung with chains. Now, she had on an acid-yellow evening dress, strapless with a puffball skirt caught in above her knees. Slender black-silk-stockinged legs ended in high-heeled suede shoes with embroidered tongues. Her shoulders were draped with very old lace sparkling with brilliants, and her hair, blue-black like hothouse grapes, was scraped into a tight coil on the top of her head secured by an ivory comb. "I hardly knew you, dear."

"Hullo, Mrs. Winstanley." Cully shook hands. "Hullo, Harold." She was wondering how anyone could bring herself to put that cardigan on even once, never mind year after year. Leaving his daughter after a stern warning glance had failed to connect, Barnaby pushed his way over to the door, where a youngish man accompanied by a vapidly pretty girl was entering the foyer.

"You made it then, Gavin?"

"We did, sir." Detective Sergeant Troy pulled down the cuffs of his sports jacket nervously. "This is my wife, Maure." Mrs. Troy moved her foot. "Ooh. Sorry. Maureen."

"Pleased to meet you." Maureen shook hands. She didn't seem especially pleased. Barnaby guessed she was about as fed up as Doris Winstanley, but without the necessity to conceal the fact. He always put a CADS poster in the staff canteen without ever making a point of his connection with the company, but his sergeant, hearing him mention Joyce's rehearsals, had put two and two together, and tickets had been purchased. Barnaby could imagine the conversation in the Troy household. Gavin believing that keeping in with the old man couldn't be bad; Maureen picturing just what sort of draggy old time she was letting herself in for. She smiled now, a glum, restrained smile, and said she couldn't half get outside a lager and lime. Embarrassed, her husband eased her nearer the auditorium steps. As he did so, he caught sight of Cully, who was making her way toward the swing door opening onto the corridor that led backstage. After a few moments Maureen set him in motion again with a savage poke in the small of his back.

"It's a pity you didn't bring a knife and fork," she said as they took their seats.

"What?" He stared at her blindly.

"You could have eaten her in the interval."

Mr. Tibbs was late, and Deidre was in a ferment of agitation. She was already regretting that she had accepted, even encouraged, his wish to attend the first night. It seemed to her now the height of foolishness. If he had a bad turn or became frightened, there would be no one to help him. She wished now she had thought of putting him next to Tom, but a gangway seat on the back row had seemed the better idea. She had been afraid he might feel threatened, surrounded by rows and rows of strangers. She clutched a program, painfully aware of the insignificant position of her own name, and the prominence of Harold's, which could not have been bolder unless burning with letters of fire.

She glanced at her watch. Where on earth could he be? She had booked a taxi for a quarter to eight, and the journey was a few minutes at the most. Then she saw a cab drawing up at the curb and hurried out into the cold night air. Mr. Tibbs alighted.

"Oh, Daddy," she cried, "I was so worried—" She broke off, gaping. Her father was wearing a short-sleeved summer shirt and cream cotton trousers and carrying a linen jacket over his arm. She had left him wearing a thick tweed suit with a cardigan for extra warmth and five pounds tucked in the breast pocket. At least, she thought, watching him hand over the note, he had remembered to switch the money. As the driver wound up his window, Deidre tapped on it and said, "Isn't there any change?"

"Do me a favor," said the man. "I had to sit ticking over for ten minutes while he changed all his clothes!"

Deidre took her father's arm, ice-cold and slightly damp, and led him through the now almost deserted foyer to his seat in row P. Fortunately the auditorium was warm, and she would make sure he got a hot drink during intermission. She left him sitting up very straight and staring with febrile intensity at the rich red curtains.

In the foyer Barnaby nodded to Earnest and followed his daughter toward the wings, easing himself past Harold, who was being gracious to a heavyweight couple in full evening regalia.

The ladies' dressing room was only being used by four people and, the actress playing Katherina Cavalieri also being part of the stage staff, now held only three. Joyce Barnaby in a puritan gray dress and snowy-white fichu was pressing powder on her nose. Kitty twitched and twirled about in her seat, clattering her bottles and jars and mumbling her opening lines with so much fervor they might have been a rosary. Rosa sat, apparently serene, in the chair nearest the electric fire. She had dressed and made up with sublime disregard as to the requirements of her character. Far from appearing plain and severe, her face, splendidly orchidaceous, could have been that of a turn–of–the century *poule de luxe*. Eyelids shimmered like the insides of a mussel shell, and her plummy lips glistened. She wore a large hat from which a bunch of cherries hung down, lying against her damask cheek. Perfect speckled crimson ovoids, they could have been the eggs of some fabulous bird. There were two magnificent bouquets from Harold for his leading ladies. Joyce (small parts/wardrobe) had a bunch of wintersweet and hellebores tied with a velvet ribbon from her husband. On the back of a chair between Rosa and Joyce hung Kitty's "baby."

The door opened. Cully put her head round briefly, said "Neck and leg break," and vanished. Barnaby was close behind. "Good luck, everyone." Joyce slipped out into the corridor and hugged him. He kissed her cheek. "Good luck, Citizen of Vienna, Maker of the Cakes, and Noises Off."

"I've forgotten where you are."

"Row C in the middle."

"I'll know where not to look, then. Is Cully behaving herself?"

"So far."

Barnaby found the men's dressing room charged with emotion. Only Esslyn, wearing the memories of past first nights like invisible gongs, appeared calm. Other actors were laughing insecurely or prowling about or wringing their hands or (in the case of Orsini-Rosenberg) all three at once. Colin called "Beginners: Act One," and pressed the buzzer. Emperor Joseph shouted, "The bells! The bells!," and let forth screams of maniacal laughter. Barnaby mumbled, "The best of British," and withdrew, backing into Harold, who then leaped into the center of the room with a clarion call of ill-reasoned confidence.

"Well, my darlings—I know you're all going to be superb. . . ."

Barnaby melted away. Passing through the wings, he saw Deidre already in position in the prompt corner. In the light from the anglepoise lamp he thought she appeared distressed. Colin stood by her side. Barnaby gave them both the thumbs-up. He spotted Nicholas waiting behind the archway through which he would make his first entrance. The boy's face looked gray in the dim working light and was pearled with transparent beads of sweat. He bent down, picked up a glass of water, and drank, then he clutched the struts of the archway with shaking hands. Better you than me, mate, thought the chief inspector. He had just made his way to row C and settled next to his daughter when Harold followed, flinging open the pass door to the left of the front row with a quite unnecessary flourish, then turning to face the audience as if expecting a round of applause simply on the grounds of his existence. Then he sat in the center of the row, and the play began.

Things went wrong from the word go, and everyone, as they came off, blamed the lighting. Tim and Avery, now sweating in the box, had been so totally wrapped up in their daringness and so entranced by the fact that they were, at long last, going to do their very own thing, that they had taken no account of the effect a whole new spectrum of light and color might have on the cast. Actors became slow and muddled, as well they might. Even Nicholas, who was prepared for the change, was badly thrown and found it hard to recover. And his first scene, full of four-letter words, nearly brought him to a standstill.

At first the residents of Causton, determined to show that they were as *avant garde* as the next man, boldly took this profanity in their stride, but when Mozart said he wanted to lick his wife's arse, one honest burgher, muttering loudly about "toilet humor," got up and stomped out, his good lady bringing up the rear. Nicholas hesitated, wondering whether to wait until they had disappeared or carry straight on. His indecision was not helped by hearing Harold clearly call "peasants!" after the departing couple. As Nicholas stumbled again into speech, all the Rabelaisian relish had vanished from his voice. He felt morbidly self-conscious, almost apologetic, as if he had no right to be on a stage at all. He was sharply aware of Kitty, floundering unsupported by his side, proving the truth of Esslyn's snide predictions. After his first exit, he stood in the wings sick with disappointment, listening to Salieri, word perfect, roll smoothly and woodenly on.

For the first time ever, Nicholas asked himself what the hell a grown man was doing standing drenched in nervous sweat, wearing ludicrous clothes, his face covered with makeup, and a daft wig on his head, waiting to step through a canvas door into a world having only the most tenuous connection with reality.

Act I did not improve. The tape of Salieri's march of welcome as reworked by Mozart started too soon. Fortunately the lid of the pianoforte hid the fact that Nicholas had not had time to actually reach the keys. At least, he thought as he sat down, I haven't fallen over my sword.

In the *Seraglio* scene Kitty, rushing across the stage crying, "Well done, pussy-wussy," to her Wolfgang, caught her foot in a rug and ended up hanging onto the Emperor's arm in an effort to remain upright. Franz Joseph laughed and broke up everyone else. Only Esslyn and Nicholas remained in character and straight-faced.

On Barnaby's right Cully slid slowly downward, her shoulders beneath the black lace trembling slightly, and covered her face with her hands. Three seats in front and to the left, he saw Doris Winstanley glance anxiously at her husband. Harold's profile was rigid, his lips clamped tightly together. Then a light so brilliant it seemed impossible the stage and four walls could contain it shone. This was accompanied by a stellar explosion of glorious sound from the C Minor Mass, then everything faded to a predawn gray. Esslyn finished his final speech, crammed his mouth with sweetmeats, and strode off.

Barnaby watched Harold propel himself up the aisle two steps at a time, then rose himself and turned to his daughter. "Would you like a drink?"

"Oh, Dad." She got up slowly. "I wouldn't have missed that for the world. What's my eye makeup like?"

"Runny."

"I'm not surprised. We did a cod panto at the Footlights last year, but it wasn't a patch on that." She followed him up the aisle. "It must be some sort of a record when you go to the theater and the best thing onstage is the lighting. Oh . . . oh . . ."

"Don't start gurgling again."

"I'm not . . ." She snuffled into her hanky. "Honestly."

As they drew level with the back row of seats and the exit doors, Barnaby saw Mr. Tibbs. He was leaning forward, holding the back of the seat before him. He looked grubby and abstracted, like a saint at his devotions. Barnaby, who hadn't seem him for nearly two years, was shocked at his physical deterioration. His skin was like tissue paper and salt white. Blue corded veins pulsed on his forehead. Barnaby greeted him and received a smile of singular sweetness in reply, although he was convinced the old man had no idea who it was that spoke to him. Three young people sitting between Mr. Tibbs and the wall kept saying "Excuse me" very politely, but he did not seem either to hear or to understand, and eventually they climbed over the row of seats in front and got out that way.

The clubroom was packed. Cully dug out a wisp of lace and a mirror from her jet-encrusted reticule, spat in the hanky, and wiped away a runnel of mascara. When Barnaby brought her wine, she nodded across at the lighting box on which Harold was tapping more and more urgently. Then he put his lips to the door-jamb and hissed. The door remained closed. Clamping his success-ful impresario's smile into position, Harold backed away and moved once more into the center of the room, where Cully caught his arm.

"Wonderful lighting," she said. "Brilliant. Tell Tim I thought so."

"There's . . . there's no need for that!" cried Harold, put-put-ting like a faulty two-stroke. "Tim is simply a technician. No more, no less. *I* design the lighting for my productions."

"Oh. Really?" Cully's tone, though exquisitely polite, posi-tively curdled with disbelief. Barnaby took her arm and hustled her away.

"I shan't bring you out again."

"You used to say that when I was five."

"You don't improve. Drink up." Barnaby made an irritated tch as Cully lowered her delightful nose into the glass and sniffed. "What's wrong with it?"

"Nothing. If you like paraquat and crushed bananas."

Sergeant Troy approached, trailing his resentful wife, and Barnaby forced a smile. "Enjoying yourself, Gavin?"

"Not bad, is it, sir?" He spoke to Barnaby, but his eyes were on Barnaby's companion. "I mean for amateurs." He continued to stare until the chief inspector was forced to introduce them.

"Your daughter." Barnaby appreciated Troy's poleaxed demea-nor. Each time Cully returned home, he was newly amazed that such an elegant, sassy creature should be the fruit of his loins. "I'm surprised we haven't run into each other before, Cully."

"I'm at Cambridge. Final year."

Yes, you would be, thought Mrs. Troy, reflecting tartly on the unequal distribution of gifts come christening time.

"Oh—this is my wife, Maure," said Troy, and the two girls touched hands.

"More what?" said Cully.

"Troy," said Maureen, with a flinty spark in her eye.

Once more Barnaby led his daughter out of trouble. As they backed away, he nearly stepped on Tim, who nipped out of the box, looked quickly around the room, and hurried down the stairs. Meanwhile Harold had stormed through the wings shooting glances of disgust at the stage staff—who alone, during the disastrous first half, had hardly put a foot wrong—and was now in the men's dressing room impresaroing like mad to powerful effect.

"Never... *never* in all my years in the business," bawled Harold, "have I seen such a grotesque display of mind-boggling incompetence. Not to mention complete lack of verismo. All of you were corpsing. Except Salieri."

"Do you mind?" said Nicholas angrily. "I certainly wasn't."

"We were thrown by the lighting," said Emperor Joseph. Unfortunately adding, "Fabulous though it was."

"You should be used to my lighting by now," squawked Harold, puce with rage.

Nicholas, jaws agape, stared at his director. He had wondered how Harold would react to Tim's defiant behavior. He had visualized everything from freezing instant dismissal to temper tantrums and violent exhibitionism. What he had never considered, would never have considered in a hundred years, was that Harold would calmly annex the new lighting and represent it as his own.

"All you'll catch that way is flies, Nicholas," said Harold. "I shall say nothing more now. You all know you've let me down. Yes—you too, Mozart. There's no need to look at me like that. Where is your sword?"

"Oh." Tardily, Nicholas realized why he had not fallen over it at the piano. "Sorry."

"Sorry is not enough. I want an improvement—no, I want a transformation—from everyone here in Act Two. You can do it. I've seen you all turn in marvelous work. So go back out there and show them what you're made of." He spun around, and a moment later they heard him haranguing the distaff side next door.

"That's all we need," murmured Van Swieten. "A little touch of Harry on the night."

"That man's his own worst enemy."

"And when you think of the competition."

Boris made some tea in polystyrene cups, asking as he

wielded the kettle, "D'you think I should make some for Esslyn and his crapulous cronies?"

"Where are they, anyway?"

"Last I saw, he was in the wings rubbishing Joycey yet again about the cakes. God, David—you messy devil—"

"Sorry." David Smy seized a paper-towel roll and mopped up his tea. "I didn't know it was there."

"I saw them all go into the bog."

"Ooo..." Boris waved a limp wrist. "Troilism, is it? Bags I Cressida?"

"Never. You can say all sorts about Esslyn, but I don't think anyone seriously thinks he's gay."

Just then the three subjects of their conversation appeared in the doorway. They stood very still, their shadows taking a dark precedence, and the overheated, stuffy place suddenly seemed chilly. It was immediately obvious that something was very wrong. The Everards wore looks of sly anticipation, and Esslyn, eyes glittering, darted his head forward in an avid, searching way. The head seemed to Nicholas to have become elongated and slightly flattened. A snake's head. Then he chided himself for such exaggerated speculations. A trick of the light surely, that was all. Pure fantasy. As must be the idea that Esslyn was looking at him. Searching *him* out. Nevertheless, Nicholas's throat was dry, and he sipped his tea gratefully.

Esslyn sat down and started to retie his stock. Always self-contained, he now appeared almost clinically remote. But the overcareful movements of his hands, the tremor of his jaw only partially controlled by his clenched lips, and that terrible soulless glitter in his eye told their own tale. No one in the dressing room remained unaware that the company's leading man was boiling with suppressed rage.

Boris collected the cups in painstaking silence, and the odd remark, uneasily spoken, shriveled as soon as uttered. When the buzzer sounded, there was an immediate exodus, with everyone easing their way cautiously around Esslyn's chair. As he left, Nicholas looked back and caught a following glance so malign he felt his stomach kick. Convinced now that his earlier perceptions were not merely imagination, he turned hurriedly away, but not before he noticed that Esslyn had removed all his rings.

Why this should strike him as ominous, Nicholas could not understand. Perhaps it was simply that, given the man's present volcanic mien, any slight deviation from the norm gave cause for concern. Nicholas joined the other actors in the wings and stood quietly, a little apart, running over his next scene and forcing his mind to reenter the eighteenth century.

With seconds to go, Deidre peeped out into the auditorium. She had taken her father a cup of coffee and had toyed with the idea of putting a little brandy in it (he had seemed so tense and still quite cold) but, not knowing how it might interact with his tablets, had decided against the idea. Now, she watched him, staring eyes unnaturally bright, perched on the very edge of his seat as if preparing for imminent departure. What a terrible mistake it had been to allow him to come. She had almost called a taxi during the intermission to take him home, but feared for his safety if he was left alone in the house until eleven o'clock.

Colin touched her arm and she nodded, her attention now all on the opening of Act II. Esslyn was already in position, a gray shape humped over the back of his chair. As she prepared to raise the curtain, he lifted his head and looked into the wings, and there was on his face an expression of such controlled ferocity that Deidre, in spite of the distance between them, automatically stepped back, bumping into Kitty. Then she cued Tim's box, the house lights went down, and the play began.

Esslyn turned to the audience and said, "I have been listening to the cats in the courtyard. They are all singing Rossini."

Silence. Not just lack of laughter. Or a stretch of time punctuated only by the odd cough or rustle or movement of feet, but absolute total silence. Esslyn stepped down to the footlights. His eyes, glittering pinpoints of fire, raked the audience, mesmerizing them, gathering them close. He spoke of death and hatred with terrible, thrilling purpose. In the back row Mr. Tibbs whimpered softly. His hair seemed to stir softly on his neck, although there was not the slightest breeze. In the wings knots of actors and stagehands stood still as statues, and Deidre rang the bell for Constanze's entrance.

Most actors love a good row onstage, and the argument between Mozart's wife and Salieri had always gone well. Now, Kitty screamed, "You rotten shit!," and belabored her husband with her fists. She had her back to Deidre, who was thus facing Esslyn and watching in mounting horror as he seized his wife by the shoulders and shook her, not with the simulated fury that he had shown in rehearsals but in a wild rage, his lips drawn back in a snarl. Kitty's screams, too, became real as she was whirled round and round, her hair a golden stream whipping across her face, her head on its slender support snapping back and forth with such force it seemed impossible her neck would not break. Then he flung her so violently from him that she staggered across the stage and was only halted by smacking straight into the proscenium arch.

Deidre, appalled, looked at Colin. Her hand hovered near the curtain release, but he shook his head. Kitty stood for a moment, winded, fighting for breath, then she sucked in air like a drowning man, took two steps, and fell into Deidre's arms. Deidre led her to the only space in the crowded wings, next to the props table, and pulled up one of the little gilt chairs. She lowered the girl gently into it, handed her clipboard to Colin, and took Kitty's hand in hers.

"Is she all right?" Nicholas came up and whispered. "What the hell's going on?"

"It's Esslyn. I don't know . . . he seems to have had some sort of brainstorm. He just started throwing her about."

"Christ."

"Can you sit with her while I get some aspirin?"

"I'm on in two secs."

"Get one of the ASMs, then. Kitty, I shan't be a minute, okay?"

". . . *my back* . . . ahh . . . God . . ."

Deidre ran to the ladies' dressing room. The first-aid box kept always on the windowsill in the far corner behind the costume rail was not there. Frantically she started searching, pulling the actresses' day clothes—Rosa's fur coat, Joyce's looped gray wool—flinging various dresses and skirts aside. She knelt down, hurling shoes and boots out of the way. Nothing. And then she saw it. Sticking out from behind Rosa's wig stand. She grabbed the box and the aspirin, struggling with the screw top. It seemed impossibly stiff. Then she realized it was a "child proof" cap that you needed to push down first. Even as she shook out three tablets, she recognized the futility of what she was doing. Aspirins were for trivial ailments. A headache, a rise in temperature. What if Kitty's spine was damaged? What if every second's delay increased the dreadful danger of paralysis? At the least, she might be about to lose the baby . . . Deidre suddenly felt afraid. She should have ignored Colin and stopped the play. Asked if there was a doctor in the house. It would be her fault if Kitty never walked again. She forced this dreadful possibility from her mind and murmured, "Water...water." There were various mugs and polystyrene beakers scattered about, all with dirty brown puddles in the bottom. Deidre seized the nearest mug, rinsed it out, half filled it with cold water, and ran back to the wings.

The first thing she heard was Nicholas's voice from the stage. This meant the first scene was over, the set change effected, and scene 2 well under way. She had been longer than she thought. She hurried over to the props table, but the chair where she had left Kitty was empty. Deidre crossed to Colin, who, on her mouthed "Where is she?" mouthed back "Toilet."

Kitty was walking up and down the tiled floor when Deidre entered. Walking stiffly, stopping every few steps to ease her shoulders, but still, thank God, walking. Deidre proferred the aspirin and the mug, only to be met with a flood of invective the like of which she'd never heard in her life. The fact that it was aimed at Kitty's husband and Deidre just happened to be in the firing line hardly lessened the shock. The language left her face burning, and she "sshh'd" in vain. Some of the words were familiar from the text of *Amadeus,* and one or two more from the odd occasion when Deidre had been compelled to use a public lavatory, the rest were totally unfamiliar. And they had a newly minted ring, as if normal run-of-the-mill abuse could not even begin to do justice to Kitty's fury, and she had been compelled to create powerfully primed adjectives of her own.

"*Please...*" cried Deidre in an urgent whisper. "The audience will hear you."

Kitty stopped then, adding just one more sentence in a very quiet voice. "If he lays a finger on me again," she said, "I'll fucking kill him."

Then, still moving slowly and stiffly, she went, leaving Deidre staring after her openmouthed, the three aspirins, already sweatily crumbling, in the palm of her hand.

Barnaby and Troy, like the rest of the audience, were aware of the extraordinary change that had come over *Amadeus* in the second half. It seemed to them at the time that this was entirely due to the actor playing Salieri.

In Act I he had given a capable if rather stolid performance. In Act II his whole body seemed alive with explosive energy, which it seemed to barely contain. You would not have been surprised, thought Barnaby, if sparks had flown when he clapped his hands or struck the boards with his heel. The very air through which he stalked, trailing clouds of inchoate rage, seemed charged. Maureen Troy thought she might not have missed *Coronation Street* for nothing, and Barnaby became aware that his daughter was now sitting up and leaning forward in her seat.

Salieri's startling transformation did not help the play as a whole. The rest of the cast, instead of interacting with him as they had done previously (albeit with varying degrees of convincingness), now seemed to have become quite disengaged, moving cautiously within his orbit and avoiding eye contact even when indulging in direct speech.

Nicholas waited for his cue, gazing into the brilliantly lit arena. He was tense but not alarmed. He responded to the crackling energy that, even in the wings, he could feel emanating from Esslyn, in a very positive way. He felt his own blood surge in response. He knew he could match, even overmatch, the other man's power. His mind was clear; his body trembled pleasingly with anticipation. He stepped onstage and did not hear Emperor Joseph whisper as he drifted by, "Watch him."

And if he had heard, Nicholas would have paid no mind. He had no intention of pussyfooting about. For him, always, the play came first. So he stepped boldly up to Salieri, and when Esslyn said, "I commiserate with the loser" and held out his hand, Nicholas gladly offered his own. Esslyn immediately stepped in front of the boy, masking him from the audience, gripped Nicholas's hand in his own, and squeezed. And squeezed. Harder. And harder.

Nicholas's mouth stretched involuntarily wide in silent pain. His hand felt as if it were being wrapped in a bunch of savagely sharp thorns. Esslyn was smiling at him, a broad jackal grin. Then, just as Nicholas thought he might faint with agony, Esslyn suddenly let go and sauntered to the back of the stage. Nicholas gasped out a reasonable approximation of his next few lines and managed to get across to the piano and sit down. The Venticelli entered, and Mozart, who had no more to say, took this opportunity to examine his hand. It was already puffing up. He straightened the fingers gently one at a time. The back of the hand was worse than the palm. Covered in tiny blue bruises, with the skin actually broken in several places. The whole hand looked and felt as if someone had been trying to hammer thumbtacks into it. At the end of the scene he made his exit. Colin approached him in the wings.

"Deidre thinks we ought to stop it."

Nicholas shook his head. "I can cope. Now I know."

"Let's have a look." Colin stared at the hand and drew in his breath sharply. "You can't go on like that."

"Of course I can." Nicholas, having got over the immediate shock of the attack, was now, despite the pain, rather relishing this opportunity to display his cool professionalism. He was a trouper. And troupers trouped no matter what. Deidre touched his arm and whispered, "What happened?"

"His rings." Nicholas held out his hand. "I thought he'd taken them off, but he'd just turned them round."

"Bloody hell," muttered Boris, peering over Deidre's shoulder. "You won't play the violin again in a hurry."

"But why?" asked Deidre, and Nicholas shrugged his ignorance.

Onstage Salieri shouted his triumph. *"I filled my head with golden opinions—yes, and this house with golden furniture!"* and the whole set was suffused with soft, rich amber light. Gilded chairs and tables were carried on. Beside Nicholas, Joyce Barnaby stood holding a three-tier cake stand painted yellow. Like everyone else, she looked anxiously at him.

Nicholas nodded reassuringly back, attempting to appear both calm and brave. In fact, he was neither. He felt intensely excited, rather alarmed, and very angry. He strove to suppress the anger. The time to let that rip would be afterward. Now, he had to face the challenge of the next half hour. He would have more scenes alone with Salieri, but only one where they had physical contact (another handshake), and that handshake he would make sure to avoid. And the man could hardly do him any serious physical harm in front of a hundred people.

In the audience, his exquisite daughter raptly attentive by his side, Barnaby's nostrils widened and twitched. The smell in the theater was a smell he recognized. And so he should. It had been under his nose for a large part of his working life. A hot, burned smell, ferocious and stifling. The whole place stank of it. The smell of violence. He withdrew the larger part of his attention from the play and glanced about him. Everyone was still and quiet. He could see Harold's profile, bulging with pleasure mixed with disbelief. His wife looked simply frightened. Others sat eyes wide, unblinking. One woman savaged her bottom lip, another had both fists knuckling her cheeks. Barnaby turned his head slightly. Not every gaze was out front. Sergeant Troy, alert—even wary—was also looking about him.

Behind them in the back row Mr. Tibbs gripped the back of the seat in front of him and pushed away from it so hard that it seemed his backbone must impress the wall behind. His face showed terrible anticipation mixed with a craven appeal for mercy. He looked like a child, innocent of wrongdoing, who awaits harsh punishment.

Barnaby redirected his attention to the stage and the source of his unease. Esslyn was like a man possessed. He seemed to be never still. Even when he withdrew to the back of the stage and rested in the shadows, energy seemed to pulse through and around him as if he stood on a magnetic field. Barnaby would be glad when the play was over. Although he could think of no reason why Joyce should be at risk, he would be happy to see *Amadeus* concluded and whatever raging grievance Esslyn had sorted out in the proper manner. It was obviously something to do with Kitty.

She reentered now, bulkily pregnant, leaning heavily on Mozart's arm. She looked neither crushed nor beaten. Her curtsey to Salieri was a mere ironic sketch, her mouth a hard line and her eyes flashing. When she said, "I never dream, sir. Things are unpleasant enough to me awake," her voice, though raw and bruised, surged with acrimony. Barnaby glanced at his watch (about twenty minutes to go) and attempted to relax, giving himself up to the ravishing music of *The Magic Flute*. How entrenched, how impregnable must Esslyn's malice be that it could remain undiminished in the presence of such glorious sound.

Now, clad in a long gray cloak and hat, the top half of his face concealed by a mask, Salieri, harbinger of doom, moved stealthily across the stage to where Mozart, madly scribbling over sheets of paper, was working, literally, to a deadline, composing his own requiem.

Nicholas worked in a cold fever of exhilaration. Even though he had spent the evening in a more or less constant state of anxiety, there had been enough luminous moments to convince him that, as far as Mozart was concerned, he was on the right track. Whole sections had almost played themselves and seemed to be newly created moment by moment, as if the whole grinding discipline of rehearsal had never been. I can do it! Nicholas thought, dazed with jubilation. A dark figure moved in the doorway of his pathetic apartment and came to stand behind him.

Afterward, recounting the scene for Barnaby's benefit, Nicholas found it impossible to describe precisely the exact moment when the simulated terror with which he had acknowledged Salieri's phantasmagoric appearance fled and the real thing took its place. Perhaps it was when Esslyn first laid a bony hand upon his shoulder and breathed searing, rancorous breath over his cheek. Perhaps it was when the other man cut their first move and flung aside a chair that Nicholas had cunningly re-sited as a possible barrier between them. Or was it when he whispered, "Die, Amadeus... die"?

Automatically at this point Nicholas, as he had done at each rehearsal, dropped to all fours and crawled underneath the shrouded table that doubled as a writing desk and bed. The table was permanently set flush to the proscenium arch, and Colin had stapled the heavy felt cover to the floor on either side. So when Esslyn crouched at the entrance and his cloak blotted out the opening like great gray wings, Nicholas was trapped.

He crawled back as far as he was able in the dark, tiny space. He felt suffocated. What air there was, was thick with the musty staleness of the cloth and the reek of jackal breath. Esslyn curled back his lips in a hideous parody of a smile. And Nicholas realized that his earlier conviction (that he could come to no harm under the gaze of a hundred assorted souls) was a false one. He believed now that Esslyn would not be bound by the normal man's rational fear of discovery. Because Esslyn, Nicholas decided, was stark staring bonkers.

Now, the other man's hand, knuckledustered with silver spikes and hard, violating stones, reached for Nicholas's throat. And Nicholas, cutting the rest of the scene, yelled Kitty's cue: "*Oragna figata fa! Marina gamina fa!*" He heard her footsteps on the other side of the cloth and her first line, "Wolfie?" Esslyn withdrew his hand, his arm, his shoulders, and, finally, his vile grimace. By the time Nicholas crawled out, Salieri had retreated once more to the shadows.

"Stanzerl..." Nicholas clung to Kitty. She supported him, helping him to climb onto the table, arranging his pillows. His death scene (his marvelous death scene on which he had worked so hard) went for nothing. He gabbled the lines, his eyes constantly straying over Kitty's shoulder to the figure, furled all in gray, waiting in the dark. When Nicholas had died and been thrown without ceremony into his pauper's grave (a mattress concealed behind the fireplace) he lay there for a few moments, then crawled off into the wings. He found his way to the chair by the props table and fell into it, resting his head against the wall.

Expecting instant attention and sympathy, he was surprised when no one paid him any mind, then realized that they could hardly have known what was going on beneath a covered table. Time enough to tell them afterward. He became aware that his other hand, or at least the thumb, was hurting like hell. He held it up, but the light was so dim that he could see only the outline. He hurried downstairs, on the way up passing Deidre, who cried, "Watch out!" and held a kettle of steaming water out of his way.

In the bright lights of the men's dressing room, he discovered a great splinter rammed down the side of his nail. The surrounding flesh already had a gathered, angry look. He held it under the hot tap for a few moments, then looked around for a pair of tweezers. Occasionally an actor would have some for applying wisps of false hair or eyebrows. But he had no success. He tried next door, knocking first.

"Oh," Rosa exuded kind concern. "You poor lamb. I've got some twizzies. Hang on." She riffled in her box. "Have you put anything on it?"

"No. Just given it a rinse."

"Here we are." Rosa picked up some tweezers smeared with greasepaint. "Let's have a look, then."

Nicholas handed over his thumb while eyeing the surgical appliance with some disquiet. "Shouldn't we sterilize them or something?"

"Good Lord, Nicholas. You want to enter the profession, you'll have to learn to take something like this in your stride."

Nicholas, who had never seen the willingness to embrace septicemia as one of the more obvious qualities a young actor might find useful, jibbed at this robust assertion.

"There." Rosa extracted the splinter with surprising gentleness, then rummaged in her handbag, produced a grubby Band-Aid, and peeled off the shiny backing. "How did you come to pick it up, anyway?" Nicholas told her. "Oh, how you exaggerate."

"I do not. He went straight for the jugular." But even as he spoke, Nicholas was aware of a watering down of his conviction. The cozy air of normalcy in the dressing room and the fact that no one in the wings had noticed anything untoward were encouraging a slight feeling of unreality about his recollections. But there was one thing that was true and very real. Nicholas said, "And he shook the living daylights out of Kitty."

"Did he?" Rosa smiled and wrapped the Band-Aid extra tenderly around her companion's thumb. "Naughty boy." Nicholas rightly assumed that this reproof was intended for Esslyn rather than himself, although it seemed astonishingly mild under the circumstances. "I expect he discovered," continued Rosa creamily, "that she was having an affair."

"Bloody hell! How did you know that?"

"Common knowledge, darling."

Nicholas, swamped by guilt, sat contemplating his throbbing hand. This was all his fault. If he hadn't told Avery and Tim, it would never have got out. So much for Avery's promises. And for all he knew, Tim had blabbed as well. They were both as bad as the other. "Pair of gossipy old queens," he muttered.

"Sorry?"

"Tim and Avery."

"Well, really, darling," continued Rosa, "if you feel like that about homosexuals, you may just be entering the wrong profession. I understand there's at least one in every company."

Nicholas stared at her severely, no longer grateful for the Band-Aid. How would she know what there was in every company? Swathed in her nylon wrapper with its collar of molting cerise ostrich feathers. Playing the leading lady, regurgitating chunks of past performances, trailing shreds of ersatz glamor as false and tawdry as last year's tinsel. The Latimer, thought Nicholas savagely, was the perfect place for her, along with the other poseurs and has-beens and never-would-be's and deadweights. Conveniently he forgot past kindnesses. The patience and encouragement shown to a neophyte who hadn't known a claw hammer from a codpiece. The support and refuge offered when he had suddenly left home. He only knew that he was sick of the whole narcissistic bunch. He jumped up, startling Rosa.

"I'm going to watch the end. Coming?"

"I don't think so, angel," replied Rosa, batting her false lashes, gluey with mascara. "I have seen it all before."

In the wings actors were gathering for the call. Nicholas, last in the queue (Esslyn being already *in situ*), lined up by Emperor Joseph and said, "What a night."

"Carry on up the Schönbrunn, lover."

David Smy passed them carrying his valet's tray with the razor, wooden dish of soap, folded towel, and china bowl complete with rising steam. One of the ASMs pushed Salieri's wheelchair on, and David followed. He put his tray down on a little round table, took his master's will as instructed, and retired to the back of the stage to amend his signature. Salieri picked up the razor, stepped down to the footlights, and spoke, directly and passionately, to the audience.

"*Amici cari*. I was born a pair of ears. It is only through hearing music that I know God exists. Only through writing music that I could worship . . ."

In the wings Joyce prepared to step forward. Behind her the Venticelli hovered ready for their final entrance.

". . . To be owned . . . ordered . . . exhausted by an *Absolute* . . . And with it all meaning . . ."

Maureen Troy, although not actually sorry the end was nigh, found herself experiencing a shade of disappointment. Because she definitely fancied that bloke playing the wop. Just her mark. Tall, dark, and handsome, and old enough to have a grown-up daughter in the cast if Maureen's program was anything to go by. Maybe the evening wasn't going to be a total bust after all. Her husband's shifty glances in Cully Barnaby's direction had not gone unnoticed, and two could play at that game. Maybe she could wangle an invite round the back and introduce herself.

". . . now I go to become a ghost myself. I will stand in the shadows, when you come to this earth in your turn . . ."

Cully, on the other hand, had been impressed by Mozart. Obviously inexperienced and somewhat all over the place, he had still given an energetic and very sensitive performance, with touches of real pathos. She found herself wondering about the actor. How old he was. How serious about the theater.

"And when you feel the dreadful bite of your failures—and hear the taunting of unachievable uncaring God—I will whisper my name to you. Salieri: Patron Saint of Mediocrities!"

Tim in his box said, "Truth will out." Avery smiled, and Harold ran over his first-night speech. Tom Barnaby still sensed a slide toward misrule and sat upright and unrelaxed. In the back row Mr. Tibbs had lost the theater entirely, and wandered in a dark wood pursued by demons and the howling of wolves.

"And in the depths of your downcastness you can pray to me. And I will forgive you. *Vi saluto.*"

Esslyn lifted the razor and, with one dramatic sweep, drew it across his throat. It left a bright red line. He stood for a moment frowning down at the blade, unexpectedly scarlet. He swayed forward, then jerked himself upright as if with great effort. The keeper of the cakes bustled cheerfully on with the breakfast tray. Salieri took a step to meet her. She stared at him, her mouth shaped to a silent O, then she dropped the tray and caught him as he fell. Then she screamed. Shrieks of pure terror. Over and over again. While the bright blood flowed over her snowy fichu and dove-gray skirt onto the boards beneath.

ENTER THE BROKER'S MEN

Barnaby was out of his seat and onto the stage within seconds. Troy followed hard on his heels.

"Get the curtain down!" Deidre looked blindly at and through him. *"Get it down."*

There was a sweep of velvet plush as Colin released the holding mechanism cutting off the grisly tableau from the audience's startled and excited gaze. Barnaby looked to his wife. She was standing absolutely rigid, her face blank, her eyes tightly closed. Esslyn, his life ebbing, hung around her neck with almost balletic grace, like a dying swan.

Troy slipped his hands under the man's armpits and lowered him with infinite pointless care to the floor. Barnaby stepped outside the curtain. No need to say, "Could I have your attention please?" The conversation ceased as if by magic.

"I'm afraid there's been an accident," he said calmly. "If you'd remain in your seats for a few moments, please. Do we have a doctor present?"

No one spoke. Tim had put up the house lights, and Barnaby noticed Harold's empty space and the swinging door by row A. Cully's seat was also unoccupied. He stepped back onto the stage where Sergeant Troy, knife-creased trousers stained crimson, was kneeling, his head turned to one side, his ear almost touching Esslyn's lips. The sergeant's mouth was pursed, and his brow pleated with the effort of concentration. He felt an exhalation; cold, infinitely frail, and heard one exhausted sound. The narrow red line was now a gaping incision, and Esslyn's eyes were glazed. A moment later his life was over. A great crack of thunder, ludicrously apt, was heard, then the patter of rain on the roof. Troy stood up.

"Hear anything?"

"'Bungled,' sir. As near as I could get."

"Right. Take the stage door, would you? Colin—over there in the check shirt—will show you where it is. No one in or out."

The sergeant disappeared. Barnaby looked round. In the wings, next to a clutch of fifth-formers huddled together for comfort in a suddenly alien landscape, Rosa's husband held her hand. The chief inspector crossed to them.

"Earnest, I need some temporary help. Would you go to the foyer, please? Notify the station what's happened on the pay phone. Don't let anyone leave. Won't be for long."

"I would, Tom, but I feel I should stay with Rosa."

"No, no. Do as Tom says." Rosa wore a clown face, makeup crudely drawn on a chalky background. "I'll be all right, really."

"Shall I ask them to send help?"

"They'll know what to do."

Earnest, still looking rather uncertain, left them both. By now the wings were full of actors, and the stage deserted. Barnaby noticed with some relief that his wife had lost her terrible frozen stillness and was weeping in their daughter's arms. Colin returned, and Barnaby asked him for a box or carrier bag and something to cover the body. Colin tipped some flexible cord and electrical connections out of a shoe box and gave it to Barnaby, who placed it over the razor, which was lying near Esslyn's right hand. A curtain was found, and Barnaby covered the corpse, stepping carefully around the blood, which was still seeping outward. It had made a large stain, pear-shaped with an extra bulge on one side, like an inverted map of Africa. The curtain was hideously inappropriate, being covered with rainbows and balloons and teddy bears having a grand time. Barnaby took the key to the men's dressing room from the board, ran downstairs (closely shadowed by Harold), locked it, and returned the key to Colin.

"You seem to be taking a lot upon yourself," said Harold. Alone among the shocked and haggard faces, his shone with lively indignation.

"What's it all for, Tom ... all this ... ?" said Colin, gesturing with the key. "I mean, a terrible thing has happened, but it was an accident. ..."

"You're probably right," answered Barnaby. "But until I get

a clearer picture, there are certain precautions it's only sensible to take."

"I must say, I don't see why," retorted Harold. "All this showing off. Ordering people about, barging here and there, locking the place up. Who the hell do you think you are?"

"I'm just going to have a word with the audience," continued Barnaby. "Explain what is going on. We shouldn't have to keep them too long."

"You most certainly will not have a word with the audience!" cried Harold. "Any words to be had will be had by me. This is *my* theater. I'm in charge here."

"On the contrary, Harold," replied Barnaby, and his voice made him a stranger to them all. "Until further notice, *I* shall be in charge here."

Half an hour had passed. Reinforcements had arrived. The audience had their names and telephone numbers taken and, with a single exception, had gone off to spread the news to family and friends considerably more excited than when they arrived, which, as one elderly gentleman said while buttoning up his overcoat, made the evening a first in more ways than one.

One of the half-dozen worried parents waiting outside to take the fifth-formers home had been allowed to enter and was now acting as chaperon in the women's dressing room while they were being gently questioned. Registration numbers in the parking garage and adjacent streets had been noted, and a constable was positioned in the pouring rain outside the main door. Another sat onstage on the Emperor Joseph's throne with the humped gay curtain.

In the clubroom Deidre was trying to persuade her father to drink some coffee. When she had first fled up the aisle to him just after the curtain fell, she had been horrified to see his staring eyes and wildly gesturing hands. His legs, too, had been shaking and twisting, and he drummed his feet like a runaway horse. People sitting nearby were either ignoring him, looking sympathetic, or, in the case of the teenagers in the same row, laughing hysterically. Deidre, tears of pity pouring down cheeks still pale with shock, gradually managed to soothe him into some sort of quiescence. Now, he jiggled and joggled his mug and splashed coffee all over the settee. Deidre spoke softly, reassuringly, to him while he stared over her shoulder. He had just started to make a toneless droning sound when the door opened and a young man with bristly red hair and a sharp, narrow face entered. He wore a sports jacket, and his trousers were marked with dreadful stains.

"You Miss Tibbs? The DCI would like a word."

"I'm sorry," said Deidre. "I don't think I can leave my father."

"I'm not offering you a choice, miss."

"Oh." Deidre got hesitantly to her feet. She wondered if she could be talked to in the clubroom, then quickly realized what a stupid idea that was. The last thing she wanted now that her father was calming down a little were questions that might recall the climax of the play.

"Could you . . . perhaps stay with him?"

"Sorry." Troy held the door open, adding glibly, "He'll be okay. Right as rain." He closed the door and led her firmly downstairs.

Deidre felt a little better when she entered the ladies' dressing room and realized the detective chief inspector was going to be Tom. She asked if he'd be very long, as she was anxious to get her father safely home.

"No longer than I can help, Deidre. But the quicker we can sort this business out, the better. I'm sure you'll want to help us all you can."

"Of course I do, Tom. But I just don't understand how anything like this could have happened. It worked perfectly well at rehearsals."

"When did you actually check the props this evening?"

"Just before the half. About twenty past seven, I suppose."

"And the tape was in place then?"

"Of course. Otherwise I would have—" She broke off then, her eyes widening. "Oh my God, you don't mean . . ." Her stare was a mixture of horror and disbelief. "You can't!"

"What did you think had happened?"

"I assumed it had rubbed thin. Or got torn."

"I'm afraid not. Completely removed."

Deidre said "My God!" again, and buried her head in her hands. After a few moments she looked up and said, "Who on earth could have done such a terrible thing?"

Barnaby gave her a moment more, then said, "Where was the tray with the razor kept?"

"On the props table. At the back, out of the way. It only goes on once, you see. Right at the end."

"And it's fairly dark in the wings?"

"Yes. A certain amount of light spills out from the stage, of course, although the flats cut off a lot. And I've got an anglepoise in my corner. For tape and lighting cues. Not that I needed to give any of those. Tim was doing his own thing. He's been threatening to for years, but no one thought he ever would."

"Did you see anyone touch the tray or anything on it during the evening?" Deidre shook her head. "Or anyone hovering about in that area who shouldn't have been?"

"No. But then I wouldn't, Tom. *Amadeus* has got nearly thirty scenes. We don't have a second to think. Oh, there was Kitty, of course. And Nicholas. He sat down there for a minute after his last exit."

"Tell me about Kitty first."

"Well, you must have seen what happened in Act Two. I don't know what it looked like from the front ..."

"Pretty savage."

"I wanted to stop the whole thing, but Colin disagreed. When Kitty came off, she could hardly stand. I sat her down next to the table." Noticing an intensification of watchfulness in Barnaby's expression, Deidre added quickly, "But she didn't stay. I went down to the dressing room to get her a drink and an aspirin."

"How long do you think you were away?"

"Several minutes. First I couldn't find the aspirin, then I couldn't get the top off, then I had to wash a mug. Then I panicked. You can imagine." Barnaby nodded, imagining very well. "When I got back, Kitty had gone, and I found her in the toilet."

"How did she react to what had happened?"

"She was terribly angry. Furious. She ... well, she cursed a lot. Then she said, 'If he touches me again, I'll—'" Deidre broke off. She looked around the room at the bottles and jars and showy bouquets and at a good-luck card sporting a large black cat who had obviously completely failed to get the hang of its required function. "Sorry, Tom. I don't remember what she said after that."

"Deidre." Deidre made eye contact with a coffee jar, a jar of artificial sweetener, and one of powdered milk. "Look at me." She managed a quick glance, timorous almost pleading. "This isn't a practical joke we're investigating."

"No."

"So what did Mrs. Carmichael say?"

Deidre swallowed and took a deep breath. "'If he touches me again...'" The rest of the sentence was smothered in a whisper.

"Speak up."

"'I'll kill him.' But she didn't mean it," Deidre rushed on. "I know she didn't. People say that all the time, don't they? Mothers to their children in the street. You're always hearing them. It doesn't mean anything, Tom. And she was probably worried about the baby. She hit the pros arch with a terrible smack."

"Where did she go when she left the toilet?"

"Back to the wings. Joycey was standing by to put her padding on. And I followed. She didn't go near the table again, I'm positive."

"Do you have any idea why Esslyn should have acted the way he did?"

"No—I can't understand it. He was perfectly all right till the interval."

"You haven't heard any gossip?"

"Gossip? About what?"

"Perhaps... another man?"

"Oh, no, I shouldn't think so. Kitty was pregnant, you see."

He was certainly meeting them tonight, thought Sergeant Troy, resting his ball-point against the pad borrowed from the constable on pavement duty. First the old gaffer upstairs singing his cracked old song halfway up Delilah Street, now the droopy-bottomed daughter who apparently believed that once you'd got one in the oven you hung a no-trespassing sign around your neck. In fact, as Troy knew to his philandering benefit, it was the one time you could hold open house with nobody having to foot the bill. He covered his mouth with the back of his hand to conceal an involuntary twitch of derision.

"Now you know the tape was deliberately removed, do you have any idea how this could have been done?" Deidre's features seemed to gather themselves together in the center of her face, so great were her efforts at concentration. Barnaby said, "No hurry."

"I just can't think, Tom. The risk. It was so sharp." Suddenly she saw David's fingers, quick and deft, wrapping the razor.

"What is it?"

"Nothing." Before he could persist, Deidre improvised. "I mean—it was so dangerous, it couldn't have been done in the dark. And although the wings and stage were brightly lit till curtain up, it couldn't have been done then, either, because of the chance they might have been seen."

"Who was the first to arrive after you?"

"Colin and David."

"Did you tell them you'd done the check?"

"I told Colin."

"But if they were together, that means you told them both." Deidre's gaze reconnected with the powdered milk. "Do you remember who came next?"

"Not really, Tom. Half a dozen people arrived together. Rosa and the Everards... and Boris. All the ASMs were in on the half."

"Did anyone ask if you'd done your check?" Barnaby knew this question to be rather futile. The last thing the person who doctored the razor would wish to do was draw attention to himself. But he felt it still had to be put. Deidre shook her head. "Did you leave the stage area at any time?"

"Yes. I went to the dressing rooms to call the quarter. Then I fetched my ASMs from the clubroom and I went to meet my father. This was just before eight o'clock. He was late." Reminded, she half rose, saying, "Is that all, Tom? He's waiting, you see."

"In a moment." Reluctantly, Deidre reseated herself. "Did you like Esslyn, Deidre?" She hesitated for a minute, then said, "No."

"Do you have any idea at all who might have done this?"

This time there was no hesitation. "Not at all, Tom. To be honest, I don't think anyone liked him very much, but you don't kill someone just because of that. Do you?"

The question was not lightly put. It was flooded with such intense appeal that Deidre seemed to be seeking reassurance that the police had perpetrated a shocking misconstruction and that the tape had managed to fly away of its own accord. Barnaby's unconsoling reply was never made. There was a knock at the door, and the constable who had been sitting with the body popped his head round the door and said, "Dr. Bullard's arrived, sir."

Meanwhile, next door in the scene dock, the company, while still shocked, was starting to bounce back. Some more than others, naturally. But hushed whispers had already gone the way of solemn looks and reverential head shakings. Now ideas and suggestions were being mooted, but in tones of bashful solemnity out of respect for Kitty's grief.

Not that this was much in evidence. She sat on a workbench staring crossly at Rosa and tapping her foot with irritation. The first Mrs. Carmichael, her mouth loose and frilly, wept continuously. Her makeup now resembled a Turner sunset. You would have thought that she, not Kitty, was the widow. Earnest, who could have gone home ages ago, remained by her side. Joyce, her blood-soaked clothes hidden behind a screen with Cully's ruined dress, sat holding her daughter's hand and wearing her husband's topcoat. Cully was wrapped in several yards of butter muslin that she had found in a basket. Nicholas, who could not take his eyes off her, thought she looked like an exquisite reincarnation of Nefertiti.

All of them had been searched quickly and efficiently, and although it had been no more than the brisk, impersonal going-over anyone gets at an airport, Harold had taken umbrage and threatened to write to his member of Parliament.

"If a man's been stupid enough to cut his own throat," he had cried indignantly, "I don't know what on earth the police expect to gain by subjecting my people to this humiliating procedure."

None of his people had really minded, but they had all been equally puzzled by the need for such a step.

"I really don't see," said Bill Last, lately Van Swieten, "why they've locked up the men's dressing room. My car keys are in there. And my wallet. Everything."

"Right," said Boris, who chain-smoked and was desperate for a drag.

"I don't see why they want to talk to us at all," complained Clive Everard. "We're not responsible for checking the props. It's obviously Dreary's fault. Took the tape off for some reason. Forgot to put it back again."

"Typical," said his brother.

"It is not at all typical," said David Smy angrily. "Deidre's very capable."

"Hear, hear," from Nicholas.

Kitty, who had caught sight of Deidre being escorted by

Troy, said, "She's been in there a hell of a time, though. I'd say it looks quite promising."

"What an unkind thing to say," protested Avery. "Honestly. I thought adversity was supposed to bring out the best in us."

"You can't bring out what isn't there," said an Everard.

"Bastard," said Kitty.

Still, the same thought had struck them all, save one. It would be nice if Deidre had just been careless. Problem solved. And in a not too uncomfortable manner. Quite neat and tidy, really. Then they could all get changed and go home to bed.

But it was not to be. Harold bustled in, quite unsubdued by his forced incarceration, all asimmer with tendentious self-esteem. "I've just been questioning the uniformed halfwit in the foyer," he began, "as to why we are all being treated in this tyrannical fashion and why half my theater seems to be out of bounds, and he was totally unforthcoming. Mumbled something about protecting the scene in a case like this, and when I said, 'a case like what?' he said I should have a word with the DCI. 'Easier said than done, my man,' I replied. Tom is on the stage at the moment," he continued, looking accusingly at the chief inspector's wife, "with a complete and utter stranger who is cutting away—*cutting away* at that magnificent blue brocade coat. What with that and Joyce messing up her costume, you can imagine what my bill will be like."

"That's show business," murmured Tim. "Start the evening with Mozart, end up with *Götterdämmerung*."

"And when I tried to ask Tom what he thought he was playing at, he told me to come down here and wait with the others. And an obnoxious youth with red hair practically strongarmed me down the stairs. If there is one thing I cannot stand it's high-handedness."

Harold gazed at the ring of incredulous faces and was struck by one showing a remarkably uncontrolled use of color. "And what on *earth*," he concluded, "is the matter with Rosa?"

Above their heads Jim Bullard crouched beside the body, and Barnaby watched him as he had done more times than he cared to remember.

"Cause of death's plain enough. Don't need a pathologist for this one."

"Quite."

"Extraordinary thing to do. Slash your throat in front of a theater full of people. I know actors are exhibitionists, but you'd think there'd be some limits. At least there's no argument as to the time of death. Was he on anything?"

"Not that I know of."

"Well, the PM'll show that up. Right." He rose, dusted his knees, and repacked his bag. "You can get him shifted. No scene-of-crime people yet?"

"I'm scratching round. Davidson's at his Masonic dinner. Fenton's gone to the Seychelles..."

"Coo. Well, I'm off back to the U.S. of A. If there's any *Dallas* left..."

"Before you go, Jim, I wonder if you'd have a look at Mr. Tibbs. He's the father of the girl who just went through. Upstairs in the clubroom."

"What's the matter with him?"

"He's mentally ill. I think what happened tonight might've, well, pushed him just that bit nearer the edge. He looked very ill."

"I will, of course, Tom, but I haven't got anything with me to give him. You'd be better getting in touch with his own— God! What on earth is that?"

A terrible cry. An awful, keening cry shot through with desolation and woe. Then rapid running and, through the open doors at the top of the aisle, they saw Deidre fly past and disappear into the foyer below.

Outside it was still raining. Freezing needles of rain that could burrow through the warmest cloth, never mind a thin summer shirt and cotton trousers. (He had left his linen jacket behind.) Rushing blindly onto the pavement carrying the abandoned jacket over her arm, Deidre bumped into a young policeman, caped and helmeted, getting soaked in the pursuance of his duty. He caught her arm.

"I'm sorry. No one's allowed to leave."

"Tom's finished with me—the chief inspector, that is. Have you seen an old man?" A little crowd opposite glumly standing beneath a cluster of bright umbrellas perked up at this sign of activity. "He's got white hair...*please.*" She clutched at the constable frantically, rain and tears intermingling on her cheeks. "He's ill."

"Slipped through my fingers a few minutes ago. Racing he was. No coat or anything."

"Oh, God!"

"He went up Carradine Road. Wait, if you hold on, I'll get in touch . . ."

But he spoke to the night air, for Deidre had run away. He saw her a moment later racing across the shining wet tarmac, her dress already soaked, her face a livid green-blue in the glow from the traffic lights. Then she was gone.

Rosa was interviewed next. Supported by Earnest as far as the dressing-room door, she subsided opposite Barnaby in an excitation of cerise fluff.

"You must ask me anything, Tom," she cried, and her voice, though brave, was a rill of sorrows. "Anything at all."

"Thank you," said the chief inspector, who fully intended to. "Can you think of anyone who might have wished to harm your ex-husband?"

"Absolutely not," Rosa replied promptly. But the look that followed implied that the speed with which her interlocutor had approached the nub of the matter might be considered a bit short on finesse. "Everyone liked Esslyn."

Barnaby raised his shaggy eyebrows. His eyes shone with a gleam at once caustic and humorous. The gleam implied that he quite understood she felt she had to say things like that, and now she'd said them, perhaps they could cut the obsequies and get down to the nitty-gritty. Maybe even flirt with the truth a little. "That is," continued Rosa, acknowledging the proposition, "on the whole. Of course, he was terribly unhappy."

"Oh?"

"Kitty, you see." She gave him a slightly suggestive yet shaded look, as if she were acknowledging Kitty's guilt from behind a veil. "A shotgun wedding is never a good start, is it? And of course once she'd got him safely hooked, she started to play around."

"Who with?"

"That's not really for me to say."

"I quite understand."

"David Smy."

"Goodness."

"Of course it might just be a rumor."

"It was Esslyn's child, though?"

"We all assumed so." The verb's emphasis was beautifully judged. "Poor little mite."

Barnaby changed tack, deliberately hardening his voice. "How did you feel, Rosa? After your divorce?"

Rosa's pose fell away. Her naked face showed plain through its rioting complexion. She looked cornered. And older. "I... really don't see... what that has... has to do with anything, Tom." She took a deep breath and seemed to be fighting for control.

"Just background."

"Background to what?"

"One never knows what might be helpful."

Rosa hesitated, and her feathers trembled. Barnaby appreciated her predicament. It was one that every person he interviewed would be in right up to their neck. For the first time in his life all the people connected with the case (for case he was sure there would prove to be) were known to him, and the history of their present and past relationships even better known to his wife. Which made all the usual subterfuges, evasions, white lies, black lies, half-truths, and deliberate attempts to lead him astray rather futile. Advantage Barnaby. For once.

"To be absolutely honest, Tom..." She paused, resting a crimson nail against her nose as if checking it for rapid growth.

"Yes?" murmured Barnaby/Gepetto.

"I was angry at first. Very angry. I thought he was making a terrible mistake. But by the time the *decree nisi* came through, I had changed. I realized that, for the first time in years, I was free." She flung her arms wide, narrowly missing Harold's flowers. Her sailor's gaze raked the far horizon. "Free!"

"And yet you remarried so quickly."

"Ah." The gaze became wary, contracted from the hemispheric, and swept the floor. "Love conquers all."

They were back in fantasy land, observed Barnaby to himself, but he let it ride. For now. And fantasies were not entirely unrevealing. He repeated his first question.

"Well, Tom, I don't know about anyone wanting to kill Esslyn, but Nicholas came down here just before the final curtain with a splinter in his thumb and said that Esslyn had tried to kill *him!*" Barnaby received this dramatic pronouncement with irritating self-control. "Under the table," continued Rosa. "In the requiem scene. And he'd already damaged Nicholas's hand."

"Oh," said Barnaby. Then, disappointing her: "If we could return to the razor. Did you see anyone touching it or handling the tray who shouldn't have been?"

"No. And I'll tell you why." She looked with deep solemnity at both men. "When I'm acting... when I'm in that state of high concentration that we in the profession must be able to summon if the performance is going to work, I see nothing—but *nothing*—that isn't measurably relevant to my part."

"Even when you've no lines?" asked Barnaby.

"Especially then. *Sans* words, there's only the action of the drama to anchor the emotions."

"I understand." Barnaby nodded, matching her gravity. Troy, unimpressed, wrote on his borrowed pad, "Saw nothing suspicious at props table."

"What time did you arrive this evening, Rosa?"

"On the half. I went straight to my dressing room and didn't come out till my first entrance. About ten minutes into Act One."

Barnaby nodded again, then sat, silent, drumming his fingers absently against the arm of his chair. As the moments passed, Rosa shifted uneasily. Troy, long familiar with the chief's technique, simply anticipated.

"Rosa." Barnaby gathered himself and leaned forward. "It is my belief that, far from welcoming your freedom at the time of your divorce and wishing Esslyn well in his second marriage, you fought to keep your own going and have hated him ever since he left you."

Rosa cried out then, and covered her clown's mouth with her fingers. Her hands shook, and sweat rolled down her face. Barnaby sat back and watched the actorish deceit evaporate, leaving, oddly now that truth was present, doubt and childlike bewilderment.

"You're right." Having said this she sounded almost relieved. She paused for a long time, then started to speak, stopping and starting. Feeling her way. "I thought it would fade, especially after I remarried. And Earnest is so good. But it persisted, eating at me. I wanted a child, you see. He knew that. He denied me. Persuaded me against it. And then to give one to Kitty." She produced a handkerchief and rubbed at her face. "But the amazing thing, Tom—and I do mean this, I really do—is that all the hatred's gone. Isn't that extraordinary? Just as if someone somewhere pulled a plug and let it drain away. It doesn't seem possible, does it? That something so strong it was poisoning your life could simply disappear. Like magic."

After a few moments' silence, during which Barnaby mulled over Rosa's excellent motive for murder, he indicated that she was free to go. She stood for a moment at the door, looking, in spite of her cheap flamboyant robe and rampaging complexion, not entirely ridiculous. She seemed to be searching for some concluding remark, perhaps with the idea of ameliorating her former harshness. Eventually, almost as if memory had caught her by surprise, she said, "We were young together once."

Barnaby next interviewed Boris, who twitched and shook his way through the questions until Sergeant Troy, from pure pity, offered him a cigarette. Boris insisted that he had seen no one handle the razor all evening, and could not imagine why anyone would want to kill Esslyn. All the other bit-part actors came and went, saying the same thing. As each one left the scene dock, they were followed by a cry of fury as Harold protested against this disgraceful reversal of the natural order of precedence.

One scene-of-crime man arrived closely followed by Bill Davidson, untimely wrenched from his Masonic revels. After a briefing, they went about their business, working through the men's dressing room first and releasing it for occupation. Cully took her mother home, Esslyn left for the county morgue, and Barnaby called for the Everards.

Clive and Donald came prancing in, their eyes aglow with anticipation, trailing clouds of *schadenfreude*. They were still made up, and their pointilliste complexions were the peculiar tea-rose pink of old-fashioned corsets. Barnaby chose to see them together, knowing their habit of egging each other on to ever more indiscreet and racy revelations. Now, preening and clucking like a couple of cassowaries, they circled the two chairs cautiously a couple of times before perching. They stared beady-eyed at Sergeant Troy and his notebook, and he stared boldly but uneasily back.

The sergeant liked men to be men and women to be glad of it. Here was a pair he couldn't place at all. He always boasted he could tell a faggot a mile off, but he wasn't at all sure about this particular combo. He decided they had probably been neutered at an early age and, having pinned them down to his satisfaction, heard Barnaby ask if they could think of anyone who would wish to harm the dead man and flipped over to a new page.

"Quite honestly," said Clive Everard, taking a keen, deep

breath, "it'd take less time to tell you who wouldn't wish to harm him. I shouldn't think there's anyone in the company hasn't come up against Esslyn at some time and been the worse for it."

"If you could be a little more specific."

"If it's *specific* you want—" They exchanged glances glittering with spite. "Why not start with Deidre. He was telling this wonderful story in the dressing room—"

"—positively hilarious—"

"About her father—"

"Laughter and applause—"

"And suddenly there she was in the doorway. She must have overheard Esslyn call the old man senile—"

"Which of course he is."

"But d'you think she'll admit it? Absentminded... disoriented... poorly..."

"*Poorly,*" cackled Donald. "So what more natural than that she had a stab at getting her own back. Oops... Freudian slip there. Sorry." He didn't look sorry. His smile was as bright as a new penny as he added, "And of course who would have a better opportunity?"

"This happened when she called the quarter?" asked Barnaby, recalling Deidre's distressed appearance as he had passed through the wings.

"That's right. Would you care to hear the story?" Clive added politely.

"No," said Barnaby. "Anyone else?" Then, when they appeared to be savoring a multitude of possibilities: "What about Nicholas?"

"Ahhh, you've snuffed out that little *contretemps*. Esslyn'd just discovered that his little kitten was having an affair."

"And I'm afraid," murmured Donald, looking with shy regret at Sergeant Troy, "that it was rather our fault."

"Not that we thought he'd react anything like he did."

"Heaven forbid."

"I mean, his complacency is legendary."

"Undentable."

"So who," asked Barnaby, "was she supposed to be having an affair with?"

"Well, we heard from Rosa who got it from Boris who got it from Avery who got it from Nicholas that it was David Smy."

"And where did Nicholas get it from?"

"My dear, apparently he actually saw them," cried Donald. "Going at it like the clappers in Tim's lighting box."

Barnaby supposed stranger things had happened. Himself, he would not have thought that Kitty, whose winsome appearance masked, he felt sure, a self-serving duplicitous little nature, would have fancied the rather stolid David. Mind you, if she was looking for a change, no one could have been a greater contrast to Esslyn.

"And as he was our friend," said Donald with an unctuous wriggle, "we felt he ought to know."

"So we told him."

"In the middle of a performance?"

"Well, you know what an old pro he is... was. Nothing fazed him." No need to ask how Barnaby knew precisely when. Act II spoke for itself. "Or so we thought."

"But my God—the effect!"

"We didn't take his ego into account, you see. He's like Harold. Sees himself as a prince... or a king. And Kitty belonged to him. No one else was allowed to touch."

"Lèse-majesté."

"He went white, didn't he, Clive?"

"Quite white."

"And his eyes blazed. It was really frightening. Like being a messenger in one of those Greek plays."

"Where you hand over the bad news, then they take you outside and rearrange your innards with a toasting fork."

"He got hold of my arm. I've still got the marks, look." Donald rolled back his sleeve. "And he said *who?*"

"Just the one word, *'who?'*"

"And I looked at his face and I looked at my arm and I thought, Well *I'm* not going to be the one to tell him who."

"Friendship can be taken just so far."

"Absolutely," said Barnaby, ignoring his nausea and giving an encouraging smile. "So...?"

"So I said," continued Donald, "better ask Nicholas. And before I could say another word—"

"Before either of us could say another word—"

"He'd stormed off. And I never had a chance to add, "'He's the one who knows.'"

"And we realized once we'd got down to the dressing rooms that Esslyn'd got hold of the wrong end of the stick and thought that Nico was actually the man!"

"And you didn't feel like disabusing him?"

"The place was packed, Tom." Clive sounded reproving, if not scandalized. "You don't want everyone knowing your business."

Even Troy, so impassive in his role of bag-carrier that suspects occasionally thought he had entered a period of hibernation, choked back an astonished laugh at this astounding example of doublethink. The Everards turned and studied him carefully. Clive spoke.

"He's not writing all this down, is he?"

Deidre ran on. And on. She seemed to have been running for hours. Her legs and feet ached, and a savage wind repeatedly plastered strips of soaking-wet hair over her eyes and mouth. She felt, from the soreness of her throat and totally clogged mucous membranes, that she must be crying, but so much water was pouring down her cheeks that it was impossible to be sure. Her father's now-sodden coat, still clutched to her bosom, felt as heavy as lead. She peeled her hair away from her face for the hundredth time and staggered into the doorway of McAndrew's Pharmacy. Her heart leaped in her breast, and she tried to take long, deep breaths to calm it down. She averaged about one in three, the rest being broken by deep, shuddering sobs.

She rested between the two main windows. On her left stacks of disposable diapers and Tommy Tippee teething rings all supported by surging polystyrene worms. On her right a display of carboys, cans of grape concentrate, and coils of lemon plastic tubing like the intestines of a robot. (Be Your Own Fine Wine Merchant.)

Deidre moved to the edge of the step and stared up at the arch of the black thundering sky, a soft anemone violet when she had first left home. The stars in their courses, never all that concerned with the welfare of the human race, tonight looked especially indifferent. Through the rivulets making their way down Deidre's glasses, individual stars became blurred, then elongated into hard, shining lances.

She had been running in circles. Starting in the High Street, then working outward in concentric rings. She had looked in all the shop entrances and checked Adelaide's and the Jolly Cavalier, although a public house was the last place she would normally expect to find her father. In both places bursts of laughter had followed her wild appearance and speedy withdrawal. She scurried round and round, obsessed by the idea that she was just missing him. She saw him, old and cold and drenched to the skin, just one street ahead or a hundred yards behind or even in a directly parallel path concealed only by a house or dark gathering of trees.

Twice she had called in at home, checking every room and even the garden shed. The second time she had been terribly tempted by the still faintly glowing embers in the kitchen grate to take off her wet clothes and make some tea and just sit by the fire for a while. But minutes later, she was driven out to the streets again, afraid she would never find him yet compelled by love and desperation to keep on trying.

So now she stood, her hand pressed against her pounding heart, her skin stinging under the arrowheads of rain, unable to take another step. Not knowing which way to turn. She tormented herself with pictures of her father lying in a gutter somewhere. Or huddled against a wall. No matter that, having covered every gutter and every wall, if he had been, she would have long since discovered him. The ability to think rationally vanished the moment she had stepped into the clubroom and seen the empty chair, and blind panic took its place. She pressed her face against the cold glass and stared into the window.

Once more she turned her face toward the savage constellation of stars. God was up there, thought Deidre. God with His all-seeing eye. He would know where her father was. He could direct her if He chose. She locked her fingers together and prayed, choking on half-remembered fragments of childhood incantations: "Gentle Jesus . . . now I lay me down to sleep . . . in Thee have I trusted . . . neither run into any kind of danger . . ." Numb with cold, her hands pressed against each other in an urgency of supplication as she stared beseechingly upward.

But nothing changed. If anything, the great wash of iridescent stars looked even more distant, and the milky radiance of the moon more inhumanly bright. On one of Deidre's lenses a rivulet spread sideways; the lance became a stretched grin.

She recalled her father's years of piety. His simple confidence that he was loved by his Lord. Overlooked always by that luminous spirit and safe from all harm. Slowly anger began to course through her veins, unfreezing her blood, thawing out her frozen fingers. Was this to be his reward for years of devotion? To be allowed to slide into madness, then abandoned and left to caper about in the howling wind and rain like some poor homeless elemental? A wave of anguish swept over her. Followed by feelings of fury directed at a God she was no longer sure even existed. She stepped out of her shelter into the torrential rain and shook her fist at the heavens.

"You!" she screamed. "You were supposed to be looking after him!"

The police escort, alerted by the constable outside the Latimer, had just missed Deidre several times. Now, Policewoman Audrey Brierley gave her companion a nudge and said, "Over there."

Deidre had stopped yelling by the time they got out, and just stood with sad resignation awaiting their approach. Very gently they persuaded her into the car and took her home.

After showing in Tim and Avery, Troy pointedly moved his chair several feet away. Then he sat, legs protectively crossed, giving off waves of masochistic fervor, his breathing ostentatiously shallow. One might have thought the air to be thick with potentially effeminate spores, a careless gulp of which might transform him from a sand-kicker supreme to a giggling, girlish wreck.

Avery, aware of the antagonism, typically became overhelpful, even ingratiating. Tim calmly shifted his chair so that his back was toward the sergeant and ignored him throughout the interview. In reply to Barnaby's opening question, they agreed they had arrived on the half, gone up to the clubroom, and had a glass of Condrieu accompanied by Nicholas, who'd had a bitter lemon. Then they'd drifted around to the dressing rooms in what Tim called, "a whirl of insincere effusion and fake goodwill." They did not touch the razor or notice anyone else doing so. They entered the box at ten to eight and stayed there.

"You came out at the intermission, surely?"

"Well, no," said Avery.

"Not even for a drink?"

"We have our own wine. Tim won't drink Roo's Revenge."

"I was perhaps mistaken then...?" Barnaby's voice trailed off mildly.

"Oh! I did dash to the loo," said Tim. "Once the coast was clear."

"Yes. Splendid lighting."

"Our swan song."

"Was that the actors' loo off the wings or the public?" asked Barnaby.

"The actors'. There was a queue in the clubroom."

"Can you think of any reason," continued Barnaby, "why anyone would wish to harm Esslyn?"

Avery started to flutter, like a young bird trying to get off the ground. Fatally he glanced at Troy, receiving in return a look of such poisonous dislike that it took him a full five minutes to recover. Nervously he rushed into speech. "He wasn't an easy person. Expected everyone to defer all the time, and most of us did. Except for Harold, of course. I quite liked him myself—"

"Oh, for heaven's sake, Avery!" interrupted Tim. "We're both in the clear. We were in the box. There's no need to be such a bloody toady."

Avery looked disconcerted, then relieved. "I hadn't thought of that. 'Phew,' as they say." He mopped his forehead with an emerald-green Paisley hankie. "Well, if that's the way of it, I don't mind admitting that I thought Esslyn was an absolute shit. And so did everyone else."

Tim laughed and felt the blade of Troy's attention in the small of his back. Barnaby said, "Some more than others, perhaps?"

"People often weren't bold enough to show it."

"Or careless enough."

"Pardon?" Avery looked puzzled but willing, like a puppy who hasn't quite got the point of a trick but is prepared to give it a try.

"He means," said Tim dryly, "that this was probably some time in the planning."

Troy resented the speed of this connection. His own thought processes, though he liked to think he got there in the end, were less wing-footed. Queers were bad enough, he thought, stabbing at the page with his ball-point, but clever queers ...

"You wouldn't like to make a guess who is responsible?"

"Certainly not," said Tim.

"Avery?"

"Oh ..." As if called upon unexpectedly to make a speech, Avery half rose in his seat, then sank back again. "I'd have thought Kitty. I mean, she can't have enjoyed being married to Esslyn. He was over twice her age and about as much fun as a night out with the tontons macoutes. And of course they were heading for trouble as soon as the baby came."

"Oh? Why was that?"

"Esslyn would have been so jealous. He couldn't bear not to be the center of attention, and babies need an awful lot of looking after. At least," he added, it seemed to Barnaby a trifle wistfully, "so I understand."

"You knew she was having an affair?"

"So Nicholas told us." Avery blushed and looked rather defiantly across at his partner. "And I, for one, don't blame her."

Neither of them could think of anything else at the moment that might be of help, so Barnaby let them go, turning to his sergeant as the door closed and saying, "Well, Troy. What do you think?"

Troy knew that it was not his opinion of homosexuals that was being solicited. There had been a particularly repulsive example of the species in a case the previous year at Badger's Drift, and Troy's suggestions as to how the man's activities might be curtailed had been very frostily received. His chief was funny like that. Hard as iron in many ways. Harder than the iron men who thought they could never be broken and were now serving their time. Yet he had these peculiar soft spots. Wouldn't come out and condemn things that everyone knew to be rotten. Probably his age, thought Troy. You had to make allowances.

"Well, sir—I can't think of any reason why either of them should have been involved. Unless the dead man was queer, and that's why his missus screwed around. But from what I've heard, he seemed to have had a steady stream of tarts on the go."

Barnaby nodded. "Yes. I don't think his heterosexuality is in question."

"And those Everards, just slimy little time-servers."

"That seems to be the general opinion. Right—let's have Nicholas."

The sergeant paused on his way out. "What shall I tell that little fat geezer? Every time I go in and it's not for him, he nearly wets himself."

"Tell him"—Barnaby grinned—"tell him the dame always comes down last."

*   *   *

Scenes of crime had worked their way through the wings and were now tackling the stage. To save time, Colin and David Smy had been released and told to present themselves at the station the next morning. Barnaby was interviewing Nicholas.

He had always liked the boy, and quickly became aware that Nicholas was enjoying the drama of the situation while feeling rather ashamed of himself for doing so. Which, thought Barnaby, was one up on certain other members of the company, who had taken in the enjoyment while stopping well short of the shame. Having ascertained that Nicholas knew and saw nothing in relation to the tampering with the razor, Barnaby asked if he could think of any reason why anyone would wish to harm Esslyn.

"You've never acted with him, have you?" said Nicholas, with a strained laugh. He was blushing with nerves and anxiety.

"I advise you to keep facetious remarks like that to yourself," said Barnaby. "A man has died here tonight."

"Yes . . . of course. I'm sorry, Tom. It was just nerves. Panic, I suppose."

"What have you got to be panicky about?"

"Nothing!"

Barnaby paused for a moment, letting his impassive gaze rest on Nicholas. Then he exchanged a look with Sergeant Troy. Anything could have been read into that look. Nicholas, already a bundle of quivering apprehension, felt his spine turn to jelly.

Barnaby could not have seen (no one could have seen) what had happened to him onstage under the table. But if he had, he would never believe the attack to be entirely unmotivated. Who would? And if Esslyn appeared to have a reason for attacking Nicholas, might Nicholas not be supposed to have a reason for killing Esslyn? How airy-fairy now, thought Nicholas, did his reasoning seem that the other man was temporarily mad. Nicholas could see himself drawn into a whole area of emotional muddle and mess with questions and counterquestions all under that basilisk eye. (Could this be old Tom?) Thank God no one else had seen the confrontation. All he had to do was not get rattled and he'd be fine.

"What have you done to your hand?"

"What hand?"

"Let's have a look." An irritated grunt. "The other one, Nicholas."

Nicholas held out his hand. Barnaby regarded it silently. Troy allowed himself a low whistle.

"Nasty," said the chief inspector. "How did you manage that?"

"Stung."

"What by?"

"A wasp."

"A wasp's nest in the wings? There's novelty."

"I did it yesterday."

"Ah." Barnaby smiled and nodded, as if he found this suspiciously unsound explanation quite satisfactory, then said, "I understand it was you who started the rumor of Kitty's infidelity."

"It wasn't a rumor," retorted Nicholas hotly. "I know I was wrong to tell Avery, and I'm very sorry, but it wasn't a rumor. I actually saw her in the lighting box with David Smy."

"You're sure?"

"Yes. They were the only two people in the building."

"Apart from yourself."

"Well . . . of course."

"So we only have your word for it that anyone was with Kitty."

"She'd hardly have been reeling and writhing about up there on her own."

"But she might have been there with you."

"*Me!*"

"Why not? I'd have thought you were a much more likely contender than David." Nicholas looked more trapped than flattered.

"Why on earth would I want to tell tales about myself? It doesn't make sense."

"You might have wanted things out in the open."

"That's nonsense."

"What happened to your hand, Nicholas?"

"I *told* you."

"Forget the wasps. It's November, not mid-July. What happened to your hand?"

"I don't remember. . . ."

"All right. What happened to your thumb?"

"A splinter." Nicholas seized gladly at this opportunity to give a brief and truthful reply.

"When?"

"Tonight."

"How?" Barnaby's look became more concentrated, and Nicholas closed his eyes against the glare.

"I've forgotten . . ."

"Nicholas." Nicholas opened his eyes. The glare was muted now. Tom looked slightly more like his old self. Nicholas, who hadn't realized he was holding his breath, let it out gratefully; his backbone unjelled a little; his shoulders relaxed.

"Yes, Tom?"

"Why did you believe that Esslyn was trying to kill you?"

Nicholas gasped as if a pail of cold water had been thrown in his face. He struggled to regain his equilibrium and formulate a sensible reply. At the moment his brain seemed unraveled, nothing but kaleidoscopic fragments. All he could do was stall.

"What?" He tried a light laugh. It came out a strangled croak. "Where on earth did you get that idea?" Rosa. Of course. He had forgotten Rosa. Tom had stopped looking like his old self. He spoke.

"I've been sitting in this chair for a very long time, Nicholas. And I'm getting very tired. You start messing me about, and you'll find yourself in the slammer. Got that?"

Nicholas swallowed. "Yes."

"Right. The truth, then."

"Well . . . my hand . . . he did that with his rings. Turned them all facing inward and squeezed tight. Then, near the end of the play when I crawl under the table, he came after me. His cape cut all the light off. I was trapped. Then he tried to strangle me. . . ." Nicholas trailed lamely off. Barnaby leaned forward and studied his lily-white throat. "Oh—he didn't actually touch me."

"I see," said the chief inspector. "He tried to strangle you. But he didn't actually touch you."

Nicholas fell silent. How could he convey the feelings he had experienced during those dreadful minutes when, half-paralyzed with fear, he had shrunk away from Esslyn's jackal breath and groping, bony fingers. He stumbled into speech, explaining about cutting a page and a half and bringing Kitty on.

"And you really believe that it was only her entrance that stopped him attacking you?"

"I did then . . . yes."

"But temporarily?"

"I'm sorry?"

"Obviously anyone really determined balked at one attempt will look for an opportunity to make a second."

"That didn't occur to me. I just felt that if only I could get offstage, I'd be safe."

"You really expect me to believe that?"

"I know it sounds unlikely, Tom."

"It sounds bloody ridiculous! How much more likely that you come off frightened and angry. Take the razor, nip off to the loo, remove the tape, and bingo! You get him before he gets you. Problem solved."

"*That's not true.*"

"Cop a plea of self-defense," said Barnaby cheerfully, "get off with three years."

"No!"

"Why go straight to the props table?"

"I just sat down for a second. I felt shaken. I'd got this splinter. It hurt like hell. I went down to the men's dressing room." Nicholas could hear the sentences clattering out through chattering teeth. Each one less convincing than the one before.

"Anyone see you?"

"... I don't know ... yes ... Rosa ..."

"What on earth was Rosa doing in the men's dressing room?"

"She wasn't. I couldn't find any tweezers, so I went next door."

"Who was in the men's, then?"

"No one." Barnaby tutted. "But ... if I'd been messing with the razor, I'd have taken the tape off, then gone straight back, surely? To put it back before it was missed."

"Oh, I don't know. If I'd been messing with the razor, I'd have made sure I had a good excuse to be downstairs and someone saw me going about my lawful business."

"You don't think I rammed that splinter down my thumb on purpose? It was bloody agonizing." Nicholas plucked at the square of grubby Band-Aid. "Do you want to have a look?"

Barnaby shook his head, then slowly got to his feet. "See if you can rustle up some tea, Sergeant. I'm parched."

Nicholas waited for a moment and, when Barnaby made no attempt to continue the conversation, also got shakily to his feet ... "Is that all, then, Tom?"

"For now."

"D'you think"—Nicholas appeared almost to gag on the words—"I ought to find a solicitor?"

"Everyone should have a solicitor, Nicholas," said Barnaby, with gently smiling jaws. "You never know when they're going to come in handy."

It was about ten minutes later, when Nicholas was putting on his coat, that the odd thing struck him. Barnaby had not asked the first question that even the most inexpert of investigators must surely have put. And the chief inspector, as Nicholas's still twitching nerve ends could testify, was far from inexpert. He had not asked Nicholas why Esslyn would wish to kill him. There must be a reason for this very basic omission. Nicholas did not believe for a moment it was either lack of care or forgetfulness. Perhaps Barnaby thought he already knew. In which case he knows a darn sight more than I do, thought Nicholas. He decided to look into this further, and retraced his steps to the ladies' dressing room.

Long afterward, when she was able to look back with some degree of equanimity on the first night of *Amadeus* and its shocking aftermath, Deidre marveled at the length of time it had taken her to realize that there was only one place where her father felt safe and cared for when she was absent. Only one place where he could possibly be.

The day center, Laurel Lodge, was nearly a mile from the middle of town. Two custard-yellow minibuses, Phoenix One and Phoenix Two, collected the elderly and infirm at their homes and ferried them to and from the center each weekday. So Mr. Tibbs knew the way. In fact, it was not complicated. You just took the B416 as if you were going to Slough, then tapered off on a side road toward Woodburn Common. The distance could be covered in about an hour. Or less, if you were running your heart out and pacing yourself against dark, unreasoned fears.

Deidre remembered the center when she had been hunched over the electric fire in the kitchen being urged by the policewoman to swallow some hot, sweet tea and try not to worry. Now, she sat once more in the back of the Escort warmed by the drink and above all by the knowledge that the hopeless, misdirected floundering was over and that they were definitely on their way to where her father would be waiting. She struggled to keep calm, knowing that her attitude was bound to affect the situation when they met.

She couldn't help worrying, of course. For instance, the place was locked up and there was no caretaker on the premises, so Mr. Tibbs would not have been able to get in. This observation, when first made, had considerably threatened Deidre's equilibrium. For the building, thoughtfully, even lovingly designed so that its inhabitants would get the benefit of all the light and sunshine available, was made almost entirely of glass. And what if her father, frenziedly searching for Mrs. Coolidge (or Nancy Banks, who made such a fuss over him) harmed himself by hammering on those heavy slabs or, worse, seized a stone from the garden and tried to smash the doors? Suppose he then tried to squeeze through gripping the jagged raw edges . . . ?

At this point Deidre would wrench her mind from such dreadful fancies and once more wrestle her way toward comparative tranquillity. But the idea would not easily be vanquished, and when the car drew up outside Laurel Lodge, and the dark glass structure loomed apparently undisturbed, she felt a great rush of relief.

The iron gates were locked, a token restraint merely, as the grounds were surrounded by a brick wall barely a yard high. The rain had stopped, but there was still a high howling wind. As Deidre staggered across the gravel, her coat streamed out behind her and her cries of "Daddy, where are you? It's Deidre" were blown back into her mouth as soon as uttered. Constable Watson had a flashlight in his hand, and was testing all the doors and windows and bellowing "Mr. Tibbs?" in what seemed to Deidre a very authoritative, even threatening manner. He disappeared around the side of the building shining his light into each of the five transparent boxes; the workroom and kitchen, the rest room and office, the canteen. Then he came back shouting "He's not here," and Deidre, uncomprehending, yelled back, "Yes, yes . . . somewhere."

She waved at the surrounding garden, and the man followed the movement with his flashlight. The beam swept an arc of brilliant light over the surrounding lawns and shrubbery. A band of green-gold conifers, waving and soughing like the sea, leaped into sight, then vanished as the flashlight moved on. The flower beds were empty brown sockets, and the shrubs that gave the place its name creaked in the bitter whirling wind. (Deidre had always hated the laurels. They were so coarse and melancholic, and their leathery spotted leaves made her think of the plague.)

She seized PC Watson's arm, gasped, "We must search," and started pulling him toward the nearest dark mass of shrubbery. He resisted, and Deidre, turning back, was just about to redouble her efforts when the blistering roar of the wind ceased. The strife-torn trees rustled and groaned for a few moments more, then settled into silence.

Surprisingly—for they were half a mile from the nearest habitation—a dog barked. This was followed by another sound, which, although muffled by the hedge of Leylandii conifers, was unmistakably a human voice. It was calling out, not in any panic-stricken way but with a sonorous, tolling necessity, like a town crier. Deidre moaned, "The lake!," and flew in the general direction from which the recitations had come. Her companion followed, trying to light her with his flashlight, but she was running so fast and zigzagging so wildly back and forth that he kept losing her. Once she tripped, fell into a flower bed, and scrambled up, her hands and clothes plastered with mud.

In fact, the lake was not a lake at all but a reservoir. A vast natural hollow that had been extended and shaped into a rectangle, then edged with masonry and planted all about with reeds and other vegetation. People were allowed to sail on it in the summer, and it was home to a large variety of birds and small mammals. Nearby was a concrete building surrounded by a high wire fence with a sign attached. It showed a yellow triangle with a jagged arrow and a man lying down and read DANGER OF DEATH. KEEP OUT. Just as Deidre arrived, the moon, so white it appeared almost blue in the icy air, sailed serenely out from behind a bank of dark cloud. It illuminated an astonishing sight.

Mr. Tibbs was standing rigidly upright in an oarless rowing boat in the very center of the reservoir. His arms were flung wide and, as his fingers were almost precisely aligned with the perfect circle of the reflected moon, he seemed to be holding a new, mysterious world in the palm of his hand. His trousers and shirt were torn, his hair stuck out wildly in all directions, and his forearms and chest were scratched and bleeding. But his face as he stared upward was stamped with such ecstatic bliss that it was as if he saw streams of celestial light pouring from the very gates of paradise.

Mr. Tibbs had an audience of one. A rough-haired, rather shabby brown-and-white mongrel with a plumed tail. He sat bolt upright, his head cocked to one side in an attitude of strained attention, his ears pricked. He paid no attention when the others crashed into view, but kept his eyes (brown and shiny as beechnuts) firmly fixed on the figure in the boat.

"I saw a mighty angel come down from heaven!" cried Mr. Tibbs. "Clothed with a cloud. And a rainbow was upon his head! And his face was as it were the sun. And his feet as pillars of fire!"

While the constable used his radio to organize assistance, Audrey Brierley was hanging on to a struggling Deidre. "We're getting reinforcements, love," she said urgently. "And an ambulance. They'll be here in no time. *Please* calm down. There's nothing you can do. If you get in there, that'll be two people we'll have to pull out. Twice the trouble, twice the risk. Now you don't want that, do you?" Deidre stood still then. "Good girl. Try not to worry. He'll be cold and wet, but he's in no real danger."

"If any man have an ear, let him hear," clarioned Mr. Tibbs. Then he flung out his arm in a wide sweep encompassing his human audience of three, the concrete hut, and the scrupulously attentive canine, and fell into the water.

Deidre screamed, Policewoman Brierley hung on anew, and Constable Watson peeled off his heavy tunic, got rid of his boots, and dived in. He kicked out with great difficulty (his trousers were immediately saturated), cursing the fate that had put him on late turn. He attempted a strong crawl toward the dark outline of the boat, and each time he turned his head, a little of the water, freezing cold and tasting richly of mud and iron, slopped into his mouth. He grabbed what he thought was his quarry, only to find himself clutching a huge skein of slimy weed. He swam further in. On his limited horizon the water lapped and bobbed against the sky. Mr. Tibbs's descent had fractured the immaculate circle of the moon, and it now lay in broken bars of silver around the policeman's head. He could hear wails from Deidre interspersed with barks from the dog, which, now that the declamation had ceased and the action had started, was running excitedly round in circles.

The policeman reached Mr. Tibbs, hooked an arm around the old man's neck, and turned him around. To the anguished Deidre, wringing her hands on the bank, her father seemed to spin with graceful ease, but to Jim Watson it was like hauling a hundred-pound sack of potatoes. Thank God, he thought, feeling his arms wrenching in their sockets, the old man wasn't thrashing about. Indeed, Mr. Tibbs seemed quite unaware that there was any danger in his position at all. He drifted beatifically, cruciformly, on his back. With his rigid, unnatural smile and spreading white hair, he looked like the corpse of a holy man floating in the Ganges. PC Watson plodded on. His arm was almost beating the water in his efforts to keep them both afloat.

Then Mr. Tibbs decided he had had enough and announced his approach to the next world. "We are coming, Lord," he cried, and made the sign of the cross, poking PC Watson savagely in the eye.

"Christ!" exclaimed the unfortunate constable as an agonizing pain exploded behind his forehead. Mr. Tibbs, no doubt encouraged by this sign of solidarity, twisted himself out of the policeman's grasp, placed his hands on his rescuer's shoulders, and sank them both. Jim Watson held his breath, kicked his way violently to the surface, took a fresh lungful of air, and dived again, bringing up Mr. Tibbs.

"Ohhh..." wailed Deidre. "We must *do* something."

"He'll be all right." PW Brierley sounded more confident than she felt. The two pale faces were still a long way from the edge.

"Can't you go in and help?"

"Then there'd be two of us round his neck."

"I thought everyone in the police had to be able to swim."

"Well they don't," snapped Audrey Brierley, unpleasantly aware that her uniform was wet and filthy, her hat lost somewhere in the bushes, her tights in shreds, and that she was screamingly, ragingly, desperately dying for a pee. She moved slightly forward, extending her fingertips another inch. The inch that might make all the difference. She said, "Hang onto my legs."

The dog, as if sensing that the situation was now completely out of his control, had crouched quietly down and was looking back and forth from the couple on the edge to the couple in the water with increasing degrees of anxiety.

PC Watson had been unable to seize Mr. Tibbs with his former neat precision and, having awkwardly grabbed at his shoulder, was now lugging rather than towing him. The policeman's muscles ached almost beyond endurance with the double effort of trying to steer them both to the bank and keep Mr. Tibbs's head above the water. Also, the old man's benign attitude had become transformed, no doubt due to his being snatched from the jaws of death against his will, to one of extreme truculence. He flailed his arms and legs about, and gave little wheezy hoots of crossness. Kevin Lampeter, the ambulance driver, said afterward it was as if someone were trying to drown a set of bagpipes. He arrived just after the police reinforcements, who had brought a coil of rope and had drawn PC Watson and his burden to safety.

Deidre immediately flung herself on her father, supporting him and calling his name over and over again. But he shrank away as if from an unkind stranger. The ambulance men persuaded him onto a stretcher, and the bedraggled group limped, staggered, or, in the case of the dog, trotted briskly toward the waiting vehicle. The wall was negotiated with far less ease than previously. PC Watson, a blanket around his shoulders, climbed heavily into the back of the ambulance, and Mr. Tibbs, all the light fled from his countenance, went next. The dog, attempting to follow, was sternly rebuffed.

"You'll have to take him up front."

"Oh, but he's not—" said Deidre, bewildered. "I mean. . . . I don't know. . ."

"If you could hurry it up, please, dear. The sooner we get the old man to a hospital, the better."

Deidre climbed into the cab, but the dog had got there first. When she sat down, he bounded onto her lap, unfurled his plume tail, wrapped it neatly around his hindquarters, and stared intently out of the window all the way to Slough.

Kitty settled herself composedly. She inspected her pretty face, flirted her curls a bit, and accepted a cup of tea from Sergeant Troy with a look that was as good as a wink and then some. Barnaby assumed her sangfroid to be genuine. Given her present position as suspect number one, this argued either great cunning, absolute innocence, or absolute stupidity. Of the three, Barnaby was inclined to favor the latter. He started with formal condolences.

"A terrible business this, Kitty. You must be dreadfully upset."

"Yeah. Terrible. I am." Kitty's azure glance slid sideways and fastened, sweet and predatory, on Troy's carrot-colored crown. He looked up, met the glance, flushed, smirked, and looked down again.

"Do you have any idea who might have wanted to harm your husband?"

"Could've been any number of people. He was an absolute pig."

"I see." He was obviously not going to have the same problem with the second Mrs. Carmichael that he had had with the first. "You would include yourself among that number?"

"Definitely."

"But it wasn't you who removed the tape?"

"Only because I didn't think of it first." Bold madam, thought Troy. And get a load of those sweet little oranges.

"Did you and Esslyn arrive together?"

"Yes. I went straight to the dressing room. Got dressed and made up. All of a twitch and tremble I was. Ask Joycey."

"That was a savage bit of business in Act Two," said Barnaby, circling closer.

"Bastard. Nearly broke my back."

"I understand he'd just discovered you'd been having an affair."

"*An affair.*" Dismay, indignation, and comprehension jostled for position on Kitty's foxy face. "So that was what set him off. How the hell did that get out?"

"You were seen."

"Charming. Nosy buggers." She scowled. "Where was I seen?"

"In the lighting box."

"Oh, no." Kitty laughed then. A blowsy, coarse chuckle. "Poor old Tim. He'll be furious."

"Would you care to tell me who the man is?"

"But—" She stopped. Her face, spontaneously surprised, became smooth and guarded. "Not really. You seem to be doing very well on your own. I'm sure by this time tomorrow you'll know his name, what he has for breakfast, and the size of his socks. Not to mention the length of—"

"Yes, all right, Kitty," interrupted Barnaby, noticing his sergeant's look of rollicking appreciation.

"In any case, it wasn't what you'd call an affair. Not a real steamer. More of a frolic . . . all very lighthearted, really."

"Did you expect your husband to see it like that?"

"I didn't expect my husband to find out, for godsake!"

"Who do you suppose told him?"

"His little muckrakers, I should think. They're never happier than when they're turning over a nice big stone and mixing up the ooze. He relied on them for all the juicy bits."

"I understand that after this violent scene onstage, you rested for a while in the wings—"

"Hardly for a while."

"—next to the props table. In fact, almost on top of the tray with the bowl of soap and the razor."

"I was only there a second."

"A second is all you would need," said Barnaby. "It's obvious that whoever messed with the razor took it away to do so. And almost the only place where it could have been tampered with undisturbed was a locked lavatory cubicle." His voice tightened. "I understand it was in the ladies' where Deidre found you."

"Where'd you expect her to find me? In the gents'?"

"And that you then said that if Esslyn touched you again, you would kill him." Kitty stared, suddenly whey-faced with shock.

"What a brilliant lot. Gossips. Spies. Peeping Toms. And now a bloody tipster. You wait till I see her. Little cow!"

"You mustn't blame Deidre," said the chief inspector, feeling that the least he could do was save the wretched girl from a further stream of opprobrium. "You were overheard. In the wings."

"Well? So what?" Kitty was quickly regaining her balance. "You saw what happened onstage. What d'you think I'd say? We must do this more often? In a pig's eye."

Her voice was steely and laced with bravado. Barnaby, remembering the coquettish, adoring glances directed at her husband and her other cute wriggling little ways, could only reflect wryly on the commonly held assumption that Kitty couldn't act for beans.

"Anyway," she continued, her eyes bright and astute, "if I'd been in the loo taking the tape off, I'd hardly start shouting to the world that I was thinking of killing him."

"Stranger things have happened. You could have been perpetrating a double bluff. Assuming that we would think exactly that."

"Oh, come on, Tom. You know me. I'm not that clever."

They stared each other out. Kitty, her cornflower blue eyes dark with anger, was thinking she'd find out who had spotted her in the lighting box, and when she did, they'd wish they'd never been born. Barnaby was wondering if she had genuinely not known the reason for Esslyn's sudden explosion of rage. Had she really been sitting in the scene dock for (he checked his watch) the best part of two hours with Nicholas, also the recipient of Esslyn's violence, without coming to any conclusions? They must surely have discussed it. He supposed if the Everards had kept their mouths shut, this could be the case. Was Kitty a bored young wife playing around? he wondered. Or was she a calculating harpy who had snagged a financially secure older husband and then wished to be rid of him? Was the removal of the tape an impulsive act? Or planned for some time? If so, Barnaby asked himself (as he was to do over and over again in the coming days), why on earth should it be done on the first night? He became aware that Kitty was leaning forward in her seat.

"You're not sticking this on me, Tom," she said firmly.

"I have no intention of 'sticking' this on anyone, Kitty. But I intend to find out the truth. So be warned."

"I don't know what you mean. I've nothing to hide." But her cheeks colored suddenly, and she did not look at him.

"Then you've nothing to fear."

After a longish pause during which Kitty recollected herself to the extent that she was able to send a second slumberous glance in Troy's direction, she got to her feet and said, "If that's all, a person in my condition should have been in her lonely bed hours ago."

"Quite a girl," said Barnaby as the door closed behind her.

"Anybody for a gin and tonic?" murmured the sergeant, hopefully memorizing the telephone number at the top of Kitty's statement. Then he added, "Maybe they were in it together. Her and her bit of crackling."

"The thought had occurred to me. We'll see how he checks out tomorrow."

Troy scanned his notes briefly, then said, "What now, sir?"

Barnaby got up and collected his coat. "Let's go and find the big white chief."

Barnaby had hardly set foot in the scene dock before Harold, incandescent with rage, sprang before them like a greyhound in the slips. "So there you are!" he cried, as if to a pair of recalcitrant children. "How dare you leave me while one and then the other of the company is interviewed? It's not as if you aren't aware of my position. How am I supposed to keep control when they see me constantly passed over like . . . like the boot boy!"

"I'm sorry you're upset, Harold," said Barnaby soothingly. "Please . . . sit down." He indicated a rustic arbor on which dusty blue paper roses were impaled. Reluctantly, simmeringly, Harold lowered himself.

"You see," continued the chief inspector, "everyone has had a story to tell. Sometimes these are mutually supportive, sometimes they contradict each other, but what I need at the end of the day is the viewpoint of someone who knows the group through and through. Someone perceptive, intelligent, and observant, who can help me to draw all the information together and perhaps see some underlying pattern in this dreadful affair. This is why I left you until the last." He looked concernedly at Harold. "I thought you'd understand that."

"Of course, Tom. I sensed that something like that was behind it all. But I would have appreciated a discreet word. To have been kept informed."

Barnaby's look of regret deepened. Troy, sitting just to the side of Harold in a deck chair (Relatively Speaking) watched with proprietorial pleasure. You could almost hear the steam hissing out of the old geezer (or geyser, revised the sergeant wittily), and see self-importance taking its place. Next would come complacency, the most fertile ground for the forcing of revelation. (Not fear or anger, as is commonly supposed.) Troy tried to catch his chief's eye to indicate his appreciation of the maneuver, but without success. Barnaby's concentration was total.

Actors, thought the sergeant, wearing the shade of a contemptuous smile. You'd have to get up early to find one to match the D.C.I. He had as many expressions to his face and shades to his voice as a mangy dog had fleas. He could imitate the dove and the scorpion and even the donkey if he thought it would serve his ends. More than once Troy had seen him shaking his head in apparent dumb bewilderment while witnesses feeling secure in his incomprehension happily babbled on, quite missing the echo of the turnkey's tread. And he had a special smile seen only at the moment of closing in. Troy practiced that smile sometimes at home in the bathroom mirror and frightened himself half to death. Now, Barnaby was congratulating Harold on the excellence of his production.

"Thank you, Tom. Not an easy play, but I pride myself on a

challenge, as you know. I wasn't *altogether* delighted with Act One, but the second half was a great improvement. So intense. And then to end like that . . ." He clicked his tongue. "And of course any sort of screw-up, people immediately blame the director."

"I'm afraid that's the case," agreed Barnaby, marveling at Harold's grasp of the essentials. "You were hardly backstage at all, I believe?"

"Not really. Went through on the five to wish them all *bonne chance*—well, you were directly behind me, I believe? Then again in the intermission to tell them to pull themselves together."

"And you saw no one behaving suspiciously in the wings?"

"Of course not. If I had, I would have stopped them. We had five more performances, after all. And Saturday's sold out."

"Do you have any idea who might have tampered with the razor?"

Harold shook his head. "I've thought and thought, Tom, as you can imagine. There might be someone in the company who's got it in for me but . . ."—he gave a perplexed sigh—"I can't possibly think why."

"Or Esslyn."

"Pardon?"

"It could be said that Esslyn had been sabotaged just as successfully as your production."

"Oh. Quite." Harold pursed his lips judiciously, implying that although this was a completely new slant on the situation, it was not one he was prepared to reject out of hand. "You mean, Tom, it might have been something personal?"

"Very personal, I'd say." Troy, almost alight with enjoyment, leaned back too hard in his deck chair and broke the strut. By the time he had sorted himself out, Barnaby had reached the four-dollar question. "Did you have any reason for wishing Esslyn Carmichael harm?"

"*Me?*" squeaked Harold. "He was my leading man. My star! Now, I shall have to start all over again, training Nicholas."

"What about his relationships with the rest of the company?"

"Esslyn didn't really have relationships. His position made that rather difficult. I have the same problem. To hold authority, one must keep aloof. He always had a woman in tow, of course."

"Not since his recent marriage, surely?"

"Perhaps not. I'm sure we'd all know. I'll say this in Esslyn's favor—he never attempted to conceal his infidelities. Not even during his years with Rosa."

Quite right, thought Troy, flicking over his page. What's the point of having it if you don't flaunt it?

"She seemed very distressed, I thought."

"Rosa could always weep to order."

"In fact," insinuated the chief inspector, "far more so than the present incumbent."

"Ah." In an ecstasy of enlightenment Harold slapped himself about the jowls like S. Z. (Cuddles) Sakall. "In other words, *cherchez la femme*. Could be, could be. He was the sort to make enemies, mind you. Selfish to the core."

Barnaby had always believed it was possible to judge the love and respect in which the newly deceased was held by the width of the gap between the immediate, almost inevitable reaction of shock and distress (even if only on the "every man's death diminishes me" principle) and the point at which the dead party's failings could be discussed with something approaching relish. In Esslyn Carmichael's case, the gap was so narrow it would hardly have accommodated one of Riley's whiskers.

"But in spite of that, you got on with him?"

"I get on with everyone, Tom."

"Personally and professionally?"

"They're intertwined. Esslyn didn't always accept my suggestions easily, but there was never any question of compromise. There can only be one leader."

Harold's disdain for accurate introspection and his airbrushed memory were certainly working overtime tonight, observed Barnaby. Or perhaps he genuinely believed that Esslyn had dutifully carried out the instructions of his imperator—which argued a hazy grip on reality, to say the least.

"Returning to the question of motive, you have to remember," continued Harold, borrowing the obituarist's subtle shorthand when describing arrogant insensitives, "that he didn't suffer fools gladly. But then"—a smug smile peeped through the silvery boscage—"neither do I."

When Harold had been dismissed and left, apparently without noticing that he had neither given an overview nor pulled any threads together, Barnaby returned to the now scrupulously investigated and empty wings and took the reel of tape from a box on Deidre's table. He wound it twice around the handle of her microphone, then removed it by slicing it through with a Stanley knife. He gave it to Troy. "Chuck that down the toilet." Then he stood listening to the repeated flushings and gushings till his sergeant returned.

"Can't be done, chief."

"Tried the ladies' as well?"

"And upstairs. And the disabled."

"Well, the search proved none of them were concealing it. Scenes of crime didn't turn it up. So . . ."

"Out the window?"

"Right. And with this wind and rain, it could be halfway to Uxbridge by now. Still, we might be lucky. It could've caught up somewhere. Have a look in the morning. I've had enough for one night."

As they made their way up through the deserted auditorium, Troy said, "Why did you leave him till last, sir? Old fat 'n' hairy?"

"I don't like the way he speaks to people." Then, when Troy still looked inquiring: "He thinks everyone's there to do his bidding. Takes them for granted, gives them no thanks, and talks to them like dirt. I didn't think it would do him any harm to be at the end of the queue for once."

"Think it'll do him any good?"

"No. Too far gone."

"I think he's round the twist."

"All theatricals are round the twist, Troy," said Barnaby, tugging at the doors that led to the foyer. "If they weren't, they'd get out of the business and into real estate."

It seemed to take forever for Mr. Tibbs to be seen by all the people who had to have a look at him. Deidre gave the few details that were to be entered on his admission card, and was then told to wait in reception. She had been there over an hour when a nurse came and said she could see her father for a sec just to say good night.

Mr. Tibbs lay, neatly swaddled, in the iron rectangle of his hospital bed. He did not respond to her greeting, but stared straight ahead humming something atonal. His cheeks were flushed bright red.

"Nurse!" called Deidre, anxiety overcoming her innate wish not to be any trouble. "I think he's got a fever."

"We've given him something for that. He'll be asleep soon."

The nurse bustled up with a steel bedpan and started drawing the curtains of the bed next door. "You'll have to go now."

"Oh." Deidre backed away. "Yes. I'm sorry. I'll ring in the morning."

"Make it latish. The rounds will be over then, and we can tell you how he's been and where he's going."

"Won't he stay here then?"

"No. This is just emergency admissions."

"I see . . . well . . . good night then," said Deidre to some orange folds of fabric. "And thank you."

After a final look at her father, who already seemed to be part of another world, Deidre drifted back to the reception area. A young man was in the middle of a conversation, phone clamped to his ear supported by his shoulder. He said "Just a sec" to Deidre and went on talking. "Don't talk to me about Miss Never on Sunday," he said. "I saw her in the Boltons last night and she spent every other second in the john." He listened for a moment, sucking his cheeks. "If promises were piecrusts, dear, she'd be in crumbs up to her armpits." He was very dark. Deidre wondered if he could possibly be Italian. After he had hung up, she explained that she was now ready to go home.

"No can do, I'm afraid. Transport's for emergencies only."

"B . . . b . . . but . . ." Deidre stammered in her distress. "I live miles away."

"That's as may be, love. What would we do if there was a pileup on the motorway and you were out joyriding in the ambulance?"

"You've got more than one, surely. . . ."

"Sorry. Those are the rules."

Deidre stared blankly at him. In the close, hot air of the vestibule, her still-damp clothes started to steam. She was swaying from exhaustion. Now that her father was being safely cared for, all her emotions—fear, love, terror, despair—tumbled away. She was benumbed almost to the point of nonexistence.

"The buses start up at seven . . . you could have a little shuteye." He felt sorry for her, no doubt about that. She looked really zonked out. "If it was up to me, dear . . ." He always said that, it made them feel better. Made him feel better, too, come to that. "Or I could call you a taxi."

"A taxi." It wasn't a question. She just repeated it like a child learning a lesson. Deidre struggled to think. The machinery of memory, like all her other physchological and physiological functions, seemed to have ground to a halt. A taxi meant money. She put her hands carefully into each of her pockets. She had no money. With great effort she forced herself to print a memory on the blank screen of her mind. She saw herself running from the Latimer. She was wearing her coat, and her hands were empty. That meant her bag must still be at the theater. So (her brows fretted with the effort of working out the next step) if she took a cab there, the driver could wait while she picked up her bag, then she could pay him and he could drive her home. Deidre, her face gray with exhaustion, labored over the details of this simple plan but could find no flaw.

"Yes," she said. "A taxi."

"Be double time," said reception, cheerfully dialing. "After twelve, you see."

Deidre declined the offer to relax on a settee while she was waiting, feeling that once she sat down, she would simply keel over and never get up. As it was, she could not understand how her legs supported her body. They felt as if they were made of broken pieces of china insecurely glued together. The car came almost immediately. The driver, a middle-aged man, regarded Deidre with some alarm.

And indeed she was an alarming sight. Her face was deathly pale, her eyes—dull and staring—were black-ringed. Her damp clothes showed patches of mud, and somewhere during the course of the evening she had lost a shoe. She was also (the cabbie could not help noticing) minus a handbag. This fact, combined with her bizarre appearance—he had already decided she was some sort of hippie—gave rise to the quite natural apprehension that his fare might not be forthcoming. Once reassured on this point, he offered his arm, which she did not ignore as much as not seem to see, and they left the building together.

"Animals is extra," he said when they reached the car.

"What?"

"He is yours, ain't he?" The man nodded at a small dog who had been patiently waiting outside the main doors and was now trotting alongside.

"Oh..." Deidre hesitated, looking down at the creature. The gargantuan task of trying to explain her lack of comprehension as to his background, ownership, and reason for being here was quite beyond her. "Yes."

The roads were almost deserted, and they covered the twelve miles to Causton in under twenty minutes. It was not until they drew up outside the Latimer that the large snag in Deidre's plan became apparent. There was no sign of life. The building was dark, the policeman outside had gone. Deidre stood on the pavement, having realized that not only were her house keys in her bag, so also were her keys to the Latimer.

The cabbie, all his suspicions reawakened, tooted his horn. Deidre moved toward the theater noticing as she did so a tall, gangling scarecrow of a figure with wild spiraling hair suddenly reflected in the glass. She pushed on one of the doors. It didn't move. She leaned on it then with both hands, more for support than anything else, and felt it shift slightly. Then she pushed with all her might. It was like trying to roll a giant boulder up a hill. Deidre stepped into the darkened foyer. Surely, she thought, there must be someone still here, or why would the door be unlocked? Perhaps, with all the hubbub (light years ago, it now seemed), they'd just been forgotten. At least she would be able to get her bag. She regarded the dim outline of the steps leading, like a cliff face, to the auditorium, and the immense reaches of carpet to be covered before she could start to climb.

She took the first step. And tottered two more. Then light flooded the foyer as the auditorium doors swung open and two figures emerged. Dazzled, Deidre saw the still-moving doors fly slowly up into the air. The steps followed. Then she felt the sudden hard thud of the floor against the back of her head.

EXIT,
Pursued by a Bear

The Barnabys were at breakfast. Cully was enjoying some fresh pineapple and Greek yogurt. Barnaby was squaring up to the wobbly challenge of a half-cooked egg, and Joyce was putting two sprigs of *virburnum bodnantense* in a glass vase on a tray.

She was feeling very tired, but much calmer than she had expected. She was still living with the moment when Esslyn turned and, with the thin red weeping line across his throat, had put his hands on her shoulders and stared disbelievingly into her eyes. But she had talked about it over and over again to Cully, which had helped, and then, when he had finally come home at two o'clock bringing Deidre, to Tom. But as for offering any constructive ideas as to the reason for that terrible death, or on how or when the tape could have been removed, Joyce was as uninformative as the rest of the company. She felt keenly frustrated that this should be so. This was the first time in their long and happy marriage that she had been directly involved in one of her husband's cases and in a position where, it might be supposed, she could be of some help. But waiting in the scene dock, intensely aware of her companions, when she had brought each of their names individually to the forefront of her mind and tried to imagine that it belonged to a murderer, all she experienced were mounting feelings of incredulity. She could not believe that even the hateful oily Everards could have set in motion such a formidably final train of events.

Tom had been neither surprised nor disappointed at her response. He knew how much she had to do during the course of the play and how little time was spent standing around and had

had no expectations in that direction. What he hoped for was that, in casting her mind back over the weeks of rehearsal and clubroom conversation as he suggested, Joyce might remember a remark, an expression, a reaction that, put into the later context of Esslyn's demise, might prove to be significant. Now, tuning in once more to the early morning conversation (still about *Amadeus*), she heard Cully say that at least Harold couldn't complain on his first night about lack of verismo. Unbowed under her father's criticism that such a remark showed a certain lack of sensitivity, she then asked if he thought the culprit was the merry widow in cahoots.

"Possibly."

"I bet it is. Like in all those *films noirs. The Milkman Always Comes Twice.*"

"Don't be rude, Cully."

"Alternatively," said Barnaby, shaking out a tablet, "it seems to be even-stevens on Diedre."

"Poor Diedre," Joyce said automatically. Then she tutted at her husband's pill-taking, which she insisted on regarding as an amusing affectation.

"You ought to stop saying that. Everybody ought."

"What do you mean, dear?" asked her mother.

"This persistent attitude toward her as an object of pathos."

"It's understandable," argued Joyce. "She's had a very sad life. You've had all the advantages. You should be kinder."

"Since when does having all the advantages make you kind? You and Dad are sorry for her. That's awful—so patronizing. Pitying people isn't a kindness. It makes them supine. And those who seek it don't deserve respect." Barnaby looked at his bright, beautiful, clever daughter as she continued, "Last time I was home, Mum was going on about her losing some weight and getting contact lenses. I mean, it's so sentimental. The Cinderella bit. Deidre's quite interesting and intelligent enough as she is. I should think she could wipe the floor with the lot of them at the Latimer given half a chance. She's got a grasp of stage management that would put Cardinal Wolsey to shame." She added, as her mother took down a jar of instant coffee, "Don't give her that, for godsake. It's going to be hard enough waking up this morning as it is. Use one of my filters."

Joyce took one of the Marks and Spencer individual coffee filters out of its box and set it on a cup. Cully always brought what she called protective rations home with her. One of the reasons her father looked forward to her visits so much. Now, she said, "Could I have the vegetable lasagne tonight? It's in the freezer."

"I'm doing a *bouillabaisse*."

"Oh, Ma—don't be silly."

"It's all in here." Joyce indicated a book lying open near the breadboard. "Very plainly explained. I'm sure I shall cope perfectly."

Cully finished her pineapple, crossed to her mother, and picked up the book. "*Floyd on Fish?* It's not like you to be seduced by the telly."

"Oh, I didn't buy it. Harold gave it to me."

"*Harold?*" said her husband. "Harold wouldn't give you the fluff from his navel."

"He didn't buy it, either. It turned up at the theater anonymously. *Toast...*"

Cully snatched the bread from the jaws of the toaster in the nick of time, saying, "What a peculiar thing to give to a place that doesn't sell food."

"I don't think it was for the theater. It was addressed to him personally."

"When did it arrive?" asked Barnaby.

"Oh, I don't know." Joyce put some butter in a saucer. "A few days ago." The coffee drip-dripped through the fine-meshed gauze, its fragrance mingling with the scent of the *Viburnum*.

"Let's have a look." Cully brought the book over, hissing "Burn it" in her father's ear as she put it close to the egg, which had now congealed almost to the stage where he might just feel able to put a little in his mouth. He opened the book. There was no inscription.

"Did it come through the post?"

"No. Pushed through the letter box. So Diedre said."

"Fancy." Barnaby slipped the book in his pocket.

"Tom! What about the *bouillabaisse*?"

"A delight I fear we shall all have to postpone, my love." Barnaby got up. "I'm off."

As he left, he heard his daughter say, "Have you got the phone number of that boy who played Mozart?" and Joyce reply, "Open the door, Cully."

Joyce bore the tray upstairs, put it down outside the spare room, and knocked gently.

Deidre had slept and slept. Even now, hours after she had been helped to bed after drinking a hot rum and lemon toddy, she was barely conscious. Sometimes she heard a voice, but very distantly, and occasionally chinking and chiming sounds that seemed to be part of a dream. She resisted wakefulness, already faintly aware that it was pregnant with such dismay that reaching it would make her long for oblivion again.

Joyce opened the door and crept in. She had already looked in twice, and found the girl so deeply asleep she had not had the heart to disturb her.

When Tom had brought Deidre home, she had been in a terrible state. Soaking wet and covered in mud, her face scratched and tearstained. Joyce had taken her temperature, and between them they had decided that she was simply distressed and exhausted and that there was no need to call out a doctor. Tom, when paying off the taxi, had discovered the starting point of Deidre's journey, and Joyce had already rung the hospital before breakfast, hoping to have some cheerful news with which to wake the girl. But they had been very cagey (always a bad sign) and, when she admitted she was not a close relative, simply said he was as well as could be expected.

Now, she crossed to the side of the bed and watched consciousness wipe the look of sleepy confusion from Deidre's face. Once awake, Deidre sat up immediately and cried, "I must go to the hospital!"

"I've rung them. And the gas office. I just said you were a bit off color and wouldn't be coming in for a couple of days."

"What did they say? The hospital?"

"He's doing . . . reasonably well. You can ring as soon as you've had breakfast. It's nothing too complicated." Joyce laid the tray across Deidre's knees. "Just a little bit of toast and some coffee. Oh—and you're not to worry about your dog. He's being looked after at the station."

"Joyce . . . you're so kind . . . you and Tom. I don't know what I would have done last night . . . if . . . if—"

"There, there." Joyce took Deidre's hand, thought the hell with being patronizing, and gave her a hug. "We were very glad to have the chance to take care of you."

"What lovely flowers . . . everything's so nice." Deidre lifted her cup. "And delicious coffee."

"You've Cully to thank for that. She didn't think the instant was good enough. The nightie, too."

"Oh." Deidre's face darkened. She looked down at her voluminous scarlet flanneled arms. She had forgotten Cully was home. She had known the Barnabys' daughter since the child was nine years old, and was well aware of Cully's opinion of the CADS, having heard it thoroughly bruited during her early teens. Now she was acting at Cambridge, no doubt she would be even more scathing. "I don't think I can manage any toast."

"Don't worry—you have only just woken up, after all. But I expect you would like a bath?" Joyce had done no more previously than sponge Deidre's face and hands while the girl had stood in front of the basin swaying like a zombie.

"Please. . . . I feel disgusting."

"I've put out some clothes for you. And some warm tights. I'm afraid my shoes'll be too small. But you could probably squeeze into my wellies." Joyce got up. "I'll go and run your bath."

"Thank you. Oh, Joyce—did they find out after I'd gone— the police, I mean—who had . . .?" Joyce shook her head. "I still can't believe it." Deidre's face quivered. "What a terrible night. I'll never forget it as long as I live."

"I don't think any of us will," replied Joyce. "You might like to ring the hospital while you're waiting for your bath. I've left the number by the phone."

After Joyce had gone, Deidre found her glasses, put them on, and sat on the edge of the bed staring into the dressing-table mirror. Cully's gown billowed around her like a scarlet parachute. It was the red of wounds and freshly killed meat. Hearing the water start to gush reminded Deidre of the reservoir. She gripped the edge of the bed. In her mind the two images juxtaposed: Esslyn's throat gaped anew. Blood came—a trickle, a stream, a torrent, pouring into the reservoir, turning the water crimson. Her father fell again from his boat, disappeared, and surfaced, his face shining, incarnadined. He did this over and over, like a mechanical doll. Oh, God, thought Deidre, I'm going to see those two things for the rest of my life. Every time I stop being busy. Every time I close my eyes. Every time I try to sleep. For the rest of my life. Futilely she covered her eyes with her hands.

"Hi." Deidre jumped up. Cully stood in the doorway, pencil-slim, an eel in blue jeans. She also wore a T-shirt inscribed *"Merde! J'ai oublié d'éteindre le gaz!"* "You look much nicer than I ever did in that thing, Deidre. Do keep it."

That's a dig at my size if ever I heard one, Deidre observed to herself. She replied primly, "No, thank you. I have several pairs of pajamas at home." Then she thought, what if Cully was simply trying to be kind? How brusque and ungrateful I must sound.

"Okay." Cully smiled, unoffended. She had perfect teeth, even and brilliantly white like a film star's. Deidre had read once that very white teeth were chalky and crumbled easily. It seemed a small price to pay. "I just came to say that I got some super bath oil for my birthday from France. Celandine and Marshmallow— and it's on the bathroom windowsill. Use lots—it really makes you feel nice." Cully turned to go, turned back, and hesitated.

"Terrible business, last night. I'm so sorry. About your father, I mean."

"He'll be all right," said Deidre quickly.

"I'm sure he will. I just wanted to say."

"Thank you."

"Not sorry about Esslyn, though. He was an outbreak of rabies and no mistake. If I were queen, I'd order dancing in the streets."

When Cully had gone, Deidre rang the hospital and was told that her father was resting, that he was being seen that afternoon by a specialist, and they would prefer her not to visit until the following day. On receiving the assurance that he would be told she had rung and given her love, Deidre made her way to the bathroom rather guiltily relieved that she had a whole day to rest and recover before the stress of a visit.

She measured out a careful thimbleful of *Essence de Guimauve et Chélidoine,* tipped it in, then stepped into the faintly scented water. Then, as she lay back letting go, floating away, sliding away, vanishing, her mind emptied itself of ghastly memories, and a new idea gradually, timidly drifted to the surface. It was an idea too appalling really to be given credence, yet Deidre, tensing a little with not unpleasurable alarm, braced herself to consider it.

Cully's intemperate phrases when referring to the previous night's disaster had shocked Deidre deeply. She had been brought up to believe that you never spoke ill of the dead. As a child, she had assumed that this was because, given half a chance, the dead would come back and savage you. Later she modified this apprehension to include the understanding that a) if you only said nice things about them, they might put in a good word for you when your turn came, and b) it just wasn't honorable to attack people who couldn't answer back.

Now, hesitant and half-fearful, she prepared to examine—even acknowledge—an emotion she had always prayed would be forever absent from her heart. She recalled Esslyn's behavior to his fellow actors. His condescension and spite, his indifference to their feelings, his impregnable self-esteem and swaggering coxcombry. His laughter and sneers about her father. Holding her breath, lying rigidly, fists clenched in the perfumed bath, Deidre faced, more or less boldly, a terrible new perception about herself. She had *hated* Esslyn. Yes. Hated him. And, even worse, *she was glad that he was dead.*

White-faced, she opened her eyes and stared at the ceiling. Waiting for a sign of God's displeasure. For the thunderbolt. When told as a child that every time she told a lie He got one out and it was only His all-forgiving love that stopped Him firing it off with all deliberate speed, she had tried to picture this celestial weapon of retribution, but all her young mind could come up with was the bolt on the kitchen door magnified a thousand times and painted shining bronze. Nothing even remotely similar crashed punitively through the Barnabys' bathroom ceiling.

At the recognition that it never would and that she could be glad that Esslyn was no longer in a position to cause anyone pain or distress without fear of divine retribution, a tremendous wave of something far too powerful to be called relief broke over Deidre. She lay dazed, still faintly incredulous at this new truth. She felt as if someone had removed a great yoke from her shoulders or heavy chains from her legs and feet. Any minute now, she might drift up to the unriven ceiling. She felt weak but far from helpless. She felt weak in the way the strong must sometimes do. Not endemically, but accepting the need of occasional rest and refreshment. She wished now she had eaten her toast.

After a few somnolent minutes more, she turned on the hot tap and reached for the Celandine and Marshmallow elixir. If a thimbleful had this effect, reasoned Deidre, what could half a cupful do?

Barnaby, having perused his scenes-of-crime reports and witnesses' statements, sat gazing at his office wall, lips pursed, gaze vacant, to a casual observer miles away. Troy, having seen all this before, was not deceived. The sergeant sat on one of the visitor's chairs (chrome tubes and tweed cushions) and stared out of the window at the dark rain bouncing off the panes.

He was dying for a cigarette but did not need the restraint of the no-smoking sign on the back of the door to stop him lighting up. He was used to being closeted all day with a clean-air freak. What really bugged him was that the chief had been a fifty-a-day high-tar merchant in his time. Reformed smokers (like reformed sinners) were the worst. Not content, thought Troy, with the shining perfection of their own lives, they were determined to sort out the unregenerate. And with no thought at all as to the possible side effects of their actions. When Troy thought of all that fresh cold air rushing into poor little lungs denied their protective coating of nicotine, he positively trembled. Pneumonia at the very least must be waiting around the corner. He insured himself against this eventuality by lighting up in the outer office, in the toilet, and anywhere at all the second Barnaby was off the premises. As a sop to all the haranguing, he had changed from unfiltered to filtered, flirting with Gitanes Caporal along the way. He admired the idea of a French cigarette more than the things themselves, and when Maureen had told him they stank like a polecat on the razzle he had not been sorry to give them up.

Troy had read through the statements but not the scenes-of-crimes reports. He had also been present an hour ago when the Smys were interviewed. David had arrived first and stated, in an even and unflurried manner, that he had not removed the tape from the razor or seen anyone else do so. His father had said the same, but much less calmly. He had blushed and blustered and stared all over the place. This did not mean that he was culpable. Troy was aware that many innocent people, finding themselves being formally questioned in a police station, become overwhelmed by feelings of quite unfounded guilt. Still, Smy senior had been in a state. Troy became aware that Barnaby was making a vague rumbling sound. He gathered his wits about him.

"That last word, Sergeant."

"Sir."

"'Bungled'. . . . Odd, wouldn't you say?"

"Yes. I've been thinking about that." Troy waited politely for a nod of encouragement, then continued, "Was someone supposed to do something, and they bungled? And was the throat-cutting the result? Or was it Carmichael who bungled? I mean, I assume he was doing what he should have been doing? What he did when they all . . . practiced?"

"Rehearsed. Yes. Everyone seems to agree the last scene ran as usual."

"So what could the bungle have been? I did wonder actually if he took the tape off himself."

"No. He was the last person to commit suicide."

"What I meant is, if he took it off for some cock-eyed reason of his own. Maybe to get someone into trouble. Then, in the heat of the moment—acting away with all that music and everything—just forgot. Maybe he was trying to say, "'I've bungled.'"

"A bit unlikely." Troy looked so crestfallen that Barnaby added, "I haven't come up with anything, either. But he struggled to tell us something with his dying breath. It must have a point. And a very important one, I'd say. We'll just have to poke away at it. This"—he slapped his scenes-of-crimes report sheets, "has one or two surprises. For a start, the razor, supposedly checked by Deidre and further handled by Sweeney-whoever-it-was, only has one set of prints. We'll check it out, of course, but they must be those of the murdered man. We all saw him pick it up and use it. Now as Deidre would have no reason for wiping her own off—"

"Unless, sir, she could see we'd think that. And wiped them for that reason?"

"I doubt it." Barnaby shook his head. "That argues a degree of cunning that I just don't think Deidre has. And I've known her for ten years. Apart from anything else, she has very strict ideas of right and wrong. Quite old-fashioned for someone her age."

"Well—that still leaves us plenty to play with."

Barnaby was not so sure. In spite of the large amount of people milling around both on and off the set, he believed the razor renovator would be found within the handful of people intimately known to the dead man. He thought it highly unlikely, for instance, that an evil prankster would be discovered among the youthful ASMs, although he had their statements on file should he wish to follow up the idea. Nor did he feel he was in with much of a chance with the small-part actors, three of whom had no previous knowledge of the dead man, having only joined the company for *Amadeus*. Although keeping an open mind on both these available options, Barnaby actually chose to cleave tightly to his core of hard-line suspects. Chief of whom, he surmised aloud, must be the widow.

"An armful of spontaneous combustion there, sir."

"So they say."

"And I wouldn't be surprised if the current bun might not be the husband's. Women are a faithless lot." Troy spoke with some bitterness. He had been laying none too subtle siege to Police-woman Brierley for about two years, only to see her fall the previous week to a new recruit, hardly out of his rompers before he was into hers. "And as for these actors—well... you just don't know where you stand."

"Can you expand that a bit?"

"The thing is," Troy continued, "when you usually talk to suspects, they either tell you the truth or, if they've got something to hide, they tell you lies. And on the whole you know what you're dealing with. But this lot... they're all exaggerating and swanking and displaying themselves. I mean, look at that woman he used to be married to. Getting her to answer questions was like watching Joan of Arc going to the stake. Almost impossible to know what she really felt."

"You think she wasn't genuinely distressed?"

"I just couldn't decide. I'm damn glad you knew them all beforehand."

"Just because someone displays an emotion in the most effective or even stylish manner of which they're capable doesn't mean it isn't genuine. Remember that."

"Right, chief."

"And in any case, with the exception of Joyce and Nicholas, you should be able to see through them. They're all dreadful actors."

"Oh." Troy kept his counsel. Actually he had thought the show was rather good. His disappointment had been in looking at the scenery close up. All old stuff cobbled together, painted over, and held up by what looked like old clothes props. Marvelous what a bit of illumination could do. Which reminded him. "I take it Doris and Daphne are definitely out, sir? Airy and fairy in the lighting box?"

"I'm inclined to think so. Apart from the fact there's no discernable motive, they were in the wings and dressing rooms so briefly—as these statements from the actors confirm"—he tapped the pile of forms with his hand—"and also so near to the first curtain that there would simply have been no time for tinkering. The same goes for Harold. I happened to arrive at the theater when he and his wife did. He hung up his coat and started swanning around in the foyer doing his Ziegfeld number. He was there when Cully and I went to wish the cast good luck—"

"Beautiful girl that, chief. Fantastic."

"—and came down himself a minute or two later. And we all left virtually at the same time to take our seats."

"He didn't slip into the bog?" Barnaby shook his head.

"What about the intermission?"

"Same problem with time, really. He was up in the club-room for a bit, then went backstage to give them hell for lack of verismo, so my wife says. Then went back to his seat with the rest of the audience. And anyway, not only did Harold have no discernable motive for wanting Esslyn out of the way, he had very positive reasons for wanting him to stay alive. He was the only person in the group who could tackle leading roles in a moderately competent manner. He was doing *Uncle Vanya* next."

"Who's he, sir, when he's buying a round?"

"It's a Russian play."

Troy's nod was distant. It seemed to him that you could go on for a very long time indeed before you ran out of decent English plays without putting on foreign rubbish. And Communist rubbish, at that. He tuned back into the chief inspector's gist.

"I think the next thing is to give Carmichael's house the once-over. There might be something in his effects that will give us a lead. Organize some transport, will you? I'll sort out a warrant."

Rosa had a plan. She had not revealed it to Earnest despite the fact that if the plan came off, his life would never be the same again. Time enough to spring it on him if it proved to be workable. Really, it all hinged on whether Rosa had read Kitty's character correctly. And Rosa was sure she had. Kitty had always struck her as a vapid, silly little thing, frankly on the make. A good-time girl. Now she was free, rich (unless Esslyn had been singularly spiteful in drawing up his will), and still only nineteen. What on earth, reasoned Rosa, would someone in that position want with a child?

Kitty had been in the company for two years. Never during

this time had she been heard to express the slightest interest in children. Dressing-room conversation, when touching on family matters, produced only yawns. Various offspring of CADS members backstage from time to time hardly merited a glance, let alone a kindly word. So, given this lack of interest, Rosa, like the majority of people at the Latimer, assumed that Kitty had got herself deliberately pregnant only to ensnare Esslyn. Now that he was so conveniently dispatched, surely the means of ensnarement would be nothing but a hindrance? Of course, there were those with no concern for other people's children who still, when their own arrived, found them a never-ending source of wonder and delight, but Rosa believed (or had persuaded herself to the belief) that Kitty was not of that number. And it was this persuasion that had instigated her grand design.

Since Esslyn's death, Rosa had been whirling around in a veritable hodge-podge of emotions and troubled thoughts. Beneath her affected public manner she was increasingly aware of an aching pulse of sorrow. She recalled constantly the early days of her marriage, and mourned the passing of what she now believed to be a tender and passionate love. And as she dwelt on those happier days, it was as if her imagination, newly refurbished by the recent tragedy, wiped out in one blessed amnesiac stroke the years of disillusionment, leaving her with a wholesome if slightly inaccurate picture of Esslyn as sensitive, benevolent, and quite unspoiled.

It was this sentimental sleight of memory that had led her first to covet Kitty's baby. A child, Esslyn's child, alive and growing in his wife's womb, would transform her (Rosa's) barren life, making it fresh and green again. Over the past two days the idea of adoption had flickered through her mind, returned, settled, taken root, and flowered with such intensity that she had now reached the point where she was practically regarding it as a *fait accompli.*

Until she picked up the telephone. Then her previous sanguinity was swamped by a flood of doubts. Prominent among these was the idea that Kitty might decide to have an abortion. Having dialed the first three digits of the number at White Wings, Rosa replaced the receiver and pondered this alarming notion. Common sense forced her to admit that it must appear to Kitty the obvious solution. And she would have the money to go privately, so there would be no holdups. The whole thing would be simplicity itself. In and out: problem solved. The baby, vulnerable as an eggshell, all gone. She might even now be making the arrangements! Rosa snatched up the receiver again and redialed. When Kitty answered, Rosa asked if she might call in for a chat, and Kitty, as laconic as if such a request were an everyday occurrence, said, "Sure. Come when you like."

Backing the Panda out of the garage and crashing the gears with nervousness, Rosa struggled to plan out the strategy that would shape the argument she would have to present to Kitty. If it was going to be successful, she must look at the whole situation from the younger girl's point of view. Why, Kitty might well and understandably ask, should she lumber around for the next five months, getting heavier and heavier, less and less able to circulate and enjoy life, then go through the lengthy and perhaps extremely painful ordeal of giving birth, only to hand over the result of all this travail to another woman? What (Rosa could just see her sharp, calculating little eyes weighing the odds) was in it for her?

During the ten-minute drive over to White Wings, Rosa made herself answer that question to what she hoped would be Kitty's satisfaction. First she would point out the psychological as well as the physical damage that might result from an abortion. Then she would ask Kitty if she had thought of the expense involved in rearing a child. A child cost thousands. They weren't off your hands until they were eighteen, and even then, if Earnest's sister's complaints were anything to go by, you had to cough up for three more years while they went to university. "But you will have none of that financial burden," Rosa heard herself saying, "I will take care of everything."

On the other hand, once the adoption was legally formalized, she would make it clear that Kitty could continue to see the child whenever she wished. Surely, Rosa thought as she drove, far too fast, down Carradine Street, the triple thrust of her argument (huge savings, no responsibility, ease of access) must win the day. She had already forgotten her previous assumption—that Kitty's maternal instinct was minus nil—which made immediate nonsense of hook number three.

And as things turned out, none of the previous dialectic was of use anyway. Because at the moment of pressing the bell at the house and hearing it jangle in that so-familiar way in the sitting room, all Rosa's careful reasoning evaporated and she was left, trembling with the urgency of her appeal, on the doorstep. And when Kitty opened the door and said "Hi" and clicked back to the kitchen in her feathered mules, Rosa, mouth desert dry, followed floundering with uncertainty.

The kitchen was just the same. This was both a surprise and a comfort. She had been sure that Esslyn must have changed things around. That Kitty must have wanted new furniture, wallpaper, tiles. Apparently not. Rosa looked at the eggy, fat-smeared plate and the frying pan on the burner and noted the lingering fragrance of the full English breakfast. All this grease couldn't be doing the baby much good, she thought proprietorially. Which brought her back to her reasons for being there. As Kitty removed a butter dish, its contents liberally garnished with burned toast crumbs and smears of marmalade, Rosa reviewed the situation.

Momentarily she wondered if she should throw herself on Kitty's mercy. Reveal how she'd always longed for a child and that this might be her last chance. Almost immediately this idea was rejected. Kitty would just give the thumbs down. She would enjoy that. Seeing Rosa on her bed of nails. The thing to do— why hadn't she thought of it before?—was to offer money. Rosa had five thousand pounds in the bank and some jewelery she could sell. That was the way. Not to let Kitty see that she was desperate but to remain calm, even casual. Just to slip the subject almost lightheartedly into the conversation. Won't be much fun coping with a child by yourself. Or, I expect you feel differently about having a baby now that Esslyn's gone. Kitty removed more crumbs from the table by the simple expedient of sweeping them onto the floor with the sleeve of her negligee, and asked Rosa to take the weight off her feet.

As soon as she did so, Rosa felt the move was a mistake. She felt uneasy and at a disadvantage. Kitty put the frying pan on top of the dishes already in the sink and turned on the hot tap. The water hit the handle of the pan and sprayed upward and all over the tiles. Over her shoulder Kitty said, "And how's dear old Earnest?"

She always referred to Earnest in this manner, as if he were a shambling family pet on the verge of extinction. An ancient sheepdog, perhaps. Or elderly spaniel with rapidly stiffening joints. The point of such remarks, Rosa knew, had always been to force a comparison between her husband and Kitty's, the man Rosa had loved and lost. Normally it evoked a response of irritation shot through with bitterness. Now, noticing these dual emotions twitching into life, Rosa made a determined effort to repress them. Apart from not wishing to give Kitty the satisfaction of knowing she'd drawn blood, any feelings of antagonism would assuredly work against a successful outcome to the mission. And, Rosa comforted herself, whatever Earnest's shortcomings in the youth and glamour stakes, he did have the undeniable advantage of still being alive. That should give him some sort of edge, if nothing else.

She settled back a little more easily in her chair. Outside the waxen dark green leaves and scarlet berries of a cotoneaster framed the kitchen window through which the winter sun streamed, further gilding Kitty's already extremely honeyed curls. It was intensely hot. The central heating was on full blast, and Rosa sweltered in her heavy cape. Kitty was wearing a shortie cream satin nightie styled like a toga, slit almost to the waist on one side, and a spotted blue chiffon cover-up with little knots of silver ribbons. And not a knicker leg in sight, observed Rosa sourly. And her stomach still as flat as a pancake. She noticed with some satisfaction that, without her armory of blushers and shaders and pencils and lipsticks, Kitty's face looked almost plain.

Kitty dried her hands on the dish towel and, leaning against a radiator for extra warmth, turned to face her visitor. She had no intention of offering coffee or tea. Nor any other form of sustenance. Kitty did not go in for female friendships at the best of times, and certainly not with women old enough to be her mother and with a hefty ax to grind. Now, watching Rosa's greasy, large-pored nose, which seemed to Kitty to be positively quivering under the urge to poke itself into matters that were none of its business, she braced herself against what she was sure would be a great slobbery wash of false sympathy and sickly reminiscence.

Rosa took a deep breath and shuddered under her heather-mixture bivouac. She felt immobilized by the complexity of her thoughts. She saw now that she should have blurted out the reason for her visit, no matter in what garbled and emotional form, the minute she entered the house. The longer she sat in the untidy, homely kitchen (only a high chair needed to complete the picture), the more bizarre did her request appear. And Kitty was no help. She had made no welcoming gesture; not even the one regarded as virtually mandatory in any English home when a visitor calls. Realizing she had missed the boat on the instant-clarification front, Rosa had just decided to approach the subject snakily, starting with a formal expression of sympathy, when Kitty spoke.

"What's on your mind, then?"

Rosa took a huge lungful of air and, not daring to look at Kitty, said, "I was thinking now that Esslyn's dead, maybe you wouldn't feel able to keep the baby, and was wondering if I could adopt it."

Silence. Timidly Rosa looked up. As she did so, Kitty lowered her head and covered her face with her hands. She made a small sound, a little plaintive moan, and her shoulders trembled. At this Rosa, who was basically a kindhearted person, experienced a spontaneous welling up of sympathy. How callous, how imperceptive she had been to assume that, just because Kitty made no public display of sorrow, she was unmoved by the shocking fact and manner of her husband's death. Now, observing the thin shoulders shaking in despair, Rosa pushed her chair back and, awkwardly holding out her arms, made a tentative, somewhat clumsy move to comfort the sobbing figure. But Kitty shook off such consolation and crossed to the open door, where, her back to Rosa, she started to make terrible jackdaw squawks and cries.

Rooted to the spot, impotent, distressed, and self-castigating, Rosa could only wait, her hands held beseechingly, palms upward, continuing to offer solace should it be eventually required. At last the dreadful noises stopped and Kitty turned, her face puffy and red traces of tears on her cheeks, her shoulders still feebly vibrating. And it was then Rosa realized, with a tremendous shock of outrage and indignation, that Kitty had been *laughing*.

Now, shaking her head apparently with disbelief at the pricelessness of the situation, Kitty pulled a crumpled tissue from the pocket of her negligee, mopped her streaming eyes, and dropped it on the floor. Her shoulders finally at rest and her breathing quieted, she stared across at Rosa, and Rosa, still mortified but starting to get healthily angry, stared back.

Everything became very still. And quiet. A faucet dripped, making a dull, soft-spreading sound. Already, only seconds into this embarrassing and faintly ridiculous confrontation, it was getting on Rosa's nerves. She stood (she would have said stood her ground), and could think of nothing to say. In any case, she felt it was not up to her to speak. She had described why she was there, and invoked in Kitty an explosion of grotesque mirth. Now, it was up to Kitty to either explain her behavior or bring the interview to an end.

Rosa forced herself to meet that hard blue gaze. No merriment there. Indeed, now she came to think of it, there had not been much humor in those raucous hoots in the first place. They had been run through with an almost . . . almost *crowing* aggression. Yes, that was it! There had been triumph in those sounds. As if Kitty, with the battle lines hardly sketched out, was already victorious. But why was she crowing? Probably, thought Rosa, with a stab of humiliation, about the fact that she had Esslyn's first wife in a begging position. What a tale that would make to pass around the dressing rooms. Rosa could just hear it. "You'll never guess. Poor old Mrs. Earn came round the other day wanting to bring up the baby. Talk about an absolute scream. Left it too late to have any of her own. Silly old fool."

Ah, well, observed Rosa, she'd brought it on herself. Imagining Kitty's phantom gibes made her now wonder how she had ever entertained the ridiculous, misbegotten idea of adoption for a minute, never mind letting herself get to the stage where she'd actually visited the house and put the question. What in the world, queried Rosa, now devil's advocate, did she want with a child at her time of life? And dear Earnest, who had brought up three and, while doting on his grandchildren, found a half-hour-a-week romp and dandle with each a contact of ample sufficiency. How would he have coped? But there was no point in railing, she thought doughtily. What was done was done. Now, the only course open was to withdraw with as much dignity as she could muster. And she was about to do just that when Kitty closed the door.

The click sounded very loud. And rather final. Having shut the door, Kitty didn't move away but leaned back against it in what seemed to Rosa a rather threatening manner. And then she smiled. It was a terrible smile. Her narrow top lip with its exaggerated lascivious arch did not spread sideways. It lifted in the manner of an unfriendly animal, revealing pointed, sharp incisors. The light glinted on them. They looked dangerously sharp and bright. Then she stopped smiling, and that was worse. Because Rosa, distracted briefly by the sight of those alarming pale fangs, made the mistake of looking into Kitty's eyes. Brilliant azure ice. Inhuman. Suddenly the air in the room was thick and fearful. And

Rosa knew. She knew that all the joshings and suppositions and half-serious theories bandied about in the clubroom were no more than simple facts. And that Kitty had truly got rid of her husband for his money and her freedom. And that she, Rosa, was now alone with a murderess.

Rosa realized she had been holding her breath, and let it out now with great care, as if the gentle purling might snatch Kitty's attention and activate some quiescent impulse to destroy. Rosa tried to think, but all her cerebral processes seemed to have ground to a halt. She tried to move as well, and found to her horror that far from simply standing on the floor as she had supposed, she seemed to be rooted in it like a tree. Her heart thudded, and the drop of water splashed and spread. And it seemed to Rosa that the long long space between one splash of water and the next and one thud of her heart and the next was alive with the pulsating obscene hum of evil.

What could she do? First look away. Look away from those guileless, cruel eyes. Then have a go at tautening up her sagging mental faculties. If only she had told someone—anyone—that she was going to White Wings. But then, thought Rosa sluggishly, ticking over again at last, Kitty didn't know that. Bluff! That was the thing. She would bluff her way out. She would say that she had told Earnest where she was going, and that he was driving over to pick her up any minute now. Quaveringly she got the information across.

"But Rosa—how can he be? The car's out there in the drive."

Oh, but she was cunning! All that was in her voice was simple puzzlement. Rosa joined Barnaby in wondering how the hell they had all come to believe that Kitty couldn't act. Well, that was water down the drain. What next? Kitty moved away from the door, and Rosa's brain, now miraculously freed from its former coagulate state, leaped into protective action, feeding dozens of combative images across the screen of her mind.

She floored Kitty with a kung-fu kick or a straight uppercut. She pressed her to the ground and held a knife to her throat. With one immaculate Frisbee spin of a plate, she stunned her into insensibility. As the last of these comforting pictures faded, she realized that Kitty was slowly walking toward her.

"Oh, God," prayed Rosa. "Help me . . . *please*."

She felt huge and stifled, hippo-sluggish in the heat. Runnels of sweat ran over her scalp and down between her breasts, yet her upper lip and forehead prickled with chill, and her blood felt thick and unmoving. She stared at Kitty, young, Amazonian, slim as a whip with strong, sinewy arms and legs and thought again, What chance will I have?

Kitty was smiling as she came on. Not her genuine weasely smile, but a false one, painted on her lips. A simulacrum of concern. So might she have smiled at Esslyn, thought Rosa, as she wished him well on the first night, before unsheathing the means of his destruction. And then, recalling her first husband, she had a sudden, vivid impression of Earnest arriving home as he would be just now and wanting his lunch. At the thought of never seeing his dear face again, Rosa felt her blood stir and start to flow. Anger chased out fear. She went up on the balls of her feet (now miraculously unstuck) and felt her calf muscles tense. She would not go down without a fight.

Kitty was barely a foot away. It was now or never. Rosa hooded her eyes in what she hoped was a menacing fashion. And sprang.

Colin Smy sat alone in his workshop. He was cold but could not be bothered to light the heater. He held a smooth blond piece of maple in his hands, but the beauty and grain of the wood, once a certain stimulus to feelings of the deepest contentment and an amulet against despair, this morning had lost the power to move. Next to him was a cedarwood cradle. Only two days ago he had been delicately chiseling a border of leaves and flowers around the name Ben. He pushed the cradle with his finger, and it rocked on its bed of fragrant rust-colored shavings. He got up then and moved a little stiffly around the room, touching and stroking various artifacts, pressing the outlines hungrily and devouring the detail of line and marking as a man might who was on the point of going blind.

Colin picked up his chisel. The varnish on the handle had long since worn away, and it fitted the palm of his hand to such perfection that the word "familiar" was totally inadequate to describe the sensation. Colin always felt vaguely ill at ease away from his workshop and the beloved tools of his trade. Now, believing that it might be months or even years before he saw or touched any of them again, he felt a great gaping, prescient sense of loss.

He stilled the cradle and stood looking round for a moment more. Although his emotions were chaotic, his thoughts were crystal clear. Paramount was the vow he had made to Glenda when she lay dying. "Promise me," she had cried, over and over again, "that you will look after David." And he had reassured her, over and over again. Almost her last words (before "such a short while" and "good-bye, my darling") were, "You won't let any harm come to him?"

Colin had kept his promise. Since her death, David had been his world. He had given up everything and gladly for the boy. His welding job had been the first to go. So that he could take David to and from school and be available at the weekends and holidays, Colin had taken up free-lance woodwork and carpentry, at first with scant success. In material terms they'd had very little, but they had each other, and Colin had been overwhelmed with pride when his son had shown a talent far surpassing his own for carving. Two of David's sculptures stood now on his workbench. A grave old man, a sower of seed, a shallow basket in the crook of his arm and a kneeling heifer, a present for Ben, most tenderly carved, its head bowed, the horns tipped at such an eloquent angle.

After Glenda had left them, Colin put thoughts of remarriage aside. At first, grieving for his wife, this had not been difficult. Later, when occasionally meeting women he might normally have been tempted to pursue, the thought that they might not love David as he deserved or, worse, come to resent him had stopped the chase before it started. But now David was grown up and had even brought one or two girls of his own home, but the affairs had petered out, and Colin had been glad at the time. The girls had seemed a touch overconfident (one of them was almost domineering) for David. Now, of course, Colin wished to God his son had married one of them. But even then, he had to admit, if David had continued helping out at the Latimer, he would still have met Kitty.

Colin sat down again and held his aching head in his hands. When he had first heard the rumor about David and Esslyn's wife, he had been unalarmed if a little disappointed in his son. But Kitty was an attractive young woman and, like everyone else in the company, Colin was not averse to the idea of Esslyn's eye being put out. But to think it could lead to this. . . .

Last night, sick at heart, he had tried to talk to David, but when it came to the sticking point, he had lacked the courage to put his feelings of dread into plain words. Instead, he had mumbled, "Now she's free . . . I suppose . . . well . . . you'll be . . ."

"Yes, Dad." David had spoken calmly. "She's free. Although I wouldn't have wanted it to happen like this, of course."

Colin had listened, struggling with feelings of amazed disbelief. That David could speak in such a manner. In such a detached, *heartless* manner. David, who had never harmed a living thing. Who would carry spiders carefully out into the garden rather than kill them. Who, when he was ten and his hamster died, had wept for three days. When he added, "I shall have to go very carefully at first," Colin, not trusting himself to reply, had left the house and spent the ensuing hours walking round and round Causton trying desperately to come to some decision. Knowing what the right thing to do was, realizing simultaneously that he could never do it, and struggling to alight on an alternative course of action.

Because he must do something. He had experienced great alarm during his interview with Tom at the station on Tuesday morning. More alarm than David apparently, who, when asked at one o'clock how it had all gone, had just said "fine" and continued with his dinner. Although Colin's time at the station had been short, it had also been deeply disturbing. He had never thought of old Tom as being especially clever, but the sharp, piercing quality of the chief inspector's gaze—quite absent from their cozy sessions in the scene dock—had caused him to think again. Now, having got a glimpse of the measure of the man, Colin realized that Barnaby was a hunter. He would pursue; questioning, checking, rechecking, perceiving, concluding, closing in. And how well would David be able to stand up to that sort of treatment?

Before going back to work, he had told his father that he had simply denied any knowledge of razor tampering and this had been accepted, but already Colin was seeing this supposed acceptance as a clever ploy. David was so guileless. He would not see that Barnaby was only pretending to believe him. That, even now, they were probably questioning Kitty. Making her admit complicity. And she would, too. She would tell them everything to get herself off the hook.

Colin snatched up his raincoat. One of the sleeves had got tangled, and he almost growled with impatience as he tried to force his arm in. What the hell was he doing sitting here brooding, going round and round the situation while perhaps any minute . . .

He ran out, not even stopping to lock his shed, skidding on the icy pavement. He cursed his previous indecision. He had known hours ago; had known when he was walking the streets at 3:00 a.m., that there was only one course of action that he could possibly take. Because of what he had sworn to Glenda all those years ago. ("You won't let any harm come to him? Promise me?") Oh, why had he waited? Now, Colin became convinced as he slid and skittered toward the police station, that he was already too late, that sometime during the afternoon the police had fetched David from his place of work and were even now working on him, trying to break him down.

At last he hauled himself up the station steps, searing his hands on the freezing metal rail, and asked at the desk to see Detective Chief Inspector Barnaby. A pretty dark-haired policewoman told him that the inspector was out and showed him to a small room, acrid with stale cigarette smoke, where he could wait. Noticing his white face and trembling hands, she asked if he would like to talk to anyone else. Then if he would like some tea. But Colin declined both these offers, and was then left in peace studying an antitheft poster and waiting to confess to the murder of Esslyn Carmichael.

"How the other half lives, eh, chief?" muttered Troy snidely as he drove up the graceful curve of the drive leading to White Wings and swaggered into a semi-circular preparking spin, throwing up several pounds of gravel in the process. Troy drove fast, skillfully, and with care, but could not resist the flourish of a zigzag or curlicue when coming to a halt. Occasionally Barnaby felt it sensible to restrain this flamboyant behavior, and then Troy, with a piqued, almost disconsolate air, would park with such funereal exactitude that it was all his superior could do to keep a straight face. This usually lasted a few days, then exuberance gradually snuck back in. Troy regarded this pizazz as part of his style. He was very hot on style, and despised those dullards who didn't know a Cordobian reversal from an uphill start. Right now, feeling a lecture coming on, he snapped his belt and started to climb out before the chief could really get into the swing of it.

As he did so, a piercing yell came from the house. Then a series of screams. Troy raced to the baronial front door, tried it, found it locked, and pounded on it with his fists, shouting, "Open up! This is the police!" Barnaby had just joined him when a key was turned and the door swung inward. Kitty stood in the opening in a pretty blue housecoat with the most extraordinary expression on her face. She looked in a state. A bit fearful, a bit angry, but shiftingly so, as if she didn't know whether to laugh or cry. She stood in the center of the hall patting her curls and pulling a mock-horrified face.

"What's wrong?" demanded Barnaby. "Who was that screaming?"

"Me, actually..."

"Why?" An icy wind was blowing into the house. Troy shut the front door, but the blast continued. Barnaby strode into the kitchen. The back door was wide open. "Who else is here?"

"No one." She tiptoed across to the garden door and closed it. "Brrr."

"Whose car is that outside?"

"I'm going to make some coffee to calm my nerves. D'you want some?"

"Kitty." Barnaby stopped her. "What the devil's going on?"

"Well... you won't believe this, Tom, but I think I've found your murderer."

"Perhaps I can make some coffee, Mrs. Carmichael?" said Troy, with his most winning smile. "You sound as if you could do with some."

"Oh, how sweet." Kitty's unpainted lips returned the smile. Troy noticed with an uprush of excitement that beneath the lusciously lipsticked Cupid's bow he had so admired the other evening was a real one. Just as luscious and twice as sexy. "But I'd better do it," she continued. "It's all Eyetalian, the equipment... it might blow up in inexperienced hands." Although her voice barely changed, it managed to imply that she was sure Sergeant Troy's hands were anything but inexperienced, and, given the opportunity, would be more than prepared to put her theory to the test. "Shan't be a mo."

"You can talk, I assume, Kitty, while you're getting to grips with that contraption."

"'Course I can," replied Kitty, juggling water, coffee, twists of chrome and a couple of retorts. "To put it in a nutshell, Rosa just came round here and *attacked* me."

"Just like that?" asked the chief inspector, shaking his head at Troy, who seemed quite prepared to hare off and make an instant arrest.

"Just like that." She set the contraption on a low flame, clopped to the radiator, and nestled against it. "Warm me bottie. Otherwise I'll get goosebumps." She pulled the blue wrapper very tight, and at least two of the bumps leaped into prominence.

"Any idea why?"

"Jealousy. What else? She killed Esslyn because she couldn't bear to see him happy. Then she came round after me."

"But they'd been divorced for over two years. Surely if she couldn't bear to see him happy, she'd have done something about it before now."

"Ahhh . . ." Kitty shook a cigarette out of a packet. Troy's nostrils twitched in anticipation. "Before there wasn't the baby."

"Perhaps you'd better tell us from the beginning."

"Okay." Kitty, having lit her cigarette and dragged deep, coughed and said, "It's hard to credit, I know, but she had the bloody cheek to come round here and ask me when the baby was born if I'd hand it over to her and ancient Ernie."

"And what did you say?"

"I didn't actually *say* anything. To tell you the truth, it was so funny I had to laugh. And then once I started, I couldn't stop. You know how you get . . ." She winked at Troy, who, tormented enough already by the smoke from her Chesterfield, nearly collapsed under the extra strain.

"And why was it so funny?"

"Because there wasn't any baby."

There was a pause while the apparatus gurgled and googled and backfired. Then Barnaby said, "Can I just get this clear, Kitty? Are you saying that you've had a miscarriage? Or that there was never a child in the first place?"

"Never one in the first place."

"And I assume Esslyn was not aware of this?"

"Are you dumb? D'you think he'd have married me if he had been?" The smile was almost voluptuously satisfied. It said, "Aren't I clever? Don't you wish you were as smart as I am?"

Tricky little tart, thought Troy. He looked at Kitty, torn between admiration and resentment. He understood her class and stamp (he often picked up her less fortunate sisters around the bus station trying to turn a trick) without recognizing how close it was to his own. So her nerve and determination earned his grudging respect. On the other hand, she had definitely made a monkey out of one of the superior sex, and he couldn't go along with that. He couldn't go along with that at all.

"And what did you plan to do," asked Barnaby, "when your condition—or rather, lack of one—became obvious?"

"Oh—I thought a tiny tumble down the steps. Nothing too drastic. Poor little precious—" her sorrowful sigh went ill with her saucy grin—"wouldn't have had a chance."

"So your husband's death could hardly be more opportune."

"Right." Kitty poured the coffee into three opalescent mugs. "Men on the job like lots of sugar, don't they? For energy?"

"None for me, thank you." Troy asked for two sugars and plenty of milk. Barnaby accepted his drink and took a sip. In spite of the baroque extravagance of the "Eyetalian" ganglia, the coffee was absolutely disgusting. Worse even than Joyce's, and that was saying something. For some odd reason he found this rather a comfort. He was about to restart the conversation at the point where it had broken off, when Kitty did it for him.

"And when you discover who carried out the dirty deed, I shall go and thank him personally."

As Kitty drank her coffee, she stared at Barnaby over the rim of her mug. The stare was so sassy he wondered if she was aware of just how precarious her situation actually was. He returned the stare in a manner that made the weather outside seem positively summery. "You've been seemingly very frank with us, Kitty. And your refusal to pretend to any grief you do not feel does you credit. But if your belief that the world was well rid of your husband has given you any ideas about protecting his killer, or hindering our investigation in any way, I advise you to think again. Because you'll find yourself in very serious trouble."

"I wouldn't do that, Tom," Kitty said soberly, stubbing out her cigarette. "Honestly."

"As long as we've got that straight. Now to return to this business with Rosa. She'd asked for the baby, you'd had a fit of the giggles. Then what happened?"

"It was really weird. There was a terrible draft from that door"—she nodded toward the hall—"and me being only in my naughties and feeling the pinch, I went over and closed it. Then, when I turned round, she was staring at me—her eyes were positively *bulging*. Then she started shaking. She looked as if she was going to have a fit. So I thought I'd get her some water...I didn't know what to do. I mean, it's not the sort of thing that happens to you every day, is it? So I went to the sink, which meant I had to cross the room, and I was just in front of her when she jumped at me. I yelled and started to scream . . . and she ran away—"

"Just a minute. Was that when Sergeant Troy started banging on the door?"

"Is his name Troy? How romantic. No, that was the funny thing. She ran off the second I started shouting. Before we knew you were here at all."

"It doesn't sound much like a serious attempt to do you harm."

"That's a nice attitude for the police to take, I must say. I shall sue her for assault."

"That's up to you, of course."

"Actually—why are you here? With all the excitement, I never asked."

"We're continuing our inquiries, Kitty."

"Oh, Tom." She smiled delightedly. "Do you really say that? I thought it was just in the movies." She crossed to the littered pine table and pulled out two wheelback chairs. "Park yourselves, then, if you're stopping."

The two men sat at the table, and Kitty joined them. She sat quite close to Troy, and he was aware that she had not yet bathed. She gave off a warm, intimate, faintly gamey scent, redolent of nighttime retreats and assignations.

"I'd like first to ask you, Kitty," continued the chief inspector, "if you noticed anything—anything at all—in the weeks leading up to your husband's death that might assist us?"

"What sort of thing?"

"Did he talk of any plans? Any special difficulties? Problems with relationships?"

"Esslyn didn't have relationships. There was nothing of him to relate to."

"What about a break in his usual routine?"

"Well, he did pop into the office on Saturday morning. Said he had to call something in . . . and oh, yes—his costume. He brought his costume home. I've never known him to do that before."

"Did he say why?"

"Didn't want to risk leaving it in the dressing room. He really fancied himself in that coat. 'Course, in the play he starts off in a grotty old shawl and dressing gown, then flings them off and stands up looking like the Queen of Sheba, and we're all supposed to go 'ooh' and 'aaah.' He tried the whole thing on on Saturday, prancing about looking in the glass. Practically hugging himself to death, he was. Then he said what a coo... coody... something."

"*Coup de théâtre.*"

"Yeah. Whatever that is."

"A staggering theatrical effect."

"He made that all right," giggled Kitty. Then, catching Barnaby's eye, she had the grace to blush. "Sorry, Tom. Bad taste. Sorry."

"Can I pin you down on this, Kitty? It may be important. Can you remember precisely what it was he said?"

"No more than I've just told you."

"What a *coup de théâtre* it'll be."

"Yes."

"You're sure by "it" he meant this transformation in Act One?"

"Well... that's what he was talking about just before."

Barnaby, watching Kitty closely, then said, "Your husband did speak once before he died." No flicker of fear there. No spark of alarm. Just straight-forward curiosity. Damn, thought the chief inspector. And my favorite suspect, too.

"What did he say?"

"My sergeant got the sound of the word 'bungled.' That mean anything to you?"

Kitty shook her head. "Except..." Under Barnaby's look of encouragement she stumbled on. "Well... that something had gone wrong. That's what bungled means, isn't it? And it had. For Esslyn, anyway."

"Perhaps his grand *coup de théâtre.*"

"No—that's at the beginning of the play. He pulled that off all right. This was right at the end." Sharp little cookie, thought Troy, wincing as she shook out another cigarette and lit up. Catching his greedy eye, she held out the pack.

"Not on duty, Mrs. Carmichael, thank you."

"Gosh. I thought that was just hard liquor and... er... what was the other?"

"I have a warrant with me, Kitty." Barnaby got up abruptly. "I'd like to look through Esslyn's effects before I go. Especially any correspondence and personal papers."

"Help yourself. I'd better slip into something decent." They followed her into the hall, and she nodded toward a door on the left. "That's his study. See you in two ticks."

Troy watched her long, tanned legs disappear up the thickly carpeted stairs. He thought she looked like a delectable slave girl in one of those TV comedies set in ancient Rome. Where all the birds pranced around in shortie nighties and the men had brushes growing out of their helmets. He wouldn't mind chasing her round the Forum. Whu-hoo.

"Forget it, Troy."

"I'm off duty at seven, chief. Might find out something."

"The only thing you'll find out is how to stunt your growth. Now come on—let's get cracking."

They entered a small room sparsely furnished with a knee-hole desk, bookshelves, and a couple of armchairs. Troy said, "What are we looking for?"

"Anything. Everything. Especially personal."

No section of the desk was locked, but the contents proved to be meager and unexciting. Insurance. Documents for the Volvo. Mortgage and a few bills. Bank statements that showed regular standing orders and moderate monthly transfers from a deposit account. Barnaby put these aside. There were also a couple of holiday brochures. They checked the shelves of books (all on accountancy apart from a set of Dickens that looked as if it had never been opened, let alone read) and shook them open, but no sinister letter or revealing *billet doux* fell out.

Esslyn's wardrobe and the rest of the house were equally unrevealing. By the time they were ready to leave, Kitty, in a black jumpsuit, was racing away on her exercise cycle. She came down to the hall to see them out. She had brushed her hair, and it lay like pale satin against her velvet shoulders.

"Beautiful house," said Troy, putting a friendly smile in the bank for future use.

"Miles too big for little me," replied Kitty, opening the front door. "I'm putting it on the market tomorrow."

"I should make sure it belongs to you first," said Barnaby.

"What do you mean? Everything comes to me as next of kin."

"A commonly held misconception, Kitty." Then, looking at her suddenly frozen features, Barnaby patted her arm sympathetically. "I'm sure Esslyn left things in order, but I'd pop into the solicitor if I were you. Just to make absolutely sure."

He left then, and his sergeant was about to follow when Kitty laid her hand on his sleeve.

"Funny you being called Troy, isn't it?"

"Why's that, Mrs. Carmichael?" Even through the thickness of his overcoat he could feel the warmth of her fingers.

"Cause my middle name's Helen," she said with a wicked smile.

"Hold it . . . hold it."

Barnaby stopped Colin on line one, asked for some tea, and talked vague generalities until it turned up. He waited while Colin had dissolved his three sugars with a lot of active stirring, then pulled a pad and pencil toward him.

"Tea okay?"

"Yes, thank you." Colin had been in such a state waiting for the chief inspector that he hadn't really got much past picturing his own declaration of guilt. If he had, he'd certainly have envisioned a slightly more excitable reception than he had received so far.

"What did you expect, Colin?" asked Barnaby. "That I'd clap you in irons?"

Colin flushed. And felt a deep stab of alarm that the other man could read his mind so easily. He struggled to compose his expression. To set it in a mask of unconcern. "'Course not." He swallowed nervously. "I knew there'd be tea. Seen it all often enough on the box."

"Ah, yes. They only got bread and water before *Hill Street*."

Colin felt he should laugh or at least crack a smile. There was a long pause. What were they waiting for? Colin scraped his throat nervously and drank some more tea. Perhaps this was the way it worked. How they broke people down. Ordeal by silence. But what was there to break down? He'd come in to make a confession, hadn't he? Why the hell couldn't he just get on with it? The continuing quiet stampeded him into speech.

"It's been preying on my mind, Tom."

"Messing with the razor?"

"Yes. I felt I couldn't . . . um . . . live with myself so . . . I came to confess."

"I see." Barnaby nodded seriously, but without, Colin noticed, writing anything on his pad. "And why exactly did you do it?"

"Why?"

"Not an unreasonable question, surely?"

"No . . . of course not!" *Why?* Oh, God, Colin! You great fool. You haven't thought any further than the end of your bloody nose. "Because . . . he was awful to David . . . sneering and laughing at him at rehearsals. Humiliating him. I . . . decided he should be taught a lesson."

"Rather a savage lesson."

"Yes . . ."

"Disproportionately harsh, one might say." Barnaby picked up his pen.

"I didn't expect—" Colin's voice strengthened. "He was an absolute bastard to David."

"He was an absolute bastard to everyone." When Colin did not reply, Barnaby continued, "Well, what didn't you expect?"

"That he'd . . . die."

"Oh, come *on,* Colin. Why do you think there were two thicknesses of tape on the thing? What did you think would happen when they were removed and he dragged it across his throat? If you've got the guts to come and confess, at least have the guts to admit you knew what you were doing." Although Barnaby had hardly raised his voice at all, it seemed to Colin to positively boom, bouncing off each wall in turn, belaboring his eardrums. "So when did you take the tape off?"

"After Deidre checked it."

"Obviously. But when precisely?"

"Do you mean the time?"

"Of course I mean the time!"

". . . um . . . after she'd called the half, I think . . . yes. That's right. So between seven-thirty and seven-forty."

"Bit dodgy, wasn't it? Must've been quite a few people about."

"No. Deidre had gone to collect her ASMs from upstairs. All the actors were still in their dressing rooms."

"And where did you do it?"

"Pardon?"

"Where?"

". . . well . . . the scene dock."

"You'd have to be quick. What did you use?"

"A Stanley knife."

"The same one that was in the wings?"

Colin hesitated. Fingerprints, he thought. His should be all over the one in the wings, but you never knew. "No. I used my own."

"Got it with you?"

"It's in my workshop."

"And what did you do with the tape?"

"Just . . . scrumpled it up."

"And left it there?"

"Yes."

"So if we went over now, you could produce it?"

"No! Afterward . . . when I realized how terrible everything was . . . I threw it away. Down the bog."

Barnaby said, "I see," and nodded. Then he leaned back in his chair and gazed out of the window at the black and gray scudding clouds. Colin leaned back a little, too. His breathing returned to near normal; his heart stopped thundering. That hadn't been too bad. All he had to do now was remember precisely what it was he'd said (for Barnaby's pad now seemed to be quite covered with lines and squiggles) and stick to it. And that shouldn't be too difficult.

Colin glanced at the clock. To his amazement, barely ten minutes had passed since he had entered the room. The delusion that he had been shut up here blabbing away for hours must simply be put down to stretched nerves. Barnaby drained his tea. "Some more, Colin?" When the other man declined, Barnaby said, "I think I will," and disappeared.

Left alone, Colin gathered his wits. He was bound to be asked all the foregoing questions again and probably many more (although he could not imagine what they might be), but now he had got the time, method, and motive firmly tethered, he felt a lot more confident. After all, those were the basics. The crucial underpinnings to the case, and no one could prove that he wasn't telling the truth. He would stand up in court and swear. He would swear the rest of his life away, if need be.

Barnaby was a long time. Colin wondered why he hadn't just pressed the buzzer as he had before if he wanted more tea. Colin inclined his ear toward the door, but he could hear nothing but the distant rattle of a typewriter. Perhaps Barnaby was finding someone to take down a proper statement. Colin listened again; then, hearing no approaching footsteps, leaned over the desk and turned the chief inspector's pad around. It was covered with beautifully drawn flowers. Harebells and primroses. And ferns.

Alarmed, Colin slumped back in his seat. Tom had not writ-ten down a single thing! Following this realization came another, more terrible. The only reason for this must be that Tom had not believed a word that he, Colin, had said. He had been sitting there, nodding, scribbling, asking questions, and all the time he had just been playacting. Only pretending to take things seriously. Colin's leg started to tremble and his foot to jounce on the lino-leum floor. He pressed his leg hard against the chair to keep it still, then felt his mouth brim with bile. He was going to be sick. Or faint. Before he could do either, Barnaby returned, sat behind his desk, and gave Colin a concerned glance.

"You look a bit green. Are you sure you don't want another drink?"

"Some water..."

"Can we have a glass of water?" said Barnaby into his buzzer. "And I'd like some more tea."

The drinks arrived. Colin sipped his slowly. "Didn't you go out for some more tea, Tom?"

"No. To arrange some transport."

"Ah." Colin put his glass on the desk. He desperately needed time to think. Struggling to apply his attention to the matter, Colin almost immediately saw where he had gone wrong. It was in the murder motive. No wonder Tom had been disbelieving. Colin, in the chief inspector's shoes, would have felt the same. How ridiculous—to kill someone because they had been unkind to your son. And him a grown man. If only, Colin chided himself, he had prepared what he had come to say more carefully. But it was not too late. He saw now how he could put things right. And what he should have said in the first place.

"The truth is, Tom," he blurted out clumsily, "David is in love with Kitty. You've seen...you were in the audience...how violent Esslyn was toward her. He found out, you see. And I was afraid. Afraid for her and for David. He was fiendish, Esslyn. I really thought he might harm them both."

"So you spiked his guns?"

"Yes."

"Well...that sounds a bit more likely."

"Yes. I didn't say that at first, because I thought if I could keep them out of it, I would."

"Such delicacy does you credit." Barnaby drank deep of his

breakfast blend. "There's only one little snag in that scenario. Esslyn believed his wife was having an affair with Nicholas."

"*Nicholas.*"

"But of course you weren't to know that."

"Was it true?" Colin turned an eager look upon the chief
inspector.

"No. The general consensus seems to be that David was indeed the man. By the way, where was he while you were carrying
out all this jiggery-pokery?"

Colin's breath stopped in his throat. He gazed at Barnaby;
the mouse and the cat. He felt the skin on his face prickle and
knew it must be stained crimson. He opened his mouth, but no
sound came. He couldn't think. His brains were stewed. Where
was David while all this was going on? *Where was David?* Not in
the wings or (obviously) the scene dock. Not upstairs. In the
dressing room! Of course.

"In the dressing room. Anyone will vouch for him."

"Why should anyone need to vouch for him?"

"Oh—no reason. Just . . . if you wanted to check."

"I see." Barnaby completed to perfection the tight, curled tip
of the *Asplenium trichomanes.* "I feel I should tell you that we tried
to flush the tape down every loo in the theater and were completely unsuccessful."

". . . oh . . . did you? Yes . . . sorry . . . my memory . . . I threw
it out of the window."

"Well, Colin"—Barnaby put down his pen and smiled rather
severely at his companion—"I've sat at this desk and listened to
some sorry liars in my time but if I gave a prize for the worst, I
think you'd cop it."

He watched Colin's face, which had already shown every
aspect of alarm and apprehension, further suffuse with emotion. It
seemed to blow up like a balloon. The skin stretched tight across
his cheekbones and jaw, and his eyes darted around like tiny,
trapped wild creatures. He seemed to have no control over his
mouth and his lips worked in little push-pull convulsions. He
swayed in his chair as if giddy.

And giddy was what he felt. For Colin was reeling under the
force of a double-edged blow. He now saw with icy clarity that
coming to the station and making a false confession was the worst
thing he could possibly have done. Not only had he failed to save
his son, but the slightest pause for reflection must have shown him

that David would never stand silently by while his father, innocent of any crime, was arrested, perhaps imprisoned. In trying to protect the boy, Colin now saw that he had stupidly thrust him into the very heart of the crime where all the danger lay. He covered his face with his hands and moaned.

Barnaby shifted from his chair, came round to the front of the desk, and perched on the edge. Then he touched Colin on the shoulder and said, "You could be wrong, you know."

"No, Tom!" Colin turned a desolate seeking look upon the chief inspector. The look was wild with unfounded expectation. It begged Barnaby, even at this late stage, when a traitorous admission, though still unspoken, lay as solid as a rock between them, to perform a magical conjuring trick. To say it wasn't so. When Barnaby remained silent, Colin gave one terrible dry sob, racked from his gut, and cried, "You see. . . . I saw him do it. *I actually saw him do it.*"

Ten minutes later, having accepted more tea and, to some degree, composed himself, Colin told Barnaby what he had observed in the wings at the first night of *Amadeus.* He spoke in an emotionless voice, hanging his head as if deeply ashamed to be speaking at all. Barnaby received the information impassively, and when Colin had finished, said, "Are you positive he was tinkering with the razor?"

"What else could he have been doing, Tom? Looking round so furtively to make sure that no one was watching. Bending over the props table. And he actually went into the toilet, came out, and went back again."

"But you didn't see him touch it?"

"No. I was over on the other side of the stage, behind the fireplace. And of course he'd got his back to me. . . ." Colin looked up then and a tiny wisp of hope touched his voice. "Do you think . . . Oh, Tom . . . d'you think I've got it wrong?"

"I certainly think we'd better not leap to any more conclusions. One's enough to be going on with. We'll see what David has to say when he gets here."

"*David . . . here . . .* Oh, God!" Horrified, Colin rose from his seat.

"Sit down," said Barnaby, irritated. "You come in here and make a false confession. As you're not a head case, it's clear that you're protecting someone. There's only one person you'd go to those lengths for. Obviously we need to speak to that person. And here"—the buzzer sounded—"I should imagine, he is."

As the door opened, Colin quickly bowed his shoulders and buried his face once more in his hands. He did not look up as David almost ran across the room and knelt beside him.

"Dad—what is it? What are you doing here?" Getting no response, he turned to Barnaby. "Tom, what the hell's going on?"

"Your father has just confessed to the murder of Esslyn Carmichael."

"He's done what?" David Smy, absolutely dumbfounded, stared at Barnaby, then turned again to the figure crouched in the chair. He tried to move his father's head so that his face was visible, but Colin gave a fierce animal cry and burrowed ever more firmly in the wedge of his arms.

David stood up and said, "I don't believe it. I simply don't believe it."

"No," replied Barnaby dryly. "I don't believe it, either."

"But then . . . why? What's the point? *Dad.*" He shook his father's arm. "Look at me!"

"He's shielding someone. Or thinks he is."

"You stupid . . . What do you think you're playing at?" Panic streamed through David's voice. "But . . . if you know he's lying, Tom . . . that's all right, isn't it? I mean . . . that's all right?"

"Up to a point."

"How 'up to a point'?"

"Who do you think he would be prepared to go to prison for?"

David frowned, and Barnaby watched his homely face move through incomprehension, dawning apprehension, and incredulity. Incredulity lingered longest. "You mean . . . *he thought it was me?*"

"That's right."

"But why on earth would I want to kill Esslyn?"

Barnaby had heard that phrase (give or take a change in nomenclature) a good many times in his career. He had heard it ringing with guilty bluster and innocent inquiry; spoken in high and low dudgeon, afire with self-righteous indignation, and shot through with fear. But he had never before been faced with the quality of complete and utter stupefaction that was now stamped on David Smy's bovine features.

"Well," answered the chief inspector, "the general consensus seems to be because of your affair with Kitty." David's expression of disbelief now deepened to the point where he looked positively poleaxed. He shook his head from side to side slowly, as if to clear it from the effects of a blow. Barnaby said, "I should sit down, if I were you."

David collapsed into the second of the tweedy chairs and said, "I think there's been some mistake." Colin raised his head then, the disturbed agony of his gaze quieted, transmuted.

"You were seen acting suspiciously in the wings," said Barnaby. "Around the quarter."

David went very pale. "Who by?"

"We had an anonymous tip. These things have to be followed up."

"Of course." David sat silently for a moment, then said, "I was sure there was no one around."

"You don't have to say anything else!" cried Colin. "You have all sorts of rights. I'll get you a solicitor—"

"I don't need a solicitor, Dad. I haven't done anything all that dreadful."

"Do you think we could get down to exactly what you have done?" Barnaby said brusquely. "My patience is rapidly running out."

David took a deep breath. "Esslyn told this unkind story about Deidre's father. It was so cruel. Everyone laughed, and I knew she'd overheard. She was just on the stairs outside. Then I saw her afterward checking the sound deck, and she was crying. I got so angry. When she went upstairs to collect the ASMs, I got some scouring powder from the gents' and I shook it all over those little cakes he eats in Act One. I know it was silly. And I know it was spiteful and childish, and I don't care. I'd do it again."

Barnaby stared at David's stubborn face, then shifted his glance to the boy's father. Before his eyes Colin's countenance was rinsed clean of misery and despair and brightly transformed as is a child's face when a smile is "wiped" on by the back of its hand. Now, Colin was expressing a delight so intense it made him appear quite ridiculous.

"I didn't know you fancied the girl!" he cried joyously.

"I don't 'fancy' her, Dad. I care deeply for her and have for some time. I told you."

"What?"

"We were talking about her last week. I told you that I cared for someone, but she wasn't free. And we discussed it yesterday as well."

"You meant *Deidre?*"

"Who else?" David looked from his father to Barnaby and back again. His expression was stern. He had the air of a man who was being trifled with and could do without the experience. "I don't know who got this idea off the ground that I'd got something going with Kitty." Barnaby shrugged and smiled, and David continued indignantly, "It's no laughing matter, Tom. What if it got back to Deidre? I don't want her thinking I'm some sort of Don Juan." The thought of David with his shining countenance and straight blue eyes and simple heart in the role of Don Juan caused Barnaby's lips to twitch once more, and he faked a cough to cover it. "As for you, Dad . . ." Colin, looking discomfited, shamefaced, and radiant with happiness, shuffled his feet. "How did you get to know about all this, anyway?"

"We called at the house," cut in Barnaby before Colin could reply. Not that he looked capable. "I'm afraid your father drew his own conclusions from the form our questions took."

"You silly sod," David said affectionately. "I don't know how you could have been so daft."

"No," said Colin. "I don't either, now. Well . . ." He got up. "Could we . . . is it all right to go now?"

"Can't wait to see the back of you."

"Actually, Tom," David said hesitantly, "there's something I'd half meant to tell you. It seemed so vague, that's why I didn't mention it yesterday, but I've been thinking it over, and . . . as I'm here . . ."

"Fire away."

"It's very slight. So I hope you won't be cross."

"I shall be extremely cross any minute now if you don't hurry up and get on with it."

"Yes. Right. Well, you know I take the tray with all the shaving things on at the end of the play. There was something odd about it on the first night."

"Yes?"

"That's it, I'm afraid. I told you it was vague."

"Very vague indeed."

"I knew you'd be cross."

"I am not cross," said Barnaby with an ogrish grin. "All the usual things were there, I take it?"

"Yes. Soap in wooden dish. China bowl with hot water. Shaving brush. Closed razor. Towel."

"Placed any differently?" David shook his head. "Different soap, perhaps?"

"No. It's never used actually, so we've kept the same piece, Imperial Leather, all the way through rehearsals."

"In that case, David," said Barnaby rather tersely, "I'm at a bit of a loss to see what was so odd about it."

"I know. That's why I hesitated to tell you. But when I picked the tray up from the props table, I definitely got that feeling."

"Perhaps then it was something *on* the table?" asked Barnaby, his interest quickening. "In the wrong position. Or maybe something that shouldn't have been there at all?"

David shook his head. "No. It was to do with the tray."

"Well"—Barnaby got to his feet dismissively—"keep mulling it over. It could be important. Ring me if anything clicks."

Colin thrust out his hand, and the strength of his gratitude for Barnaby's white lies could be felt in the firm grip. "I'm very, very sorry, Tom, to have been so much bother."

They left then, and Barnaby stood at his office door and watched them, David striding forward looking straight ahead, Colin loping alongside in a cloud of relief so dense it was almost tangible. As they went through the exit, Colin, careful not to sound incredulous, said, "But why Deidre?"

And Barnaby heard David reply, "Because she needs me more than anyone else ever will. And because I love her."

Deidre walked up the drive toward the Walker Memorial Hospital for Psychiatric Disorders, the dog trotting at her heels. On being informed by Barnaby that he was being kept in one of the police kennels until she claimed him, Deidre had called there on her way to the hospital to put the record straight. The nice blond policewoman was in reception and asked how Deidre was feeling. Deidre asked in her turn after the constable who rescued her father, then the policewoman lifted the counter flap, said, "Through here," and disappeared. Deidre, murmuring "The trouble is, you see," followed.

The kennels were really large cages and held three dogs. Two lay mopingly on the earthen floor, the third leaped to its paws and moved eagerly forward. Deidre, repeating "The trouble is, you see," looked down at the questing black nose and soft muzzle pressed against the wire mesh. The tail was wagging so fast it was just a brown blur. Policewoman Brierley was unfastening the padlock. Now was the time to explain. Afterward, trying to understand why she hadn't, Deidre decided it was all the dog's fault.

If he had whined or complained or yapped or reacted in any other way but the way that he had, she was sure her heart could have been hardened. But what she couldn't handle was his simple confidence. There was no doubt at all in his eyes. Here she was at last, and off they would be going. And didn't she owe him something? reasoned Deidre, recalling the terrible night when he had been her father's only companion.

"Got his lead?"

"Oh...no...I came straight from the Barnabys'. I haven't been home yet."

"Shouldn't really take him without a lead." She was replacing the lock. Deidre looked at the dog. His expression of dawning dismay was terrible to behold.

"It'll be all right," she said hurriedly. "He's very well-trained. He's a good dog."

PW Brierley shrugged. "Okay. If you say so..." and opened the cage. The dog ran out, jumped up at Deidre, and started licking her hands. She signed a form for his release and they left the station together and entered the High Street. The cobbler's had some brightly colored leads and collars, and Deidre chose one of scarlet leather with a little bell. As she bent down to put it on, the man behind the counter said, "D'you want a disc for him? In case he gets lost? Do one while you wait."

"Oh, yes—please." Already, barely minutes into dog ownership, Deidre could not bear the thought of him getting lost. She gave her address and telephone number.

"And his name?"

"His name?" She thought frantically as the man stood with the drill buzzing ready. All sorts of common or garden dog's names came to mind, none of them suitable. He was certainly no Fido or Rover. Nor even a Gyp or Bob. Then she remembered the day center where she had first seen him and the name came. "Sunny," she cried. "He's called Sunny." The man engraved "Sunny," added the other details, and Deidre fixed the disc to the collar.

Now, arriving at the main hospital entrance, she wondered
what to do with him. "You can't come inside," she said. "You'll
have to wait." He listened closely. She tied his lead around an iron
foot-scraper and said, "Sit." To her surprise, he immediately lowered his ginger rump to the floor and sat. She patted him, said,
"Good dog," and went indoors.

She was immediately engulfed in a series of labyrinthine cor-
ridors and started walking with a heavy heart. When she had been
told, on ringing the general hospital to inquire when she could
visit, that her father had been transferred to "the Walker," she had
been horrified. The brooding soot-encrusted Victorian pile of
bricks had always been known locally as the fruit-and-nut house,
and, as a child, she had luridly imagined it inhabited by chained
people in white robes, raving and shrieking, like poor Mrs. Roch-
ester in *Jane Eyre*.

The reality was very different. So quiet. As Deidre continued
on past several pairs of swing doors looking for the Alice Kennedy
Baker ward you could have believed the place to be deserted.
Thick, shiny linoleum the color of cooked veal muffled every
footfall. The walls were dirty yellow, the paint cracked and peel-
ing, and the radiators, though giving out powerful blasts of heat,
were scabbed with rust.

But all these things, though depressing, were nothing compared to the deadening pall of despair that permeated the atmosphere. Deidre felt it choking her lungs like noisome fog. It
smelled of stale old vegetables and stale old people. Of urine and
fish and, most profusely, of the sickly synthetic lavender that had
been aerosoled everywhere in a futile attempt at aping normal domesticity. A nurse, crackling by in white and sugar-bag blue,
asked her if she was lost, then pointed her in the right direction.

The Kennedy-Baker ward appeared to be empty but for a
West Indian nurse sitting at a small table in the center by a telephone. She got up as Deidre entered and said the patients were in
the sun lounge. She explained why Deidre had not been consulted
over the decision to transfer her father. Apparently there was no
question of permission being sought. He was being admitted to
the Walker for his own safety and that of others. If Deidre wished
to speak to the doctor in charge of his case, an appointment could
be made.

"Your father's feeling very well, though, dear," she added as she led Deidre to the sun lounge, a bulbous growth on the far end of the ward. "Quite tip-top."

The lounge had a gray-stained haircord carpet, assorted shabby chairs, and an ill-conceived and poorly executed oil painting of its benefactress in true electric blue gazing munificently down at the assembled company. There were five people in the room; three elderly women, a young man, and Mr. Tibbs, who was sitting by the window wearing unfamiliar pajamas and a violently patterned dressing gown surely designed to stimulate rather than to soothe.

"Your daughter's come to see you, Mr. Tibbs. Isn't that nice?" said the nurse very firmly, as if expecting some denial.

Deidre pulled up a low chair with scratched wooden arms and sat down, saying, "Hullo, Daddy. How are you feeling?"

Mr. Tibbs continued to gaze out of the window. He didn't look very "tip-top." His jaw gaped in a sad, loose way and was covered in grayish-white stubble and snail trails of dried saliva. Deidre said, "I've brought you some things."

She unpacked her bag and laid his toilet articles, some soap, and Arrowroot biscuits on his lap, keeping back his special treat, a box of Turkish delight, until the last moment, to east the pain of parting. He looked at the little pile with fierce puzzlement, then picked the things up one at a time, handling them very carefully, as if they were made of glass. He obviously had no idea what they were, and tried to put the soap in his mouth. Deidre took them all away again, and put them on the floor.

"Well, Daddy," she said brightly, struggling to keep her voice on an even keel, "how are you?" Oh, God, she thought, I've asked that already. What could she say next? And what an incredible question to be asking herself. She who had spent years quietly and contentedly talking and listening to the old man in the basket chair who bore such a strange resemblance to her father. She couldn't even tell him about the dog, in case it brought back memories of that shocking night at the lake. So she just held his hand and looked around the room.

The young man in baggy flannel trousers was drumming on his knees with the tips of his fingers at tremendous speed. He sat next to an elderly woman with the hooded, gorged glance of a satisfied bird of prey. Then there was a dumpy, bald woman with warts like purple Rice Krispies who was stretching out her arms, palms inward, holding an invisible skein of wool. The third woman was just a bundle of clothing (checks and spots and stripes and patterned lisle stockings) with a tube disappearing up the skirt from which hung a plastic bag of yellow liquid. There they sat, each sealed in an impenetrable bubble of drugs and dreams. They could not even be said to be waiting, since the act of waiting acknowledged the possibility that life might be about to change. Deidre eased back her sleeve and looked at her watch. She had been in the sunshine lounge for three minutes and suddenly felt that she could stand no more. She fastened her coat and started to pull on her gloves. Her father gazed blindly out of the window. I can do nothing here, she thought. I am no help. No use. "I'll come again soon, Daddy. . . . On Sunday. . ."

She stumbled out into the ward proper. Before she had reached the swing doors, she heard her father's voice raised in song to the tune of his favorite hymn, "The Old Rugged Cross." But the words were strange and garbled, and some of them obscene.

Nicholas, invited to dinner, had arrived bursting with excitement, brandishing his letter of acceptance to Central and sporting a battered nose. He had been at the house half an hour and hadn't stopped going on about the letter, although, as far as Avery was concerned, you could have covered the subject adequately in two minutes flat and still had time for a lengthy reading from the Upanishads.

"Isn't it absolutely marvelous?" Nicholas was saying yet again.

"Enough to bring stars to your eyes." Tim smiled. "Drink up."

Avery, eggshell-brown tonsure gleaming under the spotlights, was slicing a tenderloin of pork into slices so thin they fell into soft rosy curls on the marble slab. Peanuts and chilies stood by. The fresh tomato soup was keeping warm in the double boiler. Basil, picked the previous summer and immediately frozen into an ice cube, thawed in a cup. Avery moved purposefully among his culinary arcana and drank a little Frog's Leap Cabernet Sauvignon almost content. Almost, not quite. A cloud, no bigger than a man's lie, would keep drifting across his horizon. And a tiny scene—hardly a scene even, a vignette, was stamped on his memory.

Tim and Esslyn, standing together in the clubroom, heads close, two tall, dark blades. Esslyn talking quietly. When Avery had entered, they moved apart, not guiltily (Tim never did anything guiltily), but quickly nonetheless. Avery had let several days drag by before he had casually asked what the fascinating conversation had been about. Tim had said he couldn't recall the time in question. The lie oblique. Bad enough. Avery let the matter slide. What else could he do? But then, much worse, came the lie direct.

While they were all huddling frailly in the wings, as Esslyn's life blood seeped into the boards and Harold stormed, Avery had whispered, "This will put the lighting out of his mind. P'raps we won't have to leave after all."

And Tim had said, "No. We'll definitely have to go now."

"What do you mean *now*?"

"What?"

"You said, 'We'll definitely have to go *now*.'"

"No, I didn't. You're imagining things."

"But I distinctly heard—"

"Oh, for Christ's sake! Stop nitpicking."

So, of course, Avery had stopped. Now, not quite content, he watched his love through the yellow-mottled screen of mother-in-law's tongue relaxing, toasting Nicholas.

"I must say," Avery called, making a special effort to put his fears aside, "I do miss not being able to bad-mouth Esslyn."

"I don't see why you shouldn't," replied Tim. "When he was alive, you never stopped."

"Mmm..." Avery took down a heavy iron pan, poured in some sesame oil, and added a pinch of anise. "Half the pleasure then was the chance that it would somehow get back to him."

"Tom said I ought to get a solicitor," Nicholas said suddenly. "I'm sure he thinks it was me."

"If he thought it was you, dear boy," said Tim, "you wouldn't be sitting there."

Nicholas cheered up then, and asked for the third time if they thought he would have any problem getting a grant for drama school. Avery reached for his chilies and threw a couple in. He shook and rattled his pan a little more loudly than was strictly necessary. He often did this when visitors came. Childlike, he was afraid both that they might forget he was there behind the monstera and philodendron or, if they did remember, might not appreciate just how hard he was working on their behalf.

Nicholas leaned back on a raspberry satin sofa seamed and scalloped like a great shell and drank deeply of his apéritif. He loved Tim and Avery's sitting room. It was an extraordinary mixture of downy delights such as the sofa and austere pieces of donnish severity like Tim's Oscar Woollen armchair, two low black glass Italian tables, and a stunning heavy bronze helmet lying on its side near the bookshelves. He said, "What's on the menu today, Avery?"

"Satay."

"I thought that was a method of doing yourself in." Nicholas slithered about on the shiny cushions. "Whoops! Can I have some more of this marvelous wine, Tim?"

"No. You're already all over the place. And there's some Tignanello with the meat."

"Shame!" cried Nicholas. Then: "Did you see Joycey's daughter on the first night? Wasn't she the most breathtaking thing?"

"Very lovely," said Tim.

"Those legs...and that long neck...and eyelashes...and those spectacular bones..."

"Well, you may not be the most sober person in the room, Nicholas," said Avery. "But my God you know how to take an inventory."

"Will you come and see me in my end-of-term shows?"

"How the boy leaps about."

"If asked," said Tim.

"Maybe in my last year I shall win the Gielgud medal?"

"Nicholas, you really must at least pretend to be a bit more modest, otherwise the rest of the students will positively loathe you." Avery turned his attention back to his cooking. He frazzled the pork a little, sipped some more wine, checked the soup, and peeped at his little sugar baskets with iced cherries keeping cool in the larder. Then he took hot brown twists of bread from the oven, poured the soup into a warm tureen, and tuned once more into the conversation.

Nicholas was saying that he would come back and see them in the holidays. Personally Avery believed that once the lad hit the smoke, neither of them would see or hear from him again. He called, "From me to you," and took in the tureen, the bread, and an earthenware bowl of Greek yogurt and sour cream. The talk was still of the theater.

"I don't know whether to stay on for *Vanya* or shoot off now," Nicholas was saying.

"You won't start at Central for months," said Tim.

"But I could get some sort of job and see all the plays and join a movement class or something."

"There are three marvelous parts in it," continued Tim. "And now that Esslyn's gone, you could take your pick."

"Mmm." Nicholas spooned in some more soup. "This isn't very tomatoey, Avery."

"Miss Ungrateful," retorted his host. "Still, if your taste buds are punch-drunk on monosodium glutamate, what can one expect?"

"I don't know the play," said Nicholas. "What's it like?"

"Twice as long as *Little Eyolf* but without the laughs," said Avery. "And the tap routines."

"It's wonderful. A Russian classic."

"I don't think I fancy being directed by Harold in a Russian classic. He'll have us all swinging from the samovars. I think I'll go."

"You may not be allowed to go," said Tim, "while the investigation's still going on."

"Blimey." Nicholas scraped his bowl clean and held it out for more. "I hadn't thought of that. I suppose we're all under suspicion. Present company excepted."

"We've guessed and guessed at the possible culprit," said Avery, wielding the ladle. "You don't deserve this—but answer came there none."

"The present odds-on favorite is the Everards."

"Don't talk to me about the Everards," said Nicholas, tenderly touching his swollen nose.

"That was wicked of Tom to tell you," said Tim. "I didn't think the police did that sort of thing. I thought statements were in confidence."

"What have they got?" asked Avery.

"A black eye each and one cut lip."

"Don't swagger, Nicholas."

"He asked me! Anyway—why are they on top of the list? They were the court toadies."

"Nasty position, court toady," said Avery, passing the still-warm twists. "You must get to hate the person you're sucking up to."

"Not necessarily," said Nicholas. "Weak people often respect those much stronger than themselves. They feel safe getting carried along on their coattails."

"You surely don't see the Everards as weak, Nico?" said Tim.

"Well . . . yes . . . don't you?"

"Not at all."

"I can see him wanting to get rid of *them*," continued Nicholas, "nasty little parasites. But not vice versa. I still favor Kitty."

"What about Harold?" suggested Avery.

"Of course, along with everybody else, I'd just love it to be Harold. In fact, apart from him having neither motive nor opportunity, I see Harold as the perfect candidate." Nicholas slurped his last spoonful. "This soup really grows on you, Avery."

"Well, you're not having any more," cried Avery, bearing away the empties, "or you'll have no room for the nice bits."

Avery scraped the sauce, smelling of butter and peanuts, into a boat, and took his shallow Chinese dishes from the oven. He loved using these. They had a shaggy bronze crysanthemum painted on the bottom and small blue-green Oriental figures touched with gold around the sides going about their business in a world of tiny trees and short, square white rivers, tightly corrugated, like milky squibs. Avery got such pleasure from causing all this exquisite artificiality to vanish then, as he supped, gradually exposing it again. They were the only things in the kitchen that never went into the dishwasher, and only Avery was allowed to clean them. They had been an anniversary present from Tim bought during a holiday at Redruth, and so doubly treasured. Now, he brought the bowls with their curls of crispy pork and scurried round the table, placing them before the others.

Tim said, "I do wish you wouldn't romp," and Nicholas sniffed and murmured, "Aahhh . . . gravy mix." Avery bowed his head for a moment more in relief over a job well done than in thanks for benisons received, and they all dug in. Avery passed the sauce to Nicholas, lifting it high over the candle flames.

"There's no need to elevate it," said Tim. "It's not the host."

The Tignanello was opened and poured, and Tim lifted his glass. "To Nicholas. And Central."

"Oh, yes..." Avery toasted Nicholas, who grinned a little awkwardly. "R. and F. before you're twenty-five, or I shall want to know the reason why. And don't forget—we believed in you first."

"I won't." Nicholas gave a slightly drunken smile. "And I'm so grateful for everything. The room...your friendship... everything..."

"Don't be grateful," said Tim. "Just send seats in the front row of the dress circle for all your first nights."

"Do you think then...the gods will reward me by answering my prayers?" The heavy attempt at sarcasm was only partially successful. Nicholas's voice trembled.

"Nico—you're so naive." Tim smiled. "That's the way the gods punish us—by answering our prayers."

"Oh, my—it's not going to be one of your world-weary evenings is it? I don't think I could stand that."

But Avery's response was jocular, and he appeared the picture of contentment. He beamed, and his little blue eyes twinkled. He started to relax. He had been tiptoeing about very carefully all day, because his morning horoscope, though fairly positive on the whole, had ended, "There may be friction in the home, however." But surely, reasoned Avery, by nine-thirty any respectable bird of ill omen must be safely tucked up in its nest, reading the runes for the following day.

"Is it all right?" he asked, mock-anxious.

"My love—it's absolutely marvelous." Tim reached out, and his slim El Greco fingers rested briefly, lightly on Avery's arm. Avery's face burned with the intensity of his pleasure, and his heart pounded. Tim *never* used an endearment or touched him when other people were present, and Avery had quickly learned that he must behave with the same propriety. Of course, it was only Nico but even so...

Avery breathed slowly and deeply, experiencing the spicy scents of the meat, the delicate fragrance of the jasmine in its hooped basket, the aroma of the wine, and the slightly acrid drip of the candles not just briefly in the membranes of his nose but pervasively, as if they had been injected into his bloodstream and were spreading languorously through his body. He broke a piece of bread and popped it into his mouth, and it was like the bread of angels.

The phone rang. Everyone groaned. Avery, who was nearest, pushed back his chair and, carrying his glass, went to answer it.

"Hullo?...Oh, hullo, darling."

"Who is it?" Tim mouthed, silently.

Avery pressed the secrecy button. "The Wicked Witch of the West."

"My condolences."

"Tim sends his love, Rosa."

"And mine."

"And Nicholas. We've been having the most divine—Oh, all right. I'll be quiet. There's no need to be rude. One must go through these opening civilities, otherwise one might just as well take to the hills...Shut up yourself, if it comes to that." He switched again. "Evil-tempered old crone."

The two men at the table exchanged glances. Tim's faintly humorous, rather resigned. Nicholas's wry, even a touch patronizing. A look that would never have graced his features when their friendship had first begun. They turned their attention back to Avery, whose face was avidity personified. His soft lips, delicately tinted toffee brown from the satay, were pushed forward into a thrilled marshmallow O.

"My dear!" he cried. "But didn't we always say? Well, I certainly always said...Are you sure? Well, that clinches it then... Of course I will...and *you* keep *me* posted." He hung up, took a deep swallow of his wine, and hurried back to the table. Bursting with information, he looked from Tim to Nicholas and back again. "You'll never guess."

"If there are three more irritating words in the English language," said Tim, "I've yet to hear them."

"Oh, come on," Nicholas said, rather slurrily, "what she say?"

"The police have arrested David Smy."

Avery sat back more than satisfied with the effect of his pronouncement. Nicholas gaped foolishly in disbelief. Tim's face, golden and ivory in the candle's flame, became bleached; white and gray. "How does she know?"

"Saw him. She was going to the library when a police car drew up outside the station and two cops marched him inside."

"Did he have a blanket over his head?"

"Don't be so bloody silly, Nicholas. How on earth could she have known it was David if he'd had a blanket over his head?"

"Only they do," persisted Nicholas with stolid determination. "If they're guilty."

"Well, really. Sometimes I think your thought processes should be in a medical mysteries museum."

"Leave the boy alone." Tim's voice laid a great chill over the lately so festive company. "He's had too much to drink."

"Oh . . . yes . . . sorry." Avery picked up his glass, then nervously put it down again. His exhilaration was draining away fast. Almost as he entertained this thought, the last couple of wisps evaporated. He looked across at Tim, who was not looking at him, Avery, but through him, as if he didn't exist. Avery looked down at the glistening puddle of peanut sauce, picked up his spoon, which clattered against the gilded rim of the bowl, and tasted a little. It was nearly cold. "Shall I warm this up Tim . . . do you think? Or bring in the pudding?"

Tim did not reply. He had withdrawn into himself as he occasionally did in a way that Avery dreaded. He knew Tim didn't mean this behavior as any sort of punishment. The action was so undeliberate as to appear almost involuntary, yet Avery inevitably felt responsible. He turned to their guest. "Are you ready for some pudding, Nico?"

Nicholas smiled briefly and shrugged. He looked a little sulky and deeply abashed, as if guilty of some social misdemeanor. Yet, Avery thought, it is I who have committed the solecism. How unpleasant now, how *crass,* his reception of Rosa's news appeared. With what salacious relish had he rushed to the table to relay the information, as if it were some edible goody he couldn't wait to share. If he had stopped to think, even for a moment, he must have behaved differently. After all, this was a friend they were talking about. They all liked David and his kind, unhurried ways. And now he might be going to prison. For years. No wonder Tim, extremely fastidious at the best of times, had removed his attention from such a lubricious, blubbering display.

"Well . . ." he said, forcing cheeriness into his voice, "it doesn't do to get depressed. Okay, Rosa saw him going in . . . what does that mean? He might have just been asked to help clear up one or two points. Help them with their inquiries." Avery wished he hadn't said that. He was sure he'd read somewhere that

was the official way of announcing that the police had got the
guilty party but weren't legally supposed to say so. "Just because
he was the man in the lighting box doesn't mean... well... what
else have they got to go on, after all?" (Only that he had ample
opportunity. Only that he was the man who took the razor on.
Only that his mistress was now a rich widow.) Tim was getting up.

"What... what's happening?" said Avery. "We haven't finished."

"I've finished."

"Oh, but you must have some cherries, Tim! You know
how you love them. I made them especially. In little sugar baskets."

"Sorry."

I could kill Rosa, thought Avery. Malicious, scandalmonger-
ing, interfering old bitch! If it weren't for her, this would never
have happened. And we were having such a lovely time. Tears of
disappointment and frustration sprang to his eyes. When they
cleared, Tim, wearing his overcoat and Borsalino hat, was at the
sitting room door. Avery leaped to his feet.

"Where are you going?"

"Just out."

"But *where,* Tim?" Avery hurried across and hung on Tim's
arm. His voice trembled as he continued, "You must tell me!"

"I've got to go to the station."

"...the... the police station?" When Tim nodded, Avery
cried, "What on earth for?"

But even as he asked, Avery's heart was squeezed with the
terrible cold foreknowledge of what would be Tim's reply.

"Because," said Tim, gently removing Avery's hand from
his sleeve, "I was the man in the lighting box."

Tim was sorry he had come. Barnaby had vouchsafed the information (it seemed to Tim with a certain amount of wry pleasure)
that David Smy, far from being arrested, was as free as a bird and
likely to remain so. Still, Tim's confession had been made, and he
could hardly take it back. He had assumed once this simple statement had been completed, he would be free to go, but Barnaby
seemed keen to question him further. To add to the charm of these
unwelcome proceedings, the poisonous youth with the carroty
hair was also present at his scrivenings.

"Just background, you understand, Tim," Barnaby was saying. "Tell me how you got on with Esslyn."

"As well and as badly as anyone else. There was nothing to get on with, really. He was always posing. You never knew what he truly felt."

"Even so, it's unusual for someone to belong to a group for over fourteen years and not have a single relationship of any depth or complexity."

"Oh, I don't know. Lots of men don't have close friendships. As long as Esslyn was much admired and had plenty of sex, he was content." Tim smiled. "The advertiser's dream made manifest."

"No more than human." Barnaby sounded indulgent. "Which of us can't say the same?"

Bang on target, thought Troy. Don't knock it till you've had enough. Like when you're stepping into your coffin. Troy was feeling very put out. He just couldn't cope with the revelation that the man he thought of (apparently only too appropriately) as the cocky bugger in the executive suit had had it off with Kitty. Paradoxically, his resentment against Tim was now doubled. And the way he sauntered about. . . . Look at him now . . . completely at home, mildly interested, cool as a cucumber. The dregs of society, thought Troy, should know their place and not come floating to the surface mingling with the good honest brew. Serve Kitty right if she got AIDS.

"He was never short of female company, then?" Barnaby was asking.

"Oh, no. Nothing that lasted long, though. They soon drifted off."

"You don't know of anyone in the past that he had rejected? Who might be suffering from unrequited love?"

"Anyone involved with Esslyn, whether rejected or not, suffered from unrequited love. And no, I don't."

"You must realize, I'm sure, that Kitty is our number-one suspect. Did you assist her in doing away with her husband?"

"Certainly not. There would have been no reason for me to do so. Our affair was trivial. I was already tired of it."

"Did she let anything slip while you were together that might give us some insight into this matter?"

"Not that I recall."

"Or hint at any other man?"

"No."

"To get on to Monday night—"

"I've really nothing to add there, Tom."

"Well," said Barnaby easily, "you never know. Try this. Why did the murder happen then? Why not, for instance, at one of the early rehearsals? Fewer people hanging around. No coppers present."

"The wings are never dark at rehearsal. And there's always someone there prompting. Or wanting to do a scene change."

"They're not dark at the run-through, surely. Or the dress rehearsal?" When Tim did not reply, Barnaby added, "By the way —did I congratulate you on your splendid lighting?"

"I really don't remember."

It was like touching a snail on the horns, thought Barnaby, sensing the quick (protective?) folding in of the other man's attention.

"Harold seemed quite put out."

"Did he?"

"I noticed him thumping away in the intermission on the door of your box."

Tim shrugged. "He runs on a short fuse."

"Might've been less alarming if you'd sprung these splendid illuminations before the first night."

"If I'd done that, they'd never have reached the first night."

"So Harold didn't know?"

The snail disappeared completely. Although Tim's expression remained laconic, even a tinge scornful, his eyes were disturbed and the skin seemed to tighten over his patrician nose. "That's right."

"So he got two shocks for the price of one?"

"As things turned out."

"Quite a coincidence."

"They happen all the time."

Not this time, thought Barnaby. He did not know how he knew, but he knew. Somewhere way back in the murk of his mind, so faint as to be hardly apprehended, he heard a warning rattle. This man who could not possibly have murdered Esslyn Carmichael knew something. But he met Barnaby's gaze frankly, almost dauntingly, nor did he look away.

"You're probably not aware," said Barnaby, "that Harold is claiming the new lighting plot as his own."

"Hah!" Tim laughed harshly, strainedly. His face flushed. "So that—" his laughter croaked—"so that was all we had to do. Say 'Yes, Harold' to everything. And go our own way. Just like Esslyn."

"So it seems."

"All these years." He was still laughing in a rasping, irascible way when the chief inspector let him go a few minutes later.

Barnaby had seen no point in keeping Tim there or in applying pressure at this stage. Tim was not the sort to wilt under generalized bullish cajoling. But Barnaby knew now where the pressure point was and could apply a little leverage if or when it became necessary. He turned to his sergeant.

"Well, Troy?"

"A worried man, sir," Troy replied quickly. "All right till you touched on his lights, then shut up like balls in an ice bucket. He might have been hard put to it to have done the murder, but he knows something."

"I believe you're right."

"How would it be if I had a word with his friend"—Troy arched his wrist limply—"Little Miss Roly Poly. On her own, like." He winked. "She'd soon crumble." He received in exchange for the wink a stare so icy that he all but crumbled himself.

"First thing tomorrow I want to visit Carmichael's office. And his solicitor. Get on the phone and fix it."

Nicholas had left fairly quickly after Tim, thanking Avery for the dinner, then saying on the doorstep with absolute clarity, "I'm not as think as you drunk I am."

Now, Avery sat alone. He had finished the Tignanello, pouring and gulping, pouring and gulping, at first in shock, then, steadily, in bitter loneliness and despair. After emptying the bottle, he had, in a confused state of aggressive misery jumbled up with vague ideas of retaliation, opened some Clos St. Denis, *grand cru,* that he knew Tim was keeping for his birthday. He wrestled savagely with the cork, breaking off little pieces and sloshing the wine about.

The candles in their Mexican silver rose holders guttered, and Avery blew them out. But even in the dark the room was full of memories of Tim. Avery flinched at the word "memories," and chided himself for being melodramatic. After all, Tim was coming back. But no sooner had this thought, which should have been a comfort, struck him than it was swamped by a hundred others, all permeated with the fervor of self-righteousness. Oh, yes, observed Avery to himself with a miserable snigger, no doubt he'll be coming back. He won't find anyone else like me in a hurry. Who else would cook and iron and clean and care for him with just the odd kind word for wages? And that tossed so casually into the conversation it might have been a bone to a mangy cur. Who but me would have bought a bookshop and given—*yes given,* fulminated Avery, half of it away? Whose money had furnished the house? And paid for the holidays? And he asked so little in return. Just to be allowed to love and look after Tim. And to be offered in exchange a modicum of affection. Immensely moved by this revelatory glimpse into the nobility of his soul, Avery shed a disconsolate tear.

But the tear had no sooner dried on his cushiony cheek than the cold finger of reason pointed out that, for a reasonable sum, people could be found to cook and iron and clean and that Tim had once earned an excellent living teaching Latin and French in a public school and no doubt could do so again. And that if Avery poured out all the tiger words that, at this moment, were prowling round his heart when Tim came back, he might put on his Crombie overcoat and Borsalino hat and leave again, this time forever. And in fact (Avery felt sick with apprehension), even if he made the most tremendous superhuman efforts at self-control and behaved with calmness and understanding when his lover returned, it was probably too late. Because Tim had already met somebody else.

Avery stood up suddenly and put the light on. He felt he must move. Walk about. He thought of going down to the station to meet Tim, to know the worst right away, and had seized his coat and opened the front door before he recognized what a foolish thing that would be to do. For Tim hated it when Avery "trailed around" after him. Also (Avery dropped his coat onto the raspberry bouffant sofa), his quick dash to the door had revealed him to be intensely, dizzily nauseous. He moved to the table and sat upright with difficulty, holding on to the edge. He felt as if he were trapped in a revolving door of the emotions. Having whipped rapidly and passionately through jealousy, rage, yearning fear, and concupiscence, he now seemed to be meeting them all on the way back.

Avery made a huge effort to fight free of this soggy swamp

of wretchedness. He drank several large glasses of Perrier and sat quietly struggling to compose himself. He tried to think as Tim would think. After all, what was done could not be undone. Perhaps, Avery thought tremulously, I am blowing it up out of all proportion. Also, getting into this state is just what Tim would expect. Poor Tim. Sitting down there for hours at the police station and then coming home to face a raging screaming row. How remarkable, how truly amazing it would be if he were welcomed by a tranquil, smiling, naturally slightly distant but ultimately *forgiving* friend. Let him without sin, decided Avery, and all that jazz. What would be the point, after all, of railing at Tim because he was not doggedly faithful? It's because he's so completely unlike me, realized Avery, now quite mooney with sentiment, that I love him so. And how proud he will be when he sees just how well I can actually handle things. How mature and wise, how detached, he will find me in the face of this, our first real catastrophe. Avery's chest had just swelled to a pouter-pigeon prominence when he heard a key in the door, and a moment later Tim was standing before him.

Avery yelled, "You faithless bastard!" and threw one of the Chinese bowls. Tim ducked, and the bowl hit the architrave and shattered into small pieces. When Tim bent to pick them up, Avery shouted, "Leave it! I don't want it. I don't want any of them. They're all going in the trash bin!"

Ignoring him, Tim picked up the pieces and put them on the table. Then he got a clean glass from the kitchen and poured some of the Clos St. Denis. He sniffed at it and made an irritated sound, picking out a few cork crumbs.

"I was laying this down."

"Seems to be your favorite occupation."

"If you wanted to get tanked up, why on earth didn't you use the Dao? There's half a dozen bottles in the larder."

"Oh, yes—the Dao! Any old rubbish will do for me, won't it? I haven't got your exquisite palate. Your celebrated *je ne sais quoi.*"

"Don't be silly." Tim took a thoughtful swallow. "Wonderful fruit. A lot of style. Not as big as I expected."

"Well hoity fucking toity."

"I'm tired." Tim removed his muffler and coat. "I'm going to bed."

"You most certainly are not going to bed. You are going to

leave my house. And you are going to leave it now!"

"I'm not going anywhere at this hour of the night, Avery." Tim hung up his coat. "We'll talk in the morning, when you've sobered up."

"We'll talk now!" Avery leaped up from the table and stumbled over to the hall, where he stood at the bottom of the staircase barring the way. Tim turned then, made his way to the kitchen, and started filling up the coffemaker. Avery followed, crying, "What do you think you're doing?" And "Leave my things alone."

"If I'm going to stay awake, I need some strong coffee. And so, by the look of things, do you."

"What did you expect? To come home and find me all sweet reason? Clearing up after the Last Supper? Counting out your thirty pieces of silver?"

"Why are you being so dramatic?" Tim spooned the Costa Rica out lavishly. "And come and sit down before you fall down."

"You'd like that, wouldn't you? You'd love it if I fell and hit my head and died. Then you'd get the shop and the house, and you'd be able to move that bloody little tart in here. Well, you can think again, because first thing tomorrow I shall go to the solicitor's and change my will."

"You can do what you like tomorrow. For now, I should concentrate on parking your bum on something and getting this coffee down you."

Avery, allowing a moment for a disdainful pause, thus making it clear that any move he might be inclined to make would be entirely of his own choosing, made his erratic way over the kitchen floor and contemplated the north face of the Bentwood stool. Somehow he managed to clamber up and hang on, swaying like an aerial mast in a high wind.

The rich, homely smell of coffee filled his nostrils cruelly, recalling a thousand shared starts to happy days and as many intimate and gossipy after-dinner exchanges. All gone now. All ruined. He and Tim would never be happy again. Avery's eyes filled with sorrow as the utter terribleness of the situation struck him anew, and a thrill of pain stabbed clean through the deadening haze of alcohol. A needle to the heart.

As Tim passed the coffee, he folded Avery's limp, unresisting fingers around the cup, and this gesture of concern was the last straw breaking the back of Avery's anger and releasing a great gush of tears. And with the release of tears came an overwhelming need for contact and solace. He cried, "I *trusted* you..."

Tim sighed, put down his drink, pulled up a second stool, and sat next to Avery. "Listen, love," he said, "if we are going to have a heart-to-heart at this ridiculous hour of the morning, let's not start with a false premise. You have never trusted me. Ever since we started to live together, I've known that whenever we're apart, you do nothing but worry and fret over whether I'm meeting someone else or that I might one day meet someone else. Or that I've already met someone else and I'm concealing it. That is not trust."

"And you can see why now, can't you? How right I was. You said you were going to the post office."

"I went there first. Don't worry. All the books went off."

"I didn't mean that," screamed Avery. "You know I didn't."

"It was of no importance," said Tim quietly. "Not compared to us."

"Then *why?* Why risk you and me...all this...?" Avery gestured at the cozy sitting room with such vigor that he slid off his perch.

"God—you're pixilated," said Tim, helping him back up.

"I am not pissilated," wept Avery. "I mean...if it wasn't David in the box, I thought it might be Nico...or Boris. I never in a million years thought it could be you."

"I don't see why not. You know my sexual history."

"But I thought you'd turned your back on all that," said Avery. Then: *"Don't laugh."*

"Sorry."

"And why Kitty, of all people?"

Tim shrugged, remembering the combination of fragile bones and tough, sly cherubinical smile that had briefly excited him. "She was pretty, and lean...quite boyish, really...."

"She won't be boyish for long," cut in Avery. "Very unlean and unpretty she'll be."

"I wouldn't have wanted her for long," said Tim. And for a second he looked so desolate that Avery forgot who was the guilty party and almost made a move to comfort him as he would have done before the betrayal. "If it makes you feel any better," continued Tim, "it was Kitty who started it all. I think she regarded me as some sort of challenge."

"Some people don't seem to know the difference between a challenge and a bloody pushover." Avery braced himself. "How long . . . how many . . . ?"

"Half a dozen times. At the most."

"Oh, God!" Avery gasped as if from a body blow and covered his face with his hands. "And was she . . . I mean . . . has there been. . . ."

"No. No one else."

"What shall I do?" Avery rocked from side to side on his stool. "I don't know what to do."

"Why should you do anything? It seems to me more than enough's been done already. And don't blubber."

"I'm not." Avery took his little butterball fists, shiny with moisture, from his teary eyes. His pale yellow curls, limp with sorrow, looked like a ring of scrambled egg. He choked out the next words. "I don't know how you can be so heartless."

"I'm not heartless, but you know how I hate these honky tonk emotions." Tim tore a piece off the paper-towel roll and mopped Avery's face, which was crisscrossed with rivulets of tears and mucous and sweat. "And give me that cup before it's all over the floor."

"Everything's soiled . . . and . . . spoiled. I just can't bear it anymore . . ."

"I don't see how you can possibly know that until you try." This cold, sinewy reasoning brought Avery to a fresh pitch of misery. "I mean it, Tim," he cried. "You must promise me faithfully that you'll never ever *ever* again—"

"I can't do that. And you wouldn't believe me if I did. Oh, you might now, because you're desperate, but tomorrow you'd start to wonder. Any by the day after that . . ."

"But you *must* promise. I can't go on with all this insecurity."

"Why not? Everybody else has to. Your trouble is you expect too much. Why can't we just muddle along like Mr. and Mrs. Average? You know . . . doing our best . . . picking each other up if we fall . . . making allowances . . . Cloud nine's for retarded adolescents." Tim paused. "I never promised you a rose garden, as the saying goes."

"Well," said Avery, with a flash of the old asperity. "If I'm not going to have a rose garden, I shan't want all this shit, shall I?" Then, when Tim smiled his shadowy, introspective smile, Avery suddenly cried, "It'd be all right if I didn't love you so much!"

"But if you didn't love me so much, what on earth reason would I have for staying?"

Avery pondered this. Was such a remark a consolation? It seemed to imply that what he had to offer (the shop, the house, the meticulous and affectionate concern with which he went about his daily tasks) was not, after all, the reason why Tim stayed. Yet what else, worried Avery, did he have to offer? He turned the thought over. It seemed to him that the question had a catch in it somewhere, and he said so.

"There's always a catch." Tim moved back to the sitting room and collected the pieces of the Chinese bowl. "I must get some stuff tomorrow and fix this."

"That's right. Put the boot in." But Avery felt his woozy unhappiness touched by a flicker of warmth. Perhaps Tim would not be packing his bags after all. Perhaps in the morning they could open the shop and check the till and tidy the books and carefully, like the walking wounded that they were, reach out to each other for comfort. Tim came back and put the painted fragments on the kitchen table.

"I'm sorry about the dish."

"No, no. It's what I've always wanted," Tim said kindly. "A glued-together home."

"Do you remember Cornwall?"

"To my dying day. I thought I'd never get you away from that Redruth fisherman."

"Oh." Avery turned a guilty countenance toward his lover. "I'd forgotten all about that."

"I hadn't. But ... as you see ... I'm still here."

"Yes. D'you think"—Avery held out his hand—"we'll ever be really happy again?"

"Stop living in some mythical future. You can't invent happiness. It's just a by-product of day-to-day plodding along. If you're lucky."

"We have been lucky, haven't we, Tim?"

"We are lucky, you old tosspot. Best not to talk anymore now. I'm wacked."

Tim went upstairs then, leaving Avery to finish his coffee. He felt like a punching bag once the belaboring has ceased. Still vibrating with the memory and bruised. Then, because the first terror had passed and because Tim had come home and was going to stay, the concentration of despondency that had obscured Avery's fear lifted, and the cloud no bigger than a man's lie returned.

Tim's remark that he had first denied making then shrugged aside appeared suddenly to have developed an ominous gloss. For it seemed to Avery that to say "We shall certainly have to leave *now*" indicated some secret knowledge. Surely it implied that, if Esslyn had not been killed, Avery and Tim, in spite of the lighting conspiracy, would have been able to stay? Now, to add to Avery's alarm, was the information that Tim had been Kitty's lover. And it was Tim who had supplied the razor. Had he really just gone down to the john in the interval of the play? And why go downstairs at all when there were two restrooms in the clubroom?

Tim called, "What's keeping you? Come on..."

But for the first time ever Avery, even while experiencing the usual sting in the flesh, did not get up and hurry toward the source of his delight. He sat on in his disordered kitchen, getting colder and colder. And feeling more and more afraid.

It was the following day, and Harold was making one of his rare appearances at the lunch table. Usually he dined out, and Mrs. Harold, who put up the sandwiches, was quite thrown by this sudden change of plan. Her household budget was tiny, and any incursion at one point meant immediate retrenchment at another. She had found a Fray Bentos canned individual steak and kidney pudding at the back of the cupboard and had rushed out and bought some carrots out of her flower-seed money. But Harold had eaten so abstractedly that she felt she could well have given him her own lunch (boiled potatoes and two slices of luncheon meat) without him being any the wiser. Now, as he scraped up the last smear of gravy, she said, "It's not like you to come home midday, Harold."

"I'm taking the afternoon off. It's Nicholas's half day and we have to have a serious talk about his future."

"Does he know you're coming?" Harold looked blank. "I mean...have you made some arrangement?"

"Don't be silly, Doris. I don't make arrangements with junior members of the company."

"Then he might not be in."

"I can't imagine where else he would be on a dreadful day like this."

Doris looked out at the black rods of rain hammering against the kitchen window. "There's a piece of cake for sweet, Harold. If you'd like it."

Harold did not reply. He stared at his wife but did not see her yellowish-gray hair and shabby skirt and cardigan. His mind was full of his future leading man. He saw Nicholas striding the stage as Vanya and perhaps later as Tartuffe and later still as Othello or even Lear. Why not? Under Harold's expert guidance, the boy could develop into a fine actor. Every bit as good as Esslyn. Perhaps even better.

Harold had not come to this decision easily. He had toyed with Boris and even Clive Everard who gave, in his quirky posturing way, quite an interesting performance. But he was aware that the potential of both was still nowhere near that of Nicholas. The only reason Harold had considered, even briefly, an alternative was because of a certain willfulness, an antic disposition, that he had sensed strongly in the boy during rehearsals for *Amadeus*. Several times he had felt Nicholas getting away from him and glimpsed flashes of prowling energy that were disturbing, to say the least. And of course Nicholas was very saucy. But Harold was confident that he could handle it. After all, he had always managed to handle Esslyn.

"What are you going to see him about?" asked Doris.

"I'd have thought that was obvious. I have to find a replacement for Esslyn."

Mrs. Harold dutifully saw her husband off the premises and waved as he squeezed his paunch into position behind the wheel of the Morgan and backed out of the garage. A replacement for Esslyn indeed, she thought as she put the plates and cutlery in the sink. Anyone'd think he was a door handle. Or a broken teapot.

She had been deeply shocked by the reaction of Harold and the rest of the CADS to the death of their leading actor. She knew he wasn't popular (she hadn't liked him much herself), but some tears should be shed somewhere by someone. She decided to go to the funeral, and left the dishes to soak while she went upstairs to look for something dark and respectable.

Meanwhile Harold zipped up Causton High Street and parked outside the Blackbird. He planned to kill two birds and was pleased to see that Avery, who returned his greeting in a very subdued manner, and his partner were both in the shop. Harold beckoned Tim grandly to the cubbyhole and said, "I'm holding

auditions for *Vanya* on Friday evening. Dashing around and noti-
fying everyone. Is Nico in?"

"Yes but he's—"

"Good. Now—I'd be very interested to see any ideas you
might have on lighting the play." Ignoring Tim's surprised and
ironical glance, he continued, "Technically you're very capable,
and I think it's high time you were given a chance to branch out."

"Thank you, Harold."

"Nothing too fancy. It's Russia, don't forget." On this enig-
matic note, Harold whisked aside the chenille curtain and heaved
himself up the wooden stairs.

Nicholas was sitting on the floor declaiming. The gas fire was
on, and the room was warm and cozy. Cully Barnaby was curled up
on the bed drinking coffee. Play scripts littered the floor, and Nicholas was reading from the Harrison translation of the Aeschylus:
"Down, down, down he goes, and falling knows nothing, nothing.
A smother of madness clouds round the victim. The groans of
old—" As Harold appeared in the doorway, Nicholas broke off, and
he and Cully looked at the intruder rather coolly.

"Ah," said Harold, missing the coolness but spotting the appellation. "I'd have expected to see you reading *Uncle Vanya*."

"Why, Harold?"

"The auditions are on Friday." Harold would have preferred
this conversation without Tom Barnaby's daughter sitting in. She
had been, in his opinion, although quite a good actress, a nasty,
self-opinionated little girl, and she didn't improve with age. Harold cleared his throat.

"I'm sure you will be very proud . . . very excited to hear that
I have chosen you out of all the company to succeed Esslyn as my
leading man." Harold could see from the expression on Nicholas's
face that he should perhaps have led up to this revelation more
subtly. The boy looked deeply alarmed. Reassuringly Harold
added, "You're too young for Vanya, of course, but if you work
hard, with my help I know you'll be a great success."

"I see."

So overwhelmed was Nicholas with emotion that he choked
out the words. Then he added something else, but the girl chose
that precise moment to indulge in a fit of coughing, and Harold
had to ask Nicholas to repeat himself. When he did so Harold,
openmouthed with dismay, tottered to the nearest chair and fell
into it.

"Leaving?"

"I'm going to Central."

"Central what?"

"Central School of Speech and Drama. I want to go into the theater."

"But . . . you're *in* the theater."

"I mean the real theater."

The force of Harold's response lifted him clean from his seat. He gave a great cry in which rage and incredulity and horror were equally intermingled. Nicholas paled and climbed hurriedly to his feet. Cully stopped coughing.

"How dare you!" Harold walked across to Nicholas, who stood his ground but only just. "How dare you! My theater is as real . . . as true . . . as fine as any in the country. *In the world.* Do you have any idea who you're talking to? What my background is? I have heard the sort of applause for my work in what you are pleased to call the real theater that actors would sell their souls to achieve. Stars have clamored to work for me. Yes—stars! If it weren't for circumstances completely beyond my control, do you think I'd be working in this place? With people like you?"

The final sentence was a tormented shout, then Harold stood, panting. He appeared bewildered and ridiculous, yet there was about him the tatters of an almost heroic dignity. He looked like a great man grown overnight too old. Or a warrior on whose head children have placed a paper crown.

"I'm . . . I'm sorry . . ." Nicholas stumbled into speech. "If you like, I could stay for *Vanya* . . . I don't have to go to London immediately."

"No, Nicholas." Harold stayed the boy's words by a simple gesture. "I would not wish to work with anyone who did not appreciate and respect my directorial gifts."

"Oh. Right. I might come along and audition anyway . . . if that's okay?"

"Anyone," replied Harold, magisterially breaking upstage right, "can audition."

After he had left, the two young people smiled at each other, celebrating their meeting and mutual admiration.

"Will you go on Friday?" asked Cully.

"I think so. He might've calmed down by then."

"Then I shall, too."

"You wouldn't."

"Why not? I'm not due back till the end of January. And I'd give anything to play Yelena. We can always work our own way."

"Gosh—that'd be fantastic."

Cully parted her lovely lips and smiled again. "Wouldn't it though?" she said.

Barnaby and Troy were in the office of Hartshorn, Weatherwax, and Tetzloff. Their Mr. Ounce, who handled Esslyn Carmichael's affairs, was being affable if slightly condescending. Entertaining the police, his manner implied, was not what he was used to, but he hoped if it was thrust upon him, he could behave as well as the next man.

But if Barnaby had hoped to discover some sinister undertow to the murdered man's life in his solicitor's office, he was unlucky. Mr. Ounce could reveal little more than did the arid contents in the desk at White Wings. Barnaby had been unlucky at the bank as well. No suspiciously large sums of money ever leaked in or out of the Carmichael account, all was depressingly well ordered, the balances no more and no less than one would have expected. The only thing remaining was the will, which he was about to hear read. (He had offered to apply in the proper manner and go to a magistrate, but Mr. Ounce had graciously waived the necessity, saying he was sure time was of the essence.)

The document was brief and to the point. His widow would get the house and a comfortable allowance for herself and the child as long as she carried out her maternal duties in a proper manner. Carmichael Junior would get the full dibs on reaching twenty-one, and in the event of the child's demise everything, including White Wings, went to the brother in Ottawa. Mr. Ounce replaced the stiff ivory parchment folds in a metal deeds box and snapped the lock.

"Neatly tied up," said Barnaby.

"I must confess my own fine Italian hand was somewhat to the fore there, Chief Inspector." He rose from his old leather swivel chair. "We can't let the ladies have it all their own way, can we?"

"Blimey," said Troy, when they were back in the station and warming themselves up with some strong coffee. "I wouldn't mind being a fly on the wall when Kitty hears that."

Barnaby did not respond. He sat behind his desk tapping his nails against each other. A habit to which he was prone when deep in thought. It drove Troy mad. He was just wondering if he could sneak out for a quick drag when his chief gave voice.

"What I can't get, Sergeant, is the timing. . . ." Troy sat up. "There are dozens of ways to kill a man. Why set it up in front of a hundred witnesses . . . taking risks backstage . . . tinkering with a razor . . . when all you have to do is wait and catch him on some dark night?"

"I feel that's rather a strike against Kitty, myself, chief. Trying it at home, she'd be the first person we'd suspect."

"A good point."

"And now we've flushed the lover out," Troy bounded on, encouraged, "*and* discovered that he was the one who supplied the razor in the first place. I bet he even suggested the tape—"

"I think not. I've asked a lot of people about that. The general consensus seems to be that it was Deidre."

"Anyway, there he is with the perfect alibi, leaving Kitty to carry the can. That sort always do."

"I don't know. It's a bit obvious."

"But . . . excuse me, sir . . . the times you've said the obvious is so often the truth."

Barnaby nodded. The observation was a fair one. As was Troy's implication that the familiar unheavenly twins lust and greed were once again probably the motivating power behind a sudden death. So why did Barnaby feel this case was different? He didn't welcome this perception, which seemed to him at the moment to lead absolutely nowhere, but it would not be denied. He saw now, too, that his previous knowledge of the suspects, which he had regarded from the first as an advantage, could also work against him. It was proving well nigh impossible to make his mind the objective mirror it should be if he was to appreciate what was really going on. His understanding of Kitty's character, his liking for Tim and the Smys, his sympathy for Deidre, all were gradually forcing him into a corner. At this rate, he observed sourly to himself, I'll hardly have a suspect left.

And then there was *Floyd on Fish*. He picked it out of his tray and fanned the pages yet again. The thing had been through the works at the lab. It was no more and no less than what it purported to be, and smothered with dozens of assorted prints. Now, why the hell should someone send Harold, who had not the slightest interest in cooking, a recipe book? Why was it given anonymously? Troy, asked for his ideas, had been worse than useless. Just given one of his excruciating winks and said, "Very fishy, chief." Joyce said Harold had seemed to be genuinely puzzled by its arrival, assumed it to be a gift from an unknown admirer, and promptly given it away. Barnaby couldn't see a single way in which it might be connected with the case, but it was certainly odd. A loose end. And he didn't care for loose ends, although, as the case looked at the moment like a bundle of cooked spaghetti, he supposed another one more or less didn't much signify.

Troy was clearing his throat, and Barnaby retrieved his wandering thoughts and raised his eyebrows. "If we're leaving sex and cash out, chief, I suppose the other big one would be that he'd got something on somebody and they wanted to keep him quiet." Barnaby nodded. "I know we didn't find any surprises in his account, but it could still have been blackmail. He could've been stashing it abroad."

"Mmm . . . it's an appealing idea. The trouble is, it doesn't fit the nature of the beast."

"Sorry, sir . . . I'm not quite with you on that one." Troy was frowning; a little anxious about being found wanting, but determined to have each step quite clear before proceeding to the next. He never pretended that he understood what Barnaby was getting at when he didn't, and the chief inspector, knowing how his sergeant longed to give the impression of keeping up or even leaping ahead, respected this veracity.

"I just don't think Carmichael was the type. It's not that he was a nice man—far from it—but he was completely self-absorbed. He had no interest in other people's affairs, or the sheer energetic nastiness a successful blackmailer needs."

"Jealousy then, chief? Him being the leading light and all that. Maybe somebody else wanted a go?" Even as he voiced this suggestion, Troy thought it was probably a nonstarter. Although he had quite enjoyed *Amadeus*, he thought the actors a load of pimpish show-offs. Personally he wouldn't have thought any of them had the guts to skin a rabbit, never mind putting somebody in the way of cutting their own throat. Still, he had been wrong before (Troy saw his willingness to admit to possessing this almost universal human weakness as a sign of real maturity) and might well be so again. "Perhaps they were all in it together, sir? Like that film on a train . . . where everybody had a stab at the victim. A conspiracy."

Barnaby raised his head at this and looked interested. Interested but glum. Troy remembered a phrase from the early morning news and essayed one of his witticisms.

"A putsch-up job, sir?"

"What?"

"Put up—it's a joke, chief. A sort of play on words. Putsch up—put up . . . "

Barnaby was silent for a minute, then spoke slowly. "My God, Troy. You might just be right."

Gratified, the sergeant continued, "It was in one of these banana republics—"

"It's so near . . ."

"That's what I said. Put and—"

"No, no. I'm not talking about that. Perhaps . . . let me think. . . ."

Barnaby sat very still. A nebulous possibility, no more than a glimmer, flickered into his mind. Flickered and was gone. Came back, solidified a bit, was gently tested.

"I wonder," continued Barnaby, "perhaps Esslyn gave us the reason for the murder. At least"—he groped toward the next words slowly—"he gave it to Kitty. She didn't have the wit to see the implication behind what he said, but I should have. There's no excuse for me."

Troy, appreciating that he also hadn't had the wit and that there was no excuse for him, either, regarded his boots sulkily. Barnaby got up and started to pace around, then sent his sergeant for some more coffee. Troy disappeared into the outer office and helped himself from the Cona.

When he returned to the inner sanctum, the DCI was gazing out the window. Troy put the mugs on the desk and returned to his seat. When Barnaby turned, he was struck by the paleness of the chief inspector's countenance. Pale but lively. No sooner had one expression, hopeful elation, registered than it was chased away by disbelief, which in turn gave way to a jauntiness that was almost debonair, dissolving into puzzlement.

"You've . . . got something then, sir?" asked Troy.

"I don't know. It's all out of whack . . . but it must be. I just can't see *how*."

Fat lot of good that is then, opined Troy silently. The old sod always did this when he believed a case was shifting toward a conclusion. He would say that all the information so far obtained was as available to Troy as it was to him and that the sergeant should be perfectly capable of coming to his own assessment. The fact that this remark was a perfectly valid one in no way lessened the sergeant's chagrin every time he heard it. Now, he noticed Barnaby was looking at him rather oddly. Then, to his alarm, the chief walked around the desk, came up to Troy's chair, bent down, and brought his lips close to the younger man's ear. Bloody hell, thought Troy, preparing to leap for the door. Who'd have thought it? Barnaby moved his mouth, breathed faintly, and returned to his seat. Troy produced a handkerchief and mopped his face.

"Well, sergeant," Barnaby said, in a blessedly masculine and unseductive manner. "What did I say?"

"Bungled, sir."

"Aaahhh..." It was a long, slow hiss of satisfaction. "Nearly, Troy. A good guess. Nearly...but not quite."

Bangles? thought the sergeant. Burgled? Boggled? Buggered? (Back to Doris and Daphne.) Or how about bonbons? Hey ...how *about* bonbons? The bloke was eating sweets all through the play. Or there was borrowed. That fitted. The razor was borrowed. All the dead man's clothes were hired. Wasn't much like bungled, though. *Fumbled.* Something had been fumbled. That was more like it. Meant practically the same thing, after all. As no revelation appeared to be forthcoming from the horse's mouth, Troy decided to settle for "fumbled." He looked across at Barnaby, who seemed to have gone into a trance. He was staring over Troy's left shoulder, the light of intelligence quite absent from his eyes.

But his mind was whirring. Like a chess player, he moved his figures around. On the black squares (the wings, the stage, the dressing rooms) and on the white (the lighting box, the clubroom, the auditorium). He forged likely and unlikely alliances and guessed at possible repercussions. He imagined mirrored reflections of his suspects, hoping that way to surprise a familiar face in secret revelatory relaxation. And gradually, by way of improbable juxtaposition, glancing insights, and hard-won recall of certain conversations, he arrived at an eminently workable hypothesis. It fitted very well. It made perfect sense and was psychologically sound. It explained (almost) everything. There was only one slight snag. The way things stood at the moment, what it hypothesized (who had murdered Esslyn Carmichael and why) could not possibly be anywhere near the truth. He muttered that fact aloud.

Near what truth? wondered Troy, still smarting over his inability to figure out Barnaby's earlier insights. Now, the chief was rumbling again. Rumble, rumble. Mutter, mutter.

"There *had* to be an audience, Troy. We've been looking at things from quite the wrong angle. It wasn't a hazard—it was an essential. So that everyone could see what he was doing."

"What, Carmichael?"

"No, of course not. Use your nous." Barnaby picked up a ball-point and started scribbling. "And don't look so affronted," he continued, not looking up. "Think, man!"

While Troy thought, Barnaby reflected minutely on the times and the names and positions he had jotted down. If everyone was where they said they were at the times they said they were, doing what they said they were doing, then he was up a creek. So someone was lying. Fair enough. You expected murderers to lie. But when you had a theater full of people prepared to stand by what was, after all, the evidence of their own eyes and back him up then you were in a real bind. Especially when two of the eyes were your own.

But he knew he was right. He knew in his blood and in his bones. Over the years he had come to this point in a case too many times to be mistaken. Details might be unclear, practicalities elusive, methodology right up the Swanee, but he knew. The backs of his hands prickled, his neck in the stuffy, overheated office crawled with cold. He knew and could do nothing.

"Oh, fuck it, Troy!" The sergeant jumped as Barnaby's fist hit the desk. "I'm bloody hemmed in. Nobody can be in two places at once . . . can they?"

"No, sir," replied Troy, feeling for once on pretty safe ground. He was not displeased to see Barnaby foxed. You could put up with just so much swaggering about. Now, there were two of them without a bloody clue. He watched his chief's fierce frown and tightly clamped jaw. Any minute now, the little brown bottle would appear. And here it was. The chief inspector shook out two indigestion tablets and chased them down with cold coffee. Then he sat and stared at his piece of paper for so long that the neat black letters became meaningless.

"This is where," he said to Troy, "if I were a religious man, I should start praying for a miracle."

And—such is the wickedly unfair tilt of things in a world where a monk can spend his life on his knees and never get a nibble—for Tom Barnaby, sometimes profane, moderately decent, frequent faller by the wayside, the miracle occurred. Buzz, buzz. He picked up the phone. It was David Smy. Barnaby listened for a moment, responded "You're quite sure?" and replaced the receiver.

"Troy," he said, presenting an awesome countenance. "When all this is over, remind me to send a hefty check to a worthwhile cause."

"Why's that then, chief?"

"Strokes of luck like this must be paid for, sergeant. Otherwise whoever's sending them gets annoyed."

"So what did they say? Whoever it was."

"If you remember," said Barnaby with a smile so broad it seemed to touch his ears, "David thought there was something odd about the tray he took on."

"But he described it all and there wasn't."

"Quite right. But you'll recall from his statement that as it was a personal prop he gave the tray a quick look-see about the five. Now, the razor that Young supplied and that the murdered man used to cut his throat had a mother-of-pearl design of flowers and leaves on one side of the handle and a little line of silver rivets on the reverse. The reason David Smy thought there was something odd when he entered the wings with it lying sunny-side down on his tray was because he noticed the rivets."

"So?"

"When he gave the tray the once-over just before eight, *the rivets were not there.*"

"Then"—Troy picked up the inspector's excitement—"there were two?"

"There were two."

"So all our problems with the time . . . ?"

"Gone. The whole thing's wide open. It could have been tinkered with any time between when Deidre checked it and ten o'clock, when David took it on."

"So . . . whoever it was left the substitute, took the tape off, and slipped the original back in his or her own good time."

"Precisely. I'd thought of that option, of course, but assumed no one would dare risk leaving the tray on the props table minus the razor for more than a few minutes, even with the wings dark. But, as we now see, they didn't have to."

"So you're no longer boxed in, sir?" Troy struggled hard not to sound peevish. He didn't wish to appear mean-spirited, but really, the way information fell into some people's laps was beyond a joke. Then he recalled that some of the kudos at the end of a successful case always fell on the bag-carrier and cheered up. "So we've got a full house, then? Anybody could have done it?"

"I think we'll have to except Avery Phillips. He didn't come out of the box till after the murder. But apart from him, yes... anybody." He got up, suddenly full of vim and vigor, and grabbed his coat. "I'm going to sort out a warrant. Get the car round."

"We looking for the other razor, sir?"

"Yes. I expect whoever it is has had the sense to chuck it by now, but you never know. We might strike lucky."

By the time Barnaby returned from Superintendent Penrose's office, Troy, sub-Burberry tightly belted, had brought the car round.

"Where to first, chief?"

"We'll start at the top and work our way down."

Deidre opened the front door of the house and stepped inside. It was eerily quiet. She had always thought of her father's presence as a silent one; now, she realized it instigated many subtle sounds. The creak of his armchair, the soft rub of his clothes against the furniture, the snatched papery rustle of his breath. She took off her coat and Sunny's leash and hung them in the dingy hall, then walked to the kitchen, where she stood uncertainly, looking at the dishes that had been sitting in the sink, gravied and custard-streaked, for the past four days. They looked as much a fixture as the spotted chrome taps and grubby roller towel. Best to keep busy, the medical social worker had said, and Deidre knew this was good advice. Even as she stood there, she saw herself sweeping and polishing and dusting. Hanging gay new curtains, placing a bright geranium on the windowsill. But vivid as these pictures were, they paled beside a concomitant weight of ennui so great that after a few more minutes attached to the hearth rug, she began to believe she would never move again.

Sunny, who had gone in for the most dashing leaps and runs when they were out, had already sensed the situation and now sat quietly at her feet. Deidre picked up her copy of *Uncle Vanya,* interleaved and crammed with production ideas and sketches for the set. One of the nicest things during her stay with the Barnabys had happened on Wednesday morning, when she had discussed the theater for hours with Cully, at first tentatively, then, as her companion responded with great interest, more and more enthusiastically. They had talked through lunch (extraordinarily inedible) and well into the afternoon, in fact right up to the time Deidre had had to leave for the hospital. She couldn't understand now why she had ever thought Cully sneering and standoffish.

Sunny made a hopeful sound, stretching his lips in that strange manner that dogs have; half yawn, half grin. Deidre started guiltily. He had not eaten all day, and had made no complaint till now. There were three cans of meat and a large bag of Winalot in her bag, and she put some food on a plate, then filled his stone dish marked DOG with clean water. She left the sound of steady lapping behind as she climbed the stairs.

In her father's room she started automatically to make his bed, then stopped, sharply recalled to the complete pointlessness of her task. She looked around, a fall of green blanket in her arms, taking in the bottle of medicine and little bottles of pills on the bamboo table; the Bible open at the First Book of Kings showing an engraving of Elijah being delicately fed by ravens; two pieces of Turkish delight in a saucer.

Gradually, and with the deepest apprehension, she absorbed the full enormity of what had happened. Her father was not poorly or a little unstable or susceptible to queer turns. He had Alzheimer's disease and was a danger to himself and others; the balance of his mind disturbed. Deidre had a sudden vision of some old-fashioned scales and an impersonal hand dishing out wholesome grains of sanity with a little brass scoop. They were white and clean like virgin sand. Into the other shallow metal saucer was poured a hot dark flux of irrationality until the saucer overflowed and the chaste pale granules were first swamped, then quite washed away, in the black froth of madness.

Deidre bowed her head. She swayed and momentarily fought for breath. But she did not sit down. And she did not cry. She stood for five full minutes in a tumult of misery and sorrow, then started to strip the bed and fold up the sheets and blankets. She opened the window and, as the cold air rushed in, realized for the first time how stuffy the room was. Fearful of her father's health once October had arrived, she had kept the window tightly closed. "That'll blow the cobwebs away," he would say when she opened it again in May. Having put the bedding in a neat pile, Deidre picked up the wastebasket and swept all bottles into it together with his carafe and glass. The Bible she snapped shut and replaced on the bookshelf.

She worked mechanically, under no illusion that her activities could even begin to ease, let alone transform, her situation. But (the social worker had been right in this respect) as she continued to go briskly from one simple task to the next, generating her own momentum, she became aware that the procedure did offer some slight degree of comfort. And—even more important —was getting her through the period she had dreaded most, her first time alone in Mortimer Street.

She shook the two rugs in the backyard and noticed how threadbare the dark red-and-blue Turkish one was. She rolled it up and pushed it in the trash bin. Then she carried the bedding downstairs and put it by the front door. She would have the sheets washed, the blankets cleaned, and give the lot to the Salvation Army. She cleaned and polished for the next hour, until the room shone and smelled fragrantly of beeswax and Windowlene. She replaced the single mat and put Mr. Tibbs's tortoiseshell hairbrush and comb and leather cuff-link box away in the chest of drawers. Then she leaned against the windowsill and sighed with something like satisfaction.

The room looked clean, neat, and would have appeared to a casual visitor quite impersonal. Deidre completed her task by dusting the pictures. Two Corot reproductions, a text (TRUST IN THE LORD) garlanded with pansies and ears of wheat and framed in burnt pokerwood, and "The Light of the World." Deidre flicked the dust from the first three while they were *in situ,* then took down the Holman Hunt and studied it pensively. The figure that had given comfort to her childish hurts and sorrows and had seemed to stand loving guard when she slept now appeared nothing more than a sentimental dreamer, a paper savior impotent and unreal, standing in his flood of insipid yellow light. She fought against the pity that always gripped her at the sight of the crown of thorns; she fought against insidious false comfort.

Running downstairs again, holding the picture away from her almost at arm's length, Deidre hurried through the kitchen to the back garden and once more lifted the lid of the trash bin. She dropped "The Light of the World" inside and, replacing the cover, turned away immediately, as if that sad, calm, forgiving gaze might pierce the metal and catch her own. And she had no sooner gone back upstairs than the upbeat energy, the essential driving feeling that she was tackling a job well done, drained away. Now, looking at the poor denuded room with all traces of her father so firmly erased, Deidre was appalled. She was behaving as if he were dead. And as if his memory must always bring pain and never solace. She apologized aloud as if he could hear, and brought out his brush and comb and link box and replaced them on the bamboo table. Then she returned to the backyard and retrieved the painting.

She stood, indecisive and shivering in the cold air, with "The Light of the World" in her hands. She did not want to take it back inside, but felt now that it was out of the question that it should be destroyed. In the end she put it in the shed, placing it carefully on an old enamel-topped table beside the earth-encrusted flowerpots, balls of green twine, and seed trays. She closed the door gently as she left, not wishing to advertise her presence and invoke Mrs. Higgins.

Deidre had only seen her neighbor once since Monday evening, when she had called in briefly to collect any mail. Mrs. Higgins had been all agog with many a "fancy" and "poor Mr. Tibbs—out of the blue like that." Deidre had reacted tersely. "Out of the blue" had seemed to her an especially fatuous remark. Terrible things surely came out of the gray, or out of a deep, transforming black. At the realization that there would be no more little envelopes or lugubrious sighs and miserable forecasts when she arrived home from the Latimer, Deidre's spirits lifted once more.

She returned to the kitchen, where Sunny, curled up in front of an empty grate, immediately got up and ran to meet her. She crouched down and buried her face in his sparkling cream and ginger ruff. Glancing at the mantelpiece, she realized there were three hours before she needed to leave for the Chekhov auditions. How slowly the clock seemed to be ticking. Of course, there was plenty to do. All those dishes, for a start. Perhaps Sunny might like another walk. And she still hadn't unpacked her case. It occurred to Deidre suddenly how much *time* there seemed to be when you were unhappy. Perhaps this leaden comprehension that each minute must last for at least an hour was what people meant by loneliness. Time turning inward and then standing still. Well—she'd just have to get used to it and soldier on. She was turning on the hot-water faucet when the doorbell rang.

She decided not to go. It was probably one of her father's

so-called friends who had heard the news and, after cutting him dead for the past eighteen months, was now calling to see if there was anything he could do. Or Mrs. Higgins, dewlaps aquiver with curiosity. It wouldn't be the Barnabys. Although warmly pressing her to stay, Joyce had left it that Deidre would get in touch if she wanted any further help. The bell rang again, and Sunny started to bark. Deidre dried her hands. Whoever it was, was not going away. She opened the front door. David Smy stood on the step clutching a bunch of flowers.

"Oh!" Deidre stepped back awkwardly. "David... What a ...Come in...that is...come in. What a surprise. I mean, what a *nice* surprise..." She chattered nervously (no one from the company had ever visited her at home before) as she led him to the kitchen. On the threshold she remembered the state of the place, backed away, and opened the door of the sitting room.

"Please...sit down...how nice...how lovely to see you. Um...can I get you anything...some tea?"

"No thank you, Deidre. Not at the moment."

David sat, as slowly and calmly as he did everything, on the Victorian button-backed nursing chair, and removed his corduroy cap. He had on a beautiful dark green soft tweed suit that Deidre had never seen before, and looked very smart. She wondered where on earth he was going. Then he stood up again, and Deidre fluttered to a halt somewhere between the piano and the walnut tallboy.

David's flowers were long-stemmed apricot roses, the flowers shaped like immaculate candle flames. The florist had assured him that in spite of being scentless and unnaturally uniform, they were the finest in the shop and had been flown in from the Canaries only yesterday. David, starting as he meant to go on, had bought every bloom in the bucket (seventeen) at a cost of thirty-four pounds. Now, he held them out to Deidre, and she closed the gap between them, reaching out hesitantly.

"Thank you... that is kind. Actually, I've already been to the hospital, but I'll be going again on Sunday. I'm sure my father will love them. I'll just get a vase."

"I don't think you quite understand, Deidre." David stopped her as she turned away. "The flowers are not for your father. They're for you."

"For...for *me*? But...I'm not ill...."

David smiled at this. He further narrowed the gap between

them and bent upon her a look of such loving kindness that she all but burst into tears. Then he stretched out his green tweedy arm and drew her to him.

"Ohhh..." breathed Deidre, hope and disbelief shining equally in her eyes. "I didn't...I didn't know...I didn't understand..."

She did weep then; little sobs of joy. Sunny, much concerned, started to whimper. "It's all right." She bent down and patted him. "Everything's all right."

"I didn't know you had a dog."

"It's a long story. Shall I tell you? Perhaps while we have some tea—" She turned toward the door, but David drew her back.

"In a moment. I've been waiting a long time to do this. And we have the rest of our lives to have some tea." And then he kissed her.

She nestled once more against his shoulder, and his arm tightened. It was not a white-feathered arm, and it was certainly not twelve feet tall, yet such was the feeling of exhilarating comfort, for a moment it seemed to Deidre that she might have been enclosed in a tightly furled wing.

Rosa sat in the middle of row D, feeling disappointed. She had been convinced there would be an "atmosphere" at the audition for *Vanya*. Surely the unseemly departure of the company's previous leading man would mark the proceedings in some way? Slightly lowered tones perhaps; a nice hesitancy in putting oneself forward for the unexpectedly vacant title role. But no, everything was proceeding as usual. Actors striding on and off the stage, Harold pontificating, Deidre at her table. David Smy was in the back row next to his father with a piebald dog on his knee, and Kitty, who had had quite a bit of fun running away from Rosa with mock squeals of fright, was now leaning against the proscenium arch and sulking. She had come down not to read but to have a nice cozy chat with Nicholas, only to find him deep in conversation with Joycey's showy daughter.

Joyce herself, hoping for the part of Marina, the elderly nurse, was waiting in the wings with Donald Everard. Clive, to everyone's surprise, had cheekily taken to the stage to try for Telyegin. Boris, having just given Astrov's "idle life" speech, was drinking Kanga's piddle, and Riley rested on Avery's bosom darting many a snappy glance over his shoulder at the dog in the back row, suspecting some planned territorial infringement.

When Clive had finished, Cully Barnaby stepped forward to read for Yelena, and Rosa sat up. No reason why the child shouldn't make an attempt, of course. There was no denying that she was marginally nearer to the character's age (twenty-six) than Rosa, or that, as a youngster, she'd had quite a little way with her onstage. Still . . . Rosa half settled back and waited, uneasy.

"You're standing by the window," called Harold. "You open it and talk, half looking out. From 'my dear—don't you understand' . . . page two one five."

Then Cully moved, not as Rosa had expected, toward the window at the back of the set, still in place from *Amadeus,* but right down to the footlights, where she pushed against an imaginary casement and leaned out, her lovely face stamped with irritated melancholy. She began to speak in a rich, sharp voice, vivid as an ache and not at all in the musical "Chekhovian" manner the CADS thought proper. Her anger flowed into the auditorium, powerful and bitter. Rosa, chilled to the marrow, felt her heart tumble out of its place and bounce against her ribs.

But Cully was hardly into the speech when two men appeared at the swing doors under the exit sign and walked, with measured tread, down the aisle. So unflurried and even was their stride (neither fast nor slow), so closely did the younger man emulate the bearing of his companion, that there was something almost comic in their sudden appearance. They might have been making an entrance in a musical comedy. Until you looked at the first one's face.

Cully faltered, read one more line, stopped, and said, "Hello, Dad."

"Well, *really,* Tom . . ." Harold got up. "Of all the times. We're auditioning here. I hope this is important."

"Extremely. Where are you going?" Tim had climbed out of his seat.

"To open some wine."

"Sit down please. What I have to say won't take long." Tim sat down. "Perhaps everyone onstage and in the wings could come to the stalls. Save me screwing my neck round."

Nicholas, Deidre, Joyce, and Cully clambered down from the stage. Donald Everard followed and slid into the seat next to his twin. The young detective in the raincoat sat on the steps leading from the stage, and Barnaby walked to the pass door at the end of row A, turned, and surveyed them all. Joyce, sitting next to her daughter, shivered as the cold, impersonal beam of her husband's attention swept around the stalls. She felt suddenly alienated, and watched his profile tighten and become almost hawkish, with increasing feelings of distress. By the time he began to speak, she felt she was looking at a complete stranger. There was absolute quiet. Even Harold had fallen silent, though not for long, and Nicholas, innocent though he might be, thought, This is it, and experienced a thrill of alarm so strong it made him feel almost sick.

Barnaby began by saying, "I felt it only fair to keep you abreast with the current investigations pertaining to the Carmichael case." What a tease, thought Boris. As if the police ever kept a suspect abreast of anything. Tom's setting something up. "And I'd like to talk for a moment if I may about the character of the murdered man. It has always been my belief that an accurate assessment of the victim's personality is the first step in an inquiry of this kind. Random killing apart, a man or woman is usually done away with because of what they think or believe or say or do. In other words, because of the sort of person they are."

"Well, I hope we're not going to waste much time going over that," interrupted Harold. "We all know what sort of person Esslyn was."

"Do we? I know what the general opinion was. I went along with it myself—why not? Until now, I'd no reason to go into the matter in any detail. Oh, yes, we all knew what sort of person Esslyn was. Eminently fanciable, vain, strong-willed, solipsistic, a wow with the ladies. But when I tried to get to grips with this character, I found he simply wasn't there. There were outward signs, of course. Certain narcissistic posturings and Casanovian pursuits, but beyond this . . . nothing. Now why should this be?"

"He was shallow," said Avery. "Some people just are."

"Perhaps. But there is always more to any one person than what they choose to reveal. So I asked questions and listened to the answers and examined my own perceptions a bit more closely, and gradually a very different picture began to emerge. First, perhaps, we can look into the question of women. There is no doubt that he was loved, and very truly loved, by one." His glance fell on Rosa, and her mouth folded tightly into a controlled line. "She accepted him for what he was. Or what she thought he was."

"There's no thought about it!" cried Rosa, her voice raw. *"I knew him."*

"But who else ever cared? When I tried to pin this down, I got varying replies. Esslyn himself naturally fostered the illusion that they all cared. That, like Don Juan, he had no sooner had his way with one blossom than he moved on to pluck the next, leaving a trail of broken hearts. But I could find no actual proof of this. It was all hearsay, very vague. I did, however, come across one or two interesting comments. 'Nothing ever lasted very long for Esslyn,' and 'They used to get fed up and drift off.' *They,* you'll notice—not *he.* Certainly when he finally did break up his marriage for a pretty girl, she'd left him within the month. And his second wife had no love for him at all."

Kitty's eyes, already quite tarnished with crossness, glowered. Barnaby guessed at a recent visit to Mr. Ounce.

"And why was it such a piece of cake for her to lead this man, who supposedly had the pick of the bunch, to the altar by simply lying about a pregnancy?"

There was an audible intake of breath from several people at this revelation, and Rosa made a thick, choking sound. The Everards whickered like excited horses.

"To move on to his position as an actor. In this company, he was top dog. A big fish in a little pond—"

"I beg leave to take issue there, Tom. This theater is—"

"Please." Harold subsided reluctantly. "A little pond. True, he had leading roles, but he did not have the talent, the perception, or the humility to make anything of them. Neither did he have the ambition to look for pastures new. There are bigger groups in Slough or Uxbridge where he might have stretched himself, but he never showed the slightest inclination to do so. Perhaps because he may not have found another director quite so amenable."

"Amenable!" cried Harold. "Me?"

"There are many people I know who regarded his refusal to take direction as revealing supreme confidence. I disagree. It is putting yourself in a director's hands, trying different ways of working, taking risks, that shows an actor's confidence. And I gradually came to the conclusion that ambition and self-assurance were two things that Esslyn Carmichael had very little of."

He got a lot of puzzled looks at that, but none of actual disbelief. More than one person seemed to find the idea feasible. Rosa, while looking a little mystified, also nodded.

"And yet . . ." Barnaby left his position at the pass door and walked slowly up the aisle. Every head followed. "There were certain signs that this aspect of his personality was undergoing some sort of change. The feeling I picked up during questioning was that over the last few months, he had become openly argumentative, querying or defying Harold and castigating the only other actor in the company who was any serious threat." Nicholas looked rather pleased at that remark, and gave Cully a wide smile. "Now," continued Barnaby, "why should that be?"

The company recognized the question as purely rhetorical. No one spoke. In fact, two people looked so deeply disturbed you could have been forgiven for thinking that they might never speak again. "I believe that once we know the answer to that, we shall know why he was murdered. And once we know why, we shall know who."

Troy found his mouth was dry. At first guarded and resentful of his chief's deductive progress, he had sat outside the circle with a slightly defiant air, knowing his place, showing his detachment disdainfully. Now, in spite of himself totally gripped by the thrust of Barnaby's narrative, he leaned forward, caught in the storyteller's net.

"I'd like to jump to the first night of *Amadeus,* and the drama within the drama. I'm sure you all know by now that rumor and misinformation were running rife, and that Kitty and Nicholas were both attacked by Esslyn during the course of the evening." At this indication that his previous declaration had been validated, Nicholas looked even more pleased. "This naturally put them high on the list of suspects. In any case, I'm afraid the widow of a murdered man is usually thrust into this unenviable position. Kitty had the motive—he'd discovered she was unfaithful, and once the baby had 'disappeared' would perhaps have turned her out. And she had the perfect opportunity—"

"I didn't kill him!" shouted Kitty. "With all the witnesses I'd got to physical cruelty, I could've got a divorce. And maintenance."

"That sort of procedure can take a long time, Kitty. And not always end to your advantage."

"I never touched the bloody thing."

"Certainly your prints were not on the razor, but then neither were anybody else's until the dead man picked it up. But then, the most inept delinquent knows enough to wipe the handle of a murder weapon clean. Even so, all my instincts set themselves against this simple solution."

Kitty and Rosa engaged glances. Triumph and disappontment sizzled back and forth.

"I also decided that David, Colin, and Deidre were in the clear, and in each case for pretty much the same reasons. I've known them all a long time, and although I'd never be foolish enough to say that none of them are capable of murder, I very much doubt if they were capable of this *particular* murder. But of course they did have the opportunity. And this was my real stumbling block. Because, until earlier this evening, it seemed all the wrong people had the opportunity and all the right people had none."

"What happened earlier this evening, then?" asked Harold, who had been quieter for longer than anyone present could ever remember.

"I discovered there were two razors."

The remark fell into the silence like a stone. Ripples of emotion spread and spread. Some faces looked eager, some were flushed and serious, one turned ghastly pale. Avery, noticing, thought, Oh, God—he knows something. I was right. Then, not caring whether or not he was publicly rebuffed, he took his lover's hand and squeezed it; once for comfort and twice for luck. Tim didn't even notice.

"This, of course, opened up the whole thing. Almost anyone could have taken it, left the substitute, removed the tape when it was convenient, and then slipped the original back."

"Who's the 'almost,' Tom?" asked Nicholas.

"Avery. He didn't return to the wings till the play was over. Now I knew how," continued Barnaby, "I was left with the two whys. Why should anyone wish to murder Esslyn in the first place and, much more puzzling, why choose to do it in front of over a hundred people? Frankly, I still haven't understood the second, but I have become quite sure about the first."

Now, he retraced his steps and, once again, every head, as if yoked together on one invisible string, turned. He leaned back against the thrust of the stage, hands in pockets, and paused. The old ham, observed Cully admiringly. And I thought I got it all from me mum.

"Putting aside the motives we first thought of—namely, passion and money—we are left with a third, equally powerful and, I believe, the correct one. Esslyn Carmichael was killed *because of something he knew.* Now, our investigation has proved that, unless he's been ordering his affairs with special cunning, there have been no large sums of money coming his way, and that seems to rule out using this knowledge for financial coercion. But a blackmailer's demands can be other than monetary. He can put sexual pressure on people, or he can use his secret to obtain power. I thought the first, as he was so newly married and, according to his imperceptive lights, quite satisfied, was unlikely. Yet how much more unlikely, given my understanding of his character as lacking ambition and confidence, was the latter. And yet I became more and more certain that it was in this area of investigation that my solution lay.

"Like all of you, I'm sure I have thought of this murder as a theatrical one. Although on this dreadful evening reality crept upon the stage in certain unpleasant ways, we all knew, until the very last minute, that we were watching a play. Esslyn wore makeup and costume, he spoke lines, and executed moves that he had rehearsed. Whoever killed him was a member of the company. It seemed so plain that everything centered on the Latimer that I hardly took into account the rest of Esslyn's life—the larger part of it, after all. It was Kitty who reminded me that from nine till five Monday to Friday Esslyn Carmichael *was an accountant.*"

At this point Tim covered his chalk-white countenance with his hands and lowered his head. Avery put an arm around his shoulders. As he did so, his mind became crowded with bathetic images. He saw himself visiting Tim in prison every week, even if that meant for years. He would bake a cake with a file inside. Or smuggle in a rope beneath his poncho. At the thought of prison food, Avery felt his tummy start to churn. How would Tim survive?

"If you remember, Kitty"—Avery forced his attention back to what Tom was saying—"I asked you if you had noticed any change recently in your husband's routine, and you said he had gone to work the Saturday morning before he died. I don't know, Rosa, if you recall . . . ?"

"Never." The first Mrs. Carmichael shook her head. "He was quite firm on that. Said he had enough of facts and figures during the week."

"He had gone to the office, Kitty told me, to 'call something in.' A strange phrase, surely. One you'd be more likely to hear from the lips of a gambler than an accountant. Or a debt collector. Because that's what the phrase means. You 'call in' a debt. And I believe this is what Esslyn was about to do. What was owed and for how long we don't know. But he had apparently decided that it had gone on long enough."

"But, Tom," interrupted Joyce, her voice harsh and nervous, "you said he was killed because he knew something."

"And also"—Nicholas took advantage of the breach— "owing someone money isn't much fun, but it's not the end of the world. Certainly not worth killing for. I mean, the worst that can happen is you get taken to court."

"Oh, there was much more than that at stake. To discover precisely what, we have to go back to the point I reached earlier and ask again what happened several months ago—six, to be exact—to give Esslyn the confidence to start throwing his weight about?"

Barnaby paused then, and the silence lay ripe with suspicion and stabbed by startled looks. At first dense, it slowly became more lightsome, gathering point and clarity. Barnaby was never sure who first fingered the Everards. Certainly it was not him. But, as if telepathically, first one head, then another, pointed in their direction. Nicholas spoke.

"He got himself a pair of toadies."

"I see nothing wrong—" rushed in Clive Everard.

"Neither do I," said Donald.

"—in becoming friendly with—"

"—in *devotedly* admiring—"

"—even venerating—"

"—someone of Esslyn's undoubted talents—"

"—and remarkable skills."

"You bloody hypocrites." Barnaby's voice was so quiet that for a moment people glanced around, uncertain from where that damning indictment had arisen. Troy knew, and his adrenaline shot up. Barnaby walked to the edge of the row in which the brothers were sitting and said, still softly, "You malicious, wicked, meddling, evil-minded bastards."

Pasty-faced, their nostrils pinched in tight with alarm, the Everards shrank closer together. Kitty gazed at them with dawning horror, Cully, unaware that she was gripping Nicholas's arm very tight, half rose from her seat. Avery's expression of misery was suddenly touched with a glow of hope. Joyce felt she would choke on the suspense, and Harold was nodding. His head wagged back and forth as if it were loose on his shoulders, like the head on those gross chinese Buddhas found sometimes in antique shops.

"You've no call to speak to us like that," cried one of the Everards, recovering fast.

"Since when has it been against the law to admire an actor?"

"*Admire.*" Barnaby almost spat out the word, and the volume of his voice increased tenfold. He pushed his angry face close to theirs. "You didn't admire him. You *despised* him. You laughed at him. You sported with him. You led him around like a bear with a ring through its nose. And he, poor bugger, never having had a friend in his life, thought no doubt that this was what friendship was. Court toadies? Quite the reverse. Whatever that might be."

"*Éminences grises?*" suggested Boris.

"And directly responsible for his death."

At this, Donald Everard flew out of his seat. "You heard that!" he screamed, flapping his arms at the rest of the gathering. "That's slander!"

"We shall sue!" shrieked his brother. "You can't go around saying we killed Esslyn and get away with it."

"We've got witnesses!"

"All these people!"

"I didn't say you had killed him," said Barnaby, stepping back from these hysterics with an expression of deep distaste. "I said I believed you were responsible for his death."

"It's the same thing."

"Not quite. As you'll realize if you'll stop flinging yourselves about and settle down to think about it." When they had reluctantly, with many an injured cluck and toss of a gel-stiffened crest, reseated themselves, Barnaby carried on. "So we now have a puppet, a hollow man with someone pulling his strings. And what do they do, oh so subtly, so slyly, these puppeteers? At first they encourage intransigence. I can just hear it . . . 'You're not going to take that, are you? You're the leading man . . . don't you realize how powerful you are? They couldn't do anything without you.'" But after a few weeks that rather modest mischief starts to pall. They've gone about as far as they can go with that one. So they look around for something more interesting, and I suspect it was about this time that Esslyn shared with them the information that was to instigate their grand design and lead directly to his death.

"In fact, it was something my sergeant said in the office today that pointed me in the right direction." His sergeant, suddenly in the spotlight, attempted to look intelligent, modest, and invaluable. He also managed a surreptitious wink at Kitty, who promptly winked back. "He's given to making feeble, atrociously unfunny jokes," continued Barnaby (Troy immediately looked less intelligent), "the latest being a play on the word 'putsch,' but, as these things sometimes do, it reminded me of something very similar from a recent interview. I don't know if you remember, Kitty . . . ?"

Suddenly addressed, Kitty, who was still ogling Troy, blushed and said, "Sorry?"

"You told me that Esslyn spoke to you of the dramatic effect he intended to make on the first night."

"That's right, he did."

"And because he was admiring himself in his costume, you assumed that he referred to his own transformation."

"No—you said that, Tom. When you explained that funny French bit." Barnaby almost repeated the phrase, making it a question, and Kitty said, "That's right."

"Are you sure?"

Kitty looked around. Something was amiss. People were staring at her. She suddenly felt cold. What had she done that they should stare so?

"Yes, Tom, quite sure. Why?"

"Because what I just said was not the same phrase." So near though, and it had taken him two days to get it. "What I said— what *Esslyn* said—was '*coup d'état*.' A seizing of power."

"Oh, God—" The fragment of sound from Deidre was almost inaudible, but David immediately handed the dog to his father and took her hand.

"Twice a phrase was misheard or misinterpreted. And in both instances the correct readings would have provided vital clues."

"What was the other, Tom?" asked Boris, the only member of the group who seemed relaxed enough to speak.

"Esslyn tried to tell us with his dying breath of the plan that had undone him. Only one word, and that word was thought to be 'bungled.' But I performed a simple experiment earlier today, and I'm now quite sure the word in fact was '*Uncle*.' And that if time had been granted him the next word would have been

'*Vanya.*' Isn't that right, Harold?" Harold's head continued to nod like a Chinese Buddha.

"Did you not pick up the razor as you went through the wings, remove the tape in the interval, wipe the handle with your yellow silk handkerchief, and put it back on the tray? And while you had it in your pocket, did you not put this in its place?" He produced an old-fashioned razor from his pocket and held it aloft.

There was a terrible pause. Everyone looked at each other, shocked, excited, horrified by this revelation. Joyce covered her eyes with her hands and gave a muffled cry.

"Yes, that's right, Tom," said Harold pleasantly.

"And with an audience prepared to swear you never left your seat, you would be in the clear."

"Certainly that's how I envisaged it. And it all seemed to work terribly well. I can't imagine how you spotted the substitution." Barnaby told him. "Imagine that," continued Harold ruefully. "And I always thought David rather a slow-witted boy."

David did not seem to take offense at this, but his father glared at the back of Harold's head, and Deidre flushed angrily.

"I shall have to have a firm word with Doris about letting you root among my private possessions."

"She had no choice in the matter. We served a warrant."

"Hm. We'll see about that. Well, Tom, I expect now you know how, you'd like to know why?" Barnaby indicated that he would indeed, and Harold rose from his seat and started pacing in his turn, thumbs hooked into his vest pocket, the DA making his closing speech.

"To elucidate this rather annoying matter, we have to go back some considerable time. In fact, fifteen years, to the building of the Latimer and the formation of my present company. Money was short. We had a grant from the council, but not nearly enough for something that was to become the jewel in Causton's crown. And when that drunken old sot Latimer dropped dead, his successor was not nearly so sympathetic. I believe he had leftish tendencies—and cut our grant. No doubt he would have preferred to see a bingo hall. So almost from the beginning, we had cash-flow problems. And naturally one had to keep up a certain lifestyle. An impresario can't go round in a Ford Escort dressed like a shop assistant." Harold broke here, having reached the top of the stairs, wheeled dramatically, took a deep breath, and continued.

"I have an import-export business, as you may know, and

flattered myself that the hours I worked yielded very satisfactory returns. I kept my domestic expenses to a minimum and put my profits where they showed—that is, about my person and into the Latimer productions. However, healthy as these profits usually were, a huge percentage of them went to the Customs and Excise sharks for the VAT on import duty, and another great slice to the Inland Revenue. Obviously I resented this, especially when the scrap I got back in the form of a grant was slashed. So I decided to even the situation out a little. Of course, I intended to pay *some* tax and a proportion of the VAT required—after all, I'm not a criminal—but a judicious rearrangement of the figures saved me, in that first year, several hundred pounds, most of which went into *The Wizard of Oz,* our opening production. I don't know if you remember it, Tom?"

"A splendid show."

"Of course, when Esslyn prepared my accounts, I expected him to recognize my sleight of hand, but I was sure, as the company's star, he would appreciate the necessity for such a procedure. However, to my amazement, he said nothing. Just submitted them as usual. Naturally I had mixed feelings about this. On the one hand, no one wants an accountant so incompetent he can't spot a necessary juggle or two. On the other, it augured very well for the future. And so it proved. I kept back a little more every year—several thousand when I bought the Morgan—and every year no comment was made. But do you know what, Tom?"

Harold had come to rest near Barnaby. His head, which had been doing no more than gently bob in time to his movements, now began to jiggle and shake alarmingly. *"He had known what I was doing all the time.* He had known and said nothing. Can you imagine anything more deceitful?"

Barnaby, facing the murderer of Esslyn Carmichael, thought yes, he could imagine one or two things more deceitful, actually, but just said, "When did you discover this?"

"Last Saturday afternoon. I'd just got in from being interviewed at the theater. He rang and asked if he could come over. Doris was out shopping, so we had the place to ourselves. He didn't beat about the bush. Just said he was taking over direction at the Latimer starting with *Uncle Vanya,* and making an announcement to that effect after the curtain call Monday night. I said it was out of the question, he produced all these figures and said I could either step down or go to prison. I immediately spotted a third alternative, which I lost no time in carrying out. I got the duplicate razor from a shop in Uxbridge on the Monday morning. I knew Deidre's routine and that everything would have been checked long before the five. Esslyn never touched props, so I knew he wouldn't be likely to spot the substitution. I simply picked up the original as I went through the wings and, in the interval, took off the tape—"

"Where was this?"

"Well, I popped into the actors' loo, but Esslyn and his cronies were there. So I just stepped outside the stage door for a minute on my way to the dressing rooms to give them all a rollicking. Then, going back, I made the switch again. It only took a second. I used Doris's flower knife, it's very sharp. Simple."

Harold gave everyone a delighted smile, squinting at each face in turn and gloating a little in his cleverness. His beard had lost its clean, sculptural outline, and now had a disordered, almost herbaceous air.

"I knew, of course, Esslyn hadn't worked it out all by himself, especially when he owned up to sending that silly book. It was supposed to be a hint, he said. I was involved in 'fishy' business, you see. And a cookbook because I was 'cooking the books.' Well, really, he could never have thought of anything so subtle to save his life. I knew where that had come from, all right. And all the fifth-column work at rehearsals to make me seem incompetent, so the takeover would be more acceptable."

The Everards, trying to register self-righteousness and lofty detachment, merely looked as if they wished they were a thousand miles away. The rest of the company expressed surprised disgust, excitement, amusement, and, in two cases (Deidre and Joyce) shades of pity. Troy got up from his position on the steps and crossed the stage. Harold started to speak again.

"You do understand, don't you, that I had no choice? This" —he made a great open-armed gesture gathering in his actors, the theater, all of the past, and triumphs yet too come—"is my life."

"Yes," said Barnaby, "I do see that."

"Well, I must congratulate you, Tom." Harold held out his hand briskly. "And I can't say I'm sorry that all this has been cleared up. No doubt it would have come out sooner or later, but it's nice to start a new season with a clean slate. And I can assure you no hard feelings—at least on my part. And now, I'm afraid I must ask you to excuse me"—the hand returned, unshaken, to his side—"I must get on. We've an awful lot to get through tonight. Come along, Deidre. Chop-chop."

No one moved. Tom Barnaby stood irresolute, opened his mouth to speak and closed it again. He had arrested many criminals in his time, quite a few of them for murder, but he had never been faced with one who had confessed, offered to shake hands, then turned to go about his business. Or one who was so obviously mad.

"Harold . . ."

Harold turned, frowning. "You can see I'm tied up here, Barnaby. I've been reasonable so far, I'm sure you'll agree—"

"I want you to come with us."

"What—now?"

"That's right, Harold."

"Out of the question, I'm afraid. I must get *Vanya* cast tonight."

Barnaby felt Troy move, and put a restraining hand on the sergeant's arm. Apart from Barnaby's own sensibilities, which made dragging a demented, possibly screaming man out of a building and into a car a task he would hardly relish, there was the fact that his wife and daughter were present. Not to mention Deidre, who must have had more than enough of this sort of thing already. Harold was now standing waving his arms about urgently in the center of the stage. No one laughed. Barnaby prayed for inspiration, and caught Joyce's eye. Her face looked withdrawn, almost alarmed. Barnaby had never seen his "closing-in look," and had no idea how fearsome it could be. He allowed his expression to soften and saw his wife respond, warmth come back into her cheeks. Then he noticed a newspaper lying on her lap, *The Stage and Television Today,* and silently sent his thanks.

"Harold," he repeated, moving toward the director, then gently touching his arm. "The press are waiting."

"The *press.*" Harold repeated the honeyed words, then his brow darkened. "That potbellied idiot from the *Echo* . . ."

"No, no. The real press. *The Times, The Independent, The Guardian.* Michael Billington."

"Michael Billington." The blaze of hope in Harold's eyes dazzled. "Oh, Tom." Harold placed his hand on the chief inspector's arm, and Barnaby felt the weight of his exultation. "Is it really true?"

"Yes," said Barnaby, his voice rough.

"At last! I knew it would come. . . . I knew they'd remember me." Harold gazed wildly around. His face was white with triumph, and saliva, like a bunch of tiny crystal grapes, hung on his lips. He allowed Barnaby to take his arm and guide him down the steps leading from the stage. Halfway up the aisle, he stopped. "Will there be pictures, Tom?"

"I . . . expect so."

"Do I look all right?"

Barnaby looked away from the shining countenance disfigured by lunacy. "You look fine."

"I should have my hat!"

Avery got up and collected Harold's succubus and silently handed it to him. Harold put on the hat at a grotesque angle, the tail hanging over one ear; then, satisfied, continued his progress to the exit.

Troy, a few steps ahead, opened and hooked back one of the double doors and held aside the heavy crimson curtain. Harold paused on the threshold, then turned and stood for a moment to take a last look at his kingdom. He held his head a little to one side and appeared to be listening intently. On his face memory stirred, and an expression of the most intense longing appeared in his crazed eyes. He seemed to hear, from far away, a trumpet call. Then, still touched by the magic of death and dreams, he walked away. The heavy crimson curtain fell, and the rest was silence.

ANOTHER OPENING, ANOTHER SHOW

Christmas had come and gone, and the weather was far from clement. The woman who climbed out of the shiny blue Metro was wearing a full-length fur coat (beaver) and a silk-lined fur hood. She made her way across the wet pavements to the Far Horizons Travel Agency and gratefully hurried into its warmth. She pushed back the hood as she waited at the counter, revealing soft gray-blue curls, and also removed her gloves. She asked for some cruise brochures and, at the sound of her voice, the agency's only other customer, a slender girl in black, turned and spoke in some surprise.

"Doris?"

"Kitty—hullo." Doris Winstanley's response was a spontaneous smile; then, remembering past circumstances, an embarrassed silence. Kitty was far from embarrassed. She smiled back and asked Doris where on earth she was planning to sail away to.

"I'm not sure. It's just that all my life I've dreamed of going on a cruise. Of course, I never thought I'd have the opportunity."

"Don't blame you, Doris. Weather like this. You want to be careful, though."

"I'm sorry? I'm not sure . . ."

"Lounge lizards. All those charmers looking round for unattached wealthy ladies."

"Oh, I'm not at all wealthy," Doris said quickly. "But I have had a little windfall. So I thought I'd treat myself."

"Super. Are you going to stay in Causton when you come back?"

"Oh, yes. I have quite a few friends here." (Indeed, it had surprised her how many people had visited and shown genuine concern and support over the last few weeks. People who had never showed their faces when Harold was at home.) "And I'm going to let my two spare rooms to students when I come back. I've already contacted Brunel. It'll be lovely to have young people around the place again. My own children are so far away."

Doris talked on for a few minutes more. She didn't mind at all Kitty asking questions, or the brazen flavor of her advice. Doris was only grateful that Esslyn's widow was able to meet her and chat with some degree of kindness. Kitty looked very attractive, and had made no concessions to the weather. Her black suit had a miniskirt, and she seemed to be wearing neither blouse nor jumper beneath the tight-fitting jacket. She was beautifully made up, and had on a little pillbox hat with a black veil that came just to the bridge of her pretty nose and through which her pearly skin gleamed. Doris concluded her ramblings by asking Kitty what she was doing in Far Horizons.

"I'm picking up my plane tickets. I fly to Ottawa on Tuesday. To visit my brother-in-law." She adjusted the veil with rosy-tipped fingers. "He's been *so* kind. They're very anxious to console me."

"Oh," said Doris. There didn't seem to be much else she could say except, "Have a nice trip."

"You, too. And watch out for those lizards." Kitty pushed her ticket into her bag. "Now, I must rush. I've got a friend coming at seven, and I want to have a bath. See you."

Doris reflected for a moment on the unlikeliness of this assurance ever coming to pass, then she collected her pile of brochures and made her way to the Soft Shoe Café where she ordered tea and cakes. It was much more comfortable here than at home. There was hardly a stick of furniture in the place at the moment. All the tired, stained, hateful old rubbish of a lifetime had gone to the junkyard, and she would take her time replacing it. She would buy some new things and hunt for little treasures in antique shops. There would be plenty of time. And plenty of money. She had got an awful lot for the Morgan and, to her surprise, a very capable solicitor that Tom Barnaby recommended had sold the business for what seemed to Doris an enormous sum. And of course the house was in her name. Doris smiled, picked up her fork, and plunged it into an éclair.

* * *

Avery was cooking supper. They were eating in the kitchen as the surface of the dining-room table had almost disappeared under a large and beautiful working model of the set for *Uncle Vanya*. Tim had spent the last hour with a flashlight and colored cellophane, experimenting with lighting and making notes. Personally he thought the main room in the composite set looked as if it belonged to a villa in New Orleans rather than one in turn-of-the-century Russia, but there was no denying the close, enervating feel of the place, especially when the jalousies were closed and the light seeped through them and fell in dusty bars across the furniture.

"I hope you understand it's just scratch."

"So you keep saying." Tim transferred his attention to Avery's garden, wonderfully light and airy, and pictured it under a bright blue sky. Then he went to the larder, chose a bottle of Pedroncelli, and wielded the corkscrew. "What are you scratching, then?"

"Skate."

Tim poured two glasses of wine and put one by the cooker. Then he picked up *Floyd on Fish*. "I thought you said he wasn't sound."

"One mustn't be too purist in these matters. Joycey didn't want to keep it—understandable under the circs—so I took it off her hands. In fact"—he tasted the juices in the pan—"I think this is going to be rather good."

Silently Avery cursed himself for leaving the book out (it was usually at the back of the dish towel drawer). The last thing he wanted was to remind Tim of the occasion of Esslyn's death. For Tim had confessed to Avery (and Barnaby, too) that he had known about the plan to unseat Harold from its very emergence —although not about the blackmail. Assured by Esslyn that once he had taken charge, there would be no interference in the area of lighting or design, Tim had seen no reason why his original ideas should not be used in *Amadeus,* beginning on the first night.

Now, of course, he blamed himself for the outcome. If he had not kept the secret, if he had only told Avery—i.e., the entire company—Esslyn would probably be alive today. For weeks after Harold's arrest, Tim sat around the house melancholic and racked with guilt. He hardly ate and took no interest in the shop, which, in the pre-Christmas rush, nearly had Avery demented, even though Nicholas gave up his job at the supermarket to help.

On top of this, Avery had his own feelings to cope with. A certain disappointment, for instance, at the realization that Tim's seemingly brave and generous offer over the lighting had actually carried no risk at all if he knew Harold was to be deposed. But Avery nobly struggled to live with the fact that one small bubble had burst, and continued to cook ravishing meals when he wasn't scurrying around the shop and catching up on orders till midnight. But now Tim was getting better. Almost his old self. Avery drained his glass and smiled across at his companion.

"Don't slosh it down like that. It's a premier cru!"

"How you do go on." Avery lifted the skate onto an oval dish, and Riley, who had been curled on top of the Bentwood stool like a cushion, leaped (or rather thudded) to the ground. Since Sunny had started visiting the theater on a regular basis, Riley had refused to enter the building and had skulked, wet, shivering, and martyred, in the yard by the trash bins. Avery had not been able to bear this for long, and the cat was now ensconced in the house, stout, comfortable, and living the life to which, in his most far-reaching and secret dreams, he had always believed his name entitled him. Now, he padded over to his plate and attacked the fish with gusto. It was not up to the pheasant Périgord he had had last night, but he was certainly prepared to give it eight out of ten for succulence.

"I've made some brown-bread ice cream for pudding."

"My favorite."

Avery chopped some parsley over the vegetables. "But I didn't have time to shop today, so I'm afraid the baby carrots are frozen."

"My God." Tim banged down the knife with which he had been slicing a baguette. "And I understood this place had five stars."

"Not for the food, duckie." Tim laughed then. The first real laugh Avery had heard for weeks. They started to eat. "How is it?"

"Delicious."

"What do you think . . . ?" mumbled Avery.

"Don't speak with your mouth full."

Avery swallowed and drank some more wine. "It's ambrosial, this stuff. What do you think we ought to give Nico for a going-away present?"

"We've already given him *The Year of the King*."

"But that was weeks ago. Now he's staying on for *Vanya,* shouldn't we give him something else?"

"I don't see why. We hardly see him, what with rehearsals. And Cully."

"There's talent, if you like."

"Terrifying. I thought Nico was good, but she lights up the stage."

"Tim . . . you're not sorry Kitty's gone?"

"Of course not. Don't start."

"I'm not. Truly."

And, truly, he wasn't. Avery, having weathered the first really shattering blow to the relationship that was the cornerstone of his existence, now experienced, somewhere unreachably deep within his heart, a safe, abiding peace. He didn't quite understand this. It wasn't that he thought that Tim would never stray again. Or even that he might not, on some future occasion, stray himself (although this struck him as incredibly unlikely). Rather, it seemed that his personality had somehow developed an extra dimension where hurts or sharp surprises could be absorbed or even neutralized. Gratitude for this unexpected and surprising state of affairs, and for the very fact of his continuing existence, struck him anew, and he smiled.

"What are you beaming at in that fatuous manner?"

"I'm not."

"You look ridiculous."

"I was just thinking how nice it was that the good ended happily and the bad unhappily."

"I thought that was only in fiction."

"Not always," said Avery, and poured some more wine.

"Can you drop me off?"

Barnaby and Troy were about to leave the office. Troy, trench coat tightly belted, a shiny packet of cigarettes to hand, was already anticipating that first cloudy, cool lungful. Barnaby shrugged on his greatcoat, adding, "It's on your way home." When his sergeant still did not reply, the chief inspector added, "You can smoke if you like."

Blimey. In my own car. In my own time. Thanks a bloody million. Troy noticed his boss's eyebrows, which today looked more like used-up shreds of Brillo pads than ever, lift inquiringly.

"Where's the Orion, sir?"

"Joyce took it in for an MOT."

"Only I'm not going straight home . . . calling at the Golden Swans." More waggling. "It's a free house," explained Troy. "Out on the Uxbridge Road."

"That's all right by me. I could do with something wet and warm on a night like this."

"Well . . ." Red-faced, hanging on to the door handle, Troy elucidated further. "It's not really a pub—that was just a joke—they're on the bath, you see."

Barnaby looked at his sergeant. And saw. "Ah. Sorry, Troy. I'm not usually so slow on the uptake. It's been a long day."

"Yes, sir." The younger man made it halfway through the door, then turned and squared up to Barnaby in a manner both awkward and defiant. "I mean, the case *is* over."

"Oh, yes, yes. What you do off duty's your own affair." Then, when Troy still hovered: "If you're waiting for my approval, you'll stand there till daisies grow out of your arse."

"Good night then, sir."

"Good night, Sergeant." As the door closed, Barnaby called, "Give my regards to Maureen."

That reminded him of the song about Broadway, which reminded him of theaters, which reminded him of the Latimer, which reminded him of Harold, whom he was trying to forget, which he did most of the time, especially once he got into the business of the day. After all, he told himself (yet again), it was just another arrest. A bit out of the ordinary in that it was someone he knew. Also slightly out of the ordinary in that, once Harold had realized that the *crème de la crème* of British journalism had not gathered to honor him, it had taken three men to hold him down and get him into a cell. Barnaby, for the first time that he could remember in working hours, took the coward's way out and left them to it. But even in the canteen, he could still hear Harold screaming.

"Oh, Christ!" Barnaby slammed the office door and decided to walk home. A brisk trot through the snapping air should cool his blood. And calm his recollections. He strode down Causton High Street, darkness by his side. Naturally he had never expected, even as a naive young constable in the early fifties, that his policeman's lot would be an entirely happy one. He had been prepared for foulness galore, and the preparation had not been in vain. But there were occasions when all the foulnesses memory

held seemed to join together and become one great dark malodorous scab blotting out the good times, the bright times.

He strode on, crossing the road before he got to the Latimer
even though it meant he would have to cross back further on. He
didn't want to go near the place. Neither did he have any intention
of helping to paint the set for their next production, "heavenly"
though his daughter had asserted it to be. She and Joyce would be
in there now—he glanced at his watch—carrying on. He knew
he'd probably feel differently in a few days' time, perhaps even
tomorrow, but just at the moment he was sick of actors. Sick to
death of their ramshackle emotions and dissembling hearts. Of
their posturing ways and secret, gossipy gatherings.

Then, on the principle that spiteful coincidence always seeks
out those who can least tolerate it, as he moved out onto the Peli-
can crossing, the car that had stopped gave a friendly hoot and,
glancing across, Barnaby saw the Everards. Their faces were
grubby yellow under the sodium street lamps. Clive wound his
window down and called, "Hello," and Donald, who was driving,
tootled again. Barnaby continued to walk.

There must be something, he grimly thought, as he grimly
plodded on, still in a welter of miserable recall, to turn this sorry
tide of introspection. Then, felicitously, outside the Jolly Cavalier,
he stopped. The scene at that morning's breakfast table popped
into his mind. Joyce had said would he mind terribly, as she had a
packed day and had to be at the theater by seven, getting something from the Indian or Chinese for his supper. So Barnaby
pushed open the door of the Cavalier and went in.

Moving with the times, the pub offered a family/no-smok-
ing room at the back. They also did all their own cooking. Barnaby obtained a large helping of meat pie—rich steak and kidney
and flaky pastry—buttered broccoli, roast potatoes, and steamed
treacle pudding for dessert. He added a pint of real ale and took his
tray through.

The family room, living up to its name, held one small family. A thin young woman nursing a baby and a youngish man,
heavily tattooed, who was crouching in front of a cardboard box
filled with much-used toys and showing them to his three-year-
old daughter. He was speaking quietly and offering first a shabby
animal, then a doll. Their table was littered with potato-chip bags
and beer bottles. Barnaby nodded curtly (he would much rather
have had the place to himself), and sat down.

The hot, savory food was soothing, and gradually he started to relax. The little girl eventually chose a woolly lamb, took it back to their table, and offered it to her brother. He took it and dropped it on the floor. She reclaimed it and gave it back. He threw it down again. They both seemed to think this was a great joke.

Barnaby started on his pudding. He no longer wished he had the place to himself. The family about which, perhaps fortuitously, he knew nothing, seemed to offer, in a muddled way he could not be bothered to define, a kind of solace. He drained his glass and, deciding to make an evening of it, went to get another pint.

The Latimer caravan rolled on. Right now there was a rehearsal for *Uncle Vanya*. Rosa, who had seriously thought about getting off forever when she had been offered the measly part of the old nurse, was now glad that she hadn't. It had been a near thing, though, more than once. Especially when she'd been told there was no such thing as a small part, only small actors. She'd flounced out then, but had sidled back after Joycey had made her some coffee and talked about how exciting it would be. And Rosa had to admit that it was. Exhilarating, in fact. But frightening, too.

All the little technical tricks she had accumulated over the years had had to go. And that romantic husky voice the audience loved. All very well being told to use her imagination, search for the truth, and follow the syntax. Armorless, Rosa frequently felt she had never been on a stage before in her life. It was like stepping out over an abyss on a thin wire. And *tired*. She had never been so tired. When she looked back at all the leading roles that she had played, all on technique, without even getting out of breath, she marveled at her present exhaustion. Thank goodness for dear Earnest. He was such a comfort; warming her slippers by the fire, cocoa freshly made as soon as she tottered in. Rosa gathered her wits. It was nearly time for her entrance; opening Act IV.

Nicholas and Joyce sat together halfway up the stalls. They were both thinking of Cully. Nicholas, madly in love, wondered if she meant it when she said they would meet in London and, if he was in anything at Central, he was to let her know and she'd come along to cheer and shout.

Joyce, observing the sad splendor in which her daughter

moved as Yelena, marveled and was afraid. What a business she was going into. Cully knew all about theatrical uncertainties, of course; her mother had made sure of that. All about being "between engagements" and the unanswered letters and the auditions where they would let you know and never did. But like all young hopefuls, she didn't really think they would apply much to her. Joyce turned her attention to the stage, where Boris as Telyegin was holding out his arms, which were draped with a skein of wool. The ancient nurse, Marina, wound the ball slowly, holding it with great care in arthritic fingers. Her face and humped shoulders were old, but there was a robust peasant merriment in her cackling voice.

"Who'd ever have thought," whispered Nicholas, "that Rosa could turn in a performance like that."

Joyce smiled. All of them were thinking—and feeling—on their feet, alive, alive-o, re-creating moment to moment. Her ideas on her own character (Maria Voinitski) had gotten pretty short shrift. Cully had got off lightest. Not that any of them minded. Because what was happening onstage made it all worthwhile.

In the scene dock David Smy was recovering a chaise longue with olive-green patterned velvet. Sunny lay yawning by the portable gas fire. There seemed to be a lot going on at the moment, he thought, and certainly his walks were getting shorter and shorter, but he was not a dog to complain. Perhaps when the nice weather came, things would perk up.

Colin worked on a huge armoire, painting it with a walnut stain. Phoebe Glover, the ASM, would pop down and tell them when it was okay to saw and bang and generally make a racket. Colin wasn't too worried. The set was almost finished. There hadn't been any flats to paint or rostrums to drag about; it all looked so simple, yet seemed to work very well. He glanced across at David's bent head. Colin was neither a fanciful nor a religious man, but just at that moment found himself wondering if Glenda knew of their son's present happiness. Why not? Stranger things must have happened. He smiled at the thought. David looked up.

"What is it, Dad?"

"I'm parched, that's what. I'm popping up to the clubroom for a drink. Coming?"

"No. I want to get this done."

"Henpecked."

David gave a broad grin. "You want to bet?"

Upstairs they were taking a break. The cast had gathered together and were sitting, standing, or lying about on the stage. Their director rose from her seat in the back row, a tall, slim figure in a white jumpsuit, and came down to the footlights, clipboard in hand.

"That wasn't bad at all. We've a long way to go yet. Don't look like that, Rosa—what you got in Act Four was marvelous. Really very good."

There was a murmur of genuine agreement, and Rosa, proud but inexplicably shy, studied the carpet.

"I'm sure we could all do with some coffee. Phoebe?" The ASM hurried out from the wings. "Put the kettle on, there's a good girl."

"I'm just painting the candlesticks."

"Leave those for now. Go on then..." said Deidre, and she smiled. A smile with all the zing and glitter of a bold young samurai. Then she clapped her hands and cried, "Chop-chop!"